AF344320

IMAGE PROCESSING

Image Processing

Edited by
Yung-Sheng Chen

Image Processing

Edited by Yung-Sheng Chen

CBS, Edition **2017**

Published by InTech

Janeza Trdine 9, 51000 Rijeka, Croatia

Publishing Process Manager Jelena Marusic

Technical Editor InTech DTP team

Cover Designer InTech Design Team

Additional hard copies can be obtained from orders@intechopen.com

Image Processing, Edited by Yung-Sheng Chen
p. cm.
ISBN 978-953-307-026-1

Preface

Computers, imaging produces, electronic circuits, and software engineering have become very popular and common techniques in the modern society. We can find that there are more and more diverse applications of image processing in these technologies. Nowadays, multimedia applications occupy an important position in technology due to Internet development; however, the topics on image processing, which have been studied for near half a century, still remain tons of fundamentals worth in-depth researches. Generally speaking, developing image processing is aimed to meet with either general or specific needs. Specially, algorithm design is treated as the core topic of the image processing, whatever kinds of applications would benefit from good algorithms to achieve their desired goals. Besides, computer-aided diagnoses applied to medical imaging also plays an extremely significant role on the existing health care systems. Neural networks, fuzzy systems, and genetic algorithms are frequently applied to the variety of intelligent analyst applications. Speeding image processing hardware, especially, should take credit for solving problems with execution performance of appliance-based image processing as well.

There are six sections in this book. The first section presents basic image processing techniques, such as image acquisition, storage, retrieval, transformation, filtering, and parallel computing. Then, some applications, such as road sign recognition, air quality monitoring, remote sensed image analysis, and diagnosis of industrial parts are considered. Subsequently, the application of image processing for the special eye examination and a newly three-dimensional digital camera are introduced. On the other hand, the section of medical imaging will show the applications of nuclear imaging, ultrasound imaging, and biology. The section of neural fuzzy presents the topics of image recognition, self-learning, image restoration, as well as evolutionary. The final section will show how to implement the hardware design based on the SoC or FPGA to accelerate image processing.

We sincerely hope this book with plenty of comprehensive topics of image processing development will benefit readers to bring advanced brainstorming to the field of image processing.

Editor

Yung-Sheng Chen
Yuan Ze University
Taiwan, ROC

Contents

Contents

Contents

Image Acquisition, Storage and Retrieval

Hui Ding, Wei Pan and Yong Guan
Capital Normal University
China

1. Introduction

In many areas of commerce, government, academia, hospitals, and homes, large collections of digital images are being created. However, in order to make use of it, the data should be organized for efficient searching and retrieval. An image retrieval system is a computer system for browsing, searching and retrieving images from a large database of digital images. Due to diversity in content and increase in the size of the image collections, annotation became both ambiguous and laborious. With this, the focus shifted to Content Based Image Retrieval (CBIR), in which images are indexed according to their visual content.

The chapter will provide mathematical foundations and practical techniques for digital manipulation of images; image acquisition; image storage and image retrieval.

Image databases have particular requirements and characteristics, the most important of which will be outlined in this Section.

1.1 The description of CBIR

Content Based Image Retrieval or CBIR is the retrieval of images based on visual features such as colour, texture and shape (Michael et al., 2006). Reasons for its development are that in many large image databases, traditional methods of image indexing have proven to be insufficient, laborious, and extremely time consuming. These old methods of image indexing, ranging from storing an image in the database and associating it with a keyword or number, to associating it with a categorized description, have become obsolete. This is not CBIR. In CBIR, each image that is stored in the database has its features extracted and compared to the features of the query image. It involves two steps (Khalid et al., 2006):

- Feature Extraction: The first step in the process is extracting image features to a distinguishable extent.
- Matching: The second step involves matching these features to yield a result that is visually similar.

Many image retrieval systems can be conceptually described by the framework depicted in Fig. 1.

The user interface typically consists of a query formulation part and a result presentation part. Specification of which images to retrieve from the database can be done in many ways. One way is to browse through the database one by one. Another way is to specify the image in terms of keywords, or in terms of image features that are extracted from the image, such as a color histogram. Yet another way is to provide an image or sketch from which features of the same type must be extracted as for the database images, in order to match these features. A nice taxonomy of interaction models is given in (Vendrig, 1997). Relevance feedback is about providing positive or negative feedback about the retrieval result, so that the systems can refine the search.

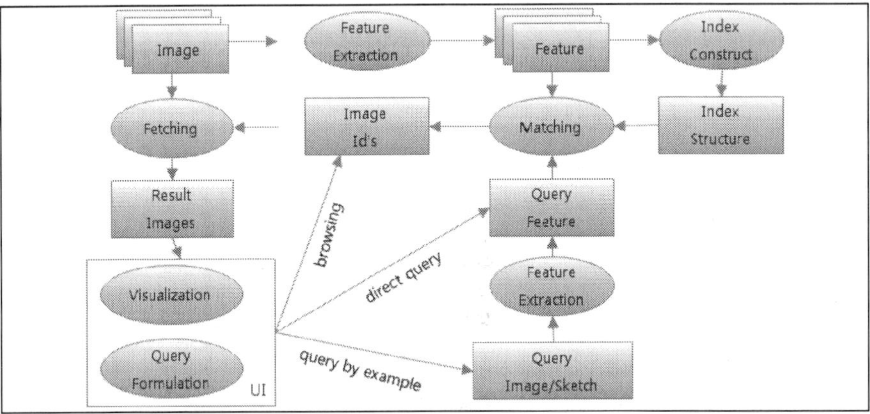

Fig. 1. Content-based image retrieval framework

1.2 A short overview

Early reports of the performance of Content based image retrieval (CBIR) systems were often restricted simply to printing the results of one or more example queries (Flickner et al., 1995). This is easily tailored to give a positive impression, since developers can chooses queries which give good results. It is neither an objective performance measure, nor a means of comparing different systems. MIR (1996) gives a further survey. However, few standard methods exist which are used by large numbers of researchers. Many of the measures used in CBIR (such as precision, recall and their graphical representation) have long been used in IR. Several other standard IR tools have recently been imported into CBIR. In order to avoid reinventing pre-existing techniques, it seems logical to make a systematic review of evaluation methods used in IR and their suitability for CBIR.

CBIR inherited its early methodological focus from the by then already mature field of text retrieval. The primary role of the user is that of formulating a query, while the system is given the task of finding relevant matches. The spirit of the time is well captured in Gupta and Jain's classic review paper from 1997 (Gupta & Jain, 1997) in which they remark that "an information retrieval system is expected to help a user specify an expressive query to locate relevant information." By far the most commonly adopted method for specifying a query is to supply an example image (known as query by example or QBE), but other ways have been explored. Recent progress in automated image annotation, for example, reduces the problem of image retrieval to that of standard text retrieval with users merely entering search terms. Whether this makes query formulation more intuitive for the user remains to be seen. In other systems, users are able to draw rough sketches possibly by selecting and combining visual primitives (Feng et al., 2004; Jacobs et al., 1995; Smith & Chang, 1996).

Content-based image retrieval has been an active research area since the early 1990's. Many image retrieval systems both commercial and research have been built.

The best known are Query by Image Content (QBIC) (Flickner et al., 1995) and Photo-book (Rui et al., 1997) and its new version Four-Eyes. Other well-known systems are the search engine family Visual-SEEk, Meta-SEEk and Web-SEEk (Bach et al., 1996), NETRA, Multimedia Analysis and Retrieval System (MARS) (Honkela et al., 1997).

All these methods have in common that at some point users issue an explicit query, be it textual or pictorial. This division of roles between the human and the computer system as exemplified by many early CBIR systems seems warranted on the grounds that search is not only computationally expensive for large collections but also amenable to automation.

However, when one considers that humans are still far better at judging relevance, and can do so rapidly, the role of the user seems unduly curtailed. The introduction of relevance feedback into image retrieval has been an attempt to involve the user more actively and has turned the problem of learning feature weights into a supervised learning problem. Although the incorporation of relevance feedback techniques can result in substantial performance gains, such methods fail to address a number of important issues. Users may, for example, not have a well-defined information need in the first place andmay simply wish to explore the image collection. Should a concrete information need exist, users are unlikely to have a query image at their disposal to express it. Moreover, nearest neighbour search requires efficient indexing structures that do not degrade to linear complexity with a large number of dimensions (Weber et al., 1998).

As processors become increasingly powerful, and memories become increasingly cheaper, the deployment of large image databases for a variety of applications have now become realisable. Databases of art works, satellite and medical imagery have been attracting more and more users in various professional fields. Examples of CBIR applications are:

- Crime prevention: Automatic face recognition systems, used by police forces.
- Security Check: Finger print or retina scanning for access privileges.
- Medical Diagnosis: Using CBIR in a medical database of medical images to aid diagnosis by identifying similar past cases.
- Intellectual Property: Trademark image registration, where a new candidate mark is compared with existing marks to ensure no risk of confusing property ownership.

2. Techniques of image acquire

Digital image consists of discrete picture elements called pixels. Associated with each pixel is a number represented as digital number, which depicts the average radiance of relatively small area within a scene. Image capture takes us from the continuous-parameter real world in which we live to the discrete parameter, amplitude quantized domain of the digital devices that comprise an electronic imaging system.

2.1 Representations for the sampled image

Traditional image representation employs a straightforward regular sampling strategy, which facilitates most of the tasks involved. The regular structuring of the samples in a matrix is conveniently simple, having given rise to the raster display paradigm, which makes this representation especially efficient due to the tight relationship with typical hardware.

The regular sampling strategy, however, does not necessarily match the information contents of the image. If high precision is required, the global sampling resolution must be increased, often resulting in excessive sampling in some areas. Needless to say, this can become very inefficient, especially if the fine/coarse detail ratio is low. Many image representation schemes address this problem, most notably frequency domain codifications (Penuebaker & Mitchell, 1993; Froment & Mallat, 1992), quad-tree based image models (Samet, 1984) and fractal image compression (Barnsley & Hurd, 1993).

Sampling a continuous-space image $g_c(x,y)$ yields a discretespace image:

$$g_d(m,n) = g_c(mX,nY) \tag{1}$$

where the subscripts c and d denote, respectively, continuous space and discrete space, and (X,Y) is the spacing between sample points, also called the pitch. However, it is also convenient to represent the sampling process by using the 2-D Dirac delta function $\delta(x,y)$. In particular, we have from the sifting property of the delta function that multiplication of $g_c(x,y)$ by a delta function centered at the fixed point (x_0,y_0) followed by integration will yield the sample value $g_c(x_0,y_0)$, i.e.,

$$g_c(x_0,y_0) = \iint g_c(x,y)\delta(x-x_0,y-y_0)dxdy \tag{2}$$

Provided $g_c(x,y)$ is continuous at (x_0,y_0). It follows that:

$$g_c(x,y)\delta(x-x_0,y-y_0) \equiv g_c(x_0,y_0)\delta(x-x_0,y-y_0) \tag{3}$$

that is, multiplication of an impulse centered at (x_0,y_0) by the continuous-space image $g_c(x,y)$ is equivalent to multiplication of the impulse by the constant $g_c(x_0,y_0)$. It will also be useful to note from the sifting property that:

$$g_c(x,y) * \delta(x-x_0,y-y_0) = g_c(x-x_0,y-y_0) \tag{4}$$

That is, convolution of a continuous-space function with an impulse located at (x_0,y_0) shifts the function to (x_0,y_0).

To get all the samples of the image, we define the comb function:

$$comb_{X,Y}(x,y) = \sum_m \sum_n \delta(x-mX,y-nY) \tag{5}$$

Then we define the continuous-parameter sampled image, denoted with the subscript s, as

$$\begin{aligned}g_s(x,y) &= g_c(x,y)comb_{X,Y}(x,y) \\ &= \sum_m \sum_n g_d(x,y)\delta(x-mX,y-nY)\end{aligned} \tag{6}$$

We see from Eq. (6) that the continuous- and discrete-space representations for the sampled image contain the same information about its sample values. In the sequel, we shall only use the subscripts c and d when necessary to provide additional clarity. In general, we can distinguish between functions that are continuous space and those that are discrete space on the basis of their arguments. We will usually denote continuous-space independent variables by (x,y) and discrete-space independent variables by (m,n).

2.2 General model for the image capture process

Despite the diversity of technologies and architectures for image capture devices, it is possible to cast the sampling process for all of these systems within a common framework.

Since feature points are commonly used for alignment between successive images, it is important to be aware of the image blur introduced by resampling. This manifests itself and is conveniently analysed in the frequency domain representation of an image. The convenience largely arises because of the Convolution Theorem (Bracewell, 1986) whereby convolution in one domain is multiplication in the other. Another technique used is to work in the spatial domain by means of difference images for selected test images. This technique is less general, though careful construction of test images can be helpful. In (Abdou & Schowengerdt, 1982), the question of the response to differential phase shift in the image was considered in the spatial domain. That study, though thorough, was concerned with bi-level images and used a restricted model for the image capture process.

2.3 Image decimation and interpolation

Interpolation and decimation are, respectively, operations used to magnify and reduce sampled signals, usually by an integer factor. Magnification of a sampled signal requires that new values, not present in the signal, be computed and inserted between the existing samples. The new value is estimated from a neighborhood of the samples of the original signal. Similarly, in decimation a new value is calculated from a neighborhood of samples and replaces these values in the minimized image. Integer factor interpolation and decimation algorithms may be implemented using efficient FIR filters and are therefore relatively fast. Alternatively, zooming by noninteger factors typically uses polynomial interpolation techniques resulting in somewhat slower algorithms.

2.3.1 Downsampling and decimation

Decimation is the process of filtering and downsampling a signal to decrease its effective sampling rate, as illustrated in Fig. 2. To downsample a signal by the factor N means to form a new signal consisting of every Nth sample of the original signal. The filtering is employed to prevent aliasing that might otherwise result from downsampling.

$$x(n) \longrightarrow \boxed{\downarrow N} \longrightarrow y(n)$$

Fig. 2. Downsampling by the factor N

Fig. 2. shows the symbol for downsampling by the factor N. The downsampler selects every Nth sample and discards the rest:

$$y(n) = Downsample_{N,n}(x) \triangleq x(Nn), \quad n \in Z \tag{7}$$

In the frequency domain, we have

$$Y(z) = ALIAS_{N,n}(x) \triangleq \frac{1}{N} \sum_{m=0}^{N-1} X(z^{\frac{1}{N}} e^{-jm\frac{2\pi}{N}}), \quad z \in C \tag{8}$$

Thus, the frequency axis is expanded by factor N, wrapping N times around the unit circle, adding to itself N times. For $N=2$, two partial spectra are summed, as indicated in Fig. 3. Using the common twiddle factor notation:

$$W_N \triangleq e^{-j2\pi/N} \tag{9}$$

the aliasing expression can be written as :

$$Y(z) = \frac{1}{N} \sum_{m=0}^{N-1} X(W_N^m z^{1/N}) \tag{10}$$

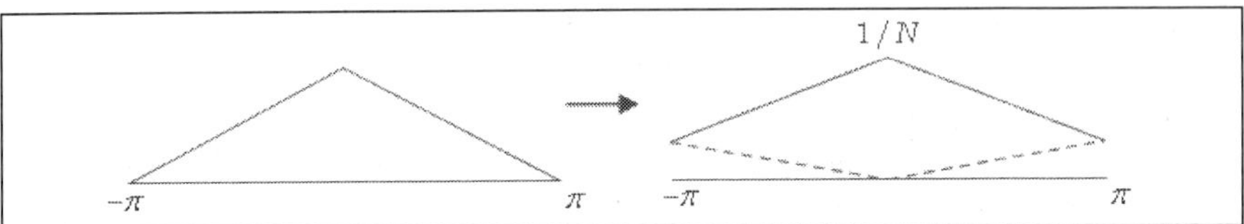

Fig. 3. Illustration of $ALLAS_2$ in frequency domain

2.3.2 Upsampling and Interpolation

The process of increasing the sampling rate is called interpolation. Interpolation is upsampling followed by appropriate filtering. $y(n)$ obtained by interpolating $x(n)$, is generally represented as:

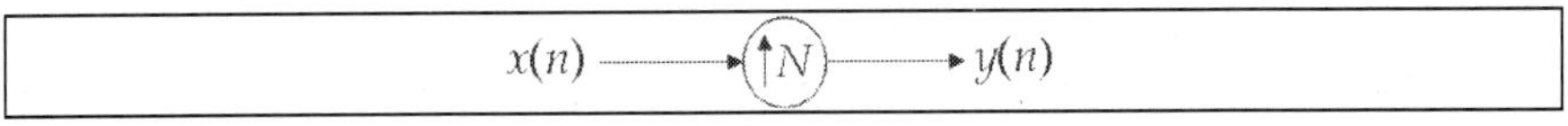

$$x(n) \longrightarrow \uparrow N \longrightarrow y(n)$$

Fig. 4. Upsampling by the factor N

$$y(n) = STRETCH_N(x) \triangleq x(Nn), \quad n \in Z \tag{11}$$

Fig. 4 shows the graphical symbol for a digital upsampler by the factor N . To upsample by the integer factor $N-1$, we simply insert zeros between $x(n)$ and $x(n+1)$ for all n . In other words, the upsampler implements the stretch operator defined as :

$$y(n) = STRETCH_{N,n}(x) \triangleq \begin{cases} x(n/N), & \frac{n}{N} \\ 0, & otherwize \end{cases} \tag{12}$$

In the frequency domain, we have, by the stretch (repeat) theorem for DTFTs:

$$Y(z) = REPEAT_{N,n}(X) \triangleq X(z^N), \quad z \in C \tag{13}$$

Plugging in $z = e^{jw}$, we see that the spectrum on $[-\pi, \pi)$ contracts by the factor N , and N images appear around the unit circle. For $N = 2$, this is depicted in Fig. 5.

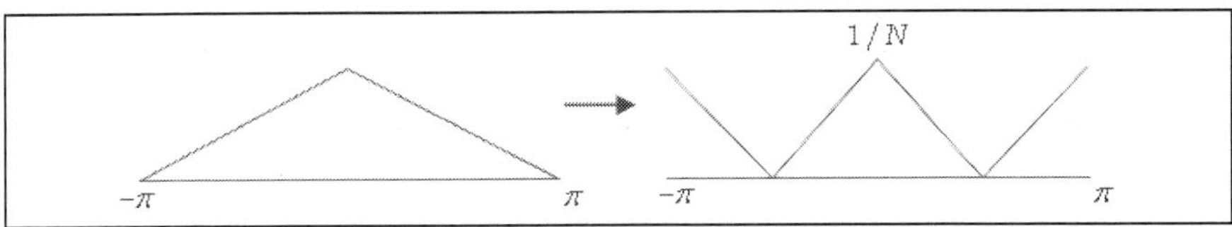

Fig. 5. Illustration of $ALLAS_2$ in frequency domain

For example, the down sampling procedure keeps the scaling parameter constant (n=1/2) throughout successive wavelet transforms so that it benefits for simple computer implementation. In the case of an image, the filtering is implemented in a separable way by filtering the lines and columns. The progressing of wavelet decompose has shown in Fig. 6. (Ding et al., 2008)

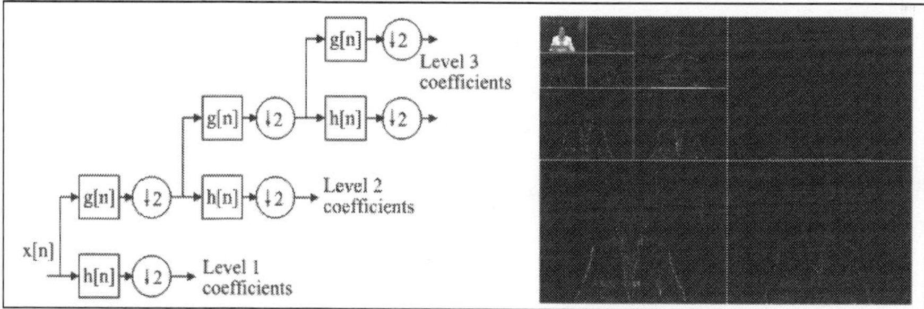

Fig. 6. 2-D wavelet decomposition. (a) : 3 level filter bank, (b): the example of wavelet decomposition

2.4 Basic enhancement and restoration techniques

The Moving Picture Experts Group (MPEG) is a working group of ISO/IEC in charge of the development of international standards for compression, decompression, processing, and coded representation of moving pictures, audio and their combination.

The process of image acquisition frequently leads (inadvertently) to image degradation. Due to mechanical problems, out-of-focus blur, motion, inappropriate illumination, and noise the quality of the digitized image can be inferior to the original. The goal of enhancement is - starting from a recorded image $c[m,n]$ to produce the most visually pleasing image $\hat{a}[m,n]$. The goal of enhancement is beauty; the goal of restoration is truth.

The measure of success in restoration is usually an error measure between the original $a[m,n]$ and the estimate $\hat{a}[m,n]: E\{\hat{a}[m,n], a[m,n]\}$. No mathematical error function is known that corresponds to human perceptual assessment of error. The mean-square error function is commonly used because:

- It is easy to compute;
- It is differentiable implying that a minimum can be sought;
- It corresponds to "signal energy" in the total error;
- It has nice properties vis à vis Parseva's theorem.

The mean-square error is defined by:

$$E\{\hat{a},a\} = \frac{1}{MN} \sum_{m=0}^{M-1} \sum_{n=0}^{N-1} \left| \hat{a}[m,n] - a[m,n] \right|^2 \tag{14}$$

In some techniques an error measure will not be necessary; in others it will be essential for evaluation and comparative purposes.

Image restoration and enhancement techniques offer a powerful tool to extract information on the small-scale structure stored in the space- and ground-based solar observations. We will describe several deconvolution techniques that can be used to improve the resolution in the images. These include techniques that can be applied when the Point Spread Functions (PSFs) are well known, as well as techniques that allow both the high resolution information, and the degrading PSF to be recovered from a single high signal-to-noise image. I will also discuss several algorithms used to enhance low-contrast small-scale structures in the solar atmosphere, particularly when they are embedded in large bright structures, or located at or above the solar limb. Although strictly speaking these methods do not improve the resolution in the images, the enhancement of the fine structures allows detailed study of their spatial characteristics and temporal variability. Finally, I will demonstrate the potential of image post-processing for probing the fine scale and temporal variability of the solar atmosphere, by highlighting some recent examples resulting from the application of these techniques to a sample of Solar observations from the ground and from space.

3. Image storage and database

With increased computing power and electronic storage capacity, the potential for large digital video libraries is growing rapidly. In the analysis of digital video, compression schemes offer increased storage capacity and statistical image characteristics, such as filtering coefficients and motion compensation data. Content-based image retrieval, uses the visual contents of an image such as color, shape, texture, and spatial layout to represent and index the image.

3.1 Statistical features

In pattern recognition and in image processing feature extraction is a special form of dimensionality reduction. Features that are extracted from image or video sequence without regard to content are described as statistical features. These include parameters derived from such algorithms as image difference and camera motion. Certain features may be extracted from image or video without regard to content. These features include such analytical features as scene changes, motion flow and video structure in the image domain, and sound discrimination in the audio domain.

3.1.1 Gaussian statistics

To understand the role of statistics in image segmentation, let us examine some preliminary functions that operate on images. Given an image f_0 that is observed over the lattice Ω, suppose that $\Omega_1 \subseteq \Omega_2$ and f_1 is a restriction of f_0 to only those pixels that belong to Ω_1. Then, one can define a variety of statistics that capture the spatial continuity of the pixels that comprise f_1.

$$T_{f_1}(p,q) = \sum_{(m,n)\in\Omega_1} \left[f_1(m,n) - f_1(m+p,n+q) \right]^2 \tag{15}$$

where $(p,q) \in [(0,1),(1,0),(1,1),(1,-1),...]$, measures the amount of variability in the pixels that comprise f_1 along the $(p,q)th$ direction. For a certain f_1, if $T_{f_1}(0,1)$ is very small, for example, then that implies that f_1 has a little or no variability along the $(0,1)th$ (i.e., horizontal) direction. Computation of this statistic is straightforward, as it is merely a quadratic operation on the difference between intensity values of adjacent (neighboring) pixels. $T_{f_1}(p,q)$ and minor variation thereof is referred to as the Gaussian statistic and is widely used in statistical methods for segmentation of gray-tone images; see [6,7].

3.1.2 Fourier statistics

$$F_{f_1}(\alpha,\beta) = \sum_{(m,n)\in\Omega_1} \left[f_1(m,n)e^{-\sqrt{-1}(m\alpha+n\beta)} \right] \times \left[f_1(m,n)e^{\sqrt{-1}(m\alpha+n\beta)} \right] \tag{16}$$

where $(\alpha,\beta)\in[-\pi,\pi]^2$, measures the amount of energy in frequency bin (α,β) that the pixels that comprise f_1 possess. For acertain f_1, if $F_{f_1}(0,20\pi/N)$ has a large value, for example, then that implies that f_1 has a significant cyclical variation of the $(0,20\pi/N)$ (i.e., horizontally every 10 pixels) frequency. Computation of this statistic is more complicated that the Gaussian one. The use of fast Fourier transform algorithms, however, can significantly reduce the associated burden. $F_{f_1}(\alpha,\beta)$, called the period gram statistic, is also used in statistical methods for segmentation of textured images; see [8,91.

3.1.3 Covariance statistics

$$K_{f_1} = \sum_{(m,n)\in\Omega_1} \left(f_1(m,n)-\mu f_1 \right)^T \left(f_1(m,n)-\mu f_1 \right) \tag{17}$$

where $\mu f_1 = \sum_{(m,n)\in\Omega_1} f_1(m,n)$, measures the correlation between the various components that comprise each pixel of f_1. If K_{f_1} is a 3×3 matrix and $K_{f_1}(1,2)$ has large value, for example, then that means that components 1 and 2 (could be the red and green channels) of the pixels that make up f_1 are highly correlated. Computation of this statistic is very time consuming, even more so than the Fourier one, and there are no known methods to alleviate this burden. K_{f_1} is called the covariance matrix of f_1, and this too has played a substantial role in statistical methods for segmentation of color images; see [10,111.

Computation of image statistics of the type that motioned before tremendously facilitates the task of image segmentation.

3.2 Compressed domain feature

Processing video data is problematic due to the high data rates involved. Television quality video requires approximately 100 GBytes for each hour, or about 27 MBytes for each second. Such data sizes and rates severely stress storage systems and networks and make even the most trivial real-time processing impossible without special purpose hardware. Consequently, most video data is stored in a compressed format.

3.2.1 JPEG Image

The name "JPEG" stands for Joint Photographic Experts Group, the name of the committee that created the standard. The JPEG compression algorithm is at its best on photographs and paintings of realistic scenes with smooth variations of tone and color.

Because the feature image of a raw image is composed of the mean value of each 8×8 block, the mean value of each block in the JPEG image is then directly extracted from its DC coefficient as the feature. The result can be easily inferred as follows:

$$J(0,0) = \frac{c(0)c(0)}{4}\sum_{x=0}^{7}\sum_{y=0}^{7} f(x,y)\cos\left(\frac{(2x+1)\times c(0)\times\pi}{16}\right)\cos\left(\frac{(2y+1)\times c(0)\times\pi}{16}\right)$$

$$= \frac{1}{16}\sum_{x=0}^{7}\sum_{y=0}^{7} f(x,y) = 4\times\frac{1}{64}\sum_{x=0}^{7}\sum_{y=0}^{7} f(x,y) = 4\times M \tag{18}$$

where $J(0,0)$ and M are the DC coefficient and mean value of the corresponding block. For the reason that a level shifting by –128 gray levels in the JPEG encoding, the real mean value of the block is $\left[\dfrac{1}{4}J(0,0)+128\right]$. The real mean values of all blocks are assigned to be the pixel values of the feature image. The size of the feature image is still $1/64$ of original JPEG image size because the DCT block size is 8×8.

3.2.2 Wavelet-compressed Images

For a wavelet-compressed image, feature image is extracted from the low-low band of the wavelet-compressed. If the one-level wavelet decomposition is used in the wavelet-compressed image, the low-low band subimage will approximate to the scaled original image. Thus, the mean value of each 4×4 block in the low-low band subimage is assigned to be the pixel value of the feature image. The pixel value of the feature image is:

$$WI_{x,y} = \frac{1}{16}\sum_{j=0}^{3}\sum_{i=0}^{3}LL_{4x+i,4y+j} \tag{19}$$

where $WI_{x,y}$ is the pixel value of feature image with coordinate (x,y), and $LL_{x,y}$ is the pixel value of low-low 8×8 band image with coordinate (x,y). The size of feature image here is $1/64$ of the original wavelet-compressed image size. If the wavelet-compressed image is compressed by three-level wavelet decomposition, then the image should be reconstructed back to the one-level wavelet decomposition first.

The feature images will be the same if they are extracted from the raw image and the JPEG image of the same image. Moreover, the mean squared error (MSE) between feature images generated from the raw image and from the wavelet-compressed image is quite small.

3.3 Image content descriptor

"Content-based" means that the search will analyze the actual contents of the image. The term 'content' in this context might refer to colors, shapes, textures, or any other information that can be derived from the frame image itself.

- *Color* represents the distribution of colors within the entire image. This distribution includes the amounts of each color.
- *Texture* represents the low-level patterns and textures within the image, such as graininess or smoothness. Unlike shape, texture is very sensitive to features that appear with great frequency in the image.
- *Shape* represents the shapes that appear in the image, as determined by color-based segmentation techniques. A shape is characterized by a region of uniform color.

3.2.1 Color

Color reflects the distribution of colors within the entire frame image. A color space is a mathematical representation of a set of colors. The three most popular color models are RGB (used in computer graphics); YIQ, YUV or YCbCr (used in video systems); and CMYK (used in color printing). However, none of these color spaces are directly related to the intuitive notions of hue, saturation, and brightness. This resulted in the temporary pursuit of other models, such as HIS and HSV, to simplify programming, processing, and end-user manipulation.

- RGB Color Space

The red, green, and blue (RGB) color space is widely used throughout computer graphics. Red, green, and blue are three primary additive colors (individual components are added together to form a desired color) and are represented by a three-dimensional, Cartesian coordinate system. The indicated diagonal of the cube, with equal amounts of each primary component, represents various gray levels. Table 1 contains the RGB values for 100% amplitude, 100% saturated color bars, a common video test signal.

	Nominal Range	White	Yellow	Cyan	Green	Magenta	Red	Blue	Black
R	0 to 255	255	255	0	0	255	255	0	0
G	0 to 255	255	255	255	255	0	0	0	0
B	0 to 255	255	0	255	0	255	0	255	0

Table 1. 100% RGB Color Bars

The RGB color space is the most prevalent choice for computer graphics because color displays use red, green, and blue to create the desired color. However, RGB is not very efficient when dealing with "real-world" images. All three RGB components need to be of equal band-width to generate any color within the RGB color cube. The result of this is a frame buffer that has the same pixel depth and display resolution for each RGB component. Also, processing an image in the RGB color space is usually not the most efficient method. For these and other reasons, many video standards use luma and two color dif ference signals. The most common are the YUV, YIQ, and YCbCr color spaces. Although all are related, there are some differences.

- YCbCr Color Space

The YCbCr color space was developed as part of ITU-R BT.601 during the development of a world-wide digital component video standard. YCbCr is a scaled and offset version of the YUV color space. Y is defined to have a nominal 8-bit range of 16–235; Cb and Cr are defined to have a nominal range of 16–240. There are several YCbCr sampling formats, such as 4:4:4, 4:2:2, 4:1:1, and 4:2:0.

RGB - YCbCr Equations: SDTV

The basic equations to convert between 8-bit digital R´G´B´ data with a 16–235 nominal range and YCbCr are:

$$Y_{601} = 0.2999R' + 0.587G' + 0.114B'$$
$$Cb = -0.172R' - 0.399G' + 0.511B' + 128$$
$$Cr = 0.511R' - 0.428C' \quad 0.083B' + 128$$

$$(20)$$

$$R' = Y_{601} + 1.371(Cr - 128)$$
$$G' = Y_{601} - 0.698(Cr - 128) - 0.336(Cb - 128)$$
$$B' = Y_{601} + 1.732(Cb - 128)$$

When performing YCbCr to R´G´B´ conversion, the resulting R´G´B´ values have a nominal range of 16–235, with possible occasional excursions into the 0–15 and 236–255 values. This is due to Y and CbCr occasionally going outside the 16–235 and 16–240 ranges, respectively, due to video processing and noise. Note that 8-bit YCbCr and R´G´B´ data should be saturated at the 0 and 255 levels to avoid underflow and overflow wrap-around problems.

Table 2 lists the YCbCr values for 75% amplitude, 100% saturated color bars, a common video test signal.

	Nominal Range	White	Yellow	Cyan	Green	Magenta	Red	Blue	Black
SDTV									
Y	16 to 235	180	162	131	112	84	65	35	16
Cb	16 to 240	128	44	156	72	184	100	212	128
Cr	16 to 240	128	142	44	58	198	212	114	128
HDTV									
Y	16 to 235	180	168	145	133	63	51	28	16
Cb	16 to 240	128	44	147	63	193	109	212	128
Cr	16 to 240	128	136	44	52	204	212	120	128

Table 2. 75% YCbCr Color Bars.

RGB - YCbCr Equations: HDTV

The basic equations to convert between 8-bit digital R´G´B´ data with a 16–235 nominal range and YCbCr are:

$$Y_{709} = 0.213R' + 0.751G' + 0.072B'$$
$$Cb = -0.117R' - 0.394G' + 0.511B' + 128$$
$$Cr = 0.511R' - 0.464G' - 0.047B' + 128$$

$$(21)$$

$$R' = Y_{709} + 1.540(Cr - 128)$$
$$G' = Y_{709} - 0.459(Cr - 128) - 0.183(Cb - 128)$$
$$B' = Y_{709} + 1.816(Cb - 128)$$

When performing YCbCr to R´G´B´ conversion, the resulting R´G´B´ values have a nominal range of 16–235, with possible occasional excursions into the 0–15 and 236–255 values. This is due to Y and CbCr occasionally going outside the 16–235 and 16–240 ranges, respectively, due to video processing and noise. Note that 8-bit YCbCr and R´G´B´ data should be saturated at the 0 and 255 levels to avoid underflow and overflow wrap-around problems.

Table 2 lists the YCbCr values for 75% amplitude, 100% saturated color bars, a common video test signal.

- HSI, HLS, and HSV Color Spaces

The HSI (hue, saturation, intensity) and HSV (hue, saturation, value) color spaces were developed to be more "intuitive" in manipulating color and were designed to approximate the way humans perceive and interpret color. They were developed when colors had to be specified manually, and are rarely used now that users can select colors visually or specify Pantone colors. These color spaces are discussed for "historic" interest. HLS (hue, lightness, saturation) is similar to HSI; the term lightness is used rather than intensity. The difference between HSI and HSV is the computation of the brightness component (I or V), which determines the distribution and dynamic range of both the brightness (I or V) and saturation(S). The HSI color space is best for traditional image processing functions such as convolution, equalization, histograms, and so on, which operate by manipulation of the brightness values since I is equally dependent on R, G, and B. The HSV color space is preferred for manipulation of hue and saturation (to shift colors or adjust the amount of color) since it yields a greater dynamic range of saturation.

3.2.2 Texture

Texture reflects the texture of the entire image. Texture is most useful for full images of textures, such as catalogs of wood grains, marble, sand, or stones. A variety of techniques have been developed for measuring texture similarity. Most techniques rely on comparing values of what are known as second-order statistics calculated from query and stored images (John et al.). These methods calculate measures of image texture such as the degree of contrast, coarseness, directionality and regularity (Tamur et al., 1976; Niblace et al., 1993); or periodicity, directionality and randomness (Liu & Picard, 1996). Alternative methods of texture analysis for image retrieval include the use of Gabor filters (Manjunath & Ma, 1996) and fractals. Gabor filter (or Gabor wavelet) is widely adopted to extract texture features from the images for image retrieval, and has been shown to be very efficient. Manjunath and Ma have shown that image retrieval using Gabor features outperforms that using pyramid-structured wavelet transform (PWT) features, tree-structured wavelet transform (TWT) features and multiresolution simultaneous autoregressive model (MR-SAR) features.

Haralick (Haralick, 1979) and Van Gool (Gool et al., 1985) divide the techniques for texture description into two main categories: statistical and structural. Most natural textures can not be described by any structural placement rule, therefore the statistical methods are usually the methods of choice. One possible approach to reveal many of the statistical texture properties is by modelling the texture as an autoregressive (AR) stochastic process, using least squares parameter estimation. Letting s and r be coordinates in the 2-D coordinate system, a general causal or non-causal auto-regressive model may be written:

$$y(s) = \sum_{r \in N} \theta_r y(s - r) + e(s) \tag{22}$$

Where $y(s)$ is the image, θ_r are the model parameters, $e(s)$ is the prediction error process, and N is a neighbour set. The usefulness of this modelling is demonstrated with experiments showing that it is possible to create synthetic textures with visual properties similar to natural textures.

3.2.3 Shape

Shape represents the shapes that appear in the image. Shapes are determined by identifying regions of uniform color. In the absence of color information or in the presence of images with similar colors, it becomes imperative to use additional image attributes for an efficient retrieval. Shape is useful to capture objects such as horizon lines in landscapes, rectangular shapes in buildings, and organic shapes such as trees. Shape is very useful for querying on simple shapes (like circles, polygons, or diagonal lines) especially when the query image is drawn by hand. Incorporating rotation invariance in shape matching generally increases the computational requirements.

4. Image indexing and retrieval

Content-based indexing and retrieval based on information contained in the pixel data of images is expected to have a great impact on image databases. The ideal CBIR system from a user perspective would involve what is referred to as semantic retrieval.

4.1 Feature-based retrieval

Object segmentation and tracking is a key component for new generation of digital video representation, transmission and manipulations. The schema provides a general framework for video object extraction, indexing, and classification. By video objects, here we refer to objects of interest including salient low-level image regions (uniform color/texture regions), moving foreground objects, and group of primitive objects satisfying spatio-temporal constraints (e.g., different regions of a car or a person). Automatic extraction of video objects at different levels can be used to generate a library of video data units, from which various functionalities can be developed. For example, video objects can be searched according to their visual features, including spatio-temporal attributes. High-level semantic concepts can be associated with groups of low-level objects through the use of domain knowledge or user interaction.

As mentioned above, in general, it is hard to track a meaningful object (e.g., a person) due to its dynamic complexity and ambiguity over space and time. Objects usually do not correspond to simple partitions based on single features like color or motion. Furthermore, definition of high-level objects tends to be domain dependent. On the other hand, objects can usually be divided into several spatial homogeneous regions according to image features. These features are relatively stable for each region over time. For example, color is a good candidate for low-level region tracking. It does not change significantly under varying image conditions, such as change in orientation, shift of view, partial occlusion or change of shape. Some texture features like coarseness and contrast also have nice invariance properties. Thus, homogenous color or texture regions are suitable candidates for primitive region segmentation. Further grouping of objects and semantic abstraction can be developed based on these basic feature regions and their spatio-temporal relationship. Based on these observations, we proposed the following model for video object tracking and indexing (Fig. 7).

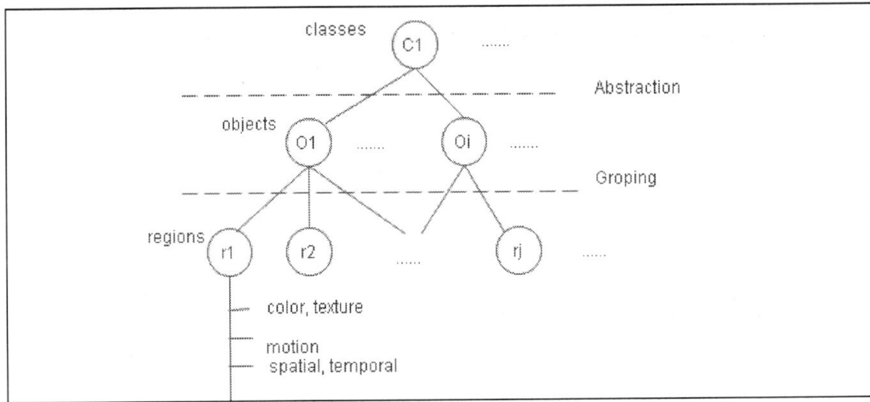

Fig. 7. Hierarchical representation of video objects

At the bottom level are primitive regions segmented according to color, texture, or motion measures. As these regions are tracked over time, temporal attributes such as trajectory, motion pattern, and life span can be obtained. The top level includes links to conceptual abstraction of video objects. For example, a group of video objects may be classified to moving human figure by identifying color regions (skin tone), spatial relationships (geometrical symmetry in the human models), and motion pattern of component regions. We propose the above hierarchical video object schema for content-based video indexing. One challenging issue here is to maximize the extent of useful information obtained from automatic image analysis tasks. A library of low-level regions and mid-level video objects can be constructed to be used in high-level semantic concept mapping. This general schema can be adapted to different specific domains efficiently and achieve higher performance.

4.2 Content-based retrieval

In this section, we will construct such a signature by using semantic information, namely information about the appearance of faces of distinct individuals. We will not concern ourselves with the extraction of face-related information, since ample work has been performed on the subject. Instead we will try to solve the problems of consistency and robustness with regards to face-based indexing, to represent face information with minimal redundancy, and also to find a fast (logarithmic-time) search method. All works on face-related information for video indexing until now have focused on the extraction of the face-related information and not on its organization and efficient indexing. In effect, they are works on face recognition with a view to application on indexing.

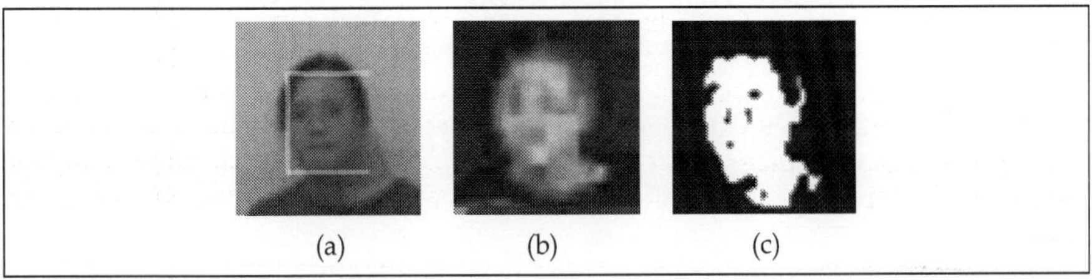

Fig. 8. Results of face detection: (a) the capture frame image; (b) result of similarity; (c) the binary result

The research on CBVIR has already a history of more than a dozen years. It has been started by using low-level features such as color, texture, shape, structure and space relationship, as well as (global and local) motion to represent the information content. Research on feature-based visual information retrieval has made quite a bit but limited success. Due to the considerable difference between the users' concerts on the semantic meaning and the appearances described by the above low-level features, the problem of semantic gap arises. One has to shift the research toward some high levels, and especially the semantic level. So, semantic-based visual information retrieval (CBVIR) begins in few years' ago and soon becomes a notable theme of CBVIR.

4.3 Semantic-based retrieval

How to bridge the gap between semantic meaning and perceptual feeling, which also exists between man and computer, has attracted much attention. Many efforts have been converged to SBVIR in recent years, though it is still in its commencement. As a consequence, there is a considerable requirement for books like this one, which attempts to make a summary of the past progresses and to bring together a broad selection of the latest results from researchers involved in state-of-the-art work on semantic-based visual information retrieval.

Several types of semantic gaps can be identified, showed in Fig. 8.:

- The semantic gap between different data sources - structured or unstructured
- The semantic gap between the operational data and the human interpretation of this data
- The semantic gap between people communicating about a certain information concept.

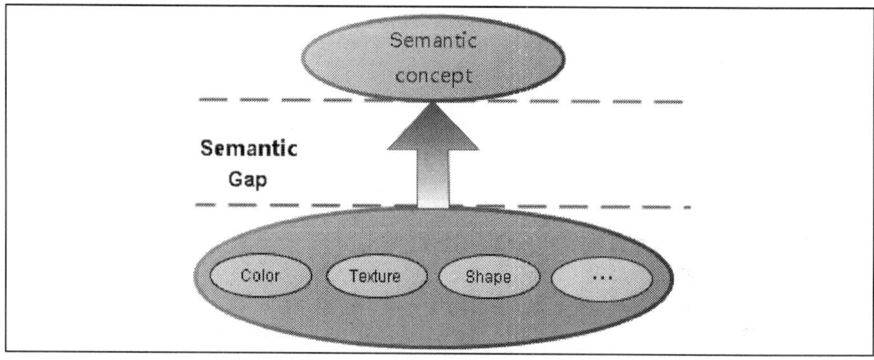

Fig. 8. Semantic Gap

Several applications aim to detect and solve different types of semantic gaps. They rage from search engines to automatic categorizers, from ETL systems to natural language interfaces, special functionality includes dashboards and text mining.

4.4 Performance evaluation

Performance evaluation is a necessary and benefical process, which provides annual feedback to staff members about job effectiveness and career guidance. The performance review is intended to be a fair and balanced assessment of an employee's performance. To assist supervisors and department heads in conducting performance reviews, the HR-Knoxville Office has introduced new Performance Review forms and procedures for use in Knoxville.

The Performance Review Summary Form is designed to record the results of the employee's annual evaluation. During the performance review meeting with the employee, use the Performance Review Summary Form to record an overall evaluation in:

- Accomplishments
- service and relationships
- dependability
- adaptability and flexibility
- and decision making or problem solving.

5. Software realization

Digital systems that process image data generally involve a mixture of software and hardware. This section describes some of the software that is available for developing image and video processing algorithms. Once an algorithm has been developed and is ready for operational use, it is often implemented in one of the standard compiled languages.

5.1 Matlab

Matlab support images generated by a wide range of devices, including digital cameras, frame grabbers, satellite and airborne sensors, medical imaging devices, microscopes, telescopes, and other scientific instruments.

Image Processing Toolbox™ software provides a comprehensive set of reference-standard algorithms and graphical tools for image processing, analysis, visualization, and algorithm development. You can restore noisy or degraded images, enhance images for improved intelligibility, extract features, analyze shapes and textures, and register two images. Most toolbox functions are written in the open MATLAB® language, giving you the ability to inspect the algorithms, modify the source code, and create your own custom functions.

5.2 OpenCV

OpenCV is a computer vision library originally developed by Intel. It focuses mainly on real-time image processing, as such, if it find Intel's Integrated Performance Primitives on the system, it will use these commercial optimized routines to accelerate itself. It is free for commercial and research use under a BSD license. The library is cross-platform, and runs on Windows, Mac OS X, Linux, PSP, VCRT (Real-Time OS on Smart camera) and other embedded devices. It focuses mainly on real-time image processing, as such, if it finds Intel's Integrated Performance Primitives on the system, it will use these commercial optimized routines to accelerate itself. Released under the terms of the BSD license, OpenCV is open source software.

The OpenCV library is mainly written in C, which makes it portable to some specific platforms such as Digital signal processor. But wrappers for languages such as C# and Python have been developed to encourage adoption by a wider audience.

6. Future research and conclusions

As content-based retrieval techniques of multimedia objects become more effective, we believe a similar semi-automatic annotation framework can be used for other multimedia database applications. The use of image sequences to depict motion dates back nearly two centuries. One of the earlier approaches to motion picture "display" was invented in 1834 by the mathematician William George Horner. In this chapter we have reviewed the current state of the art in automatic generation of features for images.

We present a semi-automatic annotation strategy that employs available image retrieval algorithms and relevance feedback user interfaces. The semi-automatic image annotation strategy can be embedded into the image database management system and is implicit to users during the daily use of the system. The semi-automatic annotation of the images will continue to improve as the usage of the image retrieval and feedback increases. It therefore avoids tedious manual annotation and the uncertainty of fully automatic annotation. This strategy is especially useful in a dynamic database system, in which new images are continuously being imported over time.

The problem of deriving good evaluation schemes for automatically generated semantic concept is still complex and open.

7. Acknowledgments

This work is supported by the research and application of intelligent equipment based on untouched techniques for children under 8 years old of BMSTC & Beijing Municipal Education Commission (No. 2007B06 & No. KM200810028017).

8. References

Michael Lew, et al. (2006). Content-based Multimedia Information Retrieval: State of the Art and Challenges, *ACM Transactions on Multimedia Computing, Communications, and Applications,* pp. 1-19

Khalid S.; Jerzy P. & Romuald M. (2006). *Content-Based Image Retrieval - A Survey,* Biometrics, Computer Security Systems and Artificial Intelligence Applications Springer, ISBN: 978-0-387-36232-8 (Print) 978-0-387-36503-9 (Online), pp: 31-44

J. Vendrig. *Filter image browsing: a study to image retrieval in large pictorial databases.* Master's thesis, Dept. Computer Science, University of Amsterdam, The Netherlands, http://carol.wins.uva.nl/~vendrig/thesis/, February 1997.

Flickner M.; Sawhney H. et al. (1995). Query by image and video content: The QBIC system. *IEEE Computer,* 28(9), pp: 23-32

MIR (1996). MTR A: Evaluation frameworks for interactive multimedia retrieval applications. Esprit working group 20039., http://www.dcs.gla.ac.uk/mira/.

Gupta A. & Jain R. (1997). Visual information retrieval. *Commun ACM,* 40(5), pp: 71–79

Feng S.; Manmatha R. & Lavrenko V. (2004). Multiple Bernoulli relevance models for image and video annotation. *In: Proc int'l conf computer vision and pattern recognition.* IEEE, Piscataway, pp: 1002–1009

Jacobs C.; Finkelstein A. & Salesin D. (1995). *Fast multiresolution image querying,* Technical report, University of Washington, US

Smith J. & Chang S-F. (1996). VisualSEEk: a fully automated content-based image query system, *In: Proc ACM int'l conf multimedia (SIGMM).* ACM, New York

Flickner M.; Sawhney H.; Niblack W.; et al. (1995). Query by image and video content: The QBIC system. IEEE Computer, pp: 23-31

Rui Y.; Huang T. S. & Mehrotra S. (1997). Content-based image retrieval with relevance feedback in MARS. *In Proc. of IEEE Int. Conf. on Image Processing '97,* pp: 815-818, Santa Barbara, California, USA

Bach J. R.; Fuller C. & Gupta A.; et al. (1996). The virage image search engine: An open framework for image management. *In Sethi I. K. and Jain R. J.; editors, Storage and Retrieval for Image and video Database IV,* vol. 2670 of Proceedings of SPIE, pp: 76-87

Honkela T.; Kaski S.; Lagus K. & Kohonen T. (1997). WEBSOM-self-organizing maps of document collections. *In Proceedings of WSOM'97, Workshop on Self-Organizing Maps,*

Espoo, Finland, pp: 310-315, Helsinki University of technology, Naural Networks Rearch Centre, Espoo, Finland

Weber R.; Schek J-J. & Blott S. (1998). Aquantitative analysis and performance study for similarity search methods in high-dimensional space. *In: Proc int'l conf very large databases,* New York, 24–27 August 1998, pp 194–205

Pennebaker W. & Mitchell J. (1993). *JPEG: Still Image Data compression Standard,* The Colour Resource, San Francisco, CA

Froment J. & Mallat S. (1992). Second generation compact image coding with wavelets. *In Chui C. K., editor, Wavelets: A tutorial in Theory and Applications,* pp: 655-678, Academic Press, San Diego, CA

Barnsley M. & Hurd L. (1993). *Fractal Image Compression,* A K Peters.

Samet H. (1984). The quadtree and related hierarchical data structures. *ACM Comp.* Surv., 16: 187-260.

Bracewell R. N. (1986). *The Fourier Transform and Its Applications.* McGraw-Hill, New York

Abdou I. E. & Schowengerdt R. A. (1982). Analysis of linear interpolation schemes for bi-level image applicatio, *IBM Journal of Research and Development,* vol. 26, pp: 667-680

Ding H.; Ding X. Q.; Wang S. J. (2008). Texture Fusion Based Wavelet Transform Applied to Video Text Enhancement, *Journal of Information and Computational Science,* pp: 2083-2090

John P. Eakins & Margaret E. Graham, *Content-based Image Retrieval: A Report to the JISC Technology Applications Program,* www.unn.ac.uk/iidr/research/cbir/report.html.

Tamura H.; Mori S. & T. Yamawaki. (1976). Texture features corresponding to visual perception, *IEEE Trans. on Systems,* Man and Cybernetics. 6(4), pp: 460-473

Niblack W. et. al. (1993). The QBIC Project: Querying Images by Content Using Color, Texture and Shape, *Proc. of the Conference Storage and Retrieval for Image and Video Databases,* SPIE vol.1908, pp: 173-187

Liu F. & Picard R W. (1996). Periodicity, directionality and randomness: Wold features for image modelling and retrieval, *IEEE Transactions on Pattern Analysis and Machine Intelligence,* 18(7), pp: 722-733

Manjunath B. S. & Ma W. Y. (1996). Texture features for browsing and retrieval of large image data, *IEEE Transactions on Pattern Analysis and Machine Intelligence,* (Special Issue on Digital Libraries), Vol. 18 (8), pp: 837-842.

Kaplan L. M. et al. (1998). Fast texture database retrieval using extended fractal features, *In Storage and Retrieval for Image and Video Databases VI* (Sethi, I K and Jain, R C, eds), Proc SPIE 3312, 162-173, 1998.

John R. Smith. (1997). *Integrated Spatial and Feature Image System: Retrieval, Analysis and Compression,* Ph.D thesis, Columbia University, 1997.

Deng Y. (1999). *A Region Representation for Image and Video Retrieval,* Ph.D thesis, University of California, Santa Barbara, 1999.

Haralick R. M. (1979). Statistical and structural approaches to texture, *Proc. IEEE.* Vol 67, pp: 786-804

Gool L. V.; Dewaele P. & Oosterlinck A. (1985). Texture analysis anno 1983, *Computerr Vision*, Graphics and Image Processing, vol. 29, pp: 336-357.

Efficient 2-D DCT Computation from an Image Representation Point of View

G.A. Papakostas[1], D.E. Koulouriotis[2] and E.G. Karakasis[2]
[1]Democritus University of Thrace, Department of Electrical and Computer Engineering
*[2]Democritus University of Thrace, Department of Production
and Management Engineering*
Greece

1. Introduction

Discrete Cosine Transform (DCT) constitutes a powerful tool in signal processing, since its first introduction (Ahmed et al., 1974). It belongs to a class of mathematical operations that includes the well-known Fast Fourier Transform (FFT), having as basic operation taking a signal and transforming it from one type of representation to another. More precisely, DCT transforms a signal from the spatial domain to the frequency space, with minimum information redundancy, since its kernel functions (cosines) comprise an orthogonal basis.

The main advantage of the DCT transform is its high energy compactness and thus the resulted DCT coefficients fully describe the signal in process. This benefit in conjunction with its implementation simplicity has inspired the scientists to use DCT as the basic transform in the well known image compression standard calling JPEG (ISO/IEC, 1994). Particularly, a 2-D version of the DCT is used to compute the projection of an image in the orthogonal basis of cosines functions, by resulting to a set of coefficients that constitutes the DCT image domain. According to the JPEG standard these coefficients are being compressed in a next step by applying a specific quantization table and an entropy coding procedure.

Besides the usage of the 2-D DCT as part of image compression algorithms, it is widely used as feature extraction or dimensionality reduction method in pattern recognition applications (Sanderson & Paliwal, 2003; Er et al., 2005; Jadhav & Holambe, 2008; Liu & Liu, 2008), in image watermarking and data hiding (Qi et al., 2008; Choi et al., 2008; Alturki et al., 2007; Wong et al., 2007) and in various image processing applications (See et al., 2007; Krupinski & Purczynski, 2007; Abe & Iiguni, 2007).

From the above it is obvious that the applicability range of the 2-D DCT is wide and increases continuously. This fact has motivated many researchers to investigate and develop algorithms that accelerate the computation time needed to calculate the DCT coefficients of an image. As a result of this massive research, many algorithms that present high computation rates were proposed (Zeng et al., 2001; Diab et al., 2002; Wu et al., 2008; Shao et al., 2008; Plonka & Tasche, 2005) and many hardware implementations were presented (Nikara et al., 2006; Tan et al., 2001) through the years.

These algorithms manage to reduce the number of operations in terms of multiplications and additions, by applying common techniques with the DFT algorithms, where optimized arithmetic methodologies and matrix operations are applied.

A completely different methodology that is making use of the image's morphology and intensities distribution, which highly improves the computational rate of the 2-D DCT, is presented in this chapter, as alternative to the conventional one. Moreover, the algorithms' nature allows the collaboration with the already existing fast methods, in order to provide high computation rates.

2. 2-D Discrete Cosine Transform

The Discrete Cosine Transform (DCT) is a popular signal transformation method, which is making use of cosine functions of different frequencies, as kernels. There are several variants of DCT with slightly modified definitions and properties, like DCT I, II, III, IV, V-VIII (Wikipedia) with the corresponding inverse formulas.

Among these types the DCT II, is usually used in image processing and compression (JPEG, MPEG), because it has strong energy compaction, meaning that a few coefficients enclose the most of the signal in process.

The $(p+q)^{th}$ order DCT-II coefficient for an NxN image having intensity function $f(x,y)$, is described by the following formulas

$$C_{pq} = \frac{1}{\rho(p)\rho(q)} \sum_{x=0}^{N-1} \sum_{y=0}^{N-1} D_p(x) D_q(y) f(x,y) \tag{1}$$

with $0 \leq p,q,x,y \leq N\text{-}1$, and

$$D_n(t) = \cos\left(\frac{(2t+1)n\pi}{2N}\right) \tag{2}$$

is the cosine kernel function of the orthogonal basis, while

$$\rho(n) = \begin{cases} N & \text{if } n = 0 \\ N/2 & \text{otherwise} \end{cases} \tag{3}$$

is a normalization factor.

According to (1) there are a lot of computations that have to be performed in calculating a set of DCT coefficients, due to the cosine functions evaluations, but most of all due to the number of image's pixels. While in the case of blocked-DCT algorithm (1) is applied to an 8x8 image block and thus the number of pixels is quite small, in the case of the global-DCT the number of pixels is increasing and is equal to the total image pixels.

A novel methodology that attempts to reduce the complexity of the above formulas by modifying these definitions in a more simple form is presented, in the next section.

3. Improved 2-D DCT computation

As it can be seen from (1), the high computational complexity of the 2-D DCT computation process, lies on the calculation of the same quantities for the entire image and thus the computation time is highly dependent on the image size by resulting to a $O(N^2)$ complexity. This fact was the main point of inspiration of investigating alternative computation methodologies to decrease the complexity by simplifying the way the operations are performed.

Recently, the authors proposed a new algorithm to accelerate the computation of Legendre moments on binary images (Papakostas et al., 2007) and generalized it in the case of gray-scale images with application on the Geometric moments (Papakostas et al., 2008), based on a new image representation scheme called Image Slice Representation (ISR).

This new image representation method is adopted and applied on the computation of 2-D DCT coefficients, in order to improve the overall computation rate, as it will be verified by appropriate experiments.

3.1 Image Slice Representation (ISR)

The main idea behind the ISR is based on a novel image perspective according to which, each gray-scale image consisting of pixels having several intensities in the range [0,255], can be completely decomposed by a finite number of image slices of different intensity.

Each slice can be defined as the following definition describes,

Definition 1: Slice of a gray-scale image, of a certain intensity f_i, is the image with the same size and the same pixels of intensity f_i as the original one, while the rest of the pixels are considered to be black.

For example let us consider the following 4x4 gray-scale image, where the pixels' intensities have been highlighted, so that the decomposition result is clear.

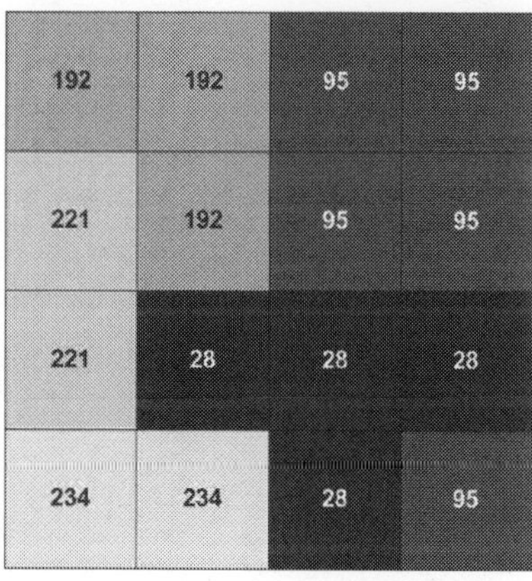

Fig. 1. Original gray-scale image, where the pixels' intensities are displayed as a number in the range [0,255].

If we consider the gray-scale image of Fig.1, as the resultant of non-overlapped image slices, having specific intensities in their pixels' positions, then we can decompose the original image to several slices, which can reconstruct it, by applying fundamental mathematical operations.

In this sense the image of Fig.1, can be decomposed to the following slices,

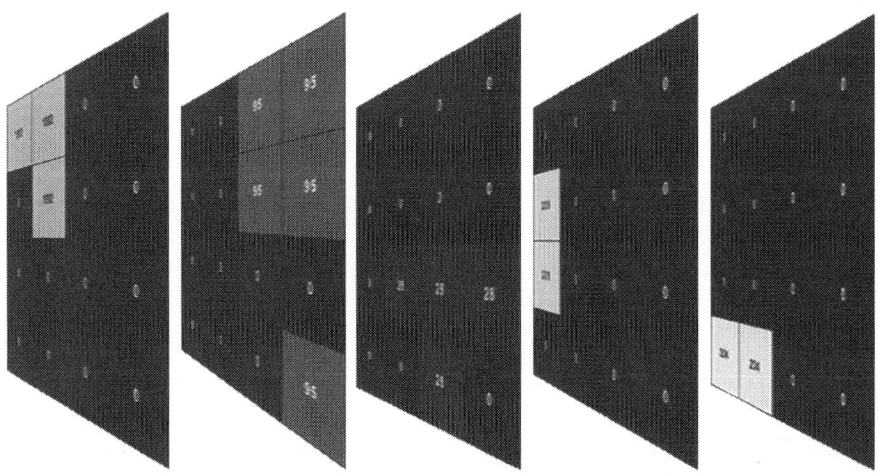

Fig. 2. Image Slice Representation of the image of Fig.1: 1st image slice of 192 intensity, 2nd image slice of 95 intensity, 3rd image slice of 28 intensity, 4th image slice of 221 intensity and 5th image slice of 234 intensity.

As a result of the Definition 1, is the following Lemma 1 and 2:

Lemma 1: Any 8-bit gray-scale image can be decomposed into a maximum of 255 slices, where each slice has pixels of one intensity value and black.

Lemma 2: The binary image as a special case of a gray-scale image consists of only one slice, the binary slice, where only the intensities of 255 and 0 are included.

The main advantage of this image decomposition is by describing a gray-scale image into a set of two-level slices of certain intensity; one can effectively apply the IBR (Papakostas et al., 2007) algorithm to compute the 2-D DCT coefficients of each binary slice and finally the total coefficients of the initial gray-scale, by superposition.

Based on the ISR representation, the intensity function $f(x,y)$ of a gray-scale image, can be defined as an expansion of the slices' intensity functions,

$$f\left(x,y\right) = \sum_{i=1}^{n} f_i\left(x,y\right) \tag{4}$$

where n is the number of slices (equal to the number of different intensity values) and $f_i(x,y)$ is the intensity function of the ith slice. In the case of a binary image n is equal to 1 and thus $f(x,y)=f_1(x,y)$.

By using the ISR representation scheme, the computation of the $(p+q)^{th}$ 2-D DCT coefficient (1) of a gray-scale image $f(x,y)$, can be performed according to,

$$C_{pq} = \frac{1}{\rho(p)\rho(q)}\sum_x\sum_y D_p(x)D_q(y)f(x,y) = \frac{1}{\rho(p)\rho(q)}\sum_x\sum_y D_p(x)D_q(y)\left(\sum_{i=1}^s f_i(x,y)\right)$$

$$= \frac{1}{\rho(p)\rho(q)}\sum_x\sum_y D_p(x)D_q(y)*\left(f_1(x,y)+f_2(x,y)+\dots+f_s(x,y)\right)$$

$$= \frac{1}{\rho(p)\rho(q)}\sum_x\sum_y D_p(x)D_q(y)f_1(x,y)+\frac{1}{\rho(p)\rho(q)}\sum_x\sum_y D_p(x)D_q(y)f_2(x,y)+\dots \quad (5)$$

$$+ \frac{1}{\rho(p)\rho(q)}\sum_x\sum_y D_p(x)D_q(y)f_s(x,y)$$

$$= f_1\left[\frac{1}{\rho(p)\rho(q)}\sum_{x_1}\sum_{y_1} D_p^1(x_1)D_q^1(y_1)\right]+f_2\left[\frac{1}{\rho(p)\rho(q)}\sum_{x_2}\sum_{y_2} D_p^2(x_2)D_q^2(y_2)\right]+\dots$$

$$+ f_s\left[\frac{1}{\rho(p)\rho(q)}\sum_{x_s}\sum_{y_s} D_p^s(x_s)D_q^s(y_s)\right]$$

$$= f_1 C_{pq}^1 + f_2 C_{pq}^2 + \dots + f_s C_{pq}^s$$

where f_i and C_{pq}^i, $i=1,2,\dots,s$ are the intensity functions of the slices and the corresponding $(p+q)^{th}$ order coefficient of the ith binary slice, respectively.

The corresponding coefficient of a binary slice C_{pq}^i, is the coefficient computed by considering a block representation of the image (Papakostas et al., 2007), as follows

$$C_{pq}^i = \sum_{j=0}^{k-1} C_{pq}(b_j) = \sum_{j=0}^{k-1} \sum_{x=x_{1,b_j}}^{x_{2,b_j}} \sum_{y=y_{1,b_j}}^{y_{2,b_j}} D_p(x)D_q(y) = \sum_{j=0}^{k-1}\left(\sum_{x=x_{1,b_j}}^{x_{2,b_j}} D_p(x)\right)\left(\sum_{y=y_{1,b_j}}^{y_{2,b_j}} D_q(y)\right) \quad (6)$$

where x_{1,b_i}, x_{2,b_i} and y_{1,b_i}, y_{2,b_i} are the coordinates of the block b_i, with respect to the horizontal and vertical axis, respectively.

The proposed methodology has already been applied to the computation of binary and gray-scale images' moments in (Papakostas et al., 2007) and (Papakostas et al., 2008) respectively, with remarkable results.

As a result of the above analysis (5) and (6), is the following Proposition 1,

Proposition 1: The $(p+q)^{th}$ order 2-D DCT coefficient of a gray-scale image is equal to the *"intensity-weighted"* sum of the same order coefficients of a number of binary slices.

3.2 Partial Image Block Representation algorithm – PIBR

Once a gray-scale image is decomposed to several slices according to the ISR method presented above, each slice can be considered as a two-level image where the IBR algorithm can be effectively applied.

While the separate application of the IBR algorithm to each slice significantly increases the overall block extraction time, a modified IBR algorithm, which extracts the image blocks in a single pass, is introduced in the sequel. This algorithm is called PIBR (Partial Image Block Representation) and consists of the same steps with the IBR, but with the extra process of extracting blocks of all intensity values.

The PIBR algorithm consists of one pass of the image and a bookkeeping process. More precisely, the algorithm is described by the following steps:

Algorithm – PIBR

Step 1.   Consider each line y of the image f and find the object level intervals for each intensity value that exists in line y.

Step 2.   Compare the intervals and blocks that have the same intensity in line y-1.

Step 3.   If an interval does not match with any block of the same intensity, then it is the beginning of a new block.

Step 4.   If a block matches with an interval of the same intensity, the end of the block is in the line y.

■

As a result of the application of the above algorithm, are several sets of rectangular blocks, having the same intensity value. After the blocks extraction, the image can be redefined in terms of blocks of different intensities, instead of individual pixels as,

$$f(x,y) = \left\{ f_i\left(x_i, y_i\right) : i = 1, 2, 3, .., n \right\} \ where \ \ f_i\left(x_i, y_i\right) = \left\{ b_{ij} : j = 0, 1, ..., k_i - 1 \right\} \quad (7)$$

where n is the number of image slices (maximum 255) and k_i is the number of image blocks having intensity i. Each block is described by two pixels, the upper left and down right corner pixels of the block.

Once the blocks of all slices are extracted, (6) can be applied to compute the 2-D DCT coefficients of each slice and then by using (5) the corresponding coefficient of the original gray-scale image.

It has to be noted that the procedure of extracting image's slices and slice's blocks, does not add significant overhead in the overall process, something which is verified by the experimental study taken place and presented in the next section.

3.3 Complexity analysis

Before proceeding with the experiments to investigate the performance of the proposed methodology in comparison with the conventional one, a detailed analysis of the algorithm's complexity is somewhat necessary in order to study its computational efficiency.

The following analysis, considers the worst case of image's intensities distribution which corresponds to the image called Chessboard defined as: *f(i,j)=0 (black) or f(i,j)=1 (white), f(i,j)≠{f(i-1,j), f(i+1,j), f(i,j-1), f(i,j+1)}.*

In the following Table 1, the computational complexity of the proposed algorithm in computing a single 2-D DCT coefficient of an *NxN* image, in the worst case, in comparison with the conventional method, in terms of the number of fundamental operations, is presented.

	Direct Method	Proposed Method
Multiplications	*10*N² + 2*	*9*N² + 4*
Additions	*3*N*M*	*3*N² + 1*
Divisions	*2*N² + 1*	*2*N² + 1*
Kernel Computations	*2*N²*	*2*N²*

Table 1. Algorithms' computational complexity.

From Table 1, it is clear that the use of the ISR can significantly reduce the number of multiplications required in order to compute a single coefficient, while the rest operations remain quite the same.

This outperformance, is reinforced in the case of multiple coefficients computation and in arbitrary images where the number of extracted blocks are smaller but with wider area.

4. Experimental study

In order to investigate the computational performance of the proposed methodology, appropriate experiments have taken place, in a 3.2 GHz PC having 1GB RAM, in C++ programming language and their results are presented in this section.

For the sake of the experiments three well known benchmark images and an artificial one have been selected, the Lena, F16, Boat and Chessboard images having 128x128 pixels size, as depicted in the following Fig.3. The images of Fig.3, is in gray-scale format but the same experiments are repeated and for their binary versions, since the usage of binary images are more suitable in real-time pattern recognition systems, where there are constraints on the amount of information that can be processed in real-time sense.

The experiments are performed in two directions: the performance of the proposed computation scheme in computing the 2-D DCT of the whole image, a common practice in pattern recognition applications where the resulted coefficients are used as discriminative features, called global-mode is investigated firstly.

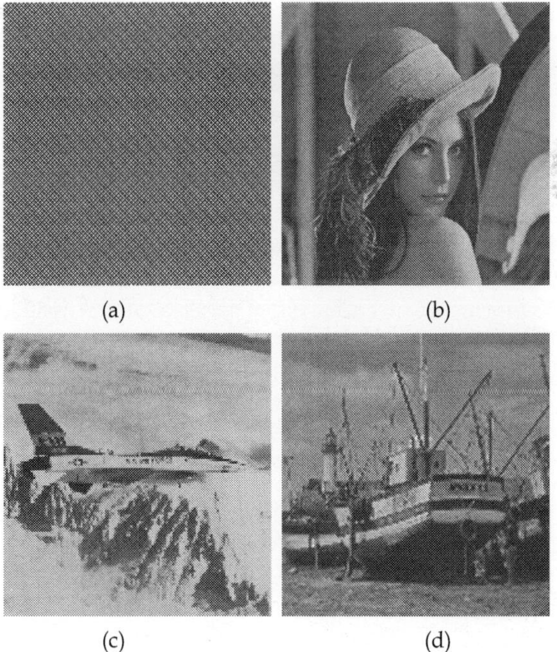

Fig. 3. Benchmark images (a) Chessboard, (b) Lena, (c) F16 and (d) Boat in gray-scale format.

In a second state, the efficiency of computing the 2-D DCT in a block-mode, meaning that the algorithm is applied in a finite number of image sub-blocks, which is a common policy in the case of image compression applications such as JPEG, and the dependency of the computation speed on the block size is derived. It has to be remarked that the complexity of the two algorithms, as already presented in section 3.3, is independent of the order (p,q) of the coefficient and thus the complexity of computing a certain number of coefficients is multiple of the corresponding complexity of one.

Direction I - *global-mode*

According to this experimental direction, the novel algorithm is applied in the entire image and its performance is compared to the corresponding of the conventional method. In the following Table 2, the computation statistics for the case of the test images are presented in details.

Operation Type	Method	Chessboard Image	Lena Image	F16 Image	Boat Image
Multiplications	*Direct*	163842	163842	163842	163842
	Proposed	147460	139263	136100	138204
Additions	*Direct*	49152	49152	49152	49152
	Proposed	49153	49103	48904	49129
Divisions	*Direct*	32769	32769	32769	32769
	Proposed	32769	31088	30449	30873
Kernel Computations	*Direct*	32768	32768	32768	32768
	Proposed	32768	31087	30448	30872
Total	*Direct*	278531	278531	278531	278531
	Proposed	262150	250655	245901	249078
Total Reduction (%)		5.88%	10.00%	11.71%	10.57%

Table 2. Performance (in number of operations) of the algorithms of computing a single DCT coefficient, for the set of all gray-scale test images.

The above results justify the theoretical analysis about the algorithms' complexity presented in section 3.3 and show that the introduced methodology requires less fundamental operations in comparison to the conventional method. Chessboard image represents the worst case image for the ISR since the number of extracted slices is very high equal to the half of image's pixels. Even in the case of the chessboard image the proposed method outperforms the traditional one, by reducing the total operations of about 5.88%, while for the other images this reduction approaches 10% in almost all cases.

Table 3, illustrates some useful performance statistics of applying ISR to the gray-scale images, such as the time needed to extract image's blocks, the number of extracted slices and the total blocks. As it can be seen from this table, the block extraction time is a fast procedure that does not add significant overhead in the whole computation and the number of extracted blocks varies depending on the image's intensities distribution.

	Chessboard Image	Lena Image	F16 Image	Boat Image
Block Extraction Time(msecs)	0.6434	0.6584	0.6912	0.6891
Num. of Blocks	16384	14708	14095	14501
Num. of Intensity Slices	2	205	211	213

Table 3. Performance statistics of applying ISR to the gray-scale benchmark images.

Since DCT coefficients are widely used as discriminative features to pattern classification applications, there is an increasing interest in implementing the process of coefficients extraction in an embedded system having a microprocessor as basic processing unit.

		Chessboard Image	Lena Image	F16 Image	Boat Image
Multiplications	*Direct*	163842	163842	163842	163842
	Proposed	147460	55330	60283	60107
Additions	*Direct*	49152	49152	49152	49152
	Proposed	49153	26881	29322	29152
Divisions	*Direct*	32769	32769	32769	32769
	Proposed	32769	13484	14746	14703
Kernel Computations	*Direct*	32768	32768	32768	32768
	Proposed	32768	13483	14745	14702
Total	*Direct*	278531	278531	278531	278531
	Proposed	262150	109178	119096	118664
Total Reduction (%)		5.88%	60.80%	57.27%	57.39%

Table 4. Performance (in number of operations) of the algorithms of computing a single DCT coefficient, for the set of all binary test images.

In these applications the need of real-time processing and resources restrictions (memory resources) constitute major issues of the software developer in implementing any time consuming algorithm such as 2-D DCT. Binary images comprise a good choice that satisfies the two above requirements and thus the study of the proposed algorithm's performance on bi-level images is of significant importance.

In this way, the gray-scale images of Fig.3 are initially converted to binary format by applying the well known Otsu's thresholding algorithm (Otsu, 1979) and the same experiments are executed in the resulted binary images. The corresponding results are presented in the above Table 4.

Table 4, shows that the efficiency of using the proposed method for binary images is significant, since it achieves 60% reduction of the total operations in comparison with the conventional method. This result is justified by the fact that in the case of binary images the number of extracted blocks is low while blocks' area is increased and thus according to (5)-(6), the whole processing is less time consuming.

The corresponding statistics of applying ISR to the binary images are depicted in the following Table 5, where it can be observed that the number of extracted blocks is small indeed.

	Chessboard Image	Lena Image	F16 Image	Boat Image
Block Extraction Time(msecs)	0.6434	0.1966	0.1778	0.1810
Num. of Blocks	16384	1394	1299	1295
Num. of Intensity Slices	2	2	2	2

Table 5. Performance statistics of applying ISR to the binary benchmark images.

Conclusively, it can be declared that the proposed methodology can be effectively applied to accelerate the computation of the 2-D DCT when the transform is applied on the entire image. While the proposed algorithm presents remarkable performance in gray-scale images, in the special case of binary images, the algorithm outperforms the conventional method totally, by making it appropriate for real-time, performance demanding applications.

Direction II – *block-mode*

Due to the high popularity of DCT in image compression methods, it is of significant importance to investigate the performance of the proposed methodology when applied on a sub-block of the image (block-mode), as it is performed in the JPEG standard.

As part of the JPEG standard, the 2-D DCT is applied on 8x8 image sub-blocks, but it is important to investigate the behaviour of the method in several dimensions of image's sub-blocks. Therefore, it is decided to study the algorithm for 2x2, 4x4, 8x8, and 16x16, sub-blocks in both gray-scale and binary benchmark images and the results are illustrated in Fig.4 and Fig.5 respectively.

Significant conclusions can be derived from these figures, about the performance of the proposed methodology when it is applied in a block-mode. The computation of 2-D DCT of an image decomposed to sub-blocks of $n \times n$ size, is accelerated by using the ISR for sub-block size greater than 8x8 considering a gray-scale format, while in binary images this acceleration occurs earlier.

Therefore, the use of the proposed methodology in the case of binary images improves the overall computation rate but when applied on gray-scale images the advantages of the method are restricted for sub-blocks greater than the 8x8 size, which is the official size used in the standard JPEG. This fact generates some questions about the efficiency of the introduced algorithm, since the usefulness of sub-block size greater than 8x8 in JPEG compression has to be studied.

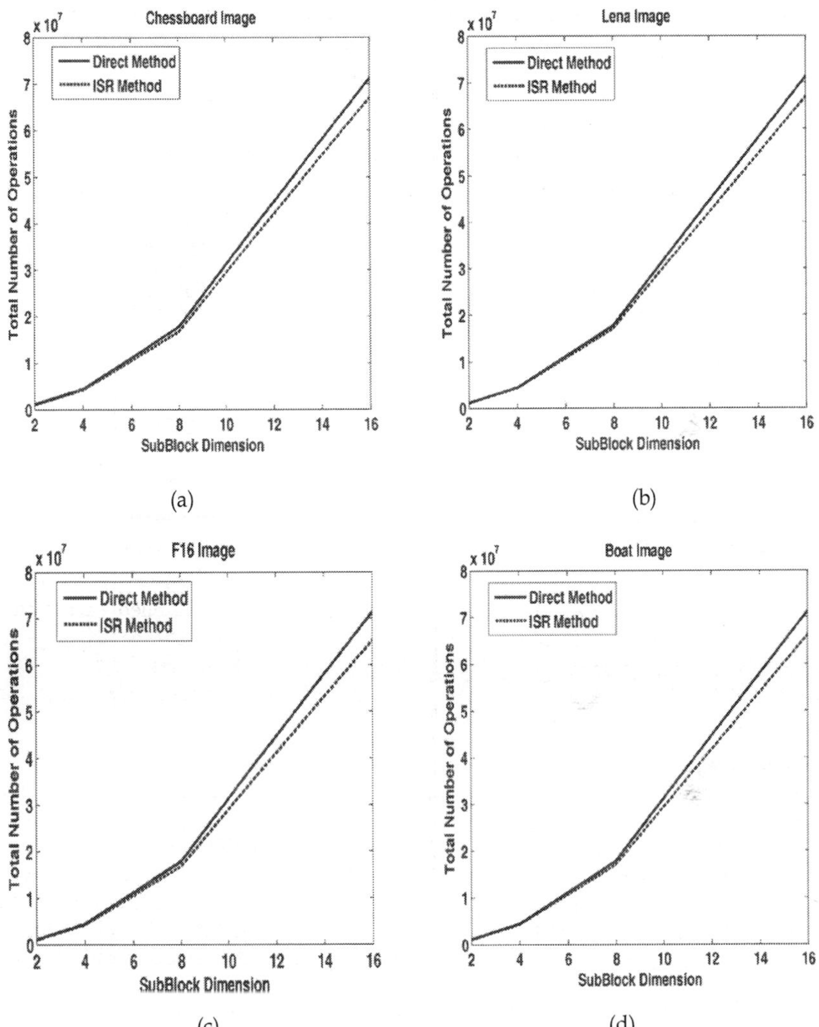

Fig. 4. Total operations in respect to sub-block size for (a) Chessboard, (b) Lena, (c) F16 and (d) Boat gray-scale images.

For this reason, it is decided to investigate the compression performance of the JPEG under variable sub-block sizes. The compression ratio for a fixed image quality (MSE – Mean Squared Error) and for 2x2, 4x4, 8x8 and 16x16 sub-block size is computed and the results are displayed in the following Fig.6. These results testify that the 8x8 sub-block size is the optimum choice regarding the compression ratio and the image quality, an observation which deals with the JPEG standard.

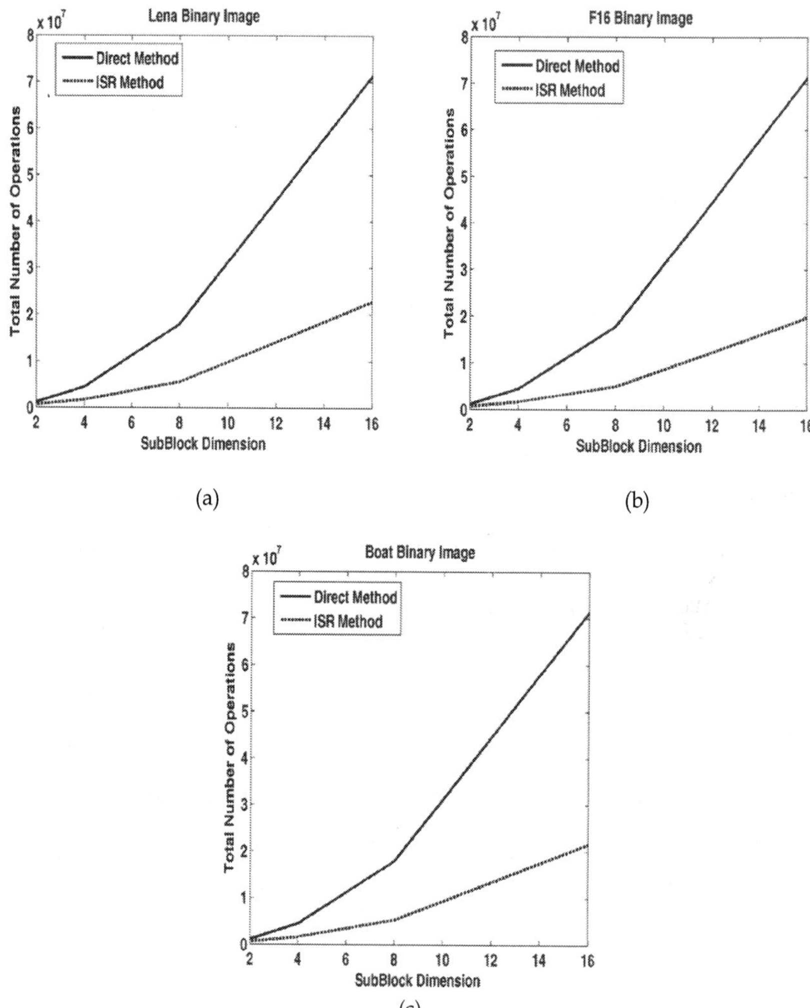

Fig. 5. Total operations in respect to sub-block size for (a) Lena, (b) F16 and (c) Boat binary images.

5. Conclusion

A novel methodology that ensures the computation of 2-D DCT coefficients in gray-scale images as well as in binary ones, with high computation rates, was presented in the previous sections. Through a new image representation scheme, called ISR (Image Slice Representation) the 2-D DCT coefficients can be computed in significantly reduced time, with the same accuracy.

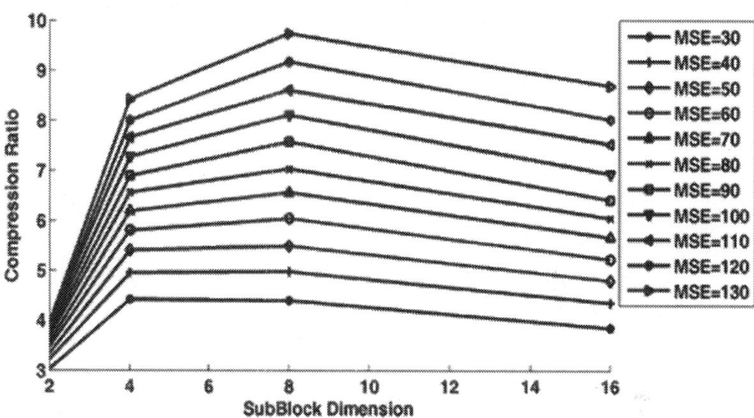

Fig. 6. Compression performance of JPEG for various sub-block sizes.

Appropriate experiments prove that the new algorithm totally outperforms the conventional method, in the case the algorithm applied on the entire image area for any image type, while in its blocked version the advantages were obvious for sub-block sizes greater than 8x8.
The experimental results are very promising and in conjunction to the capability of the methodology to collaborate with any of the existent fast algorithms, it can be a good choice for real-time and time demanding applications.

6. References

Abe, Y. & Iiguni, Y. (2007). Image restoration from a downsampled image by using the DCT. *Signal Processing*, Vol. 87, No. 10, pp. 2370–2380.

Ahmed, N.; Natarajan, T. & Rao, K.R. (1974). Discrete cosine transform. *IEEE Trans. Computers*, Vol. 23, No. 1, pp. 90-93.

Alturki, F.T.; Almutairi, A.F. & Mersereauu, R.M. (2007). Analysis of blind data hiding using discrete cosine transform phase modulation. *Signal Processing: Image Communication*, Vol. 22, No. 4, pp. 347-362.

Choi, H.J.; Seo, Y.H.; Yoo, J.S. & Kim, D.W. (2008). Digital watermarking technique for holography interference patterns in a transform domain. *Optics and Lasers in Engineering*, Vol. 46, No. 4, pp. 343-348.

Diab, C.; Oueidat, M. & Prost, R. (2002). A new IDCT-DFT relationship reducing the IDCT computational cost. *IEEE Trans. Signal Processing*, Vol. 50, No. 7, pp. 1681-1684.

Er, M.J.; Chen, W. & Wu, S. (2005). High-Speed face recognition based on discrete cosine transform and RBF neural networks. *IEEE Trans. on Neural Networks*, Vol. 16, No. 3, pp. 679-691.

ISO/IEC 10918-1, (1994). Digital compression and coding of continuous-tone still images: Requirements and guidelines.

Jadhav, D.V. & Holambe, R.S. (2008). Radon and discrete cosine transforms based feature extraction and dimensionality reduction approach for face recognition. *Signal Processing*, Vol. 88, No. 10, pp. 2604-2609.

Krupinski, R. & Purczynski, J. (2007). Modeling the distribution of DCT coefficients for JPEG reconstruction. *Signal Processing: Image Communication*, Vol. 22, No. 5, pp. 439-447.

Liu, Z. & Liu, C. (2008). Fusion of the complementary Discrete Cosine Features in the YIQ color space for face recognition. *Computer Vision and Image Understanding*, Vol. 111, No. 3, pp. 249-262.

Nikara, J.A.; Takala, J.H. & Astola, J.T. (2006). Discrete cosine and sine transforms-regular algorithms and pipeline architectures. *Signal Processing*, Vol. 86, No. 2, pp. 230–249.

Otsu, N. (1979). A threshold selection method from gray-level histograms. *IEEE Trans. Systems Man Cybernet.*, Vol. 9, pp. 62– 66.

Papakostas, G.A.; Karakasis, E.G. & Koulouriotis, D.E. (2008). Efficient and accurate computation of geometric moments on gray-scale images. *Pattern Recognition*, Vol. 41, No. 6, pp. 1895-1904.

Papakostas, G.A.; Karakasis, E.G. & Koulouriotis D.E. (2007). Exact and speedy computation of Legendre moments on binary Images. *Proceedings of 8th International Workshop on Image Analysis for Multimedia Interactive Services (WIAMIS'07)*, p.48, ISBN, Santorini – Greece, 2007.

Plonka, G. & Tasche, M. (2005). Fast and numerically stable algorithms for discrete cosine transforms. *Linear Algebra and its Applications*, Vol. 394, pp. 309–345.

Qi, H.; Zheng, D. & Zhao, J. (2008). Human visual system based adaptive digital image watermarking. *Signal Processing*, Vol. 88, No. 1, pp. 174-178.

Sanderson, C. & Paliwal, K.K. (2003). Features for robust face-based identity verification. *Signal Processing*, Vol. 83, No. 5, pp. 931-940.

See, K.W.; Loke, K.S.; Lee, P.A. & Loe, K.F. (2007). Image reconstruction using various discrete orthogonal polynomials in comparison with DCT. *Applied Mathematics and Computation*, Vol. 193, No. 2, pp. 346-359.

Shao, X. & Johnson, S.G. (2008). Type-IV DCT, DST, and MDCT algorithms with reduced numbers of arithmetic operations. *Signal Processing*, Vol. 88, No. 6, pp. 1313–1326.

Tan, T.C.; Bi, G.; Zeng, Y. & Tan, H.N. (2001). DCT hardware structure for sequentially presented data. *Signal Processing*, Vol. 81, No. 11, pp. 2333–2342.

Wikipedia contributors, Discrete cosine transform, Wikipedia, The Free Encyclopedia, http://en.wikipedia.org/w/index.php.

Wong, K.; Qi, X. & Tanaka, K. (2007). A DCT-based Mod4 steganographic method. *Signal Processing*, Vol. 87, No. 6, pp. 1251-1263.

Wu, J.S.; Shu, H.Z.; Senhadji, L. & Luo, L.M. (2008). A fast algorithm for the computation of 2-D forward and inverse MDCT. *Signal Processing*, Vol. 88, No. 6, pp. 1436–1446.

Zeng, Y.; Cheng, L.; Bi, G. & Kot, A.C. (2001). Integer DCTs and Fast Algorithms. *IEEE Tans. Signal Processing*, Vol. 49, No. 11, pp. 2774-2782.

## 3

Rank M-type Filters for Image Denoising

Francisco J. Gallegos-Funes and Alberto J. Rosales-Silva
National Polytechnic Institute of Mexico
Mexico

1. Introduction

Many different classes of filters have been proposed for removing noise from images (Astola & Kuosmanen, 1997; Bovik, 2000; Kotropoulos & Pitas, 2001). They are classified into several categories depending on specific applications. Linear filters are efficient for Gaussian noise removal but often distort edges and have poor performance against impulsive noise. Nonlinear filters are designed to suppress noise of different nature, they can remove impulsive noise and guarantee detail preservation. Rank order based filters have received considerable attention due to their inherent outlier rejection and detail preservation properties.

In the last decade, many useful techniques of multichannel signal processing based on vector processing have been investigated due to the inherent correlation that exists between the image channels compared to traditional component-wise approaches. Many applications of this technique are color image processing, remote sensing, robot vision, biomedical image processing, and high-definition television (HDTV). Different filtering techniques have been proposed for color imaging (Plataniotis & Venetsanopoulos, 2000). Particularly, nonlinear filters applied to color images have been designed to preserve edges and details, and remove impulsive noise. On the other hand, the filters based in the wavelet domain provide a better performance in terms of noise suppression in comparison with different spatial domain filters (Mahbubur Rahman & Kamrul Hasan, 2003).

The possibility to process 3D images presents a new application where it is necessary to improve the quality of 3D objects inside the image, suppressing a noise of different nature (impulsive, Gaussian noise, or may be by speckle one) that always affects the communication or acquisition process (Nikolaidis & Pitas, 2001). Multiplicative (speckle) noise is common for any system using a coherent sensor, for example, the ultrasound transducer. Other problem that is not trivial is the adaptation and implementation of the current filters, that have been investigated in different papers in the case of 2D image processing to process objects in 3D by use multiframe methods to increase the signal-to-noise ratio (SNR).

This chapter presents the capability features of robust Rank M-Type K-Nearest Neighbor (RMKNN) and Median M-Type L- (MML) filters for the removal of impulsive noise in gray-scale image processing applications (Gallegos & Ponomaryov, 2004; Gallegos-Funes et al., 2005; Gallegos-Funes et al., 2008). The proposed scheme is based on combined robust R- (median, Wilcoxon, Ansari-Bradley-Siegel-Tukey or Mood) and M-estimators, and modification of the KNN and L- filters that use the RM (Rank M-type) -estimator to calculate the robust point estimate of the pixels within the filtering window. So, such filters use the value of the central pixel within the filtering window to provide the preservation of fine details and the redescending M-estimators combined with the calculation of the rank estimator to obtain the sufficient impulsive noise rejection. Different types of influence functions in the M-estimator can be used to provide better impulsive noise suppression. We apply the proposed MML filter in SAR images which naturally have speckle noise to demonstrate that the speckle noise can be efficiently suppressed, while the sharpness and fine feature are preserved.

The robust Rank M-Type K-Nearest Neighbor (RMKNN) filters are adapted to work in color image denoising (Ponomaryov et al., 2005). We also present the 3D RMKNN and 3D MML filters which are compared with different nonlinear 2D filters which were adapted to 3D (Varela-Benitez et al., 2007a). The experimental results were realized by degraded an ultrasound sequence with different variance of speckle noise added to the natural speckle noise of the sequence. Finally, we adapt the RMKNN, MML, and different order statistics filters to work in the wavelet domain for the removal of impulsive and speckle noise in gray-scale and color image processing applications (Gallegos-Funes et al., 2007; Varela-Benitez et al., 2007b).

Another goal of this chapter is to demonstrate the possibility to implement the filters in order to process the image or sequence in real time by means of use of the Texas Instruments DSP TMS320C6701 and DSP TMS320C6711 to demonstrate that the proposed methods potentially could provide a real-time solution to quality video transmission.

Extensive simulation results with different gray scale and color images and video sequences have demonstrated that the proposed filters consistently outperform other filters by balancing the tradeoff between noise suppression, fine detail preservation, and color retention.

2. Rank M-type estimators

2.1 R-estimators

The R-estimators are a class of nonparametric robust estimators based on rank calculations (Hampel et al., 1986; Huber, 1981). We consider a two-samples of rank tests $x_1,...,x_m$ and $y_1,...,y_n$ as a two-samples with distributions $H(x)$ and $H(x+\Delta)$, where Δ is the shift of unknown location. Let $X_{(i)}$ be the rank of X_i in the pooled sample of size $N = m + n$. The rank test of $\Delta = 0$ against $\Delta > 0$ is based on the statistics test,

$$S = \frac{1}{m}\sum_{i=1}^{m} a_i\left(X_{(i)}\right) \tag{1}$$

Usually, the scores a_i are generated by the function J as follows:

$$a_i = N \int_{(i-1)/N}^{i/N} J(t)dt \tag{2}$$

The function $J(t)$ is symmetric in the sense of $J(1-t) = -J(t)$, satisfies $\int J(t)dt = 0$ and the coefficients a_i are given as $\sum_{i=1}^{n} a_i = 0$.

The median estimator can be derived from Laplace distribution function $f_0(x) = \dfrac{1}{2} e^{-|x|}$ with

function $J(t) = \begin{cases} -1 & t < \dfrac{1}{2} \\ 1 & t > \dfrac{1}{2} \end{cases}$ and is given in such a form (Hampel et al., 1986; Huber, 1981):

$$\hat{\theta}_{med} = \begin{cases} \dfrac{1}{2}\left(X_{\left(n/2\right)} + X_{\left(1+n/2\right)} \right), & \text{for even } n \\ X_{\left(\frac{n+1}{2}\right)}, & \text{for odd } n \end{cases} \tag{3}$$

where $X_{(j)}$ is the element with rank j. It is the best estimator when any *a priori* information about data X_i distribution shape and its moments is unavailable.

The Hodges-Lehmann estimator $J(t) = \left| t - \dfrac{1}{2} \right|$ is relational with Wilcoxon test and logistic

distribution function $f_0(x) = \dfrac{1}{1+e^{-x}}$. The corresponding rank estimator is the Wilcoxon R-estimator (Hampel et al., 1986; Huber, 1981):

$$\hat{\theta}_{\text{Wil}} = \underset{i \leq j}{\text{MED}} \left\{ \dfrac{1}{2}\left(X_{(i)} + X_{(j)} \right), \ i, j = 1, \ldots N \right\} \tag{4}$$

The Wilcoxon estimator is robust and unbiased. When the shape of the original data distribution is symmetrical, the such a test is known as the local asymptotically most powerful one.

Other R-estimations can be obtained by different type of functions $J(t)$. For example, the

functions Ansari-Bradley-Siegel-Tukey $J(t) = \left| t - \dfrac{1}{2} \right| - \dfrac{1}{4}$ and Mood $J(t) = \left(t - \dfrac{1}{2} \right)^2 - \dfrac{1}{12}$

determine the R-estimators (Hampel et al., 1986; Huber, 1981):

$$\hat{\theta}_{\text{ABST}} = \text{MED} \left\{ \begin{array}{ll} X_{(i)}, & i \leq \left[\dfrac{N}{2} \right] \\ \dfrac{1}{2}\left(X_{(i)} + X_{(j)} \right), & \left[\dfrac{N}{2} \right] < i \leq N \end{array} \right\} \tag{5}$$

$$\hat{\theta}_{\text{MOOD}} = \text{MED} \left\{ \begin{array}{ll} \dfrac{1}{2}\left(X_{(i)} + X_{(j)} \right), & i \leq 3 \\ X_{(i)}, & 3 < i \leq N \end{array} \right\} \tag{6}$$

2.2 M-estimators

The M-estimators are a generalization of maximum likelihood estimators (MLE) (Hampel et al., 1986; Huber, 1981). Their definition is given by a function ρ $\{\rho(X) = \ln(F(X))\}$ connected with the probability density function $F(X)$ of data samples X_i, $i = 1, \ldots, N$:

$$\theta = \arg\min_{\theta \in \Theta} \sum_{i=1}^{N} \rho(X_i - \theta) \tag{7}$$

The estimation of the location parameter θ can be found by calculating the partial derivative of ρ (with respect to θ) introducing the function $\psi(X,\theta) = \dfrac{\partial}{\partial\theta}\rho(X,\theta)$

$$\sum_{i=1}^{N} \psi(X_i - \theta) = 0 \tag{8}$$

where θ is a location parameter.

The robust M-estimator solution for θ is determined by imposing certain restrictions on the influence function $\psi(X)$ or the samples $X_i - \theta$, called censorization or trimming. The standard technique for the M-estimator assumes the use of Newton's iterative method that can be simplified by a single-step algorithm to calculate the lowered M-estimate of the average θ value (Astola & Kuosmanen, 1997)

$$\theta_{\mathbf{M}} = \frac{\displaystyle\sum_{i=1}^{N} X_i \tilde{\psi}\big(X_i - \mathrm{MED}\{\tilde{X}\}\big)}{\displaystyle\sum_{i=1}^{N} 1_{[-r.r]}\big(X_i - \mathrm{MED}\{\tilde{X}\}\big)} \tag{9}$$

where $\tilde{\psi}$ is the normalized function ψ: $\psi(X) = X\tilde{\psi}(X)$. It is evident that (9) represents the arithmetic average of $\displaystyle\sum_{i=1}^{n} \psi(X_i - \mathrm{MED}\{\mathbf{X}\})$, which is evaluated on the interval $[-r,r]$. The parameter r is connected with restrictions on the range of $\psi(X)$, for example, as it has been done in case of the simplest Huber's limiter type M-estimator for the normal distribution having heavy 'tails' (Huber, 1981)

$$\tilde{\psi}_r(X) = \min(r, \max(X,\ r)) = [X]_{-r}^{r} \tag{10}$$

Another way to derive the function $\tilde{\psi}(X)$ is to cut the outliers off the primary sample. This leads to the so-called lowered M-estimates. Hampel proved that the skipped median is the most robust lowered M-estimate (Hampel et al., 1986). Below we also use the simple cut (S) function. There exist also other well known influence functions in the literature. We also use the Hampel's three part redescending (H), Andrew's sine (A), Tukey biweight (T), and the Bernoulli (B) influence functions (Astola & Kuosmanen, 1997; Hampel et al., 1986). These functions are shown in Table 1.

2.3 RM-estimators

The proposal to enhance the robust properties of M-estimators and R-estimators by using the R-estimates consists of the procedure similar to the median average instead of arithmetic one (Gallegos-Funes et al., 2002; Gallegos & Ponomaryov 2004):

$$\theta_{\mathrm{medM}} = \mathrm{MED}\{X_i\tilde{\psi}(X_i - \mathrm{MED}\{\mathbf{X}\}), i=1,\ldots,N\} \tag{11}$$

$$\theta_{\mathrm{WilM}} = \underset{i\leq j}{\mathrm{MED}}\left\{\frac{1}{2}\big[X_i\tilde{\psi}(X_i - \mathrm{MED}\{\mathbf{X}\}) + X_j\tilde{\psi}(X_j - \mathrm{MED}\{\mathbf{X}\})\big], i=1,\ldots,N\right\} \tag{12}$$

Influence function	Formulae
Simple cut (S)	$\psi_{\mathrm{cut}(r)}(X) = X \cdot 1_{[-r,r]}(X) = \begin{cases} X, & \lvert X\rvert \leq r \\ 0, & \lvert X\rvert > r \end{cases}$
Hampel's three part redescending (H)	$\psi_{\alpha,\beta,r}(X) = \begin{cases} X, & 0 \leq \lvert X\rvert \leq \alpha \\ \alpha\cdot\mathrm{sgn}(X), & \alpha \leq \lvert X\rvert \leq \beta \\ \alpha\dfrac{r-\lvert X\rvert}{r-\beta}, & \beta \leq \lvert X\rvert \leq r \\ 0, & r \leq \lvert X\rvert \end{cases}$, where $0 < \alpha < \beta < r < \infty$.
Andrew's sine (A)	$\psi_{\sin(r)}(X) = \begin{cases} \sin(X/r), & \lvert X\rvert \leq r\pi \\ 0, & \lvert X\rvert > r\pi \end{cases}$
Tukey's biweight (T)	$\psi_{\mathrm{bi}(r)}(X) = \begin{cases} X^2(r^2 - X^2), & \lvert X\rvert \leq r \\ 0, & \lvert X\rvert > r \end{cases}$
Bernoulli (B)	$\psi_{\mathrm{ber}(r)}(X) = X^2\sqrt{r^2 - X^2} \cdot 1_{[-r,r]}(X)$

Table 1. Influence functions used in the filtering scheme to derive the robust redescending M-estimators.

Such an estimator is the combined RM-estimator. It should be noted that the RM-estimator (11) is the usual median when the function $\tilde{\psi}$ is represented by eq. (10). If the function $\tilde{\psi}$ is described by the simple cut function, it yields the skipped median. Other new RM-estimators applied below are followed from eqs. (5) and (6) (Gallegos-Funes et al., 2005):

$$\theta_{\mathrm{ABSTM}} = \underset{i\leq j}{\mathrm{MED}}\begin{cases} X_i\tilde{\psi}(X_i - \mathrm{MED}\{\mathbf{X}\}), & i \leq \dfrac{N}{2} \\ \dfrac{1}{2}\big[X_i\tilde{\psi}(X_i - \mathrm{MED}\{\mathbf{X}\}) + X_j\tilde{\psi}(X_j - \mathrm{MED}\{\mathbf{X}\})\big], & \dfrac{N}{2} < i \leq N \end{cases} \tag{13}$$

$$\theta_{\mathrm{MoodM}} = \underset{i\leq j}{\mathrm{MED}}\begin{cases} \dfrac{1}{2}\big[X_i\tilde{\psi}(X_i - \mathrm{MED}\{\mathbf{X}\}) + X_j\tilde{\psi}(X_j - \mathrm{MED}\{\mathbf{X}\})\big], & i \leq 3 \\ X_i\tilde{\psi}(X_i - \mathrm{MED}\{\mathbf{X}\}), & 3 < i \leq N \end{cases} \tag{14}$$

It is possible to expect that the robust properties of the RM-estimators can exceed the robust properties of the base R- and M- estimators. The R-estimator provides good properties of impulsive noise suppression and the M-estimator uses different influence functions according to the scheme proposed by Huber to provide better robustness, for these reasons it can be expected that the properties of combined RM-estimators could be better in comparison with R- and M- estimators (Gallegos-Funes et al., 2002; Gallegos & Ponomaryov 2004).

3. Rank M-type filters

To increase the robustness of standard filters, it is possible to employ different methods known in the robust-estimate theory, for example, the censoring or others (Astola & Kuosmanen, 1997; Peltonen & Kuosmanen, 2001). The known proposal to increase the quality of filtration via the preservation both the edges and small-size details in the image consists of the use of KNN image-filtering algorithm. Other proposal filtering schemes proposed here are the L-filter and the versions of KNN and L filters in wavelet domain.

3.1 Rank M-Type KNN filters

The following representation of the KNN filter is usually used $\theta_{KNN} = \sum_{i=1}^{n} a_i x_i \left/ \sum_{i=1}^{n} a_i \right.$ with

$$a_i = \begin{cases} 1, & \text{if } |x_i - x_c| \leq T \\ 0, & \text{otherwise} \end{cases}, \ x_c \text{ is the central pixel, and } T \text{ is a threshold (Astola & Kuosmanen,}$$

1997). If the threshold T is chosen to be twice of the standard noise deviation σ, this filter is known as the sigma filter. The KNN filter can be rewritten as $\theta_{KNN}(i,j) = \dfrac{1}{K} \sum_{m=-L}^{L} \sum_{n=-L}^{L} \psi(x(i+m,j+n))x(i+m,j+n)$ where $x(i+m,j+n)$ are the pixels in the filter window, $m,n = -L,\ldots,L$, and

$$\psi(x(i+m,j+n)) = \begin{cases} 1, & \begin{array}{l} \text{if } x(i+m,j+n) \text{ are } K \text{ samples whose values are closest to} \\ \text{the value of the central sample } x \text{ inside the filter window} \end{array} \\ 0, & \text{otherwise} \end{cases} .$$

To improve the robustness of the KNN filter that can preserve well both the edges and the fine details in absence of noise, we proposed to use the RM-estimator (11) given by $\theta_{MMKNN}(i,j) = \text{MED}\{\theta_{KNN}(i+m,j+n)\}$. So, the iterative Median M-type K-Nearest Neighbor filter can be written as (Gallegos-Funes et al., 2002; Gallegos & Ponomaryov 2004),

$$\theta_{MMKNN}^{(w)}(i,j) = \text{MED}\{h^{(w)}(i+m,j+n)\} \tag{15}$$

where $h^{(w)}(i+m,j+n)$ is a set of K_{close} values of pixels weighting in accordance with the used $\tilde{\psi}(X)$ influence function within the filter window closest to the estimate obtained at previous step $\theta_{MMKNN}^{(w-1)}(i,j)$. The initial estimate is $\theta_{MMKNN}^{(0)}(i,j) = x(i,j)$ and $\theta_{MMKNN}^{(w)}(i,j)$ denotes the estimate at the iteration w. $x(i,j)$ is the current or origin pixel contaminated by noise in the filtering window. The filtering window size is $N = (2L+1)^2$ and $m,n = -L,\ldots,L$. The current number of the nearest neighbor pixels K_{close} reflects the local data activity and impulsive noise presence (Gallegos & Ponomaryov 2004),

$$K_{close} = \begin{cases} K_{min} + aD_S, & (K_{min} + aD_S) \leq K_{max} \\ K_{max}, & \text{otherwise} \end{cases} \tag{16}$$

The parameter a controls the filter sensitivity for local data variance to detect the details. $K_{\min}$ is the minimal number of neighbours for noise removal and $K_{\max}$ is the maximal number of neighbours for edge restriction and detail smoothing. D_S is the impulsive detector, and MAD is the median of the absolute deviations from the median (Astola & Kuosmanen, 1997) which are defined as (Gallegos & Ponomaryov 2004):

$$D_S = \frac{\mathrm{MED}\left\{\,|x(i,j)-x(i+m,j+n)|\,\right\}}{\mathrm{MAD}\{x(i,j)\}} + 0.5\,\frac{\mathrm{MAD}\{x(i,j)\}}{\mathrm{MED}\{x(i+k,j+l)\}} \tag{17}$$

$$\mathrm{MAD}\{x(i,j)\} = \mathrm{MED}\left\{x(i+m,j+n)-\mathrm{MED}\{x(i+k,j+l)\}\right\} \tag{18}$$

In our experiments, a 3x3 window (i.e., $m,n=-1,\dots,1$ and $(2L+1)^2 = 9$) is applied. The algorithm finishes when $\theta^{(w)}_{\mathrm{MMKNN}}(i,j) = \theta^{(w-1)}_{\mathrm{MMKNN}}(i,j)$. The use of the influence functions mentioned above in the proposed filter (15) could provide good suppression of impulsive noise. We also propose for enhancement of the removal ability of MMKNN filter in the presence of impulsive noise to involve the standard median filter. The numerical simulations have shown that for $K_{close} > 7$ the MMKNN filter can be substituted by the *3x3 median* filter and for $K_{close} > 350$ we can use the *5x5 median* filter.

Other versions of Rank M-type K-Nearest Neighbor filters are given as follows (Gallegos-Funes et al., 2005; Ponomaryov et al., 2005),

$$\theta^{(w)}_{\mathrm{WMKNN}}(i,j) = \mathrm{MED}\left\{\frac{h^{(w)}(i+m,j+n)+h^{(w)}(i+m_1,j+n_1)}{2}\right\} \tag{19}$$

$$\theta^{(w)}_{\mathrm{ABSTMKNN}}(i,j) = \mathop{\mathrm{MED}}_{i\le j}\left\{\begin{array}{ll} h^{(w)}(i+m,j+n), & i,j\le\dfrac{N}{2} \\[2mm] \dfrac{h^{(w)}(i+m,j+n)+h^{(w)}(i+m_1,j+n_1)}{2}, & \dfrac{N}{2}<i \end{array}\right\} \tag{20}$$

$$\theta^{(w)}_{\mathrm{MOODMKNN}}(i,j) = \mathop{\mathrm{MED}}_{i\le j}\left\{\begin{array}{ll} h^{(w)}(i+m,j+n), & 3<i\le N \\[2mm] \dfrac{h^{(w)}(i+m,j+n)+h^{(w)}(i+m_1,j+n_1)}{2}, & i\le 3 \end{array}\right\} \tag{21}$$

3.2 Wavelet domain order statistics filter

This filter constitutes two filters (Gallegos-Funes et al., 2007): the filter based on redundancy of approaches (Gallegos-Funes et al., 2007) and the Wavelet domain Iterative Center Weighted Median (ICWMF) Filter (Mahbubur Rahman & Kamrul Hasan, 2003) as shown in Figure 1. For each color component of the noisy image it is necessary to apply all the steps contained in this structure. This technique applies up to 5 scaling levels for the details and only 1 scaling level for the approaches. Other operations are indicated to make clearer the wavelet analysis that it is carried out in this paper. We modify this structure in the block of the ICWMF. For that reason, the expressions used by the ICWMF to calculate the improved estimation of the variance field of the noisy wavelet coefficients will be required to indicate when and where different proposed filtering algorithms will take place to improve the performance of the proposed filter.

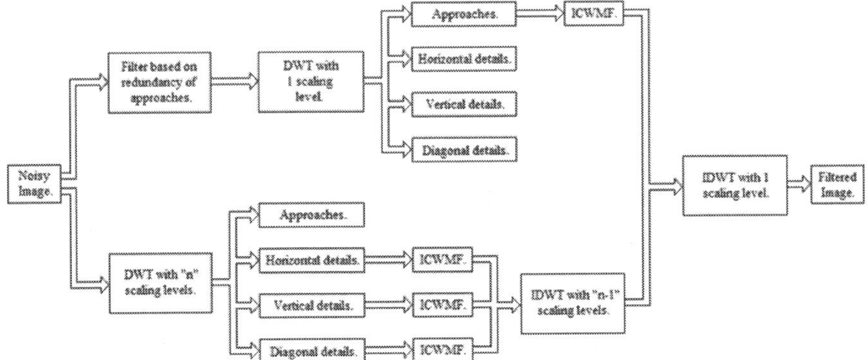

Fig. 1. Block diagram of the proposed filtering scheme of the Wavelet Domain Order Statistics Filter.

The first stage of the ICWMF that detects if a sample contains noise or not is given by:

$$\sigma_{gs}^2(k) = \begin{cases} \tilde{\sigma}_{gs}^2(k), & \text{if } \lambda_s \geq \lambda_{th} \\ med_{cw}(\tilde{\sigma}_{gs}^2(j)), & \text{otherwise} \end{cases} \qquad (22)$$

where $\tilde{\sigma}_{gs}^2$ is the variance field estimated previously, k is central sample in the filter window, j is one of the N sample contained into the window, λ_s is the standard deviation of the preliminary estimate of the signal coefficients variances $\tilde{\sigma}_s^2(k)$ in each scale, $\lambda_{th} = \sum_s \lambda_s 2^{-s} / \sum_s 2^{-s}$ is the discriminating threshold, s is the scale used in the wavelet analysis, and 2^{-s} is the weighting function (Mahbubur Rahman & Kamrul Hasan, 2003).

The *Signal dependent rank order mean* (SDROM) (Abreu et al., 1996), *Adaptive Center Weighed Median* (ACWM) (Chen & Wu, 2001), and *Median M-type KNN* (Gallegos-Funes et al., 2007) filters were applied to the proposed filter as a first detection block. But the *FIR Median Hybrid* (FIRMH) filter (Astola & Kuosmanen, 1997) was applied as a second detection block because this algorithm only constitutes the part of estimation of the noisy sample value (only if the sample was detected of this way) and the proposed filter can continue operating in all its sections in the same way. For this reason it is necessary to present the expression for the second detection block contained in the proposed filter structure (Mahbubur Rahman & Kamrul Hasan, 2003):

$$\begin{cases} med(\tilde{\sigma}_{gs}^2(j)) & \text{if } \tilde{\sigma}_{gs}^2(k) \leq \gamma\sigma_n^2 \\ \tilde{\sigma}_{gs}^2(k) + med(\tilde{\sigma}_{gs}^2(j) - \tilde{\sigma}_{gs}^2(k)) & \text{otherwise} \end{cases} \qquad (23)$$

The proposed filter uses the median algorithm represented as $med(\tilde{\sigma}_{gs}^2(j))$ to estimate the value of the central sample in a filter window if the sample is detected as noisy. It is possible to use other estimation algorithm such as the FIR Median Hybrid Filter that retains more information about the image.

3.3 Median M-type L-filter

We propose to improve the robustness of L-filter by means of use of RM-estimator (11). The representation of L-filter is $\theta_{\mathrm{L}} = \sum_{i=1}^{N} a_i \cdot X_{(i)}$ where $X_{(i)}$ is the ordered data sample, $i=1,...,N$, $a_i = \int_{-1/N}^{i/N} h(\lambda)d\lambda \Big/ \int_{0}^{1} h(\lambda)d\lambda$ are the weight coefficients, and $h(\lambda)$ is a probability density function (Kotropoulos & Pitas, 2001).

To introduce the MM-estimator (11) in the scheme of L-filter, we present the ordered data sample of L-filter as function of an influence function (Gallegos-Funes et al., 2008),

$$\theta_{\mathrm{L}} = \sum_{i=1}^{N} a_i \cdot \psi(X_i) \cdot X_i \tag{24}$$

where $N=(2L+1)^2$ is the filtering window size, $\psi(X_i) \cdot X_i$ is the ordered data sample, $\psi(u) = \begin{cases} c, & |u| \leq r \\ 0, & \text{otherwise} \end{cases}$ is the influence function, c is a constant, and r is connected with the range of $\psi(u)$.

Then, the non iterative MML filter can be obtained by the combination of L-filter (24) and the MM-estimator (11) (Gallegos-Funes et al., 2008),

$$\theta_{\mathrm{MML}} = \frac{\mathrm{MED}\{a_i \cdot [X_i \cdot \psi(X_i - \mathrm{MED}\{\vec{X}\})]\}}{a_{\mathrm{MED}}} \tag{25}$$

where $X_i \psi(X_i - \mathrm{MED}\{\vec{X}\})$ are the selected pixels in accordance with the influence function used in a sliding filter window, the coefficients a_i are computed using the Laplacian and Uniform distribution functions in $h(\lambda)$, and a_{MED} is the median of coefficients a_i used as a scale constant.

To improve the properties of noise suppression of MML filter we use an impulsive noise detector (IND) (Aizenberg et al., 2003),

$$\mathrm{IND} = \begin{cases} \text{Filtering,} & \text{if } [(D \leq s) \vee (D \geq N-s)] \wedge (|X_c - \mathrm{MED}(\vec{X})| \geq U) \\ X_c, & \text{otherwise} \end{cases} \tag{26}$$

where X_c is the central pixel in the filtering window, $s>0$ and $U \geq 0$ are thresholds, N is the length of the data, and $D=rank(X_c)$ is the rank of element X_c. The expressions $D \leq s$ and $D \geq N-s$ come from the fact that the difference between the ranks of the impulse and the median is usually large. In other words, the median is positioned in the center of data, and an impulse is usually positioned near one of its ends. The expression $|X_c - \mathrm{MED}(\vec{X})| \geq U$ has been specially developed for images that have very high corruption rate. Finally, if these conditions are true then we classify X_c as corrupted.

3.4 Wavelet Domain Median M-type L-filter

Figure 2 shows a block diagram of proposed Wavelet Domain Median M-type L (WDMML) filter (Varela-Benitez et al., 2007b). The proposed WDMML filter uses the Daubechie wavelets (Walker, 1999). We apply the proposed MML filter in the gray scale images of approaches and details obtained in the process of wavelet decomposition.

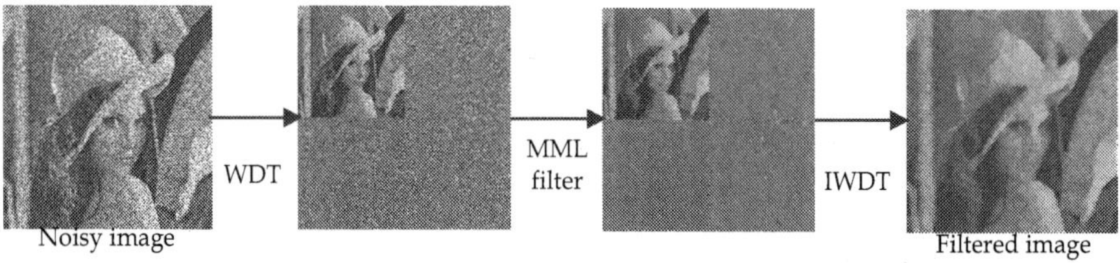

Fig. 2. Block diagram of proposed WDMML filter.

4. Overall filtering performance

The objective criteria used to compare the performance of noise suppression of various filters was the *peak signal to noise ratio* (PSNR) and for the evaluation of fine detail preservation the *mean absolute error* (MAE) was used (Astola & Kuosmanen, 1997; Bovik 2000),

$$\text{PSNR} = 10 \cdot \log\left[\frac{(255)^2}{\text{MSE}}\right] \text{ dB} \tag{27}$$

$$\text{MAE} = \frac{1}{MN}\sum_{i=0}^{M-1}\sum_{j=0}^{N-1}\left|f(i,j) - \theta(i,j)\right| \tag{28}$$

where $\text{MSE} = \frac{1}{MN}\sum_{i=0}^{M-1}\sum_{j=0}^{N-1}\left[f(i,j) - \theta(i,j)\right]^2$ is the *mean square error*, $f(i,j)$ is the original image; $\theta(i,j)$ is the restored image; and M, N is the size of the image.

In the case of color image processing, we compute the *mean chromaticity error* (MCRE) for evaluation of chromaticity retention, and the *normalized color difference* (NCD) for quantification of color perceptual error (Plataniotis & Venetsanopoulos, 2000):

$$\text{MCRE} = \sum_{i=1}^{M_1}\sum_{j=1}^{M_2}\left\|p_{i,j} - \hat{p}_{i,j}\right\|_{L_2}^2 \bigg/ M_1 M_2 \tag{29}$$

$$\text{NCD} = \sum_{i=1}^{M_1}\sum_{j=1}^{M_2}\left\|\Delta E_{Luv}(i,j)\right\|_{L_2} \bigg/ \sum_{i=1}^{M_1}\sum_{j=1}^{M_2}\left\|E_{Luv}^*(i,j)\right\|_{L_2} \tag{30}$$

where $p_{i,j}$ and $\hat{p}_{i,j}$ are the intersection points of $f(i,j)$ and $\theta(i,j)$ with the plane defined by the Maxwell triangle, respectively, $\left\|\Delta E_{Luv}(i,j)\right\|_{L_2} = \left[\left(\Delta L^*(i,j)\right)^2 + \left(\Delta u^*\right)^2 + \left(\Delta v^*\right)^2\right]^{1/2}$ is the norm of color error, ΔL^*, Δu^*, and Δv^* are the difference in the L^*, u^*, and v^* components, respectively, between the two color vectors that present the filtered image and uncorrupted original one for each a pixel (i,j) of an image, $\left\| E^*_{Luv}(i,j) \right\|_{L_2} = \left[\left(L^* \right)^2 + \left(u^* \right)^2 + \left(v^* \right)^2 \right]^{1/2}$ is the norm or magnitude of the uncorrupted original image pixel vector in the $L^*u^*v^*$ space, and $\left\| \, . \, \right\|_{L_2}$ is the L_2-vector norm.

4.1 Noise suppression in gray scale images and video sequences

The described 3x3 MMKNN, 3x3 WMKNN, 3x3 ABSTMKNN, 3x3 MOODMKNN, and 3x3 MML filters with different influence functions have been evaluated, and their performance has been compared with 3x3 *weighted median* (WM) (Bovik, 2000), 3x3 *tri-state median* (TSM) (Chen et al., 1999), 3x3 *adaptive center weighted median* (ACWM) (Chen & Wu, 2001), 3x3 *rank order mean* (ROM) (Abreu et al., 1996), 3x3 *minimum-maximum exclusive mean* (MMEM) (Wei-Lu & Ja-Chen, 1997), 3x3 *Local Linear Minimum Mean Square Error* (LMMSE) (Özkan et al., 1993), 3x3 *K-Nearest Neighbor* (KNN) (Astola & Kuosmanen, 1997), 3x3 *Ansari-Bradley-Siegel-Tukey* (ABST) (Hampel et al., 1986), 3x3 *Normalized Least Mean Squares L* (NLMS-L) (Kotropoulos & Pitas, 1996), 3x3 *Sampled-Function Weighted Order* (SFWO) (Öten & De Figueiredo, 2002), and *Modified Frost* (MFrost) (Lukin et al., 1998) filters. The reason for choosing these filters to compare them with the proposed ones is that their performances have been compared with various known filters and their advantages have been demonstrated. The runtime analysis of various filters was conducted for different images using Texas Instruments DSP TMS320C6701 (Kehtarnavaz & Keramat, 2001; Texas Instruments, 1998).

To determine the impulsive noise suppression properties of various filters the 256x256 standard test grayscale images "Airfield", "Goldhill", and "Lena" were corrupted with an occurrence rate of 20% of impulsive noise and the results obtained by the mentioned filters are presented in Table 2. One can see from the Table 2 that the proposed MMKNN and WMKNN filters have better performances in terms of PSNR and MAE criteria in comparison with the filters used as comparative in the most of cases. The processing time is given in seconds and includes the duration of data acquisition, processing and storing of data. The results reveal that the processing time values of the MMKNN filter are larger than WM, and MMEM filters but less in comparison with ACWM, LMMSE, and ROM filters and have about the same values compared to the TSM filter. The MMKNN filter with Andrew's and Bernoulli influence functions take more time than when other influence functions are used depending on the filter parameters values. For the ROM filter the processing time does not include the time for deriving weighting coefficients during the training stage and then used in this filtering scheme. The time used in its training procedure is 0.035 s approximately.

The processing time performance of the MMKNN filter depends on the image to process and almost does not vary for different noise levels; these values also depend on the complex calculation of the influence functions and parameters of the proposed filter. The proposed MMKNN algorithm can process from 16 to 19 images of 256x256 pixels per second. In the case of WMKNN filter we observe that its processing time is larger than MMKNN filter. The WMKNN algorithm can process from 10 to 14 images of 256x256 pixels per second.

In Figure 3 we present the processed images for the test image "Lena" explaining the impulsive noise suppression according to the Table 2. A zoomed-in section (upright) of each image is displayed in order to view the details.

Algorithm	Airfield			Goldhill			Lena		
	PSNR	MAE	TIME	PSNR	MAE		PSNR	MAE	
WM	22.40	10.67	0.0203	24.21	9.96	0.0203	23.58	8.67	0.0203
TSM	21.13	13.44	0.0547	23.11	12.43	0.0547	23.56	10.80	0.0547
ACWM	22.97	10.57	0.2299	24.84	10.43	0.2299	25.56	8.75	0.2299
ROM	23.08	10.42	0.0750	24.82	10.57	0.0750	25.20	9.11	0.0750
MMEM	22.69	12.23	0.0406	24.16	11.09	0.0406	24.52	9.46	0.0406
LMMSE	23.03	11.24	0.0750	24.15	11.08	0.0750	24.59	9.95	0.0751
MMKNN (S)	23.21	10.45	0.0515	25.45	9.58	0.0517	26.38	7.12	0.0515
MMKNN (H)	23.24	10.42	0.0521	25.50	9.50	0.0524	26.33	7.07	0.0521
MMKNN (A)	23.23	10.44	0.0566	25.48	9.53	0.0573	26.36	7.12	0.0557
MMKNN (T)	23.23	10.45	0.0528	25.50	9.56	0.0555	26.32	7.13	0.0528
MMKNN (B)	23.24	10.46	0.0593	25.50	9.56	0.0599	26.31	7.14	0.0588
WMKNN (S)	22.82	10.82	0.0686	25.29	9.97	0.0751	25.66	7.60	0.0757
WMKNN (H)	22.72	10.86	0.0736	25.19	10.00	0.0826	25.45	7.67	0.0814
WMKNN (A)	22.79	10.84	0.0920	25.36	9.92	0.0979	25.68	7.56	0.0944
WMKNN (T)	22.30	11.23	0.0753	24.95	10.46	0.0804	24.88	8.11	0.0775
WMKNN (B)	22.26	11.29	0.0695	24.41	10.40	0.0861	24.79	8.05	0.0838

Table 2. PSNR in dB, MAE, and Processing time values for different images corrupted by 20% of impulsive noise obtained by different filters.

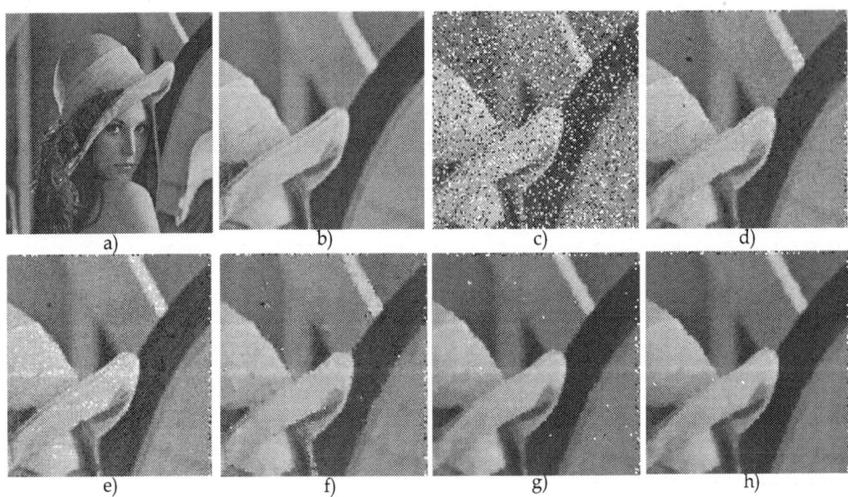

Fig. 3. Subjective visual qualities of a part of image "Lena", a) Original image, b) Zoomed-in section (upright) of (a), c) Degraded image with 20% of impulsive noise of (b), d) Restored image with the ACWM filter of (b), e) Restored image with the ROM filter of (b), f) Restored image with the LMMSE filter of (b), g) Restored image with the MMKNN (H) filter of (b), h) Restored image with the MM-KNN (B) filter of (b).

Table 3 shows the performance results in the grayscale image "Peppers" degraded with 20% of impulsive noise. We observe that the processing time values of ABSTMKNN and MOODMKNN filters are larger than the most comparison filters but the proposed filters consistently outperform other filters by balancing the tradeoff between noise suppression and detail preservation. Figure 4 depicts that the restored image by ABSTMKNN method appears to have a very good subjective quality in comparison with other methods.

Algorithm	PSNR dB	MAE	TIME
KNN	18.83	24.32	0.021380
ABST	22.61	11.10	0.038395
WM	24.68	7.81	0.020341
ACWM	25.18	9.21	0.229951
ROM	25.04	9.62	0.075008
MMEM	24.40	9.67	0.040618
LMMSE	24.75	9.70	0.075140
ABSTMKNN (S)	25.85	7.55	0.063876
ABSTMKNN (H)	25.62	7.75	0.063787
ABSTMKNN (A)	25.95	7.57	0.074301
ABSTMKNN (T)	25.51	7.75	0.063151
ABSTMKNN (B)	25.46	7.75	0.067383
MOODMKNN (S)	25.98	7.55	0.066725
MOODMKNN (H)	25.62	7.75	0.067295
MOODMKNN (A)	25.98	7.57	0.076487
MOODMKNN (T)	25.67	7.64	0.068421
MOODMKNN (B)	25.58	7.66	0.067413

Table 3. Performance results for image "Peppers".

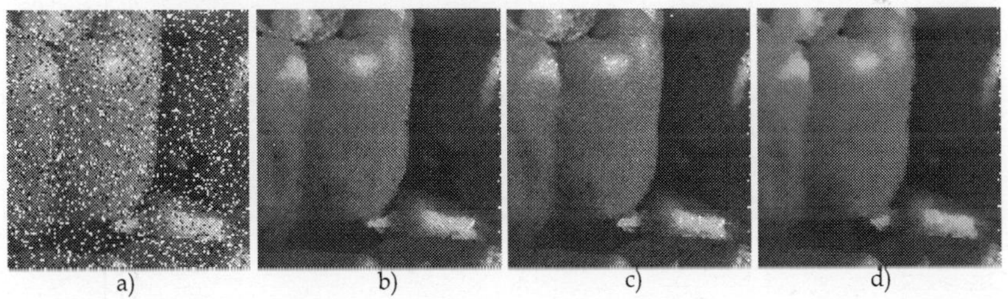

Fig. 4. Results for a part of "Peppers" image, a) Degraded image with 20% of impulse noise, b) Restored image by ACWM filter, c) Restored image by the ROM filter, d) Restored image by the ABSTM-KNN (S) filter.

The MML filter was implemented with Laplacian (L) and Uniform (U) distribution functions, and with (D) and without (ND) impulsive noise detector. Table 1 shows the performance results for "Lena" image degraded with 5% of impulsive noise and σ^2=0.05 of speckle noise. From Table 4, the proposed filter provides better noise suppression and detail preservation than other filters in the most of cases. The processing time of MML filter is less than filters used as comparative, and it takes less time when the impulsive noise detector is used. Figure 5 exhibits the filtered images in the case of 20% of impulsive noise. The restored image by proposed MML filter appears to have good subjective quality.

To demonstrate the performances of the proposed MML filtering scheme we apply it for filtering of the SAR images, which naturally have speckle noise. The results of such a filtering are presented in the Figure 6 in the case of the image "Pentagon". It is possible to see analyzing the filtering images that speckle noise can be efficiently suppressed, while the sharpness and fine feature are preserved using the proposed filter in comparison with other filters proposed in the references.

Filters	Impulsive noise = 5%			Speckle noise = 0.05		
	PSNR	MAE	TIME	PSNR	MAE	TIME
ACWM	27.73	7.35	0.2299	19.96	20.34	0.2299
ROM	27.49	7.64	0.1050	22.82	20.96	0.1050
MFrost	23.87	12.69	0.1004	24.56	10.99	0.1004
NLMS-L	24.24	11.57	0.1835	21.59	21.54	0.1835
SFWO (L)	24.94	8.38	0.1310	22.10	14.37	0.1310
SFWO (U)	15.76	32.04	0.1310	22.53	12.84	0.1310
MML (A,L,ND)	27.01	7.61	0.0815	22.78	14.21	0.0815
MML (A,U,ND)	28.03	6.13	0.0815	24.61	10.92	0.0815
MML (T,L,ND)	26.93	7.62	0.0796	22.63	14.44	0.0796
MML (T,U,ND)	28.29	5.76	0.0796	24.79	10.63	0.0796
MML (H,L,ND)	27.37	6.92	0.0804	23.12	13.53	0.0804
MML (H,U,ND)	28.40	5.56	0.0804	24.86	10.53	0.0804
MML (A,L,D)	28.62	6.01	0.0684	23.38	13.10	0.0685
MML (A,U,D)	29.10	5.51	0.0684	24.60	11.00	0.0684
MML (T,L,D)	28.59	6.04	0.0652	23.40	13.03	0.0652
MML (T,U,D)	29.23	5.34	0.0651	24.63	10.96	0.0652
MML (H,L,D)	28.75	5.83	0.0790	23.61	12.67	0.0790
MML (H,U,D)	29.33	5.16	0.0790	24.86	10.53	0.0790

Table 4. Performance results in image "Lena" obtained by different filters,

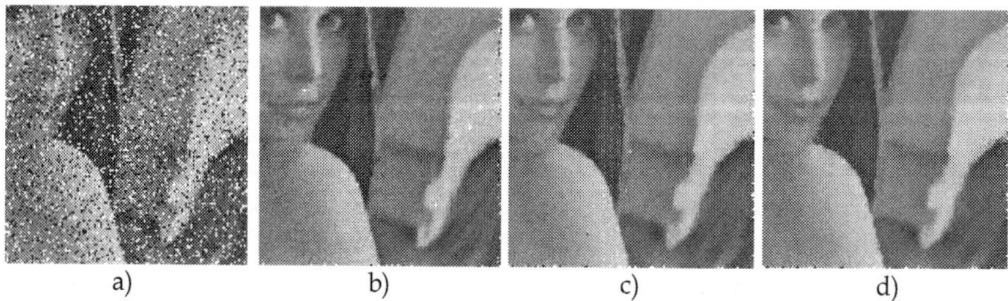

a)　　　　　　b)　　　　　　c)　　　　　　d)

Fig. 5. Filtered images with 20% of impulsive noise: a) Degraded image, b) ACWM, c) ROM, d) MML (A,L,ND).

Table 5 shows the performance results in terms of PSNR in dB and MAE for the image "Lena" degraded with 0.1 of variance of speckle noise and free of noise by use the WDMML

(S,ND,L) filter in approaches (A) and details (D) with the wavelets db1, db2, db3, and db4 with one (1) and two (2) levels of decomposition. From this Table one can see that the proposed WDMML filter provides better speckle noise suppression and detail preservation in comparison with the MML filter in the spatial domain in the most of cases. Figure 7 presents the visual results to apply the proposed filter with one and two decomposition levels in the image "Peppers". One can see from Figure 7 that the proposed WDMML filter outperforms the MML filter in the case of speckle noise.

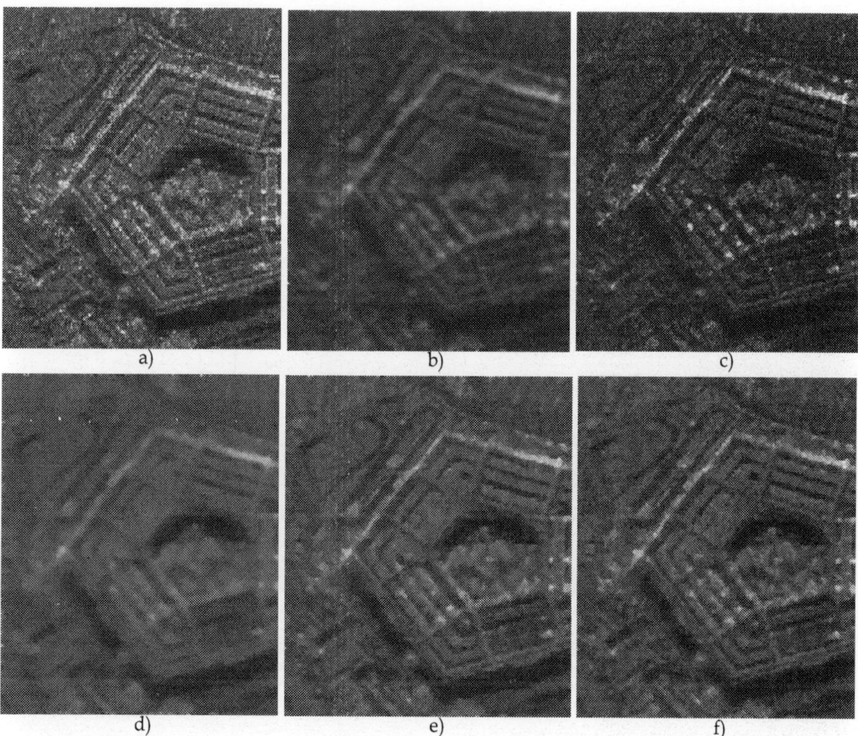

Fig. 6. Comparative results of despeckled SAR image. a) Original image "Pentagon", resolution 1m, source Sandia National Lab., b) Despeckled image with MFrost filter, c) Despeckled image with the ROM filter, d) Despeckled image with the SFWO filter, e) Despeckled image with the MML filter (S, ND, L), f) Despeckled image with the MML filter (S, D, L)

We also propose to apply the proposed filters to video signals. We process a real video sequence to demonstrate that the proposed method potentially could provide a real-time solution to quality video transmission. We investigate a QCIF (Quarter Common Intermediate Format) video sequence. This picture format uses 176x144 luminance pixels per frame and velocity from 15 to 30 frames per second. In the case of this test we used one frame of the video sequence "carphone", that was corrupted by 20% of impulsive noise. The

PSNR, MAE and processing time performances are depicted in Table 6. The restored frames are displayed in Figure 8 by using the ACWM, LMMSE, and MMKNN (H) filters. From the simulation results we observe that the proposed MMKNN and ABSTMKNN filters can process up to 33 frames of QCIF video format suppressing the impulsive noise and providing the detail preservation in real-time applications.

Filters	Free noise		$\sigma^2=0.1$	
	PSNR	MAE	PSNR	MAE
MML (S,ND,L)	29.62	3.78	22.95	13.24
WDMML (S,ND,db1,A,1)	27.84	5.09	23.35	12.24
WDMML (S,ND,db1,D,1)	31.46	3.24	20.53	18.78
WDMML (S,ND,db2,A,1)	27.90	5.11	23.60	12.15
WDMML (S,ND,db2,D,1)	32.26	3.05	20.69	18.00
WDMML (S,ND,db3,A,1)	27.92	5.24	24.02	11.77
WDMML (S,ND,db3,D,1)	32.70	2.97	20.79	17.99
WDMML (S,ND,db4,A,1)	27.87	5.27	24.33	11.28
WDMML (S,ND,db4,D,1)	33.00	2.92	20.90	18.11
WDMML (S,ND,db1,A,2)	24.83	8.32	22.46	13.57
WDMML (S,ND,db1,D,2)	27.48	5.73	22.66	13.93
WDMML (S,ND,db2,A,2)	25.40	7.61	22.94	12.85
WDMML (S,ND,db2,D,2)	28.37	5.34	23.21	13.15
WDMML (S,ND,db3,A,2)	25.24	7.89	23.14	12.59
WDMML (S,ND,db3,D,2)	28.39	5.42	23.49	12.90
WDMML (S,ND,db4,A,2)	25.06	8.21	23.38	12.47
WDMML (S,ND,db4,D,2)	28.29	5.46	23.69	12.73

Table 5. Performance results in the image "Lena" obtained by the use of WDMML filter.

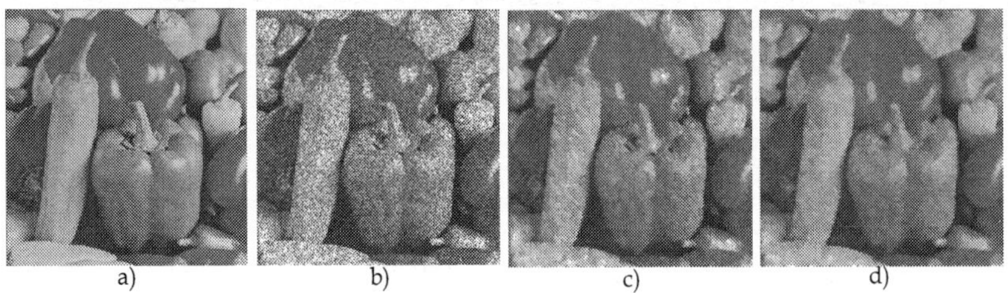

Fig. 7. Visual results in the image Peppers, a) Original image, b) Degraded image with 0.1 of variance of speckle noise, c) Restored image with MML (S,L,ND) filter, d) Restored image with WDMML filter (S,L,ND,db2,A,1).

4.2 Noise suppression in color images and video sequences

The proposed MMKNN, WMKNN, and ABSTMKNN filters were adapted to work in color image and video processing. Now, the proposed Vector RMKNN filters are called as VMMKNN, VWMKNN, and VABSTMKNN filters. These filters have been evaluated, and their performances have been compared with *vector median* (VMF) (Plataniotis &

Algorithm	"Carphone" Frame		
	PSNR	MAE	Time
WM	23.83	9.80	0.009977
TSM	21.53	13.24	0.023730
ACWM	24.34	9.79	0.093865
MMEM	23.60	11.11	0.018021
LMMSE	24.15	10.04	0.034716
MMKNN (S)	24.77	9.08	0.023773
MMKNN (H)	24.76	9.10	0.024018
MMKNN (A)	24.75	9.06	0.025717
MMKNN (T)	24.74	9.16	0.024166
MMKNN (B)	24.78	9.15	0.026760
ABSTMKNN (S)	25.07	9.44	0.027068
ABSTMKNN (H)	24.79	9.66	0.027932
ABSTMKNN (A)	25.08	9.48	0.029762
ABSTMKNN (T)	24.78	9.62	0.026815
ABSTMKNN (B)	24.88	9.62	0.028440

Table 6. PSNR values in dB, MAE, and processing time for different filters in a frame of video sequence "Carphone".

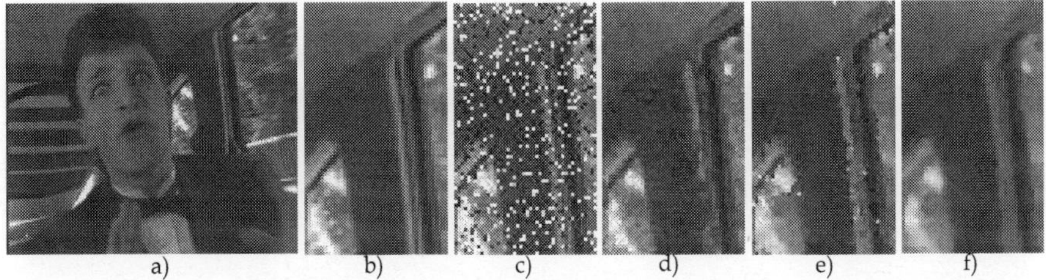

Fig. 8. Subjective visual qualities of a restored frame "Carphone" produced by different filters, a) Original frame, b) Zoomed-in section (upright) of (a), c) Degraded frame with 20% of impulsive noise of (b), d) Restored frame with the ACWM filter of (b), e) Restored frame with the LMMSE filter of (b), f) Restored frame with the MMKNN (H) filter of (b).

Venetsanopoulos, 2000), *α-trimmed mean* (α-TMF), *basic vector directional* (BVDF), *generalized vector directional* (GVDF), *adaptive* GVDF (AGVDF), *double window* GVDF (GVDF_DW), and *multiple non-parametric* (MAMNFE) (Trahanias et al., 1996; Plataniotis et al., 1997) filters.

The implementation of filters were realized on the DSP TMS320C6711 (Kehtarnavaz & Keramat, 2001; Texas Instruments, 1998) to demonstrate that the proposed filters potentially could provide a real-time solution to quality video transmission.

The 320X320 "Lena" color image was corrupted by 20% of impulsive noise. Table 7 shows that the performance criteria are often better for the proposed filters in comparison when other filters are used. Figure 9 exhibits the processed images for test image "Lena" explaining the impulsive noise suppression, and presenting the original image "Lena", image corrupted with noise probability occurrence of 20% for each color channel, and exhibiting the filtering results produced by the MAMNFE and VMMKNN filters, respectively. The proposed VMMKNN filtering appears to have a better subjective quality in comparison with MAMNFE filtering.

Algorithm	PSNR	MAE	MCRE	NCD	TIME
VMF	21.15	10.73	0.035	0.038	0.039
α-TMF	20.86	14.97	0.046	0.049	0.087
BVDF	20.41	12.72	0.043	0.045	0.065
GVDF	20.67	11.18	0.038	0.040	0.264
AGVDF	22.01	11.18	0.028	0.036	0.620
GVDF_DW	22.59	10.09	0.028	0.039	0.721
MAMNFE	22.67	9.64	0.027	0.035	0.832
VMMKNN (S)	23.15	10.00	0.033	0.034	0.296
VMMKNN (A)	23.07	10.01	0.033	0.035	0.199
VMMKNN (H)	23.05	10.04	0.033	0.035	0.199
VWMKNN (S)	22.99	10.13	0.033	0.035	0.435
VWMKNN (A)	23.00	10.08	0.033	0.035	0.756
VWMKNN (H)	22.99	10.09	0.033	0.035	0.398
VABSTMKNN (S)	22.99	10.13	0.033	0.035	0.286
VABSTMKNN (A)	22.99	10.13	0.033	0.035	0.320
VABSTMKNN (H)	23.01	10.07	0.033	0.035	0.264

Table 7. Comparative restoration results for 20% of impulsive noise for color image "Lena".

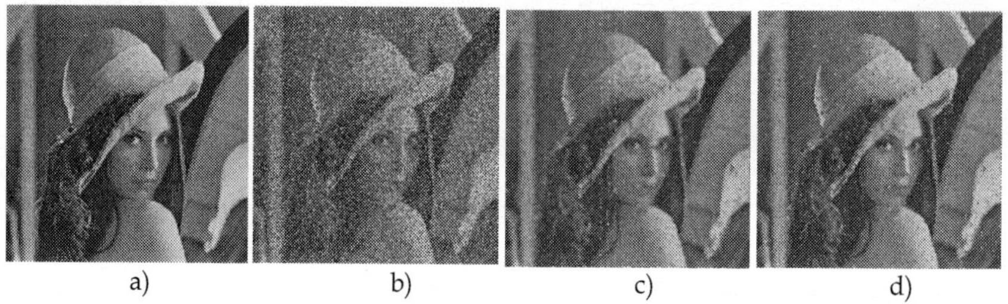

a)   b)   c)   d)

Fig. 9. Subjective visual qualities of restored color image "Lena", a) Original test image "Lena", b) Input noisy image with 20% of impulsive noise, c) MAMNFE filtering image, and d) Proposed VMMKNN (S) filtered image.

We use one frame of the video color sequence "Miss America", which was corrupted by 15% of impulsive noise. One can see in Table 8 that the performance criteria are often better for the proposed VMMKNN, VWMKNN, and VABSTMKNN filters in comparison when other filters are used in the most of cases. Figure 10 exhibits the processed frames for test image "Miss America" explaining the impulsive noise suppression. The restored frame with VMMKNN filter appears to have a better subjective quality in comparison with MAMNFE filter that has the better performance among the known color filters.

The processing time performance of the VRMKNN filters depends on the image to process and almost does not vary for different noise levels. These values also depend on the complex calculation of the influence functions and parameters of the proposed filters. From

Tables 7 and 8, one can see that the proposed algorithms can process, in the case of color images of size 320x320 pixels, up to 5 images per second, and in case of QCIF video up to 11 color frames per second in comparison with MAMNFE filter (the best comparative filter) that can process one image per second or 3 frames per second.

Algorithm	PSNR	MAE	MCRE	NCD	TIME
VMF	25.54	5.38	0.0371	0.0332	0.0153
α-TMF	24.47	6.54	0.0589	0.0251	0.0206
BVDF	22.45	7.68	0.0379	0.0329	0.1768
GVDF	23.56	9.12	0.0362	0.0308	0.1869
AGVDF	26.97	5.24	0.0308	0.0302	0.2106
GVDF_DW	26.88	5.95	0.0311	0.0249	0.7205
MAMNFE	27.01	5.82	0.0390	0.0270	0.3219
VMMKNN (S)	28.20	3.86	0.0312	0.0140	0.1109
VMMKNN (A)	28.04	3.91	0.0317	0.0143	0.0898
VMMKNN (H)	28.14	3.90	0.0315	0.0144	0.0917
VWMKNN (S)	27.27	4.48	0.0336	0.0234	0.2662
VWMKNN (A)	26.10	5.10	0.0372	0.0272	0.4599
VWMKNN (H)	26.05	5.05	0.0369	0.0271	0.2912
VABSTMKNN (S)	27.75	4.46	0.0336	0.0243	0.0929
VABSTMKNN (A)	27.56	4.68	0.0349	0.0253	0.2066
VABSTMKNN (H)	27.49	4.71	0.0350	0.0255	0.1194

Table 8. Comparative restoration results for 15% impulsive noise for a color frame of "Miss America"

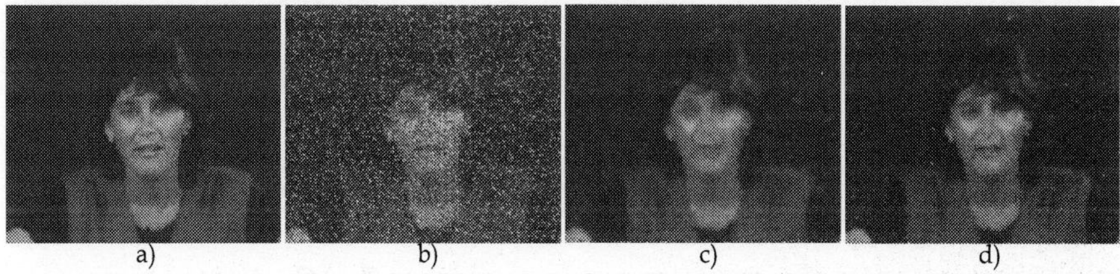

Fig. 10. Subjective visual qualities of restored color frame "Miss America", a) Original test frame "Miss America", b) Input noisy frame with 15% of impulsive noise, c) MAMNFE filtered frame, and d) Proposed VMMKNN filtered frame (A).

The proposed Wavelet Redundancy of Approaches (WRAF), Wavelet Iterative Center Weighted Median using Redundancy of Approaches (WICWMRAF), Wavelet Signal Dependent Rank-Ordered Mean (WSDROMF), Wavelet Adaptive Center Weighed Median (WACWMF), Wavelet Median M-type K-Nearest Neighbor (WMMKNNF), and Wavelet FIR Median Hybrid (WFIRMHF) Filters were compared with the *Wavelet Iterative Median* (WIMF) and *Wavelet Iterative Center Weighted Median* (WICWMF) (Mahbubur Rahman & Kamrul Hasan, 2003) filters in terms of PSNR, MAE, MCRE and NCD to demonstrate the good quality of color imaging of the proposed filters in both an objective and subjective sense.

Table 9 presents the performance results by means of use different filters in the 512x512 image "Lena" degraded with 20% of impulsive noise and with 0.2 of variance of speckle noise. From these results we observe that the proposed filters provide better impulsive and speckle noise suppression, detail preservation, and color retention in comparison with the traditional filters in the Wavelet domain. Figure 11 shows the subjective visual quantities of a restored zoom part of the color image "Lena" degraded with 0.2 of variance of speckle noise. Figure 12 presents the visual results in a part of "Mandrill" image produced by the WMMKNNF.

Filters	20% of impulsive noise				0.2 of variance of speckle noise			
	PSNR	MAE	MCRE	NCD	PSNR	MAE	MCRE	NCD
WIMF	40.6734	24.7969	0.0172	0.3294	43.7164	22.2675	0.0138	0.2617
WICWMF	40.6734	24.7969	0.0172	0.3294	43.7164	22.2675	0.0138	0.2617
WRAF	44.4936	20.8426	0.0117	0.2718	48.0338	18.2333	0.0093	0.2062
WICWMRAF	50.6952	15.8213	0.0063	0.1911	53.8602	14.1506	0.0056	0.1489
WSDROMF	50.6952	15.8213	0.0063	0.1911	53.8602	14.1506	0.0056	0.1489
WACWMF	50.6952	15.8213	0.0063	0.1911	53.8602	14.1507	0.0056	0.1489
WMMKNNF	50.6953	15.8211	0.0063	0.1911	53.8603	14.1506	0.0056	0.1489
WFIRMHF	50.6992	15.8189	0.0063	0.1911	53.8608	14.1509	0.0056	0.1489

Table 9. Performance results in the image "Lena".

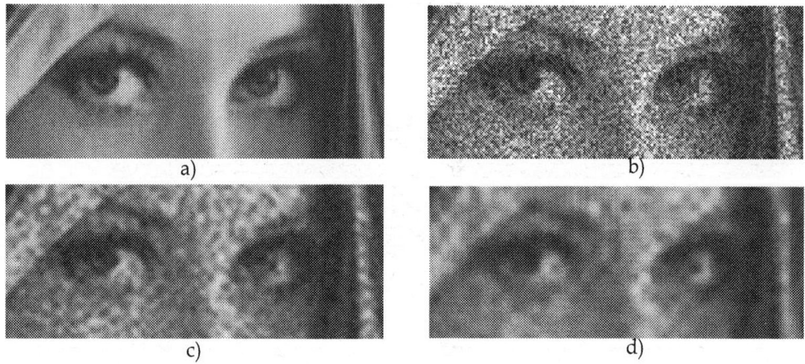

Fig. 11. Subjective visual quantities of restored zoom part of color image "Lena", a) Original image, b) Input noisy image corrupted by 0.2 of variance of speckle noise in each a channel, c) WRAF filtered image; d) WMMKNNF filtered image.

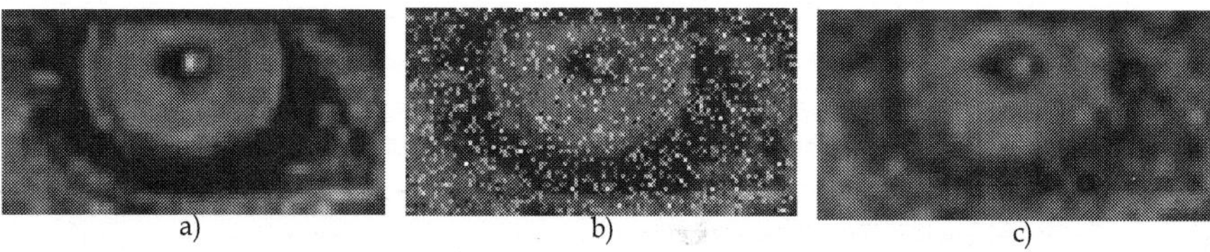

Fig. 12. Subjective visual quantities of restored zoom part of the color image "Mandrill", a) Original image, b) Input noisy image corrupted by 20% impulsive noise in each a channel, c) WMMKNNF filtered image.

4.3 Noise suppression in 3D gray scale video sequences

In this section, we propose 3D filtering algorithms to process ultrasound sequences contaminated by speckle and impulsive noise. The 3D MMKNN and 3D MML filters have been evaluated, and their performance has been compared with different nonlinear 2D filters which were adapted to 3D. The filters used as comparative ones were the *modified a-Trimmed Mean* (MATM), *Ranked-Order* (RO), *Multistage Median* (MSM1 to MSM6), *Comparison and Selection* (CS), *MaxMed, Selection Average* (SelAve), *Selection Median* (SelMed), and *Lower-Upper-Middle* (LUM, LUM Sharp, and LUM Smooth) (Astola & Kuosmanen, 1997) filters. These filters were computed according with their references and were adapted to 3D imaging.

An ultrasound sequence of 640x480 pixels with 90 frames (3D image of 640x480x90 voxels) was degraded with 0.05 and 0.1 of variance of speckle noise added to the natural speckle noise of the sequence. The performance results are depicted in Table 10 by use a frame of the sequence. From this Table one can see that the 3D MML filters provide the best results in comparison to other filters proposed as comparative. Figure 13 exhibits the visual results of restored images obtained by the use of different filters according to Table 10. In the Figure we observe that the proposed filters provide the better results in speckle noise suppression and detail preservation in comparison with other filters.

3D Filters	Speckle noise variance			
	0.05		0.1	
	PSNR	MAE	PSNR	MAE
CS	15.435	32.875	13.843	39.778
LUM Smooth	17.915	25.142	15.440	33.823
LUM Sharp	15.625	30.927	14.444	36.425
LUM	15.518	31.427	14.379	36.748
MaxMed	18.562	24.206	15.919	32.913
MATM	20.418	15.124	19.095	18.663
MSM1	20.568	17.624	18.061	23.684
MSM2	20.484	17.789	18.038	23.725
MSM3	22.421	14.206	20.261	18.456
MSM4	21.697	15.401	19.348	20.351
MSM5	19.554	20.207	16.964	27.444
MSM6	22.083	14.688	19.744	19.374
SelAve	21.182	17.647	19.192	22.814
SelMed	20.836	15.750	19.013	20.094
RO	21.587	14.520	19.802	18.179
MMKNN (S)	21.554	15.199	18.949	20.995
MMKNN (H)	21.572	15.169	19.040	20.798
MMKNN (A)	21.399	14.614	18.640	20.226
MMKNN (B)	22.658	13.309	20.075	17.819
MMKNN (T)	22.499	13.446	19.855	18.125
MML (T, U,D)	29.876	5.016	28.6175	5.7429
MML (T, L,D)	28.797	5.646	28.188	6.0194

Table 10. Performance results of different filters in a frame of ultrasound sequence degraded with speckle noise.

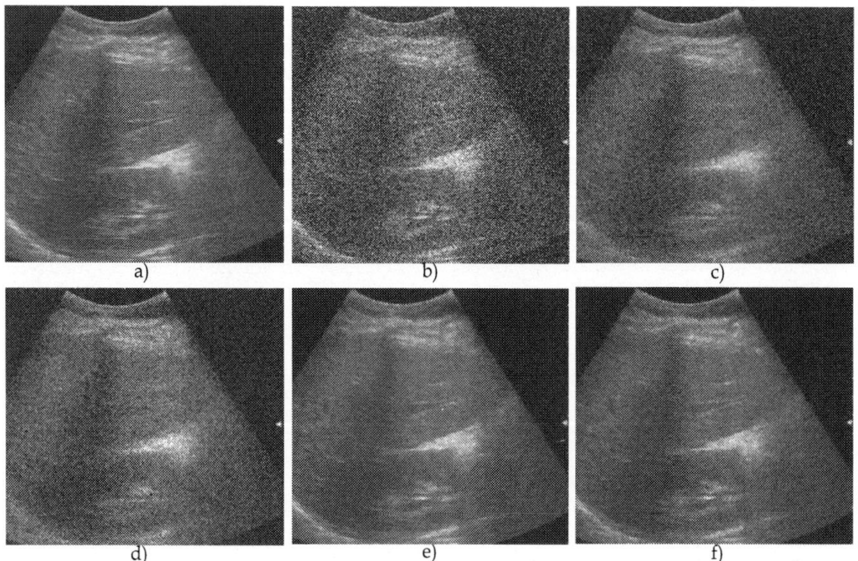

Fig. 13. Visual results in a frame of ultrasound sequence. a) original frame, b) frame degraded by 0.05 of variance of speckle noise, c) restored frame by MSM6 filter, d) restored frame by MMKNN (B) filter, e) restored frame by MML filter (T,U,D), f) restored frame by MML filter (T,L,D).

4.4 Optimal values of parameters of proposed filters

The values of parameters for the RMKNN and MML filters and influence functions were found after numerous simulations with different images and video sequences degraded with different percentages of impulsive noise and variances of speckle noise:

a. Gray scale images and video sequences: The optimal parameters of RMKNN and MML filters are: $a=4$, $K_{min}=5$, and $K_{max}=8$; and $s=3$ and $U=15$, respectively. The values for influence functions are: $r=25$, $a=40$, and $\beta=200$ for *Hampel*, $r=35$ for *Andrew*, $r=15$ *Tukey*, and $r=20$ for *Bernoulli*. Therefore, the WDMML and WMMKNNF filters use the values proposed above.

b. Color images and video sequences: The values of parameters of proposed VRMKNN filters were $0.5<a<12$, $K_{min}=5$, and $K_{max}=8$, and the parameters of the influence functions were: $r\leq81$ for *Andrew*, and $\alpha=10$, $\beta\leq90$, and $r=300$ for *Hampel*.

The processing time performance of the proposed filters depends on the image to process and almost does not vary for different noise levels; these values also depend on the complex calculation of the influence functions and parameters of the proposed filter. The processing time can change with other values for these parameters, increasing or decreasing the times but the PSNR and MAE values change within the range of ±10%, it is due that we fix the parameters to realize the real-time implementation of proposed filters.

5. Conclusions

We present the RMKNN and MML filters in spatial and wavelet domain for impulsive and speckle noise suppression in gray scale and color imaging. Extensive simulation results with different gray scale and color images and video sequences have demonstrated that the proposed filters consistently outperform other filters by balancing the tradeoff between noise suppression, fine detail preservation, color retention, and processing time.

6. References

Abreu, E., Lightstone, M., Mitra, S. K. & Arakawa, K. (1996). A new efficient approach for the removal of impulse noise from highly corrupted images. *IEEE Trans. Image Process.*, Vol.5, No.6, 1012-1025, ISSN:1057-7149

Aizenberg, I., Astola, J., Bregin, T., Butakoff, C., Egiazarian, K., & Paily, D. (2003). Detectors of the Impulsive Noise and new Effective Filters for the Impulsive Noise Reduction, *Proc. SPIE Image Process., Algorithms and Syst. II*, Vol. 5014, ISBN: 9780819448149, pp. 419-428, San Jose, Ca, USA

Astola, J. & Kuosmanen, P. (1997). *Fundamentals of Nonlinear Digital Filtering*, CRC Press. ISBN:0-8493-2570-6, Boca Raton-New York, USA

Bovik, A. (2000). *Handbook of Image and Video Processing*, Academic Press., ISBN:0121197921, San Diego CA

Chen, T., Ma, K. & Chen, L. (1999). Tri-State Median filter for image denoising. *IEEE Trans. Image Process.*, Vol.8, No.12, 1834-1838, ISSN:1057-7149

Chen, T. & Wu, H. R. (2001). Adaptive impulse detection using center-weighted median filters. *IEEE Signal Processing Letters*, Vol.8, No.1, 1-3, ISSN:1070-9908

Gallegos-Funes, F. J., Ponomaryov, V., Sadovnychiy, S., & Nino-de-Rivera, L. (2002). Median M-type K-nearest neighbour (MMKNN) filter to remove impulse noise from corrupted images. *Electron. Lett.*, Vol.38, No.15, 786-787, ISSN:0013-5194

Gallegos, F., & Ponomaryov, V. (2004). Real-time image filtering scheme based on robust estimators in presence of impulsive noise. *Real Time Imaging*, Vol.8, No.2, 78-90, ISSN:1077-2014

Gallegos-Funes, F., Ponomaryov, V., & De-La-Rosa J. (2005). ABST M-type K-nearest neighbor (ABSTM-KNN) for image denoising. *IEICE Trans. Funds. Electronics Comms. Computer Science*, Vol.E88A, No.3, 798-799, ISSN:0916-8508

Gallegos-Funes, F., Varela-Benitez, J., & Ponomaryov, V. (2008). Rank M-Type L (RM L)-Filter for Image Denoising, *IEICE Trans. Funds. Electronics, Comms. Computer Sciences*, Vol.E91A, No.12, 3817-3819, ISSN:0916-8508

Gallegos-Funes, F. J., Martínez-Valdes, J., & De-la-Rosa-Vázquez, J. M. (2007). Order statistics filters in wavelet domain for color image processing, *Proc. IEEE Sixth Mexican Int. Conference on Artificial Intelligence*, ISBN:978-0-7695-3124-3, pp.121-130, Mexico

Huber, P.J. (1981). *Robust Statistics*, Wiley, ISBN:0-471-65072-2, New York, USA

Hampel, F. R., Ronchetti, E. M., Rouseew, P. J. & Stahel, W. A. (1986). *Robust Statistics. The approach based on influence function*. Wiley ISBN:0-471-73577-9, New York, USA

Kehtarnavaz, N., & Keramat, M. (2001). *DSP System Design using the TMS320C6000*, Prentice Hall, ISBN:0-13-091031-7, Upper Saddle River, NJ, USA.

Kotropoulos, C., & Pitas, I. (1996). Adaptive LMS L-filters for noise suppression in images. *IEEE Trans. Image Process.*, Vol.5, No.12, 1596-1609, ISSN:1057-7149

Kotropoulos, C. & Pitas, I. (2001). *Nonlinear Model-Based Image/Video Processing and Analysis*, John Wiley & Sons, ISBN:0-471-37735-X, New York

Lukin, V., Melnik, V., Chemerovsky, V., Astola, J., Saarinen, K. (1998). Hard-switching adaptive filter for speckle image processing, *Proc. SPIE Mathematical Modeling and Estimation Techniques in Computer Vision*, Vol. 3457, pp. 31-42, San Diego, USA

Mahbubur Rahman, S. M., & Kamrul Hasan, Md. (2003). Wavelet-domain iterative center weighted median filter for image denoising. *Signal Processing*, Vol.83, No.5, 1001-1012, ISSN:0165-1684

Nikolaidis, N., & Pitas, I. (2001). *3-D Image Processing Algorithms*, John Wiley & Sons, ISBN:0-471-37736-8, New York, USA

Öten, R., De Figueiredo, R.J.P. (2002). Sampled-Function Weighted Order Filters. *IEEE Trans. Circuits and Systems-II*, Vol.49, No.1, 1-10, ISSN:1057-7130

Özkan, M. K., Sezan, M. I. & Murat, A. (1993). Adaptive motion-compensated filtering of noisy image sequences. *IEEE Trans. Circuits and Syst. for Video Tech.*, Vol.3, No.4, 277-290, ISSN:1051-8215

Peltonen, S. & Kuosmanen, P. (2001). Robustness of nonlinear filters for image processing. *J. Electronic Imaging*, Vol.10, No.3, 744-756, ISSN:1560-229X

Plataniotis, K. N., Androutsos, D., Vinayagamoorthy, S. & Venetsanopoulos, A. N. (1997). Color image processing using adaptive multichannel filters. *IEEE Trans. Image Process.*, Vol.6, No.7, 933-949,. ISSN:1057-7149

Plataniotis, K. N., & Venetsanopoulos, A. N. (2000). *Color Image Processing and Applications*, Springer-Verlag, Berlin Heidelberg, ISBN:3-540-66953-1

Ponomaryov, V., Gallegos-Funes, F., Rosales-Silva, A. (2005). Real-Time Color Image Processing Using Order Statistics Filters. *Journal of Mathematical Imaging and Vision*, Vol. 23, No. 3, 315–319, ISSN:0924-9907

Texas Instruments (1998). *TMS320C62x/67x Programmer's Guide, SPRU198D*, Texas Instruments Incorporated. Dallas, USA

Trahanias, P. E., Karakos, D. G., & Venetsanopoulos, A. N. (1996). Directional processing of color images: Theory and experimental results. *IEEE Trans. Image Process.*, Vol.5, No.6, 868-880, ISSN:1057-7149

Varela-Benítez, J. L., Gallegos-Funes, F. J., & Ponomaryov, V. I. (2007a). Real-time speckle and impulsive noise suppression in 3-D imaging based on robust linear combinations of order statistics, *Proc. SPIE Real-Time Image Processing 2007*, Vol.6496, ISBN:9780819466099, pp. 64960H, San Jose, USA

Varela-Benitez, J. L., Gallegos-Funes, F., Ponomaryov, V., De la Rosa Vazquez, J. M. (2007b). RM L-filters in wavelet domain for image processing applications, *Proc. IEEE Sixth Mexican Int. Conference on Artificial Intelligence*, ISBN:978-0-7695-3124-3, pp.113-120, Mexico.

Walker, J. S. (1999). *A Primer on Wavelets and their Scientific Applications*, Chapman & Hall/CRC, ISSN:0-8493-8276-9, Boca Raton-New York, USA

Wei-Yu, H. & Ja-Chen, L. (1997). Minimum-maximum exclusive mean (MMEM) filter to remove impulse noise from highly corrupted images. *Electronics Letters*, Vol.33, No.2, 124-125, ISSN:0013-5194

## 4

Removal of Adherent Noises from Image Sequences by Spatio-Temporal Image Processing

Atsushi Yamashita, Isao Fukuchi and Toru Kaneko
Shizuoka University
Japan

1. Introduction

In this paper, we propose a noise removal method from image sequences by spatio-temporal image processing. A spatio-temporal image can be generated by merging the acquired image sequence (Fig. 1(a)), and then cross-section images can be extracted from the spatio-temporal image (Fig. 1(b)). In these cross-section images, we can detect moving objects and estimate the motion of objects by tracing trajectories of their edges or lines.

In recent years, cameras are widely used for surveillance systems in outdoor environments such as the traffic flow observation, the trespassers detection, and so on. It is also one of the fundamental sensors for outdoor robots. However, the qualities of images taken through cameras depend on environmental conditions. It is often the case that scenes taken by the cameras in outdoor environments are difficult to see because of adherent noises on the surface of the lens-protecting glass of the camera.

For example, waterdrops or mud blobs attached on the protecting glass may interrupt a field of view in rainy days (Fig. 2). It would be desirable to remove adherent noises from images of such scenes for surveillance systems and outdoor robots.

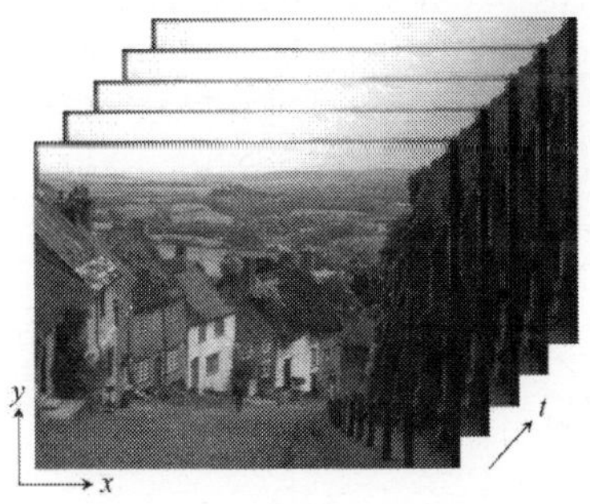

(a) Spatio-temporal image.

(b) Cross-section.

Fig. 1. Spatio-temporal image.

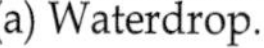

(a) Waterdrop.

(b) Mud blob.

Fig. 2. Example of adherent noise.

Professional photographers use lens hoods or put special water-repellent oil on lens to avoid this problem. Even in these cases, waterdrops are still attached on the lens. Cars are equipped with windscreen wipers to wipe rain from their windscreens. However, there is a problem that a part of the scenery is not in sight when a wiper crosses.

Therefore, this paper proposes a new noise removal method from images by using image processing techniques.

A lot of image interpolation or restoration techniques for damaged and occluded images have been also proposed in image processing and computer vision societies (Kokaram et al., 1995, Masnou & Morel, 1998, Joyeux et al., 1999, Bertalmio et al., 2000, Bertalmio et al., 2001, Kang et al., 2002, Bertalmio et al., 2003, Matsushita et al., 2005, Shen et al., 2006, Wexler et al., 2007). However, some of them can only treat with line-shape scratches (Kokaram et al., 1995, Masnou & Morel, 1998, Joyeux et al., 1999), because they are the techniques for restoring old damaged films. It is also required that human operators indicate the region of noises interactively (not automatically) (Bertalmio et al., 2000, Bertalmio et al., 2001, Kang et al., 2002, Bertalmio et al., 2003, Matsushita et al., 2005, Shen et al., 2006, Wexler et al., 2007). These methods are not suitable for surveillance systems and outdoor robots.

On the other hand, there are automatic methods that can remove noises without helps of human operators (Hase et al., 1999, Garg & Nayar, 2004). Hase et al. have proposed a real-time snowfall noise elimination method from moving pictures by using a special image processing hardware (Hase et al., 1999). Garg and Nayar have proposed an efficient algorithm for detecting and removing rain from videos based on a physics-based motion blur model that explains the photometry of rain (Garg & Nayar, 2004). These techniques work well under the assumptions that snow particles or raindrops are always falling. In other words, they can detect snow particles or raindrops because they move constantly.

However, adherent noises such as waterdrops on the surface of the lens-protecting glass may be stationary noises in the images. Therefore, it is difficult to apply these techniques to our problem because adherent noises that must be eliminated do not move in images.

To solve the static noise problem, we have proposed the method that can remove view-disturbing noises from images taken with multiple cameras (Yamashita et al., 2003, Tanaka et al., 2006).

Previous study (Yamashita et al., 2003) is based on the comparison of images that are taken with multiple cameras. However, it cannot be used for close scenes that have disparities between different viewpoints, because it is based on the difference between images.

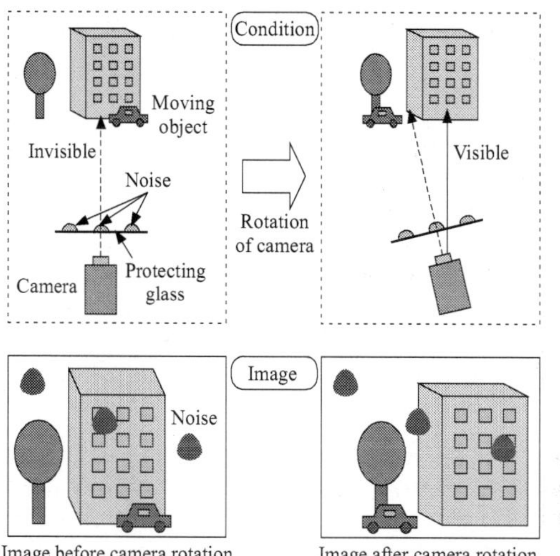

Fig. 3. Image acquisition by using camera rotation.

Stereo camera systems are widely used for robot sensors, and they must of course observe both distant scenes and close scenes. Therefore, we have proposed a method that can remove waterdrops from stereo image pairs that contain objects both in a distant scene and in a close range scene (Tanaka et al., 2006). This method utilizes the information of corresponding points between stereo image pairs, and thereby sometimes cannot work well when appearance of waterdrops differs from each other between left and right images.

We have also proposed a noise removal method by using a single camera (Yamashita et al., 2004, Yamashita et al., 2005). These methods use a pan-tilt camera, and eliminate adherent noises based on the comparison of two images; a first image and a second image taken by a different camera angle (Fig. 3). However, adherent noises cannot be eliminated if a background object is blocked by a waterdrop in the first image and is also blocked by another waterdrop in the second image.

In this paper, we use not only two images at certain two frames but all of the image sequence to remove adherent noises in the image sequence. We generate a spatio-temporal image by merging the acquired image sequence, and then detect and remove adherent noises (Yamashita et al., 2008, Yamashita et al., 2009).

The composition of this paper is detailed below. In Section 2, we mention about outline of our method. In Section 3, the method of making a spatio-temporal image is explained. In Section 4 and Section 5, the noise detection and removal method are constructed, respectively. In Section 6, experimental results are shown and we discuss the effectiveness of our method. Finally, Section 7 describes conclusions and future works.

2. Overview of noise detection and removal method

As to adherent noises on the protecting glasses of the camera, the positions of noises in images do not change when the direction of the camera changes (Fig. 3). This is because adherent noises are attached to the surface of the protecting glass of the camera and move together with the camera. On the other hand, the position of static background scenery and that of moving objects change while the camera rotates.

We transform the image after the camera rotation to the image whose gaze direction (direction of the principal axis) is same with that before the camera rotation. Accordingly, we can obtain a new image in which only the positions of adherent noises and moving objects are different from the image before the camera rotates.

A spatio-temporal image is obtained by merging these transformed images. In the spatio-temporal image, trajectories of adherent noises can be calculated. Therefore, positions of noises can be also detected in the image sequence from the spatio-temporal image. Finally, we can obtain a noise-free image sequence by estimating textures on adherent noise regions.

3. Spatio-temporal image

3.1 Image acquisition

An image sequence is acquired while a pan-tilt camera rotates.

At first (frame 0), one image is acquired where the camera is fixed. In the next step (frame 1), another image is taken after the camera rotates θ_1 rad about the axis which is perpendicular to the ground and passes along the center of the lens. In the t-th step (frame t), the camera rotate θ_t rad and the t-th image is taken. To repeat this procedure n times, we can acquire $n/30$ second movie if we use a 30fps camera.

Note that the rotation angle θ_t makes a positive direction a counterclockwise rotation (the direction of Fig. 3).

The direction and the angle of the camera rotation are estimated only from image sequences. At first, they are estimated by an optical flow. However, the optical flow may contain error. Therefore, the rotation angle is estimated between two adjacent frames by an exploratory way. Finally, the rotation angle is estimated between each frame and base frame. The detail of the estimation method is explained in (Yamashita et al., 2009).

3.2 Distortion correction

The distortion from the lens aberration of images is rectified. Let $(\tilde{u},\tilde{v})$ be the coordinate value without distortion, (u_0,v_0) be the coordinate value with distortion (observed coordinate value), and κ_1 be the parameter of the radial distortion, respectively (Weng et al., 1992). The distortion of the image is corrected by Equations (1) and (2).

$$u_0 = \tilde{u} + \kappa_1\tilde{u}(\tilde{u}^2 + \tilde{v}^2) \tag{1}$$

$$v_0 = \tilde{v} + \kappa_1\tilde{v}(\tilde{u}^2 + \tilde{v}^2) \tag{2}$$

3.3 Projective transformation

In the next step, the acquired t-th image (the image after θ_t rad camera rotation) is transformed by using the projective transformation. The coordinate value after the transformation (u_t,v_t) is expressed as follows (Fig. 4):

$$u_t = f\frac{f\tan\theta_t + \tilde{u}_t}{f - \tilde{u}_t\tan\theta_t} \tag{3}$$

$$v_t = f \frac{\sqrt{1 + f \tan^2 \theta_t}}{f - \tilde{u}_t \tan \theta_t} \tilde{v}_t \qquad (4)$$

where $(\tilde{u}_t, \tilde{v}_t)$ is the coordinate value of the t-th image before transformation, and f is the image distance (the distance between the center of lens and the image plane), respectively. The t-th image after the camera rotation is transformed to the image whose gaze direction is same with that before the camera rotation.

After the projective transformation, there are regions that have no texture in verge area of images (Black regions in Fig. 5(b)). Procedures mentioned below are not applied for these regions.

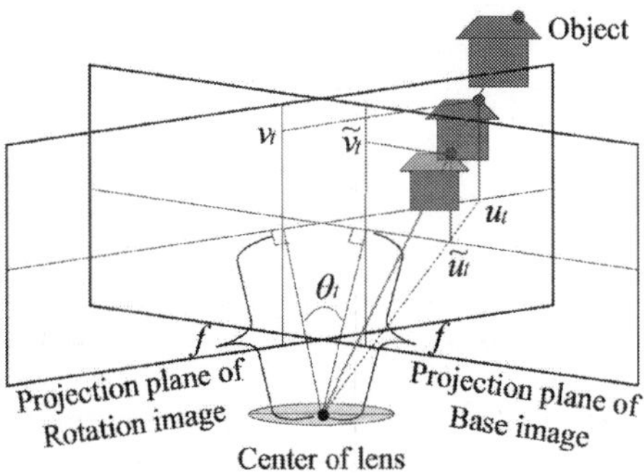

Fig. 4. Projective transformation.

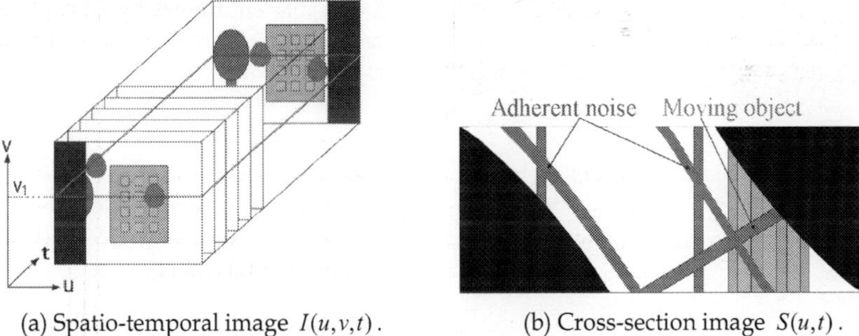

(a) Spatio-temporal image $I(u,v,t)$.

(b) Cross-section image $S(u,t)$.

Fig. 5. Spatio-temporal image.

3.4 Cross-section of spatio-temporal image

Spatio-temporal image $I(u,v,t)$ is obtained by arraying all the images (u_t, v_t) in chronological order (Fig. 5(a)). In Fig. 5(a), u is the horizontal axis that expresses u_t, v is the vertical axis that expresses v_t, and t is the depth axis that indicate the time (frame number t).

We can clip a cross-section image of $I(u,v,t)$. For example, Fig. 5(b) shows the cross-section image of the spatio-temporal image in Fig. 5(a) along $v = v_1$.

Here, let $S(u,t)$ be the cross-section spatio-temporal image. In this case, $S(u,t) = I(u,v_1,t)$.

In the cross-section spatio-temporal image $S(u,t)$, the trajectories of the static background scenery become vertical straight lines owing to the effect of the projective transformation. On the other hand, the trajectories of adherent noises in $S(u,t)$ become curves whose shapes can be calculated by Equations (3) and (4). Note that the trajectory of an adherent noise in Fig. 5 (b) looks like a straight line, however, it is slightly-curved.

In this way, there is a difference between trajectories of static objects and those of adherent noises. This difference helps to detect noises.

4. Noise detection

4.1 Median image

Median values along time axis t are calculated in the cross-section spatio-temporal image $S(u,t)$. After that, a median image $M(u,t)$ can be generated by replacing the original pixel values by the median values (Fig. 6(a)).

Adherent noises are eliminated in $M(u,t)$, because these noises in $S(u,t)$ are small in area as compared to the background scenery.

A clear image sequence can be obtained from $M(u,t)$ by using the inverse transformation of Equations (3) and (4) if there is no moving object in the original image. However, if the original image contains moving objects, the textures of these objects blur owing to the effect of the median filtering. Therefore, the regions of adherent noises are detected explicitly, and image restoration is executed for the noise regions to generate a clear image sequence around the moving objects.

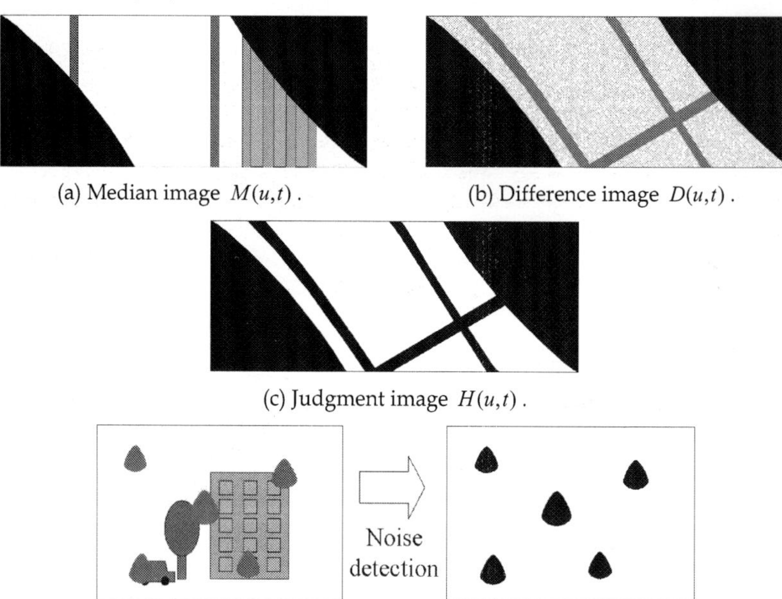

(a) Median image $M(u,t)$. (b) Difference image $D(u,t)$.

(c) Judgment image $H(u,t)$.

(d) Noise region image $R(\tilde{u},\tilde{v})$.

Fig. 6. Noise detection.

4.2 Difference Image

A difference between the cross-section spatio-temporal monochrome image and the median monochrome image is calculated for obtaining the difference image $S(u,t)$ by Equation (5). Pixel values in regions of $D(u,t)$ where adherent noises exist become large, while pixel values of $D(u,t)$ in the background regions are small (Fig. 6(b)).

$$D(u,t) = |S(u,t) - M(u,t)| \tag{5}$$

4.3 Noise region image

The regions where the pixel values of the difference images are larger than a certain threshold T_b are defined as the noise candidate regions. The judgment image $H(u,t)$ is obtained by

$$H(u,t) = \begin{cases} 0, & D(u,t) < T_b \\ 1, & D(u,t) \geq T_b \end{cases} \tag{6}$$

The region of $H(u,t) = 1$ is defined as noise candidate regions (Fig. 6(c)). Note that an adherent noise does not exist on the same cross-section image when time t increases, because v-coordinate value of the adherent noise changes owing to the influence of the projective transformation in Equation (4). Therefore, we consider the influence of this change and generate $H(u,t)$ in the way that the same adherent noise is on the same cross-section image.

In the next step, regions of adherent noises are detected by using $H(u,t)$. The trajectories of adherent noises are expressed by Equation (3). Therefore, the trajectory of each curve is tracked and the number of pixel where $H(u,t)$ is equal to 1 is counted. If the total counted number is more than the threshold value T_n, this curve is regarded as the noise region. As mentioned above, this tracking procedure is executed in 3-D (u,v,t) space. This process can detect adherent noise regions precisely, even when there are moving objects in the original image sequence thanks to the probability voting (counting).

After detecting noise regions in all cross-section spatio-temporal image $S(u,t)$, the noise region image $R(\tilde{u},\tilde{v})$ is generated by the inverse projective transformation from all $H(u,t)$ information (Fig. 6(d)).

Ideally, the noise regions consist of adherent noises. However, the regions where adherent noises don't exist are extracted in this process because of other image noises. Therefore, the morphological operations (i.e., erosion and dilation) are executed for eliminating small noises.

5. Noise removal

Adherent noises are eliminated from the cross-section spatio-temporal image $S(u,t)$ by using the image restoration technique (Bertalmio et al., 2003) for the noise regions detected in Section 4.

At first, a original image $S(u,t)$ is decomposed into a structure image $f(u,t)$ and a texture image $g(u,t)$ (Rudin et al., 1992). Figure 7 shows an example of the structure image and the texture image. Note that contrast of the texture image (Fig. 7(c)) is fixed for the viewability.

After the decomposition, the image inpainting algorithm (Bertalmio et al., 2000) is applied for the noise regions of the structure image $f(u,t)$, and the texture synthesis algorithm (Efros & Leung, 1999) is applied for the noise regions of the texture image $g(u,t)$, respectively. This method (Bertalmio et al., 2000) overcomes the weak point that the original image inpainting technique (Bertalmio et al., 2000) has the poor reproducibility for a complicated texture. After that, noise-free image can be obtained by merging two images. Finally, a clear image sequence without adherent noises is created with the inverse projective transformation.

(a) Original image.   (b) Structure image.   (c) Texture image.

Fig. 7. Image decomposition.

6. Experiment

Image sequence was acquired in a rainy day in the outdoor environment.
Figure 8(a) shows an example of the original image when the rotation speed of the camera is constant, and Fig. 8(b) shows the result of the projective transformation. In this experiment, the frame rate was 30fps, the image size was 360x240pixels, and the length of the movie was 100frames, respectively. We used a pan-tilt-zoom camera (Sony EVI-D100) whose image distance f was calibrated as 261pixel. Parameters for the noise detection were set as $T_b = 50$, $T_n = 10$.

Figure 9 shows the intermediate result of the noise detection. Figures 9(a) and (b) show the cross-section spatio-temporal image $S(u,t)$ in color and monochromic formats, respectively (red scanline in Fig. 8 (b), $v = 150$). There is a moving object (a human with a red umbrella) in this image sequence. Figures 9(c), (d) and (e) show the median image $M(u,t)$, the difference image $D(u,t)$, and the judge image $H(u,t)$, respectively. Figure 10(a) shows the noise region image $R(\tilde{u},\tilde{v})$.

Figure 11 shows the noise removal result. Figures 11(a) and (b) show the structure image after applying the image inpainting algorithm and the texture image after applying the texture synthesis algorithm, respectively, while Fig. 11(c) shows the noise removal result of the cross-section spatio-temporal image.

Figure 12 shows the final results of noise removal for the image sequence. All waterdrops are eliminated and the moving object can be seen very clearly in all frames.

(a) Original image.

(b) Original image after the projective transformation.

Fig. 8. Acquired image.

(a) Cross-section spatio-temporal image $S(u,t)$ (color).

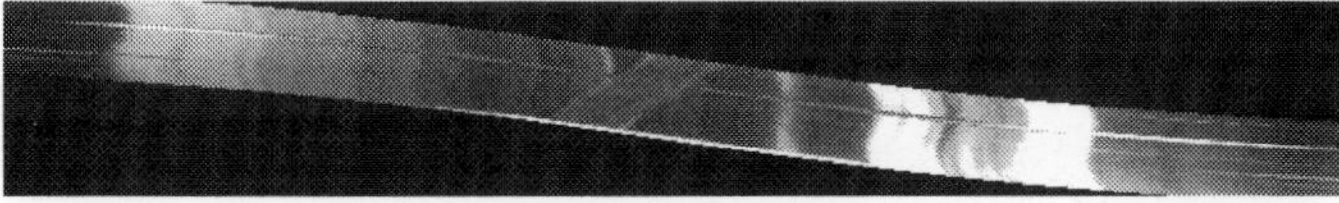

(b) Cross-section spatio-temporal image $S(u,t)$ (gray scale).

(c) Median image $M(u,t)$.

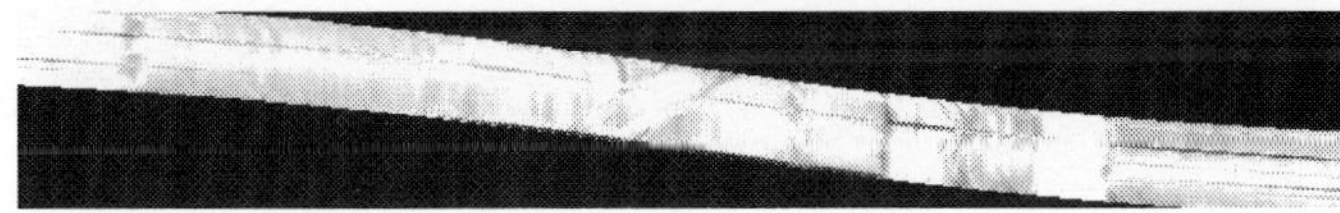

(d) Difference image $D(u,t)$.

(e) Judgment image $H(u,t)$.

Fig. 9. Results of noise detection.

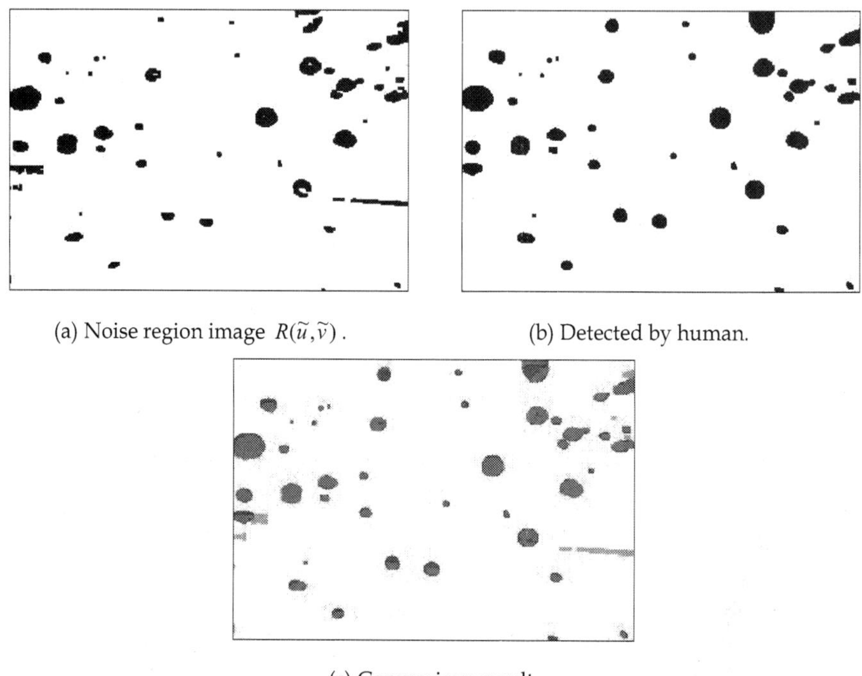

(a) Noise region image $R(\tilde{u},\tilde{v})$.

(b) Detected by human.

(c) Comparison result.

Fig. 10. Noise region image $R(\tilde{u},\tilde{v})$.

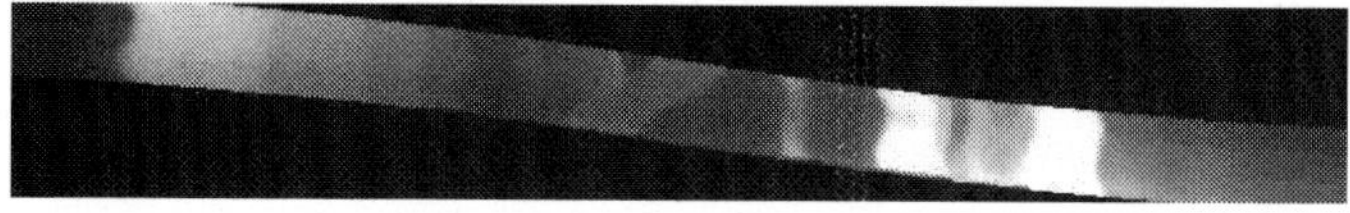

(a) Structure image.

(b) Texture image.

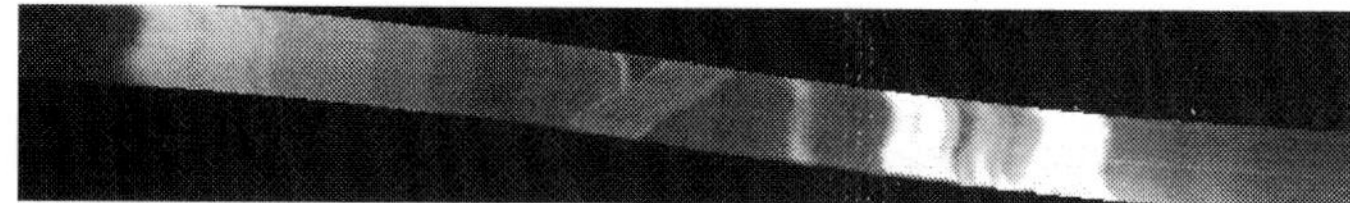

(c) Cross-section spatio-temporal image after noise removal.

Fig. 11. Results of noise removal.

To verify the accuracy of the noise detection, Fig. 10(a) is compared with the ground truth that is generated by a human operator manually (Fig. 10(b)). Figure 10(c) shows the comparison results. In Fig. 10(c), red regions indicate the correct detection, blue regions mean undetected noises, and green regions are exceeded detection regions. Actually, undetected noises are hard to detect when we see the final result (Fig. 12(b)). This is because the image interpolation works well in the noise removal step.

(a) Original image.	(b) Result image.

Fig. 12. Results of noise removal (waterdrop).

Figure 13 shows comparison results of texture interpolation with an existing method. Figure 13(b) shows the result by the image inpainting technique (Bertalmio et al., 2000), and Fig. 13(c) shows the result by our method. The result by the existing method is not good (Fig. 13(b)), because texture of the noise region is estimated only from adjacent region. In principle, it is difficult to estimate texture in several cases from only a single image. On the other hand, our method can estimate texture robustly by using a spatio-temporal image processing (Fig. 13(c)).

Figure 14 shows results of mud blob removal, and Fig. 15 shows results of waterdrop and mud blob removal, respectively.

Figure 16(a) shows an example of the original spatio-temporal image when the speed and the direction of the camera rotation is not constant, and Fig. 16(b) shows the result of the projective transformation, respectively.

Figure 17 shows the intermediate results of the noise removal. Figures 17(a) shows the cross-section spatio-temporal image $S(u,t)$. There are moving objects (walking men) in this image sequence. Figures 17(b), (c), (d), and (e) show the median image $M(u,t)$, the difference image $D(u,t)$, the judgment image $H(u,t)$, and the noise region image $R(\widetilde{u},\widetilde{v})$, respectively. Figure 17(f) shows the noise removal result from the cross-section spatio-temporal image.

Figure 18 shows the final results of noise removal for the image sequence. All noises are eliminated and the moving object can be seen very clearly in all frames.

From these results, it is verified that our method can remove adherent noises on the protecting glass of the camera regardless of their positions, colors, sizes, existence of moving objects, and the speed and the direction of the camera rotation.

7. Conclusion

In this paper, we propose a noise removal method from image sequence acquired with a pan-tilt camera. We makes a spatio-temporal image to extract the regions of adherent noises by examining differences of track slopes in cross section images between adherent noises and other objects. Regions of adherent noises are interpolated from the spatio-temporal image data. Experimental results show the effectiveness of our method.

As future works, the quality of the final result will be improved for interpolating noise regions in $S(u,v,t)$ space. As to the camera motion, a camera translation should be considered in addition to a camera rotation (Haga et al., 1997). It is important to compare the performance of our method with recent space-time video completion methods (e.g., Matsushita et al., 2005, Shen et al., 2006, Wexler et al., 2007).

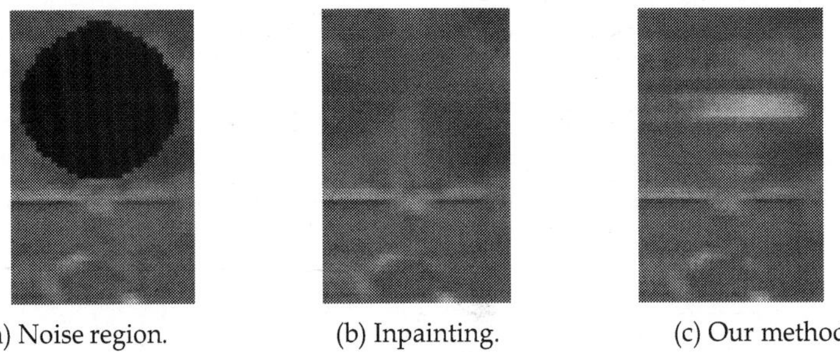

(a) Noise region.   (b) Inpainting.   (c) Our method.

Fig. 13. Comparison of noise removal results.

(a) Original image.   (b) Result image.

Fig. 14. Results of noise removal (mud blob).

(a) Original image. (b) Result image.

Fig. 15. Results of noise removal (waterdrop and mud blob).

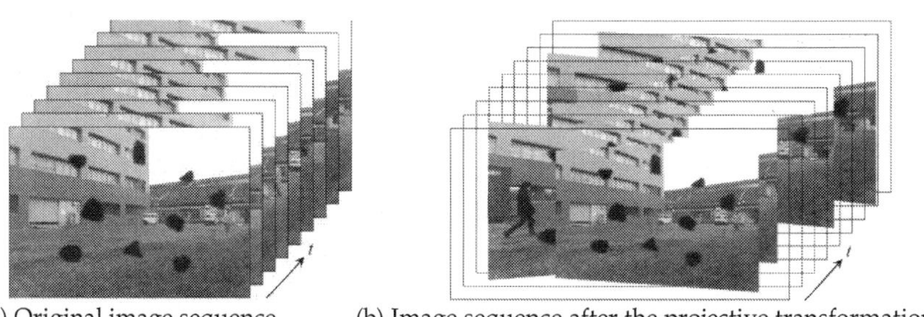

(a) Original image sequence. (b) Image sequence after the projective transformation.

Fig. 16. Image sequence when the rotation speed of the camera is not constant.

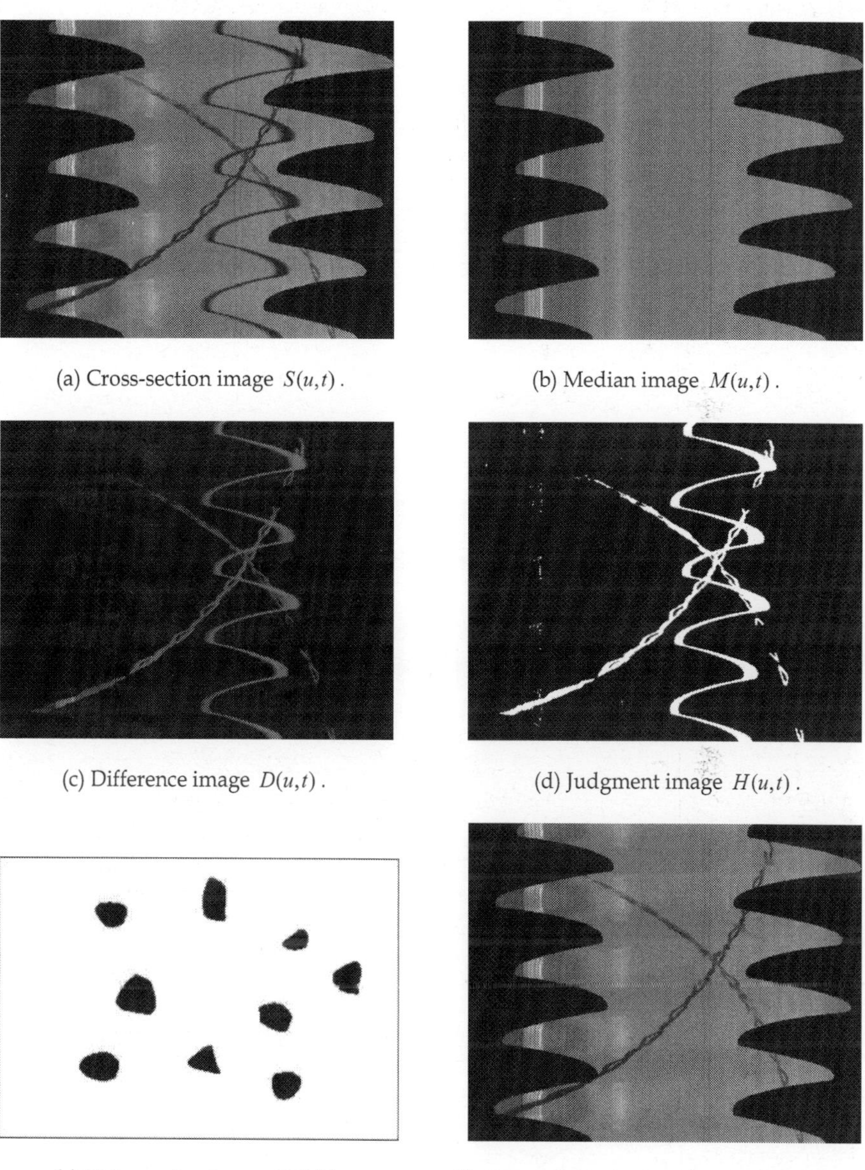

(a) Cross-section image $S(u,t)$.

(b) Median image $M(u,t)$.

(c) Difference image $D(u,t)$.

(d) Judgment image $H(u,t)$.

(e) Noise region image $R(\tilde{u},\tilde{v})$.

(f) Cross-section image after noise removal.

Fig. 17. Result of noise detection and removal (camera motion is not constant).

(a) Original image. (b) Result image.

Fig. 18. Results of noise removal (camera motion is not constant).

8. Acknowledgement

This research was partially supported by Special Project for Earthquake Disaster Mitigation in Urban Areas in cooperation with International Rescue System Institute (IRS) and National Research Institute for Earth Science and Disaster Prevention (NIED).

9. References

Kokaram, A. C., Morris, R.D., Fitzgerald, W.J. & Rayner, P.J.W. (1995). Interpolation of Missing Data in Image Sequences, *IEEE Transactions on Image Processing*, Vol.4, No.11, pp.1509-1519, 1995.

Masnou, S. & Morel, J.M. (1998). Level Lines Based Disocclusion, *Proceedings of the 5th IEEE International Conference on Image Processing (ICIP1998)*, pp.259-263, 1998.

Joyeux, L., Buisson, O., Besserer, B. & Boukir, S. (1999). Detection and Removal of Line Scratches in Motion Picture Films, *Proceedings of the IEEE International Conference on Computer Vision and Pattern Recognition (CVPR1999)*, pp.548-553, 1999.

Bertalmio, M., Sapiro, G., Caselles, V. & Ballester, C. (2000). Image Inpainting, *ACM Transactions on Computer Graphics (Proceedings of SIGGRAPH2000)*, pp.417-424, 2000.

Bertalmio, M., Bertozzi, A.L., & Sapiro, G. (2001). Navier-Stokes, Fluid Dynamics, and Image and Video Inpainting, *Proceedings of the 2001 IEEE Computer Society Conference on Computer Vision and Pattern Recognition (CVPR2001)*, Vol.1, pp.355-362, 2001.

Kang, S.H., Chan, T.F. & Soatto, S. (2002). Inpainting from Multiple Views, *Proceedings of the 1st International Symposium on 3D Data Processing Visualization and Transmission*, pp.622-625, 2002.

Bertalmio, M., Vese, L., Sapiro, G. & Osher, S. (2003). Simultaneous Structure and Texture Image Inpainting, *IEEE Transactions on Image Processing*, Vol.12, No.8, pp.882-889, 2003.

Matsushita, Y., Ofek, E., Tang, X. & Shum, H.-Y. (2005). Full-frame Video Stabilization, *Proceedings of the 2005 IEEE Computer Society Conference on Computer Vision and Pattern Recognition (CVPR2005)*, Vol.1, pp.50-57, 2005.

Shen, Y., Lu, F., Cao, X. & Foroosh, H. (2006). Video Completion for Perspective Camera Under Constrained Motion, *Proceedings of the 18th International Conference on Pattern Recognition (ICPR2006)*, Vol.3, pp.63-66, 2006.

Wexler, Y., Shechtman, E. & Irani, M. (2007). Space-Time Completion of Video, *IEEE Transactions on Pattern Analysis and Machine Intelligence*, Vol.29, No.3, pp.463-476, 2007.

Hase, H., Miyake, K. & Yoneda, M. (1999). Real-time Snowfall Noise Elimination, *Proceedings of the 1999 IEEE International Conference on Image Processing (ICIP1999)*, Vol.2, pp.406-409, 1999.

Garg, K. & Nayar, S.K. (2004). Detection and Removal of Rain from Videos, *Proceedings of the 2004 IEEE Computer Society Conference on Computer Vision and Pattern Recognition (CVPR2004)*, Vol.1, pp.528-535, 2004.

Yamashita, A., Kuramoto, M., Kaneko, T. & Miura, K.T. (2003). A Virtual Wiper -Restoration of Deteriorated Images by Using Multiple Cameras-, *Proceedings of the 2003 IEEE/RSJ International Conference on Intelligent Robots and Systems (IROS2003)*, pp.3126-3131, 2003.

Tanaka, Y., Yamashita, A., Kaneko, T. & Miura, K.T. (2006). Removal of Adherent Waterdrops from Images Acquired with a Stereo Camera System, *IEICE Transactions on Information and Systems*, Vol.89-D, No.7, pp.2021-2027, 2006.

Yamashita, A., Kaneko, T. & Miura, K.T. (2004). A Virtual Wiper -Restoration of Deteriorated Images by Using a Pan-Tilt Camera-, *Proceedings of the 2004 IEEE International Conference on Robotics and Automation (ICRA2004)*, pp.4724-4729, 2004.

Yamashita, A., Harada, T., Kaneko, T. & Miura, K.T. (2005). Virtual Wiper -Removal of Adherent Noises from Images of Dynamic Scenes by Using a Pan-Tilt Camera-, *Advanced Robotics*, Vol.19, No.3, pp.295-310, 2005.

Yamashita, A., Harada, T., Kaneko, T. & Miura, K.T. (2008). Removal of Adherent Noises from Image Sequences by Spatio-Temporal Image Processing, *Proceedings of the 2008 IEEE International Conference on Robotics and Automation (ICRA2008)*, pp.2386-2391, 2008.

Yamashita, A., Fukuchi, I. & Kaneko, T. (2009). Noises Removal from Image Sequences Acquired with Moving Camera by Estimating Camera Motion from Spatio-Temporal Information, *Proceedings of the 2009 IEEE/RSJ International Conference on Intelligent Robots and Systems (IROS2009)*, 2009.

Weng, J., Cohen, P. & Herniou, M. (1992). Camera Calibration with Distortion Models and Accuracy Evaluation, *IEEE Transactions on Pattern Analysis and Machine Intelligence*, Vol.14, No.10, pp.965-980, 1992.

Rudin, L.I., Osher, S. & Fatemi, E. (1992). Nonlinear Total Variation Based Noise Removal Algorithms, *Physica D*, Vol.60, pp.259-268, 1992.

Efros, A.A. & Leung, T.K. (1999). Texture Synthesis by Non-parametric Sampling, *Proceedings of the 7th IEEE International Conference on Computer Vision (ICCV1999)*, Vol.2, pp.1033-1038, 1999.

Haga, T., Sumi, K., Hashimoto, M., Seki, A. & Kuroda, S. (1997). Monitoring System with Depth Based Object Emphasis Using Spatiotemporal Image Processing, *Technical Report of IEICE (PRMU97-126)*, Vol.97, No.325, pp.41-46, 1997.

5

Parallel MATLAB Techniques

Ashok Krishnamurthy, Siddharth Samsi and Vijay Gadepally
Ohio Supercomputer Center and Ohio State University
U.S.A.

1. Introduction

MATLAB is one of the most widely used languages in technical computing. Computational scientists and engineers in many areas use MATLAB to rapidly prototype and test computational algorithms because of the scripting language, integrated user interface and extensive support for numerical libraries and toolboxes. In the areas of signal and image processing, MATLAB can be regarded as the de facto language of choice for algorithm development. However, the limitations of desktop MATLAB are becoming an issue with the rapid growth in the complexity of the algorithms and the size of the datasets. Often, users require instant access to simulation results (compute bound users) and/or the ability to simulate large data sets (memory bound users). Many such limitations can be readily addressed using the many varieties of parallel MATLAB that are now available (Choy & Edelman, 2005; Krishnamurthy et al., 2007). In the past 5 years, a number of alternative parallel MATLAB approaches have been developed, each with its own unique set of features and limitations (Interactive Supercomputing, 2009; Mathworks, 2009; MIT Lincoln Laboratories, 2009; Ohio Supercomputer Center, 2009).

In this chapter, we show why parallel MATLAB is useful, provide a comparison of the different parallel MATLAB choices, and describe a number of applications in Signal and Image Processing: Audio Signal Processing, Synthetic Aperture Radar (SAR) Processing and Superconducting Quantum Interference Filters (SQIFs). Each of these applications have been parallelized using different methods (Task parallel and Data parallel techniques). The applications presented may be considered representative of type of problems faced by signal and image processing researchers. This chapter will also strive to serve as a guide to new signal and image processing parallel programmers, by suggesting a parallelization strategy that can be employed when developing a general parallel algorithm. The objective of this chapter is to help signal and image processing algorithm developers understand the advantages of using parallel MATLAB to tackle larger problems while staying within the powerful environment of MATLAB.

2. Parallel MATLAB overview

The need for parallel MATLAB is presented in (Choy & Edelman, 2005) and the need for parallelizing MATLAB in particular can be summarized as follows:
1.   MATLAB is user friendly
2.   MATLAB is popular

In a survey of parallel MATLAB technologies, nearly 27 parallel MATLAB technologies were discovered. Many of these technologies are defunct, while many of these technologies are actively under development, with a large user base and active developer base. In our experience, three of these technologies stand out in terms of such factors.

In this section, we introduce three alternatives for parallel computing using MATLAB. The technologies we will be looking at are: pMATLAB+bcMPI, the Parallel Computing Toolbox (PCT) with MATLAB Distributed Computing Server and Star-P.

2.1 bcMPI

Traditionally, researchers have used MatlabMPI (Kepner & Ahalt, 2003) for parallel computing in MATLAB. bcMPI is an open source software library that is an alternative to MatlabMPI and is geared towards large, shared supercomputer centers. The bcMPI library was developed at the Ohio Supercomputer Center (OSC) to provide an efficient, scalable communication mechanism for parallel computing in MATLAB while maintaining compatibility with the MatlabMPI API (Hudak et al., 2007). The bcMPI package consists of an interface to the MPICH or OpenMPI library and a toolbox for MATLAB that implements a subset of the MatlabMPI API calls. bcMPI has been developed primarily on the Linux platform, but it has also been tested on the Mac OS-X, NetBSD and IA32 platforms. At its core, bcMPI is a C library that supports a collection of MATLAB and Octave data types. The bcMPI software architecture is as shown below:

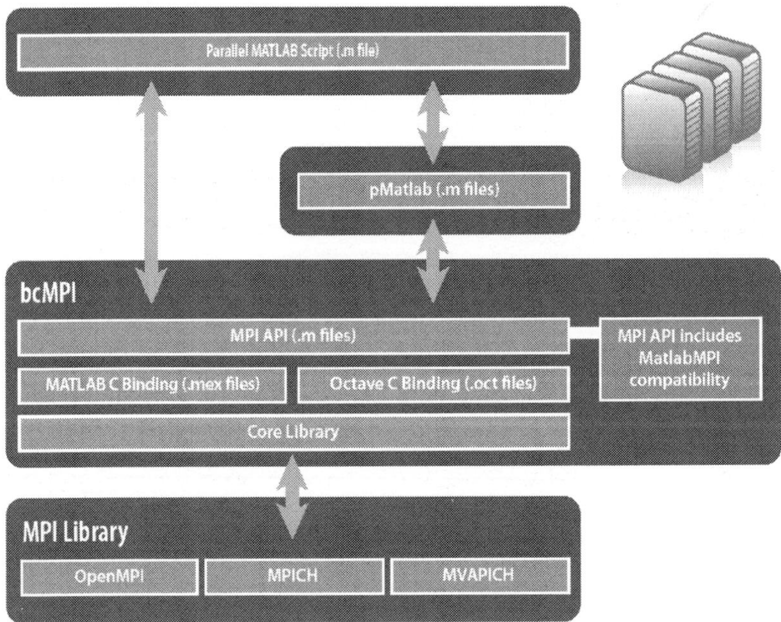

Fig. 1. bcMPI Architecture

Figure 1 illustrates the relationship between the vaious layers in the bcMPI architecture. The bcMPI library provides functions for synchronous as well as asynchronous communication between the MATLAB processes. It supports basic MPI functions as well as collective operations such as MPI_Reduce, MPI_Gather and MPI_Barrier. bcMPI also has an efficient implementation of the MPI_Broadcast function using the underlying MPI library. bcMPI has the advantage that it can use any MPI libraries even thought it has been tested actively with the OpenMPI and MPICH libraries. bcMPI interfaces with pMATLAB (a parallel MATLAB extension developed by MIT Lincoln Laboratory) (Bliss & Kepner, 2007) for distributed data processing. The combination of pMATLAB and bcMPI is denoted as pMATLAB+bcMPI. pMATLAB+bcMPI uses a layer of abstraction beyond traditional MPI calls and reduces programming complexity. With this combination, a user would not need to use explicit message passing calls to distribute data, as the pMATLAB application would perform these actions.

2.2 Parallel computing toolbox

The Parallel Computing Toolbox (PCT) along with the MATLAB Distributed Computing Server (MDCS) are commercial products offered by The MathWorks Inc. While the core MATLAB software itself supports multithreading, the PCT provides functionality to run MATLAB code on multicore systems and clusters. The PCT provides functions for parallel for-loop execution, creation/manipulation of distributed arrays as well as message passing functions for implementing fine grained parallel algorithms.

The MATLAB Distributed Computing Server (MDCS) gives the ability to scale parallel algorithms to larger cluster sizes. The MDCS consists of the MATLAB Worker processes that run on a cluster and is responsible for parallel code execution and process control. Figure 2 illustrates the architecture of PCT and MDCS

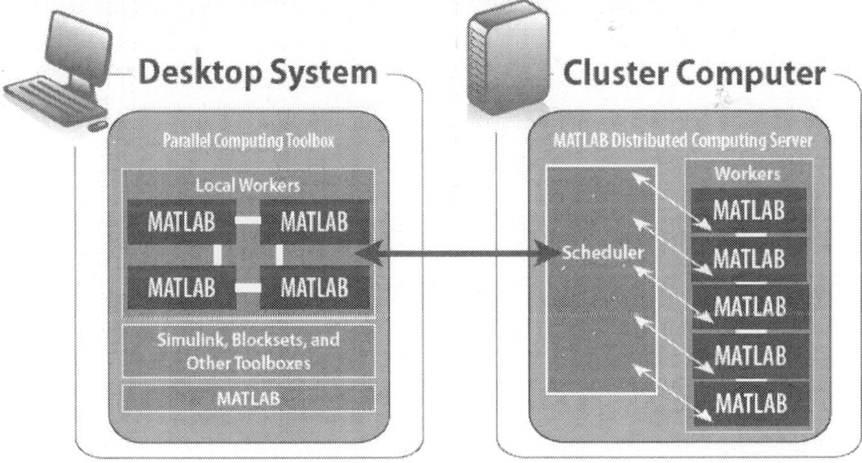

Fig. 2. The Parallel Computing Toolbox and MATLAB Distributed Computing Server

The PCT also allows users to run up to 8 MATLAB Labs or Workers on a single machine. This enables interactive development and debugging of parallel code from the desktop. After parallel code has been developed, it can be scaled up to much larger number of Worker or Labs in conjunction with the MDCS.

2.3 Star-P

Star-P is a client-server parallel computing platform for MATLAB available from Interactive Supercomputing. The architecture of Star-P is shown in the figure below:

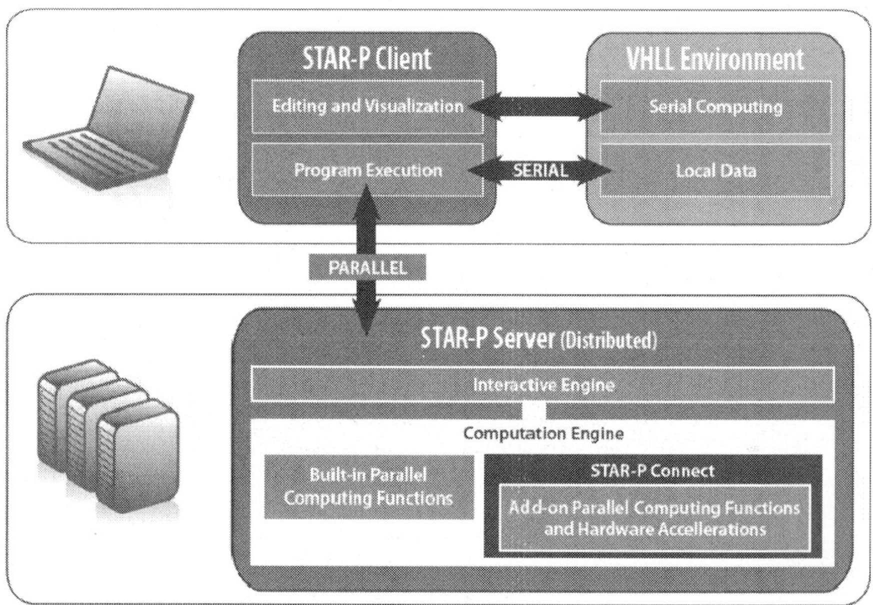

Fig. 3. Star-P Architecure

Figure 3 illustrates the structure of Star-P, and difference between the Star-P client and server. Star-P supports fine grained parallel as well as embarrassingly parallel modes of operation (these modes of operation are discussed in the next section). The biggest advantage offered by Star-P is that it eliminates the need for the developer to use explicit Message Passing Interface (MPI) message passing calls for communicating between the back-end processes. By using the "*p" construct, users can simply indicate the variables or data that are meant to be distributed over the back-end processes.

3. Parallel programming

The goals of most parallel computing algorithms include either reduction in computation time (for compute bound users) or analysis of larger data sets/parameters sweeps (for memory bound users) or some combination of both. This can also be described as a capability or capacity problem. In many cases, analysis involves small data sets, but the time required to analyze the desired data along with a wide enough parameter sweep on the same can make it impractical to run such analyses. In such (and a variety of other) cases, the use of parallel computing techniques can enable researchers to employ large numbers of processors to run comprehensive analyses in a reasonable amount of time. For example, the reconstruction of micro-CT images to generate 3D models may take up to 13 hours on a single machine. This can be reduced significantly simply by running the reconstruction algorithm in a parallel fashion. In other applications such as automated image analysis in medicine, the data sets tend to be large, with individual images ranging in the multiple gigabytes. In such cases, it may not be possible to load the data into memory and analyze the images. At the Ohio Supercomputer Center, we have observed that reading in images as large as 60000x60000 pixels in resolution on a single machine with 32GB RAM can take upwards of 30 minutes. Running simple algorithms on such large images becomes impractical, with software stability also becoming a concern. Furthermore, given many such images for analysis, the time required to run a single analysis on all images becomes impractical and parameter sweep studies become constrained by time. High resolution images obtained from tissue biopsies can be as large as 30-40GB each, and with the existing software and hardware limitation it is not possible to read in entire images on a single processor, thus leading to the problem of capability. In such cases, a simple solution is to use parallel computing in MATLAB to process parts of the image on separate processors to address problem.

Broadly, parallel algorithms can be divided into two categories: Task Parallel and Data Parallel. Task parallel (or Embarrassingly Parallel) algorithms take advantage of the fact that multiple processors can work on the same problem without communicating with each other. Typical cases of such algorithms include Monte Carlo simulations where the order of computations in a large loop are independent of each other and can be performed in any order without affecting the results. Similarly, another application ideal for task parallelism involves processing multiple datasets using the same algorithm. In such cases multiple processors can analyze subsets of the data simultaneously without the need for inter-processor communication. Data parallel (or Fine Grained Parallel) algorithms typically involve some inter-processor communication. In such algorithms the data to the analyzed is typically too large to be analyzed on a single processor. Parallel computing paradigms are used to distribute the data across processors and each processor works on a smaller chunk of the same data. In such cases, there may be some communication required between different processors that involve exchange of data to address boundary conditions. For example, a 2-D FFT of a large matrix can be carried out in a parallel fashion by splitting up the matrix across multiple processors. Based on how the data is distributed, each processor needs a small amount of data from its neighbour to complete the computations.

The maximum speed up (ratio of runtime before parallelization to runtime after parallelization) is discussed in (Amdahl, 1967). The maximum observable speedup is limited by the percent of the application that can be parallelized. The maximum percentage of the application that can be parallelized is determined by the percentage of code that must be run serially. This serial execution requirement is often due to data dependencies present in the code, or complications that may arise due to parallelization. It is important that a parallel programmer determine the maximum speed up before beginning parallelization. In certain applications regardless of parallelization technique, the required speedup may not be attainable.

In the next section, we discuss three applications that help illustrate the different types of parallel algorithms discussed here. Two of the applications being considered can be parallelized using either the task parallel or data parallel technique. One of the presented applications can be parallelized using both techniques, and a comparison is provided.

4. Application development

In this section, three applications will be presented. The aim of this section is to give real life examples of the discussed parallel MATLAB technologies in action (Krishnamurthy et al., 2008). Additionally, this section will suggest methods by which parallel MATLAB programmers can approach a given parallelization problem. The following applications have been parallelized using (1) Task Parallel (Embarrassingly Parallel) and/or (2) Data Parallel (Fine Grained Parallel) techniques.

For each of the applications developed we will concentrate on the following:

1. Application Background

    This section will give background information on the application. This section is intended to show readers the variety of problems that can be tackled using parallel MATLAB.

2. Parallelization Strategy

    This section will describe the strategy employed when parallelizing the application. Additionally, specific code examples from the serial code, and our parallel code for the same will be shown.

3. Results

    This section will demonstrate the results obtained through parallelization. This section is important in illustrating the computational benefits possible through parallelization.

4.1 Acoustic signal processing
4.1.1 Application background:

Acoustic signal processing on a battlefield primarily involves detection and classification of ground vehicles. By using an array of active sensors, signatures of passing objects can be collected for target detection, tracking, localization and identification. One of the major components of using such sensor networks is the ability of the sensors to perform self-localization. Self-localization can be affected by environmental characteristics such as the terrain, wind speed, etc. An application developed by the U.S. Army Research Laboratory, GRAPE, consists of a Graphical User Interface (GUI) for running acoustic signal processing algorithms in parallel on a cluster.

In recent experiments, several gigabytes of data were collected in 3-minute intervals. Processing each data file takes over a minute. A number of different algorithms are used to estimate the time of arrival of the acoustic signals. If the number of analysis algorithms applied to the data is increased, the processing and analysis time increases correspondingly. In order to achieve near real-time response, the data was processed in a parallel fashion in MATLAB. Since each data file can be processed independently of others, the parallelization approach was to split up processing of individual data files across multiple processors.

4.1.2 Parallelization strategy:

It was determined that this particular application could be parallellized using task parallel (Embarrassingly Parallel) techniques. Using the MATLAB profiler, it was determined that the majority of computation time was spent in the execution of a function called *process_audio()*. It was further determined that the data generated by this function was not used in other places (data independence). Thus, a task parallel approach was employed. The function *process_audio()* takes a data structure as an input. One of the fields in this structure

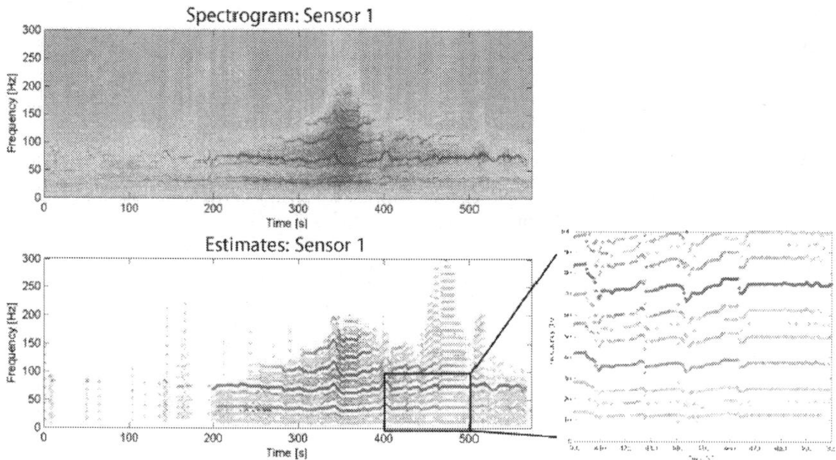

Fig. 4. Vehicle signature identified via signal processing

is *nFiles*, which describes the number of files to be run by the *process_audio()* function. A distributed array was used to distribute these indices across multiple processors. The code before and after parallelization are as follows:

```
%%%%SERIAL CODE%%%%              %%%%PARALLEL CODE%%%%

                                Alocal = A;
                                indlocal = local(indices)
out = process_audio(A)          indlocal = indlocal + [(Nfiles-size(indlocal,2)+1):Nfiles];
                                Alocal.fname = A.fname(indlocal)
                                out = process_audio(Alocal)
```

Fig. 5. pMATLAB parallelization of acoustic signal processing application

4.1.3 Results:

Results from parallelization of the GRAPE code using MDCS, bcMPI, and Star-P are presented below. In the following graphs, the primary (left) vertical axis corresponds to the total time taken by the *process_audio()* function to complete analysis on 63 data files. The secondary (right) axis displays the speedup obtained when running on multiple processors. It is also interesting to note that the modifications required to parallelize the code represented an increase of less than 1% in Source Lines of Code (SLOC).

Results for the MDCS and bcMPI tests were obtained on the Ohio Supercomputer Center's Pentium 4 cluster using an InfiniBand interconnection network. Results for the Star-P tests were obtained on the Ohio Supercomputer Center's IBM 1350 Cluster, with nodes containing dual 2.2 GHz Opteron processors, 4 GB RAM and an InfiniBand interconnection network. As the parallelization strategy is a task parallel solution that incurs no interprocess communication, a nearly linear speed-up is observed for each of the parallel MATLAB tools. It is also clear that parallel MATLAB can aid greatly in returning a timely solution to the user.

From the above results (Figures 6, 7 and 8), it is also clear that the three technologies give nearly the same speedup for a given code set. For the remaining applications, results are shown using pMATLAB+bcMPI, and similar results can be obtained by using any of the presnted tools.

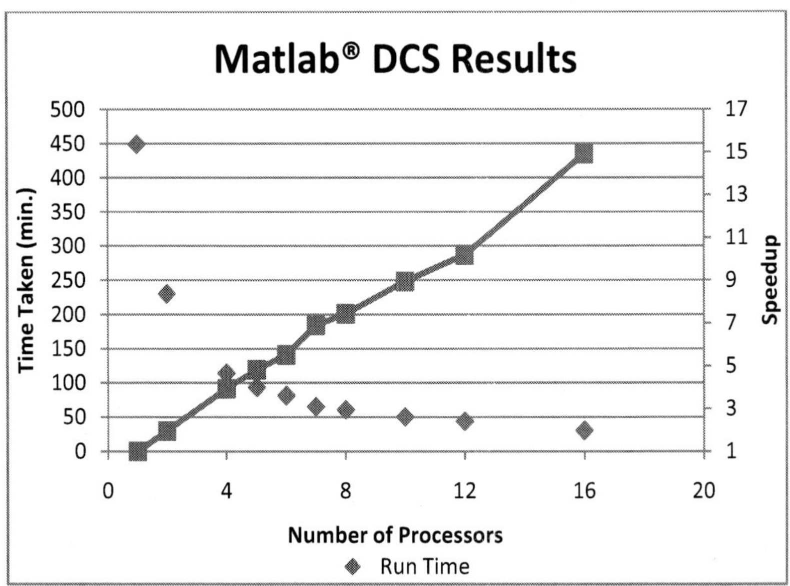

Fig. 6. MDCS Results

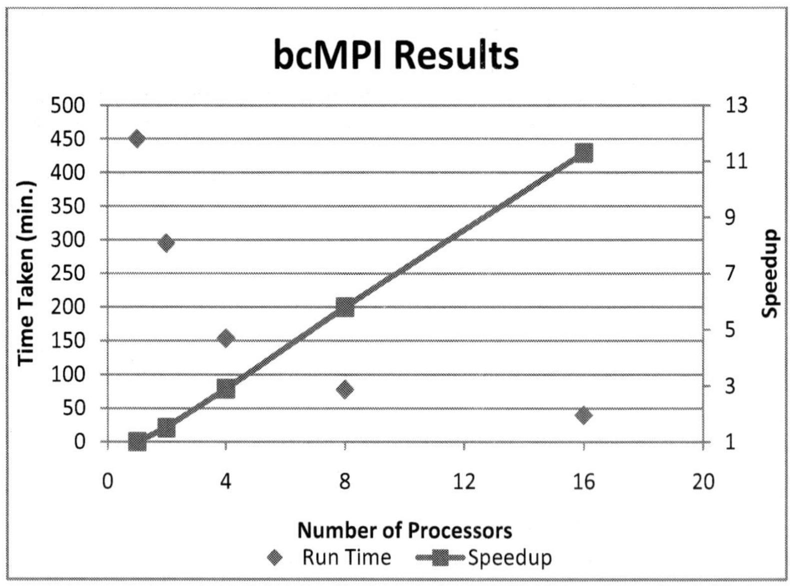

Fig. 7. bcMPI Results

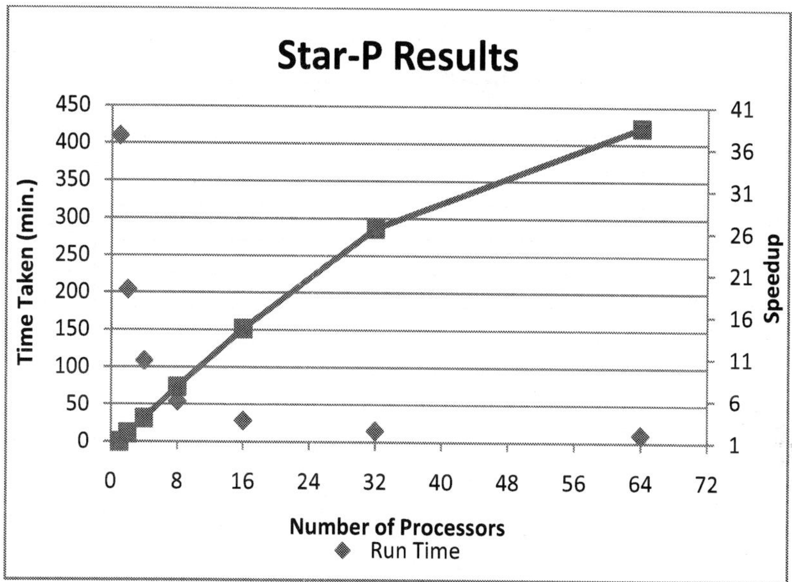

Fig. 8. Star-P Results

4.2 Synthetic aperture radar

4.2.1 Application background:

The Third Scalable Synthetic Compact Application (SSCA #3) benchmark (Bader et al., 2006), from the DARPA HPCS Program, performs Synthetic Aperture Radar (SAR) processing. SAR processing creates a composite image of the ground from signals generated by a moving airborne radar platform. It is a computationally intense process, requiring image processing and extensive file IO. Such applications are of importance for Signal and Image Processing engineers, and the computations performed by the SSCA #3 application are representative of common techniques employed by engineers.

4.2.2 Parallelization strategy:

In order to parallelize SSCA #3, the MATLAB profiler was run on the serial implementation. The profiler showed that approximately 67.5% of the time required for computation is spent in the image formation function of Kernel 1 (K1). Parallelization techniques were then applied to the function *formImage* in K1. Within *formImage*, the function *genSARimage* is responsible for the computationally intense task of creating the SAR image. *genSARimage* consists of two parts, namely, the interpolation loop and the 2D Inverse Fourier Transform. Both of these parts were parallelized through the creation of distributed matrices and then executed via pMatlab/bcMPI.

A code example is presented in Figure 9 showing the serial and parallel versions of one code segment from the function *genSARimage*. It is interesting to note that nearly 67.5% of the code was parallelized by adding approximately 5.5% to the SLOC. In the sequential code on the left of Figure 9, the matrix, *F*, needs to be divided among the processor cores to parallelize the computation. In the parallel code on the right of Figure 9, the upper shaded region shows the creation of a distributed version of the matrix, *pF*, which is distributed as contiguous blocks of columns distributed across all processors. The code within the loop remains functionally equivalent, with the parallel version altered so that each processor core processes its local part of the global array. The lower shaded region shows a pMatlab *transpose_grid* (Bliss and Kepner, 2006) operation, which performs all-to-all communication to change *pF* from a column distributed matrix to a row distributed matrix in order to compute the following inverse FFT in parallel. Finally, in the lowest shaded region, the entire pF array is aggregated back on a single processor using the pMatlab *agg* command.

```
%%%%SERIAL CODE%%%%                    %%%%PARALLEL CODE%%%%

                                       kxlocal=kx(:,(myrank*pFlocalsize(2)+1):(myrank+1)*pFlocalsize(2))
                                       KXlocal=KX(:,(myrank*pFlocalsize(2)+1):(myrank+1)*pFlocalsize(2))
F = single(zeros(nx, m));              fsmlocal=fsm(:,(myrank*pFlocalsize(2)+1):(myrank+1)*pFlocalsize(2))
                                       m = length((myrank*pFlocalsize(2) +1):(myrank+1)*pFlocalsize(2))
                                       pFmap = map([1 Ncpus], {}, [0:Ncpus-1])
                                       pF = zeros(nx,m,pFmap);
                                       pFlocal = ifft(pFlocal, [],2);
                                       pF = put_local(pF, pFlocal);

                                       Z = transpose_grid(pF);
spatial=ftshift(ifft(ifft(fftshift(F),[],2)) clear pF, pFlocal;
                                       Zlocal = local(Z);
                                       Zlocal = ifft(Zlocal, [],1);
                                       Z = put_local(Z,Zlocal);
                                       Z = agg(Z);
                                       spatial = abs(Z)';
```

Fig. 9. pMATLAB parallelization of image formation kernel

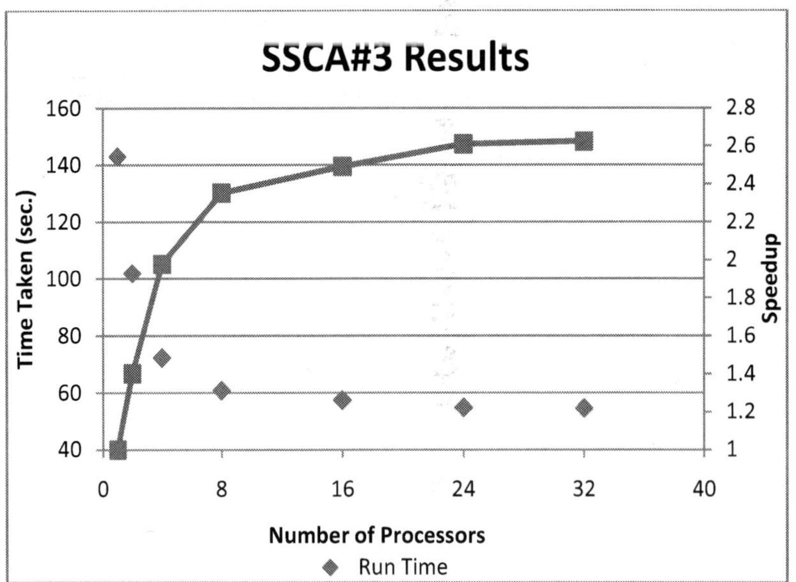

Fig. 10. SSCA#3 Results

4.2.3 Results:

The pMATLAB+bcMPI implementation of the SSCA#3 benchmark was run on an AMD Opteron cluster at the Ohio Supercomputer Center with nodes containing dual 2.2 GHz Opteron processors, 4 GB RAM and an InfiniBand interconnection network. A matrix size of 1492x2296 elements was chosen, and the runs were conducted on 1, 2, 4, 8, 16, 24, and 32 processor cores. The absolute performance times and relative speedups for image formation are given in Figure 10. The graph is presented as in the previous application.

Amdahl's law states that the maximum speedup of a parallel application is inversely proportional to the percentage of time spent in sequential execution. Thus, according to Amdahl's Law, the maximum speedup possible when parallelizing 67.5% of the code is approximately 3. In the above figure, a maximum speedup of approximately 2.6 is obtained for the 32 processor run.

4.3 Superconducting Quantum Interference Filters (SQIF)
4.3.1 Application background:

The computationally intensive signal and image processing application for this project is the modelling and simulation of Superconducting Quantum Interference Filters (SQIF) provided by researchers at SPAWAR Systems Center PACIFIC. Superconducting Quantum Interference Devices (SQUIDs) (a superconducting circuit based on Josephson junctions) and arrays of SQUIDs or Superconducting Quantum Interference Filters (SQIF) have a wide variety of applications (Palacios et al., 2006). SQUIDs are the world's most sensitive detectors of magnetic signals (sensitivity ~femto-Teslas) for the detection and characterization of signals so small as to be virtually immeasurable by any other known sensor technology. Applications such as detection of deeply buried facilities from space (military labs, WMD, etc), detection of weak signals on noise limited environments, deployment on mobile platforms, SQUID-based gravity gradiometry for navigation of submarines, biomagnetism (magnetoencephalography (MEG) and magnetocardiogram (MCG)) imaging for medical applications, detection of weapons/contraband concealed by clothing (hot spot microbolometers) and non-destructive evaluation are some of the applications based on SQUID and SQIF technologies.

Parallelization of codes that simulate SQUIDs/SQIFs are becoming extremely important for researchers. The SQIF application is intended to solve large scale SQIF problems for the study and characterization of interference patterns, flux-to-voltage transfer functions, and parameter spread robustness for SQIF loop size configurations and SQIF array fault tolerance. The SQIF application is intended to solve large scale problems relating to the field of cooperative dynamics in coupled noisy dynamical systems near a critical point. The technical background for the SQIF program can be found in (Antonio Palacios, 2006). The particular application developed was intended to run the SQIF program in an optimized fashion to either (1) reduce runtime and/or (2) increase the size of the dataset.

4.3.2 Parallelization strategy:

The MATLAB profiler was used on the supplied SQIF application to determine a course of action. Application of the MATLAB profiler on the supplied *dynamics_sqif()* function using 100 SQUIDs yielded a runtime of approximately 20 minutes. A detailed analysis showed most (approximately 88%) of the time spent in the *coupled_squid()* function. Further review of the profiler results showed a linear increase in the time taken by *dynamics_sqif()* as the number of SQUIDs (*Nsquid*) was increased. Parallelization was carried out on the *dynamics_sqif()* function.

Parallelization of code consisted of adding parallel constructs to the given SQIF application. These constructs allowed the program to be run on multiple CPUs. In the course of parallelization, developers noticed the existence of task based and data based operations in the application. Task based operations were parallelized through an embarrassingly parallel (**EP**) implementation. The data based operations were parallelized through a fine grained parallel (**FP**) solution. The application was parallelized using both of the following techniques.

1.   Task Based Parallelization (TP) – Parallelization over *length(xe)*
2.   Data Based Parallelization (DP) – Parallelization over *Nsquid*s

A brief technical background and relative merits and demerits of each implementation are given below. It is interesting to note the difference in performance for both techniques. Results of the optimization and parallelization were obtained using pMATLAB+bcMPI on the Ohio Supercomputer Center's AMD Opteron Cluster "Glenn."

<u>Task Parallel Approach</u>

This particular implementation involved a task based parallel solution. The type of parallelization implemented was embarrassingly parallel. Specifically, for this application, an approach was taken such that individual processors would perform a part of the entire task, thus making the approach task parallel in nature. The embarrassingly parallel solution, in the context of this application, involved the distribution of workload between processors for the number of points for flux calculation (*length(xe)*). For this particular implementation, parallelization efforts were carried out in the *dynamics_sqif()* function. It was determined that iterations of the loop containing "*for i = 1:length(xe)*" were independent of each other. Thus, it was determined that a number of CPUs could process different portions of the 'for' loop. For example, if there were 4 processors and *length(xe)* = 100, the loop would run such that on processor 1, *i* = 1:25, on processor 2, *i* = 26:50, etc. Thus, the approach is embarrassingly parallel in nature.

A code snippet of the added pMATLAB lines required for parallelization is shown in the following figure.

```
%%%%SERIAL CODE%%%%                %%%%PARALLEL CODE%%%%

                                   DVmap = map([1 Ncpus], {}, [0:Ncpus-1]);
                                   pDV = zeros(Nsquid, length(xe), DVmap);
                                   lngth = length(xe);
For i = 1:length(xe)               DVlocal = local(pDV);
                                   size(DVlocal)
x = series_sqif(J(j),xe(i),M,dt,   ind = zeros(1,Ncpus);
   beta_n,Nsquid,var_size,tmax);   ind(:) = ceil(double(lngth)/Ncpus);
                                   ind(1:rem(lngth,Ncpus)) = ceil(double(lngth)/Ncpus);
end                                ind(Ncpus) = (ind(Ncpus)-(sum(ind)-lngth));
                                   num_loop = ind(rank+1);
                                   t = sum(ind(1:(rank+1)));
                                   startind = t-ind(rank+1)+1;
                                   endind = startind+num_loop -1;

                                   for i = startind:endind
                                   x = series_sqif(J(j),xe(i),M,dt,
                                       beta_n,Nsquid,var_size,tmax);
                                   end
```

Fig. 11. pMatlab additions to serial code for Task Parallel Implementation

<u>Data Parallel Approach</u>

In this approach, a fine grained parallel solution is implemented. In the *dynamics_sqif()* function, there is a function call for *series_sqif()*. This function, *series_sqif()*, in turn calls *my_ode()* which in turn calls *coupled_squid()*. As has been mentioned in the application background, the majority of time is spent in the *coupled_squid()* function, due to the number of times that the *coupled_squid()* function is called. The function *coupled_squid()* creates, as an output, a matrix of size *1 x Nsquid*. Looking at this, it was decided that parallelizing over *Nsquid*s would yield improvement in overall runtime. It was observed that by making suitable modifications to *coupled_squid()*, it would be possible for different processors to work on different parts of the overall data. After creating a version of *coupled_squid()* that would allow different processors to access different parts of the data, all referring function calls were modified to make use of this parallel behavior. Thus, at the topmost level, in *dynamics_sqif()*, the function *series_sqif()* could be called by different processors with different sections of the original data. A snippet of the pMATLAB code required in the *coupled_squid()* function is shown in the following figure.

```
%%%%SERIAL CODE%%%%              %%%%PARALLEL CODE%%%%

                                xmap = map([1 Ncpus], {}, [0:Ncpus-1]);
                                x = zeros(10001, 2*NsquidsOrig, xmap);
                                xlocal = local(x);
x = series_sqif(J(j),xe(i),M,   xlocaltmp = series_sqif(J(j),xe(i),M,dt,beta_n, Nsquid,var_size,tmax,
    t,beta_n,Nsquid,var_size,tmax);             localpart, NsquidsOrig);
                                xlocal = xlocaltmp(:,locPart_x);
                                x = put_local(x, xlocal);
                                x = agg(x);
```

Fig. 12. pMatlab additions to serial code for Data Parallel Implementation

4.3.3 Results

This section discusses the results of parallelizing the SQIF application by both techniques (Task parallel and Data parallel techniques). A brief discussion about the results obtained using both techniques is also presented. In the following graphs, the primary (left) vertical axis corresponds to the total time taken by the SQIF application function to complete analysis on a fixed *NSquids*. The secondary (right) axis displays the speedup obtained when running on multiple processors.

<u>Task Parallel Approach</u>

Results for running the task parallel implementation of the SQIF application were obtained on the Ohio Supercomputer Center's AMD Opteron Cluster (glenn). Near linear speedup was obtained for increasing number of processors and constant number of SQUIDs (*Nsquid*). The following graph summarizes the results obtained by running the SQIF application at OSC with a varying number of SQUIDs, and Processors.

<u>Data Parallel Approach</u>

Results for running the data parallel implementation of the SQIF application were obtained on the Ohio Supercomputer Center's AMD Opteron Cluster (glenn). A speedup was observed, and results are graphed below. The comparison is made between different numbers of SQUIDs (*Nsquid*), and different numbers of Processors. As the parallel implementation is data parallel in nature, slight modifications were made in the actual computation.

The following graph shows the application runtime and speedup for a fixed problem size (number of *Nsquid*s). A comparison is also made between the runtimes of the task parallel solution and data parallel solution.

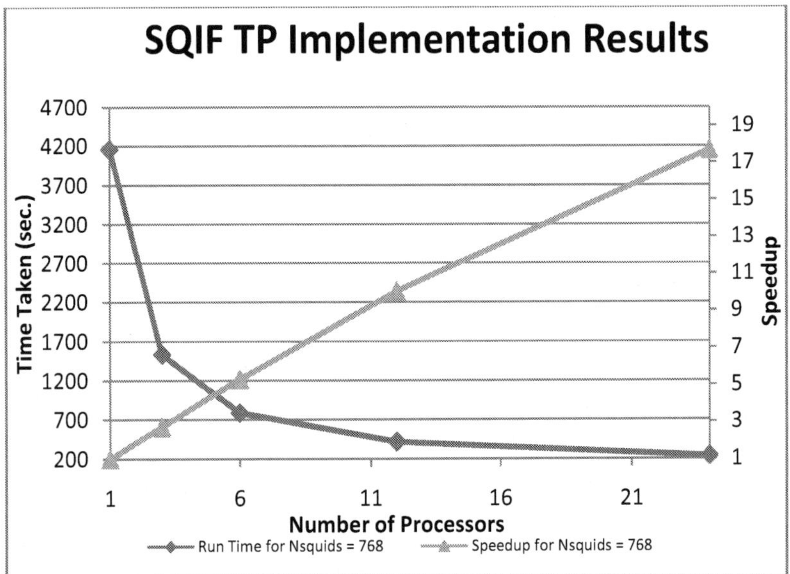

Fig. 13. Graph of TP implementation for NSquids = 768

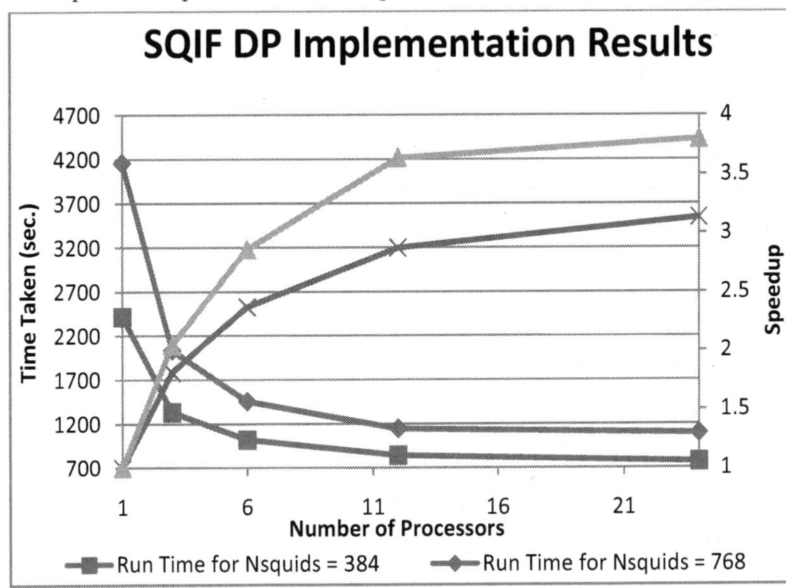

Fig. 14. Graph of DP runtimes on Glenn for Nsquids = 384 (red), 786 (blue)

From Figure 14, it is clear that there is definite speedup when using the data parallel (DP) implementation. This speedup becomes more pronounced when larger *Nsquid*s are used. In these graphs, it is interesting to note that the speedup is not linear, but is much more scalable. Also, communication overhead starts to play a large part in the results when the number of processors is greater than 24 (for the problem sizes tested).

The following graph shows the performance of parallelization over *length(xe)* when compared to parallelization over *Nsquids* for a constant *length(xe)* of 100 and varying *Nsquids*. This comparison was made on the Ohio Supercomputer Center's AMD Opteron Cluster "Glenn."

From Figure 15, it is clear that parallelization over the *length(xe)* yields far better performance than parallelization over *NSquids*. This is due to the following reasons:

1. Parallelization over *length(xe)* is embarrassingly parallel. It is expected that this approach gives near linear speedup.

2. In the parallelization over *length(xe)*, the percentage of parallelized code is nearly 99%. In the parallelization over *Nsquids*, the percentage of parallelized code is nearly 90%.

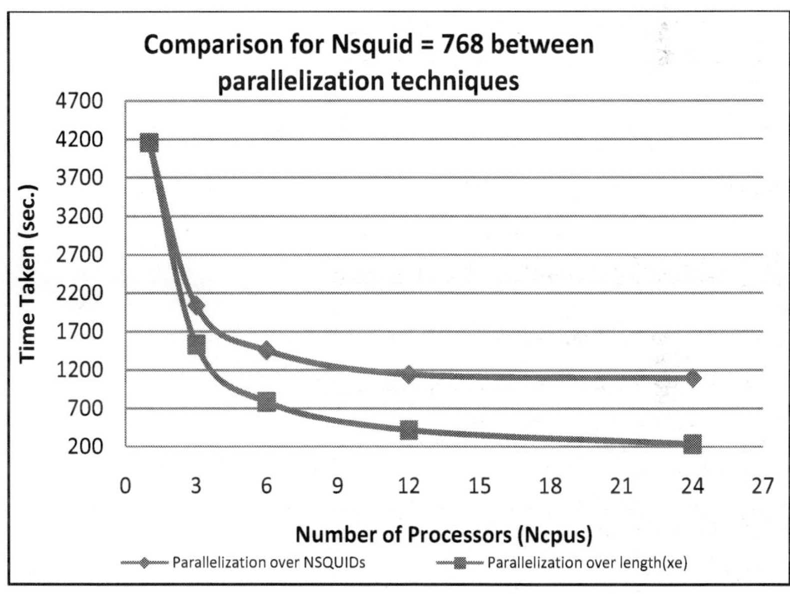

Fig. 15. Comparison between two techniques of parallelization for Nsquids = 768

Maximum speed up for both parallelization techniques:

1. By Amdahl's Law, given that parallelization is being applied to approximately 90% of the problem size, the maximum speed up one can expect is $1/(1-0.90) \approx 10$, in the case of parallelization over *Nsquids*. The maximum observed speedup is approximately 8.7 (for *Nsquids* = 14400, Number of Processors = 48).

2. By Amdahl's Law, given that parallelization is being applied to approximately 99% of the problem size, the maximum speed up one can expect is $1/(1-0.99) \approx 100$, in the case of parallelization over the *length(xe)*. The maximum observed speedup is approximately 20 (for *Nsquids* = 768, Number of Processors = 24).

5. Defining a general parallelization strategy:

In this section, a very general strategy for determining a parallelization strategy is presented. Please note that this strategy is very general in nature due to the numerous types of applications that can be parallelized.

1. **Determining what to parallelize:**
   Often, a user may use a tool such as the MATLAB profiler to determine this. The root cause of the slowdown needs to be determined. For example, if *function1()* is shown to be causing the slowdown, the lines of code within *function1()* that are causing the problem should be parallelized. If the user wants to parallelize the application for improved memory utilization, the source of memory usage should be determined, and this should be parallelized.

2. **Determining the type of parallelization:**
   In this step, the cause is analyzed by looking at data dependencies to determine whether an embarrassingly parallel strategy can be employed or whether a fine grained parallel strategy is required. In general, when parallelizing a large portion of code, embarrassingly parallel solutions are easier to code and deliver greater speedup when compared with fine grained parallel solutions. On the other hand, fine grained parallel solutions are useful when attempting to improve memory utilization in the application, as fine grained parallel solutions consist of data parallelization. Application of Amdahl's Law would also be beneficial, so that the developer understands what speedup to expect. For very few applications, parallelization may not lead to a significant speedup.

3. **Using one of the mentioned technologies to parallelize the application:**
   In our experience, all the mentioned technologies offer similar performance and usability for embarrassingly parallel applications. For fine-grained parallel applications, the user needs to look at the technologies more closely.

4. **Parallelize the application:**
   Recode the application with parallel constructs.

5. **Test the Application:**
   Verify that the parallelization gives correct results (often within a margin of error). As parallelization often modifies the calculations, the user needs to confirm that the parallelized code not only brings about a speedup or larger memory availability but also maintains the correct solution.

6. Conclusions and future work

This chapter begins with an introduction to Parallel MATLAB and its uses. From our experience, most users who require parallel MATLAB are (1) compute and/or (2) memory bound. Compute bound users often require faster time-to-solution from their MATLAB applications. Memory bound users often require the shared resources offered by using multiple processing units (more RAM, etc.). Both of these classes of users can make extensive use of parallel MATLAB technologies. Broadly, there are two techniques to parallelization (1) Task parallel (Embarrassingly parallel) or (2) Data parallel (Fine Grained parallel). Both of these techniques were described in detail, and the strategies involved with recoding an application to reflect these techniques was discussed. Three applications from the signal and image processing area were highlighted. These applications were intended to show potential users the power of parallel MATLAB, and the ease of use. Very often, for less than 5% increase in Source Lines of Code, an application can be parallelized. The applications also intended to demonstrate typical results that can be obtained by parallelizing applications using the discussed techniques. The acoustic signal processing application was parallelized using task parallel techniques, and the SSCA #3 application was parallelized using data parallel techniques. As a final application, the authors parallelized the SQIF application using both task and data parallel techniques, so demonstrate the difference between the techniques.

At the Ohio Supercomputer Center, we have had extensive experience with parallel MATLAB technologies pertaining to the Signal and Image processing area. Three parallel MATLAB technologies stand out in terms of development status: (1) bcMPI + pMATLAB (2) MATLAB DCS and Parallel Computing Toolbox, and (3) Star-P. In our experience all three technologies are equally usable, though developer preference and developer experience may play a part.

As multi-core and multi-processor systems become more common, parallel MATLAB clusters will also become more popular. MATLAB computations will be extended to Graphical Processing Units (GPUs) to harness their fast floating point arithmetic capabilities.

7. Acknowledgements

The authors would like to thank Gene Whipps (Army Research Laboratory, Adephi, MA, USA) for providing the ARL GRAPE application. The authors would also like to thank Dr. Fernando Escobar (SPAWAR Systems Center PACIFIC, Code 7113, San Diego, CA) for providing the serial SQIF code. The original SQIF application code was written by Dr. Patrick Loghini (SPAWAR Systems Center PACIFIC, Code 7173, San Diego, CA).

8. References

Amdahl, G.M., 1967. Validity of the single processor approach to achieving large scale computing capabilities. In ACM New York, NY, USA., 1967.

Bader, D.A. et al., 2006. Designing scalable synthetic compact applications for benchmarking high productivity computing systems. Cyberinfrastructure Technology Watch, 2.

Bliss, N.T. & Kepner, J., 2007. 'pMATLAB Parallel MATLAB Library'. International Journal of High Performance Computing Applications, 21, p.336.

Choy, R. & Edelman, A., 2005. Parallel MATLAB: Doing it right. Proceedings of the IEEE, 93, pp.331-41.

Hudak, D.E., Ludban, N., Gadepally, V. & Krishnamurthy, A., 2007. Developing a computational science IDE for HPC systems. In IEEE Computer Society Washington, DC, USA., 2007.

Interactive Supercomputing, 2009. StarP for MATLAB users. [Online].

Kepner, J. & Ahalt, S., 2004. MatlabMPI. Journal of Parallel and Distributed Computing, vol. 64, no. 8, pp. 997 – 1005, 2004

Krishnamurthy, A. et al., 2008. Parallel MATLAB in Production Supercomputing with Applications in Signal and Image Processing. In Conference on Parallel Processing for Scientific Computing., 2008. SIAM.

Krishnamurthy A. , Nehrbass J., Chaves J., and Samsi S., 2007. Survey of Parallel MATLAB techniques and applications to signal and image processing. IEEE International Conference on Acoustics, Speech and Signal Processing, vol. 4, 2007.

Mathworks, 2009. Parallel Computing Toolbox 4.0. [Online].

MIT Lincoln Laboratories, 2009. pMATLAB: Parallel MATLAB toolbox. [Online].

Ohio Supercomputer Center, 2009. bcMPI. [Online].

Palacios, A., Aven, J. & Longhini, P., 2006. Cooperative dynamics in coupled noisy dynamical systems near a critical point: The dc superconducting quantum interference device as a case study. Physical Review E, 74.

6

Feature Extraction and Recognition of Road Sign Using Dynamic Image Processing

Shigeharu Miyata[1], Akira Yanou[2], Hitomi Nakamura[1] and Shin Takehara[1]
[1]Kinki University, Faculty of Engineering
[2]Okayama University, Graduate School of Natural Science and Technology
[1,2]Japan

1. Introduction

At the present time, many studies are being conducted working toward the implementation of an Intelligent Traffic System (ITS). One field of this research is driving support systems, and many studies are being conducted to develop systems which identify and recognize road signs in front of the vehicle, and then use this information to notify the driver or to control the vehicle (Doermann et al., 2003; Gavrila, 1998; Hsu & Huang, 2001; Kimura et al., 2005; Mo & Aoki, 2004; Piccioli et al., 1996; Uchida et al., 2006; Uchimura et al., 2000; Yamaguchi et al., 2007).

Development of a system which can provide road information to the driver at any time is already underway. This system uses wireless communication with special narrow-band signal transmitters installed on the roadside, a technology which has already been commercialized with ETC. With the construction of this type of infrastructure, it is believed that there will be a change in the method of providing road sign information from the current method of providing visual information. However, much time will be required before this infrastructure covers all roads in local areas, and it is likely that as long as vehicles are driven by human drivers, road signs will never disappear as a means of providing traffic information.

On the other hand, the increase in traffic accidents accompanying the increasing amount of traffic has become a serious problem for society. The occurrence of traffic accidents is particularly high under special road conditions, such as at the entrance to a one-way street, sharp curves, and intersections without traffic signals. One possible countermeasure is to install "STOP," "NO LEFT TURN," and other traffic signs in order to notify the driver of the road conditions and other traffic information. However, there remains the possibility that the driver will, depending on his/her state of mind, fail to notice the sign while driving. A serious accident is possible if the driver fails to notice a sign such as "DO NOT ENTER," "STOP," or "ONLY DESIGNATED DIRECTION PERMITTED." It is said that a driver who is operating a vehicle is relying 80 - 90% on visual information to understand the environment outside the vehicle.

Predictions state that approximately 40% of traffic accidents could be prevented by reducing forward inattention among the drivers. It is possible that accidents can be prevented by utilizing an automatic road sign recognition system to provide traffic information to the driver, including information about the road in front of the vehicle. Image recognition technology which can correctly identify the external environment by means of images obtained from an on-board camera would reduce the burden on the driver and is expected to be an effective approach to driver support aimed at improving traffic safety. To date, studies have been conducted concerning development of a variety of driver support systems, primarily centered on the recognition of circular road traffic signs. However, there has been insufficient research concerning methods of recognizing road traffic signs of other shapes. In addition, previous studies have not considered changes in the signs resulting from changes in external illumination, and as a result there are problems with the effectiveness of identification and with the processing time (Inoue et al., 2003; Mastuura et al., 2002; Uchimura et al., 1998).

In order to implement a system which can recognize road signs and provide this information to the driver, both a method of identifying the areas in the camera images which contain signs and a method of recognizing the specific types of signs will be necessary. For the sign area identification method, a method using a genetic algorithm (Uchimura et al., 1998) and a method using active networks (Yabuki et al., 2000) have been proposed, and a consistent level of identification accuracy has been reported for these methods. However, the problem is the processing speed of the on-board system which is required to achieve real-time performance. Many solutions have been proposed, most of them involving identification of specific sign colors. One example is a method of identifying circular signs based on an RGB subtraction method (Mastuura et al., 2002) in order to rapidly identify the colors (specific colors) (Zin & Hama, 2005) used on the signs. For the road sign recognition method, a template matching method that is broadly used in the image processing fields, as well as improved versions of this method (Chen & Kao, 2008; Gavrila, 1998; Zhang & Ahao, 2007; Zhang, 2008), have been proposed. However the problem with these methods is that they involve a large amount of image processing, including enlargement, reduction, and rotation, which increases the processing time. With a method based on wavelet transformation or other processes for feature identification in frequency bands, accomplishing high-speed processing is highly difficult. In contrast, a method has been proposed in which the outlines of road signs contained in an image are directly identified as vectors without resizing the identified road sign image, with recognition then being performed by judgments which match the vector representations in the results (Yamauchi & Takahashi, 2003). This method has been reported to be robust in response to different image sizes and some degree of shape rotation, and also able to be carried out at high speed.

All of these proposed road sign identification and recognition methods are processes performed using an instantaneously-acquired static image, and it will be necessary for the processes to be performed for each frame if the method is to be commercialized. This means that correct recognition will not be possible in static images where temporary changes, such as a change in the light conditions or the sign being hidden by an object, have occurred. As a result, at such times an incorrect recognition result will be presented to the driver.

The method which this paper proposes assumes the use of an on-board camera, and involves processing of a moving image, allowing effective processing in cases when the sign is temporarily hidden by another object. In addition, this paper proposes a simple algorithm for sign detection and recognition that reduces the amount of required calculation. This will allow real-time processing on a software base with a general-purpose personal computer, a step which will be necessary in order to install a road sign recognition system onto a vehicle in the future. First, sign candidates are identified in the moving image based on the color-difference signals in the sign color information, and then the identified signs are recognized based on the sign external dimensions and the aspect ratio of the pattern dimensions on the sign. Nine kinds of signs, such as "STOP," "NO ENTRY" and "NO PASSAGE," were prepared, each 1/3 the size of the actual signs. Experiments were then carried out for recognition of these signs under various kinds of measurement conditions. These road signs consisted of a maximum of four colors and relatively simple designs.

2. System configuration

Figure 1 shows the configuration of the road sign detection and recognition system. The scene which included the sign was captured by a camera and sent to a computer. Then the sign recognition program, which was written by the authors of this study, analyzed the moving image, detected the sign, and recognized the sign based on the criteria described in Sec. 3. The result of this recognition was then displayed in the top left corner, and the recognized sign was shown colored using light-blue and yellow-green colors.

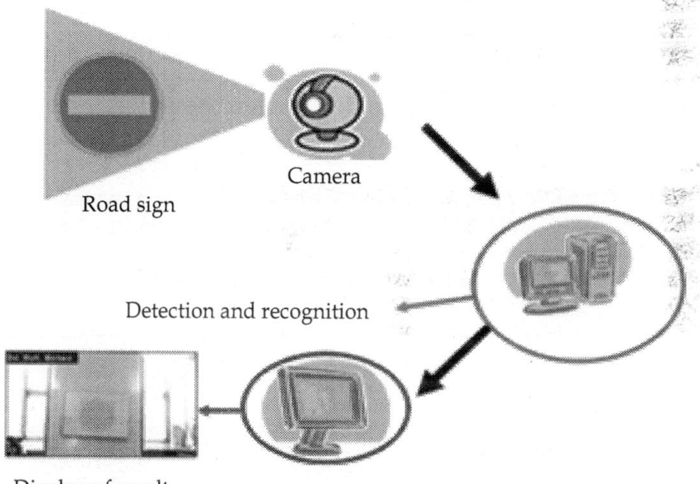

Fig. 1. Configuration of the road sign detection and recognition system, consisting of a camera, a computer, and a display

3. Configuration of the detection and recognition program

Three types of signs were used: "white on a red background," "white on a blue background," and "black on a yellow background." The configuration of the detection and recognition program is explained below, using the example of "white on a red background" signs such as "STOP," "NO ENTRY," and "NO PASSAGE," as shown in Figure 2.
The program consisted of three main function blocks: "Capture of the image," "Detection," and "Recognition and display of results," as shown in Figure 3.

Fig. 2. Examples of "white on a red background" signs.

3.1 Capture of the dynamic image

In the "Capture of the image" block shown in Figure 3, the RGB signals were converted to YCbCr color-difference signals (Miyahara & Yoshida, 1988; Rehrman & Priese, 1998) as shown in Figure 4, where Y (intensity) = 0.299R + 0.587G + 0.114R, Cb (color difference signal for blue) = 0.5B - 0.169R - 0.331G , and Cr (color difference signal for red) = 0.5R - 0.419G - 0.08B. These signals were output to the "Detection" block.

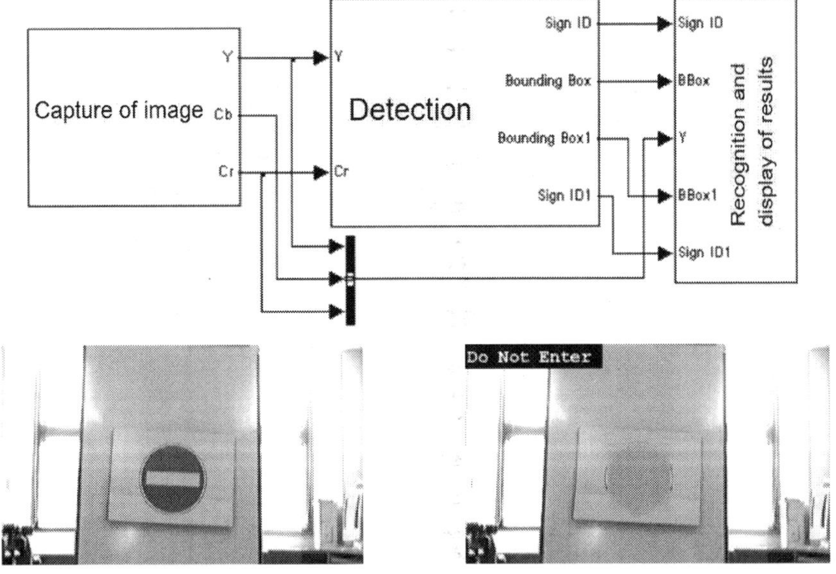

Fig. 3. The program consisted of three function blocks: "Capture of the image," "Detection," and "Recognition and display of results."

The upper and lower sides of the 320 × 240 original image were trimmed away in order to resize the image to 320 × 180. This was done because there is a low probability of signs existing in the top and bottom areas of the image.

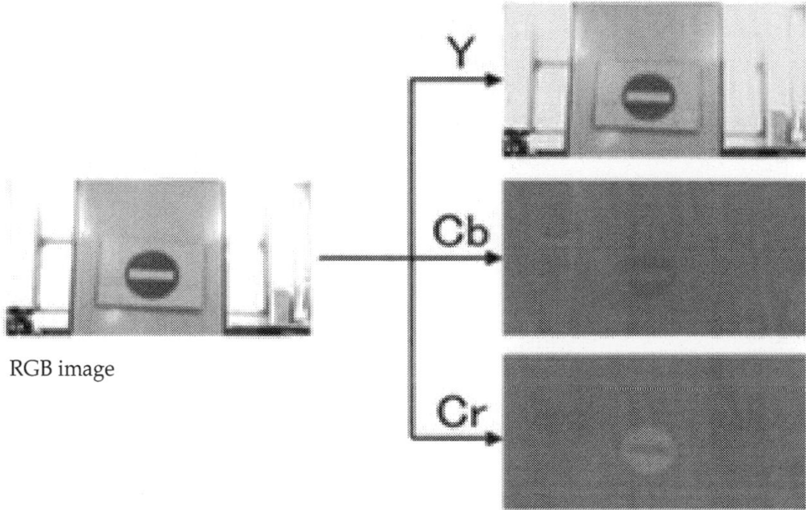

Fig. 4. Image YCrCb signals, converted from RGB signals.

3.2 Detection

The "white on a red background" signs each had a simple white pattern in the red area. In the "Detection" block, white and red areas with values that exceed the threshold values were extracted from the image by using the Y and Cr signals. The program calculated the ratio of the height of the red area to that of the white area, and the ratio of the width of the red area to that of the white area. The procedure for calculation of these ratios is described in detail below.

Images using the Y and Cr signals are shown in Figure 5. By setting the threshold value for Y to 0.57, the Y-signal image was transformed into a binary image. This binary image also included many white areas other than the one white pattern in the sign. In other words, it was not an extraction of just the sign. By setting the threshold value for Cr to 0.56, the Cr-signal image was also transformed into a binary image.

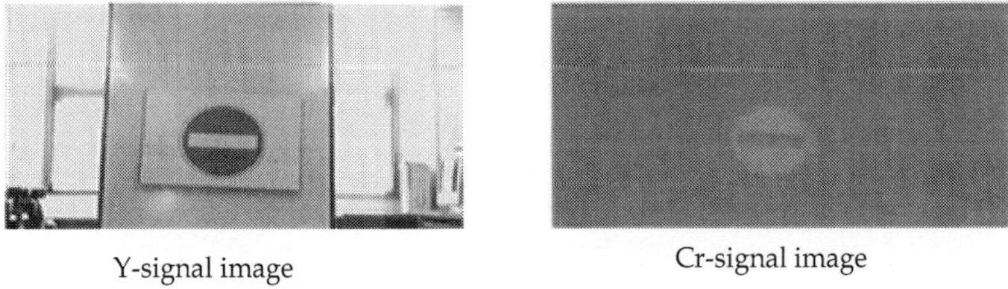

Fig. 5. Image YCrCb signals, converted from RGB signals.

The white area in the Cr-signal binary image represented the red area of the sign as shown in Figure 6(a). Dilation (enlargement) and erosion (contraction) operations were performed several times on this binary image, in which the white area of the image corresponds to the red area of the sign, until there were no black areas remaining inside this white area. Next, this image with no black area inside the sign was ANDed with the Y-signal binary image. In this way, only the white area in the sign was extracted, as shown in Figure 6(b).

(a) Red area   (b) White area

Fig. 6. Color areas of the sign.

By using the red and white areas, the ratio of the height of the red area to that of the white area (called the height ratio), and the ratio of the width of the red area to that of the white area (called the width ratio), can be calculated as shown in Figure 7. The height and width ratios for the "STOP," "NO ENTRY" and "NO PASSAGE" signs are shown in Table 1. These values are expressed as a range because the image is affected by the light conditions and/or the image processing operations.

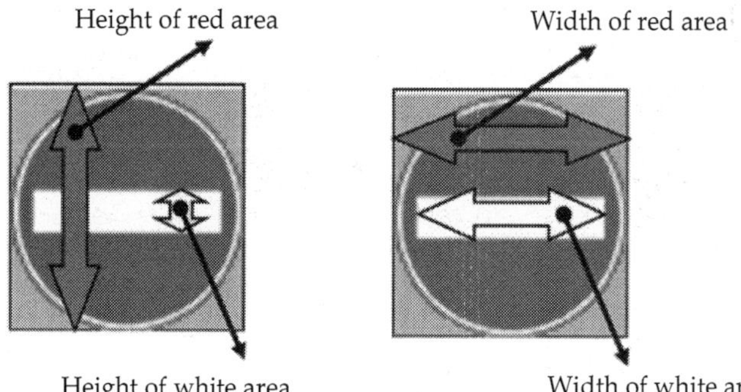

Fig. 7. Definition of height ratio and width ratio

"White on a red background" sign	Height ratio	Width ratio
STOP	0.190 - 0.233	0.532 - 0.574
NO ENTRY	0.217 - 0.241	0.821 - 0.885
NO PASSAGE	0.710 - 0.793	0.717 - 0.768

Table 1. Height and width ratios for "white on a red background" sign

3.3 Recognition and display of results

The "Recognition and display of results" block distinguished between these three kinds of signs by using the height and width ratios from the previous block. When only the height ratios were used, the ranges of the ratios for "STOP" and "NO ENTRY" partially overlapped. In contrast, because the width ratios of these three signs are different, the signs could be distinguished using only the width ratios. However, the width ratios among signs are not always different, and if recognition is restricted to just one ratio, some signs may be unrecognizable. We are certain that both of these ratios are useful when recognizing signs. The following concept was adopted for the recognition algorithm. As shown in Table 2(a), three thresholds each were set for the height and width ratios, and numbers were assigned to each of the thresholds so that the product of code "a" times code "b" corresponded to a particular sign, as shown in Table 2(b). Here, the three ranges were determined based on the ranges of measured values shown in Table 1.

Range of height ratio	a	Range of width ratio	b
≤0.18 and ≥0.81	1	≤0.18 and ≥0.91	1
0.181 - 0.7	2	0.181 - 0.8	1
0.71 - 0.8	4	0.81 - 0.9	1.5

(a)

Road Sign	A	B	Code (= a × b)
UNKNOWN	1	1	1
STOP	2	1	2
NO ENTRY	2	1.5	3
NO PASSAGE	4	1	4

(b)

Table 2. Height and width ratios for "white on a red background" sign

4. Experiment

Nine kinds of road signs, each 1/3 the size of the actual signs, were prepared. The "white on a red background" signs were "STOP," "NO ENTRY," and "NO PASSAGE." The "white on a blue background" signs were "ONLY BICYCLE," "CROSSING," and "NO ENTRY EXCEPT DESIGNATED DIRECTIONS." The "black on a yellow background" signs were "INTERSECTION," "ROAD CROSSING," and "UNDER CONSTRUCTION." Experiments were then carried out for recognition of these signs under different measurement conditions indoors and outdoors. These road signs consisted of a maximum of four colors and relatively simple designs. The signs were detected based on their color information, and were recognized based on the ratios of the component colors of the signs. The dynamic image used was a 24-bit color image of size 320 × 240 pixels. The processing time was 33 ms/frame (CPU: Pentium 4 1.6 GHz). Using the proposed processing method, the "ROAD CROSSING" sign was processed for recognition. The result was as shown below. The original RGB image shown in Figure 8(a) was first transformed into a YCrCb image. Then, threshold values were set for the Y, Cr, and Cb signals, and various kinds of processing were used to extract the yellow and black areas as shown in Figure 8(b) and (c). For the yellow area of the sign and the black area inside the sign, the processing also detected the top left corner coordinates of rectangles with heights and widths that match the extracted yellow and black areas of the sign. Each of these areas was surrounded by a square, to which a color was added. Light blue was used for the yellow area and yellow-green for the black area. The name of the sign ("ROAD CROSSING") was indicated in the top left corner, as shown in Figure 9.

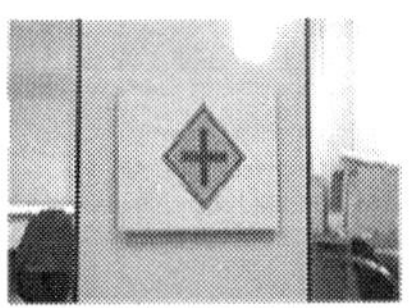

(a) Original RGB image

(b) Extracted yellow area

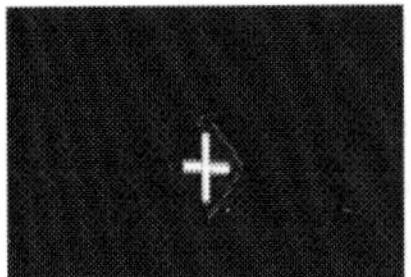

(c) Extracted black area

Fig. 8. Processed railroad crossing sign.

Fig. 9. Result displayed with colors which easily indicate the location of the recognized sign.

Displaying the recognized sign in this manner has the following advantage. If the result is not displayed, then when the recognition fails or is mistaken, the observer is unable to judge which signs were and were not recognized during the processing.

The purpose of this study was to simplify the identification and recognition algorithms and allow correct sign recognition. It showed that the system is able to satisfy this objective at the current processing time of 33 ms/frame. In comparison with methods previously proposed, this method was able to recognize a greater number of sign types while maintaining the same or better processing speed. The methods for comparison are the following.

- Reference [10] (Test environment: Pentium 1.2 GHz, Recognized signs: round signs, Processing time: approx. 0.15 s/frame)

- Reference [11]: (Test environment: Pentium 166 MHz, Identified signs: round signs, Processing time: approx. 1.5 s/frame)
- Reference [12]: (Test environment: Pentium 120 MHz, Recognized signs: round signs, Processing time: approx. 35 s/frame)
- Reference [2] (test environment: Pentium 4 2.2 GHz, Identified signs: round and triangular signs, Processing time: approx. 0.1 s/frame).

5. Conclusion

This study proposed a processing method for extracting the features of road signs and recognizing what each of these road sign means. Nine kinds of signs were used, consisting of a maximum of four colors and relatively simple designs. This method focuses on the ratio of the component colors. We verified that the method is able to correctly recognize the signs in real time. With the proposed method, good identification and recognition results were achieved with a moving image obtained under normal light conditions, and at faster processing times than the methods previously proposed.

In the future, consideration must be given to the following issues. First, recognition will be impossible if there are two signs with height and width ratios which are nearly the same. In this case, other information, such as the sign configuration, needs to be added. Second, the recognition results in this experiment deteriorated when there was an object with the same color pattern in the vicinity, and under special light conditions such as when the sign was backlit. Third, the angle of the camera with respect to the sign affects the shape of the image. Measures to address these issues need to be considered for the next step. We intend to consider new corrections and recognition methods in order to improve the recognition results for images obtained under poor photographic conditions.

6. References

Chen, C.C. & Kao, D. S. (2008). DCT-based zero replacement reversible image watermarking approach, International Journal of Innovative Computing, Information and Control, Vol.4, No.11, pp.3027-3036.

Doermann, D.; Liang, J & Li, H. (2003). Progress in camera-based document image analysis, Proc.of IC-DAR'03, pp.606-616.

Gavrila, D.M. (1998). Multi-feature hierarchical template matching using distance transforms, Proc. of IEEE International Conference on Pattern Recognition, pp.439-444.

Hsu, S. & Huang, C. (2001). Road sign detection and recognition using matching pursuit method, Image and Vision Computing, Vol.19, No.3, pp.119-129.

Inoue, Y.; Ishikawa, N. & Nakajima, M. (2003). Automatic recgnition of road signs (in Japanese), Techical report of IEICE, ITS2003-98, pp.57-62.

Kimura, S.; Tano, H.; Sakamoto, T.; Shiroma, H. & Ohashi, Y. (2005). Traversal region and obstacle detection using tilted-plane-based stereo vision (in Japanese), Journal of the Robotics Society of Japan, Vol.23, No.2, pp.59-66.

Matsuura, D.; Yamauchi, H. & Takahashi, H. (2002). Extracting circular road sign using specific color distinction and region limitation (in Japanese), IEICE Trans. D-II, Vol.J85-D-II, No.6, pp.1075-1083.

Miyahara, M. & Yoshida, Y. (1988). Mathematical transform of (R, G, B) color space to Munsel (H, V, C) color data, *SPIE visual Communication and Image Processing, visual Communication*, Vol.1001, pp.650-657.

Mo, G. & Aoki, Y. (2004). A recognition method for traffic sign in color image (in Japanese), *IEICE Trans. D-II*, Vol.J87-D-II, No.12, pp.2124-2135.

Piccioli, G.; Michieli, E. De; Parodi, P. & Campani, M. (1996). Robust method for road sign detection and recognition, *Image and Vision Computing*, Vol.14, No.3, pp.209-223.

Rehrmann, V. & Priese, L. (1998). Fast and robust segmentation of natural color scenes, *Proc. of the 3rd Asian Conference on Computer Vision*, Vol.1, pp.598-606.

Uchida, S.; Iwamura, M.; Omachi, S. & Kise, K. (2006). Category data embedding for camera-based character recognition (in Japanese), *IEICE Trans. D-II*, Vol.J89-D-II, No.2, pp.344-352.

Uchimura, K.; Kimura, H. & Wakiyama, S. (1998). Extraction and recognition of circular road signs using road scene color image (in Japanese), *IEICE Trans. A*, Vol.J81-A, No.4, pp.546-553.

Uchimura, K.; Wakiyama, S. & Fujino, M. (2000). Extraction of circular traffic sign using limited color indication (in Japanese), *IEICE Trans. D-II*, Vol.J83-D-II, No.2, pp.855-858.

Yabuki, N.; Matsuda, Y.; Kataoka, D.; Sumi, Y.; Fukui Y. & Miki, S. (2000). A study on an atumatic stop of computation in active net (in Japanese), *Technical report of IEICE*, Vol.99, No.575, pp.69-76.

Yamauchi, H. & Takahashi, H. (2003). A road sign recognition technique by tracing outline vectors, *Journal of the Institute of Image Information and Television Engineers*, Vol.57, No.7, pp.847-853.

Yamaguchi, H.; Kojima, A.; Miyamoto, T.; Takahashi, H. & Fukunaga, K. (2007). A Robust road sign recognition by superposing extracted regions from successive frame (in Japanese), *IEICE Trans. D-II*, Vol.J90-D-II, No.2, pp.494-502.

Zhang, Z. & Ahao, Y. (2007). Multiple description image coding based on fractal, *International Journal of Innovative Computing, Information and Control*, Vol.3, No.6 (B), pp.1615-1623.

Zhang, X. (2008). The improvement of a feature-based image mosaics algorithm, *International Journal of Innovative Computing, Information and Control*, Vol.4, No.10, pp.2759-2764.

Zin, T. T. & Hama, H. (2005). A robust road sign recognition using segmentation with morphology and relative color, *Journal of the Institute of Image Information and Television Engineers*, Vol.59, No.9, pp.1333-1342.

## 7

Development of Low Cost Air Quality Monitoring System by Using Image Processing Technique

C.J. Wong, M.Z. MatJafri, K. Abdullah and H.S. Lim
School of Physics, Universiti Sains Malaysia
11800 USM, Penang,
Malaysia

1. Introduction

Visual information of outdoor scenery portrays some important messages of atmospheric effects caused by light scattering, absorption and refractive-index fluctuations. These atmospheric effects are well related to some weather conditions such as air pollution, mist, haze, fog, rain and snow. In this digital age, images of outdoor scenes captured by digital camera can be processed digitally to determine these weather conditions.

In the last decade, the digital technologies have evolved at a continuously accelerating pace. This has fostered an incredible amount of research and development work on image processing technique. A number of image processing techniques are key elements of applied visual information research. In particular, image registration is a fundamental image processing technique, which has numerous applications to visual information research, in addition the more traditional application domains such as remote sensing. Other image processing techniques, such as image compression, are also relevant to the handling of large numbers of images for visual information research. Image Understanding refers to automated extraction of information from images.

In this study, we would like to develop a state-of-art image processing technique to enhance the capability of an internet video surveillance (IVS) camera for real time air quality monitoring. This technique is able to detect particulate matter with diameter less than 10 micrometers (PM10). An empirical algorithm was developed and tested based on the atmospheric characteristic to determine PM10 concentrations using multispectral data obtained from the IVS camera. A program is developed by using this algorithm to determine the real-time air quality information automatically. This development showed that the modern Information and Communications Technologies (ICT) and digital image processing technology could monitor air quality at multi location simultaneously from a central monitoring station.

2. The algorithm for image processing

In this study, we applied a unique image processing mechanism for air quality monitoring. This image processing mechanism was generated by our newly developed algorithm. We developed this algorithm based on the fundamental optical theory, such as light absorption, light scattering and light reflection. This is a skylight model, which was developed to indicate the existence of particulate matter in the air. The skylight is an indirect radiation, which occurs when the radiation from the sun being scattered by elements within the air pollutant column. Figure 1 shows electromagnetic radiation path propagating from the sun towards the digital camera penetrating through the atmospheric pollutant column.

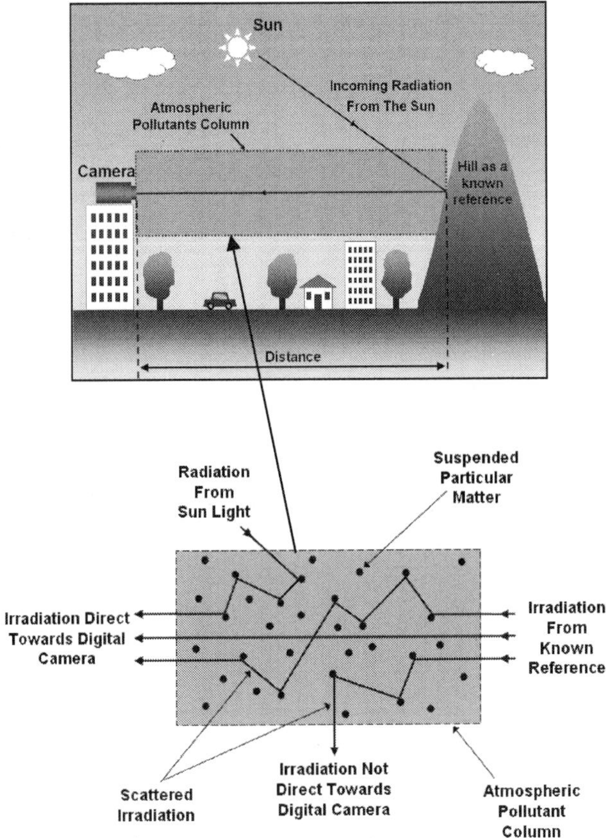

Fig. 1. The skylight parameter model to illustrate the electromagnetic radiation propagates from sunlight towards the known reference, and then reflected to propagate towards the internet surveillance camera penetrating through the interaction in atmospheric pollutant column.

Our skylight model described that the reflectance caused by the atmospheric scattering R_a was the reflectance recorded by the digital sensor R_s subtracted by the reflectance of the known references R_r.

$$R_a = R_s - R_r \tag{1}$$

In a single scattering of visible electromagnetic radiation by aerosol in atmosphere, the atmospheric reflectance due to molecules scattering, R_r is proportional to the optical thickness for molecules, τ_r, as given by Liu, et al. (1996) [10]. This atmospheric reflectance due to molecule scattering, R_r can be written as

$$R_r = \frac{\tau_r P_r(\Theta)}{4\mu_s \mu_v} \tag{2}$$

where

τ_r = Aerosol optical thickness (Molecule)

$P_r(\Theta)$ = Rayleigh scattering phase function

μ_v = Cosine of viewing angle

μ_s = Cosine of solar zenith angle

We assume that the atmospheric reflectance due to particle, R_a, is also linear with the τ_a [King, et al., (1999) and Fukushima, et al., (2000)]. This assumption is valid because Liu, et al., (1996) also found the linear relationship between both aerosol and molecule scattering.

$$R_a = \frac{\tau_a P_a(\Theta)}{4\mu_s \mu_v} \tag{3}$$

where

τ_a = Aerosol optical thickness (aerosol)

$P_a(\Theta)$ = Aerosol scattering phase function

Atmospheric reflectance is the sum of the particle reflectance and molecule reflectance, R_{atm}, (Vermote, et al., 1997).

$$R_{atm} = R_a + R_r \tag{4}$$

where

R_{atm} = atmospheric reflectance

R_a = particle reflectance

R_r = molecule reflectance

By substituting equation (2) and equation (3) into equation (4), we obtain

$$R_{atm} = \left[\frac{\tau_a P_a(\Theta)}{4\mu_s \mu_v} + \frac{\tau_r P_r(\Theta)}{4\mu_s \mu_v} \right]$$

$$R_{atm} = \frac{1}{4\mu_s \mu_v} \left[\tau_a P_a(\Theta) + \tau_r P_r(\Theta) \right] \tag{5}$$

The optical depth, τ given by Camagni and Sandroni, (1983) as expressed in equation (6), (7) and (8).

$$\tau = \sigma \rho s \tag{6}$$

where

τ = optical depth
σ = absorption
s   = finite path

$$\tau = \tau_a + \tau_r \tag{7}$$

$$\tau = \tau_a + \tau_r \tag{8}$$

Equations (7) and (8) are substituted into equation (5). The result was extended to a three bands algorithm as equation (9).

$$R_{atm} = \frac{1}{4\mu_s\mu_v}\left[\sigma_a\rho_a sP_a(\Theta) + \sigma_r\rho_r sP_r(\Theta)\right]$$

$$R_{atm} = \frac{s}{4\mu_s\mu_v}\left[\sigma_a\rho_a P_a(\Theta) + \sigma_r\rho_r P_r(\Theta)\right]$$

$$R_{atm}(\lambda_1) = \frac{s}{4\mu_s\mu_v}\left[\sigma_a(\lambda_1)PP_a(\Theta,\lambda_1) + \sigma_r(\lambda_1)GP_r(\Theta,\lambda_1)\right]$$

$$R_{atm}(\lambda_2) = \frac{s}{4\mu_s\mu_v}\left[\sigma_a(\lambda_2)PP_a(\Theta,\lambda_2) + \sigma_r(\lambda_2)GP_r(\Theta,\lambda_2)\right]$$

$$P = a_0 R_{atm}(\lambda_1) + a_1 R_{atm}(\lambda_2) \tag{9}$$

where
P =   Particle concentration (PM10)
G =   Molecule concentration
$R_{atm}(l_i)$ =   Atmospheric reflectance, $i = 1, 2$ are the band number
a_j =   Algorithm coefficients, $j = 0, 1$ are then empirically determined.
Equation (9) showed that PM10 was linearly related to the reflectance for band 1 and band 2. This algorithm was generated based on the linear relationship between τ and reflectance. Retalis et al., (2003), also found that the PM10 was linearly related to the τ and the correlation coefficient for linear was better that exponential in their study (overall). This means that reflectance was linear with the PM10. In order to simplify the data processing, the air quality concentration was used in our analysis instead of using density, ρ, values.

3. Image processing methodology

3.1 Equipment set up
The remote monitoring sensor used in this air quality monitoring study is an Internet Video Surveillance (IVS) camera. This camera was used to monitor the concentrations of particles less than 10 micrometers in diameter. It is a 1.0 mega pixel Charge-Couple-Device CCD camera, allows image data transfer over the standard computer networks (Ethernet networks), internet. Figure 2 shows the IVS camera used in this study.

Fig. 2. Internet Video Surveillance (IVS) camera used in this study was installed at the top floor of School of Physics in Universiti Sains Malaysia.

Figure 3 showed the schematic set-up of the IVS camera used in this study. This set-up can provide a continuous, on-line, real-time monitoring for air pollution at multiple locations. It is used to capture outdoor images continuously, and these images can be processed by using our own developed algorithm. By using this image processing method, it is able to immediately detect the present of particulates air pollution, in the air and helps to ensure the continuing safety of environmental air for living creatures.

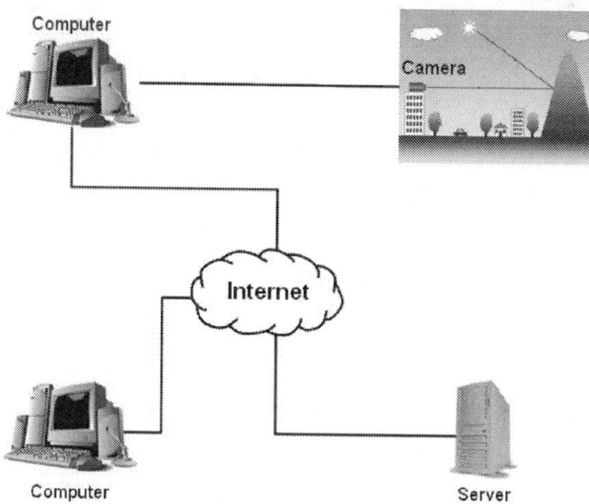

Fig. 3.The schematic set-up of IVS camera used as remote sensor to monitor air quality for this study

3.2 Study location

The camera was installed outside the wall of the Engineering Physics Laboratory at the top floor of School of Physics in the campus of Universiti Sains Malaysia at Penang, Malaysia. The location is at longitude of 1000°17.864′ and latitude of 50°21.528′ as shown in Figure 4, which is showed by the satellite map of the location to install the mentioned sensor. In this study, green vegetation is used as our reference target (Figure 4 & Figure 5).

Fig. 4. The satellite image to show the location of internet video surveillance camera, which was installed outside the wall of Engineering Physics Laboratory in School of Physics at Universiti Sains Malaysia

4. Image processing and results

A sample of digital images captured by the internet video surveillance camera on 11 May 2007 from 8.00 am to 5.30 pm is showed in Figure 5. The target of interest is the green vegetation grown on a distant hill. These digital images were separated into three bands (red, green and blue). Digital numbers (DN) of each band for this target were determined from the digital images. The IVS camera can be calibrated by using an ASD handheld spectroradiometer, then we will obtain equations 10, 11 and 12. These equations were used to convert these DN values into irradiance.

The coefficients of calibrated digital camera are

$$y_1 = 0.0005x_1 + 0.0432 \tag{10}$$

$$y_2 = 0.0006x_2 + 0.0528 \tag{11}$$

$$y_3 = 0.0003x_3 + 0.0311 \tag{12}$$

where

y_1	=	irradiance for red band ($Wm^{-2}\ nm^{-1}$)
y_2	=	irradiance for green band ($Wm^{-2}\ nm^{-1}$)
y_3	=	irradiance for blue band ($Wm^{-2}\ nm^{-1}$)
x_1	=	digital number for red band

Fig. 5.The digital image captured by internet video surveillance camera in this study, the reference target of green vegetation also shows in this photograph.

x_2 =   digital number for green band
x_3 =   digital number for blue band
An ASD handheld spectroradiometer was used to measure the sun radiation at the ground surface. The reflectance values was calculate using equation (13) below.

$$R = \frac{y(\lambda)}{E_s(\lambda)}$$ (13)

where
$y(\lambda)$ = irradiance of each visible bands (Wm^{-2} nm^{-1})
$E_s(\lambda)$ = sun radiation at the ground surface using a hand held spectroradiometer (Wm^{-2} nm^{-1})
The reflectance recorded by the IVS camera was subtracted by the reflectance of the known surface (equation 1) to obtain the reflectance caused by the atmospheric components. The relationship between the atmospheric reflectance and the corresponding air quality data for the pollutant was established by using regression analysis. The correlation coefficient (R^2) between the predicted and the measured PM10 values, and root-mean-square-error (RMS)

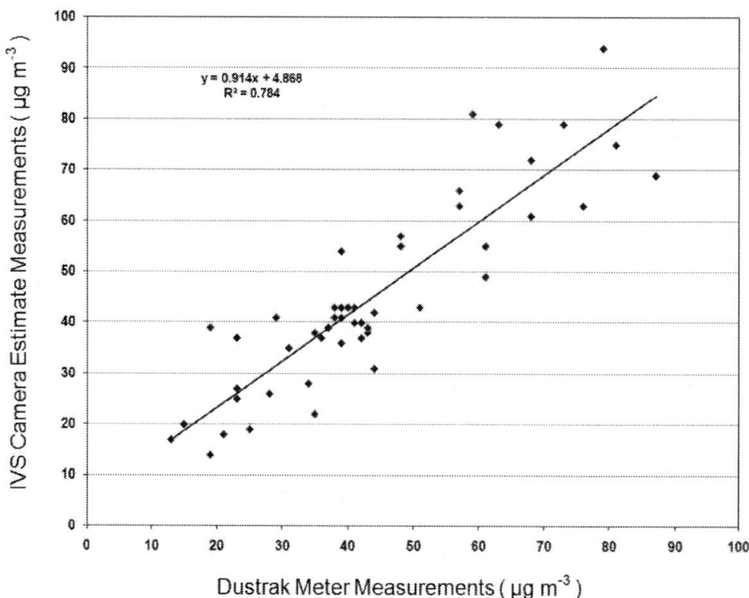

Fig. 6. Correlation coefficient and RMS error of the measured and estimated PM10 (µg/m3) value for calibration analysis on IVS camera

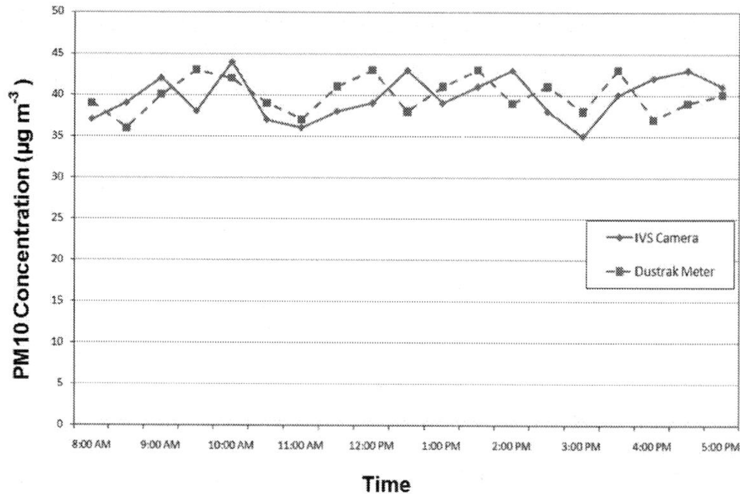

Fig. 7. Graph of PM10 concentration versus Time (11 May 2007)

value were determined. Figure 6 shows the correlation graph of the estimated measurement for IVS camera with the actual measurement from Dusttrak meter. The correlation coefficient (R^2) produced by the IVS camera data set was 0.784. The RMS value for IVS camera was $\pm 3 \, \mu g/m^3$.

The temporal development of real time air pollution in a day measured by IVS camera and a Dusttrak meter is shown at Figure 7. The data were obtained on 11 May 2007 from 8.00am to 5.30pm.

5. Conclusion

Traditionally the air quality monitoring systems are involved with high set-up cost and also high operating cost. These have become the major obstacles for setting up more air quality monitoring systems at multi location. The purpose is to give an indicator to human for preventing the air quality become worst and worst. In this study, we have showed that the temporal air quality can be monitored by our own developed image processing technique. This technique is using the newly developed algorithm to process the image captured by the internet video surveillance camera. It produced real time air quality information with high accuracies. This technique uses relatively inexpensive equipment and it is easy to operate compared to other air pollution monitoring instruments. This showed that the IVS camera imagery gives an alternative way to overcome the difficulty of obtaining satellite image in the equatorial region and provides real time air quality information.

6. Acknowledgements

This project was supported by the Ministry of Science, Technology and Innovation of Malaysia under Grant 01-01-05-SF0139 "Development of Image Processing Technique Via WirelessInternet for Continuous Air Quality Monitoring", and also supported by the Universiti Sains Malaysia under short term grant "Membangunkan Algoritma Untuk Pengesanan Pencemaran Udara Melalui Rangkaian Internet". We would like to thank the technical staff who participated in this project. Thanks are also extended to USM for support and encouragement.

7. References

Liu, C. H.; Chen, A. J. & Liu, G. R. (1996). An image-based retrieval algorithm of aerosol characteristics and surface reflectance for satellite images, International Journal Of Remote Sensing, 17 (17), 3477-3500.

King, M. D.; Kaufman, Y. J.; Tanre, D. & Nakajima, T. (1999). Remote sensing of tropospheric aerosold form space: past, present and future, Bulletin of the American Meteorological society, 2229-2259.

Fukushima, H.; Toratani, M.; Yamamiya, S. & Mitomi, Y. (2000). Atmospheric correction algorithm for ADEOS/OCTS acean color data: performance comparison based on ship and buoy measurements. Adv. Space Res, Vol. 25, No. 5, 1015-1024.

Vermote, E. ; Tanre, D. ; Deuze, J. L. ; Herman, M. & Morcrette, J. J. (1997). 6S user guide Version 2, Second Simulation of the satellite signal in the solar spectrum (6S), [Talian laman web], [02/08/2005].

http://www.geog.tamu.edu/klein/geog661/handouts/6s/6smanv2.0_P1.pdf.

Camagni, P. & Sandroni, S. (1983). Optical Remote sensing of air pollution, Joint Research Centre, Ispra, Italy, Elsevier Science Publishing Company Inc.

## 8

Remote Sensed Image Processing on Grids for Training in Earth Observation

Dana Petcu[1], Daniela Zaharie[1], Marian Neagul[1], Silviu Panica[1],
Marc Frincu[1], Dorian Gorgan[2], Teodor Stefanut[2] and Victor Bacu[2]
[1]West University of Timisoara
[2]Technical University of Cluj Napoca
Romania

1. Introduction

Remote sensing involves techniques that use sensors to detect and record signals emanating from target of interest not in direct contact with the sensors. Remote sensing systems integrate cameras, scanners, radiometers, radar and other devices, and deal with the collection, processing, and distribution of large amounts of data. They often require massive computing resources to generate the data of interest for their users.

Nowadays, remote sensing is mainly applied to satellite imagery. Satellites have proven in the last two decades their powerful capabilities to allow the Earth observation on a global scale. This observation is currently used in strategic planning and management of natural resources. The applications based on satellite data are often encountered in at least six disciplines: (1) agriculture, forestry and range resources in vegetation type, vigor and stress, biomass, soil conditions, or forest fire detection; (2) land use and mapping for classification, cartographic mapping, urban areas, or transportation networks; (3) geology for rock types, delineation, landforms, or regional structures detection; (4) water resources for water boundaries, surface, depth, volume, floods, snow areal, sediments, or irrigated fields detection; (5) oceanography and marine resources for marine organisms, turbidity patterns, or shoreline changes detection; (6) environment for surface mining, water pollution, air pollution, natural disasters, or defoliation detection.

Current applications involving satellite data needs huge computational power and storage capacities. Grid computing technologies that have evolved in the last decade promise to make feasible the creation of an environment, for these kinds of applications, which can to handle hundreds of distributed databases, heterogeneous computing resources, and simultaneous users. Grid-based experimental platforms were developed already at this century's beginning with a strong support from NASA and ESA.

In this context, the chapter presents for the beginners an overview of the technological challenges and user requirements in remote sensed image processing, as well as the solutions provided by the Grid-based platforms built in the last decade. Section 2 starts with a short description of the basic principles of the satellite imagery, the technical problems and state of the art in solving them. It points also the fact that the training activities in Earth observation are not following the intensity of the research activities and there is a clear gap between the request for specialists and the labor market offer.

For initiated readers, Section 3 of this chapter presents a complex case study: the solutions provided by the recent developed platform, namely GiSHEO, in what concerns the image processing services, workflow-based service composition, and user interaction combined with e-learning facilities.

For experts, Section 4 presents the results obtained by applying the services offered by the GiSHEO platform in order to assist archaeologists in identifying marks corresponding to buried archaeological remains.

2. Problems in satellite imagery and current solutions

The following section shortly presents the basic principles in satellite imagery and the existing solutions for fast response to its high request for resources of various kinds: computational, storage, or human.

2.1 Remote sensed image processing – basic principles

Remote sensing data measures reflected or emitted radiation from surfaces in different parts of the electromagnetic spectrum like visible, ultraviolet, reflected infrared, thermal infrared, microwave and so on.

Multiband or multispectral data consist of sets of radiation data that individually cover intervals of continuous wavelengths within some finite parts of the electromagnetic spectrum. Each interval makes up a band or channel. The data are used to produce images of Earth's surface and atmosphere or to serve as inputs to complex analysis programs.

An image is produced by radiation from ground areas that are samples for a larger region. The radiation varies depending on the reflectance, absorption or emittance properties of the various ground objects. The sampling area varies from a square meter to a squared kilometer depending on the sensor position and accuracy. Each radiation measure is associated with a gray level tone when is displayed on a computer output device. Usually a sampled area corresponds to a pixel on a display.

The multiband data collected by one sensor have differences from one band to another. The constant band to band response for a given feature or class of materials is interpreted as its spectral signature (a plot of wavelengths versus an intensity function like reflectance). If three bands are each assigned to one of the primary colors, blue, green, and red, a color composite is obtained.

Nowadays, hyperspectral sensors are making accurate and precise measurements of individual materials using spectrometers operating from space. The resulting data set produces a detailed spectral signature.

The most simple image processing operations that are performed on satellite data, named transforms in (Mather, 2004), are those allowing the generation of a new image from two or more bands of a multispectral or multi-temporal image. It is expected that the final image has properties that make it more suited to a particular purpose than the original one or ones. For example, the numerical difference between two images collected by the same sensor on different days may provide information about changes that have occurred between the two dates, while the ratio of the near-infrared and red bands of a single-date image set is widely used as a vegetation index that correlates with the difficulty to measure variables such as vegetation vigor, biomass, and leaf area index (see details in (Mather, 2004)). We should note that change detection is the most common used for satellite imagery, being important, for example, in meteorological studies and disaster management.

The more complex image processing concepts and methods involved in satellite imagery are dealing with spectral transforms, including various vegetation indices, principal components and contrast enhancement, independent component analysis, vertex component analysis, convolution and Fourier filtering, multiresolution image pyramids and scale-space techniques such as wavelets, image spatial decomposition, image radiometric and geometric calibration, spatial decomposition, thematic classification using traditional statistical approaches, neural networks, or fuzzy classification methods, image modeling, two-dimensional time series modeling, image fusion for better classification or segmentation, or multi-image fusion.

Several recent books are aiming to present in details the digital image processing procedures and methodologies commonly used in remote sensing. Books like (Jong & Meer, 2005; Schowengerd, 2007; Chen, 2007; Chen, 2008) are covering most of the above described topics. Other books provide an introduction view to a level meaningful to the non-specialist digital image analyst, as (Richards & Jia, 2006) does, or to the level of graduate students in the physical or engineering sciences taking a first course in remote sensing, as (Schott, 2007). The book (Borengasser et al, 2008) describes case studies for the use of hyperspectral remote sensing in agriculture, forestry, environmental monitoring, and geology. Topics for agriculture, forestry, and environmental monitoring applications include detecting crop disease, analysing crop growth analysis, classifying water quality, mapping submerged aquatic vegetation, and estimating hardwood chlorophyll content. For geology applications, topics include detecting hydrocarbons and identifying and mapping hydrothermal alteration.

2.2 Grid computing for remote sensed image processing

Remote sensing is a major technological and scientific tool for monitoring planetary surfaces and atmospheres. Practical applications focusing on environmental and natural resource management need large input data sets and fast response.

To address the computational requirements introduced by time-critical applications, the research efforts have been directed towards the incorporation of high-performance computing (HPC) models in remote sensing missions. Satellite image geo-rectification and classification are the first candidates for parallel processing. The book (Plaza & Chang, 2008) serves as one of the first available references specifically focused on describing recent advances in the field of HPC applied to remote sensing problems.

Satellite image processing is not only computational-intensive, but also storage-intensive; therefore special technologies are required for both data storage and data processing. Hundreds of gigabytes of raw sensor data are generated per day and these data must be fast processed to produce the data required by the final users. Moreover, satellite image processing also involves different types of image processing techniques and algorithms. For each type of image processing an analysis is needed in order to point out several requirements as determining a suitable processing type, data movement issues and workflow management. Furthermore, satellite image processing applications require not only the processing of large volumes of data, but also various types of resources, and it is not reasonable to assume the availability of all resources on a single system. In this context, the Grid based technologies promised to make feasible the creation of a computational environment handling not only heterogeneous computing resources, but also hundreds of distributed databases, and simultaneous users.

There are at least three reasons for using Grid computing for satellite image processing: (a) the required computing performance is not available locally, the solution being the remote computing; (b) the required computing performance is not available in one location, the solution being cooperative computing; (c) the required computing services are only available in specialized centres, the solution being application specific computing.

An early paper (Lee et al., 1996) describes a metacomputing application that integrates specialized resources, high-speed networks, parallel computers, and virtual reality display technology to process satellite imagery; the inputs of the near-real-time cloud detection code are two-dimensional infrared and visible light images from satellite sensors.

Later on, realizing the potential of the Grid computing for the satellite imagery, several projects were launched at the beginning of this century to make the Grid usage idea a reality. Within the European DataGrid project an experiment aiming to demonstrate the use of Grid technology for remote sensing applications has been carried out; the results can be found for example in the paper (Nico et al., 2003). In the same period, (Aloisio & Cafaro, 2003) presented an overview of SARA Digital Puglia, a remote sensing environment that shows how Grid technologies and HPC can be efficiently used to build dynamic Earth observation systems for the management of space mission data and for their on-demand processing and delivering to final users.

Since 2005, the GEOGrid project (Sekiguchi et al., 2008) is primarily aiming at providing an e-Science infrastructure for worldwide Earth sciences community; it is designed to integrate the wide varieties of existing data sets including satellite imagery, geological data, and ground sensed data, virtually, again enabled by Grid technology, and is accessible as a set of services. Later on, D4Science (Tsangaris et al., 2009) studied the data management of satellite images on Grid infrastructures.

The testing phase has finished with the study delivered by the European DEGREE project (DEGREE consortium, 2008) about the challenges that the Earth Sciences are imposing on Grid infrastructure, as well as several case studies in which Grid are useful.

The second stage is the one of the production environments. (Cafaro et al, 2008) describes the standard design of a current Grid computing production environment devoted to remote sensing. For example, a special service was developed in the frame of the European BEinGRID project (Portela et al., 2008) to process data gathered from satellite sensors and to generate an multi-year global aerosol information; through the use of Grid technologies the service generates data in near real time. The platform called Grid Processing On Demand, shortly G-POD (Fusco et al., 2008), aims to offer a Grid-based platform for remote processing of the satellite images provided by European Space Agency (ESA) and it offers several satellite image processing services for environmental management. G-POD has proved its usefulness of the concept for real applications like flood area detection. The platform for satellite imagery search and retrieval, called Ground European Network for Earth Science Interoperations - Digital Repositories, shortly GENESI-DR (GENESI-DR consortium, 2008), offers to an end-user an interface for digital data discovery and retrieval; raw data are processed using G-POD facilities. The Landsat Grid Prototype LGP is using Grid computing to generate single, cloud and shadow scenes from the composite of multiple input scenes, the data for which may be physically distributed; the system ingests multiple satellite scenes, calibrates the intensities, applies cloud and shadow masks, calculates surface reflectance, registers the images with respect to their geographic location, and forms a single composite scene (Gasster et al., 2008). Ongoing EGEE-3 and SEE-Grid-SCI European

Grid-based e-infrastructures projects are currently building environmental applications based on satellite data including also some of the ones provided by GENESI-DR.

The Committee on Earth Observation Satellites (CEOS), an international coordinating body for spaceborne missions for the study of the Earth, maintains a working group on information systems and services with the responsibility to promote the development of interoperable systems for the management of Earth observation data internationally. The WGISS Grid Task team is coordinating efforts of ESA, NOAA and NASA projects.

A new trend is to make use of service-oriented architectures. A Service Grid reflects the recent evolution towards a Grid system architecture based on Web services concepts and technologies. The Service Grids' potential for remote sensing has already been pointed out at the beginning of this evolution, for example in (Fox et al., 2005). Wrappers are used to encapsulate proprietary image processing tools as services and furthermore allowing their usage in more complex applications. This is the road taken in the last years also by small scale research platforms like MedioGrid (Petcu et al, 2008) or Grid-HIS (Carvajal-Jimenez et al, 2004) trying to support national requests for remote sensing applications.

2.3 Training in Earth Observation

The rapid evolution of the remote sensing technologies is not followed at the same developing rate by the training and high education in this field. Currently there is only a few number of resources involved in educational activities in Earth Observation. One of the most complex is EduSpace (ESA, 2007).

Recognizing the gap between research or production activities and the training or education ones, a partnership strategy for Earth Observation Education and Training was established in 1999 for an effective coordination and partnership mechanism among CEOS agencies and institutions offering education and training around the world. The key objective is to facilitate activities that substantially enhance international education and training in Earth observation techniques, data analysis, interpretation, use and application. In this context, the CEOS Working Group of Education, Training and Capacity Building is collecting an index of free Earth observation educational materials (CEOS, 2009).

3. Grid-based platform for remote sensed image processing – GisHEO

We have developed recently a platform, namely GiSHEO (On Demand Grid Services for Training and High Education in Earth Observation (GiSHEO Consortium, 2008)) addressing the issue of specialized services for training in Earth observation. Special solutions were proposed for data management, image processing service deployment, workflow-based service composition, and user interaction. A particular attention is given to the basic services for image processing that are reusing free image processing tools, like GDAL or GIMP.

Our aim is to set up and develop a reliable resource for knowledge dissemination, high education and training in Earth observation. In order to answer to the on-demand high computing and high throughput requirements we are using the latest Grid technologies. A special features of the platform is the connection with the GENESI-DR catalog mentioned in the previous section.

Contrary to the existing platforms providing tutorials and training materials, GiSHEO intends to be a living platform where experimentation and extensibility are the key words.

The platform design concepts were shortly presented in (Panica et al., 2009) and the details about the e-learning component can be found in (Gorgan et al., 2009). In this section we shortly present the architecture and technologies that are used and then we are going in details related to the basic image processing services and interfaces.

3.1 Platform architecture

While the Grid is usually employed to respond to the researcher requirements to consume resources for computational-intensive or data-intensive tasks, we aim to use it for near-real time applications for short-time data-intensive tasks. The data sets that are used for each application are rather big (at least of several tens of GBs), and the tasks are specific for image processing (most of them very simple). In this particular case a scheme of instantiating a service where the data are located is required in order to obtain a response in near-real time. Grid services are a quite convenient solution in this case: a fabric service is available at the server of the platform that serves the user interface and this service instantiates the processing service where the pointed data reside.

Figure 1 presents the conceptual view of the implemented architecture.

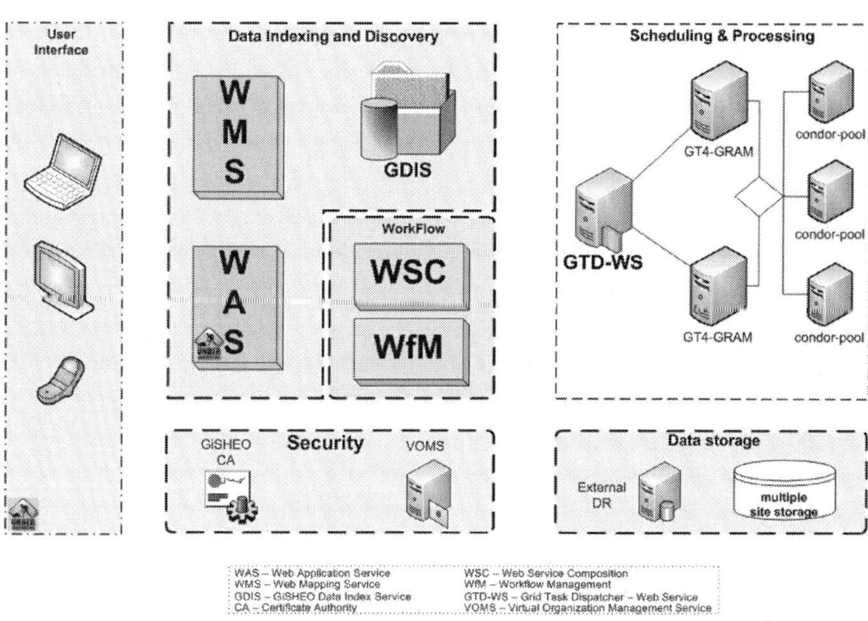

Fig. 1. GiSHEO architecture

The WMS is the standard Web Mapping Service ensuring the access to the distributed database and supporting WMS/TMS & VML. WAS is the acronym for Web Application Service that is invoked by user interface at run-time and allows workflows description. GDIS is a data index service – more precisely a Web service providing information about the available data to its clients. It intermediates access to data repositories, stores the processing results, ensures role based access control to the data, retrieves data from various information sources, queries external data sources and has a simple interface that is usable by various data consumers. The platform has distributed data repositories. It uses PostGIS for storing raster extent information and in some cases vector data. Moreover the data search is based on PostGIS spatial operators.

The physical platform is based on four clusters that are geographically distributed at four academic institutions. Due to the low security restriction between the four institutions, data distribution between the clusters is done using Apache Hadoop Distributed File System. The data transfer from and to external databases is done using GridFTP – this is for example the case of the connection with GENESI-DR database.

The Workflow Service Composition and Workflow Manager are the engines behind WAS and are connected with the tasks manager. Each basic image processing operation is viewed as a task. Several tasks can be linked together to form a workflow in an order that is decided at client side (either the teacher, or the student interface). The workflow engine is based on an ECA (Event-Condition-Action) approach since it offers much more dynamism and adaptability to changes in workflow tasks and resource-states than other classic workflow engines. In order to respond to the special requirements of the platform a rule-based language has been developed.

The GTD-WS (Grid Task Dispatcher Web Service) is a service-enabled interface for easy interoperability with the Grid environment. EUGridPMA signed certificate are required to access the full facilities of the platform.

A particular component of WAS is eGLE, the eLearning environment. It uses templates to allow teachers specialized in Earth observation to develop new lessons that uses Earth observation data.

3.2 Basic services for image processing

We divide remote sensing processing operations into two types: basic and complex. Basic operations represent basic image processing algorithms that can be applied on a satellite image (histogram equalization, thresholding etc.). Complex operations are represented by the complex image processing algorithms (i.e. topographic effect regression) or by a composition of two or more basic operations. In Grid terms this operations must be exposed using some Grid-related technologies in order to interact with other grid components. Two related technologies can be used here: Grid services and Web services.

Web services (WS) are Internet application programming interfaces that can be accessed remotely (over a network) and executed on a remote system that hosts the requested services. Grid services can be seen as an extended version of Web services.

In our platform the Web services serve as an interface for the processing algorithms. This interfaces can be accessed remotely (normally using an user interface like a Web portal) and allowing the execution on a computational Grid of different types of processing techniques (distributed or parallel) depending on each algorithm in part.

In the framework of GiSHEO project we have developed a number of basic services that are useful in Earth observation e-learning process. In the following, some of them are presented together with visual examples.

The service for grayscale conversion (Figure 2) receives as input a coloured satellite image in any desired format (TIFF, PNG, BMP etc.) and transforms the triplets of values corresponding to each pixel in a value in the range 0-255. The service for histogram equalization (Figure 3) is used to increase the global contrast of an image; the histogram of the resulting image will be flat (pixels with the same value will not be separated into new values, however, so the histogram may not be perfectly flat). The service for quantization

(Figure 4) is used for reducing the number of colours used in a image; our implementation uses a multilevel quantization.

Fig. 2. Grayscale conversion: input parameter – an image file; output - the converted grayscale image file

Fig. 3. Histogram equalization: input parameter – an image file; output – the transformed image

Fig. 4. Quantization: input parameters – image and number of gray levels; output – image

The service for thresholding (Figure 5) refers to a processing technique for image segmentation; in our implementation the user must chose a threshold (T) and this is used to compute the entire image. The service for blending images (Figure 6) is used for blending two images; different types of blending are supported. The service for image embossing (Figure 7) implements an algorithm for embossing an image.

Fig. 5. Thresholding algorithm with T=125 (input parameters - image and threshold T; the image can be TIFF, PNG, BMP etc; output - image)

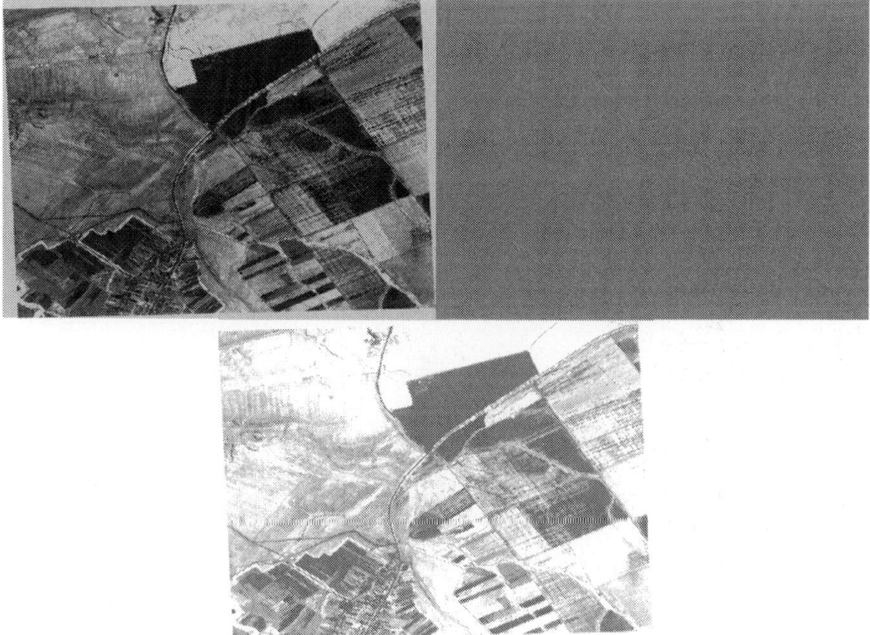

Fig. 6. Image blend: input parameters - layer | image1 | image2 | blend type (numerical value); output - blended image

The service for image transformation using a binary decision tree (Figure 8) is used for a quick image transformation using a binary decision tree to detect areas with water, clouds, forest, non-forest and scrub. The service for layers overlay is used for overlaying different layers; it has several images at inputs and produces one image. The service for vegetation

Fig. 7. Emboss service: input parameters – image | emboss level | grey level; output - image

Fig. 8. Image transform: inputs - red-band image | infrared-band image | w | c | nf | f | s, where w-water value, c-clouds value, nf-nonforest value, f-forest value, s-scrub value; output – 5-color image resulted after applying a binary decision tree algorithm

index computation is used for computing the normalized difference vegetation index (NDVI) that shows whether an area contains a live green vegetation or not; it also supports the calculation of enhanced vegetation index (EVI); the input parameters are the red-band image and near infrared-band image (default MODIS-EVI values are used L=1, C1 = 6, C2 = 7.5, and G as gain factor = 2.5).

Basic services presented above can be used as single services or composed ones (see more about Web service composition in the next subsection). Figure 9 gives an example of a resulted image in a composed execution. The input image is a standard aerial image. The applied services are the following ones: gray-scale conversion, histogram equalization, quantization and thresholding.

Fig. 9. Shape detection using a composition of several services (grayscale conversion, histogram equalization, quantization and thresholding)

3.3 Workflows and user interfaces

Processing large satellite data requires both a computational and storage effort. Usually operations on them are done in order to gain some insight on features which are not visible in the original image such as features visible at different bandwidths, changes over various time periods in ground features (floods, fires, deforestation, desertification, ice coverage), artificial or natural ground formations which are not easily distinguishable (ancient roads, fortifications, impact craters). These operations usually require two major steps before obtaining the final image(s). The first stage implies extracting relevant information from the satellite images such as geo-coding information, layers or bands. This information can be later used in the resulting image on the surface of the planet and in the actual processing step. This subsection will deal mostly with the latter step and with relevant examples.

Processing images in order to obtain relevant information usually requires several steps each of them consisting of a simple operation such as: obtaining the negative, gray level conversion, histogram equalization, quantization, thresholding, band extraction, embossing, equalization, layers subtraction etc. As it will be detailed later in this section, choosing the operations and their order depends on the desired result. This selection and ordering can be made either by the user or can be automatically generated starting from the desired output and following the chain of image combinations which lead to it. In this latter case it is up to the user to chose the solution which best fits its initial image characteristics (image type, codification, stored information). To support the user actions, we have developed a workflow language (Frincu et al, 2009) together with a set of tools for users not familiar with programming which can be used both for visually creating a workflow (Figure 10) and for automatically generate a solution given a user defined goal. The application is then responsible for converting the visual workflow into a specific language developed by us which can then be executed. After defining the workflow the user can then select a region containing one or more images on which the workflow is to be applied. The communication is asynchronously and the user can directly observe how each of the images is gradually converted by the workflow.

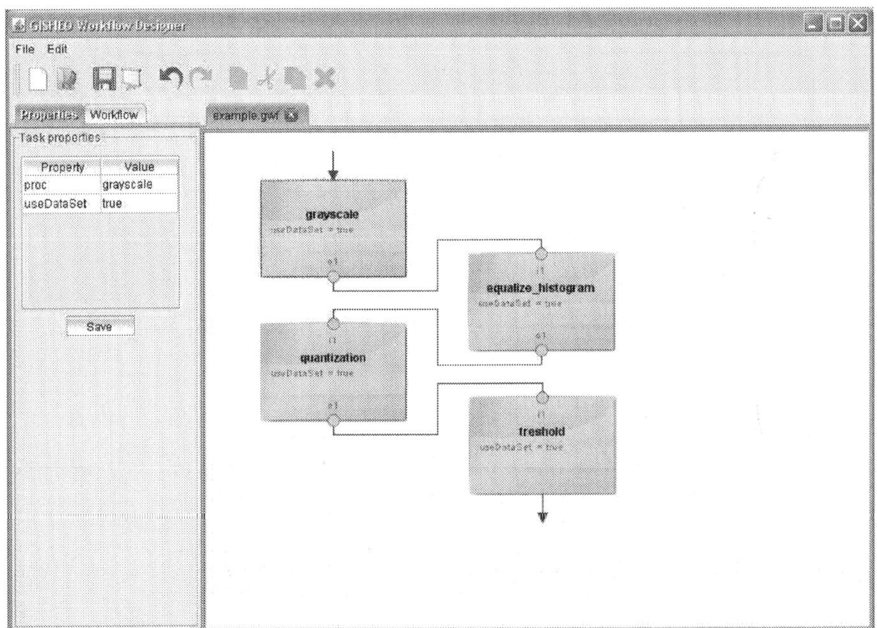

Fig. 10. Visually designing a GiSHEO workflow

In the frame of the GiSHEO project we are mostly interested in applying image transformations for historical and geographical use (see the case study from the next section). In this direction we have identified several workflows made up of basic image operations which allow the users to better observe features relevant for the two previously mentioned fields. For example in history and in particular in archaeology there is a constant need for identifying ancient sites of human settlements, fortresses or roads. Different flows of image transformations (e.g. gray level conversion, histogram equalization, quantization and thresholding) could enhance the image in order to make the marks induced by archaeological remains easier to be identified by visual inspection.

Identifying the required operations is followed by actually designing the workflow which usually implies binding them together in a certain order. Designing the workflow can be achieved in two ways either by using a visual tool such as the one presented in Figure 10, showing how a sequence of operations can be created, or by directly using the workflow language developed especially for this task which will be briefly presented in the following paragraph.

As previously mentioned visually designing the workflow is only the first step as it needs to be transformed into a language understood by the workflow engine (named in GisHEO OSyRIS – Orchestration System using a Rule based Inference Solution). The workflow language named SILK (SImple Language for worKflows) is rule based and can also be used directly by users preferring to define workflows without using the visual designer. A sequence of basic image processing operations can be defined using SILK as follows:

```
# Initial activation task
A0:=[o1:output="imageId", "instances"="1"];
# The following tasks belong to the processing workflow
A:=[i1:input, o1:output, "processing"="image grayscale(image)", "isFirst"="true"];
B:=[i1:input, o1:output, "processing"="image equalize-histogram(image)"];
C:=[i1:input, o1:output, "processing"="image quantization(image)"];
D:=[i1:input, o1:output, "processing"="image threshold(image)", "isLast"="true"];
# Compute grayscale from the initial image
A0[a=o1] -> A[i1=a];
# Apply histogramequalization to the grayscale image
A[a=o1] -> B[i1=a];
# Apply quantization to the equalized image
B[a=o1] -> C[i1=a];
# Apply thresholding to the quantized image
C[a=o1] -> D[i1=a];
```

After transforming the visual workflow in the SILK language the workflow is executed using a workflow engine and the result is sent back to the user which is able to view it inside its web portal. In Figure 11 it can be seen how a selection of four images from a geoencoded map is displayed after being processed. The sequence of operations corresponds to the sequence previously described and exemplified in Figure 10.

Fig. 11. Processed selection of four images inside the GiSHEO web interface

After obtaining the result users can than either choose another image selection or change the workflow.

As it can be noticed from the previous paragraph the user interaction module is composed of several parts including the visual workflow designer which can be used independently for creating the workflows and the web portal which allows users to select a previously defined workflows, to choose a region comprised of several images and to apply the workflow on them. The users could still use and navigate the map in search for other potential targeted images while the processing is still running. The visual designer and the engine API together with the automatic workflow generator are available on demand from the project repository.

The recent developed gProcess Platform (Radu et al, 2007), incorporated in GiSHEO platform, provides a flexible diagrammatical description solution for image processing workflows in the Earth Observation field. Abstract workflows (or Process Description Graphs (PDG)) and instantiated workflows (or Instantiated Process Description Graphs (IPDG)) are the workflows that can be defined using the gProcess Platform. Both workflows representation is based on DAGs. The PDG is a pattern definition of the workflow because it contains only the conceptual description of the workflows. On the other hand, the IPDG representation is linked to specific input data or resources. Based on this only the IPDGs can be executed in the Grid infrastructure. For describing workflows, we are using different types of nodes. The input data or data resources are used to specify satellite images or data values (int, float, string data types). The data resources are inputs for operators, sub-graphs and services. Operators are algorithms implemented to run over the Grid. The difference between operators and services is related to the way in which these nodes are executed in the Grid environment. Sub-graphs are used to integrate graphs that may have been developed by others and they can be used to define a hierarchical representation of the algorithm. We adopted an XML based representation as a persistent storage solution for the processing graphs. For every graph node, we defined an XML tag and a series of attributes that defines the nodes.

As a future development of the gProcess Platform, we intend to add the possibility to define in workflows some control structures like *for* or *if* statements. This will involve the ability of creating more complex image processing algorithm for execution over the Grid.

The gProcess architecture (Figure 12) is based on the client-server model. The server side enables the access to the Grid infrastructure using a set of services (EditorWS, ManagerWS, ExecutorWS and ViewerWS). The User Oriented Application Level and Application Level are encapsulated in the client side. The Client Java API accomplishes the access to the server side; this layer creates a transparent invocation level to the server side services. User Oriented Application Level exposes a set of user interaction components (EditorIC, ManagerIC, ViewerIC). The complex functionality is developed by using the Application Level, which combines the editor, manager and viewer functionality.

Each of the Web services exposed by the gProcess Platform is managing different functionality. The EditorWS provides information that is used to describe workflows, like the list of operators, the available sub-graphs or services, what satellite images can be used, etc. The EditorIC component that supports the user's editing operations for the workflow development uses this Web service. The interactive workflow design, the visualization of the workflow at different levels (by expanding or contracting sub-graphs), or user editing tools are developed using this interaction component.

Different information related to the existing workflows (PDGs or IPDGs) are exposed by the ManagerWS. Another functionality of this Web service is related to the interaction with the gProcess repository to integrate new operators, services, sub-graphs, to include new workflows or to access already designed workflows. The ManagerIC component can be used to instantiate workflows to different data resources (satellite images), to manage the model resources (operators, services, sub-graphs). The operator integration and monitoring user interface are implemented in Flex.

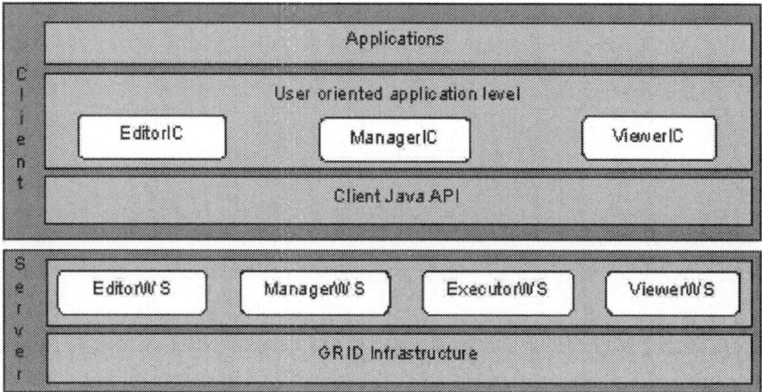

Fig. 12. gProcess platform based architecture

The instantiated workflows (IPDGs) can be executed over the Grid by using the ExecutorWS. Another important functionality of this Web service is the monitoring support for the executing workflows. An internal data structure that maps the workflow definition is created, and it is used to submit the operators to execution.

GProcess Operators Integration. The atomic component that implements a specific functionality is integrated in the gProcess platform like an operator. Currently a basic set of image processing operators are included in the gProcess operator's repository. The gProcess Platform supports the integration of user-developed operators. The operators must be written in Java and they have to extend a base class. The workflow description (the IPDG file) contains only the id from the repository. At execution time, the data from the database is retrieved and used to submit the operator to execution. An operator can have multiple input data resources. In the database, we store an invocation pattern that is used at the execution time. For example for the add operator, the pattern can be the following: OperationExec [Add-?,?,?]. The OperationExec represents the class that is executed. The *Add* represents the operator name. The last "?" specify the output and the other "?" characters are specifying the inputs. At execution time, this pattern is replaced with the execution command, for example: *OperationExec [Add-omania_b2.tif,romania_b3.tif, add_result.tif]*.

In the graphical user interface (Figure 13), in order to integrate a new operator to the repository, the user must complete the following steps. The general information section must be completed with the operator name and also with a short description of the operator. In the input section, the user can select the input type for each data resource that is needed by that operator. In the same manner in the output section, the user can select the output type. In the upload tab, the user must select the executable class for the operator and also the dependencies that are required at execution time. After completing these steps, the user can define workflows by using the newly added operators.

Workflow example – EVI algorithm. The Enhanced Vegetation Index is used to enhance the vegetation signal by reducing the atmosphere influences. The input data for the algorithm are satellite images. Based on a set of processing steps the algorithm highlights the vegetation areas. The input resources are the NIR, Red and Blue spectral bands. The basic formula is:

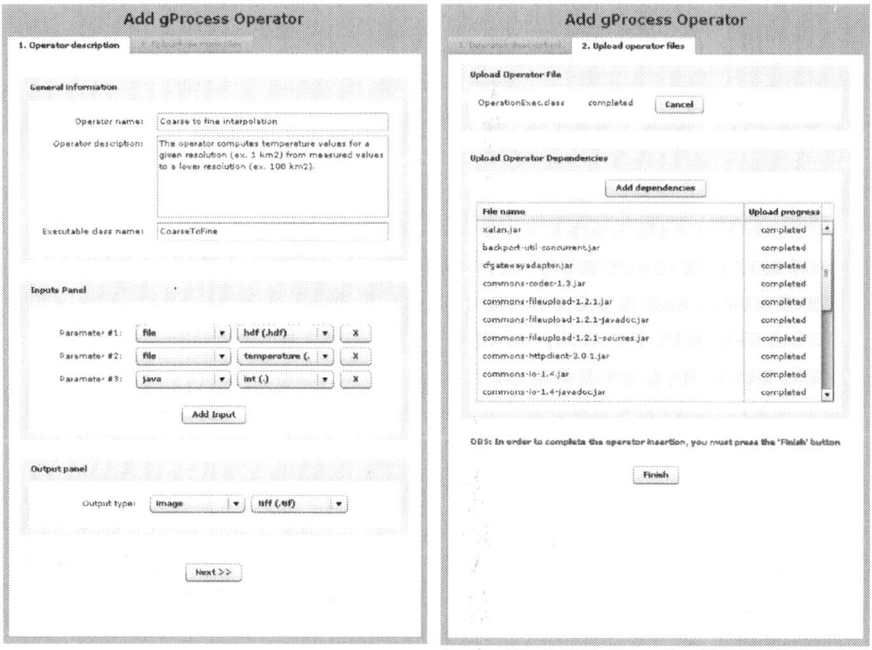

Fig. 13. gProcess interface for integration of new operators

$$\frac{2.5 * \left(NIR - RED\right)}{NIR + 6 * RED + 7.5 * BLUE + 1}$$

In order to design the workflow for this algorithm we have to identify the atomic components, and to rewrite the formula using the available operators. Since we have only binary operators for addition, subtraction, etc. the new formula is the following:

$$\frac{2.5 * \left(NIR - RED\right)}{\left[NIR + \left(6 * RED\right)\right] + \left[\left(7.5 * BLUE\right) + 1\right]}$$

In Figure 14 we exemplify the EVI graphical representation of the workflow.
A sample from the XML definition of the workflow is the following:

```xml
<?xml version="1.0" encoding="UTF-8"?>
<Workflow>
<Nodes>
 <Resource id="1" name="B4" description="NIR spectral band">
  <LocalResource path="romania_B4.tif" />
  <PostConditions>
   <Output idTypeDB="3" />
  </PostConditions>
 </Resource>
 ...
```

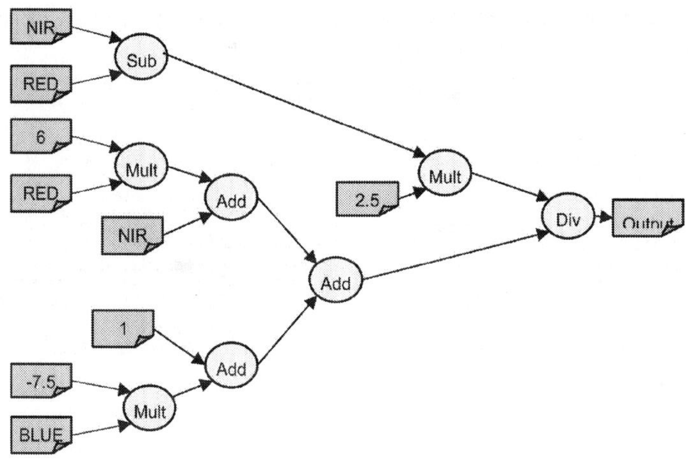

Fig. 14. EVI workflow

```
<Operator id="3" name="Sub" description="" idDB="2">
  <Preconditions>
    <Input id="1"/>
    <Input id="2"/>
  </Preconditions>
 </Operator>
...
<Operator id="15" name="Div" description="" idDB="4">
  <Preconditions>
    <Input id="3"/>
    <Input id="14"/>
  </Preconditions>
</Operator>
</Nodes>
<Groups>
</Groups>
</Workflow>
```

The processing result is presented in Figure 15 for a particular example.

Monitoring interface. The ExecutorWS is the component that, based on a user selected IPDG, submits the jobs to execution. The monitoring component from this Web service updates the database with the current execution status for each node from the workflow description. The monitoring interface (Figure 16) displays this monitoring information, node name, start time, end time, execution status (waiting, submitted, running or completed). If the job is completed then the result can be visualized (if the result is an image), or it can be downloaded.

3.4 E-learning components

The aim of the eGLE application is to provide the non-technical specialists in Earth observation with an environment that will allow them to search and retrieve information

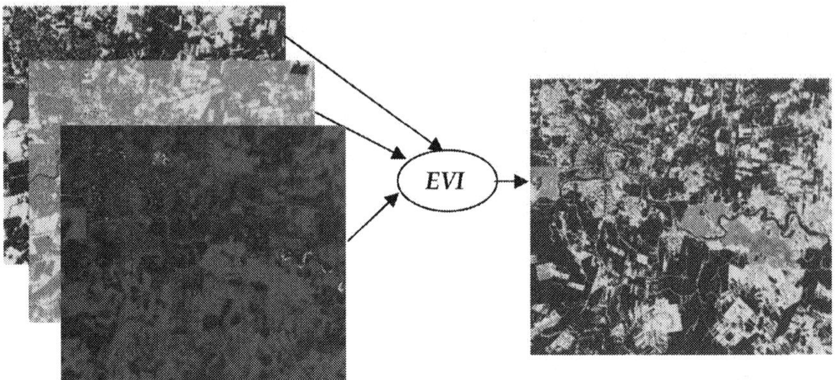

Fig. 15. EVI example: the satellite pseudo-colored spectral bands, and the pseudo-colored image result

Interpolation Processing Panel

Processing information

Processing ID:	250
HDF file:	MOD15A2.A2003001.h19v04.005.2007263165529.hdf
Temperature file:	t2m.CRU.ICTP.ref.nc
Time settings:	December 1986 - March 1987
Last refresh:	10 April 2009, 15:08:25 (refresh every 10 seconds)

Time info	Node name	Start time	End time	Status	Options
1987, March	20_Rescale	2009-04-10 14:50:13	2009-04-10 15:07:14	Completed	🖫 ●
1987, March	19_CoarseToFine	2009-04-10 14:50:14	2009-04-10 15:00:37	Completed	🖫
1987, January	9_CoarseToFine	2009-04-10 14:50:14	2009-04-10 15:04:36	Completed	🖫
1987, February	14_CoarseToFine	2009-04-10 14:50:15		RUNNING	
1987, February	15_Rescale	2009-04-10 14:50:15		READY	
1987, January	10_Rescale	2009-04-10 14:50:15		RUNNING	
1986, December	4_CoarseToFine	2009-04-10 14:50:13	2009-04-10 14:59:43	Completed	🖫
1986, December	5_Rescale	2009-04-10 14:50:15	2009-04-10 15:08:06	Completed	🖫 ●

View slideshow   Change settings

Fig. 16. Monitoring graphical user interface

from distributed sources, launch large scale computations on massive data over Grid networks and create lessons based on these pieces of information in a transparent manner. The interface of the eGLE Environment is focused on simplicity in order to be easy to use by average computer users, but the functionalities implemented must allow the launching of complex Grid operations with minimum restrictions.

There are three main steps that a teacher must complete in order to create a Grid based lesson and they are described in what follows.

Step 1. Acquire the information needed for the lesson. In a transparent manner, without having any knowledge over the location of the data or the protocol needed to access it (HTTP, FTP, GFTP etc.), the teacher is able to browse and search for information based on keywords, time intervals or latitude-longitude defined areas. This modality of information search and retrieval will be available at first only for public, non-secured repositories, as the secured access problem is a more complex issue that requires some specific user knowledge and actions. Another type of information that the teacher can include into the lesson are the results of his own computations executed over the Grid. Through the platform visual tools included in the eGLE interface, the teacher can describe his own PDGs, create iPDGs, and launch them in execution, monitor the execution progress and access the results without possessing any technical information related to Grid.

Step 2. Organize and display the lesson content. Once the information needed for the lesson is acquired, the teacher should be able to setup the lesson structure, to organize logically the information and to define the desired display settings (e.g. text size and color). As the amount of data included into the lesson can be very large (satellite images, videos, files with measured values etc.) or may be accessible only at runtime (the custom computations launched by students) the offline lesson development using dedicated desktop applications is not an option. The eGLE Platform provides the teacher with all the functionalities needed to create the visual appearance of the lesson through the usage of visual containers like *tools*, *patterns* and *templates*.

Tools are visual and functional elements specialized on a certain content type (image, video, text, graph etc.) and represent the atomic parts (smallest division) of the lesson. They are developed by the programmers and integrated into the eGLE platform in order to be used by teachers through the environment interface. The tools are concerned with data retrieval and display mechanisms and provide only an API that can be used to customize their settings (specify the data to be accessed and displayed – image, video etc., modify their visual appearance – width, height, text color, text size etc) according with the content they are specialized on.

Patterns represent visual containers and logical information organizers. They can be created directly by the teachers at authoring time (Fig. 17, Select Pattern) through a wizard like interface that will allow them to customize their visual appearance (ex. number of columns). On each column of a pattern can be integrated a different tool that will be chosen on the second step of the wizard (Fig. 17, Select Tools). Once a pattern is created, it can be reused by the teacher (or by other teachers) with the same visual settings but with different tools included.

Templates are visual containers and patterns collections that define the general layout and settings at lesson global level. The visual attributes defined at template level will provide unitary visual formatting throughout the entire lesson, and can be overridden at pattern or tool level if necessary.

Step 3. Data binding and user interaction description. After creating a pattern and selecting the desired tools to be integrated into the lesson, the teacher has the opportunity to specify the instantiated data that will be displayed in each tool by moving to the step 3 of the wizard (Fig. 17, Edit content). At this point each tool will display visual user interface

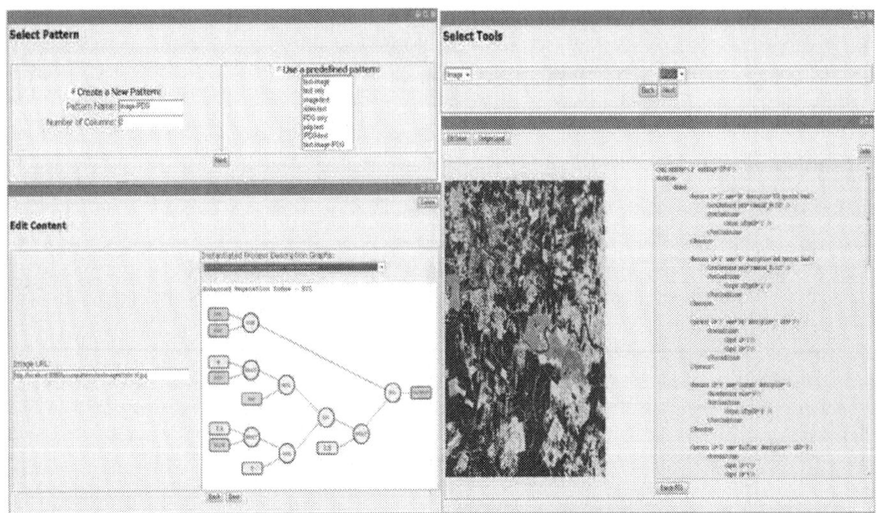

Fig. 17. Wizard steps that helps the teacher to define patterns and instantiate tools

components that are specific to the tools data type (text area for text tools, PDG/iPDG information for graph displaying tools etc.). For example the PDG component will connect to the server and retrieve a list of available PDGs in the idea that the user could use a previously defined workflow. In the same manner, the iPDG specialized tool will provide the user with necessary user interface components that will allow him to search and retrieve the information necessary to execute the iPDG over the Grid.

For some of the tools, at this point the teacher will have the ability to specify a certain student interaction level. For example, the student could receive the right to launch Grid computations on certain data sets. From this point of view, the eGLE platform aims to implement three different lesson scenarios:

- *Static lessons*: the student cannot modify the displayed information. Nevertheless, he may be granted the ability to control slideshows, videos or multimedia content.
- *Dynamic data lessons*: the students can launch specific Grid computations (described through a non-modifiable PDG) with input data sets that are predefined by the teacher at authoring time. All the available options will be displayed using a list component while the processing result will be automatically included into the lesson in a specific area chosen by the teacher.
- *Dynamic workflow lessons*: the students are granted the ability to modify a predefined PDG. For security reasons, the elements that can be added to the graph will be chosen at authoring time by the teacher, but the student will have the ability to describe any processing graph using the provided components. After finishing the workflow description the user could be allowed to launch the computation over the Grid on a specific data set or on several data sets, also predefined by the teacher.

When all the required settings are completed, the user may advance to the step four of the wizard which provides a preview of the content chosen.

4. Case study: remote sensing processing services for research in archaeology provided by GiSHEO

Remote sensing techniques proved to be useful in non-intrusive investigation of archaeological sites by providing information on buried archaeological remains (Gallo et al., 2009; Lasaponara & Masini, 2007). The presence of different remains in the ground can generate different marks identifiable in high resolution panchromatic and/or multispectral images: crop marks, soil marks, shadow marks and damp marks (Gallo et al, 2009). The crop marks are determined by the particularities of vegetation above different kind of remains. The crop above wall foundations is negatively influenced because of lack of water in soil while the crop above buried pits or ditches is positively influenced because of soil nutrients. The soil marks consist of changes of the soil colour or texture. Both crop and soil marks can be identified from panchromatic images and different spectral bands (for instance crop marks are easier to be identified by using red and near infrared bands). The main steps in extracting marks related to archaeological remains are described in the following.

Step 1. Data preparation. This step can consist in rectifying the distortions in the image and/or in fusing data corresponding to panchromatic of different spectral bands (Lasaponara & Masini, 2007). Particularly useful in identifying crop marks are the vegetation indices and other thermal parameters which can be computed from different spectral bands (e.g. red and near infra red bands).

Step 2. Applying image enhancement techniques. In order to emphasize the marks of buried remains, the images are processed by applying basic techniques. Since a good contrast is very important in making different marks easily to identify by the human eye, the contrast enhancing techniques (contrast stretching or histogram equalization) are frequently used in processing archaeological images (Aqdus et al., 2008). Other techniques frequently used to detect crop and soil marks is edge detection, edge thresholding and edge thinning (Lasaponara & Masini, 2007). In the case of multispectral images an important processing step is that of computing the principal components which help in identifying changes in surface variability.

Step 3. Extracting knowledge from processed images. Automatic identification of archaeological sites from digital images is a difficult task, since the small anomalies induced by the buried remains are usually hidden by stronger marks corresponding to the structures currently existing on the ground (roads, constructions, trees, rocks etc). Therefore the final identification and interpretation of the marks should be made by the expert by visually inspecting the enhanced image and by corroborating his observations with additional information (e.g. historical maps, current roads network etc).

The case study we conducted aimed in experimenting with different workflows of enhancement operations applied to high-resolution panchromatic images. The images correspond to several sites in Timis county, Romania where on ground research proved the existence of different remains, e.g. clusters of pits, tombs, roman fortifications etc. Different sequences of operations have been applied on a set of images selected by an archaeologist who also interpreted and validated the results.

The results obtained for three images are presented in Figs. 18, 19 and 20, respectively. In all cases we were looking for soil marks. The results in Fig. 18 were obtained by first converting the initial image in gray scale and then applying contrast stretching (Fig. 18a) or histogram equalization (Fig. 18b). For the image presented in Fig. 19a besides the contrast enhancing

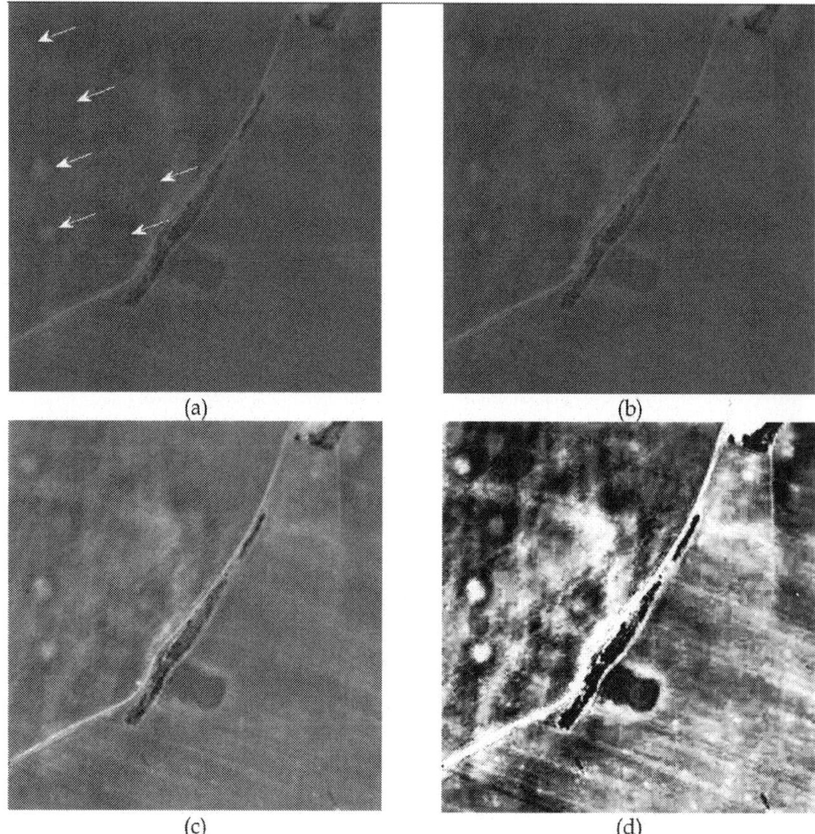

(a)   (b)

(c)   (d)

Fig. 18. Soil marks enhancement (pits cluster and ancient square delimitation) (a) Original image with position of pits marked by arrows (b) Gray level image (c) Gray level image enhanced by contrast stretching (c) Gray level image enhanced by histogram equalization.

operations (Figs. 19b and 19c) a sequence of several operations has been also applied (Fig 19d). The workflow used in this case consisted in a sequence of six operations: gray scale conversion, histogram equalization, edge detection (Sobel filter), thresholding, inversion and erosion.

In the case of the image presented in Fig. 20a besides contrast enhancement by histogram equalization (Fig. 20b) we also applied an emboss filter to the gray scale image (Fig. 15c) followed by histogram equalization (Fig. 20d).

These examples just illustrate the possibility of enhancing panchromatic images by applying flows of basic image processing operations. Thus tools allowing the construction of workflows of simple operations or just the selection of predefined workflows could be useful in training of students in landscape archaeology. Further work will address to construct the support for extracting archaeological marks from multispectral images.

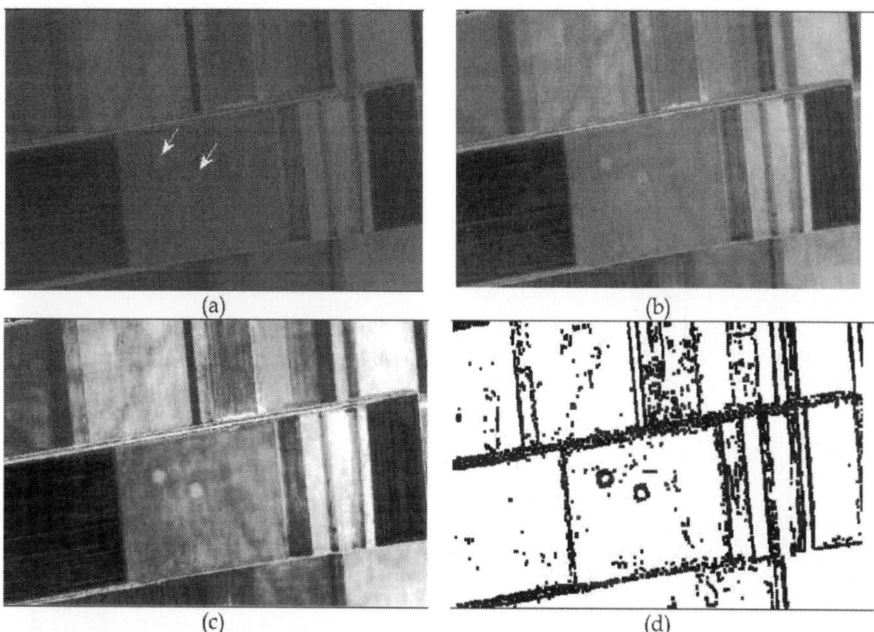

Fig. 19. Soil marks enhancement (burial mounds) (a) Original image with positions of burial mounds marked by arrows; (b) Gray scale image enhanced by contrast stretching; (c) Gray scale image enhanced by histogram equalization; (d) Result of a sequence of operations on the gray scale image: histogram equalization, edge detection, thresholding, inversion, erosion.

7. Conclusion

In order to respond to the need of training and high education platforms for Earth Observation, a Grid-based platform for satellite imagery has been recently developed and its services are exposed in this paper. The development is far from being complete. Complex services are envisioned to be constructed in the near future and intensive tests and comparisons with other approaches are planned to be performed in the next year.

8. References

Agdus, S.,A.; Drummond, J. & Hanson, W.S. (2008). Discovering archaeological crop marks: a hyperspectral approach. *The Intern. Archives of the Photogrammetry, Remote Sensing &Spatial Information Sciences*, XXXVII (B5), Beijing(2008), pp. 361-366,ISSN1682-1750

Aloisio, G. & Cafaro, M. (2003). A dynamic Earth observation system. *Parallel Computing* 29-10, pp. 1357–1362, ISSN 0167-8191

Borengasser, M.; Hungate, W.S. & Watkins R. (2008). *Hyperspectral Remote Sensing: Principles and Applications*, CRC Press Taylor & Francis, ISBN 978-1-56670-654-4, Boca Raton

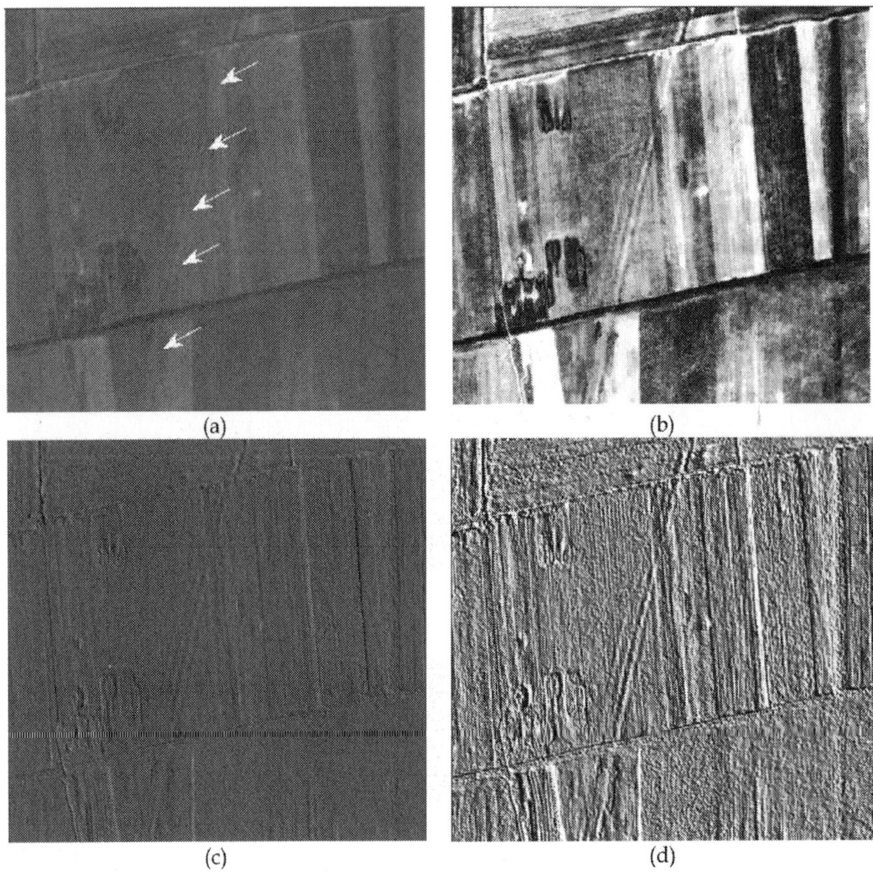

(a)   (b)

(c)   (d)

Fig. 20. Soil marks enhancement (roman fortifications) (a) Original image with linear fortification marked by arrows; (b) Gray scale image enhanced by histogram equalization; (c) Embossed gray scale image; (d) Embossed gray scale image enhanced by histogram equalization.

Cafaro, M.; Epicoco, I.; Quarta, G.; Fiore, S. & Aloisio, G. (2008). Design and implementation of a Grid computing environment for remote sensing. In: *High Performance Computing in Remote Sensing*, 281–305, Chapman&Hall/CRC, ISBN 978-1-58488-662-4

Carvajal-Jimenez, C.L.; Lugo-Beauchamp, W. & Rivera, W. (2004). Grid-HSI: using Grid computing to enable hyper-spectral imaging analysis. In: *Procs.3rd Intern. Conf. Communications, Internet&Information Technology*, Hamza. M.H. (Ed.), pp. 583-588, ISBN 0-88986-445-4, St. Thomas, USA, Nov. 2004, IASTED/ACTA Press, Calgary

CEOS (2009). Working group on education, training and capacity building – WGEdu Overview. Available at http://oislab.eumetsat.org/CEOS/webapps/

Chen C.H. (Ed.) (2007). *Signal and Image Processing for Remote Sensing*. CRC Press, Taylor & Francis Group, ISBN 978-0-8493-5091-7, Boca Raton

Chen C.H. (Ed.) (2008). *Image Processing for Remote Sensing*. CRC Press, Taylor & Francis Group, ISBN 978-1-4200-6664-7, Boca Raton

DEGREE consortium (2008). Earth Science White Paper on Grids. Available at http://www.eu-degree.eu/DEGREE/internal-section/wp6/DEGREE-D6.1.2_v2.8.pdf

ESA (2007). EDuspace The European Earth observation Web site for secondary schools.. Learning with Earth Observation. Europe from Space. Disaster Monitoring. Global Chage. Available at http://www.eduspace.esa.int/

Frincu, M.E.; Panica, S.; Neagul, M. & Petcu, D. (2009). Gisheo: On demand Grid service based platform for EO data processing, *Procs.HiperGrid'09*, ISSN: 2066-4451, Romania, May 2009, Volume 2, pp. 415–422. Politehnica Press, Bucharest.

Fox, G.; Pallickara, S.; Aydin G. & Pierce M. (2005). Messaging in Web service Grid with applications to geographical information systems. In: *Grid Computing: A New Frontier of High Performance Computing*. Grandinetti L. (Ed.), pp. 305–331, ISBN 978-0-444-51999-3, Elsevier, Amsterdam.

Fusco, L.; Cossu, R. & Retscher, C. (2008). Open Grid services for Envisat and Earth observation applications. In: *High Performance Computing in Remote Sensing*, Plaza A. &Chang C.(Eds.),237–280,Chapman&Hall/CRC,ISBN978-1-58488-662-4,Boca Raton

Gallo, D.; Ciminale, M.; Becker H. & Masini N. (2009). Remote sensing techniques for reconstructing a vast Neolithic settlement in Southern Italy. *Journal of Archaeological Science* 36, Issue 1 (January 2009), pp. 43-50, ISSN 0305-4403

Gasster, S.D.; Lee, C. A. & Palko, J.W. (2008). Remote sensing Grids: Architecture and implementation. In: *High Performance Computing in Remote Sensing*, Plaza A. & &Chang C.(Eds.),203–236,Chapman&Hall/CRC,ISBN978-1-58488-662-4,Boca Raton

GENESI-DR Consortium (2008). Ground European network for Earth Science interoperations – Digital repositories. Available at http://genesi-dr.eu

GiSHEO Consortium (2009). On-demand Grid services for high education and training in Earth observation. Available at http://gisheo.info.uvt.ro.

Gorgan D.; Stefanut T. & Bacu V. (2009). Grid based training environment for Earth observation. In: *Advances in Grid and Pervasive Computing*, LNCS 5529, Abdennadher, N. & Petcu, D. (Eds.), pp. 98-109, ISBN 978-3-642-01670-7, Springer, Berlin.

Jong, Steven M. de; Meer, Freek D. van der (Eds.) (2005). *Remote sensing image analysis:: including the spatial domain*. Series: Remote Sensing and Digital Image Processing, Vol. 5, Kluwer Academic Publishers, ISBN 1-4020-2559-9, Dordrecht

Lasaponara, R. & Masini, N. (2007). Detection of archaeological crop marks by using satellite Quickbird multispectral imagery. *Journal of Archaeological Science*, Vol. 34, Issue 2 (February 2007), pp. 214-221, ISSN 0305-4403

Lee, C.A.; Kesselman, C. & Schwab, S. (1996). Near-realtime satellite image processing: metacomputing in CC++. *IEEE Computer Graphics & Applications*, Vol. 16, Issue 4 (July 1996), pp. 79-84, ISSN 0272-1716

Mather, P. M. (2004). *Computer Processing of Remotely-Sensed Images: an Introduction*. John Wiley & Sons Ltd, ISBN 978-0470849194, Chichester, UK

Masini, N.; Rizzo, E.; Lasaponara, R. & Orefici, G. (2008). Integrated remote sensing techniques for the detection of buried archaeological adobe structures: preliminary results in Cahuachi (Peru). *Advances in Geoscience,* 19 (2008), pp. 75-82, ISSN 1680-7340

Nico, G.; Fusco, L. & Linford, J. (2003). Grid technology for the storage and processing of remote sensing data: description of an application. *Procs. SPIE:* Fuhisada H. et al. (Eds.) vol. 4881, no. 677 (April 2003), pp. 677–685, Agi Pelagia, Greece, Sept. 2002.

Panica, S.; Neagul, M,; Petcu, D.; Stefanut, T. & Gorgan, D. (2009). Desiging a Grid-based training platform for Earth observation. In: *Procs. SYNASC 08,* pp. 394-397, ISBN: 978-0-7695-3523-4, Timisoara, Sept. 2008, IEEE Computer Press, Los Alamitos

Petcu, D.; Gorgan, D.; Pop, F.; Tudor, D. & Zaharie, D. (2008). Satellite image processing on a Grid-based platform. *International Scientific Journal of Computing,* vol. 7, issue 2 (August 2008), pp. 51-58, ISSN 1727-6209

Plaza A. & Chang C. (Eds.) (2008). *High Performance Computing in Remote Sensing.* Chapman & Hall/CRC, Taylor & Francis Group. ISBN 978-1-58488-662-4, Boca Raton

Portela, O.; Tabasco, A.; Brito, F. & Goncalves, P. (2008). A Grid enabled infrastructure for Earth observation. *Geophysical Research Abstracts,* Vol. 10 (2008), ISSN 1607-7962

Radu, A., Bacu, V. and Gorgan, D.: Diagrammatic description of satellite image processing workflow. *Proc. SYNASC07.* pp. 341-348, ISBN 0-7695-3078-8, Timisoara, Sept. 2007, IEEE Computer Press, Los Alomitos

Richards, J. A. & Jia, X. (2006). *Remote Sensing Digital Image Analysis: An Introduction.* Springer-Verlag, ISBN: 978-354064-860-4, New York.

Schott J. R. (2007). *Remote Sensing: The Image Chain Approach.* 2nd edition, Oxford University Press, ISBN 978-019517-817-3,, Oxford, USA

Schowengerdt R.A. (2007). *Remote Sensing: Models and Methods for Image Processing,* 3rd Edition, Academic Press, Elsevier Inc., ISBN 978-0-12-369407-2, Burligton, USA

Sekiguchi, S.; Tanaka, Y.; Kojima, I.; Yamamoto, N.; Yokoyama, S.; Tanimura, Y.;. Nakamura, R.; Iwao, K. & Tsuchida, S. (2008). Design principles and IT overviews of the GEOGrid. *IEEE Systems Journal,* Vol.2, No.3 (Sept.2008), 374-389, ISSN 1932-8184

Tsangaris, M.; Kakaletris, G.; Kllapi, H.; Papanikos, G.; Pentaris, F.; Polydoras, P.; Sitaridi, E.; Stoumpos, V. & Ioannidis, Y. (2009). Dataflow processing and optimization on Grid and cloud infrastructures, *Bulletin of the Technical Committee on Data Engineering,* Vol. 32, No. 1 (March 2009), pp. 67-74, IEEE Computer Society

## 9

Ballistics Image Processing and Analysis for Firearm Identification

Dongguang Li
School of Computer and Security Science
Faculty of Computing, Health and Science
Edith Cowan University
2 Bradford Street, Mount Lawley,
Western Australia 6050

1. Introduction

The identification of firearms from forensic ballistics specimens is an exacting and intensive activity performed by specialists with extensive experience. The introduction of imaging technology to assist the identification process of firearms has enhanced the ability of forensic ballisticians to conduct analyses of these specimens for identification.

The positive identification of ballistics specimens from imaging systems are important applications of technology in criminal investigation [1] [2] [3] [4]. While the image capture methodology for persons and forensic ballistics specimens is similar, the process of identification for each is dependent upon the level of certainty required for the identification.

The forensic identification of ballistics specimens relies on the detection, recognition and ultimate matching of markings on the surfaces of cartridges and projectiles made by the firearms [5]. Traditional methods for the comparison of these marks are based on incident light microscopy. The image formed from the oblique illumination of the mark gives a representation of the surface of the specimen in the region of the mark [6]. This representation is critically dependent on the material of the surface on which the marks have been made, and the geometry and intensity of the illumination system. The assessment by the ballistician of the similarity between comparable marks on respective ballistics specimens from crime scenes and test firings will be based on the expertise and experience of the technologist. Thus the traditional method of matching markings has inherent difficulties, and entails an element of subjectivity [7].

The need for firearm identification systems by police services continues to increase with greater accessibility to weapons in the international contexts. The characteristic markings on the cartridge and projectile of a bullet fired from a gun can be recognized as a *fingerprint* for identification of the firearm [8]. Forensic ballistics imaging has the capacity to produce high-resolution digital images of cartridge cases and projectiles for matching to a library of ballistics images [9]. However, the reliance upon imaging technologies makes identification of ballistics specimens both a demanding and exacting task, where the control of the error of measurement in the imaging technique must not allow compromise of integrity of the identification process.

The analysis of marks on bullet casings and projectiles provides a precise tool for identifying the firearm from which a bullet is discharged [1] [10]. The characteristic markings of each cartridge case and projectile are released ready for analysis when the gun is fired. More than thirty different features within these marks can be distinguished, which in combination produce a "fingerprint" for identification of the firearm [11]. This forensic technique has wide application in the world of forensic science, and would play a vital part in legal evidence in the case where firearms are involved.

Projectile bullets fired through the barrel of a gun will exhibit extremely fine striation markings, some of which are derived from minute irregularities in the barrel, produced during the manufacturing process. The examination of these striations on land marks and groove marks of the projectile is difficult using conventional optical microscopy. However, digital imaging techniques have the potential to detect and identify the presence of striations on ballistics specimens.

Given a means of automatically analyzing features within such a firearm "fingerprint", identifying not only the type and model of a firearm, but also each individual weapon as effectively as human fingerprint identification can be achieved. Due to the high demand of skill and the intensive nature of ballistics identification, law enforcement agencies around the world have expressed considerable interest in the application of ballistics imaging identification systems to both greatly reduce the time for identification and to introduce reliability (or repeatability) to the process.

Several ballistics identification systems are already available either in a commercial form or in a beta-testing state. The two major international ballistics imaging systems are manufactured by the IBIS Company in Montreal, Canada and the FBI (Drugfire) in USA. A Canadian company, Walsh Automation, has developed a commercial system called "Bulletproof", which can acquire and store images of projectiles and cartridge cases, and automatically search the image database for particular striations on projectiles. However the user must match the impressed markings or striations on the projectiles. This inherent limitation of the system with respect to projectiles has prohibited its use. The biometric imaging and ballistics imaging expertise at Edith Cowan University (ECU) in Australia have developed the next generation of digital imaging and surface profiling information systems for forensic ballistics identification, for solving weapon related crime in Australia and in the international context. The Fireball Firearm Identification System was developed at ECU after the initial research conducted by Smith [1][9] and Cross [1], and later by an ECU software team [12]. The Fireball System was acknowledged as the leading small ballistics identification system in the world [13]. The Fireball has the capability of storing and retrieving images of cartridge case heads, and of interactively obtaining position metrics for the firing-pin impression, ejector mark, and extractor mark. The limitation of this system is that the position and shape of the impression images must be traced manually by the user. For the time being, we still have unsolved problems on projectiles imaging, storing and analyzing although the system has been put in use for nine years already. The efficiency and accuracy of the FireBall system must be improved and increased.

The research papers on the automatic identification of cartridge cases and projectiles are hardly found. L.P. Xin [14] proposed a cartridge case based identification system for firearm authentication. His work was focused on the cartridge cases of center-firing mechanisms.

And he also provided a decision strategy by which the high recognition rate would be achieved interactively. C. Kou et al. [15] described a neural network based model for the identification of chambering marks on cartridge cases. But no experimental results were given in their paper. Using a hierarchical neural network model, a system for identifying the firing pin marks of cartridge cases images automatically is proposed in this paper. We mainly focus on the consideration of rim-firing pin mark identification. A significant contribution towards the efficient and precise identification of cartridge cases in the further processing, such as the locating and coding of ejector marks, extractor marks and chambering marks of cartridge cases will be made through this system. The SOFM neural network and the methods of image processing in our study is described briefly in Section 4.

The identification of the ballistics specimen from the crime scene with the test specimen is traditionally conducted by mapping the marks by visual images from a low-powered optical microscope (Fig. 1). The selection of features within the identifying mark is chosen for their apparent uniqueness in an attempt to match both crime scene and test specimens. A decision is made whether the same firearm was responsible for making the marks under examination on the crime scene and test ballistics specimens. The selection of the mark or set of marks for examination and comparison is a critical step in the identification process, and has the capacity to influence subsequent stages in the comparison process [2].

Fig. 1. Landmarks and groove marks of a fired projectile

However, optical and photonic techniques have the capability of a quantum improvement in quality of images for comparison, and as a result will enhance reliability and validity of the measurements for matching images. The line-scan imaging (Fig. 2) and profilometry techniques [2] [3] each contribute to the information base that will allow identification of firearms from matching crime scene and test fired ballistics specimens.

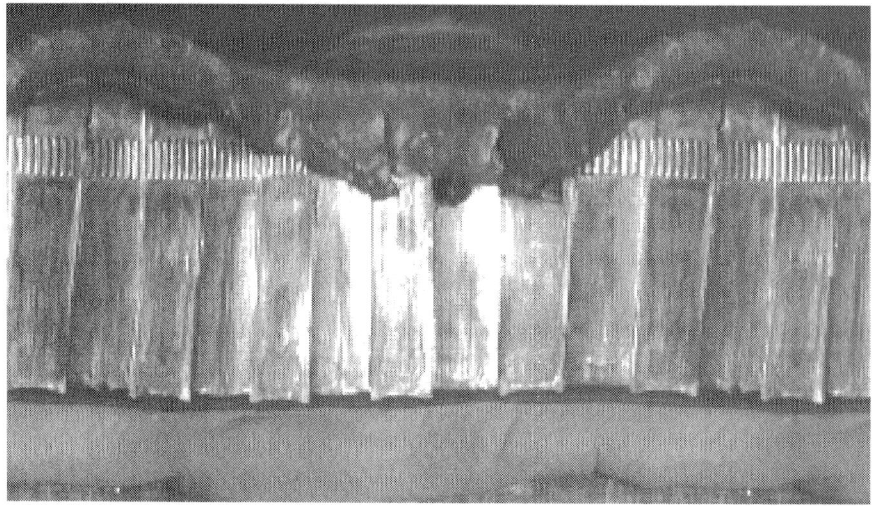

Fig. 2. Linescan image of fired projectile

The development of the line-scan technique [2] [16] [17] for ballistics specimens has the capacity to produce images for the spatial distribution of identification signatures on cylindrical projectiles and cartridge cases. This is achieved by maintaining the surface of the specimen at focus for the rotational scan of the cylinder. However, the production of high resolution images of the cylindrical ballistics specimens are still required for comparison and hence identification.

The difficulties associated with traditional imaging of forensic ballistics specimens are numerous, and include the smallness of the samples, the nature of the surfaces for the cartridge cases (brass) and for the projectiles (lead). As well the features used for identification have low contrast, the cylindrical shape of the cartridge cases, and the distorted shapes of the projectiles (after striking objects) all causing focus problems for image formation.

In this chapter, a new analytic system based on the Fast Fourier Transform (FFT) for identifying the projectile specimens captured by the line-scan imaging technique is proposed. The system gives an approach for projectiles capturing, storing and automatic analysis and makes a significant contribution towards the efficient and precise identification of projectiles. Firstly, in Section 2, the line-scan imaging technique for projectile capturing is described. Secondly, the analytic approach based on FFT for identifying the projectile characteristics and the experimental results are presented in Section 3. The artificial intelligent techonologies are applied to the ballistics image classification and identification in Section 4. In Section 5, the image database systems are discussed in details. Some online image procissing and visualizition applications are covered in Section 6. Finally, suggestions on the further research and conclusion are given in Section 7.

2. Line-scan imaging technique for projectile capturing

The proposed analysis system for identifying firearms based on the projectiles images is composed of three parts (shown in Fig. 3), and each part is described in detail in following sections.

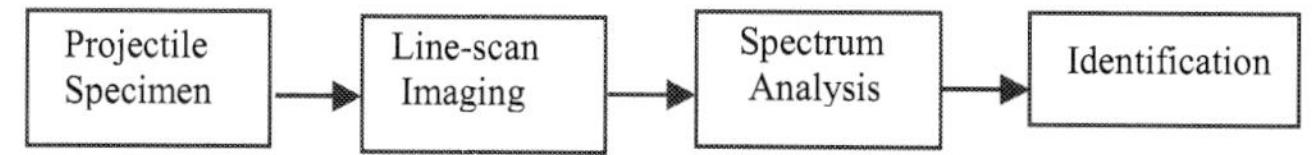

Fig. 3. The proposed analysis system for firearm identification based on projectiles

2.1 Line-scan Imaging

Due to the expected high contrast imaging involved in imaging the cylindrical shapes of ballistics specimens, the traditional optical microscopy technique is inherently unsuitable. As the specimen is translated and rotated [17], it is difficult to maintain image quality using oblique lighting on a cylindrical surface at low magnification microscopy. However, in order to obtain the surface information from a cylindrical shaped surface, a line-scan imaging technique is used by scanning consecutive columns of picture information and storing the data in a frame buffer so that a 2D image of the surface of the cylindrical specimen is produced.

The precursor-imaging device to the line-scan camera is the periphery camera, which consists of a slit camera with moving film in order to 'unwrap' cylindrical objects by rotating them on a turntable [18]. Relative motion between the line array of sensors in the line-scan camera and the surface being inspected is the feature of the line-scan technique. To achieve this relative motion, the cylindrical ballistics specimen relative to the stationary line array sensors are rotated [17][18][19][20].

Due to the line-scan technique, all points on the imaging line of the sample are in focus. This is because the cylindrical ballistics specimen is rotated about an axis of rotation relative to a stationary line array of sensor. Thus, during one full rotation of the cylindrical ballistics specimen, all points on the rotating surface will be captured on the collated image. [17].

The line-scan imaging analysis system for projectiles in our study is shown in Fig. 4. The stepper motor rotates with 360 degrees/2400 steps, namely 0.15 degree each step. The 0.15 degree stepper motor is used in order to acquire sufficient details from the surface of the projectile. For example, a projectile with a diameter of 5-15mm has a perimeter range of 15-50mm roughly. With 2400 steps a round the lowest resolution of the line-scan image will still be 2400/50=48 lines per mm. A CCD camera (Sony, Model DXC-151AP) is used instead of the traditional camera used in [17] [18]. The graphic capturing card installed in the PC has an image size of 320 × 240 pixels. A ring light source (Leica 30120202) is adopted, which can provide uniform lighting conditions [21]. The optical system used was just a standard optical microscope (Leica MZ6).

Being quite different from the method used in [17] [18], the procedure in our line-scan imaging approach is as follows:

1. With the stepper motor's every step
2. the CCD camera captures the current image of projectile specimen and
3. sends the image to Graphic card in PC;
4. The middle column of pixels in this image is extracted and saved consecutively in an array in the buffer on PC, and

5. steps 1. and 2. are repeated until the whole surface of the projectile specimen is scanned;
6. The array in the buffer is used to produce a 2-D line-scanned image for the whole surface of the projectile.

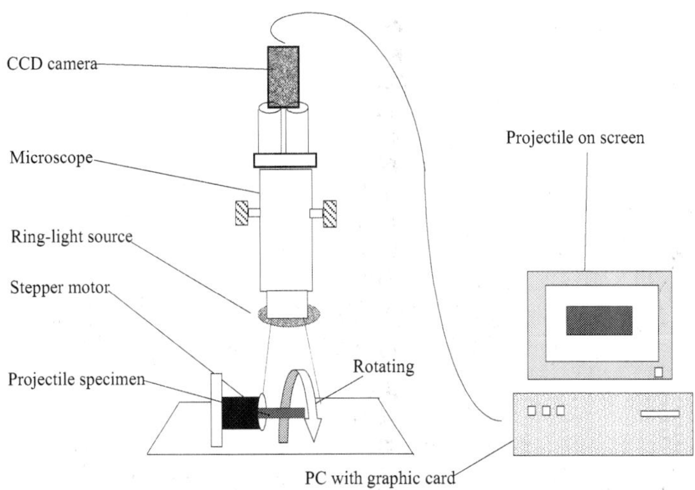

Fig. 4. The line-scan imaging and analyzing system

The resolution of the line-scan image is dependent on,
- the rotational degree per step of the stepper motor
- the resolution of CCD camera
- the resolution of graphic capturing card
- the columns captured at each step in step

By adjusting the length of each step of the stepper motor and the number of columns captured in each step to meet forensic investigation requirements, the resolution of the line-scanned image of projectile specimen could be manipulated. The resolution required to detect the major striations on land marks and groove marks is not necessary to be very high. The line-scan image resolution is set by the rotational steps and sizes of the projectile specimen.

2.2 Projectile specimens and their line-scanned images

The projectile specimens in our study, provided by Western Australia Police Department, are in four classes and belong to four different guns. They are:
1. Browning, semiautomatic pistol, caliber 9mm.
2. Norinco, semiautomatic pistol, caliber 9mm.
3. and 4. Long Rifle, semiautomatic pistol, caliber 22 (5.59mm).

Through the use of the line scan imaging technique as discussed in Section 2.1, all the projectile specimens in our study are recorded under the same conditions (e.g light conditions, the stepping angle of the stepper motor etc...). All the landmarks and groove marks of projectile specimen are captured and displayed in the line scanned image through adjusting the stepping angle of the stepper motor by just one full rotation (360 degrees).

Fig. 5. Four classes of line-scanned images of projectiles in our study (with code: a, 101; b, 201; c, 301; d, 401)

Line-scanned images of four classes of projectile specimens in our study are shown Fig. 5. For the purpose of firearm identification, what we are looking at in these images are some unique features such as land mark width, groove mark width, and their orientations. Obviously there are many more different features (visible or hidden) in the different images. All those features form a unique combination for each every weapon as a set of fingerprints for that particular weapon.

2.3 Image pre-processing for FFT analysis

In a practical application, the quality of the line-scanned image of a projectile specimen can be affected and noised by many factors such as the lighting conditions, the materials of the specimen, the original texture on the surface of specimen, and the deformed shapes. Strong noise and damage in the line-scanned image may result, and this would mean difficulties in extracting and verifying the important features used for identifying the individual specimen, such as the contours, edges, the directions and the width (or distance) of land marks and groove marks. To eradicate or minimize the effects mentioned above, the following image pre-processing operations are applied to the line-scanned images obtained in Section 2.2.

A general function of image preprocessing is the contrast enhancement transformation [22]. Low-contrast images can be a result of poor lighting conditions, lack of dynamic range of the imaging sensor, and a wrong setting of lens aperture during image acquisition. Increasing the dynamic range of gray levels in the image being processed is the idea behind contrast enhancement. In our study, the images are often blurred to a certain extent due to the reason of the strong reflection from the metal surface. The landmarks or groove marks may be hidden within. Thus, the contrast enhancement transformation is used upon the images obtained in Section 2.2. We perform a simple contrast enhancement by linearly expanding the contrast range by assigning the darkest pixel value to black, the brightest value to white, and each of others to linearly interpolated shades of grey in the image. The operation is automated when acquiring the images with a CCD camera. In the line-scanned images, only the regions that include the landmarks and groove marks are useful for analyzing and identifying the characteristics of the projectile specimens. Thus, we only select the regions in images that are necessary and useful to our study. The images (the effective regions in original images) shown in Fig. 6 are transformed versions corresponding to the images in Fig. 5 by the region selecting and the contrast enhancement transformation. One of the most important roles in the identification system is feature extraction. There are many ways to perform edge detection. However, the most may be grouped into two categories, Gradient and Laplacian. The gradient method detects the edges by looking for the maximum and minimum in the first derivative of the image. The Laplacian method searches for zero-crossings in the second derivative of the image to find edges. For detection of edge and lines in our line-scan images of projectiles, various detection operators can be used. Most of these are applied with convolution masks and most of these are based on differential operations. We pick up the first derivatives [22] as the images features. For a digital image, Sobel operators in vertical and horizontal directions (shown in Fig. 7 with 3×3 window) are the most popular powerful masks used to approximate the gradient of f at coordinate (i, j). In our experiments, we adopt the Sobel operators to extract the contours and edges of the land and groove marks on line-scanned images of projectile specimens, which convolves the images with the Sobel masks to produce the edge maps of the four line-scan images shown in Fig. 8. Because the directions of the land and the groove marks of the projectile specimens are mostly along 90 degrees in the line-scanned images,

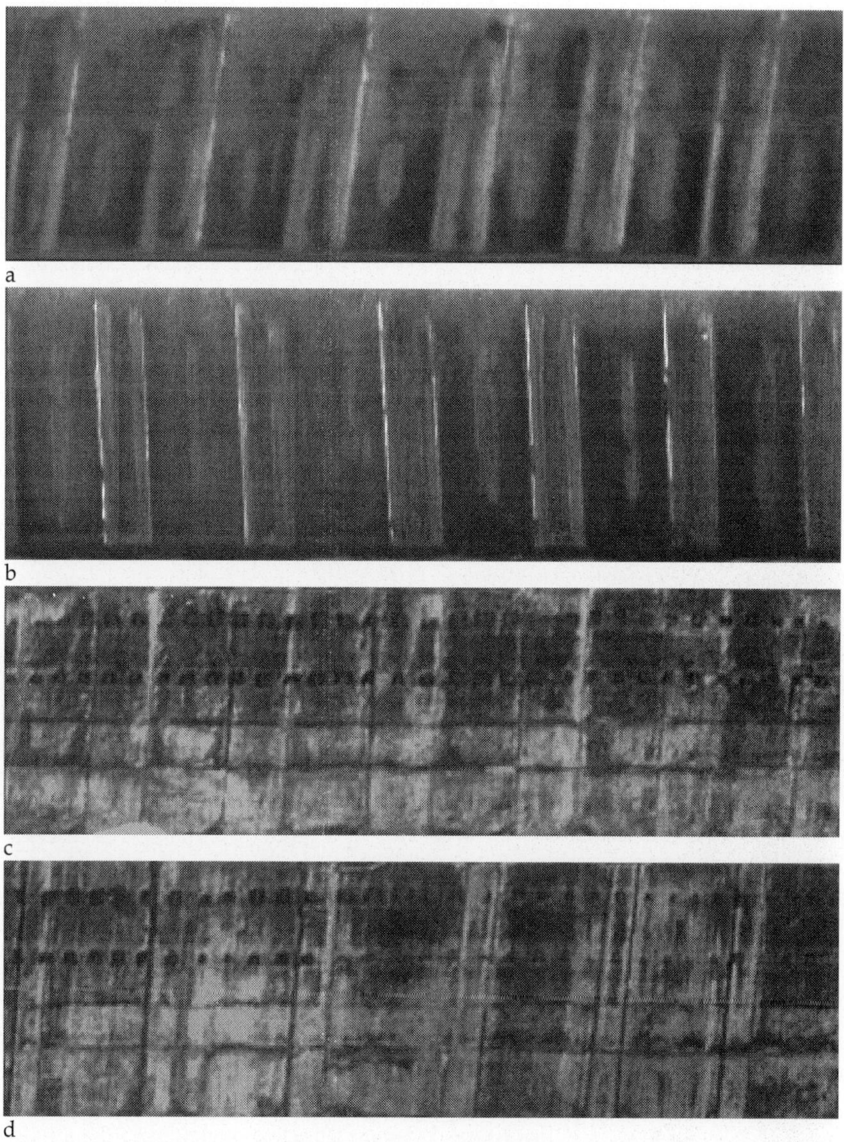

Fig. 6. Contrast enhancement results (a, b with size 400×110, and c, d with size 400×100)

-1	-2	-1
0	0	0
1	2	3

-1	0	1
-2	0	2
-1	0	3

Fig. 7. Sobel masks in vertical and horizontal directions

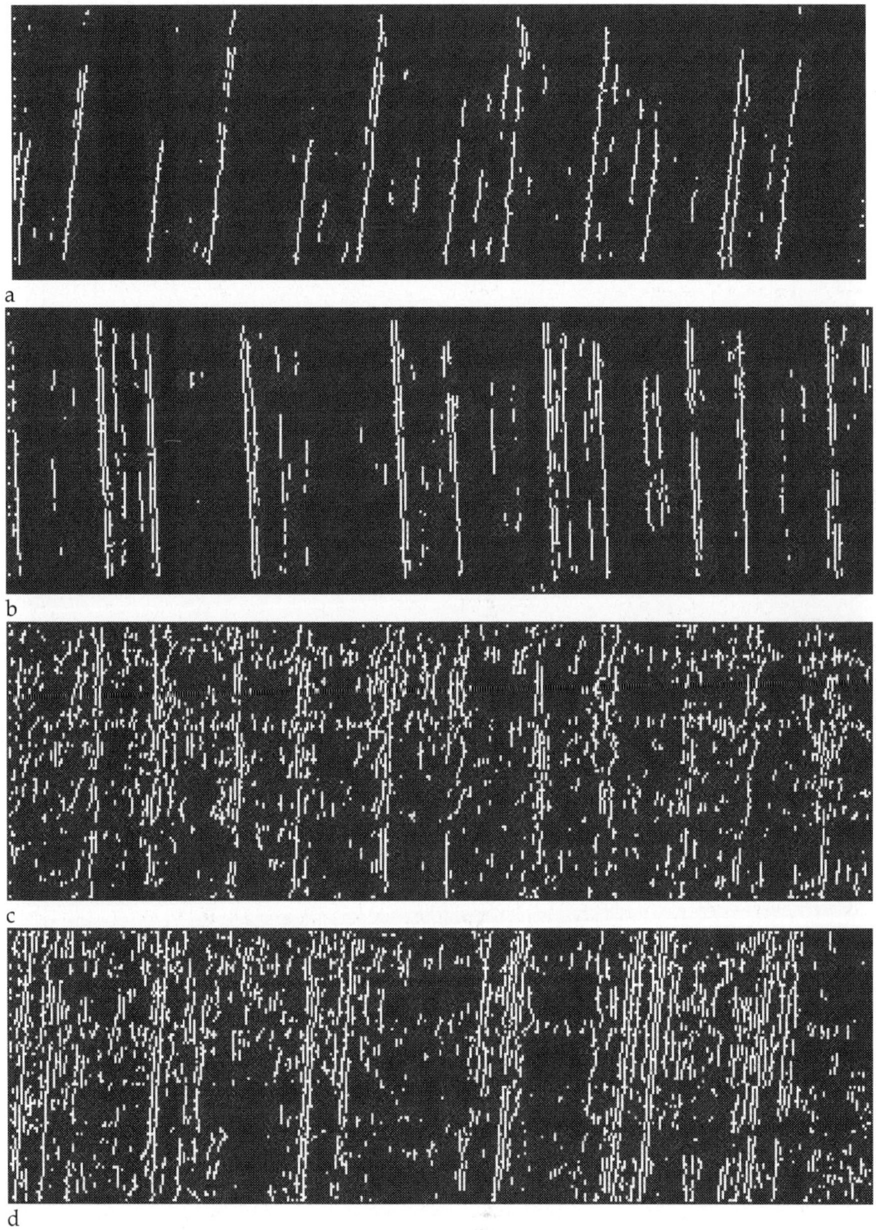

Fig. 8. The contours and edges extracting using Sobel operator in vertical direction

we only adopt the vertical direction mask (Fig. 7) for extracting the features of the line-scanned images. Through an observation of Fig. 8 in which there are lots of noises and disconnection on the land and groove marks, the conventional spatial techniques are not suitable for the nature of locally. Hence, a FFT-based analysis for projectiles is introduced.

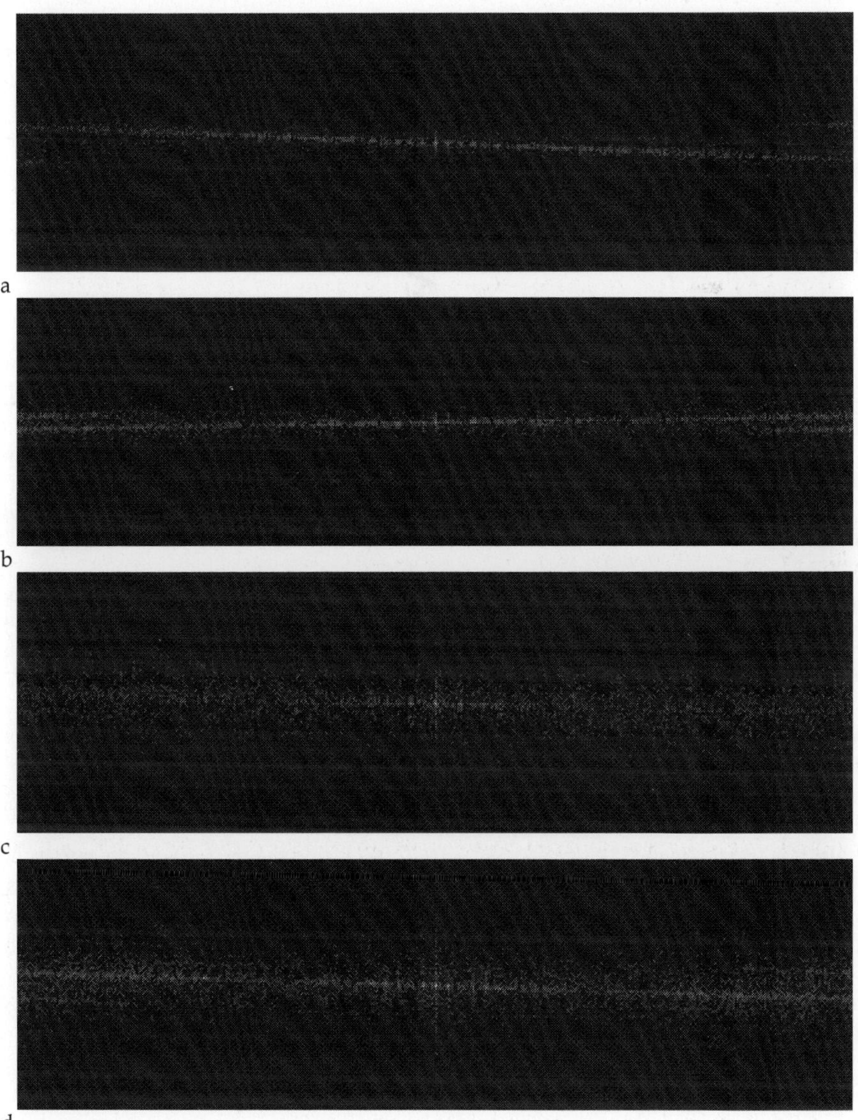

a

b

c

d

Fig. 9. Fourier transformation results of the images in Fig. 8

3. FFT-based analysis

3.1 FFT and spectrum analysis

The Fourier transform of a two-dimensional, discrete function (image), $f(x,y)$, of size $M \times N$, is given by the equation

$$F(u,v) = \frac{1}{MN} \sum_{x=0}^{M-1} \sum_{y=0}^{N-1} f(x,y) e^{-j2\pi(ux/M + vy/N)} \tag{1}$$

where $j = \sqrt{-1}$, for all $u = 0, 1, 2, \cdots, M-1$, $v = 0, 1, 2, \cdots, N-1$. We define the Fourier spectrum by the equation

$$|F(u,v)| = \left[R^2(u,v) + I^2(u,v)\right]^{1/2} \tag{2}$$

where $R(u,v)$ and $I(u,v)$ are the real and imaginary parts of $F(u,v)$, respectively.

For describing the directionality of periodic or almost periodic 2-D patterns in an image, the Fourier spectrum is ideal. As easily distinguishable as concentrations of high-energy burst in the spectrum, these global texture patterns are generally not convenient to detect with spatial methods because of the local nature of these techniques. In the feature extraction process some of texture descriptors are considered both in Fourier and spatial domains. It is noticed that some of spatial domain descriptors can be used with success for geology recordings where the image appears to be very similar to the one in this research [23].

For the specific research interests in this study we only consider a set of features of the Fourier spectrum that are used for analyzing and describing the line-scanned images of projectiles:

1. Principal direction of the texture patterns are shown by prominent peaks in the spectrum.
2. Fundamental spatial period of the patterns are shown by the location of the peaks in the frequency plane.
3. Some statistical features of the spectrum.

By expressing the spectrum in polar coordinates to yield a function $S(r,\theta)$, where S is the spectrum function, and r and θ are the variables in this coordinate system, detection and interpretation of the spectrum features just mentioned often are simplified. For each direction θ, $S(r,\theta)$ is a 1-D function $S_\theta(r)$. Similarly, for each frequency r, $S_r(\theta)$ is a 1-D function. Analyzing $S_\theta(r)$ for a fixed value of θ yields the behavior of the spectrum (such as the presence of peaks) along a radial direction from the origin, whereas analyzing $S_r(\theta)$ for a fixed value of r yields the behavior along a circle centered on the origin. A more global description is obtained by integrating (summing for discrete variables) these functions [22]:

$$S(r) = \sum_{\theta=0}^{\pi} S_\theta(r) \tag{3}$$

and

$$S(\theta) = \sum_{r=1}^{R_0} S_r(\theta) \tag{4}$$

where R_0 is the radius of a circle centered at origin.

The results of Equations (3) and (4) constitute a pair of values $\left[S(r), S(\theta)\right]$ for each pair of coordinates (r, θ). We can generate two 1-D functions, $S(r)$ and $S(\theta)$, that constitute a spectral-energy description of texture for an entire image or region under consideration by varying these coordinates. Furthermore, descriptors of these functions themselves can be computed in order to characterize their behavior quantitatively, which can be used as ballistics features for firearm identification.

3.2 FFT-based analysis, identification and experimental results

The following section discusses in detail some characteristics and descriptors of the line-scanned images for identification of projectiles using the radius spectrum and angular spectrum.

We know that the slowest varying frequency component ($u = v = 0$) corresponds to the average gray level of an image. The low frequencies correspond to the slowly varying components of an image as we move away from the origin of the transform. In a line-scanned image of projectile specimen, for example, these might correspond to the land and groove marks which are large in scale and regular in shape. Moving further away from the starting point, the higher frequencies begin to correspond to faster and faster gray level changes in the image. These are the small or irregular marks and other components of an image characterized by abrupt changes in gray level, such as noises. Now we focus our attention on the analysis of low frequencies in the radius and angle spectrum of line-scanned images.

Shown in Fig. 10 a, b, c and d, are the plots of radius and angle spectrum corresponding to images in Fig. 9 a, b respectively. The results of FFT clearly exhibit directional 'energy' distributions of the surface texture between class one and two. Comparing Fig. 10 a to b, the plots on the radius spectrum, six clear peaks in the range of low frequencies (r <20) can be observed on the former whilst the latter has only three peaks in the same range and is smooth in shape, this indicates that 'energy' of the class one specimen is distributed in several permanent positions, and also reveals that the class one specimen has a coarse surface texture and the wide land and groove marks, while the surface texture of class two is fine and the smaller widths of land and groove marks.

The angular spectrums (Fig. 10 c and d) display a great distinctness in position of prominent peaks between class one and two. With respect to the measurement coordinate, further study reveals that the angular spectrum can clearly indicate the angular position of periodic grooves or scratches on the surface. It can be seen from the angular spectrum there is a maximum peak at about 81 degrees in Fig. 10 c. This is indicative of scratches (the land or groove marks) oriented 81 degrees to the surface of the projectiles, while the maximum peak in Fig. 10 d sits at about 95 degree. Furthermore, a second prominent peak of about 100 degrees (corresponding to small or shallow marks on the projectile's surface) can be seen on the former plot. However, it is noted that the second peak of Fig. 10 d is at about 85 degree.

By examining quantitative differences of spectrums using a set of features, the characteristics of projectile specimen surface textures can also be revealed.

To compare and analyze the spectrum differences between the two classes easily, a set of features is used, and the quantitative results are shown in Table 1 (where, r_1 and a_2, Max; r_2 and a_3, Mean; r_3 and a_4, Std; r_4 and a_5, Max: Median; and a_1, Position of maximum peak).

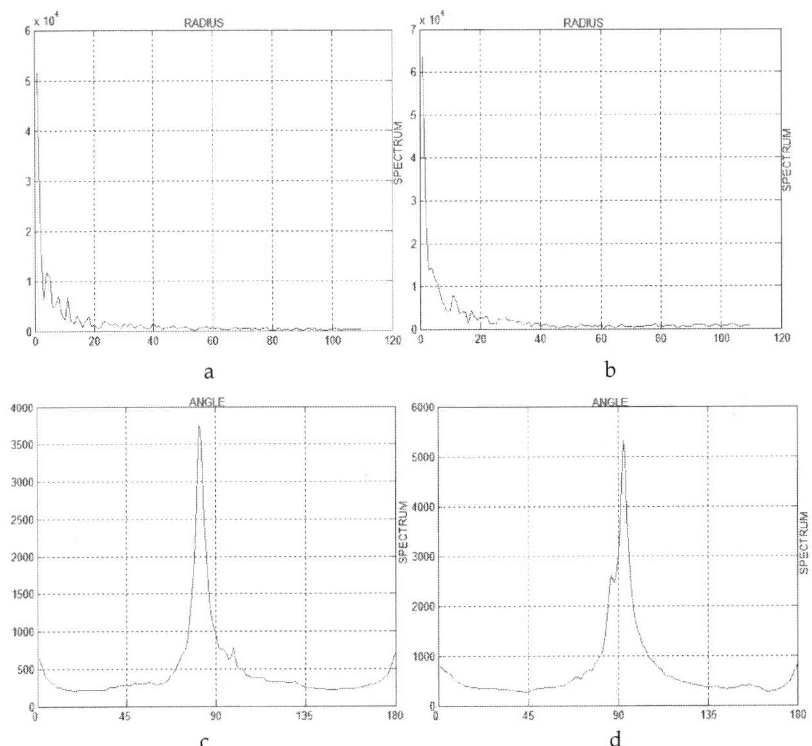

Fig. 10. Radial spectrum (a, b) and Angular spectrum (c, d) of the images (a, b) in Fig. 9

As observed from Table 1, the Max, Mean, and Std of class one are relatively smaller than class two, while the relative variation for radio between Max and Mean is greater. The difference between prominent peaks (corresponding to the orientations of land and groove marks) of class one and two is 14 degrees. All this goes to show that FFT spectrum analysis, in the form of quantification, can reveal characteristic and directional surface textures of the projectile specimen.

Class	Code	Radial spectrum				Angular spectrum				
		r_1	r_2	r_3	r_4	a_1	a_2	a_3	a_4	a_5
1	101	51517	1728	5372	29.81	81	3753	475.2	546.2	7.898
2	201	63646	2538	6809	25.07	95	5308	697.9	794.7	7.600

Table 1. Radial spectrum and angular spectrum statistics results of Fig. 9 a and b

After obtaining the initial significant results, the 12 more experiments involving 12 new projectile specimens fired by 12 different weapons are carried out. Those 12 specimens are among the four classes of weapons discussed in the section 2.2 and coded in Fig. 5 (4 in class 1, code 102-105; 2 in class 2, code 202-203; 3 in class 3, code 302-304; and 3 in class 4, code 402-404). Table 2 lists all the experimental results based on the total 16 projectile specimens in our study.

Class	Code	Radial spectrum				Angular spectrum				
		r_1	r_2	r_3	r_4	a_1	a_2	a_3	a_4	a_5
1	101	51517	1728	5372	29.81	81	3753	475.2	546.2	7.898
	102	51162	1591	5187	32.16	81	3709	437.6	545.6	8.487
	103	51200	1520	5087	33.68	81	3583	418.2	509.8	8.571
	104	51556	1699	5348	30.34	81	3589	467.3	514.1	7.685
	105	62715	1962	6299	31.96	81	4219	539.5	617.8	7.827
2	201	63646	2538	6809	25.07	95	5308	697.9	794.7	7.600
	202	64381	2738	7038	23.51	95	5257	752.9	777.7	6.990
	203	64059	2545	6707	25.16	95	5193	700.0	794.0	7.419
3	301	63959	2899	6942	22.06	86	2514	724.7	451.9	3.469
	302	64448	2478	6889	26.01	86	2714	719.4	445.5	3.774
	303	64288	2743	7090	23.43	86	2517	685.8	439.9	3.669
	304	63694	3011	6999	21.23	86	2750	752.7	512.8	3.657
4	401	76059	4040	8554	18.27	79	4965	1010	787.8	4.916
	402	76406	5026	8982	15.20	79	4972	1256	835.6	3.959
	403	75607	3735	8035	20.23	79	4897	933.9	753.3	5.249
	404	76796	3786	8498	20.28	79	4135	946.3	738.6	4.371

Table 2. Radial spectrum and angular spectrum statistics results based on the specimens in our study

By observing Table 2 and recalling that the calibers of class one and two are the same, and so are the class three and fours, we can easily identify the projectiles into a class using the features listed in Table 2. For example, all the values of r_4 for class one are greater than 28.0, while for class two, none is greater than 26.0. In order to identify the firearms to the level of the single gun we treat each every row of the table 2 as a set of fingerprints from that gun. The characteristics (r_1-r_4 and a_1- a_5) we used in spectrum analysis can be formed as a set of features vectors for building an artificial intelligent (AI) system for the automatic firearm identification based on the spent projectiles. Several AI algorithms are under investigation to best use the spectrum characteristics as searching criteria in the existing FireBall firearm identification database.

4. SOFM and cartridge case image processing

It is hard to find research papers on the automatic identification of cartridge. A cartridge cases based identification system for firearm authentication was proposed by Le-Ping Xin [14]. His work was focused on the cartridge cases of center-fire mechanism. And he also provided a decision strategy from which the high recognition rate would be achieved interactively. A neural network based model for the identification of the chambering marks on cartridge cases was described by Chenyuan Kou et al. [24]. But no experiment results were given in their paper.

In this section a proposed hierarchical firearm identification model based on cartridge cases images is shown. The following parts, describe respectively, the structure of the model, the training, testing of SOFM, and decision-making strategy.

4.1 SOFM neural network

The basic classifying units in our identification system is picked as the Self-Organizing Feature Map (SOFM) neural networks. The SOFM has been applied to the study of complex problems such as speech recognition, combinatorial optimization, control, pattern recognition and modeling of the structure of the visual cortex [25], [26], [27] and [28]. The SOFM we used is a kind of un-supervised neural network models, it in effect depicts the result of a vector quantization algorithm that places a number of reference or codebook vectors into a high-dimension input data space to approximate defined values between the reference vectors, the relative values of the latter are made to depend on it to its data set in an ordered fashion. When local-order relations are each other as if there neighboring values would lies along an "elastic surface". This "surface" becomes defined as a kind of nonlinear regression of the reference vectors through the data points [29], by means of the self-organizing algorithm.

We employ the standard Kohonen's SOFM algorithm summarized in Table 3, the topology of SOFM is shown in Fig. 11.

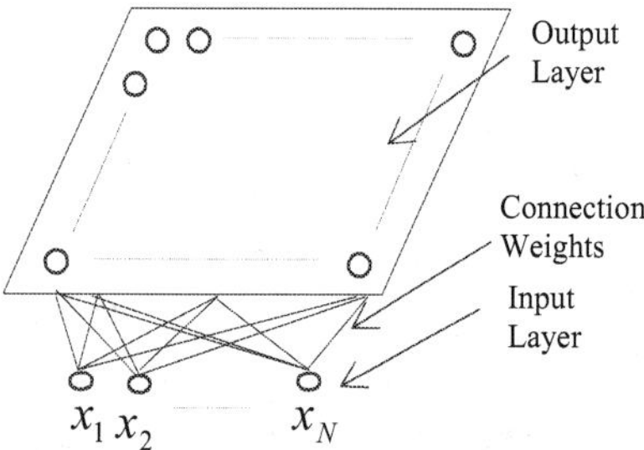

Fig. 11. The topology of SOFM

4.1.1 Identification model

The system proposed comprises of three stages as shown in Fig. 12, the preprocessing stage as mentioned in Section 2 and Section 3, the classification stage based on neural networks involving two levels SOFM neural networks and the decision-making stage. In our study, the two levels SOFM neural networks are:

The first level has one SOFM neural network (as shown in Fig. 11) labeled by $SOFM_0$ which acts as a coarse classifier among the training (or testing) patterns presented to it. The training or learning processing is the same as that mentioned in Section 4.1.2, which belongs to the unsupervised learning type.

Comprising several child SOFM networks denoted by $SOFM_i$ $i = 1, 2, \cdots, n$, where n is the number of child SOFM networks is the second level of neural networks, making fine identification among the patterns classified by $SOFM_0$ (or the output of $SOFM_0$).

4.1.2 Training

In our study, The training or learning processing for $SOFM_0$ is identical to that mentioned in Table 3, which belongs to the type of unsupervised learning (we use the images of C to train the $SOFM_0$. The number of neurons in input layer is 48×196, corresponding to the size of

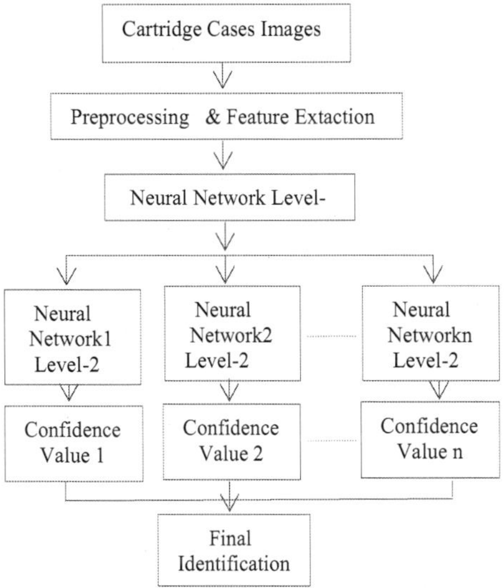

Fig. 12. The proposed identification system

windows normalized (as mentioned before). In the training phase, when a neuron of output layer is inactive for a period of time, it is removed from the network. If a neuron is not chosen frequently as the winner over a finite time interval, it may be considered inactive. After being trained, the neurons, which are active with high output value in the output layer of $SOFM_0$, stand for the classes to which the training images (or the testing specimens) belong. Due to the result of classification of $SOFM_0$ in our study, the training set C has been parted into several subsets. Combination of these subsets in a proper manner achieve training sets for the SOFMs at the second level. When the positions of two classes in the output layer are very close or overlapping the second level SOFM neural networks are generated. The training sets are formed by combining the twoclass patterns for those that are close or overlapping. This training process is identical to that of $SOFM_0$.

4.1.3 Testing

The testing procedure for firearm identification system is as follows:

Step 1. Using a selected testing cartridge case image from the testing set T, present this testing pattern to the first stage of the identification system--the preprocessing stage.

Step 2. Select a type of window from all types in turn, and move this window over the testing pattern processed in Step1 at every location by every pixel horizontally and vertically, pick up the sub-images.

Step 3. Using Formula (5) calculated the confidence values for each sub-image, to do this, present all the sub-images to the $SOFM_0$ in turn, and then to $SOFM_i$ by the result of $SOFM_0$. Return Step2 until all type windows are used up.

Step 4. These confident values are presented to the third stage which is the decision making stage, and using Formula (6) and (7), the final result for the testing cartridge case image is calculated.

4.1.4 Decision-making strategy

For the reasons of noise, lighting conditions, and the trademarks on the head of cartridge cases images, the following situation could generally be encountered in the testing phase:

a. For a testing cartridge case image, when a type of detecting window is used over the image, more than one sub-image under this type window is classified to include a firing pin mark.

b. For a particular testing cartridge case image, when all types of windows are used over the pattern, more than one sub-image under the different windows is classified to include a type of firing pin mark.

To improve the performance and accuracy, we use a final decision-making mechanism in the decision-making stage to solve these problems mentioned above, defining a Confidence Function $D(i, j)$ for the testing pattern i to the jth class which measures the ratio between the testing pattern distance to the weight vectors and the average distance of training patterns to the weight vectors, as follows:

$$D(i, j) = D(j) / D(i, j),\qquad(5)$$

where $dist(j)$ is the average distant when all the training patterns, which belong to the jth class, are tested with the jth type window, $dist(i, j)$ is the distant resulted when the ith testing pattern is tested using the jth type window. Defining a decision-making rule as follows: $i \in \text{Class } K$, if

$$D(i, k) = \min_j \{D(i, j) > \Delta_j\}, j = 1, 2, \cdots n,\qquad(6)$$

where $\Delta_j \quad j = 1, 2, \cdots n$, is an appropriate threshold selected for the class j by experiments. In General, the unbalance in the neural network for each class results from the unbalanced distribution of training patterns we get in the pattern space. Hence, Δ_j for every class is not unique.

Defining a rejection rule as follows, testing pattern i is rejected by all classes, if

$$D(i, j) < \Delta_j, j = 1, 2, \cdots n,\qquad(7)$$

where $\Delta_j \quad j = 1, 2, \cdots n$, is same as in Formula (6).

4.2 Image processing for feature extraction

Contrast Enhancement: The contrast enhancement transformation [30] is one of the general functions in image preprocessing, and function is expressed in Equation (8). Lack of dynamic range in the imaging sensor, or even wrong setting of a lens aperture during image acquisition can all lead to low-contrast images. To increase the dynamic range of the gray levels in the image being processed is the main idea behind contrast enhancement. The image shown in Fig. 13b is transformed by contrast enhancement.

Polar Transaction: Another useful tool in the stage of image preprocessing is polar transformation. In our study, the polar transformation can bring us some advantages: In the test phase, we only move the detecting windows over the testing images in direction of horizontal and vertical rather than rotating the testing images or the detecting windows. This will decrease the numerical error and increase the efficiency. We can get more informations about the testing images under the Polar systems. Some images that have similar shapes may be different in shapes and be distinguished in Polar Systems.

Step1: Initialize the weights for the given size map. Initialize the learning rate parameter, neighborhood size and set the number of unsupervised learning iterations.

Step2: Present the input feature vector $x = [x_1, x_2, \cdots, x_n, \cdots, x_N]$ in the training data set, where x_n is the n th element in the feature vector.

Step3: Determine the winner node c such that $\|x - w_c\| = \min_i \{\|x - w_i\|\}$

Step4. Update the weights, w_i's, within the neighborhood of node c, $N_c(t)$, using the standard updating rule: $w_i(t+1) = w_i(t) + \alpha(t)[x_n - w_i(t)]$, where $i \in N_c(t)$.

Step5: Update learning rate, $\alpha(t)$, and neighborhood size, $N_c(t)$. $\quad \alpha(t+1) = \alpha(0)\{1 - t/K\}$; $N_i(t+1) = N_i(0)\{1 - t/K\}$, where K is a constant and is usually set to be equal to the total number of iterations in the self-organizing phase.

Step6: Repeat 2-5 for the specified number of unsupervised learning iterations.

Table 3. The Unsupervised SOFM Algorithm

Fig. 13. Low-contrast image, a. Result of contrast enhancement, b. Result of threshold, c.

$$f(x) = \begin{cases} \dfrac{y_1}{x_1} x, & x < x_1 \\[2ex] \dfrac{y_2 - y_1}{x_2 - x_1}(x - x_1) + y_1, & x_1 \le x \le x_2 \\[2ex] \dfrac{255 - y_2}{255 - x_2}(x - x_2) + y_2, & x > x_2 \end{cases} \tag{8}$$

Feature Extracting: Feature extracting plays an important role in recognition system. In the real application, the time consuming feature extracting technique is also a crucial factor to be considered. So we pick up the morphological gradient [30] of the images processed by the two steps mentioned aboved as the images features. We deal with digital image functions of the form $f(x,y)$ and $b(x,y)$, where $f(x,y)$ is the input image and $b(x,y)$ is a structuring element , itself a subimage function.

Gray-scale dilation of f by b, denoted $f \oplus b$, is defined as

$$(f \oplus b)(s,t) =$$
$$\max\{f(s-x,t-y)+b(x,y)\,| \tag{9}$$
$$(s-x),(t-y) \in D_f;(x,y) \in D_b\}$$

where D_f and D_b are the domains of f and b, respectively.

Gray-scale erosion of f by b, denoted $f \ominus b$, is defined as

$$(f \ominus b)(s,t) = \frac{\min\{f(s+x,t+y)-b(x,y)\,|}{(s+x),(t+y) \in D_f;(x,y) \in D_b\}} \tag{10}$$

where D_f and D_b are the domains of f and b, respectively.

The morphological gradient of an image, denoted g, is defined as

$$g = (f \oplus b) - (f \ominus b). \tag{11}$$

The firing mechanism of the weapon is generally of two types: the firing pin is either rim-firing mechanism or center-firing mechanism, as shown in Fig. 14. The firing pin mark of cartridge case is formed when the bullet is fired. It is one of the most important characteristics for identifying the individual firearm. A variety of firing pins marks have been used in the manufacture of firearms for the rim-firing cartridge cases. In our study, the cartridge cases belonged to six guns can be classified into six types by shape of firing pin marks (shown in Fig. 15).

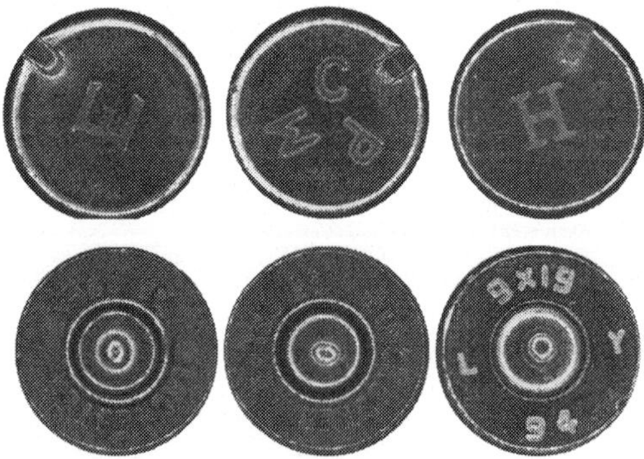

Fig. 14. Rim-firing, first row; Center-firing, second row.

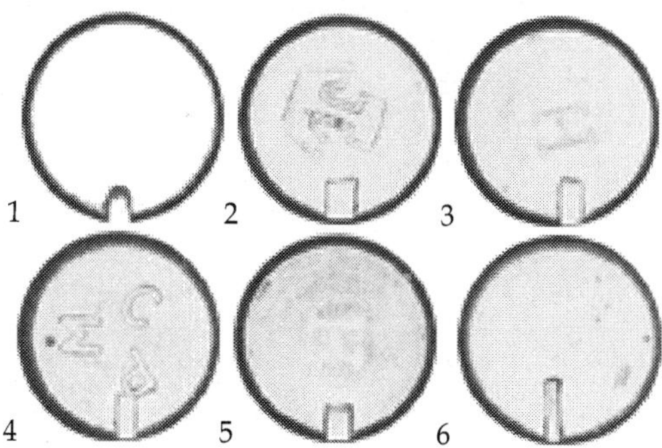

Fig. 15. Six type of cartridge cases images

In the real application, all the images of cartridge cases are obtained through the optical microscope. So some information such as the depth of the impression will be dismissed. Other factors such as the lighting conditions, the material of cartridge cases, and the stamp letters of manufacturer can bring strong noise into the cartridge cases images or damage the shapes of the cartridge cases images. All these would bring many difficulties to feature extracting and identifying. The lighting conditions for the image capturing of cartridge case is crucially importance. In order to produce high contrast of striation (firing-pin mark) on the cartridge cases, the illuminator must be installed at an angle of greater than 45 degree from normal to the plane of the head of the cartridge [1].

The 150 rim-fire cartridge cases, which are belonged to six guns, provided by the Western Australia Police are captured through the optical microscope, one image for each, formed 150 BMP files in gray scale size by 244×240 pixels, and classified into six types by shape of firing pin marks. They are: 1. U-shaped pin mark, 2. Axe-head pin mark, 3. Rectangular (Short) pin mark, 4. Rectangular (Long) pin mark, 5. Square pin mark, 6. Slant pin mark. Examples of the six types are shown in Fig. 15 (The numbers below these figures labeled the class number associated with each cartridge cases). We choose 50 images including the images of all the six guns randomly to form the set C_0 and form the testing set T for the rest images. Then, the images of set C_0 are processed through the image processing and feature extraction stage (shown in Fig. 16) discussed in Section 4.2.

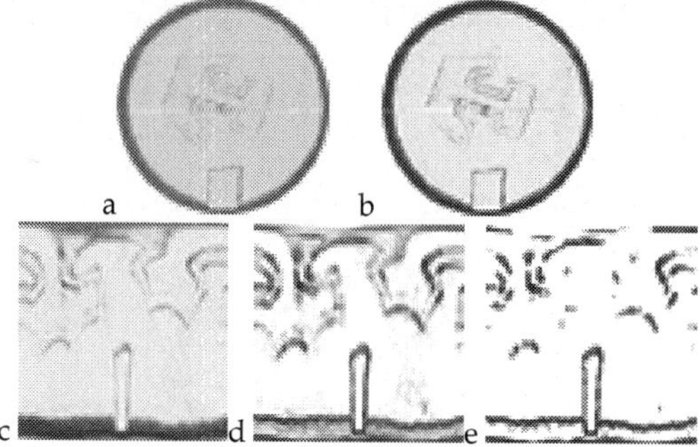

Fig. 16. The original image a, the contrast stretching b, the polar transformation c, the morphological gradient d, the threshold e.

Having been finished the above transformations for the images of every type, we need a "window" operation:

First, windows, size by $n_i \times m_i$ pixels, are used to copy the sub-images---the firing pin marks of the cartridge cases images processed before, where i stands for the label of the class to which the firing pin marks belong. Table 4 shows the sizes of six type windows associated with six type firing pin marks. Second, the images (the firing pin marks) within these six type windows are copied into windows with size normalized by 48×196 pixels to meet the need of having unified input units of SOFM. This process is shown in Fig. 17. To make our model have some robustness to slight variations in the testing cartridge case images, we used the methods as previously described to process a part of our image, we use the following methods: a. Shifted up to two pixels by the direction left, right, up, and down. b. Scaled by factor 0.95 and 0.90. All the images we obtained through the processes mentioned above, along with the number of 350, are combined into a training set C for the model based on SOFM, which will be discussed in the following section.

Type 1	20×96	Type 2	20×96
Type 3	20×120	Type 4	24×116
Type 5	20×120	Type 6	24×168

Table 4. The Size (in pixels) of Six Type Windows

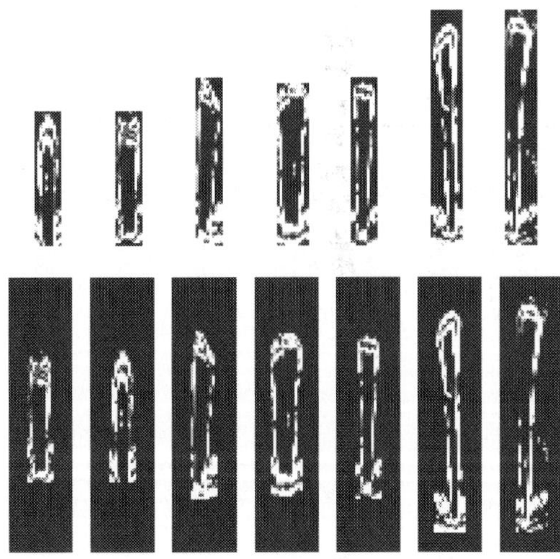

Fig. 17. Six type of firing pin marks within windows with size normalization. The first row shows the six firing pin marks within six type windows. The second row shows the firing pin marks within windows with size normalization.

4.3 Experimental results

In our study, we use the following experimental parameters (shown in Table 5) for $SOFM_0$, Level 2 SOFMs and get experimental results over Training set C .

The neurons of the output layer of $SOFM_0$ are divided into six areas separately, through which the specimens of each class are represented, when the training phase is finished. For the three training sub-networks of the second level, the training set C is divided into three subsets by the fact: the distribution area of each class is not balanced, some classes are near, and others are apart, in following manner:

Subset c_1 including images labeled with class 1 and 2, is selected as the training set of $SOFM_1$,
Subset c_2 including images labeled with class 3 and 5, is selected as the training set of $SOFM_2$,
Subset c_3 including images labeled with class 4 and 6, is selected as the training set of $SOFM_3$.

	Input Layer	Output Layer	$\eta(0)$	$\Lambda_i(0)$
$SOFM_0$	48×196	9×9	0.60	7
$SOFM_1$	48×196	3×3	0.05	2
$SOFM_2$	48×196	5×5	0.05	3
$SOFM_3$	48×196	5×5	0.05	2
	training pattern	right rate	error rate	rejection rate
	350	100%	0%	0%

Table 5. Experimental Parameters for $SOFM_0$, Level 2 SOFMs and Results over Training set C

We have the experiment results over testing set T as follows:

Testing pattern	Right rate
100	97.0%
Rejection rate	Error rate
3.0%	0%

Table 6. Experiments Results

4.3.1 Analysis of experiment results

From the results of Table 6, we can see that the Identification model in our study can make the combination of location and identification of a firing pin mark of a cartridge case images into one stage. It further shows that the model proposed has high performance and robustness for the testing patterns in the following aspects: In the location and identification of firing pin marks: it has high accuracy. Some testing results under Cartesian co-ordinates are shown in Fig. 19. Having robustnesses to the noise patterns, to the damaged and deformed patterns shown in Fig. 19(8-13). Having some robustnesses to the scaled patterns.

For some patterns, we can still see that there are rejections, these rejections are caused mainly by the following reasons: the high noise on the cartridge images; the letters of trademark on the cartridge images; the similitude of one pattern with others in some location.

4.3.2 Further work

In order to improve our model to achieve higher performance, we will do some further research in the following aspects:

In order to improve the quality of image capturing and preprocessing. Another aim of further work would be to extract some fine features with more complex techniques to represent the patterns (training or testing). Thirdly, it is our aim to integate multiple classifier combination using different feature sets.

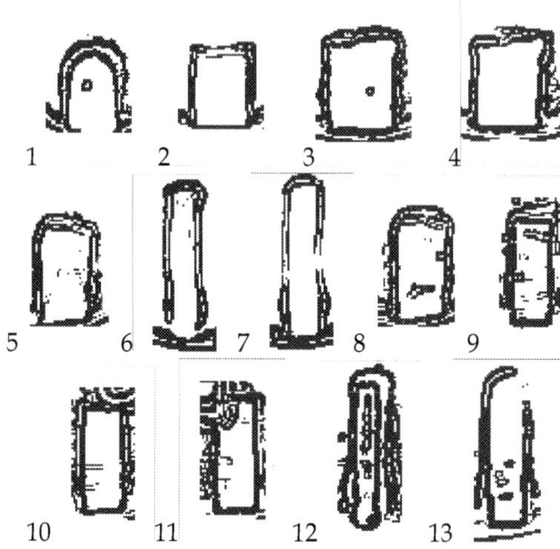

Fig. 19. Some right identification results of testing set T

5. The stand-alone ballistics image database system

A few systems for firearm identification have been developed around world. These includes DRUGFIRE [4], developed by Federal Bureau of Investigation, USA, IBIS[5], developed by Forensic Technology, a division of the Walsh Group, and FIREBALL, developed by Edith Cowan University (ECU) and National Institute of Forensic Science (NIFS) in Australia [1]. These systems integrate digital imaging, database and networking technologies to enhance the capabilities of the forensic firearm examiner.

The FIREBALL firearm identification system is developed as recognizing the need for a low-cost alternative to other established systems. Furthermore, the system is tailored to Australian conditions.

The initial FIREBALL system is a stand-alone system. Each state police department store information in its individual system. Every 3-6 months individual information will be redistributed national wide through CD-ROM. This strategy delays information sharing that is necessary for crime investigation. The stand-alone system also brings the problem for access control and information security.

To overcome shortfalls of the stand-alone system, a web based Fireball is also in progress. The following sections will briefly describe the stand-alone Fireball system and details web applications for querying, visualizing and processing images from Fireball image database on-line.

Fireball is a projectile and cartridge case comparison and image storage database software package developed by Edith Cowan University (ECU), Perth, Australia, and supplied to the National Institute of Forensic Science (NIFS) for the storage of forensic ballistics data by Australian Police Departments. This includes data on firearms, ammunition, fired cartridges cases and projectiles. The system is designed to be a preliminary identification procedure.

Class characteristics of projectile and cartridge cases only are obtained and stored by this system. Class characteristics are gross identifying features that are identical on all cartridge cases and projectiles fired from a particular make and model of firearm (eg. firing pin mark shape).

The information stored in FIREBALL includes data on firearms, ammunition, spent cartridge cases and projectiles. a Graphics User Interface (GUI) is incorporated in FIREBALL, which allows the user to obtain precise ballistics metrics of cartridge case class characteristics (ie. firing pin mark, extractor mark and ejector mark positions) by a simple point-and-click method using the mouse and an on-screen digital image of the head of the cartridge case. Once the class characteristics have been obtained, a search of the database will provide a hit list of corresponding firearms. The system is offered as a preliminary identification procedure, as the technique involves identification by class characteristics

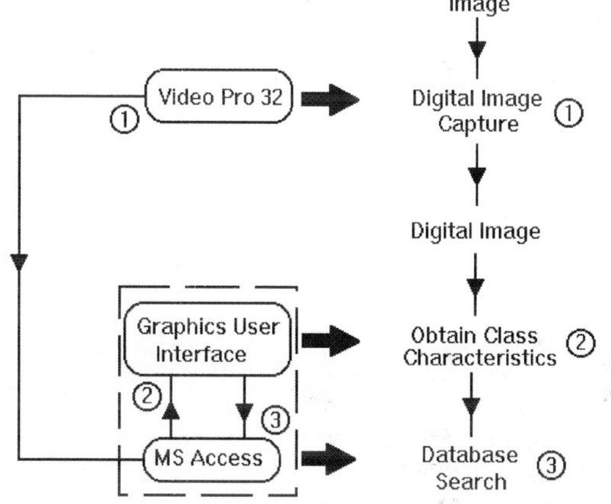

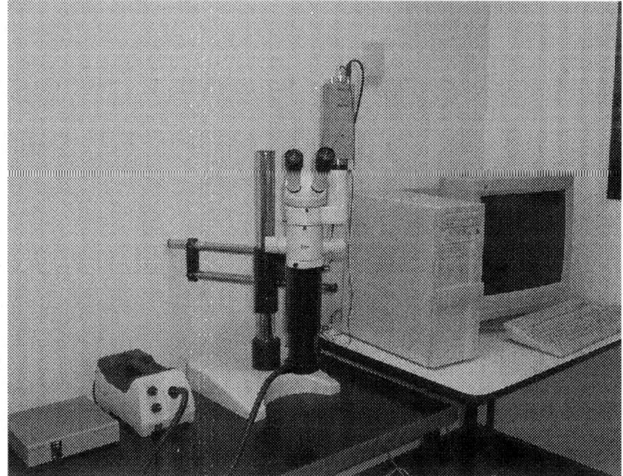

Fig. 20. FIREBALL structural schematic diagram and a photo of hardware.

only. FIREBALL is a tool that the ballistics expert can use to narrow down their field of search quickly and easily.

The FIREBALL system is comprised of image capturing software, custom designed graphics user interface (GUI) and Microsoft Access relational database (See Fig. 20).

Step 1 in the above figure is the image capture process. This sub-process is external to the FIREBALL database; therefore it is seen separate user interface. Step 2 is the GUI process of obtaining class characteristics. The GUI is custom software implemented separately to MS

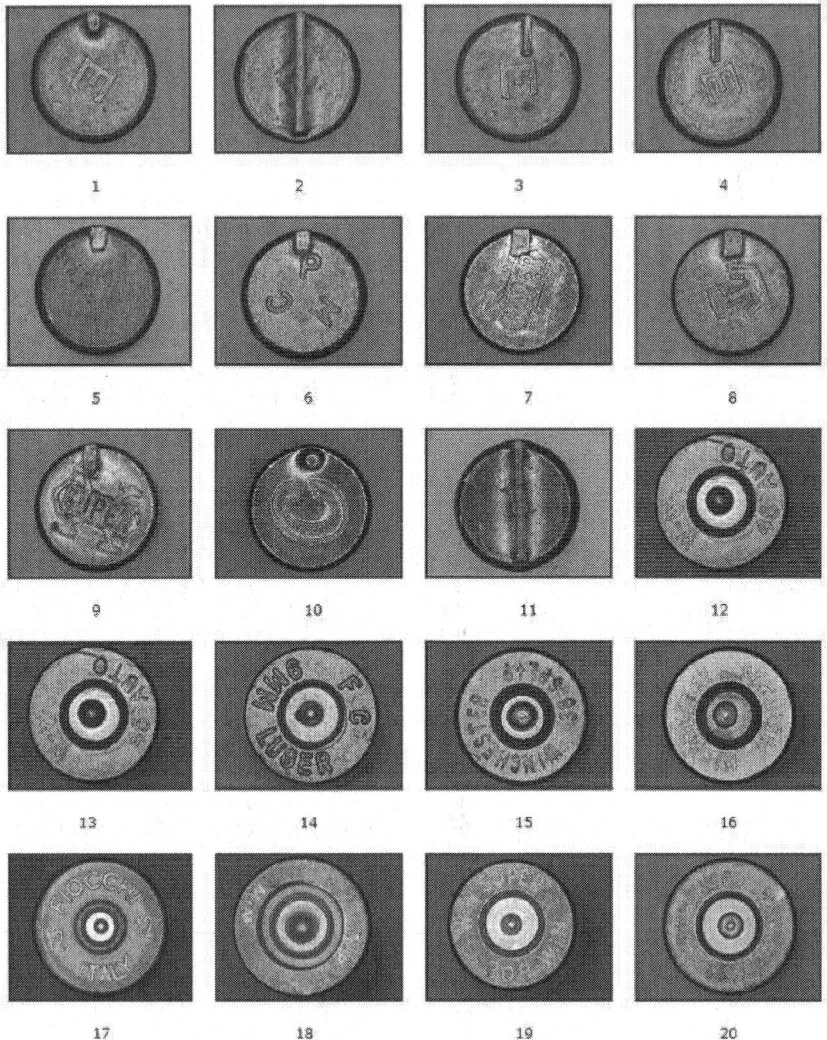

Fig. 21. Captured cartridge case images

Access; but to the end user the GUI software appears to be part of the database package. This is due to the GUI software being initiated and controlled from the database itself. The database search is implemented when control is returned to the database (ie. step 3). Fig. 21 shows some of acquired images of cartridge case heads in our database.

6. Web-based image processing and visualization

To overcome the limit and inconveience in infromation sharing arround the country, we are moving the system on-line. Applications have been developed to query the image database and display results on-line.

The original MS Acess database has be migrated to Oracle database to facilitate the database security and scalability. Since image data from all states wil be stored in this central database, MS Access may not be able to accomendate the amount of the data and the on-line transactions.

After migration, the image data are stored in an Oracle database as LOB datatype, which can store unstructured data and is optimised for large amounts of such data. Oracle provides a uniform way of accessing large unstructured data within the database or outside. We employ Oracle Objects for OLE (OO4O) and ASP for client to access the data including image data stored in BLOBs.

Fig. 22 shows the web interface for clients to query, search, and update the database.

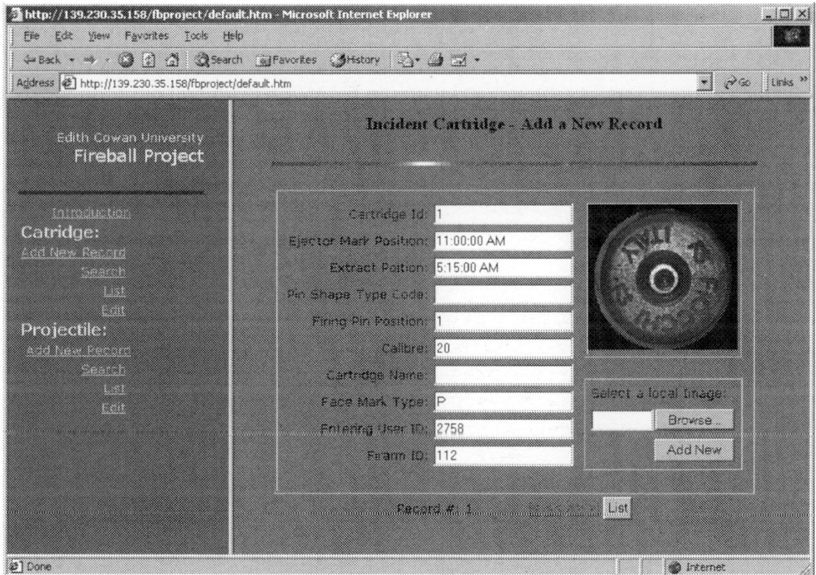

Fig. 22. Web Interface of the Fireball on-line system

The database query uses Oracle *OraDynaset* object that permits browsing and updating of data created from a *SQL SELECT* statement. An *OraDynaset* object represents the result set of a SQL SELECT query. It is essentially a client-side scrollable and updatable cursor that allows for browsing the set of rows generated by the query it executes.

This object provides transparent mirroring of database operations, such as updates. When data is updated via the Update method, the local mirror image of the query is updated so that the data appears to have been changed without reevaluating the query. The same procedure is used automatically when records are added to the *Dynaset*. Integrity checking is performed to ensure that the mirrored image of the data always matches the actual data present on the Oracle database.

To display the image on the Web retrieved from the database, we may use HTML tag <img src=location/filename>.

However, the image data is actually stored in the database instead of a file. To overcome this burden, we use the method provided by ASP, *request.binaryWrite()* method. First, we compiled a ASP code to retrieve the image data from the database and write the image data as binary using *request.binarywrite()* to the web form to display the image. The cartridge case image shown in figure 3 is obtained in this way.

In general, the acquired image shows randomises in orientation, position and noise in the background. It is necessary to reduce the background noise and normalise the orientation, position and size of the image. If these simple image processing can be done on-line, that will bring much convenience.

We used ActiveX control techniques to realise the on-line image processing. The client retrieves the image data from the server database to the client browser. After processing, the image data is saved back to the database.

The first step of the image pre-processing is to find the cartridge case area in the image. Because of the good illumination and focusing, the acquired image has higher brightness in the cartridge case area than that in the rest. There is a clear edge around the cartridge case area. The edge detection should be an efficient way to detect cartridge case.

The proposed method employs Sobel Edge Operator [31] for detecting edges. At each point in the image a vertical slope and a horizontal slope are calculated. The maximum value of the two slopes is taken as the output value of that pixel. A threshold was chosen according to the average slope of the edge magnitude to eject noise edges. Fig. 23 shows the edges detected using Sobel edge operator. Strong edges are obvious. The outside circular edge defines the cartridge case area.

The feature extraction is performed based upon the result of the edge detection. Since the bottom of the cartridge case appears as a large circle, after edge detection, we use "direct least squares fitting of ellipses" [32] to fit the cartridge case edge data set.

This fitting algorithm provides an efficient method for fitting ellipses to scattered data. It solves the problem naturally by a generalized eigensystem and is extremely robust and computationally efficient. It should be possible to use the same algorithm for the active control in our proposed automatic image acquisition system.

After extracting the cartridge case area, we can manipulate the image, such as cleaning the background, centralising and rotating the image. These can all be done by clicking buttons in a Web browser.

Suppose the centre of the cartridge case and that of the image are (X_c, Y_c) and (X_i, Y_i), the spatial transformation of

$$\begin{cases} x' = x + X_i - X_c \\ y' = y + Y_i - Y_c \end{cases}$$

will take the cartridge to the center of the image. Figure 24 and 25 show the cartridge case image before and after centralising.

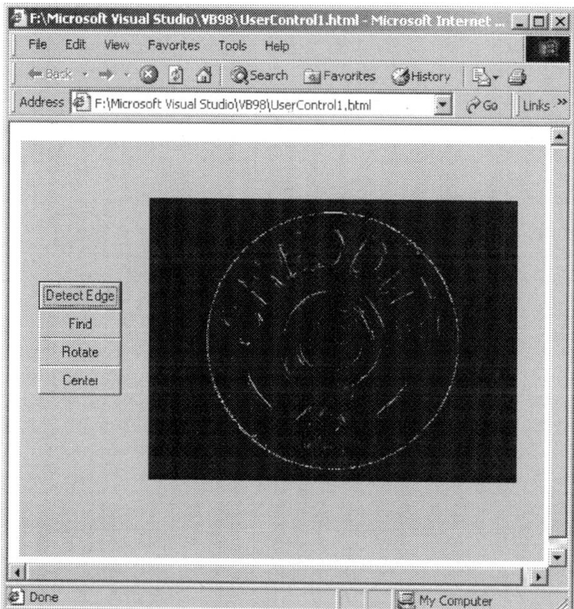

Fig. 23. Edges detected by Canny edge detection.

Fig. 24. The original Image

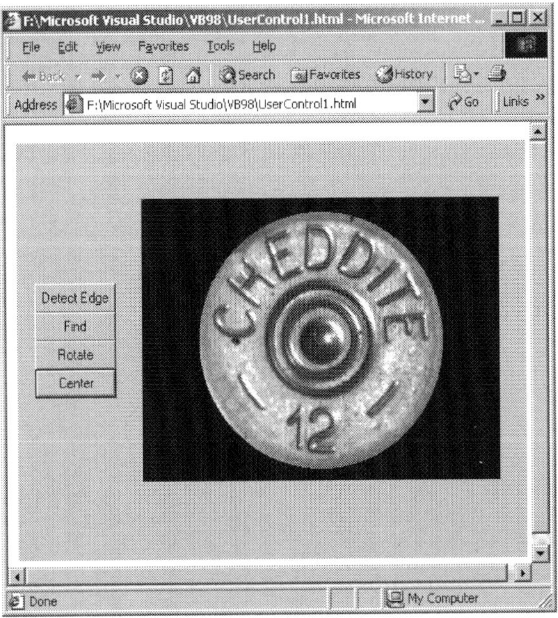

Fig. 25. The image after moving cartridge case to the center

7. Discussion and conclusion

Firearm identification is an intensive and time-consuming process that requires physical interpretation of forensic ballistics evidence. Especially as the level of violent crime involving firearms escalates, the number of firearms to be identified accumulates dramatically. The demand for an automatic firearm identification system arises.

This chapter proposes a new, analytic system for automatic firearm identification based on the cartridge and projectile specimens. Not only do we present an approach for capturing and storing the surface image of the spent projectiles at high resolution using line-scan imaging technique for the projectiles database, but we also present a novel and effective FFT-based analysis technique for analyzing and identifying the projectiles. This system can make a significant contribution towards the efficient and precise analysis of firearm identification based on projectile ballistics. The study demonstrates that different types of land and groove marks generated by different guns have distinctive surface textures, and spectral analysis can be used to measure and identify these textures effectively. Never have we seen before, a method such as this, that can study line-scanned images of projectile specimens so effectively. The method can overcome the difficulties involved with descriptions in the normal spatial domain in identifying texture features formed by land and groove marks on the surface of projectiles. In recent years the Hough transform and the related Radon transform have received much attention. These two transforms are able to transform two dimensional images with lines into a domain of possible line parameters, where each line in the image will give a peak positioned at the corresponding line parameters. This has lead to many line detection applications within image processing. As the most features we are interested in from a line-scan image of the fired projectile are composed of various lines, it is possible to apply those transforms to the projectile image analysis. In the next step of our experiments we will investigate the potentials of those transforms for firearm identification.

A hierarchical neural network is used to create a firearm identification system based on cartridge case images. We focus on the cartridge case identification of rim-fire mechanism. Experiments show that the model proposed has high performance and robustness by integrating two levels; Self-Organizing Feature Map (SOFM) neural networks and the decision-making strategy.

A prototype of Web based cartridge case image database has been developed. The demonstration of querying and visualising the image data from the database on-line was successful. The proposed on-line image processing worked fine for cartridge case images.

By moving Fireball system on-line we can have following advantages:

- Real time input and update – enable input and update information to a central database quickly.
- Better data sharing – Enable users to obtain information from the latest resources in the central database.
- Easier management – Enable information to be stored in a central database that is easier to manage than many different copies stored on local PCs in various locations.

Some disadvantages are:

- The information retrieval may be slower, due to the transmission from Internet instead of retrieving data locally.
- Information security becomes a vital issue.

The significance of this research lies in the opportunity to produce the next generation of forensic ballistics digital information imaging systems for the identification of firearms. The automated imaging systems will have the capacity to provide class characteristic information directly to the firearms examiners and can significantly reduce the analytical effort needed for identification of firearms associated with ballistics specimens.

The research is innovative as it broadly extends the range of physical, optical, and photonic techniques for future examination, analysis, and comparison of test and crime scene ballistics specimens for positive identification. The traditional approach to forensic ballistics identification has essentially remained unchanged for the past century. However, forensic laboratories and Police Services now require a quantum step in precision of measurement, and speed of analysis for forensic policing. The research introduces the opportunity to explore new and innovative approaches to the examination of the surfaces of ballistics specimens in order to detect the individual markings and class characteristics that link the specimen to a particular weapon.

In firearm identification practice there are many practical difficulties. For instance the pattern of striations on a projectile are a function of an individual weapon which itself may be changed by wear, damage, oxidation and or building up of contaminants associated with the repeated use. One of solutions to overcome those difficulties is to introduce as many identifiers as we can in order to increase the reliability of the firearm identification system. Just like the human identification with fingerprints, sometimes only using one finger may result in false output although the fingerprint used is unique. By identifying more than one fingerprint (up to ten fingers) from the same person will assure the success. For the time being, more than 30 different identifiers (such as make, model, brand, and type of the weapon; and shape, size, and position of marks on the specimen) are used in firearm identification. The FFT approach with the information on the frequency domain adds more identifiers to the collection of projectile features. In particularly with deformed projectile specimens routinely examined by ballisticians the FFT approach can still reveal the features of the markings created by weapon based on the spectrum analysis.

The research is also innovative in placing the development of optical and photonic techniques in the context of forensic science. The bench mark for forensic ballistics imaging has been set by the commercial products of IBIS and Drugfire, and the ECU Fireball imaging system. The research has markedly extended the optical and photonic physical methods of analysis of minute markings on the surfaces of forensic specimens.

For the future research the precise measurement of these features through imaging analyses will allow discrimination between the properties of the class characteristics and individual characteristics to identify the types of weapons. The development of multi-dimensional cluster analysis models for forensic ballistics specimens will identify the type of weapons that produced these ballistics specimens through intelligent imaging. Then the matching of metrics from line-scan and profilometry will allow identification of the weapon. Thus, by mapping the crime scene specimen to the multi-dimensional ballistics data, it will be possible to provide a rapid analysis of the involvement of the firearm. The potential to reduce the labour intensive activity of traditional ballistics identification provides the opportunity for rapid response in forensic ballistics analyses. Also the opportunity will be presented for better crime detection rates by police at crime scenes.

Experiments discussed in this chapter are performed on images by 16 various weapons only. Some more detailed experiments on features of various guns of the same kind and same make will be carried out in the next step of the research.

The need for intelligence applied to high resolution digital images systems for image processing is considerable, realizing the intensive nature of comparator microscope identification of forensic ballistics specimens. The future research will determine the optimum optical conditions for imaging ballistics specimens for comparison crime scene and test specimens.

In terms of cartridge case images, our main focus was on the consideration of rim-firing pin mark identification. Through the use of a hierarchical neural network model, this study investigated a system for identifying the firing pin marks of cartridge case images. The identification model in our study incorporates the combination of location and identification of firing pin marks of cartridge case images into one stage. It shows that the model proposed has high performance and robustness for real testing patterns.

Through further processing, such as the more efficient and precise identification of cartridge cases by combination with several characteristics on cartridge case images, the efficiency of this system will also make a significant contribution towards the efficient and precise identification of ballistics specimens.

8. References

[1] C.L. Smith, and J.M. Cross, (1995): Optical Imaging Techniques for Ballistics Specimens to Identify Firearms. Proceedings of the 29th Annual 1995 International Carnahan Conference on Security Technology, pp. 275-289, Oct. 1995, England.

[2] Smith, CL. (2001a). Profile measurements as a technique for forensic ballistics identification. Proceedings of 5th Australian Security Research Symposium, July, Perth, Western Australia, 153-162.

[3] Smith, C.L. (2002). Linescan imaging of ballistics projectile markings for identification. Proceedings of IEEE 36th Annual 2002 International Carnahan Conference on Security Technology, 216-222. Altantic City.

[4] Evans, JPO, Smith, CL and Robinson, M. (2004). Validiation of the linescan imaging technique for imaging cylindrical forensic ballistics specimens. American Firearm and Toolmark Examiners Journal. In press.

[5] Nichols, RG 1997. Firearm and toolmark identification criteria: A review of the literature. *Journal of Forensic Science*, 42(30, 466-474.

[6] Bunch, SG 2000. Consecutive matching striation criteria: A general critique. *Journal of Forensic Science*, 45(5), 955-962.

[7] Bonfanti, MS and Ghauharali, RJ 2000. Visualisation by confocal microscopy of traces on bullets and cartridge cases. *Science and Justice*, 40(40, 241-256.

[8] Springer, E. 1995. Toolmark examinations – A review of its development in the literature. Journal of Forensic Sciences, 40(6), 964-968.

[9] Smith, C.L. (1997). Fireball: A forensic ballistics imaging system. Proceedings of IEEE 31st Annual International Carnahan Conference on Security Technology, October, Canberra, Australia, 64-70.

[10] R. Saferstein (ED), (1988) Forensic Science Handbook: Volume 2. Englewood Cliffs: Prentice Hall, 1988.

[11] G.Burrard, (1951): Identification of Firearms and Forensic Ballistics. London: Herbert Jenkins,1951.

[12] Li, D.G. and Watson, A.C. (1998). Ballistics firearms identification based on images of cartridge case and projectile. Proceedings of 1998 SPIE Enabling Technologies for Law Enforcement and Security Symposium, Boston, USA, November 3-5.

[13] C.L. Smith, J.M. Cross, and G.J. Variyan, (1995): FIREBALL: An Interactive Database for the Forensic Ballistic Identification of Firearms. Research Report, Australian Institute of Security and Applied Technology, Edith Cowan University, Western Australia, 1995.

[14] Le-Ping Xin, (2000): A Cartridge Identification System for Firearm Authentication, Signal Processing Proceedings, 2000. WCCC_ICSP 2000. 5th International Conference on Volume: 2, P1405-1408.

[15] Chenyuan Kou, Cheng-Tan Tung and H. C. FU, (1994): FISOFM: Firearms Identification based on SOFM Model of Neural Network, Security Technology, 1994. Proceedings. Institute of Electrical and Electronics Engineers 28th Annual 1994 International Carnahan Conference on , 12-14 Oct. Pages: 120-125.

[16] Zographos, A., Robinson, M., Evans, J.P.O. and Smith, C.L. (1997). Ballistics identification using line-scan imaging techniques. Proceedings of IEEE International Carnahan Conference on Security Technology, Canberra, Australia.

[17] C.L. Smith, Robinson, M. and Evans, P.: (2000): Line-scan Imaging for the positive identification of ballistics, 2000. IEEE International Carnahan Conference on Security Technology, 269-275. 2000.

[18] Kingslake, R., Optics in Photography. SPIE Optical Engineering Press. Bellingham, Washington, USA, 1992.

[19] Evans J.P.O., Zhu C and Robinson M.: Line-scan imaging using an area array camera, The 5th Int. Conf on Control, Automation, Robotics and Vision, pp. 1471-1475, Singapore, 1998, ISBN 981-04-0318-6.

[20] Patent number EP1418767 Line-scan imaging system in 3-D.

[21] Jun Kong, D. G. Li., A. C. Watson: A Firearm Identification System Based on Neural Network, AI 2003, Lecture Notes in Artificial Intelligence, 315-326, 2003, Springer.

[22] Rafael C. Gonzalez, Richard E. Woods: Digital Image Processing, Second Edition, Beijing: Publishing House of Electronics Industry, 2002, 7, 519-566.

[23] Pitas I.: Digital image processing algorithms, Prentice Hall, ISBN 0-13-145814-0, 1993

[24] Chenyuan Kou, Cheng-Tan Tung and H. C. FU, (1994) "FISOFM: Firearms Identification based on SOFM Model of Neural Network", Security Technology, 1994. Proceedings. Institute of Electrical and Electronics Engineers 28th Annual 1994 International Carnahan Conference on , 12-14 Oct. Pages: 120-125.

[25] T. Kohonen, (1990) "Self-organising Maps", Springer, Berlin, 1995, The self-organising Maps, Proc. IEEE 78 (9) (1990) 1464-1480.

[26] S.B. Cho, "Pattern Recognition with Neural Networks Combined by Genetic Algorithm", Fuzzy Set and System 103(1999) 339-347.

[27] T.M. Ha, H. Bunke, "Off-line Handwritten Numeral Recognition by Perturbation Method", IEEE Trans. Pattern Anal. Mach.Intell. 19(5) (1997)535 -539.

[28] P.N. Suganthan, "Structure Adaptive Multilayer Overlapped SOMs with Partial Supervision for Handprinted Digit Classification ", Proceedings of International Joint Conference on Neural Networks, WCCI'98, Alaska, May 1998.

[29] T. Kohonen, Tutorial Notes, (1993) International Symposium on Artificial Neural Networks, pp. 9-15, Dec.20-22, 1993.

[30] Rafael C. Gonzalez, Richard E. Woods, Digital Image Processing, Second Edition, Beijing: Publishing House of Electronics Industry, 2002, 7, 519-566.

[31] k. R. Castleman *Digital Image Processing, 1996, Prentice Hall, Inc.*

[32] A. W. Fitzgibbon, M. Pilu and R. B. Fisher, *"Direct least squares fitting of ellipses"*, in Proceedings of International Conference on Pattern Recognition, Vienna, 1996

## 10

A Novel Haptic Texture Display Based on Image Processing

Juan Wu, Aiguo Song and Chuiguo Zou
Southeast University
P.R.China

1. Introduction

Surface texture is among the most salient haptic characteristics of objects, which help in object identification and enhanced feel of the device being manipulated. Although textures are widely known in computer graphics only recently have they been explored in haptic. Haptic textures are used to improve the realism of haptic interaction and give cues associated with many tasks in tel-manipulation or designing machines in virtual space. The haptic texture display can help the visually impaired to experience 3D art at virtual museums and perceive the features of arts (G. Jansson et al 2003). It also can be used for home shoppers in the internet shopping.

Researchers have developed many sophisticated haptic texture display methods. The texture display methods so far involve three types of construction: 1) real surface patch presentation (S. Tachi et al 1994)(K. Hirota & M. Hirose 1995), These methods use a real contact surface, arranged in arbitrary position in a 3D space, to simulate a partial model of the virtual object. The typical system was developed by Minsky and was call the Sandpaper system. 2) multiple-pin vibratory presentation. These approach need to design specialized pin-array device which can dynamically or statically exert pressure to the skin. (Ikei et al1997) (Ikei 1998) (Masami 1998) 3) Single point sensing and contact tool driving presentation. In recently years, researchers have tried to combine the kinematics and tactile device together, so as to enrich the haptic presentation and enhance the performance the texture display(Ikei 2002). However, the developments mean more complicated and more expensive.

Under the category 3), When the operator exploring the virtual sculpture's surface by performing natural movements of his/her hand, the artificial force is generated by the interaction with the virtual surface through a haptic interface. As the interacting with the virtual textured surface will generate complex force information, so the key issue of this class of methods is to computing the contact forces in response to interactions with virtual textured surface, and applying to the operator through the force-reflecting haptic interface. This paper first presents some relevant previous work in texture force modeling, and the principle of the image based feature extraction and contact force modeling is introduced. Then an implementation of the algorithm is presented. Finally the experimental results are discussed.

2. Previous work

Hari present a method to record perturbations while dragging the tip of the PHANToM on a real surface and play back using the same device (Lederman et al 2004)(Vasudevan & Manivannan 2006). Ho et.al present a modification of 'bump maps' borrowed from computer graphics to create texture in haptic environments (C.-H. Ho et al 1999). This method involves the perturbation of surface normals to create the illusion of texture. Dominguez-Ramirez proposed that the texture could be modelled as a periodic function. Saira and Pai present a stochastic approach to haptic textures aimed at reducing the computational complexity of texturing methods (Juhani& Dinesh 2006). Fritz and Barner follow this up by presenting two stochastic models to generate haptic textures (Fritz& Barner 1996). S. Choi and H.Z.Tan study the perceived instabilities arising out of current haptic texture rendering algorithms while interacting with textured models (Choi & Tan 2004). Miguel proposed a force model based on the geometry model (Miguel et al 2004). All this contact force models can be classified into four kinds.

- A mechanical sensor-based approach.
- A geometry model-based approach
- Stochastic and deterministic models
- An image date-based approach.

The sensor-based approach using the device such as scanning electron microscope, potentially reproduces tactile impressions most precisely but a sensor equivalent to human skin is not commonly available and too expensive(Tan 2006). The geometry based approach involves intricate microscopic modelling of an object surface, requiring computation time to resolve the contact state between a finger and the surface. The stochastic and deterministic models such as sinusoid and random stochastic are simple to implement and could generate different sample of contact force and perceptually different from each other, but the produced contact force is not mapping the real textures. As to the deterministic models, the variable parameters are amplify, frequency and texture coordinate. The controllable parameters are limited and these features couldn't fully describe the characteristic of texture, such as the trend and direction of texture.

To modelling the texture force during contact with texture, the geometrical shape and material properties should be grasped. However, the precise measurement of minute shape or bumpiness is not easy since it requires special apparatus for measurement. The method of using the photograph to get the geometrical data of texture has been adopted by Ikei, in which, histogram transformation was adopted to get the intensity distribution of the image.

3. Realization of haptic texture display based on delta haptic device

Although the height profile of a surface itself is not directly the intensity of tactile sensation perceived, it is among most related data to the real stimulus. The material of object should be in some category that produces the image reflecting its height map. Based on this hypothesis, a novel image date-based texture force model is proposed. We proposed that a photo image would be equivalent to a geometrical data as long as the photo was properly taken. The image data are processed with Gauss filters and the micro-geometric feature is acquired. Based on the height map, the constraint forces in tangent and normal direction are modelled. Then, the texture force is applied to the operator by the DELTA haptic device. The principle diagram of the haptic display system is shown as Figure 1. During exploration on a surface of a virtual object, the user can perceive force stimulus from the DELTA haptic device on the hand.

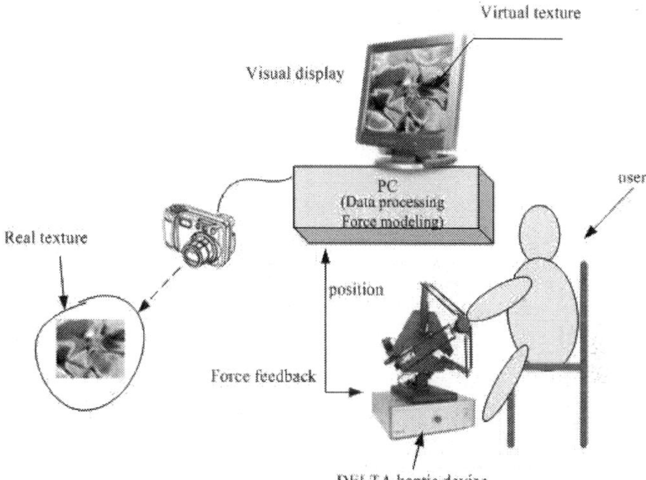

Fig. 1. A schematic representation of the haptic texture display system

3.1 Graphic to haptic

A virtual texture is presented by 3-DOF texture force. In order to simulate the contact force as if touching the real texture surface, it is proposed that the present surface texture by using a photograph. To assure the precise discrimination and high similarity to actual object textures, the feature of the image was dealt at the following step.

1. Image sampling and pre-processing. The original images were taken form digital camera. The colour image was firstly transformed into grey-scale image. To acquiring the contour of textured surface from 2D image data, the prominent problem is that an image's brightness intensity must roughly match the height map of texture protrusions. So homomorphic filtering was adopted to eliminate the effect of the non-uniform illumination.
2. In image processing, Gauss filter is a common low pass filter in the frequency domain to attenuate high frequencies and retains low frequencies unchanged. The result is to smooth the edge of the image. While to the texture image, the low frequency components usually reflect the large continuous spatial region, and the high frequency components usually reflect the edge of texture image, which are in coherence with the alternation of geometrical height in space. Here we use the uniform Gauss filter to reshape the texture image, and then the original image is minus by the filtered image, the left 'noise' denotes the texture models.

The original image is f(x,y).

a. Transforming the original image f into Fourier domain F(k,l).
b. The input image is then multiplied with Gauss filter H in a pixel by pixel fashion, that is G(k,l)=H(k,l) *F(k,l). Where H is the filter function, and G(k,l) is the filtered image in the Fourier domain.

c.   To obtain the resulting image in the real space, G(k,l) has to be re-transformed to g(x,y) using the inverse Fourier Transform.

d.   The sharp intensity changes are obtained through f(x,y)-g(x,y), which reflects the height maps of texture surface.

All the image processing is realized with MATLAB function.

As the texture height maps are acquired. The virtual texture is generated through binding the texture height map to the virtual object surface.

3.2 Haptic texture generation

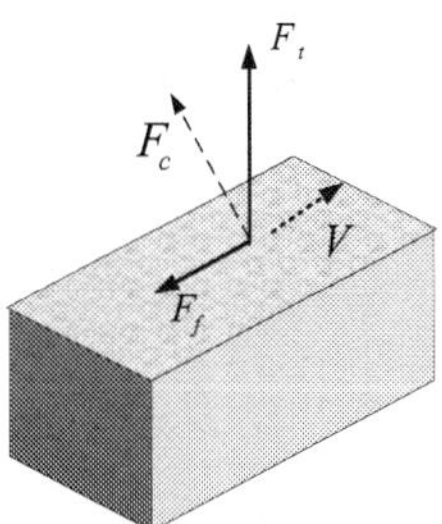

Fig. 2. Interaction force components

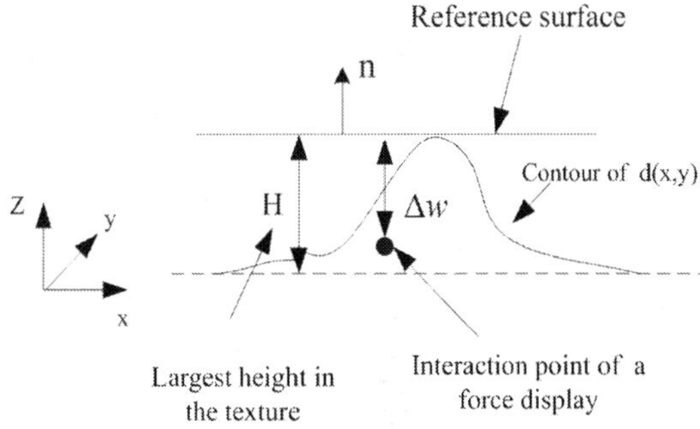

Fig. 3. the spatial coordinates of the intersection between the haptic probe (or rendering device) and the virtual object being probed

The constraint force when virtual agent (virtual finger, probe, etc.)contacting with the virtual texture surface is modelled as resultant force of texture force F_t and friction force F_f as Fig. 2 and Fig.3. The texture force is calculated as

$$F_t=k \times d(x,y) \tag{1}$$

Where k is a constant of proportionality, and d(x,y) is the height map of the texture. (x,y) is a texture coordinate within a surface. The direction of force is normal to the reference surface that forms a contour of a whole object.

The friction F_f is modelled as

$$F_f =k_1 \Delta wn \tag{2}$$

Where Δw is a depth of penetration, n is a unit normal vector and k_1 is a friction coefficient which varied with different surfaces.

$$\overrightarrow{F}_c = \overrightarrow{F}_t + \overrightarrow{F}_f \tag{3}$$

To constraint the avatar on the surface of the virtual surface, the maximum penetration depth H is given. If the depth of penetration depth is over H, then, the constraint force in normal will set to the constant value, which is within the output range of the haptic device.

3.3 Implementation and experiments

Using the techniques discussed in this paper, the texture force display system, shown in Figure 4, was composed of 3-DOF DELTA haptic device, which was able to produce the force stimulations. It was connected to a 2.66GHz Pentium PC, and graphical display on the LCD screen. During exploration on the virtual textured surface, the user can perceive variation of reactive force between the virtual probe and virtual textured surface. The screen shows the virtual space in which the red dot, an avatar representing the fingertip of the physical hand on the right, interact with a sculpture. DELTA haptic device held by the operator can reflect forces to the user whose sensations approximate the effect of exploring a real object having the same shape.

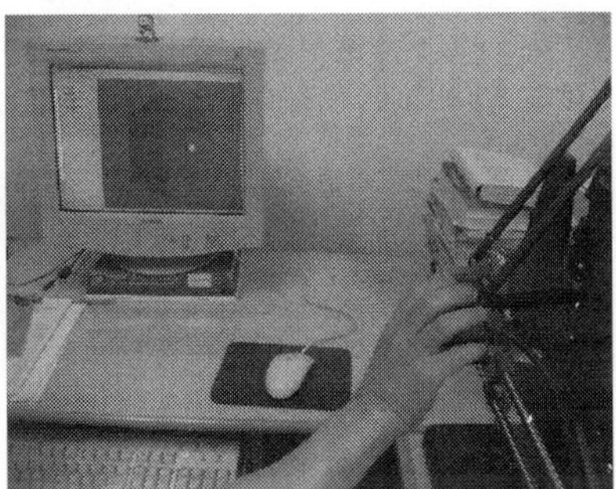

Fig. 4. the texture presentation based on DELTA haptic device

To evaluate presentation quality of the haptic texture display system, other two commonly used texture force models were compared. One is sinusoid model (Tan, 2006), the other is random stochastic model (Siira, 2006). The sinusoid model is commonly used that define the height map as

$$h(x) = A \sin(2\pi x / L) + A \tag{4}$$

Where L is the length of wave, A is the amplitude of height. The restoring force is calculated as

$$F = \begin{cases} k \times [h(x) - p_x] & when\ p_x < h(x) \\ 0 & other\ wise \end{cases}$$

Where the restoring force F always pointed up, p_z was the z-position of the stylus tip. The random stochastic model is

 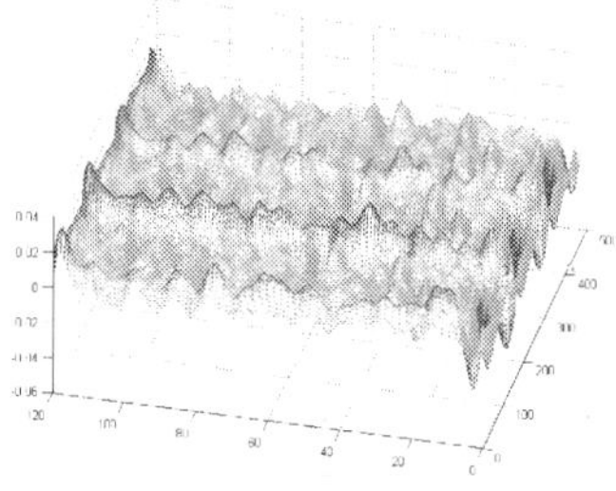

a. Metal surface and 3D height map extracted from image processing

 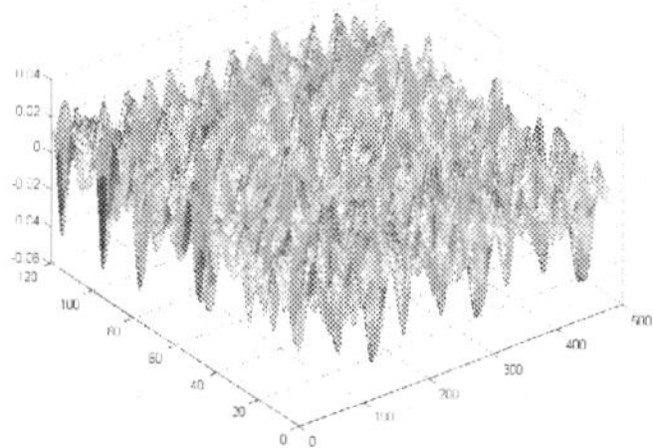

b. Stone surface and 3D height map extracted from image processing

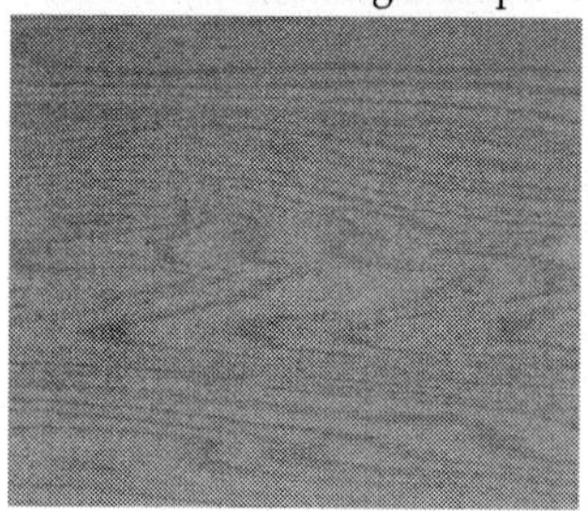 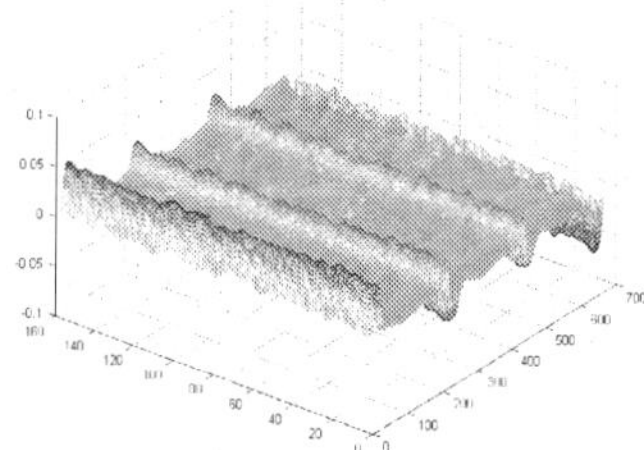

c. Wood surface and 3D height map extracted from image processing

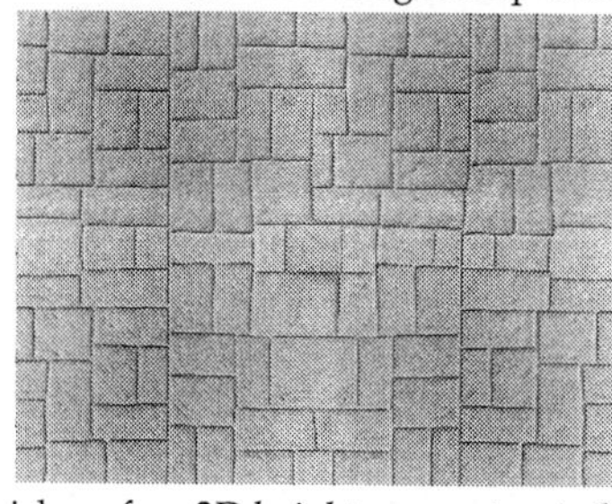 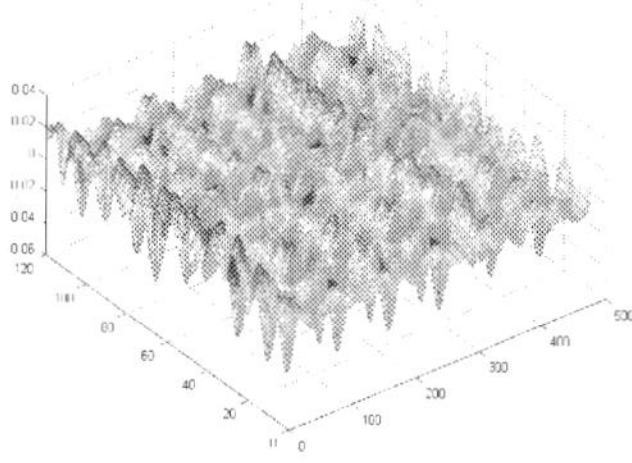

d. brick surface 3D height map extracted from image processing

Fig. 5. Sample textures used for the discrimination experiment and corresponding height maps

* Note: the unit of x and y axis is pixel, z is the contour of rough surface

$$F = k \times rand(\mu, \sigma^2)$$

Where the rand() is the white noise, produced by computer program. The adjustable parameters mean μ and variance σ, which originated from the statistical properties of the texture image sample. Higher variance produces a rougher texture. To assure that there is no texture force applied when the user is not moving, F is set to zero below a small velocity threshold.

In the psychophysical experiments, twenty subjects, 10 males and 10 female, students at the southeast university, participated. The average age was 24 years. The typical texture samples were metal, wood, brick, sand paper. The typical sample images and the corresponding profiles acquired by image processing method were shown as Fig. 5.

ISelection Experiment

This experiment is to compare the effectiveness of the texture force models mentioned above, the texture force were presented to the subjects with the models mentioned above in a random sequence. While controlling the proxy to slide over the virtual texture surface with DELTA device, subjects felt the texture force, and they were required to select which method was the most realistic one. The trials were repeated three times for different texture samples, and Table 1 shows the mean selection results.

The result indicates that the proposed model is superior to others. One explanation for this may be that the height map is originated from the real image texture, which contains more information such as orientation of the texture than other two models.

Select result (numbers). Models	Exp. 1	2	3
Our method	12	11	13
sinusoid model	7	8	7
stochastic model	1	1	0

Table 1. Comparing which method is more realistic

IIMatching Experiment

This experiment was to evaluate the proposed model's legibility. In the experiment, subjects were asked to wear the eye mask so as the process were implemented prohibiting the visual observation, four different texture samples were displayed to the subject. And then the four corresponding texture images were shown to the subject. Subject was asked to match the texture of what they saw to what they have felt previously. As human's haptic memory span is limited. For one continues haptic perception trial, the number of the samples which human can remember and identify is 3 to 6. So in this experiment, one rendered group only included four samples. Four texture samples are metal, brick, wood and brick (a, b, c, d in Fig.5). Each subject performed on the same condition for three times. The match correct rate is as table 2.

Correct (numbers) Exp. / Person.	1	2	3
Female	9	9	8
Male	9	10	9
Total	18	19	17

Table 2. Matching the haptic rendering ones with the image samples

III Recognition Experiment

This experiment is also to estimate the presentation quality of the haptic texture model. In the experiment, the haptic texture was render to the subjects with our method, and subjects were required to see a group of texture images in which the rendered one was among them, and to tell which image is the just rendered one. The number of samples in one group is 6. The correct rate of match experiment II is higher than III. It is supposed that, in experiment II, the match pairs is limited, and the human' force perception can be referred to the others samples

Correct (numbers) Exp. / Person.	1	2	3
Female	7	8	7
Male	9	8	8
Total	16	16	15

Table 3. Selecting the haptic rendered one from the image samples

4. Results and discussion

From the experiments, it implied that our model is distinctly superior to other two haptic texture models. The haptic texture render system exhibits the remarkable different reflected force to the users. One important reason is that the texture force model is from the height profile of texture image and Gauss filter is utilized. But we also have to confess that what we feel is still not what we see. Due to the complex nature of the haptic rendering pipeline and the human somatosensory system, it remains a difficult problem to expose all factors contributing to such perceptual artefacts. The haptic interface research laboratory at Purdue University has investigated the unrealistic behaviour of haptic texture. To our system, one reason for the limited matching rating is from the haptic device. As the haptic texture is implemented through the haptic device, so the performance is closely related with the device. To generate the stimuli of small texture force, the output force is controlled in the range of ±5N. However, the DELTA device has relatively large damping force compared with the magnitude of texture force, which effected the actually output of the system. On the other hand, a real stainless steel surface has an almost infinite stiffness and cannot be penetrated by the fingertip or a probe, whereas an impedance implementation of a virtual surface has a limited stiffness due to the output of the haptic device. Another reason may affect the haptic perception in our system is the mapping between the pixel coordination of the image and world coordination of haptic device. As the resolution of the image is given, the larger working space of movement means interpolation or approximation approach would be used.

5. Conclusion and future work

To rapidly and effectively modelling the textured force and simulated the haptic stimuli while the user touching the textured surface of a 3D object. The height map of the texture is acquired based on the Gauss filter in frequency domain. The texture force and friction force are modelled based on the height map. As the height map is transformed from the image data, so the processing is simple and no specialized 3D geometrical scanning device is utilized. In this system, the texture objects are regular for example cuboids and columns. In the future, more the haptic texture model could be improved to be combined with random signal based on SR (stochastic resonance) and further psychophysical experiments would be carried out to adjust the parameters. The system will be applied to the objects with irregular shape for more widely uses.

6. References

Jansson, G; Bergamasco, M& Frisoli. A. (2003)"A New Option for the Visually Impaired to Experience 3D Art at Museums: Manual Exploration of Virtual Copies" , *Visual Impairment Research*, April, 2003, vol.5, no. 1, pp. 1-12 ISSN:1388235X

Tachi.S et al..(1994) "A Construction Method of Virtual Haptic Space," *Proceedings of Fourth International Conference on Artificial Reality and Tele-Existence*, pp. 131-138, Tokyo , July,1994.

Hirota, K; Hirose. M. (1995) "Simulation and Presentation of Curved Surface in Virtual Reality Environment Through Surface Display," *Proceeding of IEEE Virtual Reality Annual International Symposium*, pp. 211-216, ISBN:0818670843, Los Alamitos, March, 1995.

Ikei, Y.; Wakamatsu, K. & Fukuda. S. (1997) "Texture Presentation by Vibratory Tactile Display", *Proceeding of IEEE Annual Virtual Reality International Symposium*, pp. 199-205, ISBN: 0818678437, New Mexico,March, 1997, IEEE, Los Alamitos

Ikei, Y.; Wakamatsu, K.&Fukuda S. (1998) "Image Data Transformation for Tactile Texture Display," *Proceedings of Virtual Reality Annual International Symposium*, pp.51-58, ISBN: 0818683627, Atlanta, March, 1998, IEEE, Los Alamitos,

Ikei, Y.; Shiratori, M. (2002) "TextureExplorer: A tactile and force display for virtual textures", *Proceedings of the 10th Symp.On Haptic Interfaces For Virtual Envir.& Teleoperator Systems.*, pp.327-334, ISBN:0769514898, Orlando, March ,2002, IEEE, Los Alamitos

Masami Shinohara; Yutaka Shimizu&Akira Mochizuki, (1998) "Three-Dimensional Tactile Display for the Blind", *IEEE Transactions on Rehabilitation Engineering*, vol. 6, no.3, September,1998, pp.249-256, ISSN: 10636528

Lederman, S.J. et al. (2004) "Force variability during surface contact with bare finger or rigid probe". *Proceedings of 12th international symposium on Interfaces for virtual environment and teleoperator system*, pp.154-160, ISBN: 0769521126, Chicago, March, 2004, IEEE, Los Alamitos

Vasudevan, H. Manivannan, M, (2006) "Recordable Haptic textures", *Proceedings of IEEE International Workshop on Haptic Audio Visual Environments and their Applications*, pp.130-133, ISBN: 1424407613, Ottawa, November, 2006, IEEE, Piscataway

C.-H. Ho, C. Basdogan & M. A. Srinivasan. (1999) "Efficient point-based rendering techniques for haptic display of virtual objects." *Presence*, October, 1999, vol. 8, no. 5, pp. 477–491, ISSN:10547460.

Juhani, Siira, Dinesh, K. Pai, (2006)"Haptic Texturing - A Stochastic Approach.", *Proceedings of IEEE International Conference on Robotics and Automation*, pp.557-562, ISBN: 0780395050, Orlando ,May, 2006, IEEE, Piscataway

Fritz, J.P., Barner, K.E. (1996) "Stochastic Models for Haptic Texture". *Proceedings of SPIE The International Society for Optical Engineering*, pp34-44, ISSN : 0277786X , Boston, November,1996, SPIE, Bellingham

Choi, S; H. Z. Tan, (2004) "Toward realistic haptic rendering of surface textures." *IEEE Computer Graphics and Applications*, March, 2004, vol. 24, no. 2, pp. 40–47, ISSN:02721716.

Miguel; A. et al., (2004). "Haptic Display of Interaction between Textured Models". *Proceedings of IEEE Visualization Conference*, pp. 297-304, ISBN: 0780387880, Austin, October, 2004, IEEE, Piscataway

H. Z. Tan; B. D. Adelstein & R. Traylor, (2006) "Discrimination of Real and Virtual High-Definition Textured Surfaces", *Proceedings of Symposium on Haptic Interfaces for Virtual Environment and Teleoperator Systems*, pp.3–9, ISBN:9781424402267, Arlington, March, 2006, IEEE, Piscataway

## 11

Image Processing based Classifier for Detection and Diagnosis of Induction Motor Stator Fault

T. G. Amaral[1], V. F. Pires[2], J. F. Martins[3], A. J. Pires[4] and M. M. Crisóstomo[5]
*[1]Escola Superior Tecnologia de Setúbal / Instituto Politécnico de Setúbal
Institute of Systems and Robotics / University of Coimbra
[2]Escola Superior Tecnologia de Setúbal / Instituto Politécnico de Setúbal
[3]CTS-UNINOVA and Departamento de Engenharia Electrotécnica Faculdade
de Ciências e Tecnologia / Universidade Nova de Lisboa
[4]CTS-UNINOVA and Polytechnic Institute of Setúbal
[5]Institute of Systems and Robotics and DEECS / University of Coimbra
Portugal*

1. Introduction

Induction motors are one of the most widely used electrical machines. These motors play a very important role in the present industrial life. Therefore, the need to insure a continuous and safety operation for this motors, involves preventive maintenance programs with fault detection techniques. In general, condition monitoring schemes have concentrated on sensing specific failure modes. Electrical faults such as winding and rotor faults are responsible for an important percentage of total motor failures (Hadremi, 2000) (Bonnett et al., 2008). Preventive maintenance of three-phase induction motors also plays a very important role in the industrial life (Thorsen et al., 1995). This procedure requires monitoring their operation for detection of abnormal electrical and mechanical conditions that indicate, or may lead to, a failure of the system. In fact, in the last years monitoring induction motors becomes very important in order to reduce maintenance costs and prevent unscheduled downtimes. Therefore, there has been a substantial amount of research to provide new condition monitoring techniques for ac induction motors (Kliman et al., 1992) (Thomson, 1999) Several strategies have been proposed to access operation conditions of induction motors (Kliman et al., 1988) (Tavner et al., 1987) (Nandi et al. 1999) (Toliyat et al., 1985) (Riley et al., 1999) (Dister et al., 1998) (Henao et al. 2003) (Li 2006). However, the input stator currents represent the most widely used signal in identifying machine faults (Çolak et al., 2005) (Benbouzid, 2000) (Bayindir et al., 2007). There are several main reasons for this: most of the machine unbalances would reflect into the current waveform, the current is feasible and inexpensive to monitor and the monitoring technique is non-invasive. One of the most significant methods based on the analysis of the machine line currents is the motor current signature analysis (MCSA) (Schoen et al., 1995) (Çalis et al., 2008) (Thomson et al., 2001) (Bellini et al., 2001) (Pires et al., 2009). This method is based on the motor line current monitoring and consequent inspection of its deviations in the frequency domain. Another approach based on the analysis of the machine line currents is the Park's vector approach (Cardoso et al., 1995). This method is based on the identification of the stator current Concordia patterns, requiring the user to have some degree of expertise in order to distinguish a normal operation condition from a potential failure. A common fact to all of these techniques is that the user must have some degree of expertise in order to distinguish a normal operation condition from a potential failure mode. Therefore, fully automatic pattern recognition methods are required to identify induction motor stator fault. Thus some artificial intelligence tools have been introduced (Nejjari et al., 2000) (Zidani et al., 2003) (Haji et al., 2001) (Ondel et al., 2006) (Martins et al., 2007). However, many of these tools require a prior identification of the system, and only then they are able to identify some faulty situation. On the other hand, the presence of noise along with the nonlinear behaviour of the machine can make this task very difficult.

Under this context, this paper proposes new procedures for the detection of a three-phase induction motor stator fault. These procedures are based on the image identification of the stator current Concordia patterns, and will allow the identification of turn faults in the stator winding as well as its correspondent severity. The identification of the faulty phase is another important feature of the proposed algorithm.

2. Pattern recognition approach

The analysis of the three-phase induction motor can be simplified using the Clark-Concordia transformation (1).

$$C = \sqrt{\frac{2}{3}} \begin{bmatrix} 1 & 0 & \frac{1}{\sqrt{2}} \\ -\frac{1}{2} & \frac{\sqrt{3}}{2} & \frac{1}{\sqrt{2}} \\ -\frac{1}{2} & -\frac{\sqrt{3}}{2} & \frac{1}{\sqrt{2}} \end{bmatrix} \tag{1}$$

This transformation allows reducing a three-phase system into an equivalent two-phase system (with a zero-sequence component). In three phase induction motors the connection to the mains does not usually use the neutral, implying that the mains current has no homopolar component. Under this situation the three-phase induction motor $\alpha\beta$ line currents are then given by (2).

$$\begin{cases} i_\alpha = \sqrt{\frac{2}{3}}\, i_a - \frac{1}{\sqrt{6}}\, i_b - \frac{1}{\sqrt{6}}\, i_c \\ \\ i_\beta = \frac{1}{\sqrt{2}}\, i_b - \frac{1}{\sqrt{2}}\, i_c \end{cases} \tag{2}$$

Considering ideal conditions for the motor and an unbalanced voltage supply, (3) can be obtained.

$$\begin{cases} i_\alpha = \dfrac{\sqrt{6}}{2}\, I \sin \omega t \\[2em] i_\beta = \dfrac{\sqrt{2}}{2}\, I \sin\left(\omega t - \dfrac{\pi}{2}\right) \end{cases} \qquad (3)$$

Figure 1 shows the structure of the stator currents acquisition, where they are transformed into two-phase equivalents using the Clark-Concordia transformation.

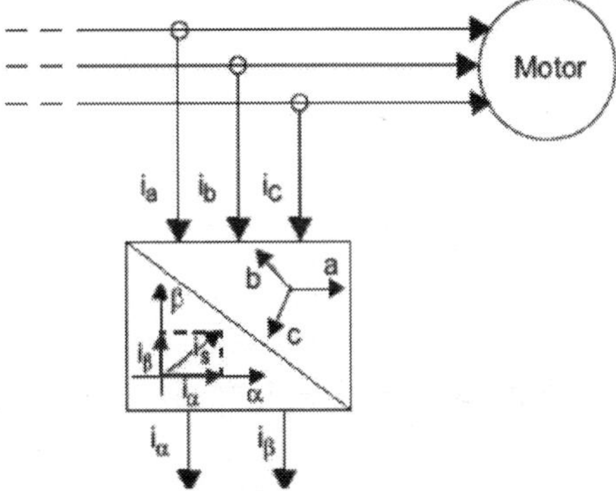

Fig. 1. Structure of the stator currents aquisition.

The obtained Clark-Concordia transformation results in a circular or an elliptic pattern, as can be seen in Figure 2. A healthy three-phase induction motor generates a circle (the radius of circle depends on load, being bigger for higher loads and vice versa). A fault in a stator

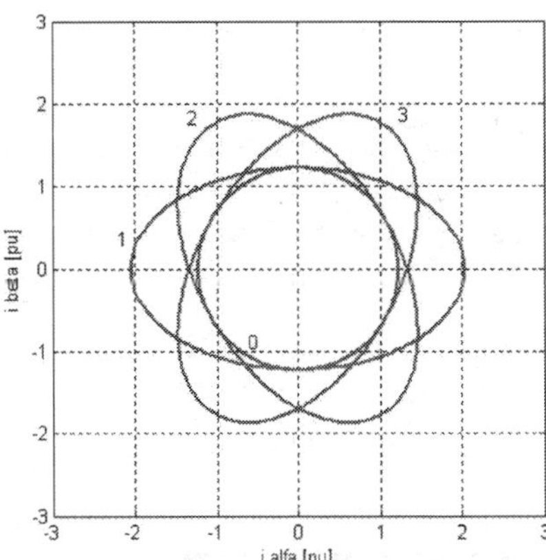

Fig. 2. Current Concordia vector pattern 0 - healthy motor, 1 - turn fault in the stator winding phase a, 2 - turn fault in the stator winding phase b 3 - turn fault in the stator winding phase c.

winding implies a distortion in the circle, assuming an elliptic pattern whose major axis orientation is associated to the faulty phase. This elliptic pattern changes according to the fault severity. For more severe faults the eccentricity of the ellipse increases.

The main idea is to implement a fully automatic pattern recognition process, which recognizes the presence of a fault, identifies the faulty phase and, furthermore, reports a severity index for that fault. The proposed algorithms deal with the diagnosis of stator winding faults by means of pattern recognition methods, based only on the acquisition of two input currents. The described algorithms will extract features of the obtained current patterns, in an automatic pattern recognition process that automatically discern the behaviour of the motor (faulty or healthy). This will allow the identification of turn faults in the stator winding and its correspondent severity.

3. Image processing based system

In order to implement a pattern recognition based fault detection, a feature-based recognition of the current stator pattern, independent of their shape, size and orientation must be obtained. Finding efficient invariants features is the key to solve this problem. Particular attention is paid to statistic moments and visual-based features obtained in the image processing system.

The proposed image-processing algorithm is divided in three stages: the image composition, the boundary representation and the feature extraction (Figure 3). The inputs for the image processing based system are the $\alpha\beta$ stator currents. The feature extraction must identify the image characteristics that can be obtained from the image composition. It was possible to verify that the obtained images for a healthy or a faulty motor are different. These differences are obtained by the feature extraction block.

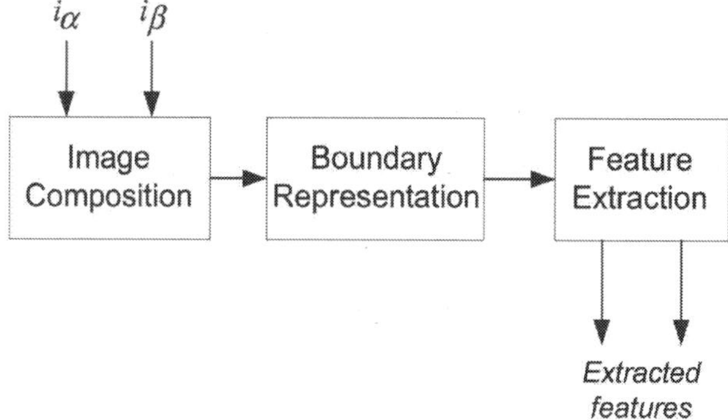

Fig. 3. Structure of the image processing based system.

3.1 Image composition

In the image composition stage, the $\alpha\beta$ stator currents are first represented as an image in order to be used in the pattern recognition method. In this way, each sample $\alpha\beta$ current value will be considered as a pixel belonging to the object contour with the coordinates (i_x, i_y) given by (4) and (5).

$$\begin{cases} i_x = round\left(\left(i_\alpha - offset\_x\right) k\right) \\[2em] i_y = round\left(\left(i_\beta - offset\_y\right) k\right) \end{cases} \qquad (4)$$

where

$$\begin{cases} offset\_x = \min\left(i_\alpha\right) - 1 \\[2em] offset\_y = \min\left(i_\beta\right) - 1 \end{cases} \qquad (5)$$

Consider an object with each pixel (i_x, i_y) as a gray level I(xi, yi). A binary image can be considered as a particular case of a grey image with I(x,y)=1 for pixels that belong to an object, and I(x,y)=0 for pixels that belong to the background. Figure 4 shows the $\alpha\beta$ stator currents represented in the image plan after the image composition process.

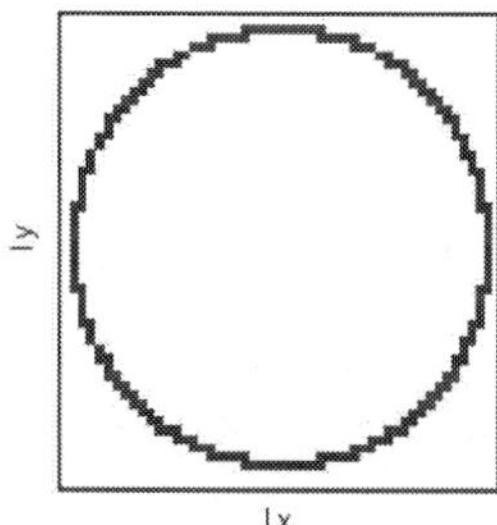

Fig. 4. Image plan for the three phase induction motor $\alpha\beta$ line currents.

3.2 Boudary representation

To implement the pattern recognition method, after the image composition it is necessary to determine the shape of the region.

To represent the boundary of the region and at the same time obtain some properties that help feature extraction the chain code algorithm is used (Ballard et al., 1982). This algorithm leads to an efficient calculation of the region area and his contour perimeter. However, the right and left upper points (tr_p, tl_p) of the region must also be obtained (Figure 5). These two points corresponds to the first and last pixels present on the first line of the region.

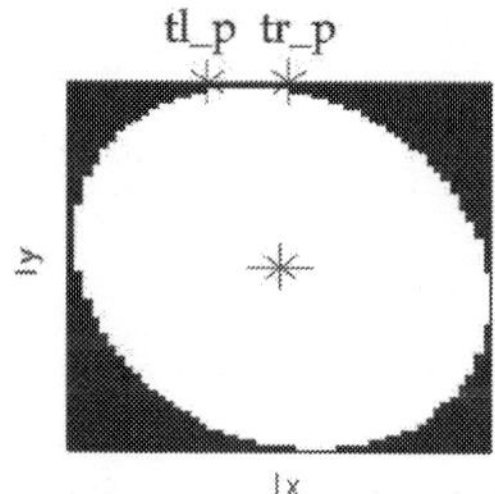

Fig. 5. Image plan for the three phase induction motor $\alpha\beta$ line currents.

4. Features extraction methodologies

The last stage of the image-processing algorithm is the features extraction. There are several feactures extraction methodologies. Here are presented two effective algorithms that can be used for the induction motor fault detection: Visual features and statistic based moments methods.

4.1 Visual features

The feature extraction stage uses the area of the object and the contour perimeter to compute the index of compactness. To obtain the distance between the xc coordinate of the gravity center of the region and the x coordinate of the mean upper point of the region it is necessary to compute the gravity center (xc, yc).

The index of compactness and the distance between the xc coordinate of the gravity center of the region and the x coordinate of the mean upper point of the region are the key features for the fault diagnosis procedure.

Assume that the pixels in the digital image are piecewise constant and the dimension of the bounded region image for each object is denoted by M×N, the visual features, area and perimeter, used to determine the I.O.C. can be obtained as (Amaral et al., 2001):

$$A(I) = \sum_{x=1}^{M}\sum_{y=1}^{N} I(x,y) \tag{6}$$

$$P(I) = \sum_{x,y} Arc_{xy} \tag{7}$$

where Arc_{xy} is the length of the arc along the object contour where x and y are connected neighbors. If the connectivity is type-4 then $Arc_{xy}=1$, otherwise $Arc_{xy}=\sqrt{2}$.

The index of compactness is then given by:

$$IOC(I) = \frac{A(I)}{P(I)^2} \tag{8}$$

Physically, the index of compactness denotes the fraction of maximum area that can be encircling by the perimeter actually occupied by the object.

The coordinate x_c of the gravity center is given by:

$$x_c = \frac{\sum_{x=1}^{M}\sum_{y=1}^{N} I(x,y).x}{A(I)} \tag{9}$$

where the y_c coordinate it is not necessary to compute.

The distance between the x_c coordinate of the gravity center of the I region and the x coordinate of the mean upper point of the region is given by:

$$dist\_x_c\_tlr(I) = x_c - \left(\frac{tl\_p + tr\_p}{2}\right) \tag{10}$$

where tl_p and tr_p are the x coordinates of the top-left and the top-right points of the region.

In Figure 6 it is represented the distance between the x_c coordinate of the gravity center of the region and the x coordinate of the mean point between the top-left and top-right points of the region I.

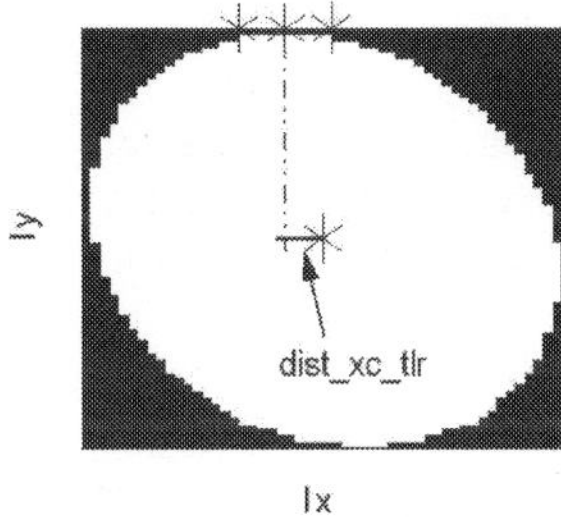

Fig. 6. Distance used in the system classifier.

4.2 Statistic moments

Another possible approach to obtain efficient invariants features is based on the use of the statistic moments algorithm. This algorithm uses the regular and the central moments to obtain the features needed for the fault diagnosis (Amaral et al., 2007). The $\alpha\beta$ stator currents are first represented onto an image in order to be used in the pattern recognition method. Again, each pixel belonging to the object contour represent each $\alpha\beta$ sample current. Considering an object with each pixel (x_i, y_i) as a gray level $I(x_i, y_i)$. The (p+q) order of the regular moment is given by:

$$m_{pq} = \sum_{i=1}^{M} I(x_i, y_i)(x_i)^p (y_i)^q \tag{11}$$

where the sum is made over the image all M pixels.

The (p+q) order of the central moment is invariant to translation and is obtained considering the origin of the object at his gravity center (12).

$$\mu_{pq} = \sum_{i=1}^{M} I(x_i, y_i)\left(x_i - \bar{x}\right)^p \left(y_i - \bar{y}\right)^q \tag{12}$$

The $\left(\bar{x}, \bar{y}\right)$ coordinates represent the gravity center of the object. These coordinates can be obtained using the regular moments of zero and first orders and are given by:

$$\bar{x} = \frac{m_{10}}{m_{00}}, \qquad \bar{y} = \frac{m_{01}}{m_{00}}. \tag{13}$$

The features used in the system recognition are the main axis angle of the $\alpha\beta$ currents pattern and it's eccentricity. The main axis angle (Figure 7) and the eccentricity can be obtained using six regular moments such as:

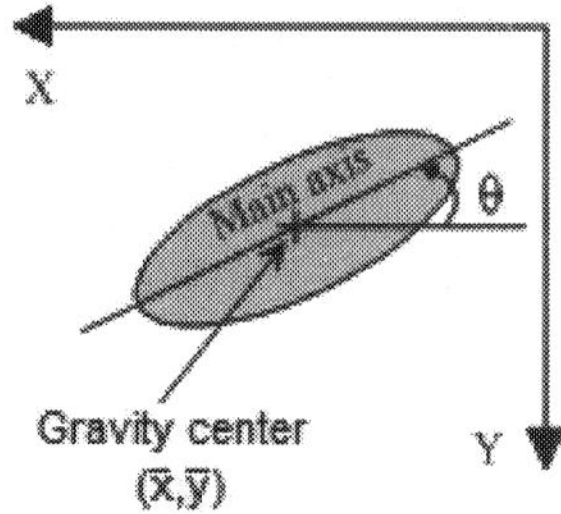

Fig. 7. Position and orientation of an object.

$$\theta = \frac{1}{2}\tan^{-1}\left(\frac{2\left(m_{00}m_{11} - m_{01}m_{10}\right)}{m_{00}\left(m_{20} - m_{02}\right) + m_{01}^2 - m_{10}^2}\right) \qquad (14)$$

$$e = \frac{1}{m_{00}}\left(m_{20} - m_{02} - \frac{m_{10}^2}{m_{00}} + \frac{m_{01}^2}{m_{00}}\right)^2 + 4\left(m_{11} - \frac{m_{10}m_{01}}{m_{00}}\right) \qquad (15)$$

These two features can be obtained more effective using only three and four central moments in the computation of the main axis angle and eccentricity, respectively. The relation between the regular and the central moments can be obtained by:

$$\begin{cases} \mu_{00} = m_{00} \\[2em] \mu_{10} = \mu_{01} = 0 \\[2em] \mu_{11} = m_{11} - \dfrac{m_{10}m_{01}}{m_{00}} \\[2em] \mu_{20} = m_{20} - \dfrac{m_{10}^2}{m_{00}} \\[2em] \mu_{02} = m_{02} - \dfrac{m_{01}^2}{m_{00}} \end{cases} \qquad (16)$$

Using these relations, the main axis angle - θ - and the eccentricity - e - can be obtained using the following equations (Ballard et al., 1982):

$$\theta = \frac{1}{2}\tan^{-1}\left(\frac{2\mu_{11}}{\mu_{20} - \mu_{02}}\right) \qquad (17)$$

$$e = \frac{(\mu_{20} - \mu_{02})^2 + 4\mu_{11}}{\mu_{00}} \tag{18}$$

A binary image can be considered as a particular case of a grey image with $I(x,y)=1$ for pixels that belong to an object, and $I(x,y)=0$ for pixels that belong to the background. Using only the sum of all pixels that belong to a 2D object, the regular and central moments equations used to obtain the two features can now be obtained as:

$$m_{pq} = \sum_x \sum_y (x_i)^p (y_i)^q, \tag{19}$$

$$\mu_{pq} = \sum_x \sum_y \left(x_i - \bar{x}\right)^p \left(y_i - \bar{y}\right)^q. \tag{20}$$

5. Neuro-fuzzy classifier

Neural networks and statistical methods are particularly well adapted for data classification. However it is also possible to use a fuzzy system for the classification problem without replacing the aforementioned methods but as a different approach to achieve the same results, with the following advantages:

- vague knowledge can be used;
- the classifier is interpretable;
- easy to implement, to use and to understand.

Since classifiers are usually derived from data, one method to obtain a fuzzy classifier is to use a neuro-fuzzy approach. The fuzzy classifier obtained by a learning procedure is called a neuro-fuzzy classifier but this "neuro-fuzzy" term strictly only applies to the creation or in the training phase. Afterwards, once the classifier is applied there only remains a fuzzy system for classification. This type of neuro-fuzzy system it is called a cooperative neurofuzzy system (Nauck et al., 1997).

The interpretation of the classifier is often illustrated by representing it in a neural network structure. Figure 8 shows the structure of the neuro-fuzzy inference system used in data classification. This figure represents the structure example of a four-layered neuro-fuzzy system with two inputs and one output. This connectionist structure effectively performs the fuzzy inferencing with some minor restrictions. In a generalized architecture for the proposed approach, there can be n nodes in first layer (input layer) and m nodes in the second layer (pattern layer) corresponding to the input and rule numbers, respectively. The number of nodes in the third layer (summation layer) depends on the number of output nodes. As it happens in the Generalised Regression Neural Network (G.R.N.N.) configuration, the number of nodes in the third layer is equal to the nodes of the output layer plus one node (Specht, D. F., 1991), (Chen, C. H., 1996), (Tsoukalas et al., 1997). Observing Figure 8, if the output layer has one output node then the third layer must have two nodes.

Each layer has a specific functionality that contributes to the equivalence of the fuzzy inference system.

The input layer consists in the input of the data values derived from the input features. The output of each node is the degree to which the given input satisfies the linguistic label associated to the correspondent node.

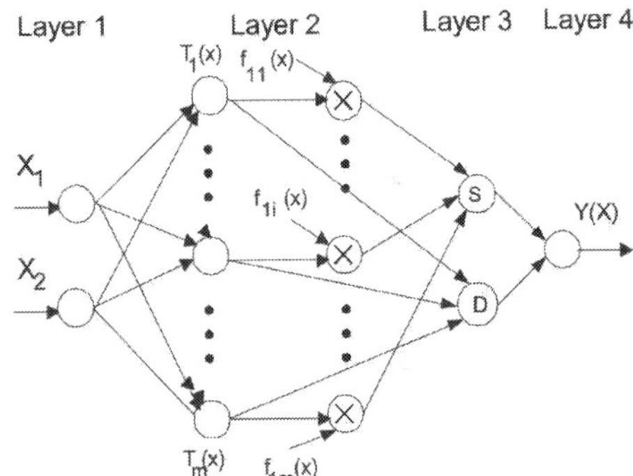

Fig. 8. Adaptive neuro-fuzzy inference system.

The pattern layer represents the rule set of the fuzzy inference system. The number of nodes in this layer it is the same as the number of rules in the fuzzy inference system. Each node, called rule node, is a special type of radial basis function processor and represents a rule where the output of each basis function unit $T_i(x_j)$ is given by equation (21).

$$T_i(x_j) = \prod_{j=1}^{n} LX_j^{(i)}(x_j) \qquad (21)$$

$LX_j^{(i)}(x)$ is the membership function of jth fuzzy set in the ith rule antecedent. Each membership function has four parameters and it can have different shapes and be asymmetric (Amaral et al., 2002b).

The summation layer has two different types of processing units: the summation and the division units. The function of the summation unit is essentially the same as the function of the output units in the radial basis function network. The division unit only sums the weighted activations of the pattern units without using any activation function. The number of the summation units is always the same as the number of the G.R.N.N. output units.

Each node in the output layer consists in a simple division of the signal coming from the summation unit by the signal coming from the division unit, as defined by equation (22).

$$u_p = \frac{\sum_{i=1}^{m} T_i(x_j)\, f_{pi}(x_j)}{\sum_{i=1}^{m} T_i(x_j)} \qquad (22)$$

p denotes the number of output nodes in the output layer.

If the fuzzy inference system has one output then the linear function $f_{pi}(x_j)$ of the firstorder Sugeno rule can be described by the following equation:

$$f_{1i}(x_j) = b_{1i_0} + b_{1i_1} x_1 + \ldots + b_{1i_n} x_n \qquad (23)$$

The number of layers of the adaptive neuro-fuzzy inference system and the function of each node in the four layers are also similar to the G.R.N.N.. Thus it was constructed an adaptive network that it is functionally equivalent to a type-3 fuzzy inference system (Takagi & Sugeno fuzzy if-then rules).

In the learning of the fuzzy inference system two learning algorithms are applied. An iterative grid partition algorithm tunes the four parameters of each antecedent membership function (Amaral et al., 2002a). The first three parameters correspond to the left, the center and the right position of each membership function and the fourth parameter to its shape. The parameters of local model $f_{1i}(x_j)$ are learned by Least Square Error (L.S.E.).

6. Results

In order to obtain experimental results it was used and induction motor with the following characteristics: 1kW, 220/380V, 50Hz. The machine load is provided by means of an electromagnetic brake and the stator currents are acquired through a personal computer data acquisition board (Figure 9). After the acquisition of the stator currents, these currents are transformed into a 2D object using the $\alpha\beta$ transformation.

Fig. 9. Experimental prototype for the proposed fault detection system.

6.1 Simulation results based on visual features

In order to verify the proposed algorithm, the fault diagnostic system was first simulated in the Matlab environment. The induction motor was initially simulated without any fault. In this case the corresponding $\alpha\beta$ vector pattern is a circle centered at the origin of the coordinates. Other simulations were considered. Initially, several tests were done in which the severity of the fault was rather small, then new tests were conducted in which the severity of the fault was higher. Table I presents the obtained results for the two features. When the induction motor has no fault the index of compactness is, approximately, 0.0726. Figure 10 presents the current vector pattern for the healthy motor, which does not present any eccentricity. For a small induction motor fault, the index of compactness decreases to 0.0720, denoting that the $\alpha\beta$ pattern exhibits some eccentricity (Figure 11). As can be seen by the results presented in Table I the distance between the xc coordinate of the region gravity center and the mean point between the top-left and top-right points of the region

(DIST_XC_TLR), is different for each phase fault, denoting this distance value the faulty phase. As long the fault becomes more severe, the I.O.C decreases and the DIST_XC_TLR increase its absolute value. In Figure 12 a severe phase fault is presented.

FAULT TYPE	I.O.C	DIST_XC_TLR
No fault	0.072666	0.13
Phase a reduced fault	0.072005	0.15
Phase a higher fault	0.028794	-1.49
Phase b reduced fault	0.072267	2.11
Phase b higher fault	0.027728	15.53
Phase c reduced fault	0.071934	-1.98
Phase c higher fault	0.028030	-14.84

Table I Simulation results

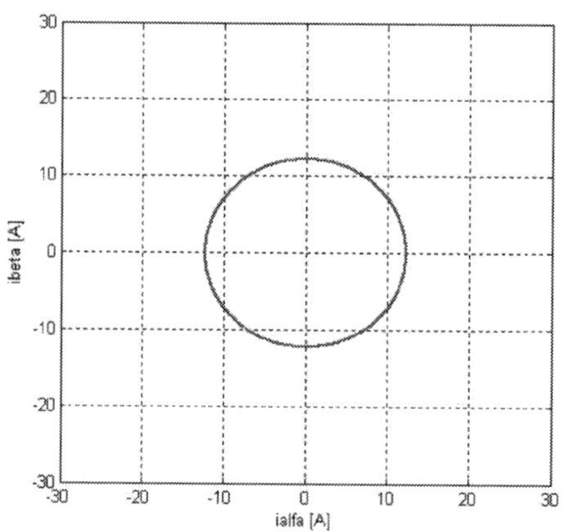

Fig. 10. Simulation result in the $\alpha\beta$ current vector pattern for the healthy motor.

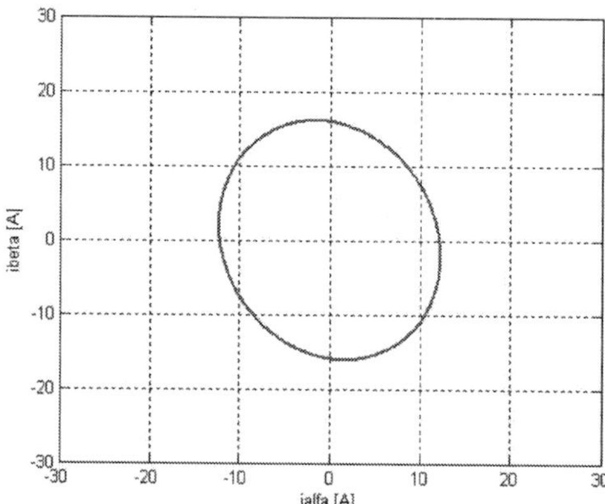

Fig. 11. $\alpha\beta$ current vector pattern for the motor with a small fault – simulation result.

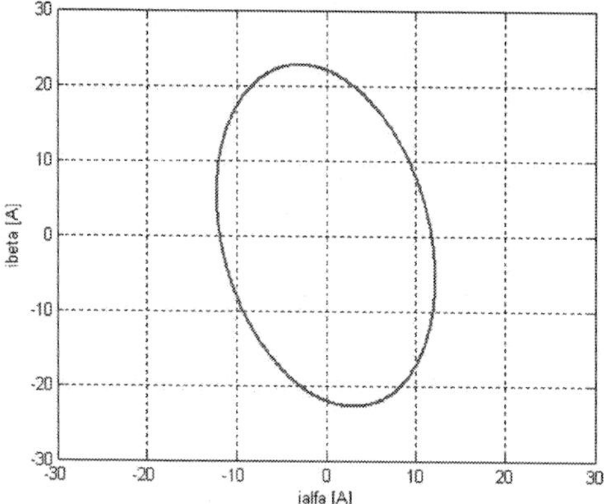

Fig. 12. Simulation result in the $\alpha\beta$ current pattern for the motor with a severe fault.

6.2 Experimental results based on visual features

The induction motor was initially operated without any fault. In this case the corresponding $\alpha\beta$ vector pattern it is practically a circle centered at the origin of the coordinates, as presented in Figure 13. This pattern slightly differs from a perfect circle pattern because the supply voltage is not a perfectly unbalanced sinusoidal system (Zidani et al., 2003). Due to this problem, the I.O.C and the DIST_XC_TLR when the induction motor presents no fault are 0.0739 and –2.45, respectively.

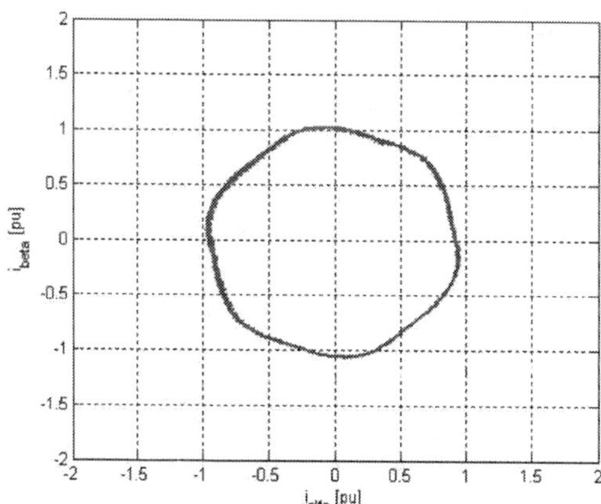

Fig. 13. Experimental result in the $\alpha\beta$ current Park's vector pattern for the healthy motor.

Figure 14 presents the corresponding $\alpha\beta$ vector representation, under an induction motor stator-winding fault. As expected, within faulty operation there is a distortion in the circle, assuming an elliptic pattern whose major axis orientation is associated to the faulty phase. In this case the I.O.C and the DIST_XC_TLR are 0.0705 and -3.95, respectively. The obtained negative distance value, indicate that the fault occurred in phase b.

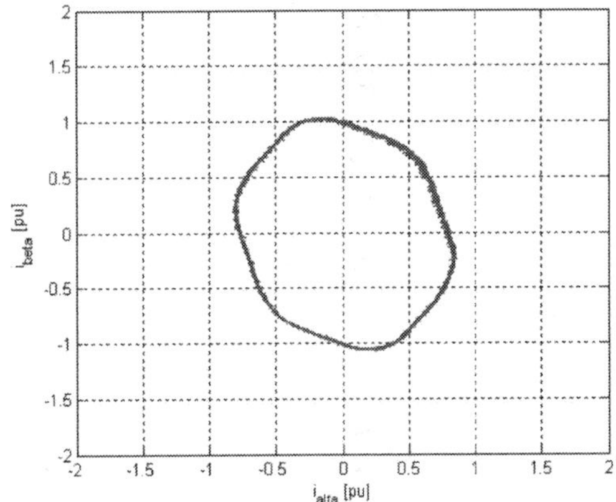

Fig. 14. Experimental result in the $\alpha\beta$ current Park's vector pattern for the motor with a small stator fault.

6.3 Simulation results based on statistic moments

In order to verify the proposed method, the system shown in Figure 9 was first simulated in the Matlab environment. The induction motor was initially simulated without any fault. In this case the corresponding $\alpha\beta$ vector pattern is a circle centered at the origin of the coordinates. Other simulations were considered. First, several tests were done in which the severity of the fault was rather small. Then new tests were conducted in which the severity of the fault was higher. Table II shows the obtained results by the statistic moments. The statistic excentricity moment when the induction motor has no fault is 0.99 (Figure 10). This means that the $\alpha\beta$ current pattern does not present any eccentricity. For a small induction motor fault (Figure 11), the statistic eccentricity moment decreases to 0.75, showing that the $\alpha\beta$ pattern exhibits some eccentricity. As can be seen by the results presented in Table II the ellipse angle is different for each phase fault, denoting this angle the faulty phase. Also the statistic moment eccentricity increases as long the fault becomes more severe (Figure 12).

	ECCENTRICITY	ANGLE [°]
No fault	0.99	45
Phase a fault	0.75	-72.4
Phase a higher fault	0.52	-70.3
Phase b fault	0.75	12.2
Phase b higher fault	0.52	10.1
Phase c fault	0.75	45
Phase c higher fault	0.52	45

Table II Simulation results

6.4 Experimental results based on statistic moments

Initially the induction motor operated with no fault and the obtained $\alpha\beta$ vector pattern differs slightly from a perfect circle. Due to this problem, the statistic eccentricity moment when the induction motor presents no fault is 0.92. When the induction motor was operated within faulty there is a distortion in the circle, assuming an elliptic pattern whose major axis orientation is associated to the faulty phase. In this case the statistic eccentricity moment is 0.78. The obtained angle value is 14.1°, denoting that the fault occurred in phase b.

7. Conclusions

In this chapter an image processing based classifier for detection and diagnosis of induction motor stator fault was presented. This system is based on the obtained stator currents and the correspondent Clark-Concordia transformation. This results in a circular or an elliptic pattern, of the Clark-Concordia stator currents. From the obtained current patterns it was used an image processing algorithm to identify if there is a motor fault. The image processing algorithm is divided in three stages: the image composition, the boundary representation and the feature extraction. For the the features extraction it was used two effective algorithms that can be used for the induction motor fault detection: Visual features and statistic based moments methods. The extract features of the the obtained current patterns allows to identify the turn faults in the stator winding and its correspondent severity. Several simulation and experimental results have been presented. From these results it was possible to verify that the proposed image based classifier can effectively be used for the diagnosis of induction motors.

8. References

Amaral, T. G.; Crisóstomo, M. M.; Pires, V. F. & Almeida, A. T. (2001). Visual Motion Detection with Hand-Eye Manipulator Using Statistic Moments Classifiers and Fuzzy Logic Approach – Study, Application and Comparation. *The 27th Annual Conference of the IEEE Industrial Electronics Society, IECON'01*, Denver, Colorado, USA, November 29 to December 2, 2001.

Amaral, T. G; Crisóstomo, M. M. & Pires, V. F. (2002a). Adaptive Neuro-Fuzzy Inference System for Modelling and Control", *The IEEE International Symposium of Intelligent Systems*, Bulgária, September.

Amaral, T. G.; Crisóstomo, M. M. & Pires, V. F. (2002b). Helicopter Motion Control Using Adaptive Neuro-Fuzzy Inference Controller. *The 28th Annual Conference of the IEEE Industrial Electronics Society, IECON'02, pp.2090-2095*, Sevilla, Spain, November 2002.

Amaral, T. G.; Pires, V. F.; Martins, J. F.; Pires, A. J. & Crisóstomo, M. M. (2007). Statistic Moment Based Method for the Detection and Diagnosis of Induction Motor Stator Fault. *International Conference on Power Engineering, Energy and Electrical Drives, POWERENG'07, pp.106-110*, Setúbal, Portugal, April 2007.

Ballard, D. H. & Brown, C. M. (1982). *Computer Vision*, Prentice-Hall.

Bayindir, R. & Sefa, I. (2007). Novel approach based on microcontroller to online protection of induction motors, *Energy Conversion and Management, vol. 48, 3, pp. 850–856*, March 2007.

Bellini, A.; Filippetti, F.; Franceschini, G. & Tassoni, C. (2001). Quantitative Evaluation of Induction Motor Broken Bars by Means of Electrical Signature Analysis,

IEEE Transactions on Industrial Applications, vol. 37, no 5, pp. 1248–1255, Sep./Oct. 2001.

Benbouzid, M. E. H. (2000). A review of induction motor signature analysis as a medium for faults detection, *IEEE Transactions Industrial Electronics, vol. 47, no. 5, pp. 984–993*, Oct. 2000.

Bonnett, A. H. & Yungb, C. (2008). Increased Efficiency Versus Increased Reliability, *IEEE Industrial Applications Magazine, pp 29-36*, Jan/Feb 2008.

Cardoso, A. J.; M. Cruz, S. M. A.; Carvalho, J. F. S. & Saraiva, E. S. (1995). Rotor Cage Fault Diagnosis in Three-Phase Induction Motors by Park's Vector Approach, *IEEE Industry Applications Conference 1995, vol. 1, pp. 642–646*, 1995.

Çalis, H. & Çakır, A. (2008). Experimental study for sensorless broken bar detection in induction motors, *Energy Conversion and Management, vol. 49, 4, pp. 854–862*, April 2008.

Chen, C. H. (1996). Fuzzy Logic and Neural Network Handbook, McGraw-Hill.

Çolak, I.; Çelik, H.; Sefa, I. & Demirbas, S. (2005). On line protection systems for induction motors, *Energy Conversion and Management, vol. 46, 17, pp. 2773–2786*, Octuber 2005.

Driankov D.; Hellendoorn H. & Reinfrank M. (1993). *An Introduction to Fuzzy Control*, Springer-Verlag.

Dister, C. J. & Schiferl, R. (1998). Using temperature, voltage, and/or speed measurements to improve trending of induction motor rms currents in process control and diagnostics, *Proceedings of the IEEE – IAS annual meeting conference, vol. 1, pp 312-318*, October 1998.

Hadremi, B. M. El (2000). A review of induction motor signature analysis as a medium for fault detection, *IEEE Transactions on Industrial Electronics, vol. 47, pp 984-993*, October 2000.

Haji, M. & Toliyat, H. A. (2001). Pattern recognition-a technique for induction machines rotor broken bar detection, *IEEE Transactions on Energy Conversion, vol. 16, no 4, pp. 312–317*, December 2001.

Henao, H.; Demian, C. & Capolino, G. A. (2003). A frequency domain detection of stator winding faults in induction machines using an external flux sensor, *IEEE Transactions on Industry Applications, vol. 39, no 5, pp. 1272-1279*, September/October 2003.

Kliman, G. B. & Stein, J. (1992). Methods of motor current signature analysis, *Electric Machines and Power Systems, vol. 20, n°5, pp 463-474*, September 1992.

Kliman, G. B.; Koegl, R. A.; Stein, J.; Endicott, R. D. & Madden, M. W. (1988). Noninvasive detection of broken rotor bars in operating induction motors, *IEEE Transactions on Energy Conversion, vol. EC-3, no. 4, pp. 873–879*, December 1988.

Li,W. (2006). Detection of Induction Motor Faults: A Comparison of Stator Current, Vibration and Acoustic Methods, *Journal of Vibration and Control, vol. 12, no. 2, pp. 165–188*, February 2006.

Martins, J. F.; Pires, V. F. & Pires, A. J. (2007). Unsupervised Neural-Network-Based Algorithm for an On-Line Diagnosis of Three-Phase Induction Motor Stator Fault, *IEEE Transactions on Industrial Electronics, vol. 54, pp. 259–264*, February 2007.

Nandi, S. & Toliyat, H. A. (1999). Condition monitoring and fault diagnosis of electrical machines - A review, *IEEE Industry Applications Conference 1999, vol. 1, pp. 197–204,* 1999.

Nauck, D.; Klawon, F. & Kruse, R. (1997). *Foundations of Neuro-Fuzzy Systems,* John Wiley & Sons.

Nejjari, H. & Benbouzid, M. (2000). Monitoring and Diagnosis of Induction Motors Electrical Faults Using a Current Park's Vector Pattern Learning Approach, *IEEE Transactions on Industry Applications, vol. 36, pp. 730–735,* May/June 2000.

Ondel, O.; Boutleux, E. & Clerc, G. (2006). A method to detect broken bars in induction machine using pattern recognition techniques, IEEE Trans. Industry Applications, vol. 42, no 4, pp. 916–923, July-August 2006.

Pires, D. F.; Pires, V. F.; Martins, J. F. & Pires, A. J. (2009). Rotor Cage Fault Diagnosis in Three-Phase Induction Motors Based on a Current and Virtual Flux Approach, *Energy Conversion and Management, vol. 50, 4, pp. 1026-1032,* 2009.

Riley, C. M.; Lin, B. K.; Habetler, T. G. & Kliman, T. G. (1999). Stator Current Harmonics and their Causal Vibrations: A Preliminary Investigation of Sensorless Vibration Monitoring Applications, *IEEE Transactions on Industry Applications, vol. 35, n° 1, pp. 94–99, January/February 1999.*

Schoen, R. S.; Habetler, T. G.; Kamran, F. & Bartheld, R. G. (1995). Motor Bearing Damage Detection Using Stator Current Monitoring, *IEEE Transactions on Industrial Applications, vol. 31, no 6, pp. 1274–1279,* November/December 1995.

Specht, D. F. (1991). A General Regression Neural Network, *IEEE Transactions on Neural Networks, vol. 2, n°. 6, pp. 568-576,* November 1991.

Tavner P. J. & Penman, J. (1987). *Condition Monitoring of Electrical Machines,* New York: Wiley, 1987.

Thorsen, O. V. & Dalva, M. (1995). A survey of faults on induction motors in offshore oil industry, petrochemical industry, gas terminals, and oil refineries, *IEEE Transactions on Industrial Applications, vol. 31, no 5, pp. 1186–1196,* September/October 1995.

Thomson, W. T. (1999). A review of on-line condition monitoring techniques for three-phase squirrel cage induction motors—Past present and future, *IEEE Symposium on Diagnostics for Electrical Machines, Power Electronics and Drives, vol. 7, pp. 3–18,* September 1999.

Thomson, W. T. & Fenger, M (2001) Current signature analysis to detect induction motor faults, *IEEE Industry Applications Magazine, vol. 7, pp. 26–34,* July-August 2001.

Toliyat, H. A. & Lipo, T. A. (1985). Transient analysis of cage induction machines under stator, rotor bar and end ring faults, *IEEE Transactions Energy Conversion, vol. 10, pp. 241–247,* June 1985.

Tsoukalas, L. T. & Uhrig, R. E. (1997). *Fuzzy and Neural Approaches in Engineering,* John Wiley & Sons, Inc..

Zidani, F.; Benbouzid, M.; Diallo, D. & Nait-Said, M. (2003). Induction Motor Stator Faults Diagnosis by a Current Concordia Pattern-Based Fuzzy Decision System, *IEEE Transactions Energy Conversion, vol. 18, pp. 469–475,* December 2003.

Zidani, F.; Benbouzid, M.; Diallo, D. & Nait-Said, M. (2003). Induction Motor Stator Faults Diagnosis by a Current Concordia Pattern-Based Fuzzy Decision System, *IEEE Transactions on Energy Conversion*, vol. 18, pp. 469–475, December 2003.

## 12

Image Processing and Concentric Ellipse Fitting to Estimate the Ellipticity of Steel Coils

Daniel C. H. Schleicher and Bernhard G. Zagar
Johannes Kepler University (Institute for Measurement Technology)
Austria

1. Introduction

In this chapter a particular image processing problem existing in quality assurance for steel industry is addressed. Since the quality standards in steel industry are ever increasing, even steel industry starts to use machine vision systems to monitor their product quality. In case of steel coils a particular figure of merit in quality is the roundness (ellipticity) or lack thereof of the coil. The mathematical correct measure of the roundness is the eccentricity $e = \frac{\sqrt{a^2 - b^2}}{a}$, with the major semi axis a and the minor semi axis b. But the fastest way for the quality inspector is just to measure a and b of the coil and calculate their ratio $\epsilon = \frac{a}{b}$. If ϵ exceeds a set limit (≈ 1.03 measured at the innermost coil layer), the coil is considered as cull. As discussed by Schleicher & Zagar (2008; 2009a) the extraction of elliptic arc segments for the ellipticity estimation and the basic concentric ellipse fitting algorithm are the main parts of the algorithm estimating the coils ellipticity. Comparing to ordinary ellipse fitting tasks that require input data distributed over the whole circumference, the estimation of the ellipse parameters using only data forming low length arcs is a much more challenging problem. To achieve a precise estimation of the ellipticity the fact of the common center of the elliptic arcs is used by the concentric ellipse fitting algorithm to estimate the center of the coil precisely. The functionality of the algorithm is show based upon of real coil images.
Indeed some error sources reduce the accuracy, which are discussed at the end of the chapter. The chapter is organized as follows: First the image acquisition system is described. Then the algorithm is explained consecutively in Sec. 3. Further sources of different errors are investigated in Sec. 4. Finally major results are presented (Sec. 5) and a conclusion (Sec. 6) is given

2. Image acquisition system

The image acquisition setup shown in Fig. 1a consists of a camera placed on a tripod, a laser trigger unit to initiate the acquisition and a laptop to store, process and view the images. A single image frame $I_{raw}(x,y)$ of the coil is acquired, when the coil transported by a lifting ramp reaches its end position triggering a light barrier. The camera is a 1/2" monochrome firewire camera (AVT Guppy 146–B) with 1392×1040 pixels. Its optical zoom is adjusted so as to image the biggest coil full frame, which has an outer diameter of 2 m. The sheet metal layers are 0.5 to 2.5 mm thick and the inner diameter of each coil is known to be 0.6 m. To ensure a circular image of a truly circular coil, the camera chip plane must be oriented parallel to the coils front side (Scheimpflug condition (Luhmann, 2003, p.147)). Figure 2 shows the camera coordinate system $\{\vec{e}_x,\vec{e}_y,\vec{e}_z\}$ in relation to the world coordinate system $\{\vec{e}_\xi,\vec{e}_\eta,\vec{e}_\zeta\}$, where the ξ, η-plane (coil front side) is kept parallel to the $\vec{e}_x$, $\vec{e}_y$-plane (camera chip). To assure the correct alignment of the camera, a spirit level was used to do the horizontal alignment ($\vec{e}_x,\vec{e}_z$-plane). Furthermore the horizontal edges of the coils carrier were used to align the rotation about the $\vec{e}_y$-axis that the coils front side is parallel to the camera chip plane. With this setup the image $I_{raw}(x,y)$ is acquired and processed by the algorithm in the next section.

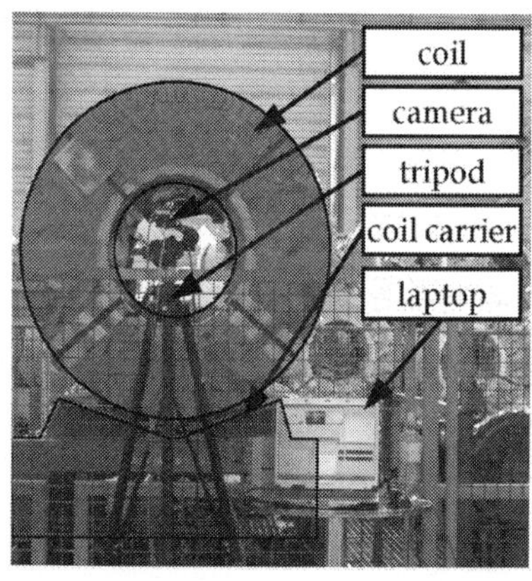

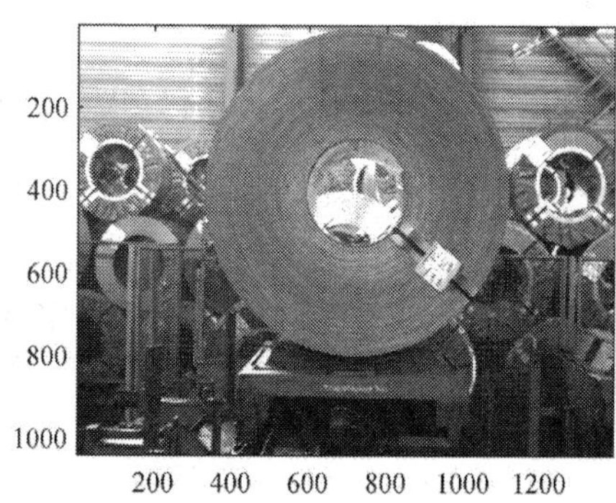

(a) The the image $I_{raw}(x,y)$ of the coil is captured by a firewire camera when the lift stops.

(b) Captured image $I_{raw}(x,y)$.

Fig. 1. Image acquisition setup (a) and typical captured image (b).

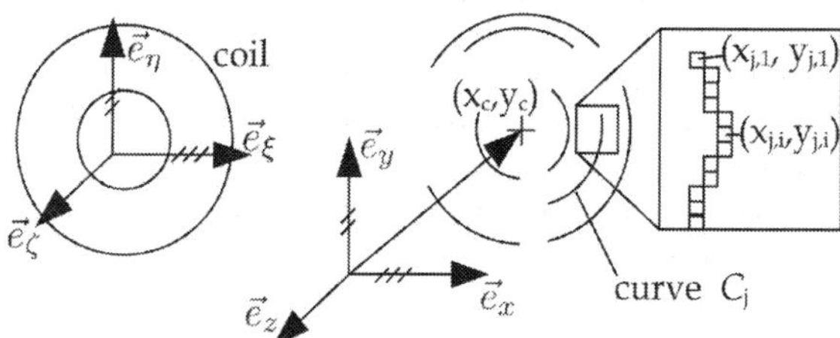

Fig. 2. The cameras $\vec{e}_x$, $\vec{e}_y$-plane is oriented parallel to the coils front side $\vec{e}_\xi,\vec{e}_\eta$ – plane.

3. Algorithm

The block diagram of the algorithm, shown in Fig. 3, reflects the structure of this section. The preprocessing, circular hough transform and extraction of all curve segments C_a are applied on the pixel level and then a reduced dataset of selected curve segments C_s is used for the ellipticity estimation.

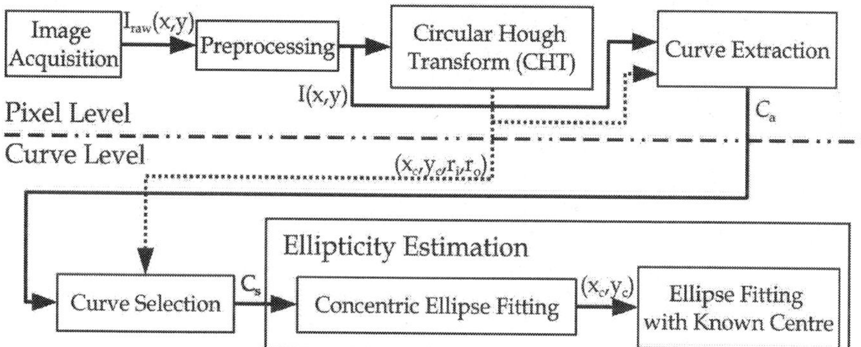

Fig. 3. Block diagram of the algorithm to estimate ellipticities. The preprocessing is done at pixel level prior to the ellipticity estimation done at curves level.

3.1 Preprocessing

The first preprocessing step is to crop $I_{raw}(x,y)$ to the region of interest, which fits the biggest coil to capture. Further the unsharp masking sharpening algorithm Eqn 1 (Jain, 1989, pp.249– 251) is used to boost the edges of the coil.

$$I(x,y) = I_{raw}(x,y) + \lambda G(x,y) \tag{1}$$

where $G(x,y)$ is the discrete Laplacian

$$G(x,y) = I_{raw}(x,y) - \frac{1}{4}\left[I_{raw}(x-1,y) + I_{raw}(x,y-1) + I_{raw}(x+1,y) + I_{raw}(x,y+1)\right] \tag{2}$$

of the raw image. The parameter λ determines the sharpening power of the algorithm. Setting λ too large leads to a very noisy image result, since the Laplacian is very sensitive to noise. Since the sharpening process is similar to a high pass filter, any influence of the inhomogeneous natural lighting is reduced.

The next important preprocessing step is the segmentation of the image into background and foreground pixels (front side highlighted in Fig. 1a). Usually this is done by comparing the actual image to a background image only (Zivkovic, 2004). Since only a single image of the coil is available this procedure can not be applied and the results of the circular hough transform are used to first find the coils center and then to segment the coils front side, which is described in the next section.

3.2 Circular Hough Transform (CHT)

The circular Hough transform (Illingworth & Kittler, 1987; Peng, 2007; Peng et al., 2007) is a transform mapping points in the x,y–plane belonging to circular slopes into parameter space. Thus filling a so called accumulator. A circle in x,y–space can be described by

$$(x - x_c)^2 + (y - y_c)^2 = r^2 \tag{3}$$

In parameter space it is then (x_c,y_c, r). This 3D parameter space can be reduced to a 2D with (x_c,y_c), we incorporate the constraint that the vectors, which are normal to the circle boundary, must all intersect at the circle center (x_c, y_c). Figure 4 illustrates this relation between the circle and its center. These normal directions can be obtained by local gray-level detection operators. The normal direction can also be expressed by

$$\tan\theta = \frac{y - y_c}{x - x_c}.$$

(4)

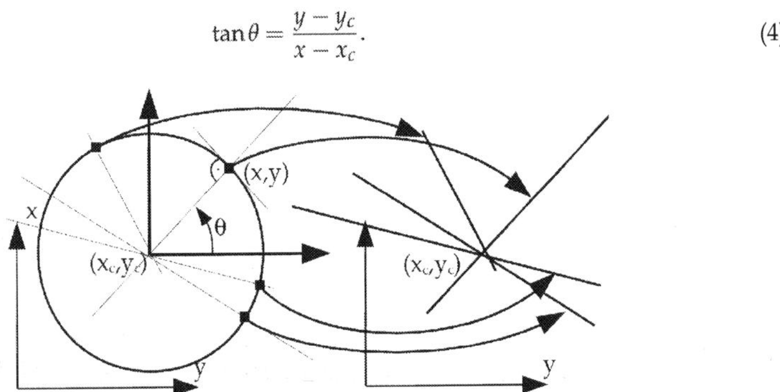

Fig. 4. Circle parameters for the circular Hough transform. The points on the circle (x,y) in image space is mapped onto a line in the accumulator.

Rearranging Eqn 4 yields

$$y_c = x_c \tan\theta + (y - x\tan\theta)$$

(5)

and transfers the problem in a form similar to the well known (line) Hough transform (HT). The accumulator of the HT, where the circles centers $(\hat{x}_c, \hat{y}_c)$ is determined by the peak, is shown in Fig. 5a. Since the determined center is only a rough estimate (denoted by ^), the center (x_c, y_c). After incorporating the circle center $(\hat{x}_c, \hat{y}_c)$ in Eqn 3, the radius can be found by histogramming, $r^2 = (x - \hat{x}_c)^2 + (y - \hat{y}_c)^2$. This histogram, also called signature curve, shown in Fig. 5b; is used to obtain an estimate for the inner radius r_i aswell as the outer

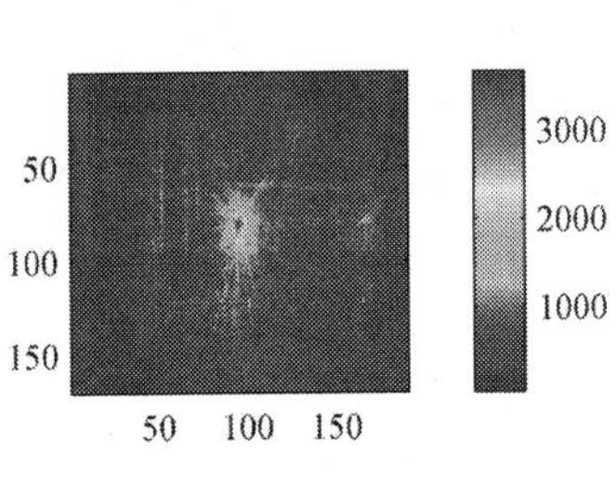

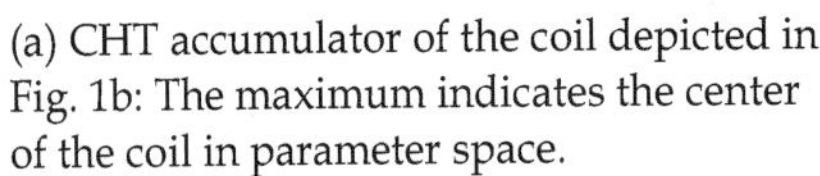

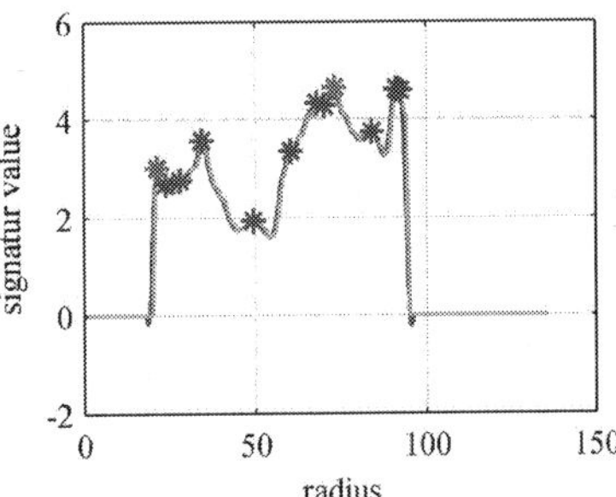

(a) CHT accumulator of the coil depicted in Fig. 1b: The maximum indicates the center of the coil in parameter space.

(b) Signature curve: Maxima indicate strong radii of circles. Signature curve (green) and smoothed signature curve (blue) with local maxima (blue asterisk) and selected maxima for inner and outer mask radius (red asterisk).

Fig. 5. Accumulator and signature curve of the CHT of sample image of Fig. 1b.

radius r_o (marked by a red asterisk). Local maxima in the signature curve are marked with a blue asterisk and signals the presence of a circular shape detected in the front side image.

To reduce the execution time of the CHT algorithm the preprocessed image $I(x,y)$ is resized (down sampled) to 150×170 pixels.

Due to the reduced image size the center estimation is only very rough, though fast. Furthermore the two stage concept causes the error of the center estimate to propagate further to the radius estimation in the signature curve. That's why the signature curve is not very reliable to return the proper real inner and outer radius, respectively. When no proper radii are found, the maximum coil size is chosen to segment the coil front side, since subsequent selection criteria will be applied to the curves before they are used for the fitting process.

3.3 Curve extraction

To extract arc curve segments at least of some of the sheet metal layers the Canny edge detector (Canny, 1986) is applied to $I(x,y)$. As a result this edge detector creates a binarized image $I_t(x,y)$ with thinned out edges. Due to the hysteresis threshold technique (Nixon & Aguado, 2002) implemented within the Canny edge detector, even weak edges are reliably extracted. As a drawback however, some edges, especially those resulting from rather weak gradients, have ramifications and squiggles that need to be taken care of.

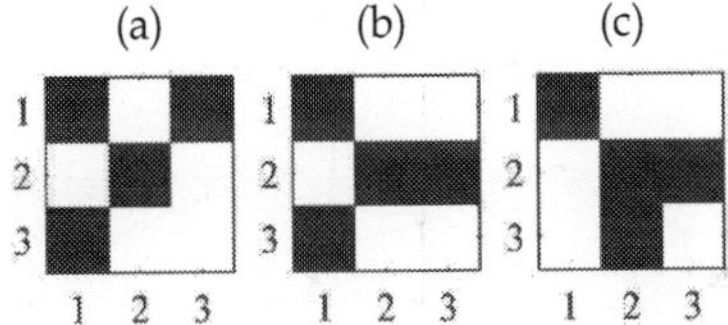

Fig. 6. Different 3 ×3 erosion masks M_1... (a), M_2... (b), M_3... (c), are used to erode all possible types of ramifications of a thinned binary image.

First the ramifications are removed by erosion (Gonzales & Woods, 2002, pp. 525–527) with the templates shown in Fig. 6 and their permutations by 0°, 90°, 180°and 270°.

$$I_c(x,y) \;=\; I_t(x,y) - \sum_{M=\{M_1,M_2,M_3\}} \sum_{\phi=\{0°,90°,180°,270°\}} I_t(x,y) \ominus \mathrm{rot}(M,\phi) \qquad (6)$$

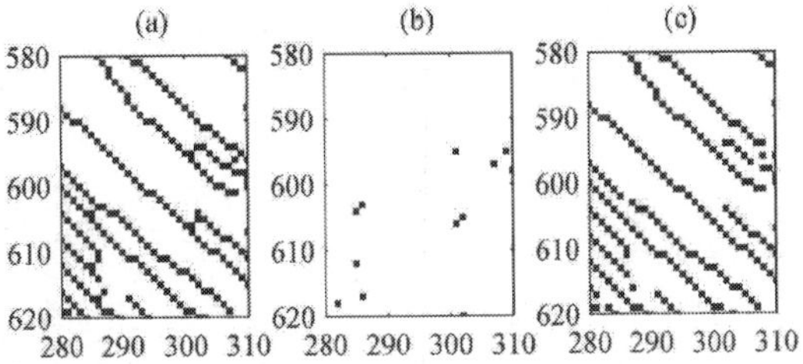

Fig. 7. (a) is a cutout of the thinned binary edge image $I_t(x,y)$, which is eroded by the templates shown in Fig. 6. (b) shows only points which are removed. (c) is the cutout of the resultant image $I_c(x,y)$ without ramifications (a)–(b)

After the erosion, the resultant image $I_c(x,y)$ contains only disrupted curve segments, which are remapped from the image matrix onto a curve set $C_a = c_1, \ldots, c_j, \ldots, c_J$, which contains all extracted curve segments denoted by c_j (See Fig. 7). The curve segment c_j is a $M \times 2$ vector containing the curve pixels coordinates.

3.4 Curve selection

Since the extracted curve set C_a also contains curves derived from the edges of the coils tapes or packaging labels, which must not be processed in the ellipticity estimation algorithm, these curves must also be remove to increase the quality of the estimators input data. Therefore figures of merits are calculated to select only those that are kept for further processing (C_s) and reject straight lines, rather short and very squiggled curves. Useful figures of merit are the curve length and the extend, which is the ratio between curve bounding box and curve length. Furthermore closed curve segments, with an eccentricity e of the ellipse that has the same second-moments as the region ($e = 0$ is actually a circle; $e = 1$ is an ellipse degenerated to a line segment) over a specific threshold (in this application 0.1 turned out to be useful), are also rejected (Rafael C. Gonzalez, 2003).

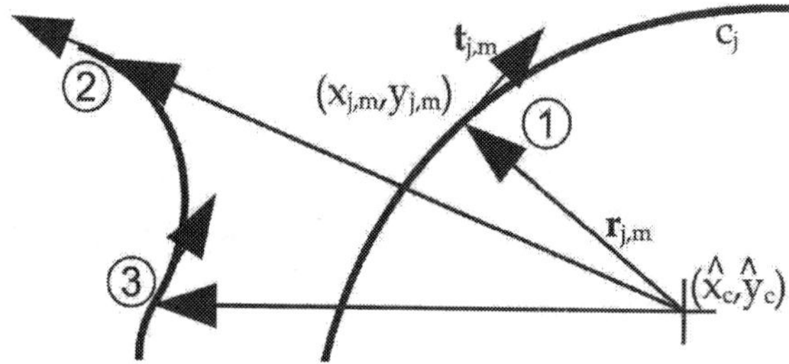

Fig. 8. The tangential vector of a circular arc is normal to the radius vector. (1) acts as a seed to an elliptic curve, (2) will be removed, (3) will be part of an elliptic curve, if it is connected to a seed point.

To select only elliptic arc segments which are part of the coil the scalar product of $\mathbf{n_r} = \mathbf{r}/|\mathbf{r}|$, the normalized radius vector, and $\mathbf{t}$, the tangential vector, is calculated for each point on each arc curve segment c_j. Figure 8 shows two curves with typical cases indicated. Concerning an ideal round coil, the scalar product $\mathbf{n_r} \cdot \mathbf{t} = 0$ for each arc segment. Since $\mathbf{n_r}$ and $\mathbf{t}$ are normalized, the range of the result of the scalar product is $[0, \ldots, 1]$. The subsequently applied hysteresis thresholding technique (Nixon & Aguado, 2002) returns only reasonable curve segments for the final ellipticity estimation algorithm.

3.5 Ellipticity estimation

To estimate the ellipticity ϵ an ellipse fit is applied to the dataset. Curve fitting is an extensive topic and even ellipse fitting is discussed in literature very detailed (Gander et al., 1994; Matei & Meer, 2000b; Leedan & Meer, 2000; Halir, 1998; Ahn et al., 2001; Nair & Saunders, 1996; Liu et al., 2006; Lei &Wong, 1999; Fitzgibbon et al., 1999; Halir, 1998).
The paper written by Gander et al. (1994), was one of the first that covered circle and ellipse fitting using least squares and iterative methods.

Figure 10 shows typical fitting results when applying the general ellipse fit algorithm to the previously extracted arc segment dataset C_s. Obviously, the common center of the coil can't be reliably determined, since the general ellipse fit algorithm is executed only for one arc segment at a time. This renders it necessary to consider additional constraints for the fitting algorithm and adopt it to use the whole dataset with all arc segments simultaneously.

In the following sections first the chosen curve fitting algorithm is described on a general way. Then the general, the simple and the new concentric ellipse fit, which incorporates the fact of the common coil center, is described in more detail.

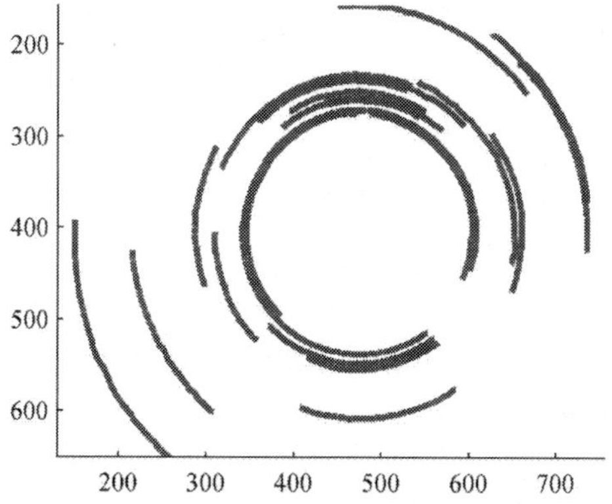

Fig. 9. Plot of the selected elliptic curve segments C_s used for the subsequent ellipticity estimation.

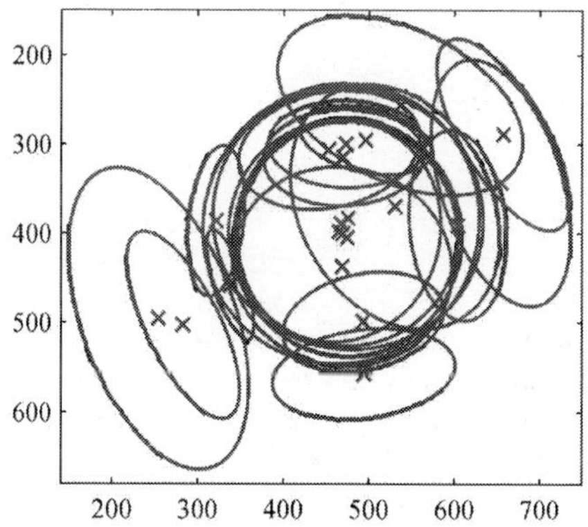

Fig. 10. Ellipse fitting of curve segments without any constraints leads to unusable results for the ellipticity estimation problem of a coil.

3.5.1 Curve fitting

Before doing the ellipse fit, a short introduction into curve fitting will be given. Therefore the same notation as proposed by Chernov (2007) will be used.

The principal equation for algebraic curve fitting is

$$\mathbf{u(x)}^\mathrm{T}\mathbf{\Theta} = 0, \tag{7}$$

with $\mathbf{u(x)} = [u_1(\mathbf{x}), \ldots, u_L(\mathbf{x})]^T$, which is the data transformed in a problem-dependent manner and $\mathbf{\Theta} = [\theta_1, \ldots, \theta_L]^T$, which contains the L unknown variables. The measured data vector $\mathbf{x} = [x_1, \ldots, x_I]^T$ is an I element long vector, assumed to represent the true data $\bar{x}_i$ corrupted by some random noise δx_i (here assumed to be normally distributed with $N(0, \sigma^2 \mathbf{I})$).

$$x_i = \bar{x}_i + \delta x_i, \quad i = 1, \ldots, I. \tag{8}$$

To estimate $\mathbf{\Theta}$ the approximate maximum likelihood (AML) method (Chernov, 2007) is used.

$$\mathcal{F}_{AML} = \sum_{i=1}^{I} \frac{\mathbf{\Theta}^T \mathbf{u}(\mathbf{x}_i) \mathbf{u}(\mathbf{x}_i)^T \mathbf{\Theta}}{\mathbf{\Theta}^T [\nabla_\mathbf{x} \mathbf{u}(\mathbf{x}_i)][\nabla_\mathbf{x} \mathbf{u}(\mathbf{x}_i)]^T \mathbf{\Theta}} \tag{9}$$

$$= \frac{\mathbf{\Theta}^T \mathbf{A}_i \mathbf{\Theta}}{\mathbf{\Theta}^T \mathbf{B}_i \mathbf{\Theta}} \to \min, \tag{10}$$

The square matrices $\mathbf{A}_i$ and $\mathbf{B}_i$ depend only on $\mathbf{x}_i$ and have the size $L \times L$.

$$\mathbf{A}_i = \mathbf{u}(\mathbf{x}_i)\mathbf{u}(\mathbf{x}_i)^T \tag{11}$$

$$\mathbf{B}_i = [\nabla_\mathbf{x}\mathbf{u}(\mathbf{x}_i)][\nabla_\mathbf{x}\mathbf{u}(\mathbf{x}_i)]^T \tag{12}$$

Using these matrices for the representation of the input data many popular schemes can be used to solve the minimization problem:

- (TAU) Taubin's fit (Taubin, 1991)
- (HEIV) Heteroscedastic errors–in–variables (Leedan & Meer, 2000; Matei & Meer, 2000a)
- (FNS) Fundamental numerical scheme (Chojnacki et al., 2001; 2005; 2004)
- (RED) Reduced scheme (Kanatani, 2005)
- (REN) Renormalization procedure (Kanatani, 2005; 1997; 2008)

All of the above algorithms were tested for the concentric ellipse fitting problem and only REN showed unstable behavior. The other algorithms only vary in execution time and achieved accuracy, which is also dependent on the maximum number of iterations and the set tolerances. For additional information about these schemes we refer to Chernov (2007). In the following sections the way to obtain the $\mathbf{A}_i$ and $\mathbf{B}_i$ matrices, $\nabla_\mathbf{x}\mathbf{u}(\mathbf{x}_i)$ and $\mathbf{u}(\mathbf{x}_i)$, respectively, will be described.

3.5.2 General ellipse fitting

A general ellipse can be described by the equation for the algebraic distance

$$F_{general}(x,y) = Ax^2 + Byx + Cy^2 + Dx + Ey + F = 0. \tag{13}$$

To obtain the unknown parameters $A, \ldots, F$ of Eqn 13 the AML method is used. Therefore the equation is written in terms $\mathbf{u(x)}$ and $\mathbf{\Theta}$.

$$\mathbf{x} = [x,y]^T; \tag{14}$$

$$\mathbf{u}(\mathbf{x}) = \left[x^2, xy, y^2, x, y, 1 \right]^T; \tag{15}$$

$$\Theta = [A, B, C, D, E, F]^T; \tag{16}$$

Further we obtain

$$\mathbf{A}_i = \mathbf{u}(\mathbf{x}_i)\mathbf{u}(\mathbf{x}_i)^T \tag{17}$$

$$= \begin{pmatrix} x_i^4 & x_i^3 y_i & x_i^2 y_i^2 & x_i^3 & x_i^2 y_i & x_i^2 \\ x_i^3 y_i & x_i^2 y_i^2 & x_i y_i^3 & x_i^2 y_i & x_i y_i^2 & x_i y_i \\ x_i^2 y_i^2 & x_i y_i^3 & y_i^4 & x_i y_i^2 & y_i^3 & y_i^2 \\ x_i^3 & x_i^2 y_i & x_i y_i^2 & x_i^2 & x_i y_i & x_i \\ x_i^2 y_i & x_i y_i^2 & y_i^3 & x_i y_i & y_i^2 & y_i \\ x_i^2 & x_i y_i & y_i^2 & x_i & y_i & 1 \end{pmatrix} \tag{18}$$

and

$$\mathbf{B}_i = \left[\nabla_{\mathbf{x}} \mathbf{u}(\mathbf{x}_i) \right] \left[\nabla_{\mathbf{x}} \mathbf{u}(\mathbf{x}_i) \right]^T \tag{19}$$

$$= \begin{pmatrix} 4x_i^2 & 2x_i y_i & 0 & 2x_i & 0 & 0 \\ 2x_i y_i & x_i^2 + y_i^2 & 2x_i y_i & 1 & 0 & 0 \\ 0 & 2x_i y_i & 4y_i^2 & 0 & 2y_i & 0 \\ 2x_i & 1 & 0 & 1 & 0 & 0 \\ 0 & 0 & 2y_i & 0 & 1 & 0 \\ 0 & 0 & 0 & 0 & 0 & 0 \end{pmatrix} \tag{20}$$

with

$$\nabla_{\mathbf{x}} \mathbf{u}(\mathbf{x}) = \left[\begin{array}{l} 2x, y, 0, 1, 0, 0 \\ 0, x, 2y, 0, 1, 0 \end{array} \right]^T. \tag{21}$$

3.5.3 Simple ellipse fitting

The denotation simple ellipse fitting (SEF) is used when the simplest form of an ellipse, with the center at the origin (0,0) and no rotation, is to be fitted. Equation 13 is then simplified to

$$F_{simple}(u,v) = Au^2 + Cv^2 + F = 0 = \frac{v^2}{a^2} + \frac{u^2}{b^2} - 1 = 0. \tag{22}$$

Here a and b are the major and minor semi axes and u and v are the coordinates related to the semi axis of the ellipse. To obtain u and v the ellipse must be centered in the origin thus:

$$v = x - x_c \tag{23}$$

$$u = y - y_c \tag{24}$$

For $\mathbf{A}_i$ and $\mathbf{B}_i$ calculated by Eqn 12 we further need

$$\mathbf{x} = [u,v]^T, \tag{25}$$

$$\mathbf{u}(\mathbf{x}) \;=\; \left[u^2, v^2, 1\right]^T, \tag{26}$$

$$\Theta \;=\; [A, C, F]^T, \tag{27}$$

and

$$\nabla_{\mathbf{x}}\mathbf{u}(\mathbf{x}) \;=\; \left[\begin{array}{c} 2u, 0 \\ 0, 2v \end{array}\right]^T \tag{28}$$

to calculate $\mathbf{A_i}$ and $\mathbf{B_i}$.

3.5.4 Concentric ellipses fitting

The concentric ellipse fit takes the whole dataset C_s of the coils elliptic arc segments into account, in contrast to the previously discussed algorithms, which use only one curve segment at a time. Thereby a highly precise center estimation is possible. To achieve this, some simplifications needs to be made:

- The rotation of the ellipses is zero.
- The ellipticity of all elliptic curve segments is equal.

For a typical coil the first assumption is justifiable since mainly the acting force of gravity determines the orientation of the semi major axis to be horizontal. Further the requirement of constant ellipticity for all elliptic curve segments doesn't hold here exactly and will cause a small error, but the center estimation is not affected by this fact (Schleicher & Zagar, 2009b).

First Eqn 13 is rewritten using the center coordinate (x_c, y_c) and the semi axes a and b.

$$\begin{aligned}
F_1(x,y) \;&=\; \frac{1}{a^2}(x - x_c)^2 + \frac{1}{b^2}(y - y_c)^2 - 1 = 0 \\[2mm]
&=\; \underbrace{\frac{1}{a^2}}_{A}\, x^2 + \underbrace{\frac{1}{b^2}}_{C}\, y^2 \underbrace{-\frac{1}{a^2}2x_c}_{D}\, x \\[2mm]
&\quad \underbrace{-\frac{1}{b^2}2y_c}_{E}\, y + \underbrace{\frac{1}{a^2}x_c^2 + \frac{1}{b^2}y_c^2 - 1}_{F} = 0
\end{aligned} \tag{29}$$

Introducing $\epsilon = \frac{a}{b}$ and factorizing $\frac{1}{b^2}$ leads to

$$\begin{aligned}
F_1(x,y) \;&=\; \frac{1}{b^2}\Big(\underbrace{\frac{1}{\epsilon^2}}_{A'}\, x^2 + \underbrace{1}_{C'}\, y^2 \underbrace{-\frac{1}{\epsilon^2}2x_c}_{D'}\, x \\[2mm]
&\quad \underbrace{-2y_c}_{E'}\, y + \underbrace{\frac{1}{\epsilon^2}x_c^2 + y_c^2 - b^2}_{F'} \Big)
\end{aligned} \tag{30}$$

Concerning Eqn 30 the newly introduced parameters $A', \ldots, E'$ are independent on b, while F' contains the curve dependent parameter b. Therefore Θ must now be written as

$$\Theta \;=\; \left[A', C', D', E', F_1', \ldots, F_j', \ldots, F_j'\right]^T \tag{31}$$

using all curve segments in the dataset C_s, which is indexed as follows: The dataset contains J curves indexed by j, where curve j has M_j points. A point on curve j is denoted by $(x_{j,m}, y_{j,m})$, where m is the index of the point ($m = 1, \ldots, M$).

$$\mathbf{x}_i \;=\; \left[x_{j,m}, y_{j,m} \right]^T \tag{32}$$
$$\tag{33}$$

When concatenating the curves to the input data vector $\mathbf{x}$ a point is addressed by index i.

$$\mathbf{x} \;=\; \left[\begin{array}{l} x_{1,1}, x_{1,2}, \ldots, x_{1,M_1-1}, x_{1,M_1}, \ldots, x_{j,1}, \ldots, x_{j,M_j}, \ldots, x_{J,1}, \ldots, x_{J,M_J} \\ y_{1,1}, y_{1,2}, \ldots, y_{1,M_1-1}, y_{1,M_1}, \ldots, y_{j,1}, \ldots, y_{j,M_j}, \ldots, y_{J,1}, \ldots, y_{J,M_J} \end{array} \right]^T \tag{34}$$

$$\;=\; \left[\begin{array}{l} x_1, \ldots, x_i, \ldots, x_I \\ y_1, \ldots, y_i, \ldots, y_I \end{array} \right]^T \tag{35}$$

Furthermore $\mathbf{u}(\mathbf{x})$ must also be extended to

$$\mathbf{u}(\mathbf{x}_i) \;=\; \left[x_{j,m}^2, y_{j,m}^2, x_{j,m}, y_{j,m}, 0, \ldots, \underbrace{1}_{1\ \text{at index}(j+4)}, \ldots, 0 \right]^T . \tag{36}$$

In the general sense we can write

$$\mathbf{u}(\mathbf{x}_i) \;=\; \left[x_{j,m}^2, y_{j,m}^2, x_{j,m}, y_{j,m}, \delta(1-j), \ldots, \delta(J-j) \right]^T . \tag{37}$$

For the gradient we obtain

$$\nabla_{\mathbf{x}} \mathbf{u}(\mathbf{x}_i) \;=\; \left[\begin{array}{l} 2x_i, 0, 1, 0, 0, \ldots, 0 \\ 0, 2y_i, 0, 1, 0, \ldots, 0 \end{array} \right]^T . \tag{38}$$

Having $\mathbf{u}(\mathbf{x}_i)$ given the matrices $\mathbf{A}_i$ and $\mathbf{B}_i$ are calculated and Θ is estimated using one of the estimators described in Sec. 3.5.1.

Out of all parameters in Θ jointly estimated the center coordinate (x_c, y_c) and parameter ϵ and b are calculated.

First the parameter vector Θ is normalized so that C is set 1. By comparison of coefficients the center coordinate (x_c, y_c) are obtained:

$$x_c \;=\; -\frac{D'}{2A'} \tag{39}$$

$$y_c \;=\; -\frac{E'}{2} \tag{40}$$

Since the other parameters ϵ and b

$$\epsilon \;=\; \frac{1}{\sqrt{A'}} \tag{41}$$

$$b \quad = \quad \sqrt{A' x_c^2 + y_c^2 - F'} \tag{42}$$

$$= \quad \sqrt{A' \frac{D'^2}{4A'^2} + \frac{E'^2}{4} - F'} \tag{43}$$

are biased due to the (invalid) assumption of equal ellipticity of all segments the simple ellipse fit (Sec.3.5.3) is done for each curve separately, using the previously estimated center coordinate (x_c, y_c).

The result of the concentric ellipse fit followed by the simple ellipse fit, where the ellipticity ϵ_j for each curve segment is calculated (shown in Fig.13) and discussed after the error analysis in Sec. 5.

4. Error analysis

In the following sections the main error sources which influence the accuracy of the estimated ellipticity will be discussed.

4.1 Aliasing

When sampling in spatial coordinates the aliasing effect (Jähne, 2002; Burger & Burge, 2006) is similar to consider as the case in the time domain. To be able to reconstruct a sampled signal the sampling frequency f_s must be larger than twice the largest occurring frequency component f_c. In case of the coil image the thinnest sheet metal layer is 0.5 mm, which means $f_c = 0.5$ mm/layer. Since the Nyquist criterion is also valid for any orientation the spatial frequencies f_c must be multiplied by $\sqrt{2}$.

$$f_{cd} = f_c \sqrt{2} \tag{44}$$

For a coil with a diameter of 2 m a minimum camera chip size of

$$\frac{2000 \text{ mm}}{0.5 \text{ mm/layer}} \sqrt{2} \cdot 1 \text{ pixel/layer} \approx 5657 \text{ pixel} \tag{45}$$

in horizontal and vertical direction, respectively, is needed. This corresponds to a 32 Mpixel camera chip. Even if we neglect $\sqrt{2}$ –factor for the diagonal layers, we still would require a camera chip with $4000 \times 4000 = 16$ Mpixel.

Luckily the small axial displacement of the sheet metal layers with respect to each other causes some shadings which can be captured very good avoiding aliasing. Also the roughly–textured cut surface of most thick sheet metal layers improves the possibility to recognize a single layer. In the worst case when a coil has thin layers, these layers appear blurred in the image.

Further the goal is still to estimate the ellipticity and not to capture each layer. Assuming that the arc segment is recognized only by its shadow which extends from one layer to the next (one pixel = 2.5 mm in this setup), the relative error for the ellipticity is bounded by

$$f_\epsilon = \frac{\Delta \epsilon}{\epsilon} = \frac{\frac{a + \Delta a}{b} - \frac{a}{b}}{\frac{a}{b}} = \frac{\Delta a}{a} = 0.67\% \tag{46}$$

with the major semi axis a = 0.3 m and the arc displacement Δa = 2.5 mm. Considering f_ϵ this error is quite large for high precise ellipticity estimation.

4.2 Camera orientation

One possible error source is the miss–orientation of the camera. As described previously the camera chip plane should be oriented strictly parallel to the coils front side. Even when the setup is build up very carefully using a spirit level and using edges of the coils carrier for the adjustment, an error free orientation can not be obtained. For a circular coil, with radius r and a misalignment angle φ, a rough error estimate can easily be obtained:

$$\Delta\epsilon = \frac{r}{r\cos\varphi} - 1 = \frac{1}{\cos\varphi} - 1 \tag{47}$$

The angle φ can have any direction, since the semi major axis of the resulting ellipse is always r and the semi minor axis is $r\cos\varphi$. Assuming $\varphi = 1°$ leads to an error of 0.0152% and even a larger angle of 5°, which should be possible to underbid when adjusting the camera, leads only to 0.55%.

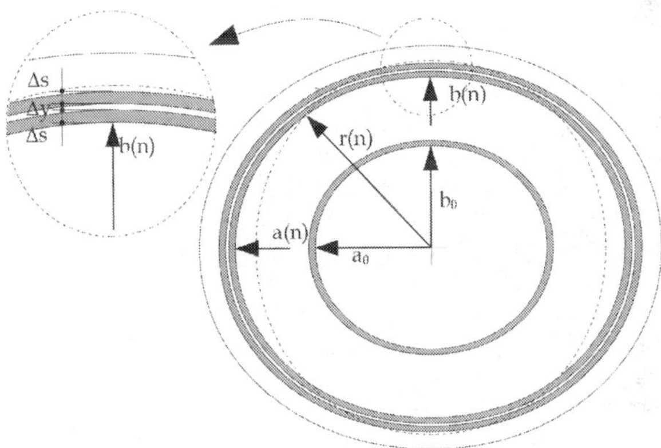

Fig. 11. Between each Δs thick sheet metal layer is a small oil gap Δy and Δx in x and y direction. a_n and b_n are the semi major and minor axes of the nth layer.

4.3 Ellipticity–radius dependency

The assumption of equal ellipticity for all arc segments made in Sec. 3.5.4 leads to a erroneous ϵ. Knowing the dimensions of the coil a simulation of the ellipticity progression can be done using the following model.

Assume an ideal circular coil with the inner radius r_i, outer radius r_o, metal sheet thickness Δs and initial oil gap Δr between the layers (see Fig.11). Approximating the layers of the coil, which in reality are forming an so–called Euler's–spiral, by concentric circular layers, the radius of the nth layer $r(n)$ is

$$r(n) = r_i + n(\Delta s + \Delta r). \tag{48}$$

The assumed maximum number of turns on the coil is

$$n_{max} = (r_o - r_i)/(\Delta s + \Delta r). \tag{49}$$

When applying a virtual vertically acting force (e.g. gravity) on this coil, it is compressed somewhat flat, the layers get elliptic and the oil gap $\Delta y(n)$ decreases in vertical direction while $\Delta x(n)$ increases in horizontal direction. Optionally, the oil gap can be modeled to be smaller at the middle layers, since there is a higher inner pressure caused by the winding action in production, by following equation:

$$\Delta y(i) = \Delta s \left[\alpha + (1 - \alpha) \frac{4(i - n_{max}/2)^2}{n_{max}^2} \right] \tag{50}$$

Or, since the oil gap is very small in ratio to the metal sheet thickness, to be a constant setting $\alpha = 1$. For the vertical minor semi axis of the coil we obtain:

$$b(n) = r_i/\beta + n\Delta s + \sum_{i=0}^{n} \Delta y(i) \tag{51}$$

where $\beta = \frac{r_i}{b(0)}$ is the compression ratio of the inner radius.

Since the mass of the circular coil m_c is equal to the mass of the deformed coil m_d, also the cut surface of the metal sheet layers must be the same ($\varrho \ldots$ density of steel, $w \ldots$ width of the coil).

$$m_c \ = \ m_d \tag{52}$$

$$\varrho w A_c \ = \ \varrho w A_e \tag{53}$$

The areas are calculated by

$$A_c(n) \ = \ \pi((r(n) + \Delta s)^2 - r(n)^2) \tag{54}$$

$$A_e(a(n), n) \ = \ \pi((b(n) + \Delta s) \cdot (a(n) + \Delta s) - b(n)a(n)) \tag{55}$$

Resolving $a(n)$ using Eqns 53, 54 and 55 we obtain

$$\epsilon(n) = \frac{a(n)}{b(n)} = f(r_i, r_o, \Delta s, \Delta y(n), \beta, n). \tag{56}$$

Figure 12 shows two simulations of the ellipticity dependency over the turn number for various coil parameter. The layer dependent oil gap $\Delta y(i)$ has the most effect on coils with thin metal sheets (see Fig. 12c vs. Fig. 12d). Generally the ellipticity decreases strongest within the first third of the radius. Setting $\Delta y(i) = 0.001$ mm and smaller gives similar results like shown in Fig. 12a. Since the exact conditions of the pressure distribution in the oil gap is unknown and no proper literature could be found considering this problem, this simulation can only give a qualitative evidence for the ellipticity progression.

4.4 Estimation errors

A comprehensive analysis of the estimation errors was done by Schleicher & Zagar (2009b), whose results are summarized in this section shortly. Using synthetic curve datasets, similar to C_s the different estimators where evaluated. First the CEF algorithm was applied onto 1500, 5000 and 20000 synthetic datasets. Then the Euclidean distance between d the true

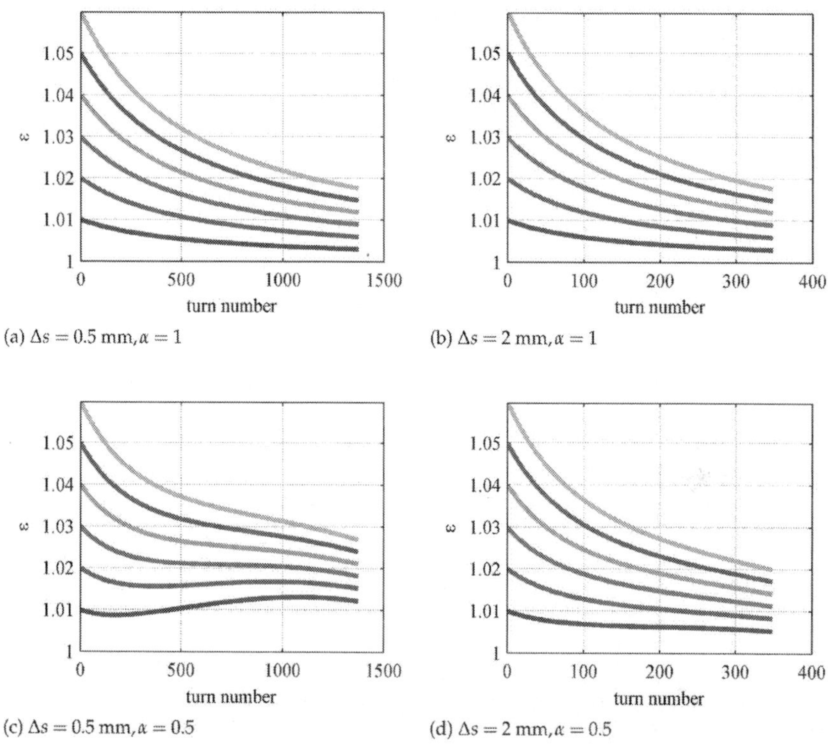

(a) $\Delta s = 0.5$ mm, $\alpha = 1$

(b) $\Delta s = 2$ mm, $\alpha = 1$

(c) $\Delta s = 0.5$ mm, $\alpha = 0.5$

(d) $\Delta s = 2$ mm, $\alpha = 0.5$

Fig. 12. Simulation of the ellipticity $\epsilon = f(n)$ for different inner ellipticities. ($\Delta y = 0.01$ mm, $r_i = 0.3$ m, $r_o = 1$ m, $\beta = (1.005, 1.010, 1.015, 1.020, 1.025, 1.030)$)

center $\bar{x}_c = (\bar{x}_c, \bar{y}_c)$ and estimated center $x_c = (x_c, y_c)$ was calculated, which corresponds to the error of the center estimation.

$$\mu_d = \mathrm{E}\{\|(\bar{x}_c - x_c|_{Alg.})\|_2\} \tag{57}$$

$$\sigma_d = \sqrt{\mathrm{Var}\{\|(\bar{x}_c - x_c|_{Alg.})\|_2\}} \tag{58}$$

With increasing number of datasets μ_d decreases, justifying and proofing that the CEF algorithm has no bias. Using the best performing HEIV algorithm an error of 0.00251 ± 0.251 pixel distance to $\bar{x}_c$ the was obtained. The variance was very similar for all algorithms and is probably limited by the quantisation of the dataset itself.

Furthermore the SEF algorithm was examined, concerning an erroneous center coordinate as input and arc segments with various center angles and lengths. The result was, that for a center displacement of $(1,1)$ (which is very large in relation to σ_d) the relative ellipticity error $f_\epsilon = \frac{\Delta\epsilon}{\epsilon}$ was smaller than $0.2 \pm 0.3\%$ for all algorithms (except Taubins) when curve segments with a length longer than $1/25$ of their circumference where used. Furthermore arcs symmetric around the ellipses apex lead to larger errors than others.

Fig. 13. Elliptic arc segments are extracted from the image of the coils front side, and used to estimate the ellipticity.

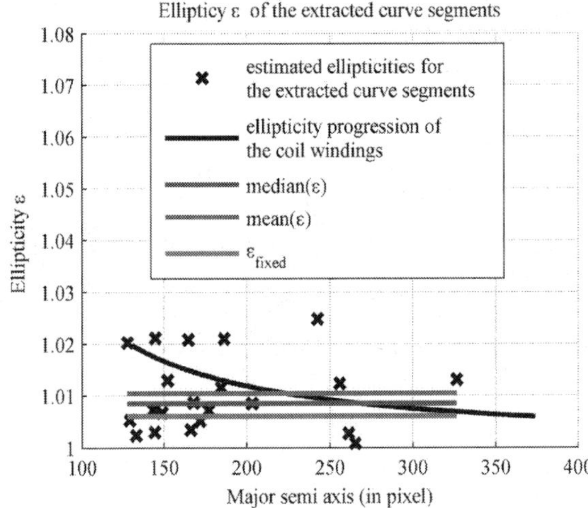

Fig. 14. The estimated ellipticities of the arc segments are plotted over the major semi axis.

5. Results

Figure 13 shows the results of the algorithm described in Sec. 3. The estimated parameters of the extracted curve segments are used to overlay the ellipses onto the image of the coils front side. Furthermore the estimated ellipticities ϵ_j are plotted over their major semi axis a_j in Fig. 14. Moreover some possible figures of merits, which could characterize the coils quality, are plotted. Depending on the extracted curve segments, the model of ellipticity progression derived in Sec. 4.3 fits more or less perfect. The main error source results from the low camera resolution, which might be changed in future when the cost of high resolution cameras decrease.

6. Conclusion

This chapter introduced the problem of ellipticity estimation on hand of a practical problem. To obtain a good ellipticity estimation proper datasets must be obtained. These datasets are generally not very easy to obtain, for which reason also the preprocessing to extract the datasets was discussed in detail. Since only arc segments could be used for the ellipticity estimation, normal ellipticy fits fail. Hence the estimation was split into two parts, first to estimate the center of the coil with the concentric ellipticity estimator and then to estimate the ellipticity of the arc segments. Using the general approach for the ellipse fit, enables also to use different solver implementations for fitting problems. When discussing the errors, it was accented that a lot of error sources affect the final result. The correct understanding of the partial errors helps to optimize the corresponding section of the algorithm.

7. Acknowledgment

At first the authors like to thank N. Chernov and Tao Peng for their support. Furthermore the authors gratefully acknowledge the partial financial support for the work presented in this paper by the Austrian Research Promotion Agency under contract grant 814278 and the Austrian COMET program supporting the Austrian Center of Competence in Mechatronics (ACCM). Last but not least the authors thank the company Industrie Logistic Linz (ILL) for its financial and technical support.

8. References

Ahn, S. J., Rauh, W. & Warnecke, H.-J. (2001). Least–squares orthogonal distances fitting of circle, sphere, ellipse, hyperbola, and parabola, *Pattern Recognition* 34(12): 2283–2303.

Burger, W. & Burge, M. J. (2006). Digitale Bildverarbeitung. *Ein Einführung mit Java und ImageJ*, 2 edn, Springer.

Canny, J. (1986). A computational approach to edge detection, *IEEE Trans. Pattern Anal. Mach. Intell.* 8(6): 679–698.

Chernov, N. (2007). On the convergence of fitting algorithms in computer vision, *J. Math. Imaging Vis.* 27(3): 231–239.

Chojnacki,W., Brooks, M. J., Hengel, A.&Gawley, D. (2001). Rationalising the renormalization method of Kanatani, *J. Math. Imaging Vis.* 14(1): 21–38.

Chojnacki, W., Brooks, M. J., Hengel, A. & Gawley, D. (2004). From FNS to HEIV: A link between two vision parameter estimation methods, *IEEE Transactions on Pattern Analysis and Machine Intelligence* 26(2): 264–268. URL: *http://www2.computer.org/portal/web/csdl/doi/10.1109/TPAMI.2004.1262197*

Chojnacki, W., Brooks, M. J., Hengel, A. & Gawley, D. (2005). FNS, CFNS and HEIV: A unifying approach, *J. Math. Imaging Vis.* 23(2): 175–183. URL: *http://www.springerlink.com/content/q1213191kjg81275/*

Fitzgibbon, A., Pilu, M. & Fisher, R. (1999). Direct least square fitting of ellipses, *IEEE Transactions of Pattern Analysis and Machine Intelligence* 1: 474–480.

Gander, W., Golub, G. & Strebel, R. (1994). Least–square fitting of circles and ellipses, *BIT* pp. 558–578.

Gonzales, R. C. &Woods, R. E. (2002). *Digital Image Processing, 2nd Edition*, Prentice Hall.

Halir, F. (1998). Numerically stable direct least squares fitting of ellipses, Proc. of the 6th International Conference in Central Europe on Computer Graphice, Visualization and Interactive Digital Media 1: 125–132.

Illingworth, J. & Kittler, J. (1987). The adaptive hough transform, *IEEE Trans. Pattern Anal. Mach. Intell.* 9: 690–698.

Jähne, B. (2002). Digitale Bildverarbeitung, 5 edn, Springer.

Jain, A. K. (1989). *Fundamentals of Digital Image Processing*, Prentice-Hall, Inc., Upper Saddle River, NJ, USA.

Kanatani, K. (1997). Statistical optimization and geometric visual inference, *AFPAC '97: Proceedings of the InternationalWorkshop on Algebraic Frames for the Perception–Action Cycle*, Vol. 1, Springer-Verlag, London, UK, pp. 306–322.

Kanatani, K. (2005). Further improving geometric fitting, Proc. 5th Int. Conf. 3–D Digital Imaging and Modeling 1: 2–13. URL: http://www2.computer.org/portal/web/csdl/doi/10.1109/3DIM.2005.49

Kanatani, K. (2008). Statistical optimization for geometric fitting — theroetical accuracy bound and high order error analysis, *Int J Comput. Vis* 80: 167–188.

Leedan, Y. & Meer, P. (2000). Heteroscedastic regression in computer vision: Problems with bilinear constraint, *Int. J. Comput. Vision* 37(2): 127–150. URL: *http://www.springerlink.com /content/w5g6738021123286/*

Lei, Y. & Wong, K. (1999). Ellipse detection based on symmetry, *Pattern Recognition Letters* 20: 41–47.

Liu, Z.-Y., Qiao, H. & Xu, L. (2006). Multisets mixture learning–based ellipse detection, *Pattern Recognition Letters* 39: 731–735.

Luhmann, T. (2003). Nahbereichsphotogrammetrie — Grundlagen, Methoden und Anwendungen, 2 edn, Wichmann.

Matei, B. & Meer, P. (2000a). A general method for errors–in–variables problems in computer vision, *In Proceedings, CVPR 2000, IEEE Computer Society Conference on Computer Vision and Pattern Recognition*, IEEE Computer Society Press, pp. 18–25.

Matei, B. & Meer, P. (2000b). Reduction of bias in maximum likelihood ellipse fitting, Pattern Recognition, 2000. Proceedings. 15th International Conference on, Vol. 3, pp. 794–798 vol.3. URL: http://ieeexplore.ieee.org/xpls/abs all.jsp?arnumber=903664 http://www.citeulike.org/user/jfmenudet/article/1639184

Nair, P. S. & Saunders, Jr., A. T. (1996). Hough transform based ellipse detection algorithm, *Pattern Recognition Letters* 17: 777–784.

Nixon, M. S. & Aguado, A. S. (2002). *Feature Extraction and Image Processing*, 1 edn, Newnes.

Peng, T. (2007). Detect circles with various radii in grayscale image via hough transform, *MATLAB Central File Exchange* .

Peng, T., Balijepalli, A., Gupta, S. & LeBrun, T. (2007). Algorithms for on–line monitoring of micro spheres in an optical tweezers-based assembly cell, *Journal of Computing and Information Science in Engineering* 7.

Rafael C. Gonzalez,Woods Richard E., E. S. L. (2003). *Digital Image Processing Using MATLAB*, Pearson Prentice Hall.

Schleicher, D. C. H. & Zagar, B. G. (2008). Image processing to estimate the ellipticity of steel coils using a concentric ellipse fitting algorithm, *Proc. of the 9th. International Conference on Signal Processing (ICSP08)*, Vol. 1, pp. 1203–1211.

Schleicher, D. C. H. & Zagar, B. G. (2009a). Ellipticity estimation on steel coils, *Proceedings of the 9th International Conference on Quality Control by Artificial Vision*.

Schleicher, D. C. H. & Zagar, B. G. (2009b). Error analysis and enhancing of the ellipticity estimation of steel coils. Accepted for IECON09.

Taubin, G. (1991). Estimation of planar curves, surfaces, and nonplanar space curves defined by implicit equations with applications to edge and range image segmentation, *IEEE Trans. Pattern Anal. Mach. Intell.* 13(11): 1115–1138.

Zivkovic, Z. (2004). Improved adaptive gausian mixture model for background subtraction, *Proceedings of the International Conference on Pattern Recognition*, Vol. 2, pp. 28–31.

13

On the Automatic Implementation of the Eye Involuntary Reflexes Measurements Involved in the Detection of Human Liveness and Impaired Faculties

François Meunier, Ph. D., ing.
Université du Québec à Trois-Rivières
Canada

1. Introduction

To this day and in spite aggressive publicity campaigns, impaired driving due to the consumption of legal/illegal drugs such as alcohol and cannabis remains a major cause of road casualties. In order to detect such impairments, police officers first rely on an array of movement coordination tests (Standard Field Sobriety Tests: SFST) which are most of the time applied at road side. If enough suspicions are raised from the first phase of tests, a second set of more reliable tests are conducted at a police station. A driver would then be subjected to an assessment by a Drug Recognition Expert (DRE) in order to determine the type of intoxication (category of drugs) a driver is under as well as his capacity to operate any type of motor vehicle.

In the present chapter as for the law enforcement community we define drugs as substance which, when taken into the human body, can impair the ability of a person to operate a vehicle safely. Drugs are mainly classified into seven categories, the Central Nervous System (CNS) depressants category includes some of the most abused drugs. Alcohol is considered the most familiar CNS depressants drug abused.

The development of the Standardized Field Sobriety Tests (SFST), which was largely done through extensive research efforts performed at the Southern California Research Institute (SCRI) (Burns, 1995); (Burns & Gould, 1997) was a critical step toward the development of the DRE procedures (Page, 2000). The DRE testing process involves twelve distinct components in which the examination of the eyes and dark room examination are parts. The examination of the eyes allows the detection of certain drugs since these drugs can produce very easily observable effects on the eyes. One of the most noticeable of these effects is the horizontal gaze nystagmus. A person under the influence of certain drugs such as alcohol usually will exhibit Horizontal Gaze Nystagmus (HGN) which is an involuntary jerking of the eyes that occurs as the eyes turn toward the side while gazing at an object. The dark room examinations can also allow the detection of certain drugs since it affects how the pupils will appear and how they respond to light stimuli. Some drugs will cause the pupils to dilate and other to constrict. By systematically changing the amount of light entering a person's eyes, one can also observe the pupil's appearance and reaction.

In order to detect drivers under the influence of substances, police officers use a standardized set of tests such as the Horizontal Gaze Nystagmus (HGN) test, the Vertical Gaze Nystagmus (VGN) test, the eye convergence test and the pupil's reaction to light tests. These tests are part of the more complete DRE procedures and are essentially applied manually by law enforcement officers to the eyes of a driver.

However, a study (Booker, 2001) analysing the effectiveness of the HGN test to detect alcohol related intoxication suggested that police officers rarely applied the HGN test according to the standard procedures, when trying to assess the degree of impairment of a driver. These inconsistencies in the administration of a test such as the HGN test could lead to erroneous diagnoses of the intoxication level of drivers.

In order to standardize the administration of the set of tests such as the HGN test involved in the DRE procedures, a first attempt to instrument the HGN test has been reported in experiments done at the Southern California Research Institute (SCRI) (Burns, 1995).

This chapter first describes the main approaches implemented in the literature to extract useful information from the eyes (pupils) of a human to allow the evaluation of his liveness and faculties. These eye-pupil related informations are mainly the involuntary reflexes such as the horizontal gaze nystagmus (HGN), eye divergence, pupil reaction to light, and the naturally occurring change of the pupil's diameter known as hippus. These involuntary reflexes are detected through the measurement of the gaze direction of the eyes while following specific visual stimuli and the pupil's diameter change resulting from the modulation of the illumination. Many researches in the field of automatic liveness and impaired faculty detection based on image processing and pattern recognition are outlined. Results of different approaches implemented in these fields are also presented. More specifically, the automatic detection of eye involuntary reflexes such as the hippus (pupil involuntary movement) and eye saccade (eye involuntary movement) are investigated in more details. The automatic detection of such eye reflexes are involved in the liveness detection process of a human which is also an important part of a reliable biometric identification system (Toth, 2005).

The present chapter also introduces existing video-based systems such as the one developed at the Southern California Research Institute (SCRI) (Burns, 1995) that are in general automating the detection of individual or few eye involuntary reflexes.

Moreover, in this chapter, a new video-based image processing system automating the implementation of the eye involuntary reflexes measurements extracted from the tests involved in the DRE procedures is proposed (Meunier, 2006; Meunier & Laperrière, 2008). This system integrates all the eye related involuntary reflexes measurements of the DRE procedures and is build around a video-based image processing system divided into three main modules, a video capturing module to grab videos of the eye movement following automatically generated visual stimuli, an image processing module that essentially extract information about the pupil such as the gaze direction and its size, a diagnosis module assesses the type of impairment of a person from the pupil's information extracted from the image processing module. This novel system must internally generate visual stimuli and captures video sequences of the eyes following and reacting to these visual stimuli. The video sequences are processed and analyzed using state of the art feature extraction techniques. In this present book chapter, the results outlined are obtained from the last updated prototype of the video-based image processing system described. This automatic human faculty assessment system tested is used in the context of alcohol related intoxication. This system was tested in experiments involving many subjects dosed to a blood alcohol concentration (BAC) in a wide range interval of 0.04% to 0.22%, and to show the efficiency of this system to detect alcohol intoxicated individuals at BAC above 0.08%. In order to demonstrate the effects of alcohol on the eye involuntary reflexes comparisons are made between pre-dose and post-dose BAC. This video-based image processing system was experimented with alcohol related intoxication for two reasons. First, the experimental data extracted in the experiments were correlated with Bulk Alcohol Concentration (BAC) measurements obtained with measurement devices such as the Breathalyser 900A or the Intoxilyser 5000 which are easy to use since they only require breath samples. Similar correlations are not so easy to perform for experiments with other drugs since blood or urine samples are often required. Second, the ethical certificates granted by the university authorities are easier to obtain in the case of alcohol workshops but far more difficult to obtain for other drug related workshops.

The present updated prototype of this video-based image processing system is an enhanced version of a previously developed automatic prototype that only implemented the HGN test (Meunier, 2006). The newly updated prototype is also a video-based image processing system but with added automated DRE tests (Meunier & Laperière, 2008). These added automated tests are the convergence test and the pupil's dark room examinations test. These added functionalities constitute an improvement over previous video-based systems (Burns, 1995); (Meunier, 2006) since these systems were dealing with fewer ocular properties limiting there ability to detect diverse intoxications. This new system also generates visual stimuli and captures video sequences of the eyes following and reacting to these visual stimuli. The ocular properties (signs) extracted from these new tests include convergence of the eyes, the pupil's reaction in room light, darkness and direct illumination.

During the step four (eye examinations) of the DRE procedures (Page, 2000) two separate eye movement examinations are conducted: the already known HGN (Meunier, 2006) and the eye convergence. During the HGN test a suspected impaired person is instructed to follow an object (pen or a pencil) that is moved horizontally in front of his eyes. During the eye convergence examination a subject is instructed to look at an object until that object is placed on the tip of the subject's nose. The step seven (Darkroom Examinations) of the DRE procedures enables the extraction of the pupil sizes. This test is administered by changing the amount of light directed to the pupils. With an alive, unimpaired healthy subject, the pupils enlarge in response to darkness and constrict to bright light. The pupils of an impaired person react differently to the light stimuli depending of the type of intoxication.

To implement the HGN and convergence tests, the automated system essentially extracts, the eye-gaze direction (angular position) of the pupils from video sequences of the eyes following visual stimuli. The analysis of these angular positions enables the detection of the saccadic motion of the eyes related to the horizontal gaze nystagmus and also the detection of the eyes convergence which in turn can enable the determination of the type of intoxication of a driver. The pupil's reaction to light is measured by extracting the radius of the pupils from video sequences of the eyes subjected to controlled illumination.

The new video-based image processing system outlined in this chapter has plenty of practical applications. As a decision support system to assist the law enforcement officers to evaluate the type of impairment of a driver, as an automatic impairment detection system to assess the capacities of an operator to operate a motor vehicle such as a bus, a subway train, a train, a plane, etc., or as a new version of ignition interlock system. This book chapter also provide a description of future research topics in the field of automatic liveness and human faculty detection.

2. Software and hardware requirements for the automatic implementation of eye involuntary reflexes measurements

The implementation of a video-based image processing system for the automation of the eye involuntary reflexes measurements requires three main modules, a video capturing module, an image processing module and a diagnosis module. The image processing module should offer some fundamental functionalities such as the segmentation of the pupils in each image frame of a video of the eye movement captured during the application of a specific DRE symptomatic test. Moreover, the gaze direction and the pupil's size are computed from the segmented pupils. The video capturing module must also provide some important functionalities. For instance, it must offer a physical environment such as a helmet or set of goggles in which the illumination devices required to test the pupillary reflexes are using the modulation of a visible spectrum light source (White LEDs). Therefore, the capturing device must be sensitive to the near-infrared (NIR) spectrum since the eyes have to be illuminated with NIR LEDs.

2.1 Software requirements: Image processing tools to extract pupil's information from images

2.1.1 Iris/Pupil region segmentation

In many researches (Ji & Zhu, 2004; Batista, 2005; Ji & Yang, 2002; Zhu & Ji, 2005; Li et al., 2004; Morimoto et al., 2000; Haro et al., 2000) the Dark/Bright pupil effect is used to segment the pupils in video images. This effect is obtained by illuminating the pupils with evenly and symmetrically distributed near-infrared (NIR) light emitting diodes (LED) along the circumference of two coplanar concentric rings. The center of both rings coincides with the camera optical axis. The bright pupils (Fig. 1 left) is produced when the inner ring centered around the camera lens is on and the dark pupil (Fig. 1 center) when the outer ring offset from the optical center is on. The pupil can be easily segmented by image subtraction (Fig. 1 right).

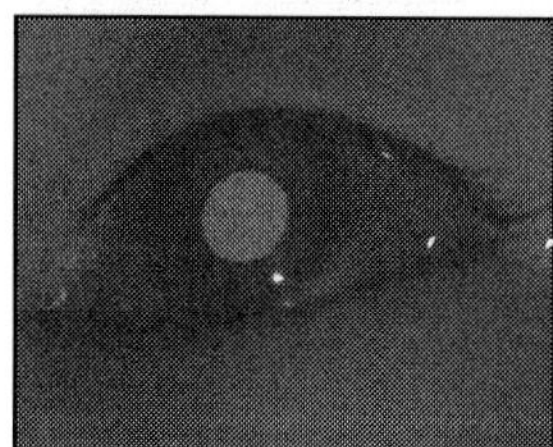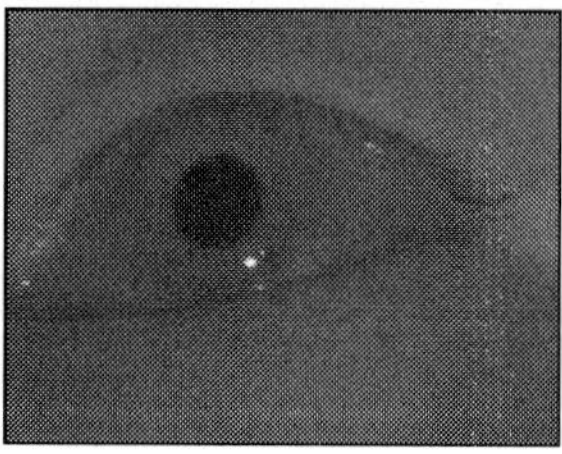

Fig. 1. Dark/Bright pupil effect and pupil segmentation.

Figure 1 (left and center) also reveals the presence of the first Purkinje image also called glint or corneal reflection. The glint is a high contrasted bright spot corresponding to the reflection of the NIR LED illuminators on the cornea surface. Since the 2D position of the glint is easy to find from frame to frame it can be useful for the estimation of the eye-gaze direction (Batista, 2005; Ohno & Mukawa, 2004; Ji & Bebis, 1999; Ji & Yang, 2002). The glint is easily detected in the dark pupil image (Fig. 1 center) using an image binary thresholding technique in the neighbourhood region of the pupils. The centroid of the segmented region of a glint is computed and gives its 2D position in an image.

The location of the eyes in a video image can also be achieved using a correlation process that maximizes the match between regions of interest (ROI) in the video image corresponding to the eyes and patterns (Fig. 2) that are reference images of an eye with different gaze directions (Matsumoto & Zelinsky, 2000; Zhu & Ji, 2005; Li et al., 2004). The results obtained from the correlation process are the 2D position of the eyes in the video image. Moreover, the patterns maximizing the match with the eye ROIs allow the estimation of the eye-gaze direction. We can also formulate the matching process as a minimization problem where the matching criterion E is the sum of squared difference errors given by:

$$E = \sum_{i=1}^{N} (I_P(i) - I_c(i))^2 \tag{1}$$

where $I_p(i)$ is the pixel value of the *ith* pixel of a given pattern image I_p, $I_c(i)$ the pixel value of an eye ROI in the current image frame, and N the total number of pixels in each pattern image and the eye ROI in the current image.

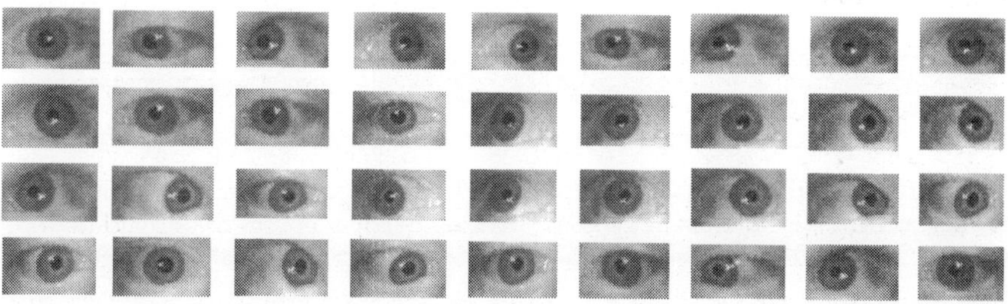

Fig. 2. Eye patterns with different eye-gaze directions.

Most of the approches implemented to locate the eyes and the pupils/irises in video image rely on the notion of image gradient (Sirohey et al., 2002; Peng et al., 2005; Ji & Bebis, 1999; Wang & Sung, 2001; Halir & Flusser, 1998; Smith et al., 2000; Li et al., 2004). The iris/sclera and iris/pupil borders exhibit a noticeable contrast that enables the detection of these borders using methods based on the image gradient. The image gradient can be expressed theoretically and numerically using the Sobel operator by:

$$\nabla I(x, y) = \left[\frac{\partial I(x, y)}{\partial x}, \frac{\partial I(x, y)}{\partial y} \right] \tag{2}$$

$$I_\theta(x, y) = \tan^{-1} \left(\frac{\dfrac{\partial I(x, y)}{\partial y}}{\dfrac{\partial I(x, y)}{\partial x}} \right) \tag{3}$$

$$\|\nabla I(x, y)\| = \sqrt{I_x^2 + I_y^2} \tag{4}$$

$$D_x = \begin{bmatrix} -1 & 0 & 1 \\ -2 & 0 & 2 \\ -1 & 0 & 1 \end{bmatrix}, D_y = \begin{bmatrix} -1 & -2 & -1 \\ 0 & 0 & 0 \\ 1 & 2 & 1 \end{bmatrix} \tag{5}$$

where ∇I is the gradient of the image $I(x,y)$ given by the image partial derivative in the x and y coordinate direction, $I_\theta(x,y)$ is the orientation of the gradient, $\|\nabla I\|$ is the magnitude of the gradient and D_x, D_y the numerical implementation of the partial derivative $\partial I/\partial x$ and $\partial I/\partial y$ of the Sobel operator. Figure 3 shows the result of the application of the Sobel operator on the dark pupil image depicted in Fig. 1 center that essentially allows the detection of the edge between the pupil/iris region. Figure 3 right shows the elliptic shape corresponding to the pupil contour. With its strong gradient the glint contour is also easy to detect.

Fig. 3. Pupil/Iris border detection (Sobel edge detection). (Left) Horizontal edge detection. (Center) Vertical edge detection. (Right) Gradient image.

The refinement of the location of the edges detected by the application of a Sobel gradient operator can be achieved using the Canny edge detection algorithm. The Canny edge detection starts by computing the gradient of an image and enhance the location of the original edges with a thinning and a thresholding phase to obtain finer edges. These refinement steps operate on the gradient magnitude computed in the linear filtering step and intend to use hysteresis thresholding on edge strength to only retain edge pixels for which the gradient magnitude reaches a maximum. Results of the application of the Canny edge detection algorithm applied to Fig. 1 center is shown in fig. 4. As the threshold value is increased, the preserved edges are stronger. With a threshold value of 60 (Fig. 4 center) the pupil /iris border is clearly observable with its elliptic shape. The glint (corneal reflection) can be also easily detected at a high threshold value and as previously mentioned is the strongest contrasted region (see Fig. 4 right).

Fig. 4. Canny edge detection algorithm. (Left) Edge detected with a threshold value of 20. (Center) Edge detected with a threshold value of 60. (Right) Edge detected with a threshold value of 80.

2.1.2 Circle/Ellipse detection and fitting

Some of the previously introduced techniques to extract iris/pupil edges and contours are used as pre-processing steps to circle/ellipse detection (Ji & Bebis, 1999; Wang & Sung, 2001; Smith et al., 2000; Li et al., 2004).

The circle/ellipse detection process can be done mainly in two different ways. A first approach (Halir & Flusser, 1998; Fitzgibbon et al., 1999) where the edge and contour pixels are fitted by a implicit second order polynomial given by:

$$F(x, y) = ax^2 + bxy + cy^2 + dx + ey + f = 0 \tag{6}$$

with the ellipse-specific constraint $b^2-4ac < 0$ and where a, b, c, d, e, f are the coeffcients of the ellipse and (x,y) the 2D position of the detected pixels at the edge/contour detection phase belonging to an elliptical 2D shape. The fitting of an ellipse to a set of 2D pixels consists in finding the coefficents of the polynomial $F(x,y)$ by a least-square minimization approach.

A second approach for circle/ellipse detection is based on the Hough transform (HT) (Guil & Zapata, 1996; Zhang & Liu, 2004). The main goal of this approach is to find the ellipse center position (x_0, y_0), the orientation of the ellipse θ and the semi-axis (a, b). Therefore, the Hough parameter space is 5-Dimensional with a parameter vector represented by $[x_0, y_0, \theta, a, b]$. The center of the ellipse can be found by searching the maxima of this Hough parameter space satisfying the following equation for each 2D pixel of the searched ellipse:

$$\frac{((x - x_0)\cos(\theta) + (y - y_0)\sin(\theta))^2}{a^2} + $$
$$\frac{((x - x_0)\sin(\theta) + (y - y_0)\cos(\theta))^2}{b^2} \tag{7}$$

where (x, y) are the edge 2D pixel coordinates, (x_0, y_0) is the ellipse center, $\theta \in [0, 2\pi]$ is the ellipse orientation, (a, b) the semi-axis lenghts.

2.1.3 Eye-gaze direction and pupil's size computation

The previously introduced Circle/Ellipse detection algorithms can be used to measure the pupil's size (diameter) and furthermore allow the measurement of the pupil's reaction to light reflexes or the hippus.

The eye-gaze estimation can be achieved by a linear mapping procedure (Ji & Bebis, 1999; Ji & Yang, 2002) using the relative position between the pupil and the glint. This mapping procedure can allow depending of the application, the estimation of the screen coordinates gazed by the eye, or the eye-gaze direction given by the horizontal and vertical pupil displacement angles. The mapping procedure is implemented by:

$$i = g \bullet w = a\Delta x + b\Delta y + cg_x + dg_y + e \tag{8}$$

with $g = [\Delta x, \Delta y, g_x, g_y, 1]$, the pupil-glint vector, where Δx and Δy are the pupil-glint displacements, g_x and g_y the glint image coordinates and $w = [a, b, c, d, e]$ the coefficients of the linear mapping equation and i the gaze region index corresponding to a given gaze direction.

The vector w is deduced through a calibration procedure that allows the modeling of the transformation from the pupil-glint matrix A to a target vector B given by:

$$A \bullet w = B$$

$$A = \begin{bmatrix} \Delta x_1 & \Delta y_1 & gx_1 & gy_1 & 1 \\ \Delta x_2 & \Delta y_2 & gx_2 & gy_2 & 1 \\ \vdots & \vdots & \vdots & \vdots & \vdots \\ \Delta x_{N-1} & \Delta y_{N-1} & gx_{N-1} & gy_{N-1} & 1 \\ \Delta x_N & \Delta y_N & gx_N & gy_N & 1 \end{bmatrix} \qquad (9)$$

During the calibration procedure a user is asked to gaze at N distinct targets on a screen while each pupil-glint image are captured. The matrix A is obtained from the computation of the pupil-glint vectors g with their corresponding target index allowing the creation of the vector B. The coefficient vector w is obtained by solving eq. (9) using a least-squares method.

Another way to compute the eye-gaze direction is through the pose-from-ellipse algorithm (Trucco & Verri, 1998; Ji & Bebis, 1999; Wang & Sung, 2001). The underlying problem consists in deducing the normal vector of a plane containing a circle shape such as an eye pupil which is depending of the eye-gaze direction imaged as an ellipse. The geometry of the pose-from-ellipse algorithm is illustrated in Fig. 5.

The image ellipse defines a 3D cone with vertex in the center of projection of the modeled pinhole camera. The orientation of the circle's plane (iris/pupil plane) is deduced by rotating the camera reference axis OXYZ in such a way that the original elliptic shape imaged in the image plane becomes a circle shape. This is achieved when the image plane is parallel to the circle plane. The equation of the 3D cone is given by:

$$ax^2 + bxy + cy^2 + dxz + eyz + fz^2 = P^T Q P = 0 \qquad (10)$$

where $P = [x, y, z]^T$ and Q is the real, symmetric matrix of the ellipse.

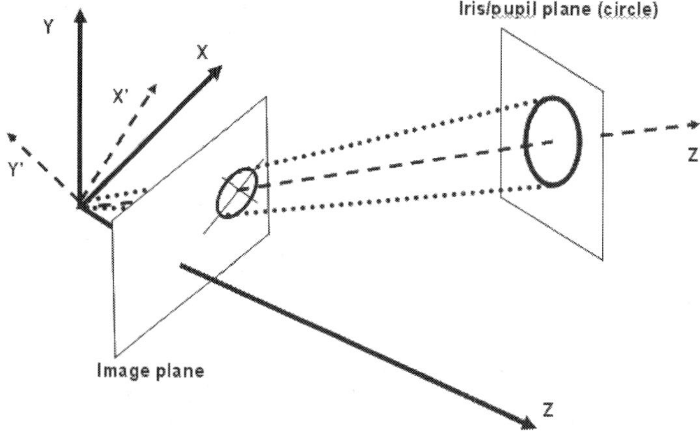

Fig. 5. Geometry of the pose-from-ellipse algorithm.

The normal n of the circle plane corresponding to the eye-gaze direction is given by:

$$R = \begin{bmatrix} e_1 \mid e_2 \mid e_3 \end{bmatrix} \begin{bmatrix} \cos\theta & 0 & \sin\theta \\ 0 & 1 & 0 \\ -\sin\theta & 0 & \cos\theta \end{bmatrix}$$

$$n = R \begin{bmatrix} 0 \\ 0 \\ -1 \end{bmatrix} = \begin{bmatrix} -R_{13} \\ -R_{23} \\ -R_{33} \end{bmatrix} \tag{11}$$

$$\theta = \pm \arctan \sqrt{\frac{\lambda_2 - \lambda_1}{\lambda_3 - \lambda_2}}$$

where λ_1, λ_2, λ_3 are the eigenvalues of Q deduced by diagonalizing the ellipse matrix Q, knowing that $\lambda_1 < \lambda_2 < \lambda_3$, and e_1, e_2 e_3 the corresponding eigenvectors.
A Hough based approach can also be used to compute the eye-gaze direction (Takegami et al., 2003). In order to compute the eye-gaze direction, the contour of each pupil is first located from video sequences. Each edge point composing a pupil's contour is assumed to be isolated. According to the Hough transform theory there could be an infinite number of ellipses that could pass through this edge point. The centers of these ellipses generate another ellipse known as a second layer ellipse. The second layer ellipse is deduced by the following expressions:

$$x = b_a.\cos\alpha \sqrt{\frac{r_0^2 - x_e^2 - y_e^2}{r_0^2}} \sqrt{\frac{x_e^2}{x_e^2 + y_e^2}} - b_a.\sin\alpha \sqrt{\frac{y_e^2}{x_e^2 + y_e^2}} + r_a \frac{x_e}{r_0}$$

$$y = b_a.\cos\alpha \sqrt{\frac{r_0^2 - x_e^2 - y_e^2}{r_0^2}} \sqrt{\frac{x_e^2}{x_e^2 + y_e^2}} + b_a.\sin\alpha \sqrt{\frac{y_e^2}{x_e^2 + y_e^2}} + r_a \frac{y_e}{r_0} \tag{12}$$

$$z = -b_a.\cos\alpha \sqrt{\frac{x_e^2 + y_e^2}{r_0^2}} + r_a \frac{\sqrt{r_0^2 - x_e^2 - y_e^2}}{r_0}$$

$$b_a = a_0 \frac{\sqrt{r_0^2 - a_0^2}}{r_0}$$

where (x_e, y_e) are the edge point coordinates, b_a is the current circle radius, r_a the distance between the cornea curvature center and the second layer ellipse, a_0 the pupil radius and r_0 the distance between the cornea curvature center and the pupil rim.
The application of the Hough transform algorithm allows the determination of the optimal pupil's center positions (x_0, y_0, z_0). These positions correspond to maximal counts in the (x, y, z) space generated by the application of eq. (12) for each pupil's contour point given their coordinates (x_e, y_e).
Since the position of the cornea curvature center is already known and the pupil's center (x_0, y_0, z_0) is deduced by the application of the Hough transform, the pupil's angular horizontal position (angle θ) can be easily computed by (Fig. 6):

$$\tan\beta = \frac{dy}{dx} \tag{13}$$

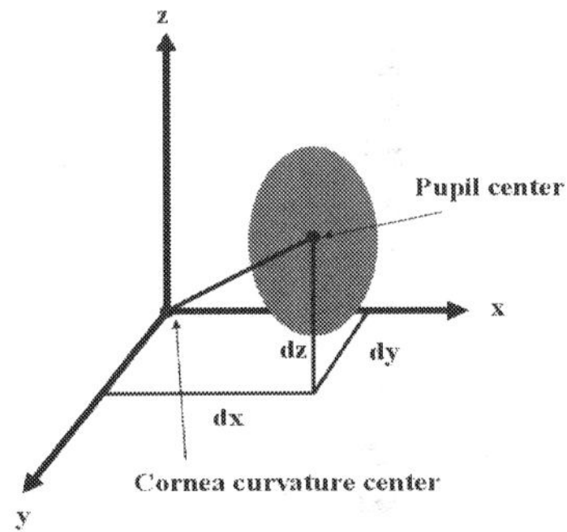

Fig. 6. Relative positions of the cornea curvature center and the pupil center.

2.2 Hardware requirements: Video-image capturing system

Few commercial and experimental systems that implement automatic detection of the eye involuntary reflexes to assess human liveness and impaired faculties actually exist. One of the first attempts to automatically apply the horizontal gaze nystagmus (HGN) test has been reported in another experiment done at the SCRI by Marceline Burns (Burns, 1995). This system also named ocular motor module (OMM) generates visual stimuli for testing eye movement. Volunteers look into a foam-lined viewport, which allows testing in complete darkness. The illumination is provided by near-infrared (NIR) light emitting diodes (LEDs). The video sequences are captured by a NIR sensitive video camera at a sample rate of 60 samples per second. The captured video sequences are further analyzed using feature extraction algorithms to obtain the eye related measurements required to implement the HGN test. The VideoNystagmoGraphy (VNG) ULMER from Synapsys is another system allowing the evaluation of vestibular functions and the detection of vertigo, dizziness and balance disorders. This system uses a near-infrared sensitive CCD camera mounted on a pair of goggles to capture the eye motion while following externally generated visual stimuli. Since the goggles maintained the eye in a dark environment during the test procedure, near-infrared light emitting diodes (NIR LEDs) are used to illuminate the eye. Another system, the Compact Integrated Pupillograph CIP from AMTech is mainly used to automatically measure the pupil dynamics such as the pupillary light reflex. This system can be useful to analyze sleep disorder and the influence of drugs on drivers. This system essentially captures and stores video images of the eye pupil dynamics during pupil's reflexes related tests. A forth system (Iijima et al., 2003), consists of a head mounted goggle equipped with a near-infrared sensitive CCD camera, a liquid crystal display allowing the investigation of eye tracking functions of neurological disease patients. The head mounted display showed visual stimuli followed by the eyes that were video captured. Image analysis of the eye movement was performed to detect eye saccades which are known to be symptomatic of Parkinson's disease.

The automatic impairment detection system implemented in more recent research (Meunier & Laperrière, 2008) is composed of the three main modules required to automatically implement a wider range of eye involuntary reflexes and is an enhanced version of a simpler system developed in previous research (Meunier, 2006). A video capturing module allows the grabbing of video sequences of the eyes following automatically generated visual stimuli. The grabbed video data are subsequently analysed by an image processing module and also a diagnosis module to allow the automatic detection of drugs and alcohol impairment. The newer version of this system is also built around the same modules. However, the video capturing module has been extensively enhanced. In order to eliminate the saccadic eye motion induced by the discrete positioning of the red Light Emitting Diodes (LEDs) (see Fig. 7) used to produce the visual stimulus a LCD flat screen and a reflective surface was installed.

With the new prototype the near-infrared (NIR) illumination system used to allow the visualization of the subject face by the NIR sensitive video-camera was also enhance to increase the coverage of the NIR LEDs beam.

The last two versions of the implemented prototype are also depicted in Fig. 8. In the previous version (Fig. 8 left) a helmet integrates the NIR sensitive camera and the automatic visual stimuli generation system. In the more recent version (Fig. 8 right), a black box integrates a LCD flat screen that projects visual stimuli in continuous motion. This version also increased the amount and coverage of the NIR illumination beam projected to subject's face which in turn enhanced the contrast of the pupils in images.

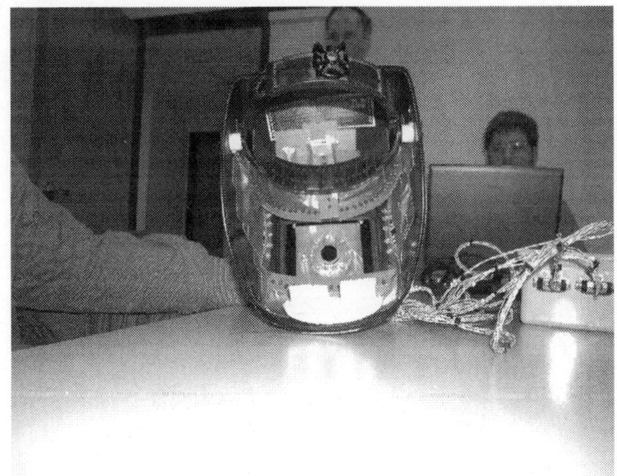

Fig. 7. A previous version of the prototype with visual stimulus produced by series of red LEDs (Meunier, 2006).

The image processing module essentially used a Hough based approach algorithm described in the previous section (Takegami et al., 2003), to extract the position (center) of the pupils in each image frame useful in the HGN and convergence tests. Since pupils correspond to darker regions in the images, pupils are easily detected by applying a simple optimal binary thresholding technique (Gonzalez & Woods, 2008).

Fig. 8. Last two versions of the prototype. (Left) Previous version with automatic generation of visual stimuli. (Right) New version with enhanced visual stimuli generation and NIR illumination.

To avoid pupil false detection, each region segmented in the thresholding phase is validated using biometric properties of the eyes and pupils (Nikolaidis & Pitas, 2000). The contour of each pupil's segmented region is also extracted. The center of each detected pupil is then computed using eq. (12) which allows the calculation of the eyes horizontal angular position (eq. (13)). These angular positions are stored on disk for further processing by a diagnosis module.

The image processing module is also used to extract the radius of the pupils measured in the pupil's reaction to light test. These measurements correspond to the radius of the fitting circles on the pupil's contours extracted from thresholded video images. The approach implemented is similar to the one reported by Toth (Toth, 2005). A Hough transform approach for fitting circles to the captured pupil's edge points contours has also been investigated. The radius of each detected pupil is also stored on disk for subsequent processing by the diagnosis module.

For the HGN test, the diagnosis module essentially performs the comparison of the pupil's angular horizontal position curves corresponding to post-dose BAC levels (BAC > 0.00%) with equivalent ideal curves at pre-dose BAC level (BAC ≈ 0.00%), to determine if a subject's BAC exceeds the tolerance limit of 0.08%.

The summation of the square difference between the pupil's horizontal angular position curves at post-dose BAC level and the approximate curves corresponding to the pre-dose BAC level are used to detect the lack of smooth pursuit and the nystagmus at maximum deviation which are two out of three visual signs obtained with the HGN test. These visual signs are known to be sufficient to establish the level of impairment of an individual intoxicated by CNS depressant drugs such as alcohol (Citek et al., 2003).

Furthermore, for the HGN test, the diagnosis module also performs a time-frequency analysis of the pupil's angular horizontal position curves at post-dose BAC levels (BAC > 0.00%), to determine the presence of pupil's saccadic motions associated with high doses of alcohol (BAC > 0.08%). This time-frequency analysis is based on a short time Fourier transform to allow a more precise localization of the saccadic motions inherent to the horizontal gaze nystagmus. Such saccadic motions tend to occur when the eyes are gazing at high horizontal deviation.

The diagnosis module also determines from the pupil's horizontal deviation curves extracted in the convergence test, if the eye-gaze direction of both eyes are converging at the same target. The horizontal deviation is computed as the difference between the pupil's horizontal position at a given time frame and the pupil's horizontal position at time 0 when a subject's eyes are gazing at reference targets placed in front of the eyes. The check for lack of convergence can provide another clue as to the possible presence of CNS depressants such as alcohol.

Ultimately, the diagnosis module assesses the response time of the involuntary reflex of the pupils triggered by changing illumination from the measured radius data extracted by the image processing module. Under ordinary conditions, the pupil should react very quickly, and constrict noticeably when a white light beam is directed to the eyes. Under the influence of certain substances such as alcohol, the pupil's reaction may be very slow. Experiments show that pupil's reaction is considered slow if it takes more than one second (roughly 30 images frames) to reach full constriction.

2.3 Alcohol workshops

The enhanced version of the video-based image processing system has been tested in alcohol workshops held at the École Nationale de Police du Québec (ENPQ). Alcohol workshops are used to train new recruits on the use of the breath analysis instruments.

Workshops usually last about 4 hours, during which volunteer drinkers are consuming alcoholic beverages and snack food for about an hour and a half. After the consumption period, the BAC of each subject is periodically measured at time intervals of 15 minutes. Pre-dose evaluations were performed at the beginning of each workshop, before the subjects start consuming alcohol.

Many volunteer drinkers were involved in the testing of the recently developed system. Subjects were recruited from the local police academy in Trois-Rivières. Each subject signed an informed consent form previously approved by the research ethical comity of the Université du Québec à Trois-Rivières.

All subjects were of legal drinking age (19-26 years), healthy and reported no sign of fatigue since the workshops were all scheduled at 11h30 in the morning.

Blood alcohol levels were assessed at each test time during each workshop using calibrated breath analysis instruments. In the course of each workshop, certified breath analysis specialists trained the recruits on how to performed BAC measurements using a Breathalyser 900A.

The automated HGN, convergence and pupil's reaction to light tests were performed with the newly implemented video-bases image processing system at the same rate of the BAC measurements.

3. Automatic eye involuntary reflexes measurements: Experimental results

The video-based image processing system introduced above to automatically assess human's faculties (Meunier & Laperrière, 2008) (see Fig. 8 right) was used to extract the pupil's horizontal angular position curves in the HGN test, the pupil's horizontal deviation curves deduced from the convergence test and the pupil's radius curves obtained from the pupil's reaction to light test, from video images sequences.

Figure 9 shows an example of the region segmentation process which reveals the pupils in an image. Figure 9 right exhibits both pupils which correspond to regions with elliptic shape. The pupil's regions segmentation operation is performed by simple binary thresholding (Gonzalez & Woods, 2008). The segmented bright regions in Fig. 9 right is related to darker regions of the original intensity image (see Fig. 9 left) such as the pupil's regions. By looking to a typical pupil's image region (see Fig. 10 left) and its corresponding intensity histogram (see Fig. 10 right) one can easily extract the threshold value used for the segmentation process. This threshold value (dashed line in Fig. 10 right) is actually the intensity value isolating the left most mode of the histogram corresponding to the pupil's intensity probability distribution. The observation of Fig. 10 left also reveals the presence of the glint (brighter region) and its intensity probability distribution corresponding to the right most mode in the pupil's image region intensity histogram (Fig. 10 right). The larger regions visible in Fig. 9 right are considered as shadow. The occurrence of shadow is a side effect of the non uniformity of the NIR illumination as well as the non uniformity of the face's surface. Nevertheless, the enhanced NIR illumination system improved the illumination pattern and allows the decrease of the shadow effect.

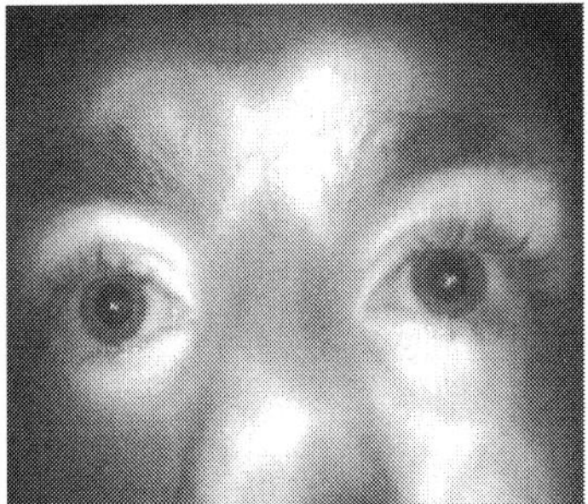 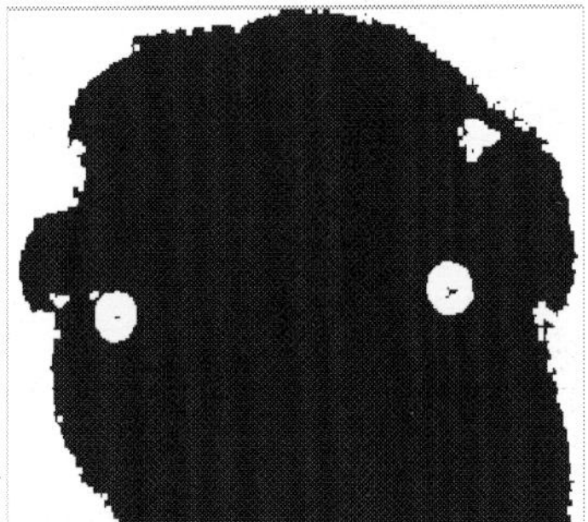

Fig. 9. Results of the pupil's segmentation process. (Left) Typical image of the pupils captured with the video-based image processing system. (Right) Segmented regions with the pupils appearing as circular shapes.

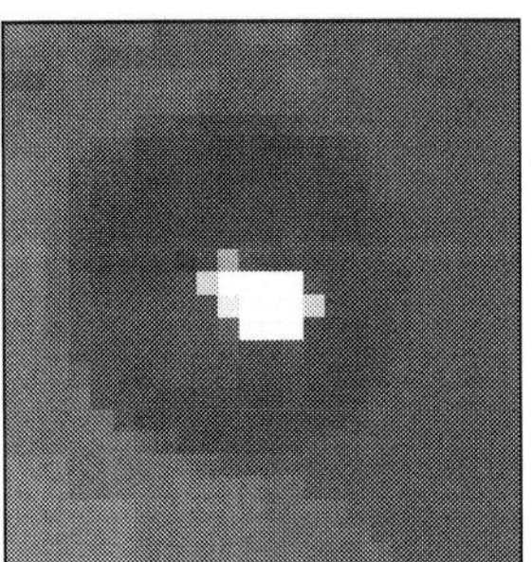 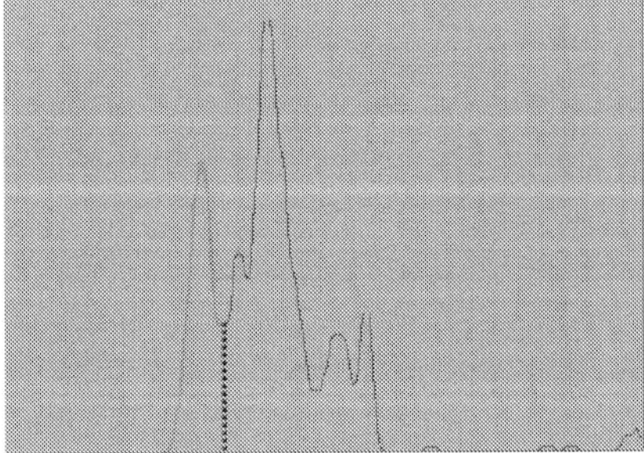

Fig. 10. Pupil's image region intensity histogram. (Left) Typical pupil's image region. (Right) Pupil's image region histogram.

These regions are eliminated at the validation stage since their respective area and shape are not compatible with pupils. Fig. 11 depicts the results of the pupil's extraction algorithm.

Figure 11 left shows the contours extracted from the segmented image (Fig. 9 right). Figure 11 right presents each pupil located by a circle with corresponding radius.

Prior to performing any comparison between the pupil's horizontal angular position curves at post-dose BAC level and the approximate curves related to the pre-dose BAC level obtained from the HGN test, we first deduced a confidence interval for the mean value of the square difference (MSD) between the pupil's horizontal angular position curves at BAC level of 0.00% and their corresponding polynomial approximations.

This confidence interval establishes a base of comparison which represents a sober state (BAC $\approx$ 0.00%). In this research we used a confidence interval with a confidence level of $1-\alpha$ = 0.90 given by $1.722439 \leq \mu_{MSD} \leq 4.681783$. Figure 12 shows a typical horizontal angular position curve of the left pupil of one of the volunteer drinkers at BAC level of 0.00% (pre-dose) following visual stimuli generated in the HGN test.

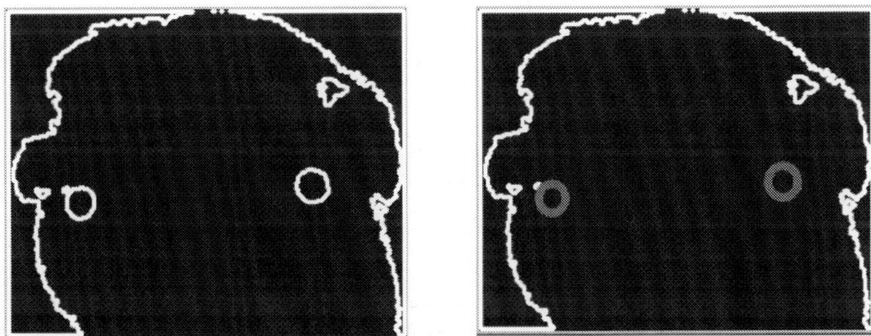

Fig. 11. Results of the pupil's position detection. (Left) Contour extracted from the segmented image. (Right) Located pupils.

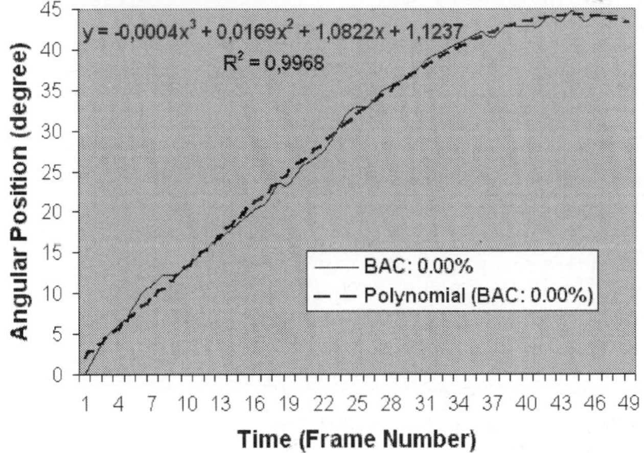

Fig. 12. Left pupil horizontal angular position curves of a subject at a BAC of 0.00% following visual stimuli in the HGN test. The continuous curve represents the extracted positions and the dashed curve its corresponding approximation polynomial.

The curves depicted in Fig. 12 are not revealing great discrepancies which is usual for healthy persons not impaired by alcohol or drugs. Such curves were used to deduce the previously mentioned confidence interval. For BAC values greater than 0.00%, the pupil's horizontal angular position curves start to show discrepancies with their related approximate polynomials. When the amplitude of the discrepancies increased sharply in saccadic fashion it means that the HGN is present.

Figure 13 shows the same curves depicted in Fig. 12 but for a subject with a BAC level of 0.22%. The differences between the curves are easily noticeable and reveal the presence of two visual signs used to assess the type of impairment of an intoxicated individual, the lack of smooth pursuit also called tracking error and the HGN. The dashed curve shown in Fig. 12 and 13 represents the ideal pupil's horizontal angular position curve associated with an unimpaired individual and is compared with the continuous pupil's horizontal angular position curve which allows the detection of the lack of smooth pursuit and also the distinctive nystagmus at maximum deviation (40-45º).

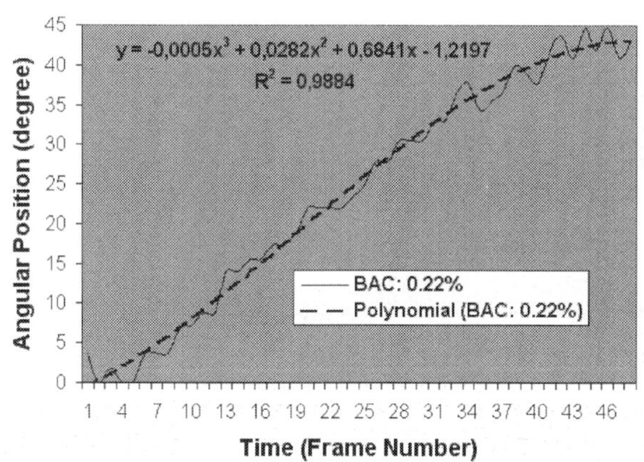

Fig. 13. Left pupil horizontal angular position curves of a subject at a BAC of 0.22% following visual stimuli in the HGN test.

Figure 14 shows the pupil's horizontal angular position curves corresponding to a BAC level of 0.09% which is within the reach of the criterion BAC level of 0.08% considering the uncertainty (10%) of the BAC measurement taken by the Breathalizer 900A. From Fig. 14 one can easily notice that the amplitude of the discrepancies between the pupil's horizontal angular position curves are much smaller at lower BAC levels and the jerking at maximum deviation is less frequent (lower frequency) and also with lower amplitude.

The pupil's horizontal deviation curves extracted in the convergence test may reveal the lack of convergence where the horizontal deviation of one eye may converge toward the tip of the nose while the other diverges away from the tip of the nose. Examples of eye's convergence and divergence are shown in Fig. 15 (left and right). Figure 16 shows a typical pupil's horizontal deviation curves corresponding to a BAC level of 0.00%. One can easily notice by observing the pupil's horizontal deviation curves in the time interval 30-60 that both eyes converge. When the lack of convergence (see Fig. 17) occurs one of the pupil's horizontal deviation curves tend to diverge from one and other in the same time interval

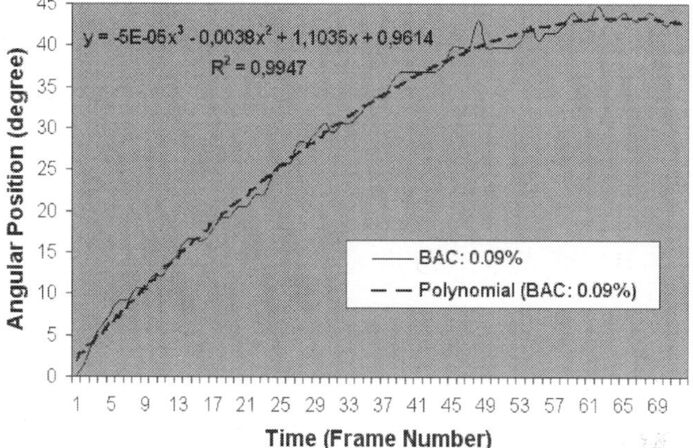

Fig. 14. Left pupil horizontal angular position curves of a subject at a BAC of 0.09%
following visual stimuli in the HGN test.

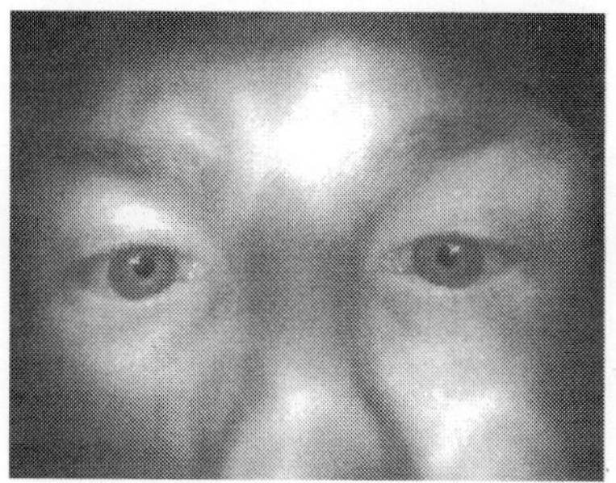 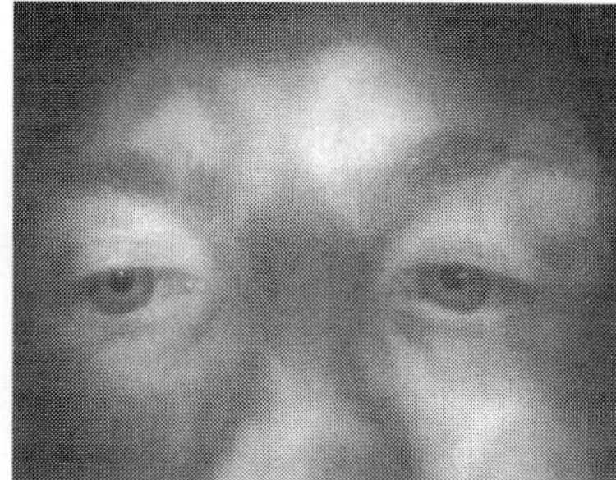

Fig. 15. Examples of eye convergence and divergence. (Left) Convergence: Both eyes are
pointing to the tip of the nose. (Right) Divergence: One eye (volunteer's right eye) is
pointing to the tip of the nose while the other is pointing away from the tip of the nose.

(30-60). In the conducted studies this phenomena was not observed for all subjects even
with fairly high BAC levels.

The pupil's reaction to light test assesses the response time of the involuntary reflex of the
pupils triggered by changing illumination. A pupil's slow reaction to changing illumination
conditions may reveal impairment caused by certain drugs such as alcohol. Figure 18
depicts the pupil's radius of the left eye of subjects with two different BAC levels subjected
to the reaction to light test. The pupil's radius is deduced from a circle/ellipse fitting
algorithm such as the one exposed previously (see section 2.1.3) and gives results such as
the ones showed in Fig. 11 right. The continuous curve was obtained with a subject at a BAC
level of 0.138%. From that curve one can deduce the response time of the involuntary reflex
of the pupil which is the elapsed time between the time the white LEDs are switched on and
the time of the pupil's full constriction. The response time deduced at this BAC level (BAC:
0.138%) is roughly 1400 ms. The response time deduced from the dashed curved (BAC:

0.00%) depicted in Fig. 18 is about 850 ms. Experiments (Page, 2000) suggest that a response time of more than 1000 ms is considered a slow reaction to light and may be linked to CNS drug related impairments.

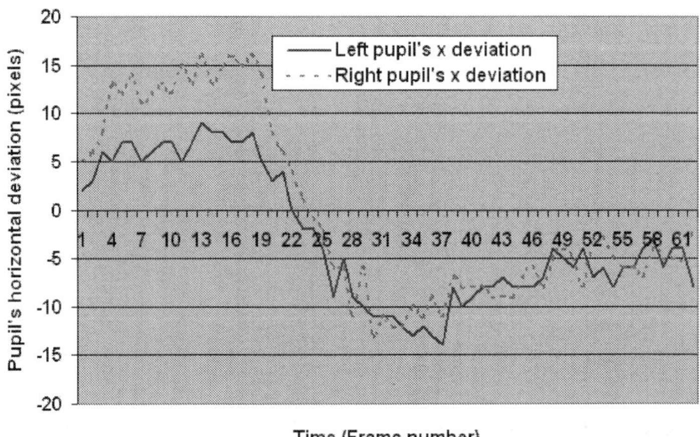

Fig. 16. Left and right pupil's horizontal deviation curves of a subject at a BAC of 0.00% following visual stimuli in the convergence test. The continuous curve represents left pupil horizontal deviation curve positions and the dashed curve the right pupil's horizontal deviation curve.

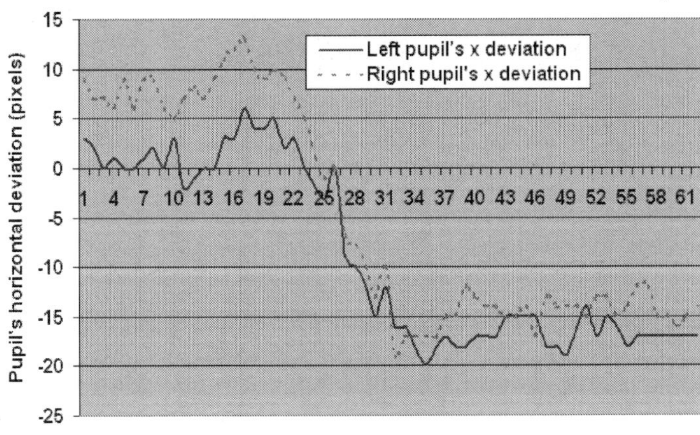

Fig. 17. Left and right pupil's horizontal deviation curves of a subject at a BAC of 0.138% following visual stimuli in the convergence test.

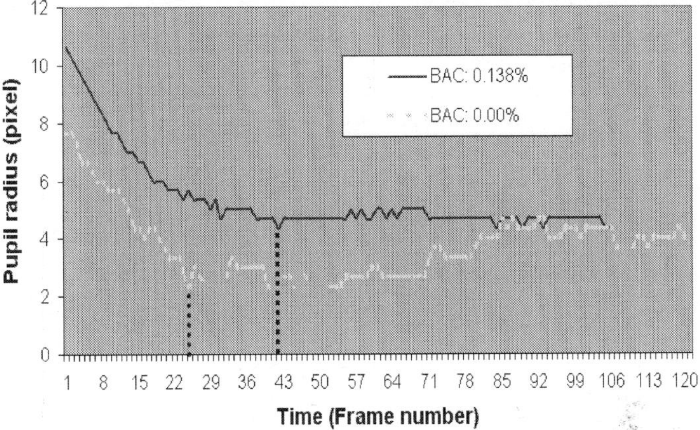

Fig. 18. Left pupil radius measured in the reaction to light test. The continuous curve
corresponds to a subject with a BAC of 0.138% and the dashed curve to a subject with a BAC
of 0.00%.

The newly developed video-based image processing system has been tested to classify a
group of subjects into one of two groups (impaired/unimpaired) based on the detection of
the four visual signs (lack of smooth pursuit and the presence of horizontal gaze nystagmus
at maximum deviation for both eyes) used in a previous study (Meunier, 2006). Other visual
signs (eye convergence, eye reaction to light) were also tested to see if they increase the
certainty of the diagnosis on a subject type of impairment. The criteria used in the
classification process (human faculty diagnosis) and their reference values are shown in
table 1. A person is considered impaired if the measured eye involuntary reflexes exceed
their reference criteria. Moreover, the criterion for impairment in the case of alcohol related
intoxication is always based on the applied BAC level of 0.08% by law enforcement
agencies.

Classification criteria	Reference values
Eye Tracking error (Mean Squared Difference: degree^2)	4,6817
HGN at maximum deviation (40-45º) (MSD: degree^2)	9,3267
Eye divergence (MSD: pixel^2)	5,0322
Reaction to light (sec)	1,0

Table 1. Classification criteria and their reference values.

The previous version of the video-based image processing system for human's faculties
assessment (Meunier, 2006) reported a classification accuracy of about 80%. The experiment
conducted with the new version of this system gives roughly the same classification rate.

One main objective of this recent study was to evaluate the efficiency of the new version of the automatic human impairment detection system especially to cope with the false negative failure rate. This figure was grossly 22 % for the previous implemented system prototype and represented the fraction of impaired subjects actually not detected. The false negative failure rate is about the same reported in the previous study (Meunier, 2006). Nevertheless, the success rate of the new system version is almost perfect for a high dose of alcohol (BAC > 0.1%). However, the failure of the classification occurs mainly at BAC levels within about 10% of the criterion (BAC $\approx$ 0.08%).

4. Discussion and future work

The results obtained in the previously presented experiment confirmed the observations made in the previous study (Meunier, 2006). These results are also consistent with other previously published experiments (Burns, 1995) on the HGN test and confirmed its validity to detect alcohol related impairments. In the more recent experiments we also used other tests such as the eye convergence and the eye reaction to light tests with the HGN test procedures. The results obtained suggest that these other visual signs are not essential for the detection of alcohol related impairments and they are not adding much discriminating power to the classification process. This observation leads us to conclude that the HGN test is the primary tool to accurately detect alcohol related impairments since the use of the visual signs associated to the darkroom examination test had little effect in the classification efficiency reported in Burns (Burn, 1995).

The implemented eye convergence test needs to be reconfigured and redesigned to improve the detection of the lack of convergence that should had been more consistently detected in alcohol related impairments encountered in the study presented here. Some volunteer drinkers mentioned during the execution of the convergence test experiencing focussing problems on the visual stimuli. In order to fully reveal the classification power of the newly implemented eye involuntary reflexes further experiments must be conducted. These experiments must also be held in the context of drug workshops in which subjects are consuming drugs such as cannabis.

Results also suggest that the automated system implemented to detect human's impaired faculties based on the eyes involuntary reflexes such as the horizontal gaze nystagmus, the eye convergence and the pupil's reaction to light needs to be improved in order to allow better detection rate at BACs near 0.08% or low level impairment. As previously stated, adding more visual signs (eye's involuntary reflexes) improved the impairment detection efficiency. Nevertheless, adding other types of information related to the DRE evaluation such as divided attention tests, examination of vital signs, examination of muscle tone to the automated impaired faculties detection process should greatly improved its efficiency. Therefore, a probabilistic framework similar to the one implemented in a research reported in the literature (Ji et al., 2006) that is based on the Bayesian networks for modeling and inferring human's impaired faculties by fusing information from diverse sources will be developed in future research. This probabilistic framework will first allow the modeling of a Bayesian networks by which the criteria maximizing the certainty of a diagnosis given on a person's faculties are chosen. Moreover, the Bayesian networks can be used to infer from the fusing information process of multiple sources the probability that a person's faculties are impaired by a given category of drugs. Figure 19 shows a first version of the Bayesian networks of the probabilistic framework dedicated to the modeling and inferring of impaired faculties.

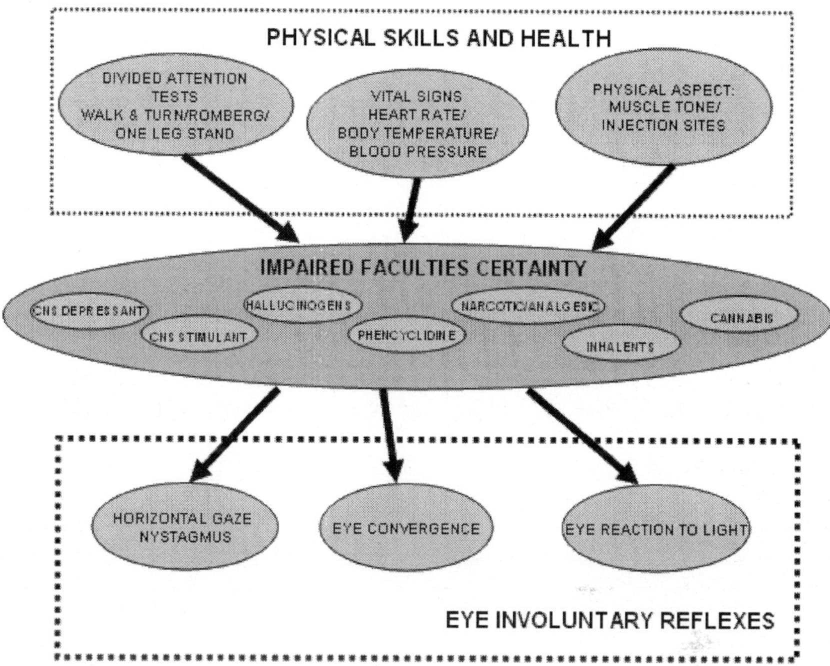

Fig. 19. Bayesian networks for modeling and inferring human's impaired faculties.

5. Conclusion

In this book chapter we outlined a new video-based image processing system implementing the HGN, eye convergence and eye reaction to light tests. This system as the one reported in a previous study (Meunier, 2006) accurately detects impairments with a success rate of about 80%. The present system is also quite efficient to detect impairments for high doses of alcohol but still needs some refinements to increase its success rate for low doses near the BAC criterion of 0.08%, the level to which the false negative failure rate is higher. The use of a probabilistic framework fusing information to improve the classification accuracy will be investigated. Nevertheless, the actual system may also be used to detect other impairments caused by drugs. By using more eye involuntary reflexes (visual signs) the newly developed video-based image processing system prototype is more versatile and can be used to detect a wide array of drug related impairments. It can also be used for the automatic detection of liveness since a living human exhibits eye involuntary reflexes such as the pupillary reflex.

The implemented automatic human faculties assessment system presented in this chapter (Meunier & Laperrière, 2008) is also useful for many other reasons. First, as an educational and interactive tool to assist trainers in alcohol workshops. Second, to document the eye's involuntary reflexes related test procedures with video sequences which subsequently can be presented in court of law to prove that an individual is under the influence of alcohol or drugs. Third, to standardize the application of these test procedures to avoid inconsistencies in its administration by law enforcement officers.

6. References

Batista, J.P. (2004). A Real-Time Driver Visual Attention Monitoring System. In: *Lecture Notes in Computer Science*, J. S. Marques et al. (eds.), Vol. 3522, pp. 200-208, Springer-Verlag, ISBN 978-3-540-26153-7, Berlin/Heidelberg

Burn, M. (1995). Oculomotor and Pupil Tests to Identify Alcohol Impairment. *Proceedings of the 13th International Conference on Alcohol, Drugs, and Traffic Safety*, Vol. 2, pp. 877-880, ISBN 0908204213, Adelaide, Australia, August 1995, Road Accident Research Unit: Adelaide University, Adelaide

Burn, M. & Gould, P. (1997). Police Evaluation of Alcohol and Drug Impairment: Methods Issues and Legal. *Proceedings of the 14th International Conference on Alcohol, Drugs, and Traffic Safety*, Vol. 2, pp. 629-634, Annecy, France, September 1997, Centre d'Études et de Recherches en Médecine du Traffic (CERMT), Annecy

Citek, K.; Ball, B.; Rutledge, D. A. (2003). Nystagmus; Testing in Intoxicated Individuals, *Optometry*, Vol. 74, No. 11, November 2003, pp. 695-710

Fitzgibbon, A.; Pilu, M.; Fisher, R. B. (1999). Direct least square fitting of ellipses. *IEEE Transactions on Pattern Analysis and Machine Intelligence*, Vol. 21, No. 5, May 1999, pp. 476-480

Gonzalez, R. C.; & Woods, R. E. (2008). *Digital Image Processing*, Prentice-Hall, ISBN 0-13-168728-X, New-York

Guil, N. & Zapata, E. L. (1997). Lower Order Circle and Ellipse Hough Transform. *Pattern Recognition*, Vol. 30, No. 10, October 1997, pp. 1729-1744

Halir, R. & Flusser; J. (1998). Numerically Stable Direct Least Squares Fitting Of Ellipses. Proceeding of the 6th International Conference in Central Europe on Computer Graphics, Visualization and Interactive Digital Media, Vol. 1, pp. 125-132, Plzen, Czech Republic, February 1998, University of West Bohemia: Campus Bory, Plzen - Bory

Haro, A.; Flickner, M.; Essa, I. (2000). Detecting and Tracking Eyes By Using Their Physiological Properties, *Proceedings IEEE CVPR 2000*, Vol. 2, pp. 163-168, ISBN 0-7695-0662-3 , Hilton Head, USA, June 2000, IEEE Computer Society

Iijima, A.; Haida, M.; Ishikawa, N.; Minamitani, H.; Shinohara, Y. (2003). Head Mounted Goggle System with Liquid Crystal Display for Evaluation of Eye Tracking Functions on Neurological Disease Patients. *Proceedings of the 25th Annual International Conference of the IEEE EMBS*, pp. 3225-3228, ISBN 0-7803-7789-3, September 2003

Ji, Q. & Bebis, G. (1999). Visual Cues Extraction for Monitoring Driver's Vigilance, *Proceedings of the Honda Symposium*, pp. 48-55, 1999

Ji, Q. & Yang, X. (2002). Real-Time Eye, Gaze, and Face Pose Tracking for Monitoring Driver Vigilance. *Real-Time Imaging*, Vol. 8, No. 5, 2002, pp. 357-377

Ji, Q. & Zhu, Z. (2004). Eye and Gaze Tracking for Interactive Graphic Display. *Machine Vision and Applications*, Vol. 15, No. 3, July 2004, pp. 139-149

Ji, Q.; Lan, P.; Looney, C. (2006). A Probabilistic Framework for Modeling and Real-Time Monitoring Human Fatigue. *IEEE Transactions on Systems, Man, and Cybernetics- Part A: Systems and Humans*, Vol. 36, No. 5, Sept. 2006, pp. 862-875

Li, L. F.; Feng, Z. R.; Peng, Q. K. (2004). Detection and model analysis of circular feature for robot vision. *Proceedings of 2004 International Conference on Machine Learning and Cybernetics*, Vol. 6, pp. 3943-3948, ISBN 0-7803-8403-2, August 2004

Meunier, F. (2006). On the Automatic Detection of Alcohol Related Driving Impairments Using a Video-Based Image Processing System: A Feasability Evaluation. *Canadian Multidisciplinary Road Safety Conference XVI*, Winnipeg, Manitoba, June 11-14, 2006

Meunier, F. & Laperrière, D. (2008). A video-based image processing system for the automatic implementation of the eye involuntary reflexes measurements involved in the Drug Recognition Expert (DRE), IEEE/ ACS international Conference on Computer Systems and Applications, pp. 599-605, ISBN 978-1-4244-1967-8, Doha, Qatar, March 31-April 4, 2008, AICCSA 2008

Morimoto C. H.; Koons, D.; Amis, A.; Flickner, M. (2000). Pupil Detection and Tracking Using Multiple Light Sources. *Image and Vision Computing*, Vol. 18, No. 4, 2000, pp. 331-335

Nikolaidis, A. & Pitas, I. (2000). Facial Features Extraction and Pose Determination. *Pattern Recognition*, Vol. 33, 2000, pp. 1783-1791

Page, T. E. (2000). The Drug Recognition Expert Police Officer: A Response to Drug Impaired Driving. *Proceedings of the 15th International Conference on Alcohol, Drugs, and Traffic Safety*, pp. 722-727, Stockholm, Sweden, May 2000, Swedish National Road Administration, Borlänge

Ohno, T. & Mukawa, N. (2004). A Free-Head, Simple Calibration, Gaze Tracking System That Enables Gaze-Based Interaction. *Proceedings of the 2004 Symposium on Eye Tracking & Applications*, pp. 115-122, ISBN 1-58113-825-3, San-Antonio, USA, 2004, ETRA 2004, San-Antonio

Takegami, T.; Toshiyuki, G.; Seiichiro, K.; Minamikawa-Tachino, R. (2003). A Hough Based Eye Direction Detection Algorithm without On-site Calibration", *Proceedings of the VIIth Digital Image Computing: Techniques and Applications*, Sydney, December 2003, pp. 459-468

Toth, B. (2005). Biometric Liveness Detection. *Biometrics*, Vol. 10; October 2005, pp. 291-297

Trucco, E. & Verri, A. (1999). *Introductory Techniques for 3D Computer Vision*, Prentice-Hall, ISBN 0-13-261108-2, Upper Saddle River, New-Jersey

Zhang, S-C. & Liu, Z-Q. (2005). A robust, real-time ellipse detector. *Pattern Recognition*, Vol. 38, No. 2, February 2005, pp. 273-287

Zhu, Z. & Ji, Q. (2005). Robust real-time eye detection and tracking under variable lighting conditions and various face orientations. *Machine, Computer Vision and Image Understanding 98,* Vol. 38, No. 1, 2005, pp. 124-154

## 14

Three-Dimensional Digital Colour Camera

Yung-Sheng Chen[1], I-Cheng Chang[2],
Bor-Tow Chen[3] and Ching-Long Huang[3]
[1]Department of Electrical Engineering, Yuan Ze University, Chungli,
[2]Department of Computer Science and Information Engineering
National Dong Hwa University, Hualien,
[3]Opto Electronics & Systems Laboratories,
Industrial Technology Research Institute, Hsinchu,
Taiwan, ROC

1. Introduction

Digital colour camera now has been a popular consumer equipment, has widely used in our daily life, and is highly suited for the next generation of cellular phones, personal digital assistants and other portable communication devices. The main applications of digital colour camera are used to take a digital picture for personal use, picture editing and desktop publishing, high-quality printing, and image processing for advanced academic research. The digital picture is a two-dimensional (2D) form with three-colour components (Red, Green, Blue). The most of efforts for a digital camera producer are focusing on the improvements of image compression, image quality, image resolution, and optical/digital zooming. However, consider the wide field of computer vision, the depth for a captured object may be another very useful and helpful information, such as surface measurement, virtual reality, object modelling and animation, it will be valuable if the depth information can be obtained while a picture is being captured. In other words, three-dimensional (3D) imaging devices promise to open a very wide variety of applications, particularly, those involving a need to know the precise 3D shape of the human body, e.g. e-commerce (clothing), medicine (assessment, diagnosis), anthropometry (vehicle design), post-production (virtual actors) and industrial design (workspace design) (Siebert & Marshall, 2000). To achieve this significant function, a novel 3-D digital colour camera has been successfully developed by Industrial Technology Research Institute, Opto Electronics & Systems Laboratories (ITRI-OES), in Taiwan. In this article, the previous works, algorithms, structure of our 3D digital colour camera, and 3D results, will be briefly presented.

To obtain 3D information of a given object, the approach may be considered in between a passive scheme and an active scheme. The widely known passive scheme is stereovision, which is useful to measure surfaces with well-defined boundary edges and vertexes. An algorithm to recognize singular points may be used to solve the problem of correspondence between points on both image planes. However the traditional stereoscopic system becomes rather inefficient to measure continuous surfaces, where there are not many reference points. It has also several problems in textural surfaces or in surfaces with lots of discontinuities. Under such an environment, the abundance of reference points can produce matching mistakes. Thus, an active system based on a structured light concept will be useful (Siebert & Marshall, 2000; Rocchini et al., 2001; Chen & Chen, 2003). In our 3D camera system, the constraint that codifies the pattern projected on the surface has been simplified by using a random speckle pattern, the correspondence problem can be solved by a local spatial-distance computation scheme (Chen & Chen, 2003) or a so-called compressed image correlation algorithm (Hart, 1998).

In our original design, the 3D camera system includes a stereoscopic dual-camera setup, a speckle generator, and a computer capable of high-speed computation. Figure 1(a) shows the first version of our 3D camera system including two CCD cameras needing a distance of 10 cm between its 2 lenses, and a video projector, where the used random speckle pattern in Fig. 1(b) is sent from the computer and projected via the video projector on the measuring object. Each of two cameras takes the snapshot from its own viewpoint, and can do the simultaneous colour image capturing. A local spatial-distance computation scheme or a compressed image correlation (CIC) algorithm then finds some specific speckles on the two camera images. Each of the selected speckles would have its position shown twice, one on each image. After establishing the statistic correlation of the corresponding vectors on the two images, the 3D coordinates of the spots on the object surface will be known from the 3D triangulation.

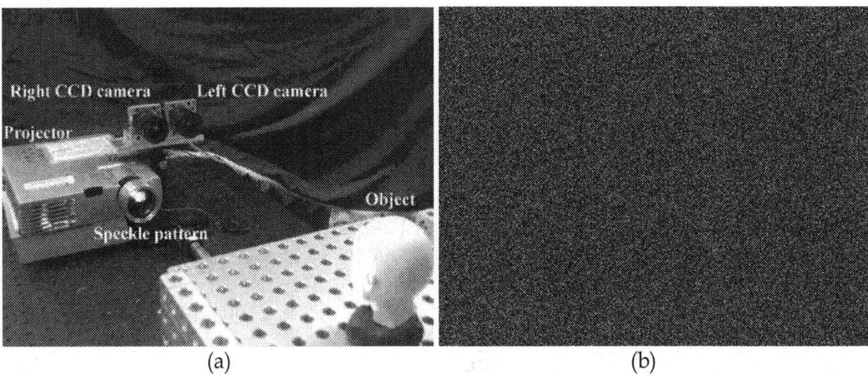

Fig. 1. (a) Our original 3D measurement system. (b) The used random speckle pattern, which is sent from the computer and projected via the video projector.

Not only the traditional stereoscopic systems (Siebert & Marshall, 2000; Rocchini et al., 2001) but also the above mentioned system (Chen & Chen, 2003) are all not easy to be used friendly and popularly due to large system scale, complicated operations, and expensiveness. Hence, to achieve the valuable features (portable, easy operation, inexpensiveness) as possessed by a 2D digital camera, we present a novel design which can be applied to a commercial digital still camera (DSC), and make the 2D camera be able to capture 3D information (Chang et al., 2002). The proposed 3D hand-held camera (the second version of our 3D measurement system) contains three main components: a commercial DSC (Nikon D1 camera body), a patented three-hole aperture lens (Huang, 2001; Chen & Huang, 2002), and a flash. The flash projects the speckle pattern onto the object and the camera captures a single snapshot at the same time. Accordingly, our 3-D hand-held camera design integrating together the speckle generating projector and the colour digital camera makes the system be able to move around freely when taking pictures.

The rest of this article is organized as follows. Section 2 reviews briefly our previous works. Section 3 presents algorithms for improving 3D measurements. The structure of our novel 3D camera is described in Section 4. Finally a conclusion is given in Section 5. Because the found 3D information should be visualized for the use, all the 3D results are currently manipulated and displayed by our TriD system (TriD, 2002), which is a powerful and versatile modelling tool for 3D captured data, developed by ITRI-OES in Taiwan.

2. Previous works

Our original 3D measurement system shown in Fig. 1(a) includes two CCD cameras and a video projector, where the used random speckle pattern shown in Fig. 1(b) is sent from the computer and projected via the video projector onto the object to be measured. In this system, to solve the correspondence problem of measuring a 3D surface, the random speckle pattern was adopted to simplify the constraint that codifies the pattern projected on the surface and the technique of spatial distance computation was applied to find the correspondence vector (or the correlation vector used in the later of this article).

To effectively perform the correspondence vector finding task, the binarization for the captured image is used in our 3D system developments. The following is our adaptive thresholding method for binarization.

Let a grey block image be defined as G having the size of $m \times m$. The correspondence problem is based on the local matching between two binary block images. Therefore it is important to determine the thresholding value TH, for obtaining the binary block image B. To overcome the uneven-brightness and out-of-focus problem arising from the lighting environment and different CCD cameras, the brightness equalization and image binarization are used. Let m^2 be the total number of pixels of a block image, and $cdf(z)$, z = 0~255 (the grey value index, where each pixel is quantized to a 8-bit data) be the cumulative distribution function of G, then a thresholding controlled by the percentile p = 0~100% is defined

$$TH_p = \left\{ z_p \mid cdf(z_p) \approx pm^2 \right\} \tag{1}$$

Thus for a percentile p each grey block image G will have a thresholding value TH_p to obtain its corresponding binary block image B, and we have

$$B(x,y) = \begin{cases} 1 & \text{if } g(x,y) \geq TH_p \\ 0 & \text{otherwise} \end{cases} \tag{2}$$

where 1 and 0 denote the nonzero (white) pixel and the zero (black) pixel, respectively. Note here that the higher the p is, the smaller the data amount having nonzero pixels.

In our previous work, our distance computation approach for finding correspondence vectors is simply described as follows. Let $B^l_{x_0,y_0}$, x_0 = 0, s, $2s$, ...; and y_0 = 0, s, $2s$, ..., be a binary block image in the left-captured image starting at the location (x_0, y_0), where s is the sampling interval from the captured image. The searched block image, $B^r_{u_0,v_0}$ starting at the location (u_0, v_0) in the right-captured image, will be in the range of u_0 in $[x_0 - R_x, x_0 + R_x]$ and

v_0 in $[y_0 - R_y, y_0 + R_y]$, where R_x and R_y depend on the system configuration. If the CCD configuration satisfies to the epipolar line constraint, then R_y can be very small. In the searching range, if a right binary block image $B^r_{u_f,v_f}$ has the minimum spatial distance $d(B^l_{x_0,y_0}, B^r_{u_f,v_f})$ between it to $B^l_{x_0,y_0}$, then the vector from (x_0, y_0) to (u_f, v_f) is defined to be the found correspondence vector.

Because the corresponding information used in the stereoscopic system are usually represented with the subpixel level, in this version of 3D system, a simple averaging with an area A of size $w \times w$ containing the found correspondence results (u_f, v_f)s is used to obtain the desired subpixel coordinate (u_f^*, v_f^*) and is expressed by

$$u_f^* = \frac{1}{N} \sum_{\forall(u_f,v_f)\in A} u_f \quad \text{and} \quad v_f^* = \frac{1}{N} \sum_{\forall(u_f,v_f)\in A} v_f \tag{3}$$

The more details of measuring a 3D surface using this distance computation scheme can be found in the literature (Chen & Chen, 2003). A result is given in Fig. 2 for illustration, where (a) and (b) show the captured left and right images; (c) displays the reconstructed 3D surface along some manipulations performed on the TriD system (TriD, 2000).

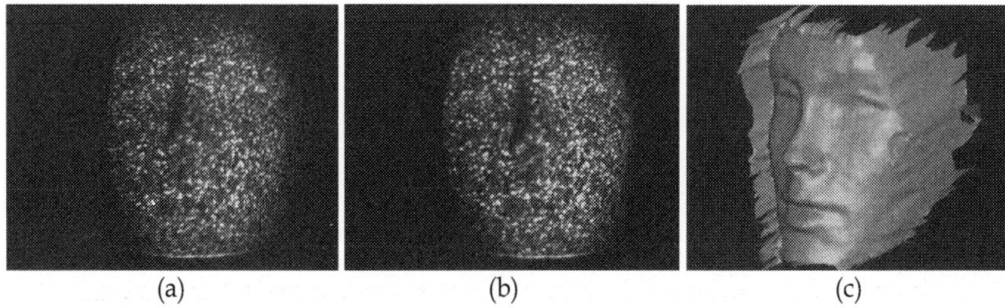

(a)   (b)   (c)

Fig. 2. (a) Left captured image, and (b) right captured image for the object shown in Fig. 1(a). The image size is 640×480. (c) The reconstructed 3D surface with the method presented in (Chen & Chen, 2003), where $p = 65\%$, $s = 4$, and a 5×5 support for subpixel compensation were used.

3. Algorithms for improving 3D measurement

In order to investigate the accuracy of 3D information, we have developed another approach different to our previous spatial distance computation for improving our system. This idea comes from the analysis of partical image velocimetry using compressed image correlation (Hart, 1998). In the following, under a hierarchical search scheme, pixel level computation and subpixel level computation combined with brightness compensation will be presented for approaching to the goal of improving 3D measurement.

3.1 Pixel level computation

A hierarchical search schem is adopted in pixel level computation. First let the left image be divided into a set of larger fixed-size blocks, and called level 1 the top layer. Consider a block B^l_1 in left image, if one block B^r_1 in right image has the best correlation then the vector

V_1 from the coordinate of B_1^l to that of B_1^r is found. Based on the facility of coarse-to-fine, the next search is confined to the range indicated by V_1 in right image and the execution time can be further reduced. Hence next, let the block image B_1^l in level 1 be further divided into four subblocks, this is the level 2. Consider the subblock B_2^l in B_1^l having the same coordinate, by the vector V_1, the correlation process is further performed only on the neighboring subblocks centered at the coordinate of B_1^r. The best correlation conducting the vector V_2 from the coordinate of B_2^l to one subblock B_2^r is found. Continue this process, if the best match is found and ended at level n, then the final vector of best correlation may be expressed as

$$V = \sum_{i=1}^{n} V_i \tag{4}$$

In order to reduce the computation time of correlation, a so-called correlation error function for an $M \times N$ image is used and defined as follows (Hart, 1998).

$$\phi_{\Delta i, \Delta j} = \frac{\sum_{m=1}^{M}\sum_{n=1}^{N}\left(I_{m,n} + I_{m+\Delta i, n+\Delta j} - \left|I_{m,n} - I_{m+\Delta i, n+\Delta j}\right|\right)}{\sum_{m=1}^{M}\sum_{n=1}^{N}\left(I_{m,n} + I_{m+\Delta i, n+\Delta j}\right)} \tag{5}$$

This function only uses addition and subtraction, thus the time reduction is expectable. Note here that the processed images Is are binarized after adaptive thresholding as described in Section 2, thus the information of Is are only either 1 or 0.

3.2 Subpixel level computation

In order to increase the accuracy of the correspondence finding, two schemes are combined for achieving this purpose. One is grey scale interpolation, the other is brightness compensation. For grey scale interpolation, a linear scheme is performed on the third layer of right image. In our study, the block size of the third layer is 8×8. The processing includes two steps as follows.

Step 1.   Use the pixel grey levels in vertical direction to interpolate the subpixel grey level, e.g., 3-point interpolation, between two neighboring pixels.

Step 2.   Based on the pixel and subpixel grey levels found in Step 1 to interpolate the subpixel grey leves in horizontal direction. In this case, the 3-point interpolation is aslo considered as example.

A comparision among pixel level, subpixel level, and after interpolation is illustrated in Fig. 3(a)-(c), respectively. Here we observe the image in Fig. 3(c) that the smoothness is improved greatly within the middle image but the randomness becomes more serious at two sides. It results from the ununiform brightness between the two CCD cameras. Hence a brightness compensation schem is presented to solve this problem.

As mentioned before for correlation error function in (5), the used correlation function (CF) may be redefined as

$$CF = \frac{I_1 + I_2 - \left|I_1 - I_2\right|}{I_1 + I_2}, \tag{6}$$

(a)   (b)   (c)

(d)   (e)

Fig. 3. Correlation results of (a) pixel level, (b) subpixel level, and (c) after interpolation. Further improved results using interpolation with (d) BC 32, and (e) BC 64.

where

$$
CF = \begin{cases} \dfrac{2I_2}{I_1 + I_2} & \text{if } I_1 \geq I_2, \\[2ex] \dfrac{2I_1}{I_1 + I_2} & \text{otherwise.} \end{cases}
\tag{7}
$$

Consider (7), if two block images I_1 and I_2 have different brightness, the correlation from I_1 to I_2 will be different to that from I_2 to I_1. Furthermore, it will be dominated by the block image having lower grey level distribution. As a result, the more uniform the two block image distribution, the higher accuracy the correlation; and vice versa. To compensate such ununiform brightness between two block images and reduce the error, a local compensation factor (LCF) is introduced as

$$
LCF = \frac{\displaystyle\sum_{(x_i, y_i) \in \text{left block}} P(x_i, y_i)}{\displaystyle\sum_{(x_j, y_j) \in \text{right block}} P(x_j, y_j)},
\tag{8}
$$

thus now (6) is modified as below and named CF with brightness compensation (BC).

$$
CF_{BC} = \frac{I_1 + LCF \times I_2 - \left| I_1 - LCF \times I_2 \right|}{I_1 + LCF \times I_2}
\tag{9}
$$

According to (9), results in Fig. 3(d) and 3(e) show that a good quality can be obtained. Here BC 32 means that 32 feature points are used in the subcorrelation. In our experiments, the accuracy can be increased 0.2-0.3 mm by the scheme of interpolation with brightness compensation; however a trade-off is that 4-5 times of computational time will be spent.

3.3 Results

Consider the two captured images shown in Fig. 2(a) and 2(b) respectively, three reconstructed results using pixel level computation, subpixel level computation, and the further improvement by interpolation with BC are shown in Fig. 4(a), 4(b), and 4(c), respectively. Obviously, the later result shows a better performance.

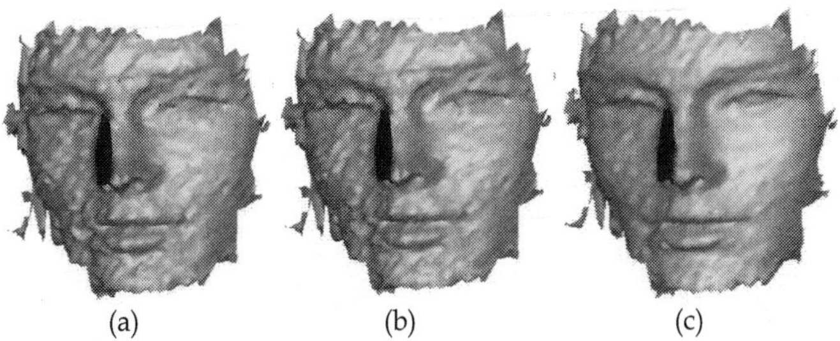

(a)(b)(c)

Fig. 4. Reconstructed results using (a) pixel level computation, (b) subpixel level computation, and (c) the further improvement by interpolation with BC.

In order to further increase the accuracy of reconstructing 3D object, a suitable method is to use a high resolution CCD system for capturing more data for an object. For example, in our system, Fig. 5(a) shows a normal resolution result with 652×512, whereas Fig. 5(b) shows a high resolution result with 1304×1024. Their specifications are listed in Table 1.

For a high resolution CCD system, due to more data to be processed we present a simplified procedure to solve the time-consuming problem. Consider the case of 1304×1024, the processing procedure is as follows.

Step 1. Down sampling. The image is reduced to a 652×512 resolution.

Step 2. Pixel level correlation with 3 levels is performed on the 652×512 image. In this step, the coarse 80×64 correlation vectors are obtained at the lowest level.

Step 3. Lift the lowest level in pixel level correlation from 8×8 to 16×16 each block, and further perform the pixel level computation on the original 1304×1024 image. Thus there are 160×128 correlation vectors to be output in this step.

Step 4. Based on the correlation vectors obtained in steps 3 and 4, the subpixel level correlation is performed to produce the final results.

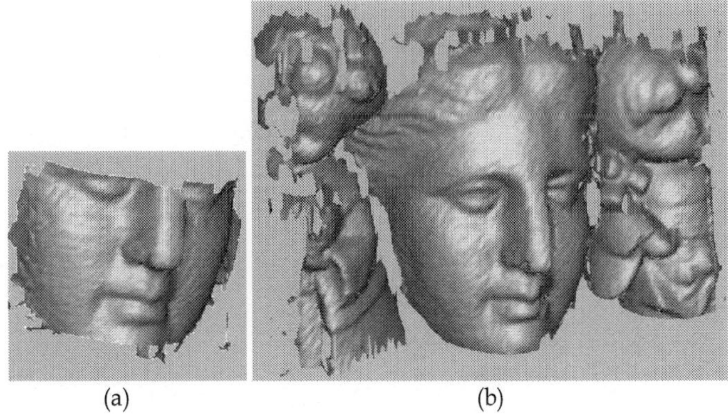

(a)(b)

Fig. 5. Examples of (a) normal resolution, and (b) high resolution.

System specification	Normal resolution system	High resolution system
Baseline (mm)	70	100
Lens (mm)	600	700
Object-CCD Distance (mm)	35	28
View Range (mm×mm)	83×62^a	180×150
Image Density Resolution	7.7×7.7^b	7.2×6.8

[a] "View Range" is defined as the (object width) × (object height).

[b] "Image Density Resolution" is defined as (image width/object width)×(image height/object height), thus the unit is (pixel/mm) ×(pixel/mm).

Table 1. Comparison between a normal and a high resolution CCD system in our study.

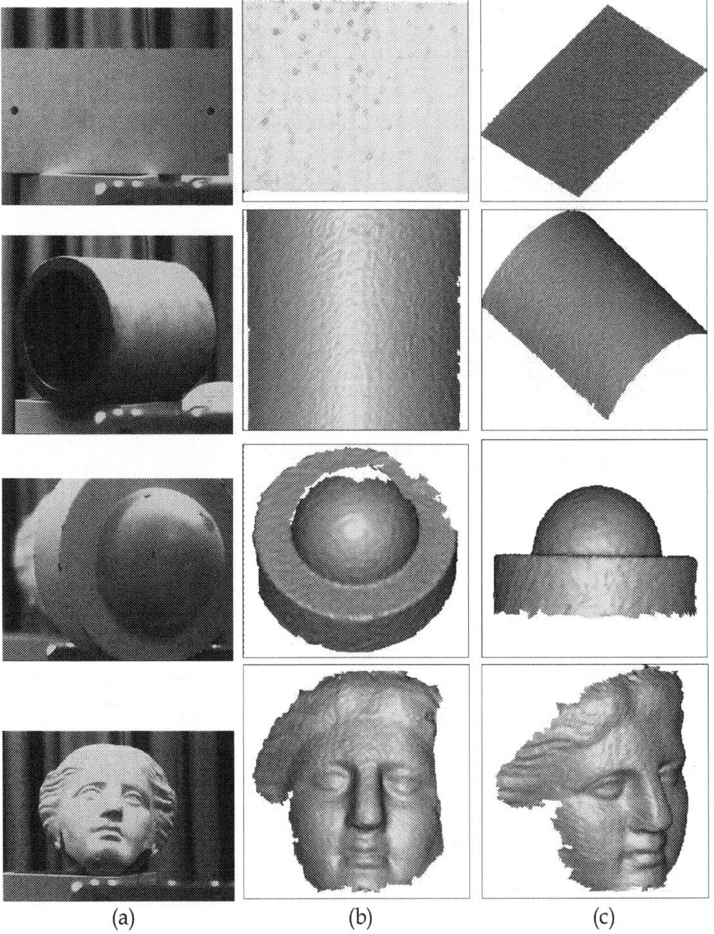

(a)   (b)   (c)

Fig. 6. Four test objects in (a), and their results with different views in (b) and (c).

For further demonstrating the quality of our algorithms, four objects in Fig. 6(a) and their reconstructed results in Fig. 6(b) and 6(c) are given. Note here that these results are only obtained from one view, thus they can be regarded as a 2.5D range image data. If multiple views are adopted and manipulated by our TriD system, the totally 3D result can be generated and illustrated in Fig. 7. As a result, a set of effective algorithms have been successfully developed for our 3D measurement system.

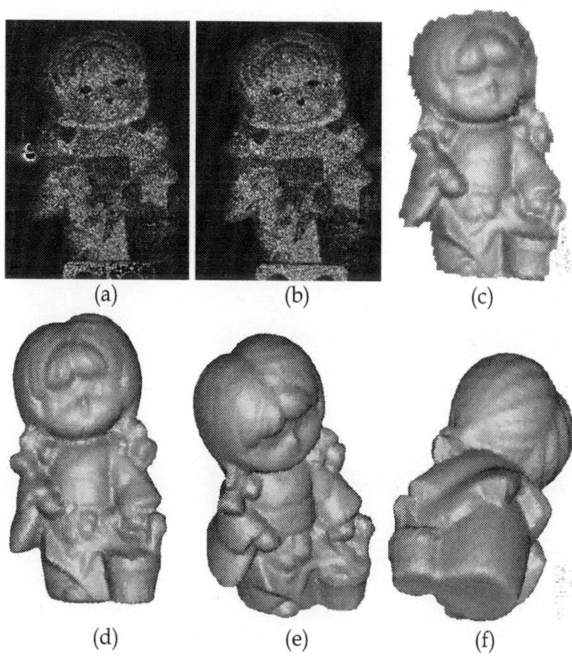

Fig. 7. Reconstructed 3D result of a doll. (a)(b) Speckled images. (c) 2.5D range image data using the speckled images. (d)-(f) Complete 3D result using many 2.5D range data.

4. 3-D Camera

The proposed 3D hand held camera contains three main components: a commercial DSC (Nikon D1 camera body), a patented three-hole aperture lens (Huang, 2001; Chen & Huang, 2002), and a flash as shown in Fig. 8(a). The flash projects the speckle pattern onto the object and the camera captures a single snapshot at the same time. To embed the 3D information in one captured image, we devise a novel lens containing three off-axis apertures, where each aperture was attached one colour filter as depicted in Fig. 8(b), so that a captured image carries the information from three different viewing directions. Since the three different images can be extracted from filtering the captured image with red, green, and blue component, respectively, the depth information may be obtained from these images by using the algorithms introduced in Section 3.

For the sake of illustrating the principle of our tri-aperture structure, an example of lens with two apertures is depicted in Fig. 8(c). Three points, P1, P2, and P3 are set on the central axis, where P2 is located at focal plane; P1 and P3 located at a far and near points with respect to the lens. The rays reflected from P2 pass through aperture A and B will intersect at the same location on the image plane, whereas P1 or P3 will image two different points. Accordingly the depth information of P1 and P3 may be computed from the disparity of their corresponding points on the image plane.

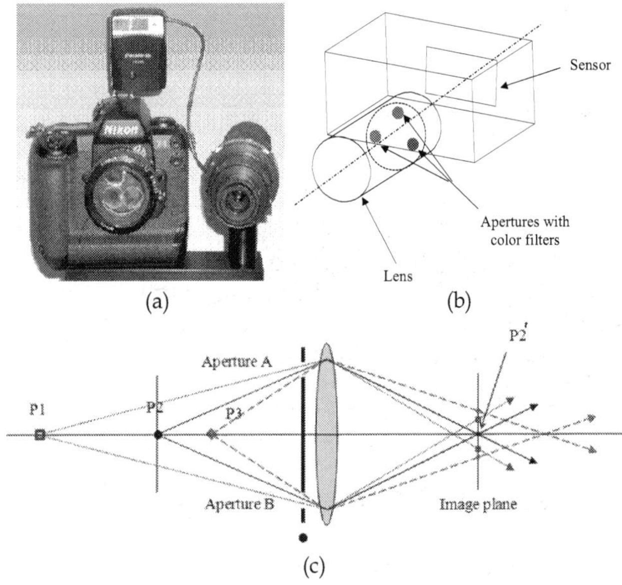

Fig. 8. (a) The newly designed version is based on a commercial digital camera (Nikon D1 camera body), a patented ring-aperture (three-hole aperture) lens depicted in (b), and a flash projecting a speckle pattern. (c) Example of lens with two apertures.

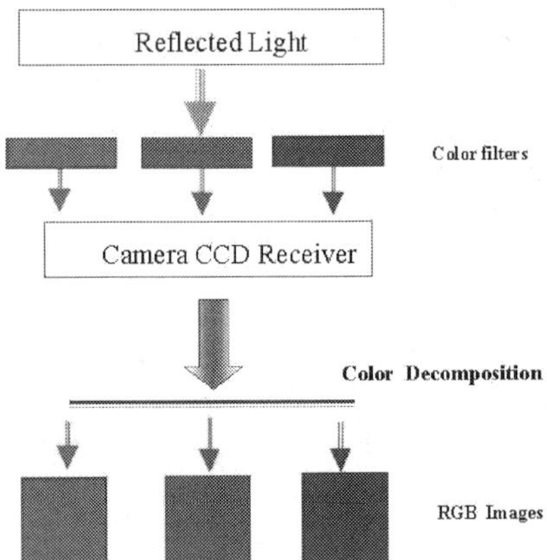

Fig. 9. Colour composition and decomposition

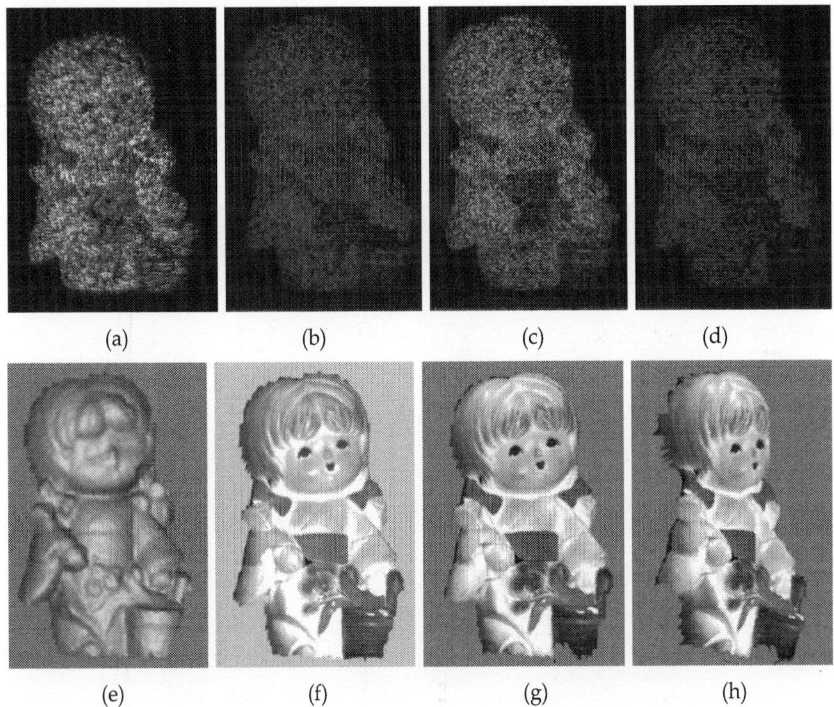

(a)   (b)   (c)   (d)

(e)   (f)   (g)   (h)

Fig. 10. (a) Image from tri-aperture lens. (b)-(d) R, G and B component obtained by separating the image from tri-aperture lens. (e) Range data. (f) Grey textured 2.5D image. (g)-(h) Colour textured 2.5D image with different view angles.

To extract the depth information from the single image, the image should be separated based on the colour filter. The colour composition and decomposition in Fig. 9 and an example shown in Fig. 10 are given for illustration. In Fig. 10(a), the image shows a mixture of R, G, B colour pixels since it merges the images from different dircection and colour filters. After colour separation process, three distinguished images based on R, G, B components are obtained as shown in Fig. 10(b)-10(d). Based on our depth computation algorithm embedded in TriD system, the range data is obtained as Fig. 10(e) shows. If a grey image is applied, we can obtain a grey textrued 2.5D image as Fig. 10(f) using a rendering process in TriD. Similarly, once a colour image is fed into our system, a colour textured 2.5D image may also be obtained as shown in Fig. 10(g) and 10(h) with different view angles. Note here that in this processing, a cross-talk problem may be rised, i.e., G and B components may corrupt the R-filtering image for example. In our study, this problem may be solved by increasing image intensity while an image is being captured.

The processing stages of our acquisition system using the proposed 3D camera are as follows. The camera captures two images of the target. The first snap gets speckled image (for 3D information computation), which will be spilt into three images based on the colour decomposition described before. Then the correlation process is used to compute depth information. The second snap gets original image (as a texture image) for further model rendering. For example, the human face of one author (Chang, I. C.) of this article is used for modelling. The speckled and texture images are captured and shown in Fig. 11(a) and 11(b), respectively. After the TriD software system, a face 3D model and its mesh model are obtained as shown in Fig. 11(c) and 11(d), respectively. This result demonstrates the feasibility of our 3-D hand-held camera system.

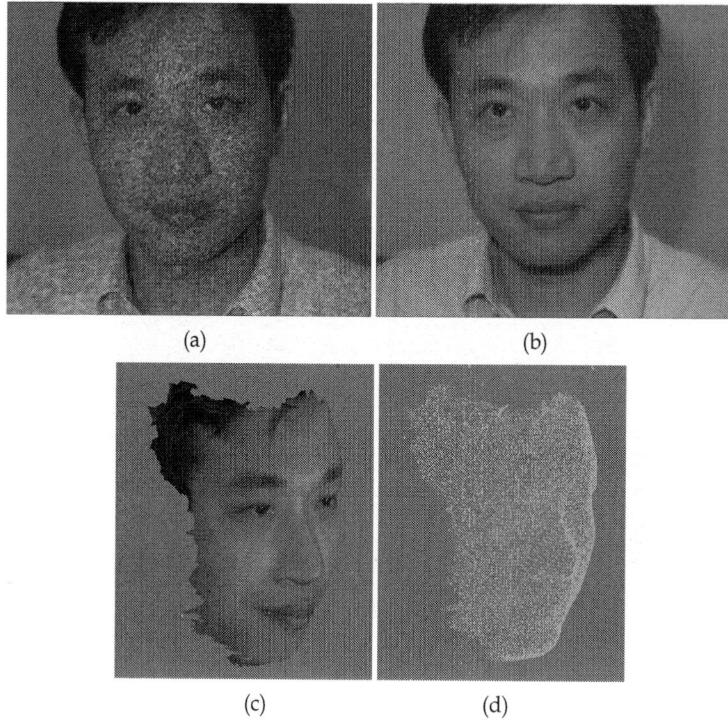

(a) (b)

(c) (d)

Fig. 11. The speckled image (a) and texture image (b) taken by our 3D hand-held camera system. The 3D face mode (c) and its mesh model (d) manipulated by our TriD system.

As described above, using the typical digital camera with our patented three-hole aperture lens along with a high accuracy calculation, the entire 3D image capturing process can now be done directly with a single lens in our 3D camera system. The three-hole aperture provides more 3D information than the dual-camera system because of their multi-view property. The depth resolution can therefore be increased considerably. Currently this 3D camera system has reached precision of sub-millimetre. The main system specifications are listed in Table 2. As a result, our 3D hand-held camera design integrating together the speckle generating projector and the colour digital camera makes the system be able to move around freely when taking pictures.

Light source	(flash) White-light random speckle pattern
CCD resolution	2000×1312
Measuring distance	500 ~ 800 mm
Measuring range	360 mm (X) × 240 mm (Y) × 80 mm (Z)
Resolution	0.18 mm (X) × 0.18 mm (Y)
Image capturing speed	1/30 second capturing time and 20 second processing time
Colour	R, G, B each 8 bits
Software	Plug-in module in *TriD* system

Table 2. System specifications in our 3-D hand-held camera design.

5. Conclusion

Three-dimensional information wanted has been an important topic and interested to many real applications. However, it is not easy to obtain the 3D information due to several inherent constraints on real objects and imaging devices. In this article, based on our study in recent years, we present effective algorithms using random speckle pattern projected on an object to obtain the useful correspondence or correlation vectors and thus reconstruct the 3D information for an object. Original two CCD cameras system has also been moved to a novel 3D hand-held camera containing a DSC, a patented three-hole aperture lens and a flash projecting random speckle pattern. Based on the manipulations of our TriD software system, our experiments have confirmed the feasibility of the proposed algorithms and 3D camera. This result guides us to a new era of portable 3D digital colour camera.

6. References

Chang, I. C.; Huang, C. L. & Hsueh, W. J. (2002). Novel three-dimensional hand-held camera based on three-aperture lens, *Proceedings of SPIE on Photonics Asia: Electronic Imaging and Multimedia Technology III*, Vol. 4925, pp. 655-662, Shanghai, China, Oct. 15-17, 2002.

Chen, B. T. & Huang, C. L. (2002). Device and methodology of capturing three-dimensional data using single len, *Patent number 154398*, Taiwan, ROC, 2002–2021.

Chen, Y. S. & Chen, B. T. (2003). Measuring of a three-dimensional surface by use of a spatial distance computation, *Applied Optics*, Vol. 42, No. 11, pp. 1958-1972.

Hart, D. P. (1998). High-speed PIV analysis using compressed image correlation, *Journal of Fluids Engineering*, Vol. 120, pp. 463-470.

Huang, C. L. (2001). Three-dimensional capturing device using single lens, *Patent number 139230*, Taiwan, ROC, 2001-2020.

Rocchini, C.; Cignoni, P.; Montani, C.; Pingi, P. & Scopigno, R. (2001). A low cost 3D scanner based on structured light, *Computer Graphics Forum, Proceedings of EUROGRAPHICS*, Vol. 20, pp. 299-308.

Siebert, J. P. & Marshall, S. J. (2000). Human body 3D imaging by speckle texture projection photogrammetry, *Sensor Review*, Vol. 20, pp. 218-226.

(2002). *TriD: Technical Report for 3D Human Modeling & Animation Application*, ver. 2.0, Opto-Electronics & Systems Laboratories, Industrial Technology Research Institute, Taiwan, ROC.

## 15

Single Photon Emission Tomography (SPECT) and 3D Images Evaluation in Nuclear Medicine

Maria Lyra
University of Athens
Greece

1. Introduction

The target of Nuclear Medicine is to provide information on the distribution of a chosen molecule in space and/or also in time, inside the human body. An image of the distribution, of a molecule of biochemical or physiological importance, within the body in a specific organ, provides information on the functioning of an organ that is valuable for medical diagnosis and for monitoring the response to the treatment of a disease.

The techniques used in Nuclear Medicine involve labelling of a specific molecule with a radioactive atom; a quantity of which is administered to the patient. The labelled molecules follow their specific biochemical pathways inside the body. The atoms used are radioactive and undergo random decay, emitting gamma ray photons. Photons are detected outside the body by the detector -NaJ(Tl) crystal- of the gamma camera.

Imaging by two-dimensional (2D) planar scintigrams has been routinely used since many years. The functional information obtained by Single Photon Emission Tomography (SPECT) is complementary to the planar images, obtained by projections of the organ under investigation. SPECT is an important tool for evaluating the functional status of the human body, emerging information by reconstructing data in slices of the total organ.

Image quality and quantitative accuracy in SPECT can be degraded by some parameters as the effects of photon attenuation and finite spatial resolution of the tomographic gamma camera system.

Volume data in nuclear medicine, by rendering and shading, give the 3 dimensional (3D) description of an organ and carry information of an organ's surface in angles around it. They are obtained by a sequence of 2D slices reconstructed from projections acquired around a 3D volume organ. Volume visualization obtains volumetric signs useful in diagnosis, in a more familiar and realistic way. Filtering, thresholding and gradient are necessary tools in the production of diagnostic 3D images.

The required input data for creation of 3D surface images is a dataset containing slice images which have been previously reconstructed from the SPECT acquisition data. These slices may be in one of several planes: transaxial, sagittal, coronal or oblique, and the orientation of the input data determine the orientation of the final 3D surface dataset. The 3D reconstruction of external surface of kidneys, lungs, liver, thyroid and heart are described here, focused on the details and precision of the final surfaces through grading.

2. Volume data in nuclear medicine

Organ volumes evaluation using planar imaging technique is a procedure often performed in nuclear medicine but faces difficulties due to structures containing radioactivity, which overlie or underlie the organ of interest. SPECT overcomes these difficulties since structures in the interior of the examined organ are separated in the reconstructed images (Rosenthal et al, 1995).

The presentation of functional volumes and activity concentrations in SPECT requires that a linear and stationary relationship exists, between the apparent activity distribution in the reconstructed image and the true distribution in the organ. However, because of the limited spatial resolution of the gamma camera, and physical processes such as photon scattering and photon attenuation, this relationship is neither linear nor stationary (Gourion & Noll, 2002).

Absolute quantification of the 3D distribution of a radionuclide within a patient has been one of the greatest challenges of Nuclear Medicine. This is difficult due to the fact that nuclear medicine images are degraded by several factors (anatomic, physical, technical factors), which limit the quantitative ability of this modality (Tsui et al, 1994).

SPECT is used in image analysis studies to extract information about areas and volumes or amounts of radioactivity in specific regions of interest. The information that derived from these studies is then applied to aid in clinical diagnoses or even to estimate radiation dosimetry or determination of volume or mass (De Sadeleer et al, 1996; Erdi et al, 1995; Pant et al, 2003;). Many methods for precise and accurate measurements of volume and the amount of radioactivity in a specific region of interest are used (Boudraa & Zaidi, 2006; Hansen, 2002a).

The set of SPECT images (slices) is used for the 3D volumetric representation of internal organs of the human body. Image based volume rendering techniques have demonstrated the improvement of rendering quality when 3D organ presentation is based on digital images as SPECT slices and some shape and functional information (Sainz et al 2003). 3D volume representation may reach photorealistic quality taking into consideration the factors that degrade slices data and affect quantitative accuracy (Zaidi, 1996b).

2.1 Data acquisition

3D images, in nuclear medicine techniques, are created by acquisition data sets in angular planes. The data are acquired by SPECT gamma camera in an arc of 180 or 360 degrees – depending on the size and the position of the studying organ- and multiple slices that can be treated as volume data are produced from the angular projections.

It is often considered that adequate compensation for the effects of physical factors, as non uniform attenuation or distance-dependent spatial resolution, requires data acquired over 2π. However, in many cases the data measured over 2π contain redundant information. Sometimes, 2π acquisition affects the quality due to effect of partially compensating attenuation of the surrounding the organ tissues. Noo & Wagner, 2001 have shown that data acquired only over π can be used to correct for the effect of uniform attenuation in SPECT and Pan et al, 2002 showed that with both non-uniform attenuation and distance- dependent spatial resolution the scanning angle can be reduced from 2π to π.

Thyroid gland is a front superficial organ and best data are collected by a 180 degrees arc acquisition, in a clockwise direction. In the case of kidneys – a posterior organ- data are acquired in a counter clock direction, over π. Similarly, because of heart position in the left part of the chest, the data for reconstruction are acquired in a clockwise direction, from -45^0 to 135^0, that is, the data are acquired over π.

Pan et al, 2001 are referred to mathematical rationales that explain that 2π measurements contain redundant information, as, in the absence of noise and other inconsistencies, the measurements of conjugate views are mathematically identical, i.e.

$$p\ (\xi,\ \varphi) = p(-\xi,\ \varphi + \pi\ ) \tag{1}$$

This is an example of the measurement of the 2D Radon transform $p\ (\xi,\ \varphi)$ of a real function over 2π, where ξ is the detector bin index and φ is the angle acquiring data.

In any cases of human organs, as lungs and liver, that their anatomic location includes front and posterior regions, the 2π geometry during data acquisition and reconstruction is necessary.

2.2 Attenuation

It is assumed that the count rate measured at a point on a planar image is equal to the sum of the count rates emerging from all the volume elements along the ray line. In reality a significant number of gamma rays will be scattered or absorbed before reaching the detector. This results in a reduction in the observed count rate at the detector:

$$N = N_1.\ e^{-\mu d} \tag{2}$$

where N is the measured count rate when N_1 is the count rate which would be measured if there were no attenuation, e is the base of the natural logarithms, d is the thickness of attenuating material through which the gamma rays must pass, and μ (attenuation coefficient) is a constant which depends on the energy of the gamma rays and the type of attenuating material. For 140 KeV gamma rays of Tc99m -*the radioisotope more used in Nuclear Medicine*- the attenuation coefficient is $\mu=0.15/cm$, for human tissue; because of scatter a value of 0.12/cm. is usually used to correct for attenuation(Rosenthal et al, 1995).

A procedure is used for correcting of the errors in reconstruction introduced by attenuation. The attenuation correction procedure is a first order method. Because of the inaccuracy of the correction procedure it is necessary to use a value less than the theoretically correct value; 0.12/cm is usually best for technetium gamma rays in man (Zaidi, 1996; Zaidi & Hasegawa, 2003).

If attenuation correction is used the system needs to know the extent of the attenuating material that is the edge of the patient. The patient outline can be calculated by the system. A threshold level is calculated, many times, as a percentage of the maximum pixel intensity for the whole planar dataset.

2.3 Volume rendering

Volume visualization in nuclear medicine is a method of extracting meaningful information from volumetric data using, manipulating and rendering a sequence of 2D slices. Volume data are 3D entities that may have information inside them or at there surface and edges at angular views that can be obtained by 3D surface rendering images in different angular views. During rendering time (Sainz et al 2008), given a new view point, the step is to determine which of the reference (acquired) views contribute to the new one and then if they overlap, combine them to produce the final volume (fig.1).

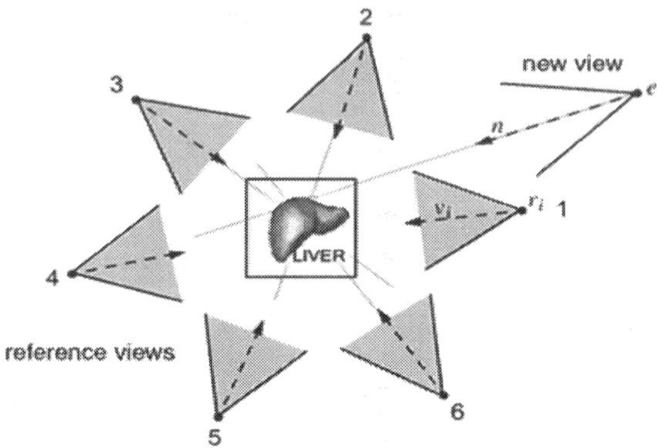

Fig. 1. Distribution of angular acquired data. Reference Views will contribute to the interpolated new view. (from Sainz et al 2008)

3D images are reconstructed by surface rendering techniques. Organ surface volumes in nuclear medicine can be made from the scientific data by outlining (threshold use) structures in the serial slices and after stacking them, surface reconstruction is done. The result of tomographic reconstructions is a set of contiguous or superposed slices in which the basic element is a voxel, since it represents volume, with the third dimension equal to one pixel. Voxels are reorganized and displayed in 3D way by labeling each voxel with information concerning the distance and the angle of its surface. Surface images are created and interpolated for any angle resulting in rotating surface images.

By gathering sufficient volume data, analysis and quantification of 3D images give valuable information in medical diagnosis. Angular measurements on body structures are often crucial for analysis of the data for diagnosis. Shaded surface images provide unique views of the three dimensional radiopharmaceutical distributions within the human body (Shin et al, 2009).

When viewed together with two-dimensional data, 3D surface images give excellent information about the location, orientation and extent of regions of isotope uptake. 3D datasets are very strong visual representations of tomographic data, and are mainly used qualitatively to help orientate the user with the tomographic slice data. This reinforces the three dimensional nature of nuclear data and strengthens the user's awareness of what the data represents and he can glean information on perfusion details for liver or cardiac studies and function information of thyroid, lungs or kidneys, from the 3D surface images.

When 3D surface images are generated, data are processed from each slice in order. This set of slice images contains information in the form of count values in volume elements, voxels, which represents the distribution of the radiopharmaceutical within the volume being imaged. The 3D surface images which are produced provide views of a specific three dimensional surface of this volume. This surface is defined by a count threshold which is applied to each of the voxels; all voxels which have count values greater than the threshold define a specific volume. The surface images display the surfaces of this volume. There are 3 possible ways in which 3D datasets can be generated: a) At a fixed count threshold, the view angle of the surface is varied to create the impression of a rotating surface, b) At a fixed viewing angle, the count threshold is varied to create a dataset which sequentially removes layers of counts from the object rather like peeling the layers from the examined organ, c) Using a fixed view angle and threshold, the distance from which the surface is viewed is varied. This enables the user to take slices through the surface image.

2.4 Thresholding

Many methods have been developed for image edge detection and most of these techniques work well in images with uniform regions, but less well in regions with greater non uniformity. Medical images are usually characterized by faded features utilizing a narrow distribution of grey-levels. Nuclear medicine images often suffer from low contrast that is further degraded by the noise introduced in the process of imaging (Razifar et al 2005). It is important to use the local contrast information as well as the overall distribution of grey-levels for obtaining meaningful regions. A large number of algorithms with many approaches have been investigated. These approaches include histogram based methods, edge and boundary detection based methods, region growing based methods, and linear feature based methods (Mortelmans et al, 1986; Russ 2006; Murli et al, 2008).

The accurate reconstruction of organ volumes from SPECT images suffers from image segmentation. Image segmentation defines the borders of the organ and allows volume measurements by counting the voxels inside (Zingerman et al 2009). The threshold has to be adapted for each case as it is dependent on the size of the organ and the contrast of the reconstructed SPECT slices.

Some threshold algorithms have been applied to minimize the difference between true and reconstructed volumes. Grey level histograms analysis has been proven a suitable technique for thresholding. Segmentation is performed with algorithms that separate object and background pixels by comparing their intensity (counts) with the mean intensity of the region. A region of interest is roughly defined by the operator to include the slices of the organ to be reconstructed.

Thresholding is one of the simplest and popular techniques for image segmentation. It can be performed based on global information that is grey level histogram of the entire image or using local information of the image. In thresholding method, to obtain automatically the optimum threshold value, an initial estimate for threshold T is selected. The image is segmented using T.(Boudraa & Zaidi, 2006). In this way two regions of pixels will be separated: R_I all pixels of the image with grey values > T and R_B the pixels of the region considered as background with values<T. By the average grey level values M_I and M_B for the regions R_I and R_B a new threshold value is computed:

$$T_N= (M_I + M_B)/2 \tag{3}$$

The main drawback of histogram-based region segmentation is that histogram provides no spatial information. Region thresholding approaches exploit the fact that pixels close to each other have similar grey values. The main assumption of this approach is that regions are nearly constant in image intensity and it is referred as a robust technique for volumetric quantification and localization of abnormal regions.

However, combining intensity and gradient data can improve histogram (Csetverikov, 2007). Better separation of objects and background pixels close to edges, give high gradients; pixels of object and background, though, have low gradients. Then, in order the result be improved, histogram high-gradient pixels are discarded. (fig.2.).

The gradient shading is used to add shading to the 3D reconstructed image Gradient shading enhances the display of surface detail.

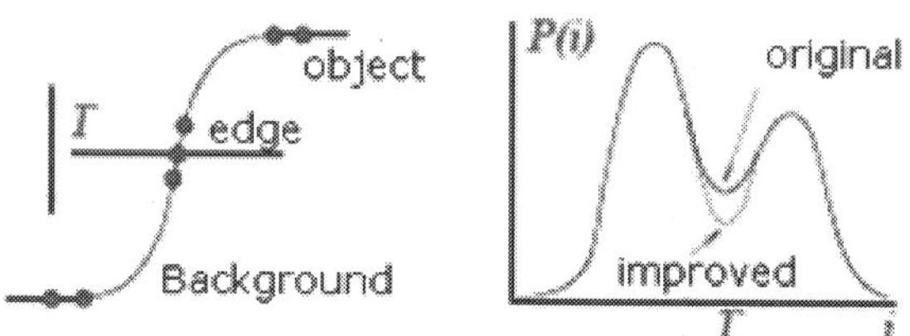

Fig. 2. Discarding high gradient pixels close to edges improves the reconstructed image. (from Csetverikov, 2007)

3. The reconstruction process

The basic reconstruction is created by the planar images, collected by the gamma camera and contain the number of gamma rays detected at each angle position on the face of the collimator. The image which is to be generated is composed of the numbers of gamma rays emitted from each of the small pixels. The data from which this are to be calculated is the sums of the counts in various rows of the pixels drawn at the angles at which images were recorded at acquisition time.

If, for example, 64 planar images in 64 x 64 matrices are acquired 360⁰ around the patient, each transaxial slice can be reconstructed from the information taken from a single row of elements (pixels) in each planar image. This information is used to calculate the values of 4096 pixels in the transaxial slice. For each angle-each planar image- there are 64 measured values, each measured value being the sum of the numbers which should appear in the reconstructed slice. The reconstruction problem is to calculate a set of numbers for the transaxial matrix the sums of which, in every direction at which a measurement was made, are equal to the measured values at that angle. In the current example there are 4096 equations (64 sums multiplied by 64 angles) containing a total of 4096 unknowns, the numbers in the pixels.

3.1 Filtering

A number of methods have been used to perform reconstructions of this type.

The method of Filtered -Back-Projection (FBP) is composed of two stages; the first is filtering of the planar image data, and the second is to back-project the filtered data to form transaxial images. The back projection is based on the inverse transformation of the geometrical model of the SPECT data acquisition. The algorithm works well for infinite number of projections, but when a limited number of projections are produced the back projection method causes "star pattern" around the reconstructed object. The star-shaped pattern and the noise are reduced by filtering the projections with a FBP algorithm (fig.3).

When the collected data are back projected, the rows with the largest numbers overlap at the position of the source, but not elsewhere. The result is that the back-projected numbers add up over the position of the source into very much larger numbers than those in other areas of the matrix.

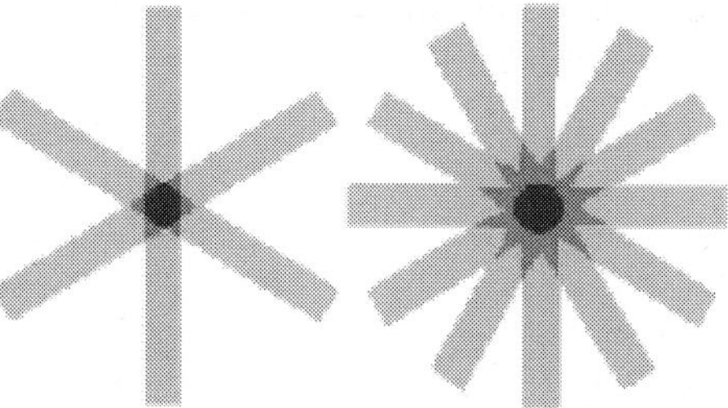

Fig. 3. Back projections of a point source created by finite numbers of projection angles; in this case "star pattern" occurs.

The difficulty with simple back-projection is that areas of the reconstructed slice which should be zero, as no radioactivity was there, are not zero. In addition there is always an increase in the numbers near the centre of the image. In order to overcome these problems, the original data are necessary to be modified by "filtering" before back-projecting.

3.1.1 Ramp filter

The modification procedure is done by filtering. This additional filtering can be performed by pre-filtering the planar data, by filtering the final reconstructed slices, or by combining a suitable filter with the back-projection filter. Because of these, it is convenient to perform the filtering on the Fourier transform of the data, rather than on the data itself.

The filter which is used is a frequency filter. It causes some spatial frequencies to be enhanced and others to be reduced. Correction for the central build-up in back-projection requires that low spatial frequencies be attenuated and high spatial frequencies be amplified.

The filter which exactly corrects for the back-projection defects is the Ramp filter (fig.4). This filter enhances high frequencies by multiplying all frequencies by a term proportional to the frequency. This "Ramp filter" compensates for the distortion introduced by back-projection but takes no account of the nature of the information being back-projected. The ramp filter may be applied in two ways; one takes account of several mathematical considerations, producing quantitative results and the other produces results with improved image contrast

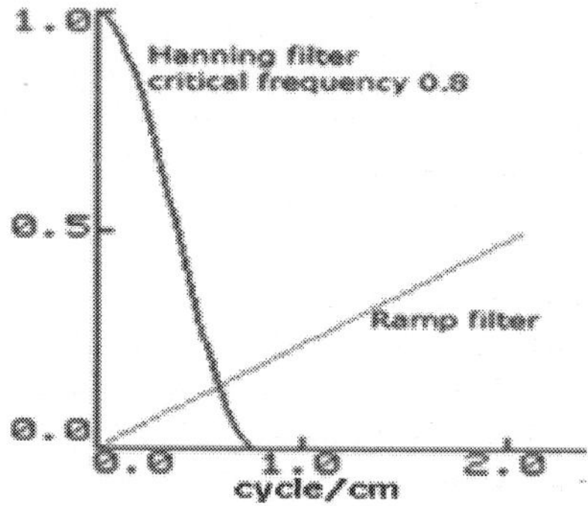

Fig. 4. High frequency information is greatly magnified by the Ramp filter. Hanning filter drops sharply to zero at a frequency (0.8 cycle/cm, in this figure) close to the limiting resolution of the gamma camera.

3.1.2 Filtering approaches

Radioactive decay is a random process, so all gamma camera data is limited by counting statistics. The statistical variations which always exist between one pixel and the next tend to disguise the true count rate being measured. This statistical noise can vary rapidly from one pixel to another according to Poisson statistics, and so contains high spatial frequencies. The information contained in these high frequencies is not real information about the patient, but contains "noise". This statistical noise is not wanted, but is always present in gamma camera images. Although it may be necessary to tolerate statistical noise in most images, there is no desire to increase the amount of noise. If tomographic data is filtered using the **Ramp** filter, all high frequency information is greatly magnified, and so therefore is the statistical noise (fig.4). For this reason the filters used in tomography are usually designed to drop sharply to zero at a frequency which corresponds to the limiting resolution of the gamma camera. Two general classes of such filters are provided, in addition to the ramp filter. The user may choose the limiting frequency at which the filter goes to zero as by **Hanning** filter (fig.4) or the relative height of the filter in the mid-frequencies when it starts to approach zero by **Butterworth** filter. Kao & Pan, 2000, have described other non-iterative methods that suppress image noise and artifacts in 3D SPECT.

Iterative reconstruction methods are also used to obtain images with good signal-to-noise ratio in nuclear medicine image reconstruction. Maximum Likelihood Expectation Maximization (ML-EM) method reduces artifacts but requires more computation time. Another iterative filtering method the Ordered Subsets Expectation Maximization (OSEM) is used in 3D SPECT reconstruction and compared to FBP. OSEM and FBP presented similar accuracy in volume measurements of myocardial perfusion (Daou et al, 2003). However, it is possible to calculate the noise constructed by FBP while this not possible by iterative methods (Hansen, 2002b). ROC analysis of OSEM and FBP techniques in lung cancer, showed that there was no significant difference in the area under the ROC curve (Son et al, 2001).

4. Surface images process

The imaged volume data which will be used for surface image generation is obtained from a set of transaxial, sagittal, coronal, or oblique slice images. Prior to the generation of the surface images, processing operations should be performed.

To improve the resolution of acquired data the maximum possible matrix size both for data acquisition and processing is used. The visual quality of the surface images improves as the voxel size decreases. Therefore, a 128 x 128 resolution acquisition would be preferred and is used for acquiring data from organs as kidneys or thyroid gland. In practice, however, many times a 64 x 64 acquisition is used with excellent results; The use of the 64 x 64 matrix offer the advantage of reduced storage requirements and processing times. Data from organs as myocardium or lungs are usually acquired in a 64x64 matrix size.

Filters used in reconstruction are also very important for the maximum transfer of information in 3D images. The choice of the filter is dependent upon the noise characteristics of the data (Yan and Zeng 2008). Since the images depict a surface, an increased amount of smoothing may be desirable without loosing surface special features, as roughness or smoothness, which may be characteristics of an abnormality of the organ. The appearance of defects at parts of the organ that are not functioning is crucial too. Lungs emboli follow up by imaging, for the perfusion improving or renal pelvis imprint are signs for the diagnosis and must be emerged in surface 3D images. A good general purpose filter for this application is the Hanning 0.8 prefilter, with a ramp backprojection filter. For high resolution data such as thyroid studies, a Butterworth filter which passes more of the middle frequencies can be used.

Zoomed reconstruction technique is used to perform a 3D zoom in the transaxial space in cases of small organs as pediatric kidneys or thyroid gland. Any tomographic slice dataset may be magnified in 3 dimensions, following reconstruction. Three dimensional magnification is recommended as it reduces the voxel size, providing improved visual image quality. Since the output images have the same resolution in pixels as the input images, magnification is limited by the possibility of excluding volumes of interest.

A magnification by a factor of 2 in all three directions is common in small organs. For example, for an initial set of 32 transaxial slices of 64x64 resolution data, as in the case of a myocardium SPECT acquisition in an 180^0 arc, the portions of the transaxial images within a certain window are magnified by double. In addition, 31 new magnified transaxial slice images are created in between each of the magnified original images. The resulting dataset will contain 63 transaxial slice images of 64 x 64 data.

It is possible to magnify the set of slices which is the result of a previous magnification, to obtain an over-all magnification factor of 4. In this study, myocardium perfusion transaxial slice data is normally magnified by a factor of 2 prior to 3D surface image generation.

In cases where multiple structures exist in the imaged volume, it may be useful to remove data which does not belong to the structure of interest by selectively remove unwanted structure from the slice images by setting selected voxel values to zero. This operation has applications in lung studies, to separate the right and left lungs or in studies of the liver where the spleen may be useful to be zeroed out. It is, also, sometimes, useful to apply in kidneys 3D surface images creation, in cases that the function of the parenchyma of one kidney is very deteriorated and the maximum intensity of one kidney is lower than 50% of the other kidney. In this case, two regions of interest are defined for the two kidneys and are processed separately. Then each kidney is reconstructed, determining the threshold as percentage of the its maximum.

4.1 Distance shading procedure

3D Surface images are created from tomographic slice data in two steps in which the images are shaded. By distance shading operation, the distance shaded surface images are produced. The detection of the surfaces occurs and this accounts for most of the processing time. The surface which will be defined for display is the surface of a volume which is obtained using a calculated count threshold. This volume contains all voxels, which have count values which are above the count threshold value. The distance surface images are created to appear as if the volume is being viewed from specific viewing planes. In the creation of 3D surface images of all the studied organs, the data of transaxial slices were used; by this selection, the orientation of the organs in the body (head/up- feet/down) is kept.

A transaxial slice image is displayed, after the application of a threshold intensity/count value so that all voxels which have count values which are greater than the count threshold are white and those below are black. The outer edge of the threshold slice is the desired surface boundary. A distance surface is generated from the entire set of slices.

The 3D image which is displayed is the surface of a volume defined by count threshold. Thus, volume contains all voxels which have count values which are above the count threshold value. For ease in application, the calculated, according to equation (3) threshold level is specified as a percentage of the maximum count level in the input slice dataset.

It is helpful when determining the appropriate threshold value for a given dataset, to create multiple surface images, from one viewing plane, changing only the threshold value from one image to the next, iteratively.

Typical threshold values are usually of the order of 40%-50% for heart, lungs and liver data. For kidneys and thyroid gland data may give a different value, ranging from 30% to 50%.

4.2 Viewing plane

The distance shaded surface images are created to appear as if the volume is being viewed from specific viewing positions. Each position is more specifically defined as an image which lies in a predefined viewing plane. These viewing planes may be positioned anywhere around the imaged volume, if the vertical axis of the viewing plane is parallel to the axis which is normal to the slice data. As the slice images are of the transaxial type, the viewing planes are positioned to view the data from the same locations as in the original projection/planar views, at any angular position about the axis (Garcia et al, 2001).

The angular position of the 3D surface images depends on the angle steps (usually 16) selected to reconstruct and view the 3D surface images, as an angle measured clockwise from a line which rises vertically from the centre of the image. Thus, if the input slices are of the transaxial type, 0 degrees corresponds to an anterior view, 90 degrees produces a left lateral view, 180 degrees produces a posterior view, and 270 degrees produces a right lateral view. A start distance value equal to zero places the viewing plane outside the entire organ volume for viewing the surface of the organ.

4.3 Gradient shading

Following, gradient shading is used to add shading to the image produced in distance shading procedure. The amount of gradient shading on a set of surface images is varied, without having to re-compute 3D distance shading images, each time. Gradient shading is expressed in percentage and is depending on the surface functionality which in this way expresses.

Gradient shading is used to enhance the display of surface detail. Garcia-Panyela & Susin, 2002 used surface reconstruction in their dynamic model to provide volume and give functionality keys about the organ. With this type of shading, the surface image brightness is a function of the local slope of the surface. This calculation is carried out on the distance surface images.

The value for the gradient surface image pixel is at a maximum when the local surface element is facing front. As the surface slopes away towards another angle, the gradient image pixel value decreases. In the limit, when the local surface element appears as an edge the gradient image pixel value is zero.

The final 3D surface images produced include the effects of both distance and gradient shading. We have computed 3D gradient shaded images from 3D distance shaded images for all human organs that we are referred in this work. We select the amount of gradient shading which will be added to a distance surface image by a gradient shading factor 10 to 20 depending on the physiology of the organ; that is abnormality of its parenchyma or its perfusion deterioration. The amount of shading to add depends on the black and white or color maps employed. A grey scale map or a color map is used as this is the way that 3D surface images produce best detailed display useful in medical diagnosis.

5. Clinical applications

The imaging system is a GE starcam AT 4000 equipped with a low energy high resolution collimator (LEHR) for acquisition of scintigraphic studies of all the organs. System collimator, used in all our studies, was this LEHR in order to achieve the most detailed data. The tomography hardware/software gamma camera facility uses the tomography ring stand, to rotate the camera around the patient during acquisition. A very fast, array processor is used to reconstruct the tomographic images. Furthermore, the whole acquisition- processing system is interfaced with a GE Xeleris 2 for fast computing and displaying planar, SPECT and 3D volume images. Elementary voxel size is determined separately. To establish this measurement, an image of two 1mm parallel line sources, 10mm apart, was created and the number of pixels between the center of the two line sources was measured. Rotating the line sources 90 degrees would provide the pixel width in the opposite direction. Pixel size was controlled weekly and in a 64x 64 matrix is approximately 6.4 mm (+-0.2).

The SPECT and 3D reconstructed images of clinical applications of the Heart, Lungs, Liver, Kidneys and Thyroid gland have been exploited and displayed. The application of this technique includes the study of parenchymatous organ (Liver, Kidneys, Thyroid gland) for possible abnormalities or for the potential assessment of organ perfusion (Heart, Lungs) in a three dimensional display. Volume images are rotated on any spatial plane and provide rich detailing of the organ surface and functional completeness. Angular appearance of body structures is often crucial for determining the medical diagnosis.

5.1 Renal studies- 3D surface images

Tc-99m DiMercaptoSuccinic Acid (Tc-99mDMSA) renal scan is the method of choice for the detection and follow-up of any possible cortical damage to the kidneys. The test is widely performed in children in order to check for any possible signs of acute pyelonephritis, scars as well as for any suspected dysplasia of the kidneys (Temiz et al 2006). Kidneys' are located in the posterior abdomen in a very small depth depending of the size, weight and age of the patient.

The usual procedure involves intravenous injection of Tc99m-DMSA and acquisition at 4 to 6 hours post-injection, of four planar images: Posterior (POST), Anterior (ANT), Right Posterior Oblique (RPO) and Left Posterior Oblique (LPO). The planar imaging (renal scanning) of the patients is followed by a SPECT study (Groshar et al, 1997; Yang et al, 2001). Tomographic imaging was carried out by data acquired in 15 sec at each of 32 positions over 180 degrees around the posterior view of the patient. The 32 angular projection views - the original data as recorded by the gamma camera- are reconstructed to get SPECT slices – transaxial, coronal and sagittal-. An acquisition magnification equal to 2 was used for planar as well as angular projections for the SPECT study. Acquisition matrix size 128x128 was used in all cases and a post reconstruction magnification equal to 2 was used in paediatric cases. In this way, 3D surface images of paediatric kidneys' were created by a final 4fold magnification to obtain the best spatial detail. FBP, Hanning with crucial frequency 0.8 and ramp filter were used in renal reconstructions. Sheehy et al, 2009, compare two filtering methods (OSEM and FBP) of reconstructing renal SPECT studies and noted that both techniques yielded identical findings for 94 of the 98 kidneys evaluated.

Lyra et al 2001, use the planar and tomographic reconstructed images for the calculation of three indices that are the ratios of counts of upper to lower, upper to middle and lower to middle part by a tomographic reconstruction technique "by parts" and they offer a quantitative comparison of the planar and tomographic images.

3D surface images have not been evaluated up to now in an angular display of surface images either as normal or pathological 3D images, where scars, renal size and renal pelvis imprint can be identified. Following figures (fig. 5.1.1, 5.1.2, 5.1.3, 5.1.4) are examples of normal and abnormal situations of the kidneys in which different qualitative signs are emerged.

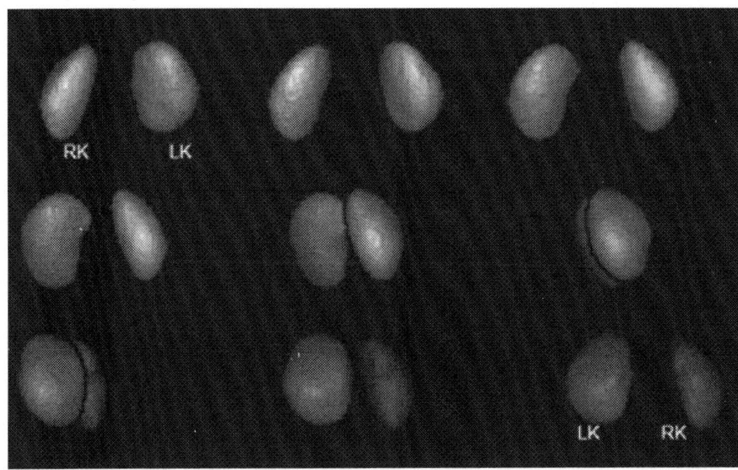

Fig. 5.1.1. 3D surface images of the normal kidneys of a child 1 year old, reconstructed for 9 angles around the body. Notice a tiny impress of right renal pelvis-Physiological sign-.

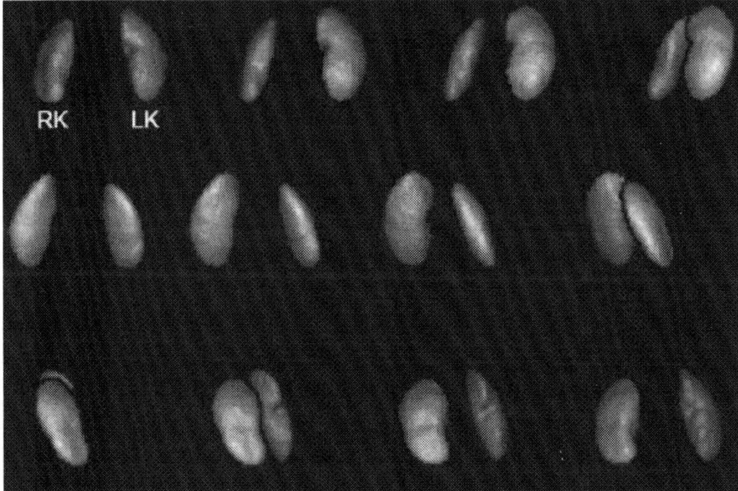

Fig. 5.1.2. 3D surface images at angular positions of a 6 months old renal study, in grey scale. Physiological impress of both renal pelvis. Reduced functioning parenchyma of the lower pole of right kidney

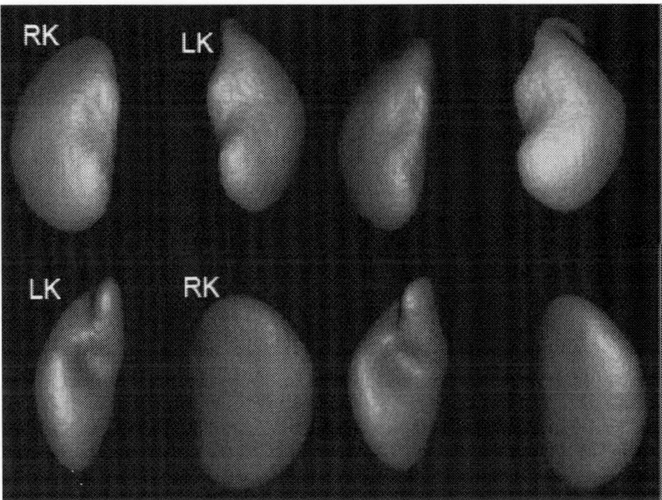

Fig. 5.1.3. 3D surface reconstructed angular images of kidneys; Deficiency of 18% of the upper pole of left kidney (scar) and central pyelocalyceal system –pyelonephritis-.

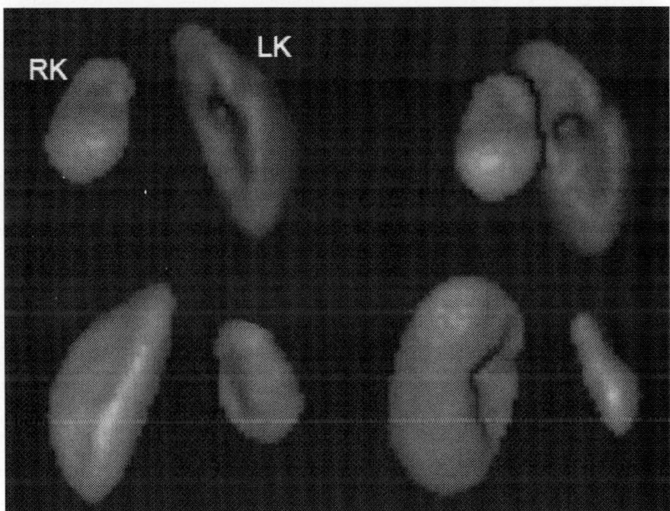

Fig. 5.1.4. 3D surface images at 4 angles; Compensatory hypertrophy of left kidney with important deficiency of the parenchyma close to pyelocalyceal system; Atrophic right kidney, with 22% of total functioning renal parenchyma.

3D display clearly offers additional valuable information. The procedure does not require any extra quantity of radiopharmaceutical to be injected to the patient, therefore the radiation burden is the same. The extra time required is in the order of 15 minutes, therefore not presenting any inconvenience for the patient.

5.2 Myocardium perfusion-3D surface images

Heart scintigraphy provides information with respect to the detection of myocardial perfusion defects, the assessment of the pattern of defect reversibility and the overall detection of Coronary Artery Disease (CAD). There is a relationship between the location and the degree of the stenosis in coronary arteries and the observed perfusion on the myocardial scintigraphy, using data of 3D surface images of myocardium. This allows us to predict the impact evolution of these stenoses to justify a coronarography or to avoid it.

The visual interpretation of Tc99m tetrofosmin SPECT myocardial perfusion images can be challenging, due to the quantity of scan information generated by the large number of normal variants, attenuation artefacts and gender differences.(García-Panyella & Susín 2002) Defects of the cardiac structure can be emerged from the 3D surface images of myocardium. Investigations on phantom studies (Matsunari et al, 2001) have been done and new method for segmentation of left ventricle (LV) for estimation of defects' size (Soneson et al, 2009) has been validated.

Our Cardiac patients had completed stress (Tc99m tetrofosmin at stress peak) and rest SPECT test by a GE Starcam 4000 tomographic gamma camera, use of 180^0 arc rotation, step and shoot, 20 sec per projection and 64x64 matrix size and magnification 2, for data acquisition. The data of the 2 sets (stress-rest) of slices were used to produce 3D surface images of myocardium for 16 angles around the body of the patient. We exploited the myocardial 3D scintigraphic data of the left ventricle, at stress and at rest, in order to recognize the cardiac volume and estimate perfusion defects as a percentage of LV myocardium mass. Co identification of myocardial perfusion images data was performed to eliminate normal morphological variances such as variances in orientation, size and shape, so that the remaining differences represent important functional differences. Dixon et al, 2004 suggest that when attenuation correction and detector resolution compensation are applied during reconstruction, patient variables do not influence the quantitative accuracy. A significant improvement in results was found with zoomed acquisitions.

3D data reconstructed by FBP, obtained at stress and at rest scintigraphic studies, used to evaluate the left ventricle deformation in both stress - rest 3D surface image series. If a significant difference is obtained in rest and stress 3D data perfusion, the location and the impact of the pathology of left ventricle myocardium are recognized. The myocardial defects have been calculated as percentage of the myocardium at rest after the estimation of the total myocardium.

The following 5 next figures (fig 5.2.1, 5.2.2, 5.2.3, 5.2.4, 5.2.5) are referred to cases that myocardium diagnosis is rely on 3D surface shaded images; 3D data obtained at stress and at rest of the LV myocardium, respectively, are analysed and the deformation of both images is evaluated , qualitatively and quantitatively.

It is expected that further significant improvement in image quality will be attained, which, in turn, will increase the confidence of image interpretation. The development of algorithms for analysis of myocardial 3D images may allow better evaluation of small and non-trans mural myocardial defects. For the diagnosis and treatment of heart diseases the accurate visualisation of the spatial heart shape, 3D volume of the LV and the heart wall perfusion play a crucial role. Surface shading is a valuable tool for determining the presence, extent and location of CAD.

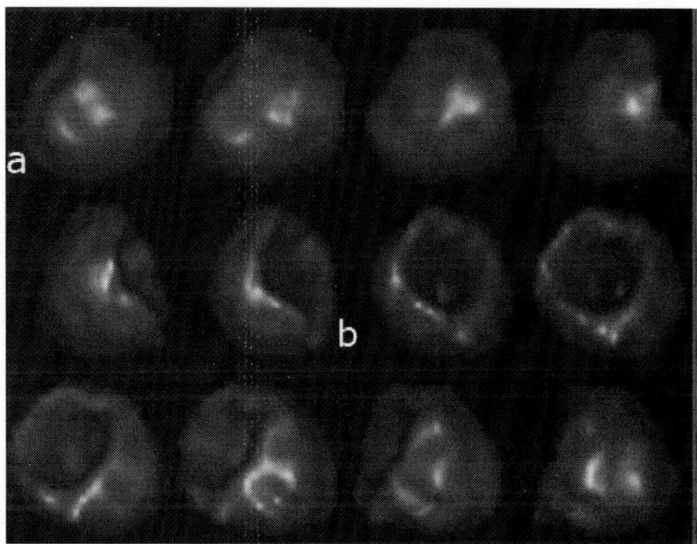

Fig. 5.2.1. 3D shaded surface display of a patient stress perfusion angular images. The study by Tc99m tetrofosmin shows normal myocardium perfusion. (a) for apex and (b) for base of myocardium. Transaxial slices were reconstructed and the created volume images show the apex at the left side. Through base we recognize the cavity of LV. No stress defect was observed and calculated as 0% of the total myocardium.

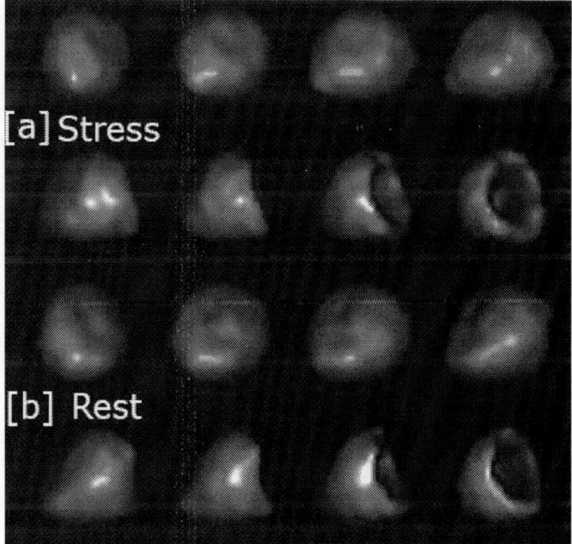

Fig. 5.2.2. Small defect at posterior- basal wall at stress (3% of the myocardium). Partial improvement at rest (2% rest defect); Threshold value 50% of maximum.

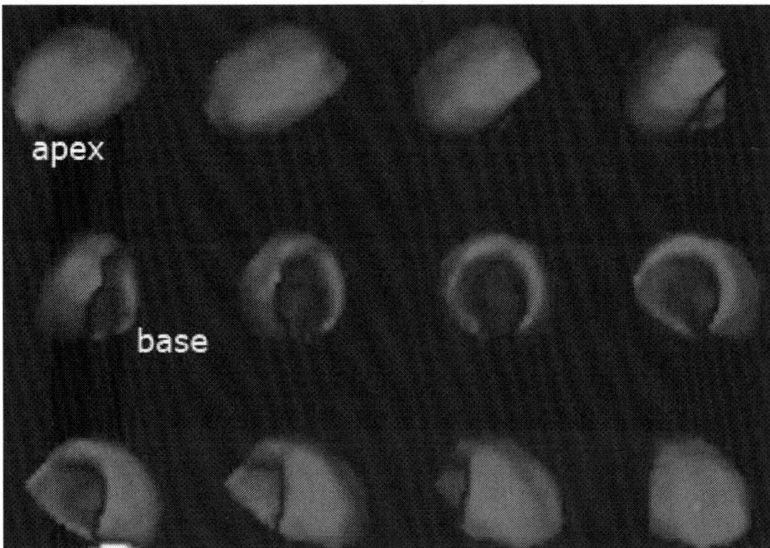

Fig. 5.2.3. 3D volume myocardium, at Rest. Permanent ischemic findings at inferior basal wall; Rest defect 8% of the total myocardium. Threshold: 50%.

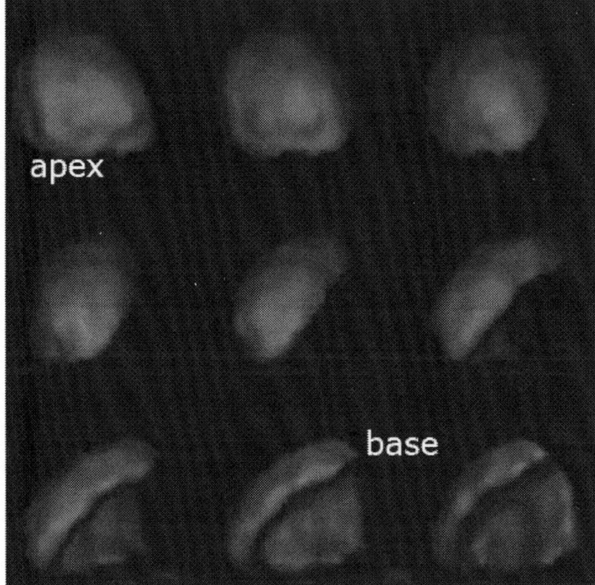

Fig. 5.2.4. 3D surface images of a male myocardium study at Rest. Permanent defect at inferior, inferior-posterior and lateral of LV. Rest defect: 28% of total myocardium volume.

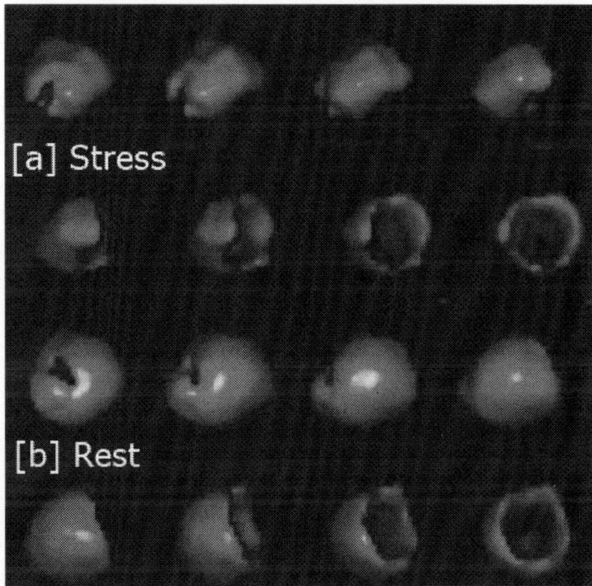

Fig. 5.2.5. Stress [a] and Rest [b] 3D surface angular images of female myocardium. Low extent permanent scar at apex wall and 4% defect at posterior – basic wall during stress. O% defect at rest.

5.3 Liver 3D surface images

Patients on the suspicion of hepatocellular disease may complete a liver scan. They are injected intravenously with Tc-99m Phytate and images are acquired 10 minutes post injection. The acquisition involved four planar images and a tomographic study of 64 planar views over a 360⁰ arc. Each SPECT angle view is preset to end in 20 sec.

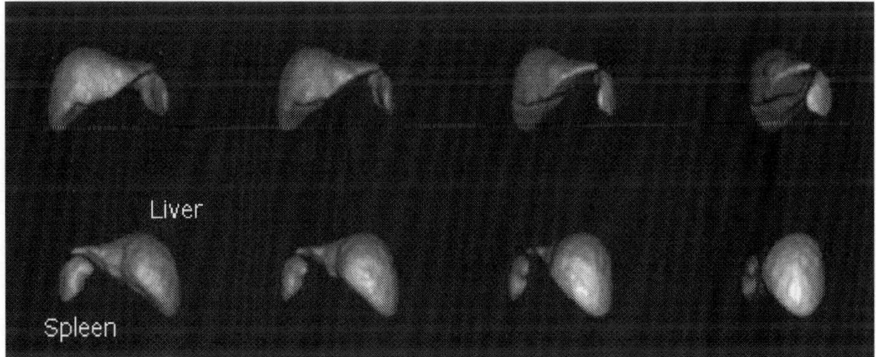

Fig. 5.3.1. 3D surface shading angular series images of liver and spleen of a 12 years old boy. Normal volume and smooth surface of both organs.

The tomographic reconstruction is performed with the FBP, Hanning 0.8 and no magnification. An image threshold calculated according to equation 3 for each specific patient and a gradient-shading factor of 20% is applied on the 3D reconstructed angular images.
3D surface images of the liver could be presented together with the planar anterior image and series of coronal views to increase the diagnostic effectiveness of the method, as information of the surface texture and volume size of this large organ together with Spleen position and size express its patho-physiology. Shin et al, 2009 present surface models of detailed structures inside and outside the liver to promote medical simulation system of the abdomen.

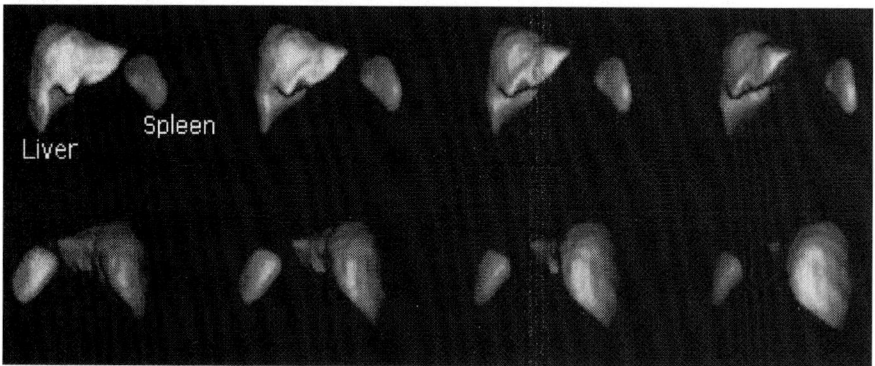

Fig. 5.3.2. 3D volume shading images of another normal variant of liver. Notice the impress of the gallbladder location in the middle of the liver, between right and left lobes (2-4 angular images).

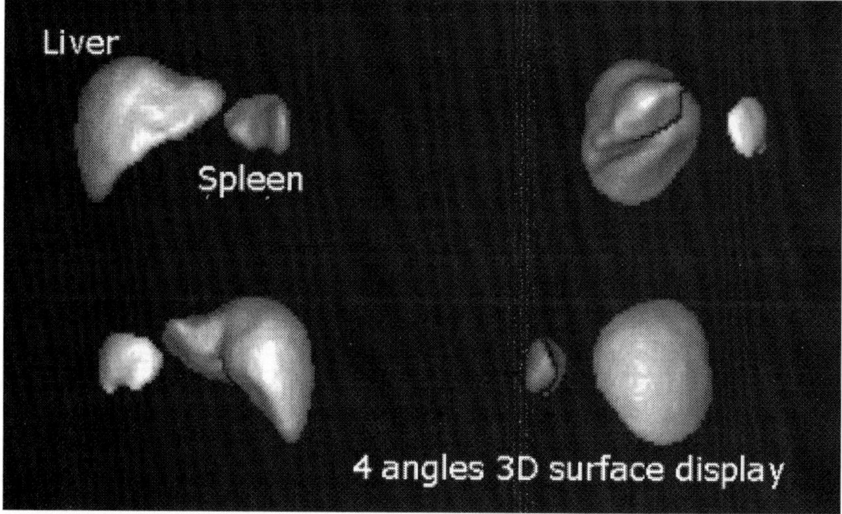

Fig. 5.3.3. 3D shading volume images of liver and spleen. Smooth surfaces of the organs. A part of the spleen is only presented (abnormal shape, image 1 and 4) due to rupture of the spleen at a recent car accident.

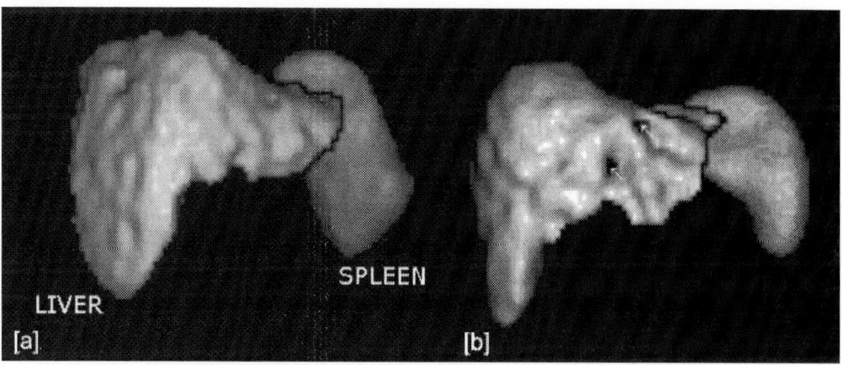

Fig. 5.3.4. The signs of the hepatocellular disease (non-homogeneous distribution in liver) are evident in the 3D volume images. Non smoothed surface of the liver (cirrhotic signs) and increased volume size of the spleen.

5.4 Lung perfusion 3D surface images

SPECT of perfusion lung study not only increases the diagnostic accuracy of the method but also permits the application of advanced image-processing techniques (Reinartz et al, 2006; Roach et al, 2008). In the evaluation of the lung status during pulmonary embolism and patient's follow up, accurate volume estimation is important. Lungs' 3D volume display, by

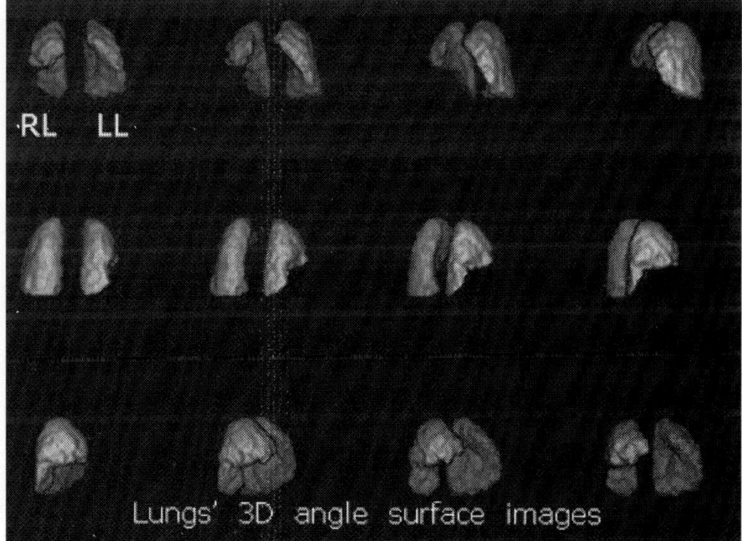

Fig. 5.4.1. Sequential 3D angular images of lungs' volume in a perfusion study. There is a large triangular defect in anterior basal and medial lobes of the right lung (RL) due to decreased blood perfusion caused by emboli (images 10, 11). Notice the cavity at left lung that accommodate heart (image 12).

reconstruction of SPECT images, can demonstrate the perfusion non-uniformity of the lungs' parenchyma.

Patterns of 3D perfusion scans with Tc-99m microspheres can provide an estimation of the extent of pulmonary embolism. Measurement of regional distribution of blood flow can help predict the consequences of lung resection or lung reduction surgery and cystic fibrosis, or radiation therapy. Four functional categories of lung pathology can be distinguished: the vascular occlusive state and the consolidative, obstructive, and restrictive states, resulting in scintigraphically detectable distortions of perfusion. Segmental or sub segmental hypo perfusion can be caused by obstruction of pulmonary vessels due to intra-or extra vascular pathology, including perfusion emboli.

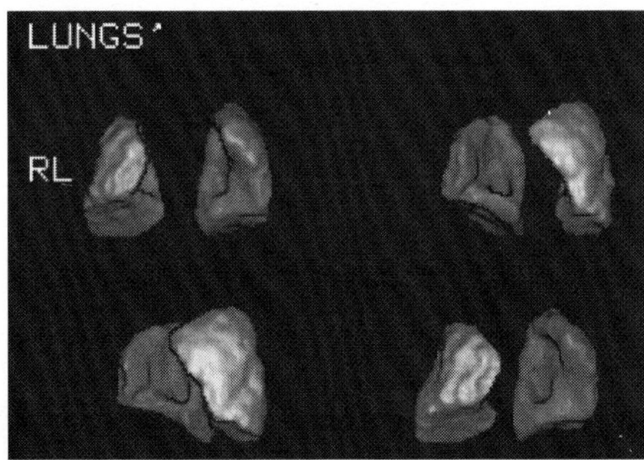

Fig. 5.4.2. 3D tomography emerges an anterior basal defect [11%], of total volume, at right lung

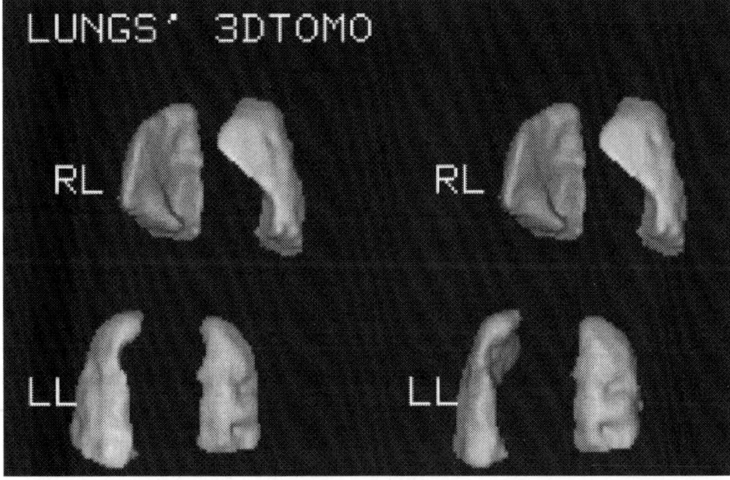

Fig. 5.4.3. Small triangular perfusion defect (5%) at the superior lobe of left lung; Similarly, two small perfusion defects at superior and lateral –basal lobes of right lung (3% each). Multiple acute lungs embolisms

A SPECT lung study can be used to estimate the lung perfusion improvement in details. Data reconstructed in transverse, coronal, sagittal slices as well as 3D surface images and series of follow up SPECT studies, after the pulmonary embolism event, must be used (Lyra et al, 2008b).

From lung perfusion SPECT data, volume of each reconstructed transverse slice can be estimated by counting the voxels inside each slice. The grey histogram edge detection program mark the lung lobe's edge and subtract background. Non-uniform attenuation compensation is performed by quantitative FBP.

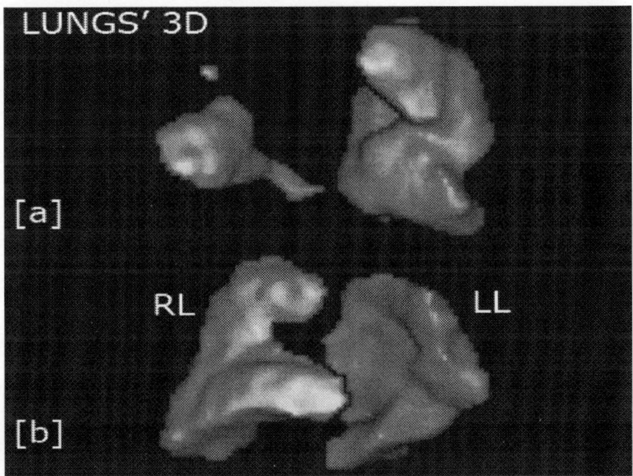

Fig. 5.4.4. Follow up 3D studies after the pulmonary embolism event, in order to estimate the lung perfusion improvement, quantitatively.
[a] Four hours post the event; Great right lobe (RL) embolism; Right Lobe volume: 23% of total Volume (both lungs)
[b] Eleven days post therapy; Right Lobe (RL) volume recovery : 49,6% of total Volume

5.5 Thyroid studies- 3D surface images

Single photon emission tomography of the thyroid gland enables improved accuracy over planar imaging in the determination of the volume, regarding the thyroid configuration variants and the difficulty of definition of the organ's borders over the surrounding background.

The accuracy of the volume estimations depends on the correct delineation of the borders of the thyroid tissue. The thersholding procedure adopted is the grey histogram thresholding and is specific for each case, in a range that start even from 20% of its maximum. Difficulties arise due to various factors including fluctuations in the background and the gland's shape and function as well as an unavoidable smoothing of the thyroid boundary during reconstruction (Zaidi, 1996a).

Tomographic images at various levels are obtained with each slice 1 pixel thick. That is, the size of the elementary voxel is one pixel in the x and y axis and 1 pixel, too, in the z direction. After correction for the contribution of background, the pixel values in a 2D transverse or coronal slice represent the radioisotope consentration within that slice.

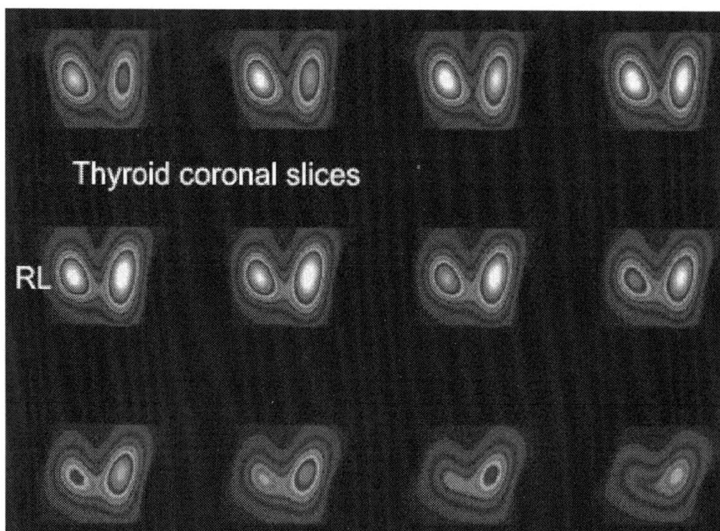

Fig. 5.5.1. A series of 16 coronal slices covering the thyroid gland thickness and showing the area of each slice.

Influence of attenuation compensation for a superficial small organ as the thyroid gland, seems not significant for volume measurements. The geometry - organ size, shape and location - varies between individuals. Volume surface displays of thyroid gland at angles show the real configuration of the gland's lobes.

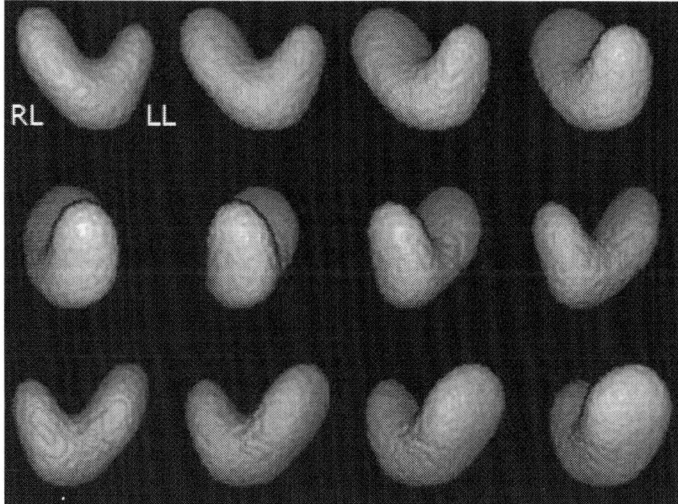

Fig. 5.5.2. 3D thyroid gland images at 16 various angles. Increased the right lobe size and high intensity at its upper pole showing a "hot" node.

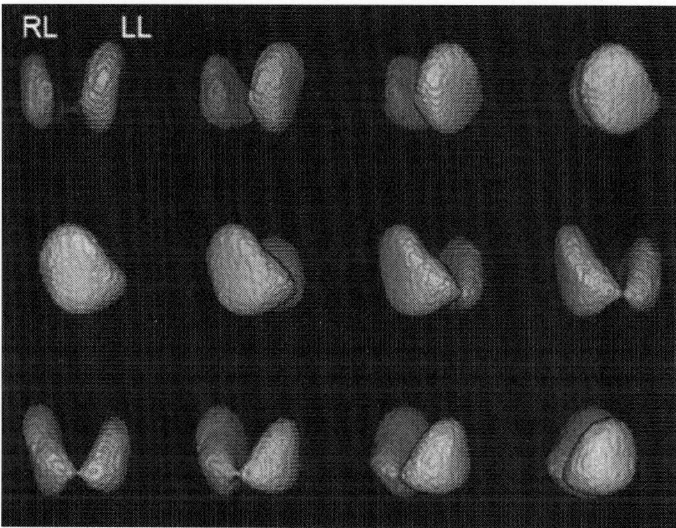

Fig. 5.5.3. Increased left lobe; butterfly shape with very thin isthus, impossible to be seen in planar scan.

A threshold to every single case is adapted as its value is dependent upon size of the imaged organ and the contrast. The thyroid lobes are enclosed with the help of regions of interest (ROI) tools for a first contouring its borders. Size of the organ, however, influences the correct threshold which correspond to a level slightly greater than the maximum fluctuation in the image background. After subtracting this level from the image, the boundary of the thyroid is delineated by the volume elements (voxels) that contain non zero counts; that is the border pixels contain counts equal to the threshold.

Gradient shading was used to surface images, by a gradient factor up to 5% low. Determination of thyroid volume leads to the calculation of the thyroid mass and the accurate activity to be administered for patient specific therapeutic purposes (Pant et al, 2003).

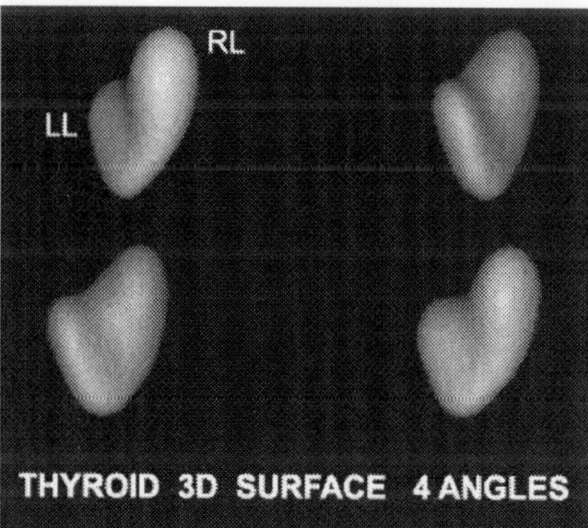

Fig. 5.5.4. Smoothed surface volume displays. Increased size of right lobe. The two lobes come close by a very thick isthus.

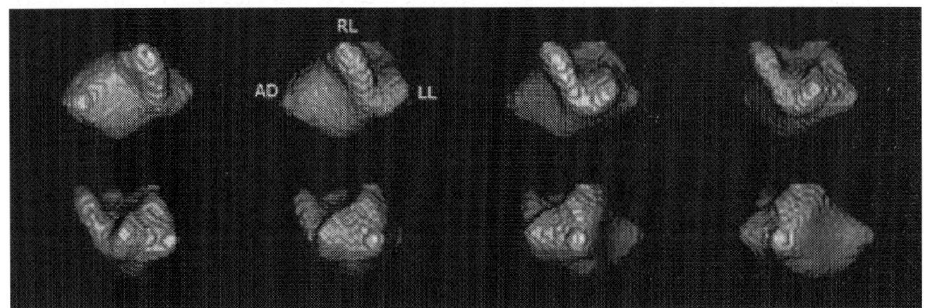

Fig. 5.5.5. The large toxic adenoma is appeared back to the right lobe. The two lobes could not be formed at all in the planar scan but are emerged in this 3D – low threshold- image.

6. Conclusion

By gathering sufficient volume data, analysis of 3D images gives valuable information to give the volume, shape and texture abnormalities of an organ (nodules in Thyroid, homogeneity of the liver surface) or defect regions' (emboli in Lungs, low perfusion in myocardium). Shading according to the gradient of the surface, results in 3D texture surface display, useful in pathologies (e.g. cirrhotic Liver).

Data sets from the above mentioned organs could also be analyzed by image processing software to take new valuable parameters. These images can be transferred in an uncompressed bitmap format and processed by Interactive Data Language (IDL) tools .The volume visualization of nuclear medicine data takes advantage of 3D texture analysis. So, in these 3D reconstructions, volumetric estimations and geometrical data measurements can be extracted; and undoubtedly they are useful in the diagnosis of organ morphological and functional abnormalities.

It is showed that 3D surface shaded images in angles, around the organ, are sensitive with the possibility to extract quantitative information for all organs that are studied. 3D imaging offers direct visualization and measurements of complex structures of the internal organs of the human body, which cannot be satisfactorily evaluated using 2D imaging.

As reconstruction methods improve in accuracy and in ability to manipulate large matrices, new threshold techniques and corrections will be used, so that perfect absolute quantitative accuracy will be brought closer.

7. References

Boudraa, A.O. and Zaidi, H. (2006) Image segmentation techniques in nuclear medicine imaging, In: *Quantitative Analysis in Nuclear Medicine Imaging*, Zaidi, H., (Ed.), (308-357), Springer, ISBN: 978-0-387-23854-8, Heidelberg, Germany

Cooke C.D.; Faber, T.L.; Areeda, J.S. and Garcia, E.V. (2001) Advanced computer methods in cardiac SPECT, Cardiac SPECT imaging, De Puey, E.G., Garcia, E.V., Berman S.D. (ed), 65-80, Lippincott Williams & Wilkins, ISBN 0-7817-2007-9,Philadelphia

Csetverikov, D. (2007), http://visual.ipan.sztaki.hu/ELTEfoliak/1-in-page/lec07_threshold_prn.pdf, *Eötvös Loránd University,Department of Informatics, Budapest, Hungary*

Daou, D.; Pointurier, I.; Coaguila, C.; Vilain, D.; Benada, A.W.; Lebtahi, R.; Fourme, T.; Slama, M.; Le Guludec, D. (2003) Performance of OSEM and depth-dependent resolution recovery algorithms for the evaluation of global left ventricular function in ^{201}T1 gated myocardial perfusion SPECT. *J Nucl Med,* Vol. 44, No. 2, 155-162, ISSN 0161-5505

De Sadeleer, C.; Bossuyt, A.; Goes E. and Piepsz A. (1996).Technetium-99m-DMSA SPECT in Normal Volunteers, *J Nuc. Med,* 1996, Vol.37, pp.1346-1349

Dixon, K.L.; Fung, A.; Celler, A. (2004) The effect of patient acquisition and reconstruction variables on myocardial wall thickness as measured from myocardial perfusion SPECT studies. *Nuclear Science Symposium Conference Record,* Vol.7, (16-22 Oct.2004), 4141-4145, DOI 10.1109/NSSMIC.2004.1466804

Erdi, Y.E.; Wessels, B.W.; Loew, M.H. and. Erdi, A.K. (1995). Threshold Estimation in Single Photon Emission Computed Tomography and Planar Imaging for Clinical Radioimmunotherapy . *Cancer Research* (Supplement) 55, December 1, 1995, 5823s.-5826s

Garcia, E.V.; Cooke C.D.; Areeda, J.S. (2001).Quantitative analysis of SPECT, *Cardiac SPECT imaging,* De Puey, E.G., Garcia, E.V., Berman S.D. (ed), 41-64, Lippincott Williams & Wilkins, ISBN 0-7817-2007-9,Philadelphia

García-Panyella O.; Susín A. (2002). Left Ventricle Volume Estimation from 3D SPECT Reconstruction, *IEEE Computers in Cardiology,* Murray, A., (Ed.), vol. 29, 621–624

Gourion, D. and Noll, D. (2002) The inverse problem of emission tomography, *Inverse Problems,* Vol.18 (2002), pp.1435–1460

Groshar, D.; Moskovitz, B.; Issaq, E. and Nativ, O. (1997). Quantitative SPECT of DMSA uptake by the kidneys: Assessment of reproducibility. *Kidney International,* Vol. 52 (1997), pp. 817−820

Hansen, C. L. (2002a). Digital image processing for clinicians, part I: Basics of image format, *Journal of Nuclear Cardiology,* Vol. 9, No. 3, 343–349

Hansen, C.L. (2002b). Digital image processing for clinicians, part II: Filtering, Journal *of Nuclear Cardiology,* Vol. 9, No. 4, 429-437

Kao, C.M. and Pan, X. (2000). Non-iterative methods incorporating priori source distribution and data information for suppression of image noise and artefacts in 3D SPECT, *Phys. Med. Biol.* 45 , pp.801-819

Lyra, M.; Skouroliakou, K.; Georgosopoulos, C.; Stefanides, C. and Jordanou, J. (2001) Single Photon Emission Computed Tomography and 3 Dimensional Quantitative Evaluation in Renal Scintigraphy, (2001*) Lecture Notes in Computer Science, Medical Image Computing and Computer-Assisted Intervention* – MICCAI 2001, *LNCS 2208,* W. Niessen and M. Viergever (Eds.):, (January 2001), 1222-1223, Springer Berlin Heidelberg, ISBN 978-3-540-42697-4, ISSN 0302-9743 1611-3349 , DOI 10.1007/3-540-45468-3_171

Lyra, M.; Striligas J.; Gavrilelli M.; Chatzigiannis, C.; Skouroliakou C. (2008a). Thyroid Volume determination by single photon tomography and 3D processing for activity dose estimation, *IEEE International Workshop on Imaging Systems and Techniques* – IST 2008, Chania, Greece, September 10–12, 2008

Lyra, M.; Gavrilelli M.; Kokona, G.; Skouroliakou, C. (2008b) Lungs SPECT image processing for volume and perfusion index estimation. *BioInformatics and BioEngineering, BIBE 2008. 8th IEEE International Conference on,* Athens, Oct. 2008

Matsunari, I.; Yoneyama, T.; Kanayama, S.; Matsudaira, M.; Nakajima, K.; Taki, J.; Nekolla, S.G.; Tonami, N.; and Hisada, K. (2001). Phantom Studies for Estimation of Defect Size on Cardiac 18F SPECT and PET: Implications for Myocardial Viability Assessment., J Nucl Med, Vol. 42 No. 10, 1579-1585

Mortelmans, L.; Nuyts, J.; Van Pamel, G.; Van den Maegdenbergh, V.; De Roo, M. and Suetens, P. (1986). A new thresholding method for volume determination by SPECT, *Eur J Nucl Med Mol Imaging,* Vol. 12, Numbers 5-6 , September 1986

Murli A.; D'Amore L.; Carracciuolo L.; Ceccarelli M.; Antonelli L. (2008). High performance edge-preserving regularization in 3D SPECT imaging, *Parallel Computing* , Vol. 34 , Issue 2, 115-132, ISSN 0167-8191 , Elsevier Science Publishers B. V, February 2008

Noo, F. and Wagner, J.M. (2001). Image reconstruction in 2D SPECT with 180° acquisition, Inverse Problems, 17, No 5, 1357-1371, PII:S0266-5611(1) 20858-2

Pan, X.; Kao, C.M.; Metz, C.; Kiselev, A.; Kiselev, E. . (2001). Image Reconstruction in 3D Short-Scan SPECT, http://cfi.lbl.gov/3D-2001/abstracts/07-02.pdf

Pan, X.; Sidky, E.Y.; Kao, C.M.; Zou, Y. and Metz, C.E. (2002). Short-scan SPECT imaging with non-uniform attenuation and 3D distance-dependent spatial resolution, *Phys. Med. Biol.,* No.47, pp.2811-2833

Pant, G.S., Kumar, R., Gupta, A. K., Sharma, S.K., Pandey, A.K. (2003). Estimation of thyroid mass in Graves' disease by a scintigraphic method, *Nuclear Medicine Communications,* Vol.24, No.7, (July 2003), 743-748

Razifar, P., Sandström, M., Schneider, H., Långström, B., Maripuu, E., Bengtsson E., Bergström, M. (2005). Noise correlation in PET, CT, SPECT and PET/CT data evaluated using autocorrelation function: a phantom study on data, reconstructed using FBP and OSEM. *Journal: Bio Medical Central (BMC): Medical Imaging 5(5),* 2005 doi: 10.1186/1471-2342-5-5.

Reinartz, P., Kaiser, H.J., Wildberger, J.E., Gordji, C., Nowak, B. and Buell, U. (2006). SPECT imaging in the diagnosis of pulmonary embolism: Automated detection of match and mismatch defects by means of image-processing techniques, *J Nucl Med,* Vol. 47, No. 6, June 2006, 968-973

Roach, P. J., Bailey, D. L., Schembri, G. P. (2008), Reinventing ventilation/perfusion lung scanning with SPECT, *Nucl Med Communications,* Volume 29, (12), December 2008, 1023-1025, ISSN: 0143-3636, DOI: 10.1097/MNM.0b013e328315efa1

Rosenthal, M.S.; Cullom, R.J.; Hawkins, W.; Moore, S.C.; Tsui, B.M.W. and Yester, M. (1995) Quantitative SPECT Imaging: A Review and Recommendations by the Focus

Committee of the Society of Nuclear Medicine Computer and Instrumentation Council, *J Nuc Med*; 36:1489-1513

Russ, J.C. (2006). *The image processing handbook,* CRC Press, Taylor & Francis group inc., ISBN 0-8493-2516-1, 5th edition, Boca Raton, Florida

Sainz, M.; Susin, A and Bagherzadeh N. (2003) MTMesh Image Based Mesh Reconstruction and Rendering IAESTED Conference in Visualization, *Imaging and Image Processing (VIIP'03)*, Hamza, M.H., (Ed.), 785-790

Sheehy, N.; Tetrault, T.A.; Zurakowski, D.; Vija, A.H.; Fahey, F. H. and Treves, S.T. (2009) Pediatric 99mTc-DMSA SPECT performed by using Iterative Reconstruction with Isotropic Resolution Recovery: Improved Image Quality and Reduced Radiopharmaceutical Activity, *Radiology*, No.251, (March 2009), 511-516

Shin, D.S.; Chung, M.S.; Lee, J.W.; Park, J.S.; Chung, J.; Lee, S.B. and Lee, S.H. (2009). Advanced Surface Reconstruction Technique to Build Detailed Surface Models of the Liver and Neighbouring Structures from the Visible Korean Human, *Korean Med Sci.* , June 2009 , Vol.24, No.3, pp.375-383

Son, H.K.; Yun, M.J.; Jeon, T.J.; Kim, D.O.; Jung, H.J.; Lee, J.D.; Yoo, H.S.; Kim, H.J. (2001) ROC analysis of ordered subset expectation maximization and filtered back projection technique for FDG-PET in lung cancer. *Nuclear Science Symposium Conference Record*, 2001 IEEE, Vol. 3, Issue, 2001, 1801 – 1805, DOI 10.1109/NSSMIC.2001.1008692

Soneson, H.; Ubachs, J.F.A.; Ugander, M.; Arheden, H.and Heiberg E. (2009). An Improved Method for Automatic Segmentation of the Left Ventricle in Myocardial Perfusion SPECT. *J Nucl Med*, Vol.50, No.2, (February 2009), 205-213

Temiz, Y.; Tarcan, T.; Onol, F.F.; Alpay, H. & Simsek, F.,(2006). The efficacy of Tc99m dimercaptosuccinic acid (Tc-DMSA) scintigraphy and ultrasonography in detecting renal scars in children with primary vesicoureteral reflux (VUR), *International Urology and Nephrology* (2006) Vol.38, pp.149–152

Tsui, B.M.W.; Zhao, X.; Frey E.C. and McCartney W.H. (1994). Quantitative single-photon emission computed tomography: Basics and clinical considerations. *Seminars in Nuclear Medicine*, Vol. XXIV, No 1, (January 1994), 38-65

Yang, J.Y.; Yang, J.A.; Seo, J.W.; Lee, S.J. (2001). The Diagnostic Value of 99mTc DMSA Renal Scan SPECT Images in Addition to Planar Image in Children with Urinary Tract Infection, *J Korean Soc Pediatr Nephrol.*, Vol.5,No.1, (April 2001),.22-29

Yan, Y., and Zeng, L.G. (2008). Scatter and Blurring Compensation in Inhomogeneous Media Using a Postprocessing Method, *International Journal of Biomedical Imaging,* Vol. 2008,(December 2008) Article ID 806705, Hindawi Publ. Corp., doi:10.1155/2008/806705

Zaidi, H., (1996a) Comparative Methods for Quantifying Thyroid Volume Using Planar Imaging and SPECT, J Nuc. Med, Vol. 37, pp.1421-1426

Zaidi, H. (1996b). Organ volume estimation using SPECT. *IEEE Transactions Nuclear Science*, Vol.43, Issue 3, June 1996, 2174-2182

Zaidi, H. and Hasegawa, B. (2003) Determination of the Attenuation Map in Emission Tomography, *J Nucl Med*, Vol. 44 No. 2, 291-315

Zingerman, Y.; Golan, H. and Moalem, A. (2009). Spatial linear recovery coefficients for quantitive evaluations in SPECT, *Nuclear Instruments and Methods in Physics Research Section A: Accelerators, Spectrometers, Detectors and Associated Equipment*, Vol. 602, Issue 2, 21 April 2009, 607-613

## 16

Enhancing Ultrasound Images Using Hybrid FIR Structures

L. J. Morales-Mendoza, Yu. S. Shmaliy and O. G. Ibarra-Manzano
Electronics Department, Guanajuato University
México

1. Introduction

The problem of saving a sharp edge with a simultaneous enhancing in the image is typical for ultrasound applications. Ultrasound imaging is a technique that is widely used in a variety of clinical applications, such as cardiology (Najarian & Splinter, 2007), obstetrics and gynecology (Jan, 2006), and others. Due to the blur and typically non Gaussian noise, an origin ultrasound image has a poor resolution. That forces researches to create image processing algorithms having a contradictive ability of cleaning the image of noise but saving its sharp edge. An overall panorama of nonlinear filtering following the median strategy has been presented by Pitas and Venetsanopoulos (Pitas & Venetsanopoulos, 1990) along with important modifications for a large class of nonlinear filters employing the order statistics. The algorithm issues for the filter design have been discussed in (Kalouptsidis & Theodoridis, 1993). In (Astola & Kuosmanen, 1997), the finite impulse response (FIR) median hybrid filters (MHF) strategy has been proposed with applications to image processing. An important step ahead has been made in (Heinonen & Neuvo, 1987; 1988), where the FIR MHF structures have been designed. In the sequel, the MHF structures have extensively been investigated, developed, and used by many authors.

Basically, hybrid FIR structures can be designed using different types of estimators. Among possible solutions, the polynomial estimators occupy a special place, since the polynomial models often well formalize a priori knowledge about different processes. Relevant signals are typically represented with degree polynomials to fit a variety of practical needs. Examples of applications of polynomial structures can be found in signal processing (Dumitrescu, 2007; Mathews & Sicuranza, 2001), timescales and clock synchronization (Shmaliy, 2006), image processing (Bose, 2004), speech processing (Heinonen & Neuvo, 1988), etc. The polynomial estimators suitable for such structures can be obtained from the generic form of the p-step predictive unbiased FIR filter proposed in (Shmaliy, 2006; 2009). Such estimators usually process data on finite horizons of N points that typically obtain a nice restoration.

In this Chapter, we first give the theory of the p-step smoothing unbiased FIR estimator of polynomial signals viewing an image as a multistate space model. We then use the polynomial solutions in the design of FIR MHF structures and justify optimal steps p from the standpoint of minimum produced errors. We show advantages of the approach employing the three generic ramp FIR solutions. Namely, we exploit the 1-step predictive filter ($p = 1$), the filter ($p = 0$), and the 1-lag smoothing filter ($p = -1$). The hybrid structures investigated are compared in terms of the root mean square errors (RMSEs) and the signal-to-noise ratio (SNR) in the enhanced image. The rest of the chapter is organized as follows: In section II, we describe the polynomial image. In section III, the gains for the optimal and unbiased smoothing FIR filters are derived. The low-degree polynomials gains for unbiased smoothing FIR filters are considered in detain in section IV. Section V is defined to design and applications of unbiased FMH structures. Finally, the concluding remarks are drawn in section VI.

2. Polynomial image model

A two-dimensional image is often represented as a $k_c \times k_r$ matrix $\mathbf{M} = \{\mu_{i,j}\}$. To provide two dimensional filtering, the matrix can be written in the form of a row-ordered vector or a column-ordered vector, respectively,

$$\mathbf{X}_r = \left[\mu_{1,1}\mu_{1,2}\cdots\mu_{1,k_r}\mu_{2,1}\mu_{2,2}\cdots\mu_{2,k_r}\cdots\mu_{k_c,1}\mu_{k_c,2}\cdots\mu_{k_c,k_r}\right]^T, \tag{1}$$

$$\mathbf{X}_c = \left[\mu_{1,1}\mu_{2,1}\cdots\mu_{k_c,1}\mu_{1,2}\mu_{2,2}\cdots\mu_{k_c,2}\cdots\mu_{1,k_r}\mu_{2,k_r}\cdots\mu_{k_c,k_r}\right]^T. \tag{2}$$

The filtering procedure is then often applied twice, first to (1) and then to (2), or vice versa. If to represent a two-dimensional electronic image with (1) and (2), then one may also substitute each of the vectors with the discrete time-invariant deterministic signal x_{1n} that, in turn, can be modeled on a horizon of some N points in state space. If x_{1n} projects ahead from $n - N + 1 - p$ to $n - p$, then the p-lag smoothing FIR filtering estimate can be provided at a current point n with a lag p, $p < 0$, as shown in Fig. 1. Referring to Fig. 1, a signal x_{1n} can further be projected on a horizon of N points from $n - N + 1 - p$, to n with the finite order Taylor series as follows:

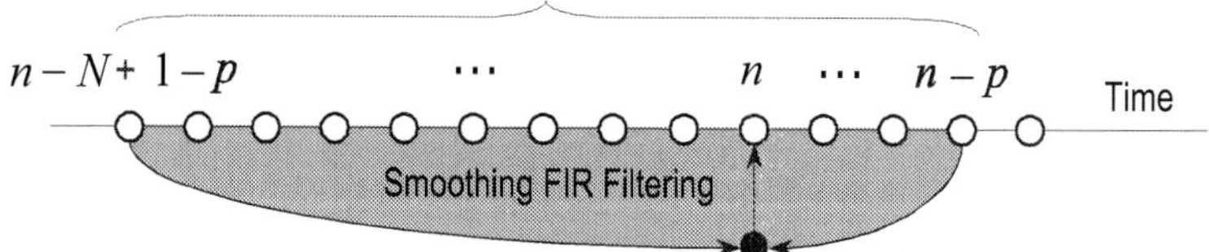

Fig. 1. Smoothing FIR filtering on a horizon of N points with a lag p, $p < 0$.

$$x_{1n} = \sum_{q=0}^{K-1} x_{(q+1)(n-N+1-p)} \frac{\tau^q (N-1+p)^q}{q!}$$

$$= x_{1(n-N+1-p)} + x_{2(n-N+1-p)}\tau(N-1+p) + x_{3(n-N+1-p)}\tfrac{1}{2}\tau^2(N-1+p)^2 +$$

$$\cdots + x_{K(n-N+1-p)} \tfrac{1}{(K-1)!} \tau^{K-1}(N-1+p)^{K-1}, \tag{3}$$

where $x_{(q+1)(n-N+1-p)}$, $q \in [0, K-1]$, can be called the signal $(q+1)$-state at $n - N + 1 - p$ and the signal thus characterized with K states, from 1 to K. Here, τ is the sampling time.

In such a model, the k-state, $k \in [1, K]$, is determined by the time derivative of the $(k-1)$-state, starting with $k = 2$. Therefore, most generally, we have

$$x_{kn} = \sum_{q=0}^{K-k} x_{(q+k)(n-N+1-p)} \frac{\tau^q (N-1+p)^q}{q!}$$

$$= x_{k(n-N+1-p)} + x_{(k+1)(n-N+1-p)} \tau(N-1+p) + x_{(k+2)(n-N+1-p)} \tfrac{1}{2}\tau^2(N-1+p)^2 +$$

$$\cdots + x_{K(n-N+1-p)} \tfrac{1}{(K-k)!} \tau^{K-k}(N-1+p)^{K-k}. \tag{4}$$

If we now suppose that x_{1n} (1) is contaminated in the measurement to be s_n with noise v_n having zero mean $E\{v_n\} = 0$, and arbitrary distribution and covariance $\mathbf{Q} = E\{v_i v_j\}$, then the model and the measurement can be represented in state space, using (4), with the state and observation equations as, respectively

$$\mathbf{x}_n = \mathbf{A}^{N-1+p} \mathbf{x}_{n-N+1-p}, \tag{5}$$

$$s_n = \mathbf{C}\mathbf{x}_n + v_n, \tag{6}$$

where the $K \times 1$ state vector is given by

$$\mathbf{x}_n = \begin{bmatrix} x_{1n} & x_{2n} & \cdots & x_{Kn} \end{bmatrix}^T. \tag{7}$$

The $K \times K$ triangular matrix $\mathbf{A}^i$, projecting the state at $n - N + 1 - p$ to the present state at n, is specified with

$$\mathbf{A}^i = \begin{bmatrix} 1 & \tau i & \tfrac{1}{2}(\tau i)^2 & \cdots & \frac{1}{(K-1)!}(\tau i)^{K-1} \\ 0 & 1 & \tau i & \cdots & \frac{1}{(K-2)!}(\tau i)^{K-2} \\ 0 & 0 & 1 & \cdots & \frac{1}{(K-3)!}(\tau i)^{K-3} \\ \vdots & \vdots & \vdots & \ddots & \vdots \\ 0 & 0 & 0 & \cdots & 1 \end{bmatrix}, \tag{8}$$

and the $1 \times K$ measurement matrix is

$$\mathbf{C} = \begin{bmatrix} 1 & 0 & \cdots & 0 \end{bmatrix}. \tag{9}$$

If we now think that the state space model (5) and (6) represents an electronic image, then we would like to find the optimal and unbiased gains for the smoothing FIR filter producing at n the estimate $\hat{\mathbf{x}}_{n|n-p}$, $p < 0$, associated with the enhanced image.

3. Smoothing FIR filtering of polynomial models

In FIR filtering, an estimate is obtained via the discrete convolution applied to measurement. That can be done if to represent the state space model on an averaging interval of some N points as shown in (Shmaliy, 2008). Referring to Fig. 1, we thus can represent the model (3) and (4) on a horizon from $n - N + 1 - p$ to $n - p$. The recursively computed forward-in-time solutions given us

$$\mathbf{X}_N(p) = \mathbf{A}_N \mathbf{x}_{n-N+1-p},\tag{10}$$

$$\mathbf{S}_N(p) = \mathbf{C}_N \mathbf{x}_{n-N+1-p} + \mathbf{V}_N(p),\tag{11}$$

where

$$\mathbf{X}_{N(p)} = \begin{bmatrix} \mathbf{x}_{n-p}^T & \mathbf{x}_{n-1-p}^T & \cdots & \mathbf{x}_{n-N+1-p}^T \end{bmatrix}^T,\tag{12}$$

$$\mathbf{S}_N(p) = \begin{bmatrix} s_{n-p} & s_{n-1-p} & \cdots & s_{n-N+1-p} \end{bmatrix}^T,\tag{13}$$

$$\mathbf{V}_N(p) = \begin{bmatrix} v_{n-p} & v_{n-1-p} & \cdots & v_{n-N+1-p} \end{bmatrix}^T,\tag{14}$$

$$\mathbf{A}_N = \begin{bmatrix} (\mathbf{A}^{N-1+p})^T & (\mathbf{A}^{N-2+p})^T & \cdots & (\mathbf{A}^{1+p})^T & (\mathbf{A}^p)^T \end{bmatrix}^T,\tag{15}$$

$$\mathbf{C}_N = \begin{bmatrix} \mathbf{CA}^{N-1+p} \\ \mathbf{CA}^{N-2+p} \\ \vdots \\ \mathbf{CA}^{1+p} \\ \mathbf{CA}^{p} \end{bmatrix} = \begin{bmatrix} \left(\mathbf{A}^{N-1+p}\right)_1 \\ \left(\mathbf{A}^{N-2+p}\right)_1 \\ \vdots \\ \left(\mathbf{A}^{1+p}\right)_1 \\ \left(\mathbf{A}^{p}\right)_1 \end{bmatrix},\tag{16}$$

where $(\mathbf{Z})_1$ means the first row of a matrix $\mathbf{Z}$. Given (10) and (11), the smoothing FIR filtering estimate is obtained as in the following.

It is known that FIR estimates can be found for each of the states separately. Following this line and utilizing N measurements from $n - N + 1 - p$ to $n - p$, the smoothing FIR filtering estimate $\hat{x}_{1n|n-p}$ of x_{1n} can be obtained at n as

$$\hat{x}_{1n|n-p} = \sum_{i=p}^{N-1+p} h_{li}(p) y_{n-i},\tag{17a}$$

$$= \mathbf{W}_l^T(p) \mathbf{S}_N,\tag{17b}$$

$$= \mathbf{W}_l^T(p) \begin{bmatrix} \mathbf{C}_N \mathbf{x}_{n-N+1-p} + \mathbf{V}_N(p) \end{bmatrix},\tag{17c}$$

where $h_{li}(p) \equiv h_{li}(N, p)$ is the l-degree filter gain (Shmaliy, 2006) dependent on N and p and the l-degree and $1 \times N$ filter gain matrix is given with

$$\mathbf{W}_l^T(p) = \begin{bmatrix} h_{lp}(p) & h_{l(1+p)}(p) & \cdots & h_{l(N-1+p)}(p) \end{bmatrix}. \tag{18}$$

Note that $h_{li}(p)$ in (17a) and (18) can be specified in different sense depending on applications. Below, we investigate this gain in the sense of the minimum bias in order to design the hybrid FIR filters.

3.1 Unbiased estimate

The unbiased smoothing FIR filtering estimates can be found if we start with the unbiasedness condition

$$E\left\{\hat{x}_{1n|n-p}\right\} = E\left\{x_{1n}\right\} \tag{19}$$

substitute x_{1n} with

$$x_{1n} = \left(\mathbf{A}^{N-1+p}\right)_1 \mathbf{x}_{n-N+1-p} \tag{20}$$

and $\hat{x}_{1n|n-p}$ with (17c). That leads to the unbiasedness (or deadbeat) constraint

$$\left(\mathbf{A}^{N-1+p}\right)_1 = \overline{\mathbf{W}}_l^T(p)\mathbf{C}_N, \tag{21}$$

where $\overline{\mathbf{W}}_l(p)$ mean the l-degree unbiased gain matrix (Shmaliy, 2006).

It can be show that the constraint (21) does not give us a direct solution for the gain matrix. Instead, one can equate the components of the row matrices in (21) and, similarly to (Shmaliy, Apr. 2009), arrive at

$$1 = \sum_{i=p}^{N-1+p} h_{li}(p)$$

$$\tau(N-1+p) = \sum_{i=p}^{N-1+p} h_{li}(p)\tau(N-1-i+p) + \sum_{i=p}^{N-1+p} h_{li}(p)$$

$$\vdots$$

$$\frac{\left[\tau(N-1+p)\right]^{K-1}}{(K-1)!} = \sum_{i=p}^{N-1+p} h_{li}(p)\frac{\left[\tau(N-1-i+p)\right]^{K-1}}{(K-1)!}$$

$$+ \cdots + \sum_{i=p}^{N-1+p} h_{li}(p)\tau(N-1-i+p) + \sum_{i=p}^{N-1+p} h_{li}(p). \tag{22}$$

Further accounting the first identity in the remaining ones of (22) leads to the fundamental properties of the p-lag unbiased smoothing FIR filter gain:

$$\sum_{i=p}^{N-1+p} h_{li}(p) = 1$$

$$\sum_{i=p}^{N-1+p} h_{li}(p) i^u = 0, \quad 1 \le u \le l. \tag{23}$$

A short matrix form (23) is thus

$$\overline{\mathbf{W}}_l^T(p)\mathbf{V}(p) = \mathbf{J}^T, \tag{24}$$

where

$$\mathbf{J} = \left[\underbrace{1 \quad 0 \quad \cdots \quad 0}_{N} \right]^T \tag{25}$$

and the p-lag and $N \times (l+1)$ Vandermonde matrix is specified by

$$\mathbf{V}(p) = \begin{bmatrix} 1 & p & p^2 \\ 1 & 1+p & (1+p)^2 \\ 1 & 2+p & (2+p)^2 \\ \vdots & \vdots & \vdots \\ 1 & N-1+p & (N-1+p)^2 \end{bmatrix}. \tag{26}$$

Now note that the inverse $\left[\mathbf{V}^T(p)\mathbf{V}(p)\right]^{-1}$ always exists. Then multiply the right-side of (24) with the identity matrix $\left[\mathbf{V}^T(p)\mathbf{V}(p)\right]^{-1}\mathbf{V}^T(p)\mathbf{V}(p)$, discard $\mathbf{V}(p)$ from the both sides, and finally arrive at the fundamental solution for the gain,

$$\overline{\mathbf{W}}_l^T(p) = \mathbf{J}^T\left[\mathbf{V}^T(p)\mathbf{V}(p)\right]^{-1}\mathbf{V}(p) \tag{27}$$

that can be used for unbiased FIR filtering of polynomial models. Because no restriction is imposed upon p, the gain (27) can be used for FIR filtering with $p = 0$, smoothing FIR filtering with $p < 0$, and predictive FIR filtering with $p > 0$.

3.2 Unbiased polynomial gain

Although (27) is an exact and simple solution for unbiased FIR estimation, there is an inconvenience in using the Vandermonde matrix acquiring large dimension when N is large. On the other hand, we still have no idea about the gain function $h_{li}(p)$. To find this function, the following fundamental property can be invoked from the Kalman-Bucy filter theory: the order of the optimal (and unbiased) filter is the same as that of the system. This property suggests that the kth state of the model characterized with K states can unbiasedly be filtered with the $l = K - k$ degree FIR filter (Shmaliy, 2006). In other words: the first state x_{kn}, $k = 1$, of the K-state model can unbiasedly be filtered, smoothed, and predicted with the gain of degree $l = K - 1$.

Most generally, following (Shmaliy, 2006), we thus can represent the filter gain with the degree polynomial

$$h_{li}(p) = \sum_{j=0}^{l} a_{jl}(p)i^{j} , \qquad (28)$$

where $l \in [1, K]$, $i \in [p, N - 1 + p]$, and $a_{jl}(p) \equiv a_{jl}(N, p)$ is still unknown coefficient.

Substituting (28) to (27) and rearranging the terms lead to a set linear equations, having a compact matrix form of

$$\mathbf{J} = \mathbf{D}(p)\boldsymbol{\gamma}(p), \qquad (29)$$

where

$$\mathbf{J} = \begin{bmatrix} \underbrace{1 \quad 0 \quad \cdots \quad 0}_{K} \end{bmatrix}^{T} , \qquad (30)$$

$$\boldsymbol{\gamma} = \begin{bmatrix} \underbrace{a_{0(K-1)} \quad a_{1(K-1)} \quad \cdots \quad a_{(K-1)(K-1)}}_{K} \end{bmatrix}^{T} , \qquad (31)$$

and a short symmetric $l \times l$ matrix $\mathbf{D}(p)$ is specified via the Vandermonde matrix (26) as

$$\mathbf{D}(p) = \mathbf{V}^{T}(p)\mathbf{V}(p)$$

$$= \begin{bmatrix} d_{0}(p) & d_{1}(p) & \cdots & d_{l}(p) \\ d_{1}(p) & d_{2}(p) & \cdots & d_{l+1}(p) \\ \vdots & \vdots & \ddots & \vdots \\ d_{l}(p) & d_{l+1}(p) & \cdots & d_{2l}(p) \end{bmatrix} . \qquad (32)$$

The component for (32) is defined by

$$d_{m}(p) = \sum_{i=p}^{N-1+p} i^{m} , \quad m = 0,1\ldots 2l , \qquad (33)$$

$$= \frac{1}{m+1}\left[B_{m+1}(N + p) - B_{m+1}(p)\right], \qquad (34)$$

where $B_{n}(x)$ is the Bernoulli polynomial.

An analytic solution to (29), with respect to the coefficients $a_{jl}(p)$ of the polynomial (28), gives us

$$a_{jl}(p) = (-1)^j \frac{M_{(j+1)1}(p)}{|\mathbf{D}|},\tag{35}$$

where $|\mathbf{D}|$ is the determinant of $\mathbf{D}(p)$ that turns out to be p-invariant, and $M_{(j+1)1}(p)$ is the minor of $\mathbf{D}(p)$.

Determined $a_{jl}(p)$ and $h_{li}(p)$, the unbiased smoothing FIR filter of the polynomial signal x_{1n} is provided as follows. Given a discrete time-invariant polynomial state space model, (5) and (6), then the p-lag unbiased smoothing FIR filtering estimate of the model x_{1n} having K states is obtained at n on a horizon of N points using the data s_n taken from $n - N + 1 - p$ to $n - p$, $p < 0$, by

$$\hat{x}_{1n|n-p} = \sum_{i=p}^{N-1+p} h_{(K+1)i}(p) s_{n-i},\tag{36}$$

$$= \overline{\mathbf{W}}_l^T(p)\mathbf{S}_N,\tag{37}$$

where $\overline{\mathbf{W}}_l(p)$ is specified with (18), $h_{li}(p)$ with (28) and (35), and $\mathbf{S}_N$ is the data vector (13).

3.2.3 Properties of the polynomial gain

The l-degree and p-lag polynomial gain $h_{li}(p)$ has the following fundamental properties:

- Its range of existence is

$$h_{li}(p) = \begin{cases} h_{li}(p) & p \le N-1+p \\ 0 & \text{otherwise} \end{cases}.\tag{38}$$

- The gain has unit area and zero moments as follows, respectively,

$$\sum_{i=p}^{N-1+p} h_{li}(p) = 1,\tag{39}$$

$$\sum_{i=p}^{N-1+p} h_{li}(p)i^u = 0,\; 1 \le u \le l.\tag{40}$$

- Its energy, referring to (39) and (40), calculates

$$\sum_{i=p}^{N-1+p} h_{li}^2(p) = \sum_{i=p}^{N-1+p} h_{li}(p) \sum_{j=0}^{l} a_{jl}(p)i^j$$

$$= \sum_{j=0}^{l} a_{jl}(p) \sum_{i=p}^{N-1+p} h_{li}(p)i^j$$

$$= a_{0l}(p), \tag{41}$$

where $a_{0l}(p)$ is the zero-order coefficient in (28).

3.3 Estimate variance

For the zero-mean measurement noise v_n having arbitrary distribution and covariance, the variance of the unbiased smoothing FIR filtering estimate can be found via the mean square error (MSE)

$$J = E(x_{1n} - \hat{x}_{1n|n-p})^2$$

$$= E\left[x_{1n} - \overline{\mathbf{W}}_l^T(p)\mathbf{C}_N\mathbf{x}_{n-N+1-p} - \overline{\mathbf{W}}_l^T(p)\mathbf{V}_N(p)\right]^2$$

$$= E\left[\left(\mathbf{A}^{N-1+p}\right)_1\mathbf{x}_{n-N+1-p} - \overline{\mathbf{W}}_l^T(p)\mathbf{C}_N\mathbf{x}_{n-N+1-p} - \overline{\mathbf{W}}_l^T(p)\mathbf{V}_N(p)\right]^2. \tag{42}$$

Embedded the unbiasedness (21) and accounted for the commutativity $\overline{\mathbf{W}}_l^T\mathbf{V}_N = \mathbf{V}_N^T\overline{\mathbf{W}}_l$, the MSE (42) represents the variance

$$\sigma^2(p) = E\left[\overline{\mathbf{W}}_l^T(p)\mathbf{V}_N(p)\right]^2$$

$$= E\left[\overline{\mathbf{W}}_l^T(p)\mathbf{V}_N(p)\overline{\mathbf{W}}_l^T(p)\mathbf{V}_N(p)\right] = \overline{\mathbf{W}}_l^T(p)E\left[\mathbf{V}_N(p)\mathbf{V}_N^T(p)\right]\overline{\mathbf{W}}_l(p)$$

$$= \overline{\mathbf{W}}_l^T(p)\mathbf{\Phi}_V(p)\overline{\mathbf{W}}_l(p). \tag{43}$$

In an important special case when v_n is a white sequence having a constant variance σ_v^2, (43) becomes

$$\sigma^2(p) = \overline{\mathbf{W}}_l^T(p)\mathrm{diag}\underbrace{\left[\sigma_v^2 \quad \sigma_v^2 \quad \cdots \quad \sigma_v^2\right]}_{N}\overline{\mathbf{W}}_l(p) = \sigma_v^2 g_l(p), \tag{44}$$

where the noise power gain (NG) $g_l(p)$ is specified by (Heinonen & Neuvo, 1987)

$$g_l(p) = \overline{\mathbf{W}}_l^T(p)\overline{\mathbf{W}}_l(p) \tag{45a}$$

$$= \sum_{i=p}^{N-1+p} h_{li}^2(p) \tag{45b}$$

$$= a_{0l}(p). \tag{45c}$$

and states that reducing noise in the estimate, by diminishing $g_l(p)$, means reducing $a_{0l}(p)$.

4. Low degree polynomial gains for unbiased smoothing FIR filters

Typically, smoothing of images is provided on short horizons with low-degree polynomials. Below, we derive and investigate the relevant unique gains for the uniform, linear, quadratic and cubic models covering an overwhelming majority of practical needs.

4.1 Uniform model

A model that is uniform over an averaging horizon of N points is the simplest one. The relevant image is characterized with single state and the filter gain is represented, by (36), with the 0-degree polynomial as

$$h_{0i}(p) = h_{0i} = \begin{cases} \frac{1}{N} & p \le N - 1 + p \\ 0 & \text{otherwise} \end{cases}. \tag{46}$$

By (45c), the NG of this filter becomes p-invariant, namely $g_0(p) = g_0 = 1/N$. Because this gain is associated with simple averaging, it is also optimal for a common task (Smith, 1999): reducing random noise while retaining a sharp step response. No other filter is better than the simple moving average in this sense. However, this gain is not good in terms of the estimate bias that reaches 50% when the model behaves linearly. Therefore, the best smooth is obtained by this gain at a centre of the averaging horizon, namely when $p = -(N-1)/2$.

4.2 Linear model

For linear models, the p-lag gain, existing from p to $N - 1 + p$, becomes ramp

$$h_{1i}(p) = a_{01}(p) + a_{11}(p)i, \tag{47}$$

having the coefficients

$$a_{01}(p) = \frac{2(2N-1)(N-1) + 12p(N-1+p)}{N(N^2-1)}, \tag{48}$$

$$a_{11}(p) = -\frac{6(N-1+2p)}{N(N^2-1)}. \tag{49}$$

At a centre of the averaging horizon provided with $p = -(N-1)/2$, the ramp gain degenerates to the uniform one (46),

$$h_{1i}\left(N, -\frac{N-1}{2}\right) = g_1\left(N, -\frac{N-1}{2}\right) = h_{0i} = g_0 = \frac{1}{N}. \tag{50}$$

With this lag, the ramp gain (47) is thus optimal with its zero bias and minimum possible noise produced by simple averaging. It can be shown that an increase in $|p|$ from 0 to $(N-1)/2$ results in reducing the ramp gain negative slope. As stated by (50), the lag $p = -(N-1)/2$ can degenerate this gain to the uniform one (46) featured to simple averaging. Further increase in $|p|$ from $(N-1)/2$ to $N-1$ produces an opposite effect: the gain slope becomes positive and such that, with $p = -N+1$, the gain function looks like symmetrically reflected from that corresponding to $p = 0$. Definitely, an ability of the ramp gain of becoming uniform with $p = -(N-1)/2$ must affect the noise amount in the smooth. An investigation of the noise reduction can be provided using the NG

$$g_1(p) = a_{10}(p) = \frac{2(2N-1)(N-1) + 12p(N-1+p)}{N(N^2-1)}. \tag{51}$$

Instantly one realizes that noise in the smooth has lower intensity than in the filtering estimate ($p = 0$). Indeed, when p ranges as $-N + 1 < p < -(N-1)/2$, the NG traces below the bound produced by $p = 0$. A situation changes when $|p|$ exceeds $N - 1$. With such values of the lag, the NG rises dramatically. One should not be surprised of this fact, because smoothing with lags exceeding and averaging horizon is nothing more than the backward prediction producing noise lager than in the filtering estimate.

4.3 Quadratic model

For the quadratic model, the gain of the unbiased smoothing FIR filter becomes

$$h_{2i}(p) = a_{02}(p) + a_{12}(p)i + a_{22}(p)i^2 , \tag{52}$$

in which the coefficients are defined as

$$a_{02}(p) = 3\frac{\begin{array}{c}\left(3N^4 - 12N^3 + 17N^2 - 12N + 4\right) + 12(N-1)\left(2N^2 - 5N + 2\right)p \\ + 12\left(7N^2 - 15N + 7\right)p^2 + 120(N-1)p^3 + 60p^4\end{array}}{N\left(N^2 - 1\right)\left(N^2 - 4\right)} , \tag{53}$$

$$a_{12}(p) = -18\frac{\begin{array}{c}\left(2N^3 - 7N^2 + 7N - 2\right) + 2\left(7N^2 - 15N + 7\right)p \\ + 30(N-1)p^2 + 60p^4\end{array}}{N\left(N^2 - 1\right)\left(N^2 - 4\right)} , \tag{54}$$

$$a_{22}(p) = 30\frac{\left(N^2 - 3N + 2\right) + 6(N-1)p + 6p^2}{N\left(N^2 - 1\right)\left(N^2 - 4\right)} . \tag{55}$$

As well as the ramp gain (47), the quadratic one (52) has several special points. Namely, by the lags

$$p_{21} = -\frac{N-1}{2} + \sqrt{\frac{N^2 - 1}{12}} , \tag{56}$$

$$p_{22} = -\frac{N-1}{2} - \sqrt{\frac{N^2 - 1}{12}} , \tag{57}$$

this gain degenerates to the ramp one and, with $p = -(N-1)/2$, it becomes symmetric. At the middle of the averaging horizon, $p = -(N-1)/2$, the gain (52) simplifies to

$$h_{2i}\left(N, -\frac{N-1}{2}\right) = \frac{3}{4}\frac{3N^2 - 7 - 20i^2}{N\left(N^2 - 4\right)} . \tag{58}$$

The NG associated with the quadratic gain (52) is given by

$$g_2(p) = a_{02}(p), \tag{59}$$

where $a_{02}(p)$ is described with (53).

Unlike the p-lag ramp gain (47) having a lower bound for the NG at $1/N$, the relevant bound for the p-lag quadratic gain (52) ranges upper and is given by

$$g_{2\min} = \frac{3\left(3N^2 - 2\right)}{5N\left(N^2 - 1\right)},$$

(60)

This value appears if to put to zero the derivative of $g_2(N, p)$ with respect to p and find the roots of the polynomial. Two lags correspond to (60), namely,

$$p_{23} = -\frac{N-1}{2} + \frac{1}{2}\sqrt{\frac{N^2 + 1}{5}},$$

(61)

$$p_{24} = -\frac{N-1}{2} - \frac{1}{2}\sqrt{\frac{N^2 + 1}{5}}.$$

(62)

Like the ramp gain case, here noise in the smooth is lower than in the filtering estimate, if p does not exceed and averaging horizon. Otherwise, we watch for the increase in the error that can be substantial.

4.4 Cubic model

The p-lag cubic gain can now be derived in a similar manner to have a polynomial form of

$$h_{3i}(p) = a_{03}(p) + a_{13}(p)i + a_{23}(p)i^2 + a_{33}(p)i^3$$

(63)

with the coefficients defines as

$$a_{03}(p) = 8\frac{\begin{aligned}&\left(2N^6 - 15N^5 + 47N^4 - 90N^3 + 113N^2 - 75N + 18\right)\\&+ 5\left(6N^5 - 42N^4 + 107N^3 - 132N^2 + 91N - 30\right)p\\&+ 5\left(42N^4 - 213N^3 + 378N^2 - 288N + 91\right)p^2\\&+ 10\left(71N^3 - 246N^2 + 271N - 96\right)p^3\\&+ 5\left(246N^2 - 525N + 271\right)p^4 + 1050(N-1)p^5 + 350p^6\end{aligned}}{N\left(N^2 - 1\right)\left(N^2 - 4\right)\left(N^2 - 9\right)},$$

(64)

$$a_{13}(p) = -20\frac{\begin{aligned}&\left(6N^5 - 42N^4 + 107N^3 - 132N^2 + 91N - 30\right)\\&+ 2\left(42N^4 - 213N^3 + 378N^2 - 288N + 91\right)p\\&+ 2\left(213N^3 - 738N^2 + 813N - 288\right)p^2\\&+ 4\left(246N^2 - 525N + 271\right)p^3 + 1050(N-1)p^4 + 420p^5\end{aligned}}{N\left(N^2 - 1\right)\left(N^2 - 4\right)\left(N^2 - 9\right)},$$

(65)

$$a_{23}(p) = 120 \frac{\left(2N^4 - 13N^3 + 28N^2 - 23N + 6\right) + 2\left(13N^3 - 48N^2 + 58N - 23\right)p + 2\left(48N^2 - 105N + 58\right)p^2 + 140(N-1)p^3 + 70p^4}{N\left(N^2 - 1\right)\left(N^2 - 4\right)\left(N^2 - 9\right)} , \tag{66}$$

$$a_{33}(p) = -140 \frac{\left(N^3 - 6N^2 + 11N - 6\right) + 2\left(6N^2 - 15N + 11\right)p + 30(N-1)p^2 + 20p^3}{N\left(N^2 - 1\right)\left(N^2 - 4\right)\left(N^2 - 9\right)} . \tag{67}$$

As well as the ramp and quadratic gains, the cubic one demonstrates several important features, including an ability of converting to the quadratic gain. The special values of p associated with this gain are listed below

$$p_{31} = -\frac{N-1}{2} + \frac{1}{10}\sqrt{5\left(3N^2 - 7\right)}, \tag{68}$$

$$p_{32} = -\frac{N-1}{2} + \frac{\sqrt{105}}{210}\sqrt{33N^2 - 17 + 2\sqrt{36N^4 + 507N^2 - 2579}} , \tag{69}$$

$$p_{33} = -\frac{N-1}{2} + \frac{\sqrt{105}}{210}\sqrt{33N^2 - 17 - 2\sqrt{36N^4 + 507N^2 - 2579}} , \tag{70}$$

$$p_{34} = -\frac{N-1}{2} - \frac{\sqrt{105}}{210}\sqrt{33N^2 - 17 - 2\sqrt{36N^4 + 507N^2 - 2579}} , \tag{71}$$

$$p_{35} = -\frac{N-1}{2} - \frac{\sqrt{105}}{210}\sqrt{33N^2 - 17 + 2\sqrt{36N^4 + 507N^2 - 2579}} , \tag{72}$$

$$p_{36} = -\frac{N-1}{2} - \frac{1}{10}\sqrt{5\left(3N^2 - 7\right)} . \tag{73}$$

The lags p_{31}, $p = -(N-1)/2$, and p_{36} convert the cubic gain to the quadratic one. These lags are therefore preferable from the standpoint of filtering accuracy, because the quadratic gain produces lower noise. The lag p_{32}, $p = -(N-1)/2$, and p_{35} correspond to minima on the smoother NG characteristic. The remaining lags, p_{33} and p_{34}, cause two maxima in the range of $-N + 1 < p < 0$.

The NG corresponding to the cubic gain (63) is given by

$$g_3(p) = a_{03}(p) . \tag{74}$$

where $a_{03}(p)$ is specified with (64). It can be shown that this NG ranges above the lower bound

$$g_{3\min} = \sqrt{\frac{3(3N^2 - 7)}{4N(N^2 - 4)}} \tag{75}$$

and, with p = const, it asymptotically approaches $g_3(N, 0)$, by increasing N. As well as in the quadratic gain case, noise in the cubic-gain smoother can be much lower than in the relevant filter ($p = 0$). On the other hand, the range of uncertainties is broadened here to $N = 3$ and the smoother becomes thus lower inefficient at short horizons. In fact, when the gain (74) exceeds unity, the 3-degree unbiased smoothing FIR filter loses an ability of denoising and its use becomes hence meaningless.

4.5 Generalizations

Several important common properties of the unbiased smoothing FIR filters can now be outlined as in the following. Effect of the lag p on the NG of low-degree unbiased smoothing FIR filters is reflected in Fig. 2. As can be seen, the NG of the ramp gain is exactly that of the uniform gain, when $p = -(N - 1)/2$. By $p = p_{21}$ and $p = p_{22}$, where p_{21} and p_{22} are specified by (61) and (62), respectively, the NG of the quadratic gain degenerates to that of the ramp gain. Also, by $p = p_{31}$ (68), $p = -(N - 1)/2$, and $p = p_{36}$ (73), the NG of the cubic gain degenerates to that of the quadratic gain. Similar deductions can be made for higher degree gains.

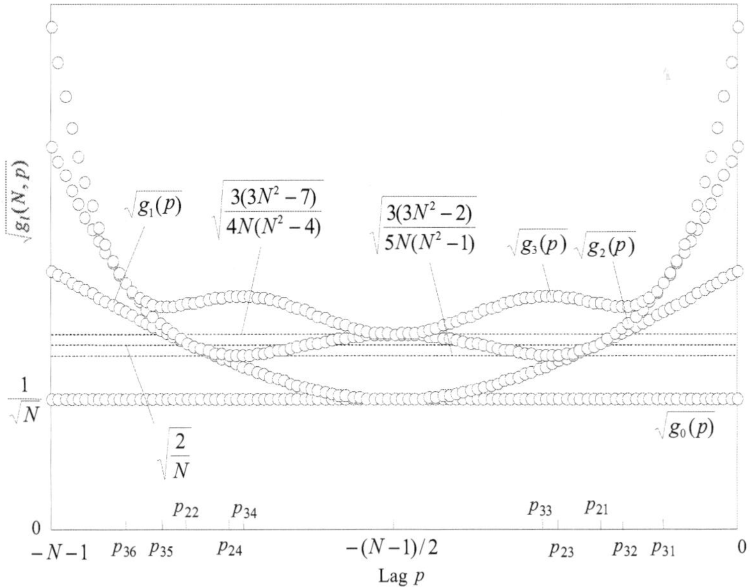

Fig. 2. Effect of a lag p, $p < 0$, on the NG of the low-degree unbiased smoothing FIR filters.

The following generalization can now be provided for a two-parameter family of the l-degree and p-lag, $p < 0$, unbiased smoothing FIR filters specified with the gain $h_{li}(p)$ and NG $g_l(p)$:

i.   Any smoothing FIR filter with the lag p lying on the averaging horizon $-(N-1) < p < 0$, produces smaller errors then the relevant FIR filter with $p = 0$.

ii.   Without loss in accuracy, the l-degree unbiased smoothing FIR filter can be substituted, for some special values of p, with a reduced $(l-1)$-degree one. Namely, the 1-degree gain can be substituted with the 0-degree gain for $p = -(N-1)/2$, the 2-degree gain with the 1-degree gain for $p = p_{21}$ and $p = p_{22}$, and the 3-degree gain with the 2-degree gain, if $p = p_{31}$, $p = -(N-1)/2$, or $p = p_{36}$.

iii.   Beyond the averaging horizon, the error of the smoothing FIR filter with $p < -N + 1$ is equal to that of the predictive FIR filter with $p > 0$.

iv.   The error lower bounds for the smoothing FIR filters with the ramp gain, g_{1min}, quadratic gain g_{2min}, and cubic gain, g_{3min}, are given by, respectively,

$$g_{1\min} = \frac{1}{N}, \tag{76}$$

$$g_{2\min} = \left.\frac{3(3N^2-2)}{5N(N^2-1)}\right|_{N\gg1} \approx \frac{9}{5N}, \tag{77}$$

$$g_{3\min} = \left.\frac{3(3N^2-7)}{4N(N^2-4)}\right|_{N\gg1} \approx \frac{9}{4N}, \tag{78}$$

v.   With large N, error in the l-degree smoother for $p = -N + 1$ are defined by

$$g_l(N,-N+1)\big|_{N\gg1} \approx \frac{(l+1)^2}{N}. \tag{79}$$

The initial conditions can hence be ascertained using the ramp and quadratic gains with the NGs $\approx 4/N$ and $\approx 9/N$, respectively.

vi.   By increasing N for a constant p such that $p \ll N$, the error in the smoother asymptotically approaches the error in the relevant unbiased FIR filter with $p = 0$.

5. Design and applications of unbiased FMH structures

In this section, we employ the above derived p-dependent gains in order to design efficient hybrid structures suitable for biomedical applications, specifically for ultrasound image processing. Every image is considered as an array of two signals, $\mathbf{x}_r$ and $\mathbf{x}_c$, as showed in (1) and (2), respectively, and processed as in the following. First, we filter out noise in the row vector and then reconstruct the image. Next, the partly enhanced image is decomposed to the column vector, the filtering procedure is applied once again, and the fully enhanced image is reconstructed. For the sake of minimum errors in the enhanced image, all of the above designed low-degree polynomial gains have been examined in the FMH structure. Namely, we employ all p-dependent, the ramp gain (47), the quadratic gain (52), and the cubic one (63). Two metrics, namely the signal-to-noise ratio (SNR) and the root mean square error (RMSE) have been used for the quantitative evaluation of the filter efficiency. It is known that FMH structures can be designed to have k substructures and that a number of such substructures needs to be optimized that is a special topic. Postponing the optimization problem to further investigations, we mostly examine in this Chapter the basic FMH structure and demonstrate the effect of a number of sub-blocks.

5.1 Basic FIR median hybrid structure

Figure 3 sketches the block diagram of the basic FIR median hybrid (FMH) structure developed in (Heinonen & Neuvo, 1987) to maximize the SNR in the row and column vectors. Here, the input signal y_n is filtered with 2 FIR filters. The forward FIR filter (FIR^{FW}) computes the points on a horizon to the left from the point n. In turn, the backward FIR filter (FIR^{BW}) processes data on the same length horizon lying to the right from n. The estimates are hence formed as, respectively,

$$\hat{x}_n^{FW}(p) = \sum_{i=p}^{N-1+p} h_{li}(p) y_{n-i} \, , \tag{80}$$

$$\hat{x}_n^{BW}(p) = \sum_{i=p}^{N-1+p} h_{li}(p) y_{n+i} \, , \tag{81}$$

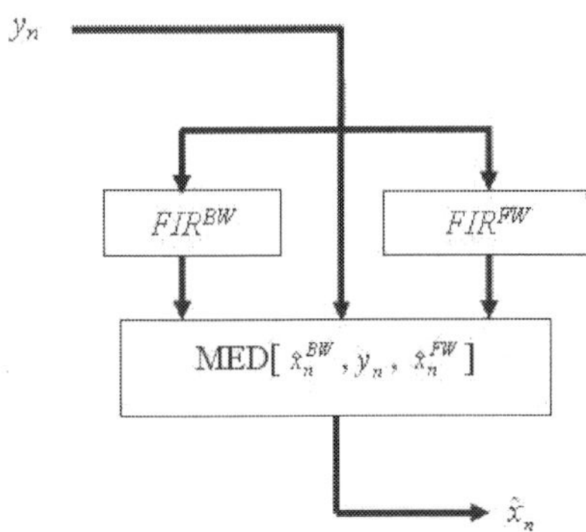

Fig. 3. Block diagram of the basic FIR median hybrid (FMH) structure.

The output signal $\hat{x}_n(p)$ is obtained using the nonlinear operator called the "median". In the median structure MED[$\hat{x}_n^{BW}(p)$, y_n, $\hat{x}_n^{FW}(p)$] (Fig. 3), the input y_n and the outputs of the FIR filters, $\hat{x}_n^{BW}(p)$ and $\hat{x}_n^{FW}(p)$, play the role of entries. Following the median filter strategy, the output $\hat{x}_n(p)$ becomes equal to the intermediate value that is stated by the operator

$$\hat{x}_n(p) = \text{MED}\left[\hat{x}_n^{BW}(p), y_n, \hat{x}_n^{FW}(p)\right] \, . \tag{82}$$

Note that the best filtering result can be obtained if one sets properly the smoother lag p or prediction step p in the FIR filters. Because the basic structure shown in Fig. 3 is commonly unable to obtain nice image enhancing, owing to a small number of the entries, a more sophisticated FIR FMH structure exploiting different p would provide better performance.

In this Chapter, we employ the combined FIR FMH structure with $k > 1$ as shown in (Heinonen & Neuvo, 1987).

5.2 SNR and RMSE metrics

Image enhancement can quantitatively be evaluated using the SNR and RMSE metrics. Given the discrete image mapping $x_n(i,j)$, where $i \in [1,P]$ and $j \in [1,Q]$, and the relevant enhanced and reconstructed mapping $\hat{x}_n(i,j)$, the SNR can be estimated (in dB) by

$$SNR_{dB} = 10\log_{10}\left(\frac{\sum_{i=1}^{P}\sum_{j=1}^{Q}[x(i,j)]^2}{\sum_{i=1}^{P}\sum_{j=1}^{Q}[x(i,j)-\hat{x}(i,j)]^2}\right), \tag{83}$$

In turn, the RMSE in the enhanced image can be estimated with

$$RMSE = \sqrt{\frac{1}{PQ}\sum_{i=1}^{P}\sum_{j=1}^{Q}[x(i,j)-\hat{x}(i,j)]^2} . \tag{84}$$

Below, we apply these metrics to ultrasonic images.

5.3 Simulation and numerical evaluations

For further investigations, we chose a renal ultrasound image shown in Fig.4. This image has been obtained under the conditions accepted in (K. Singh & N. Malhotra, 2004) and (Levine, 2007). A part of the image having 250×320 pixels of size within the rectangular area (Fig. 4) has been processed. We call this part the origin and show in Fig. 5.

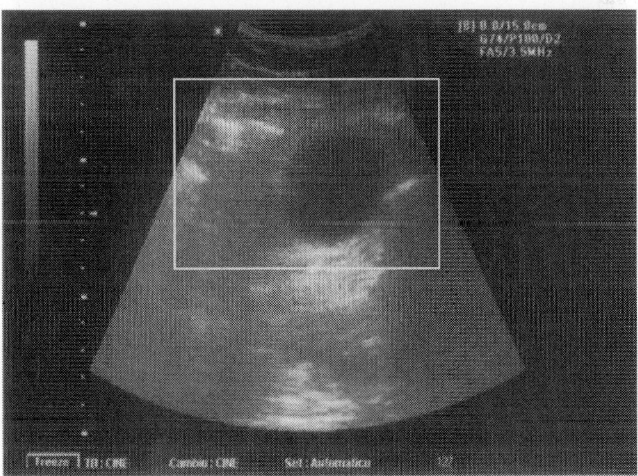

Fig. 4. The original ultrasound image.

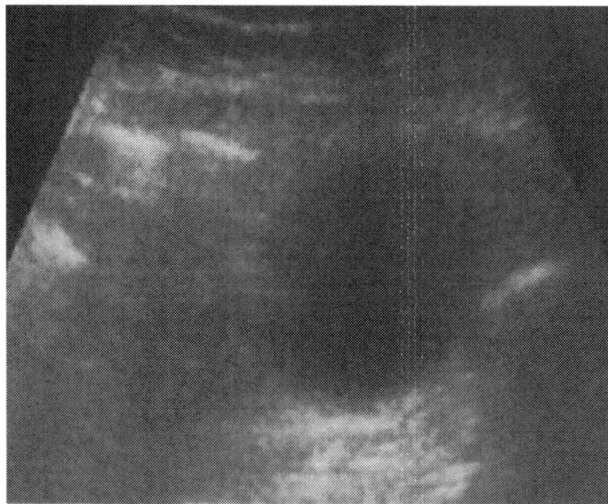

Fig. 5. A Section of the original ultrasound image of 250 × 320 pixels.

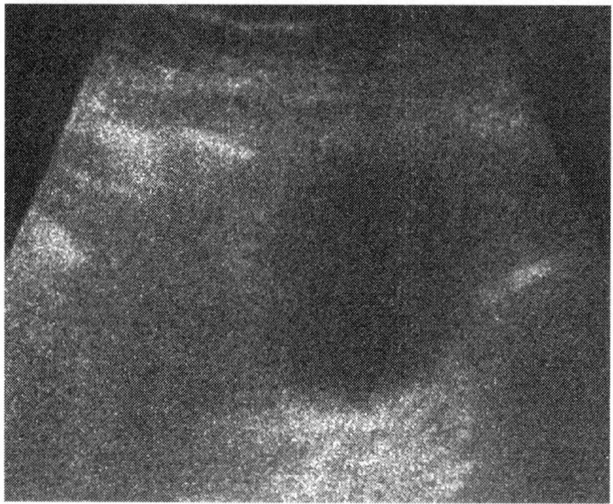

Fig. 6. A contaminated image (Fig. 5) with speckle noise and Gaussian noise, both having the variance $\sigma^2 = 0.01$.

The image was then intentionally contaminated with Gaussian noise and speckle noise, both having the variance $\sigma^2 = 0.01$, is shown in Fig. 6. To examine and exhibit an efficiency of the basic FIR FMH structure, we chose the following parameters: the number of points in the average, $N = 11$, the filter degree, $l = 1$, and the p parameter $p \in [-1, 1]$. The reader must be aware that determination of a certain set of the parameters is a special topic of optimization (minimizing both the SNR and the MSE) of the enhanced image.

Figure 7 shows us what is going on with the image if we let in the hybrid structure $p = 1$ (one-step predictive FIR filtering). In turn, Fig. 8 and Fig. 9 give us the pictures provided with $p = 0$ (FIR filtering) and $p = -1$ (unit-leg smoothing FIR filtering). One can deduce that a visual comparison of Fig. 7 – Fig. 9 does not reveal dramatic enhancements and a numerical analysis is in order. We apply such an analysis below postponing the results to several tables.

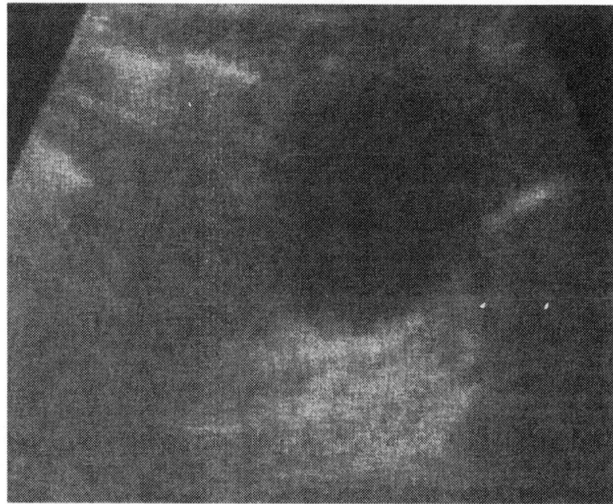

Fig. 7. An enhanced ultrasound image with $N = 11$, $l = 1$, and $p = 1$.

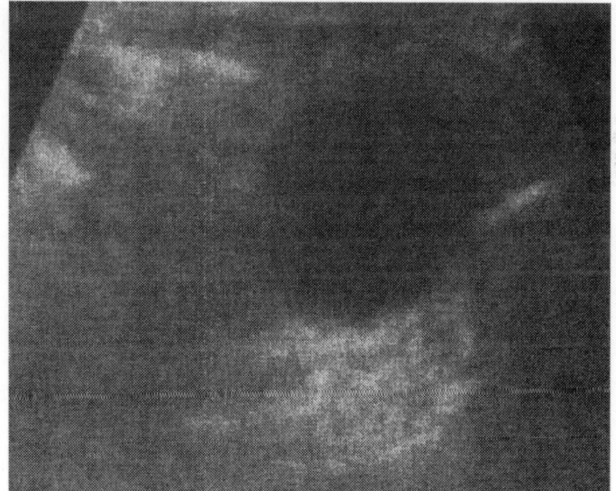

Fig. 8. An enhanced ultrasound image with $N = 11$, $l = 1$, and $p = 0$.

5.4 Analysis and discussions

In order to evaluate numerically the trade-off between the different filtering solutions employed in the FIR FMH structures, we use the SNR metric (83) and the RMSE metric (84) and apply them both to the reconstructed images obtained with different number k of sub-blocks, p-parameters, and degrees of the FIR filters, $l \in [0, 3]$, allowing $N = 11$.

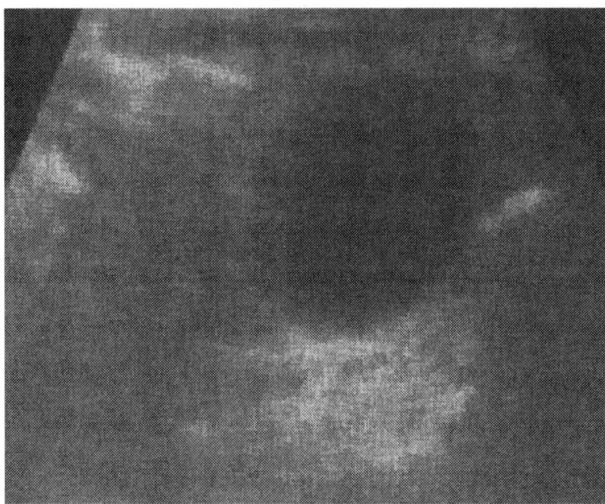

Fig. 9. An enhanced ultrasound image with $N = 11$, $l = 1$, and $p = -1$.

Fig. 10 and Fig. 11 show the RMSE and SNR as functions of p and Table 1 gives us several particular values of these measures. As can be seen, each of the degrees, $l \in [1, 3]$, allows obtaining both the maximum SNR and minimum RMSE. It is also seen that extremes of these functions are placed in the range of negative p. Specifically, it was revealed that the minimum errors are obtained with the $p = -1$ lag of the smoothing filter (Table 1). The latter speaks in favor of smoothing FIR filters for FMH structures, contrary to the predictive ones implemented in (Heinonen & Neuvo, 1987).

Effect of the FIR filter degree l on the RMSE and SNR is demonstrated in Table 2 for $p = -1$, $p = 0$, and $p = 1$. One can observe that the ramp filter ($l = 1$) produces minimum RMSEs and maximum SNRs in each of the cases, although the errors are minimum when $p = -1$. The quadratic gain ($l = 2$) and the cubic gain ($l = 3$) produce a bit worse results and simple averaging ($l = 0$) is not a rival with its large RMSE and small SNR. We thus infer that

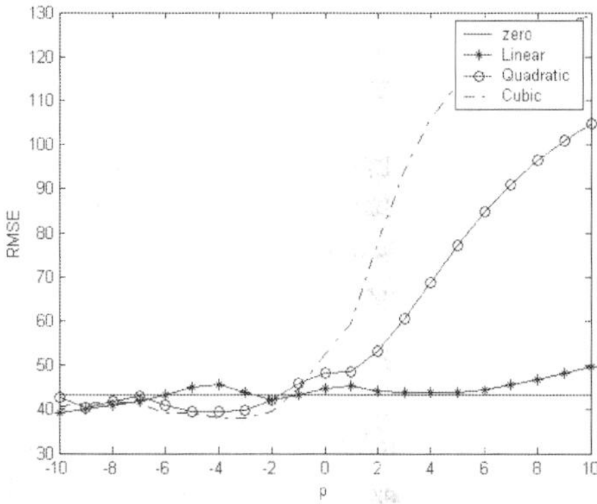

Fig. 10. RMSE in the enhanced image vs. p with $N = 11$, $k = 1$, $-5 \leq p \leq 5$, and $0 \leq l \leq 3$.

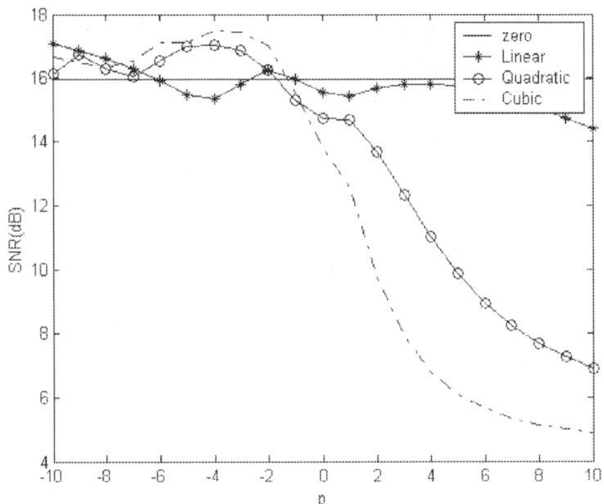

Fig. 11. SNR in the enhanced image vs. p with $N = 11$, $k = 1$, $-5 \leq p \leq 5$, and $0 \leq l \leq 3$.

	$p = -3$	$p = -2$	$p = -1$	$p = 0$	$p = 1$	$p = 2$	$p = 3$
RMSE	43.78	**42.24**	43.31	44.83	45.25	44.31	43.87
SNR (dB)	15.83	**16.24**	15.96	15.57	15.46	15.70	15.81

Table 1. Quantitative evaluation with $N = 11$, $k = 1$, and $l = 1$.

$p = -1$	$l = 0$	$l = 1$	$l = 2$	$l = 3$
RMSE	**43.24**	43.31	45.87	44.88
SNR, dB	**15.97**	15.96	15.31	15.55

$p = 0$	$l = 0$	$l = 1$	$l = 2$	$l = 3$
RMSE	**43.24**	44.83	48.33	52.63
SNR, dB	15.97	**15.57**	14.74	13.81

$p = 1$	$l = 0$	$l = 1$	$l = 2$	$l = 3$
RMSE	**43.24**	45.25	48.49	59.27
SNR, dB	**15.97**	15.46	14.70	12.56

Table 2. Quantitative evaluation with $N = 11$, $k = 1$, and $p \in [-1, 1]$.

complex FIR FMH structures need to be optimized in the sense of the minimum RMSE over l and p simultaneously and that there is an optimal solution behind each of such structures.

The next important point for the optimization is the k of the sub-blocks. At a first glance, every new sub-block should reduce errors in the median filter, because the latter acquires more entries to make a decision. Indeed, in our experiment illustrated in Fig. 12 and Fig. 13 this deduction has not been confirmed: an increase in k from 1 to 3 results in these figures in the RMSE reduction and increasing the SNR. Table 3 gives us extreme points of these functions in the p-domain.

Effect of noise on the RMSE and SNR in the enhanced image has been investigated by changing the noise variance. Fig. 14 and Fig. 15 give an idea about such an influence. First, we arrive at an almost self-obvious conclusion that the RMSE rises and the SNR diminishes when the noise variance increases. That is neatly seen in Fig. 14 and Fig. 15. What has appeared to be lesser expected is that the RMSE minimum and the SNR maximum both remove to the range of larger p since the variance increases. In fact, we watch in Fig. 14 for the RMSE minimum at $p = -1$ with $\sigma^2 = 0.02$ and at $p = 1$ with $\sigma^2 = 0.08$. Certainly this effect needs more investigations as being affecting the optimal set of parameters.

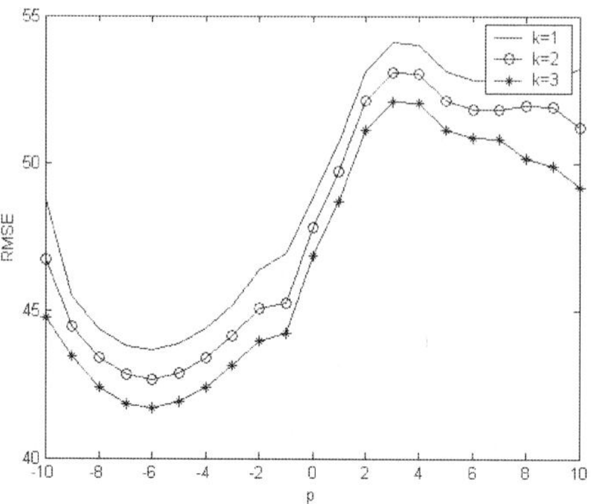

Fig. 12. RMSE in the enhanced image vs. p with $N = 11$, $l = 1$, $-5 \leq p \leq 5$, and $1 \leq k \leq 3$.

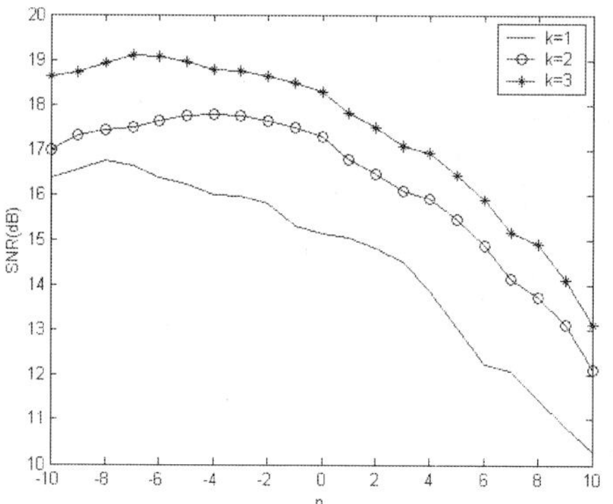

Fig. 13. Sketches of SNR vs. p with $N = 11$, $l = 1$, $-5 \leq p \leq 5$, $1 \leq k \leq 3$.

	$k = 1$	$k = 2$	$k = 3$
RMSE$_{min}$	15.13	17.29	**18.27**
SNR$_{max}$ (dB)	48.85	47.74	**46.63**

Table 3. Quantitative evaluation with $N = 11$, $l = 1$, and $p = -1$.

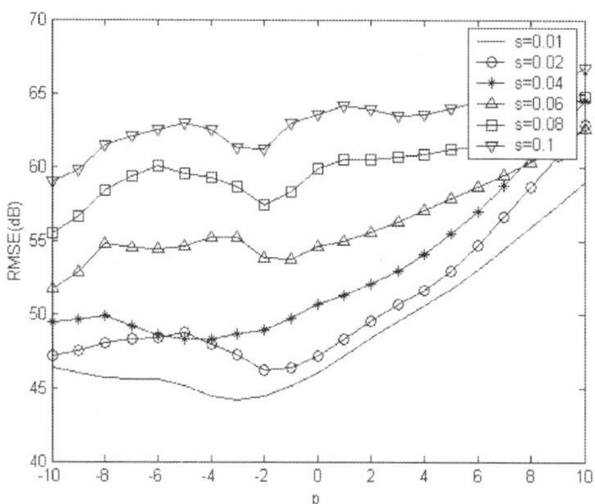

Fig. 14. RMSE vs. p with $N = 11$, $l = 1$, $k = 1$, $-5 \leq p \leq 5$, and $0.01 \leq \sigma^2 \leq 0.1$.

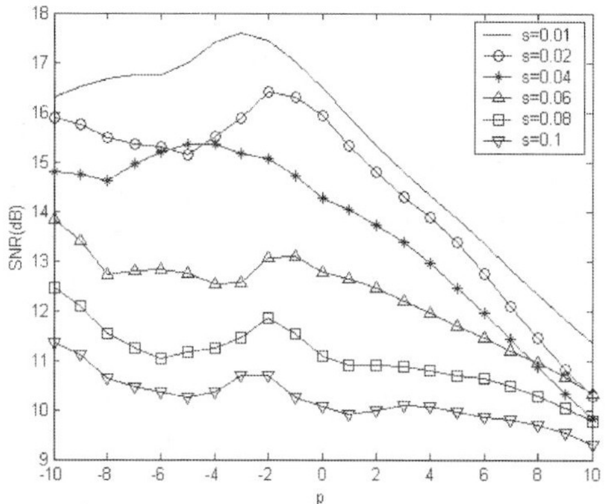

Fig. 15. SNR vs. p with $N = 11$, $l = 1$, $k = 1$, $-5 \leq p \leq 5$, and $0.01 \leq \sigma^2 \leq 0.1$.

6. Conclusion

In this chapter, we developed the theory of smoothing FIR filtering and applied the results to the design of FIR median hybrid filters in order to enhance ultrasound images. General smoothing filter gain has been derived in line with the most widely used low-order ones. We propose an unbiased solution. The gain for the unbiased smoother had been developed in the unique polynomial form that does not involve any knowledge about noise and initial state, thus having strong engineering features. It has been shown experimentally that, as a rule of thumb, the smoothing FIR filters with $p < 0$ allow for lower RMSEs and larger SNRs in the enhanced image. On the other hand, our experiments reveal that predictive filtering solutions earlier used in (Heinonen & Neuvo, 1987) in ultrasound image processing (Morales-Mendoza et. al, 2008, 2009) produce large errors.

7. References

K. Najarian and R. Splinter, *Biomedical Signal and Image Processing*. New York: CRC Taylor & Francis, 2007.

J. Jan, *Medical Image Processing, Reconstruction and Restoration: Concept and Methods*. Florida USA: CRC Taylor & Francis Press, 2006.

I. Pitas and A. Venetsanopoulos, *Nonlinear Digital Filters – Principles and Applications*, Kluwer Academic Publishers, 1990.

N. Kalouptsidis and S. Theodoridis, *Adaptive system Identification and signal processing Algorithms*, Prentice Hall, 1993.

J. Astola and P. Kuosmanen, *Fundamentals of Nonlinear Digital Filters*, CRC Press, 1997.

P. Heinonen and A. Neuvo, FIR median hybrid filters, *IEEE Trans. on Acoustic, Speech, and Signal Processing*, vol. 35, no. 6, pp. 832-838, June 1987.

P. Heinonen and A. Neuvo, FIR-median hybrid filter with predictive FIR substructures, *IEEE Trans. on Acoustic, Speech, and Signal Processing*, vol. 36, no. 6, pp. 892-899, June 1988.

Dumitrescu; B. *Positive Trigonometric Polynomials and Signal Processing Applications*, Springer, Dordrecht, ISBN 978-1402051241, 2007.

Mathews; V. J. & Sicuranza ; G. L. *Polynomials Signal Processing*, John Wiley & Sons, New York, ISBN 978-0471034148, 2001.

Y. Shmaliy, An unbiased FIR filter for TIE model of a local clock in applications to GPS-based timekeeping, *IEEE Trans. on Ultrasonic, Ferroelectrics and Frequency Control*, vol. 53, no. 5, pp. 862-870, May 2006.

T. Bose, F. Meyer, and M.-Q. Chen, *Digital Signal and Image Processing*, J. Wiley, New York, 2004

Y. Shmaliy, An unbiased p-step predictive FIR filter for a class of noise-free discrete time models with independently observed states, *Signal, Image & Video Processing*, vol. 3, no. 2, pp. 127-135, Jun. 2009.

Y. Shmaliy, Optimal gains of FIR estimators for a class of discrete-time state-space models, *IEEE Signal Processing Letters*, vol. 15, pp. 517-520, 2008.

Y. Shmaliy, Unbiased FIR filtering of discrete-time polynomial state-space models, *IEEE Transactions on Signal Processing*, vol. 57, no. 4, pp. 1241-1249, Apr. 2009.

S. W. Smith, *The Scinetist and Engineer's Guide to Digital Signal Processing*, 2nd Ed., California Technical Publishing, 1999.

D. Levine, *Ultrasound Clinics*, ELSEVIER INC., Boston USA, 2007.

K. Singh & N. Malhotra, *Step-by-Step Ultrasound in Obstetrics*, Mc-Graw Hill, 2004.

L. J. Morales-Mendoza, Y. Shmaliy, O. G. Ibarra-Manzano, L. J. Arceo-Miquel and M. Montiel-Rodriguez, Moving Average Hybrid FIR Filter in Ultrasound Image Processing, *Proceeding of 18th International Conference of CONIELECOMP*, ISBN: 0-7695-3120-2, pp. 160 – 164, Cholula, Pue. Mexico, March 2008.

L. J. Morales-Mendoza, Y. Shmaliy and O. G. Ibarra-Manzano, An analysis of Hybrid FIR Structures in application to Ultrasound Image Processing, *Proceeding of 1st International Conference of WSEAS*, ISBN: 978-960-474-071-0, pp. 344-349, Houston Tx, USA, May 2009.

## 17

Automatic Lesion Detection in Ultrasonic Images

Yung-Sheng Chen[1] and Chih-Kuang Yeh[2]
[1]Department of Electrical Engineering, Yuan Ze University, Chungli,
[2]Department of Biomedical Engineering and Environmental Sciences
National Tsing Hua University, Hsinchu,
Taiwan, ROC

1. Introduction

One of the promising clinical needs of acquiring ultrasonic images is in the detection of the possible lesions. Several methods for ultrasonic image segmentation have been proposed in the literature, such as edge based (Aarnink et al., 1994), texture based (Richard & Keen, 1996), active contour based (Hamarneh & Gustavsson, 2000; Akgul et al., 2000), semi-automatic approaches (Ladak et al., 1999; Ladak et al., 2000), and so on. The edge and texture based methods usually cannot provide a high quality segmentation results due to the speckle interference of ultrasonic images. The active contour models required an initial seed point and utilized a closed contour to approach object boundary by iteratively minimizing an energy function. It is usually a time-consuming scheme; and has poor convergence to lesion boundary concavity due to inherent speckle interference thus it cannot accurately contour the irregular shape malignant tumor. The semi-automatic approach uses model-based initialisation and a discrete dynamic contour with a set of control points so that an estimation of the prostate shape can be interpolated using cubic functions. A good survey can be found in the literature (Abolmaesumi & Sirouspour, 2004), in which the authors presented an integrated approach combining probabilistic data association filter (PDAF) with the interacting multiple model (IMM) estimator to increase the accuracy of the extracted contours. Recently, we also presented a semi-automatic segmentation method for ultrasonic breast lesions (Yeh et al., 2009). The main idea of this method is that an effective scheme of removing speckle noise was applied for the segmentation of ultrasonic breast lesions, which was performed with an iterative disk expansion method (Chen & Lin, 1995).

Base on the above brief survey, as a result, automatically detecting and extracting lesion boundaries in ultrasound images is rather difficult due to the variance in shape and the interference from speckle noise. Even several methods have been proposed for approaching to this goal, however they usually cannot be applied for the whole image; and need a selected region of interest (ROI) or an initial seed for processing. To overcome this problem, a fully automatic approach is presented in this article, which can detect the possible lesions in a whole ultrasonic image.

2. Proposed approach

The main idea of our approach is from the concept of contour map onto earth surface, where a mountain and the valley around the mountain may be distinguished with a contour line. In ultrasonic image, a possible lesion may be imaged as a mountain. Since it is usually with a poor quality and the lesion may be with a various size, in our approach a median filtering with estimated circular-window size is first used for forming a smoothed image. A proper circular-window for median filter is necessary. That is, a proper small window should be used in the case of small lesions, and vice versa. Furthermore, to avoid the zigzag effect, a squared window should not be used.

The darker region belonging to a lesion is another useful cue in ultrasonic image processing. Hence intuitively, if an ultrasonic image is divided into two regions: darker and brighter regions, assuming a lesion located in the darker region is reasonable. To perform such segmentation, a mean or median value of the given image can be used as a threshold, which can be referred to as a mean-cut or median-cut scheme, respectively, therefore M-cut named generally in this paper. Since a lesion may be of large or small; and it may be located in the newly divided darker region or brighter region, the M-cut scheme will perform continuously until a stopping condition satisfies. In our study, the stopping condition is defined as follows.

$$\left| M_{\mathrm{brighter}} - M_{\mathrm{darker}} \right| < TH \tag{1}$$

Where M_{brighter} and M_{darker} represent the M-value of brighter and darker region, respectively; and TH is a defined threshold value. If a stopping condition occurs, then the previous undivided one may represent a possible lesion.

Because the stopping condition may occur at either darker or brighter region, to check the stopping condition a binary tree structure (BTS) having several nodes is adopted in our approach. Based on the BTS, each segmented part will be regarded as a new image and fed into the BTS for analysis, and thus be regarded as a new node. A 3-level node sequence starting at node 0 for a BTS is illustrated in Fig. 1. After the BTS segmentation, all possible lesions' regions will be located and indicated by the ending nodes. To facility the final possible lesions' regions easily identified, a postprocessing will be useful. In the following subsections, the main parts of our approach namely, segmentation, binary tree structure, and postprocessings will be detailed.

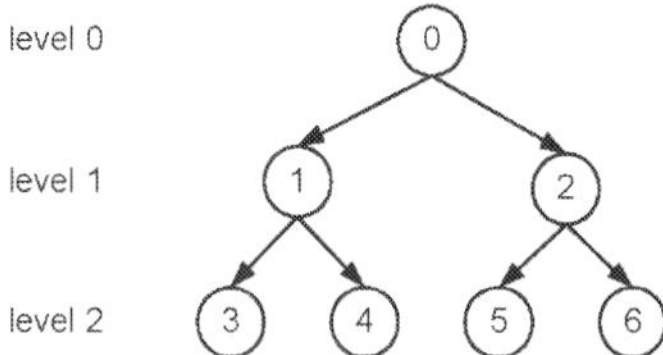

Fig. 1. Illustration of a 3-level BTS.

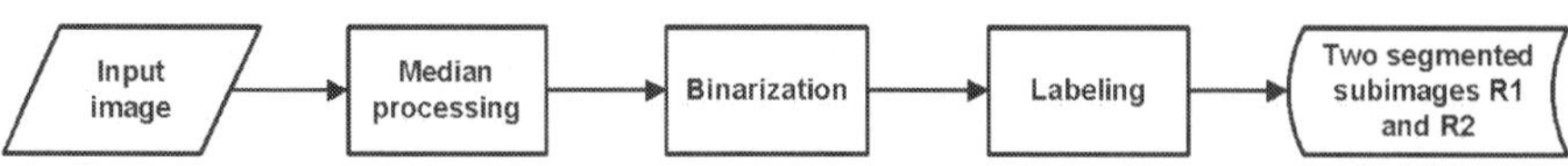

Fig. 2. Segmentation procedure.

2.1 Segmentation

The segmentation procedure is designed simply and depicted in Fig. 2. It is mainly composed of three consecutive processes: median processing, binarization, and labelling; and then yields two segmented subregions, R_1 and R_2. Here R_1 and R_2 denote the darker and brighter subimages, respectively. In other words, R_1 is the region containing the largest labelled area based on the binarized image, whereas R_2 is the rest region of subtracting R_1 from the input image. An ultrasonic image containing a lesion is given in Fig. 3 for illustrating each step of our algorithms.

At the step of median process, the significant concern is to decide the radius r of a circular window. In our study, we confine the r value between $r_{\min}$ to $r_{\max}$ for dealing with the concerned lesion's size. If a small lesion appears, the r value approaches to $r_{\min}$, and vice versa. Hence we defined a size ratio to represent the lesion's size information, i.e., $sr = n_o / n_t$, where n_o denotes the possible object's rectangular size, and n_t the half-size of the image. Here we assume a possible lesion is located in the upper region of the image, and thus the $r_{\min}$ is used for median processing and then a rough segmentation is performed to estimate the representing object's region. In this study, the sr is also ranged between $sr_{\min}$ and $sr_{\max}$. Based on these definitions, a proper r with respect to sr can be expressed by

$$r = \begin{cases} r_{\min} & sr < sr_{\min} \\ r_{\max} & sr > sr_{\max} \\ r_{\max} - \dfrac{(r_{\max} - r_{\min})(sr_{\max} - sr)}{(sr_{\max} - sr_{\min})} & \text{otherwise} \end{cases} \qquad (2)$$

In our experiments, $[r_{\min}, r_{\max}] = [5, 30]$ and $[sr_{\min}, sr_{\max}] = [0.006, 0.25]$ are empirically used. Based on the presented method, the estimated object's region is obtained in Fig. 3(b), where the estimated r value is 18. After the median processing with $r = 18$, a binarized image can be obtained as shown in Fig. 3(c) by the found median grey value 57. Further applying labelling process, the largest region can be extracted as Fig. 3(d) shows. Even the obtained region in Fig. 3(d) is nonuniform due to the speckle property of an ultrasonic image, it is easily smoothed by applying a circular-median process. Based on the presented segmentation procedure as depicted in Fig. 2, two segmented subregions R_1 and R_2 are finally obtained as shown in Fig. 3(e) and 3(f), respectively, which will be further processed by our BTS scheme.

2.2 Binary tree structure

From the segmented R_1 and R_2 subimages, we can find an obvious lesion located in R_2 image. It means that the segmentation should be further performed for R_2 image to approach the target. However, for general case, we should deal with for both R_1 and R_2 since the lesion may appear in both. Consider the BTS principle defined previously and refer to the 3-level BTS illustration in Fig. 1, R_1 and R_2 images are now represented by node 1 and 2, respectively at level 1, and will be processed continuously. If any node satisfies the stopping condition defined in (1), then it represents a possible lesion detected and the line along this node will not be proceeded. This process is continued recursively until the node number is smaller than 0 referred to the illustration in Fig. 1. In our experiments, $TH = 5$ is selected empirically. The whole BTS algorithm can be detailed in Fig. 4.

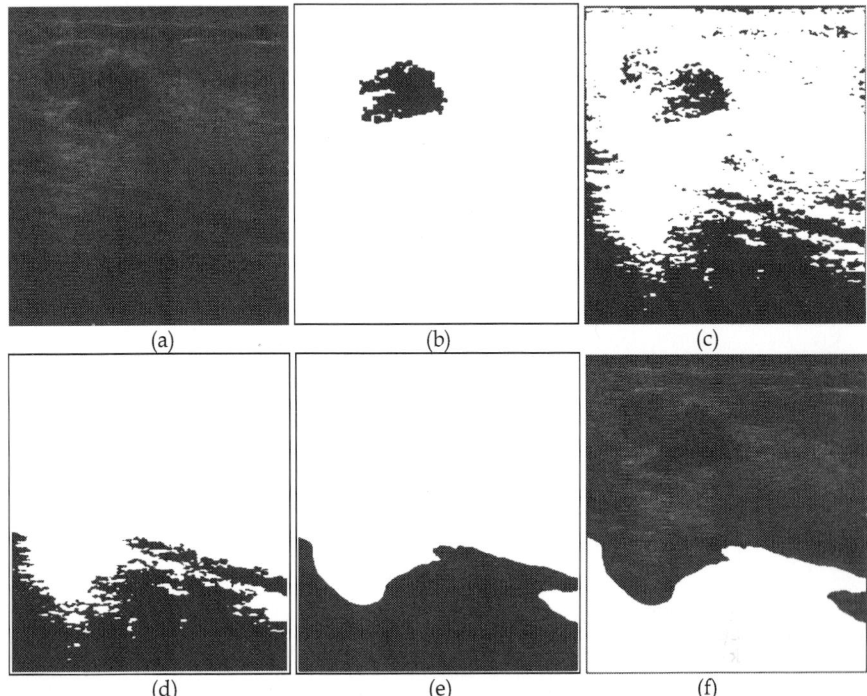

Fig. 3. (a) An ultrasonic image containing a lesion. (b) The estimated object's region from the upper image. (c) Binary result. (d) The largest labelled region. (e), (f) Segmented R_1 and R_2 subimages.

Let k be the node number. Refer to Fig. 1, for node 0 (original image), we will have two son nodes denoted node 1 and node 2. It can be formulated as: for node k, it has two son nodes: node $2k+1$ and node $2k+2$. Based on this formulation, for example, two son nodes of node 2 ($k=2$) are node 5 and node 6 as addressed in Fig. 1.

Because of the recursive operations of BTS, the backward node indexing is also needed. That is, for node k, its father node will be

$$\text{node} \begin{cases} (k-1)/2 & \text{if } k \text{ is odd,} \\ (k-2)/2 & \text{otherwise.} \end{cases} \tag{3}$$

In the BTS algorithm of Fig. 4, the tc[k] is used to count the passing times for the k-th node. Each node can be visited two times at most, one is forward and the other is backward.

After the BTS processing, for the current example, we obtain the following ending nodes: 3, 4, 12, 23, 24, 56, 111, 112, 57, 118, 235, 236, 30, 59, 121, 245, 246. The tree structure of these ending nodes denoted by black colour is depicted in Fig. 5. The detailed information including size and mean grey value of each node (subimage) are given in Table 1(a), which will be further used in postprocessings. Here size means the total non-white pixels of the corresponding subimage.

```
k=0;       //the k-th node for processing, starting at 0
tc[]=0;    //passing times of the k-th node for further checking
td[]=0;    //saving the mean-value-difference between two segmented
           //subimages divided from the k-th subimage.
tg[]=255;//mean grey value of the k-th subimage, initially 255.
to[]=0;    //label if the k-th node is ended (1) or not (0)

BTS(){
  if (k<0)
    return;

  md=td[k];
  if (md==0){
    segmentation(r);    //m1, m2: mean grey value of darker and
                        //brighter subimages.
    if (m1>0 && m2>0)
      md=|m1 - m2|;
    else
      md=0;

    td[k]=md;
    if (md>=TH){
      tg[2k+1]=m1;
      R      save the corresponding darker subimage R ;
       2K+1                                           1
      tg[2k+2]=m2;
      R      save the corresponding brighter subimage R ;
       2K+2                                            2
    }
  }
  tc[k]++;

  if (md<TH || tc[k]>2){
    if (md<TH)
      to[k]=1;

    if (k%2 != 0)
      k=(k-1)/2;
    else
      k=(k-2)/2;
  }
  else{
    if (tc[k]==1)
      k=k*2+1;
    else
      k=k*2+2;
  }

  BTS();
}
```

Fig. 4. BTS algorithm.

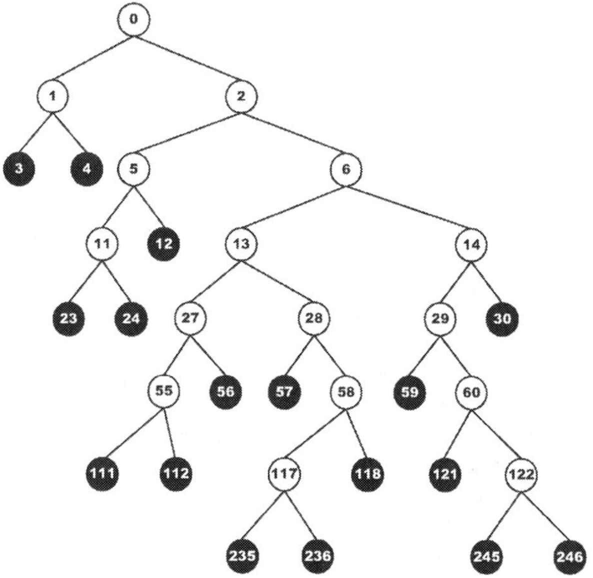

Fig. 5. The tree structure of ending nodes 3, 4, 12, 23, 24, 56, 111, 112, 57, 118, 235, 236, 30, 59, 121, 245, 246, denoted by black colour.

Node	Size	Mean grey value
3	23505	43
4	21401	52
12	5388	63
23	1297	47
24	2355	53
56	2817	65
111	782	54
112	1957	61
57	2992	65
118	16773	72
235	355	49
236	2088	63
30	41095	87
59	2575	69
121	1484	57
245	589	60
246	18721	76

(a)

Node	Size	Mean grey value
245	589	60
23	1297	47
24	2355	53
59	2575	69
57	2992	65
12	5388	63

(b)

Table 1. (a) Size and mean grey information of each node for tree structure in Fig. 5. Here size means the total non-white pixels of the corresponding subimage. (b) Reduced nodes' information after applying Rule 1. They are ordered by size in ascent for the further use of Rule 2.

2.3 Postprocessings

In clinical application, doctor may adjust ultrasonic equipments for enhancing an ultrasonic image so that the lesion can be observed, analyzed, and located for assessment. Similarly, so far, based on our segmentation and BTS algorithms, a set of possible lesion's regions (nodes) has been addressed. However there are some non-lesion's regions also included. They may be an ignorable shadow or insignificant lighting phenomenon and can be regarded as non-lesion's regions. Hence we described two rules below for filtering out these nodes.

- *Rule 1:* For a node, if the size is smaller than a specified value, e.g., 200 in our experiments, the node is removed. In addition, if a region connecting to the boundary of the original image region, it is also removed. For the current example, after applying this rule, we obtain a reduced nodes' information as shown in Table 1(b). Only six nodes are remained. Note here that they are ordered by size in ascent for the further processing of Rule 2.

- *Rule 2:* For a node a, if the subimage's region ranged by the outer-most convex boundary is covered by that of other node, say b, then we say $a \subset b$ and the node a can be removed. To explain this operation, we give an illustration as follows. Consider the information of nodes 23, 24, and 12, the size order of them is $size_{23} < size_{24} < size_{12}$. Their corresponding subimages are shown in Fig. 6(a), 6(b), and 6(c) respectively. Based on this rule, we check the outer-most boundary information between two subimages, the inclusion relationship may be easily identified. After performing this procedure, we have the relationships:

$$\begin{cases} \text{node } 23 \subset \text{node } 24 \\ \text{node } 23 \subset \text{node } 12 \\ \text{node } 24 \subset \text{node } 12 \end{cases} \tag{4}$$

Thus nodes 23 and 24 can be removed and node 12 remained. This inclusion results can be easily understood by contouring all the regions in an image as illustrated in Fig. 7. After the checking procedure of Rule 2, the total number of nodes is further reduced to four, that is, 245, 59, 57, and 12.

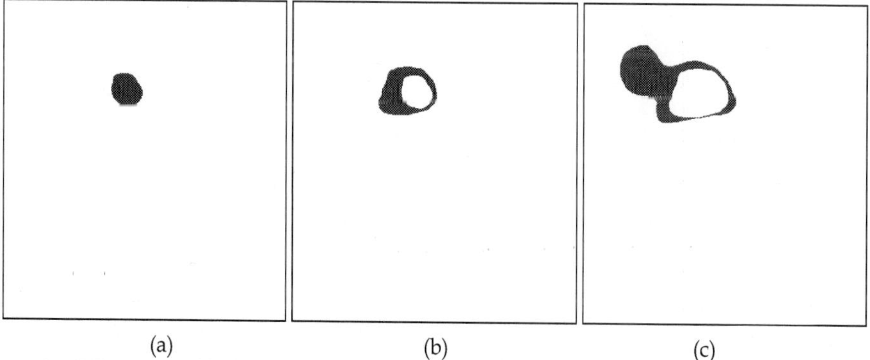

(a)   (b)   (c)

Fig. 6. The corresponding subimages of (a) node 23, (b) node 24, and (c) node 12.

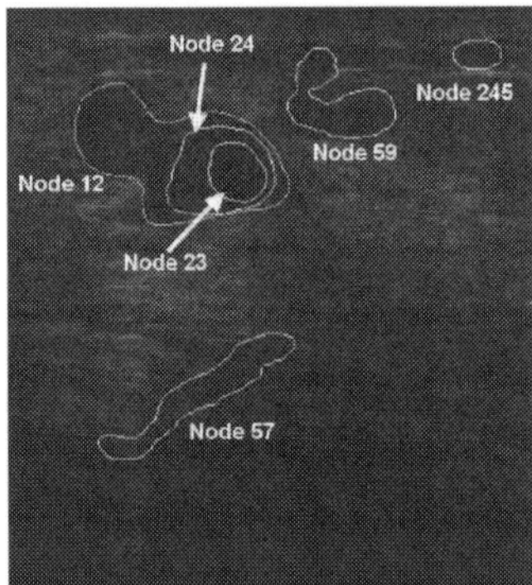

Fig. 7. Contouring all the regions in an image for illustrating the inclusion results.

The final steps of postprocessings are to sort the nodes depending on the possibility of a node belonging to a lesion and to display the lesion detection result. It is reasonable that if a region in the given image showing a higher possible lesion, it should have a higher contrast; otherwise to identify a lesion is somewhat difficult. Hence we define a so-called contrast ratio (cr) to index the possibility of a lesion. Given a node 1, its father node is easily addressed according to (3) and thus indexing to the node 2 which complements to node 1 since node 1 and node 2 are two segmented regions from their father node. Let g_1, g_2, and g_f be the mean grey values of node 1, node 2, and their father node, respectively. Three parameters $d_1 = |g_1 - g_f|$, $d_2 = |g_2 - g_f|$, and $avg = (g_1 + g_2)/2$ are defined to formulate the following contrast ratios.

$$cr_1 = \frac{d_1}{avg}$$

$$cr_2 = \frac{d_2}{avg}$$

$$cr_3 = \frac{d_1 + d_2}{avg}$$

Here cr_1 considers the contrast between node 1 and the father node; cr_2 considers the contrast between node 2 and the father node; and cr_3 considers the contrast between two son nodes and the father node. Thus our totally contrast ratio (cr_{total}) is combined by the above three terms.

$$cr_{total} = (cr_1 \times cr_2 \times cr_3)K = \frac{d_1 d_2 (d_1 + d_2)}{avg^3}K \tag{5}$$

Since the lesion tends to a darker region and possesses a higher contrast, the higher of numerator and the lower of denominator in (5) will derivate a higher cr_{total} and thus show a higher lesion possibility at this node. Here constant K is used to facilitate the numeric manipulation, 65536 is used in our program. Take node 12 at the current example as an illustration, its mean grey value is $g_1 = 63$, we can find its father node, node 5 ($g_f = 58$), and the other node 11 ($g_2 = 51$). Thus according to (5), we have $cr_{total}^{12} = 148.63$ for node 12; the next is $cr_{total}^{245} = 50.02$ for node 245; and so on. Along the descent order of cr-index, we show the final detected results in Fig. 8. Obviously, the most significant lesion is detected and placed at first.

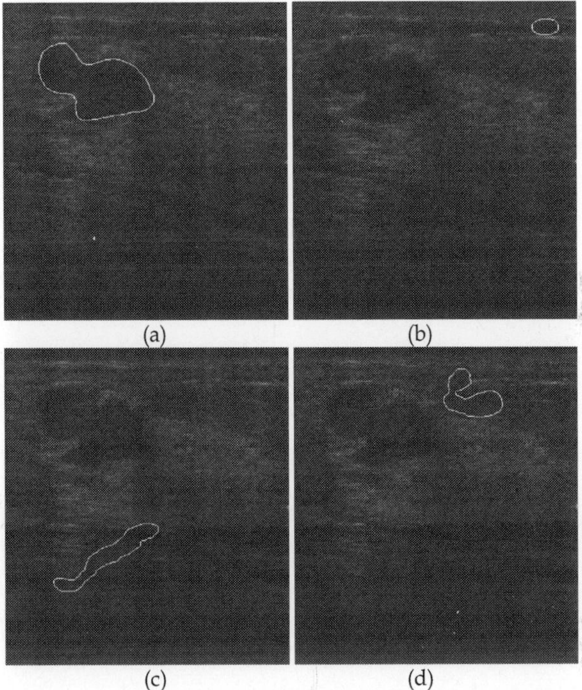

Fig. 8. The final detected results are shown by the descent order of cr-index. The most significant lesion is placed at first (a).

3. Results and discussion

So far, we have detailed our approach for automatically lesion detection in ultrasonic images with a series of illustrations. From the ordered display of results such as Fig. 8 shows, the most significant targets will be placed firstly in order. This facilitates the clinical applications and assists doctor's quick assessment for the lesion. However, some other quasi-lesion regions (may not be a lesion) may also be listed in our approach like Fig. 8(b)-(d), this is a trade-off between results and fully automatic detection in our original study motivation. In order to further confirm the feasibility of our approach, other results are given in Fig. 9. Here only the first place of detected regions in each image is displayed.

Since our approach can detect all possible lesion's regions and list them in a significant order, it implies that multiple-lesion detection can be performed. Consider an ultrasonic image having multiple-lesion in Fig. 10(a), there exist two obvious lesions. Intuitively, the detection of lesions in such an image is of difficulty due to the un-uniform brightness property and the influence of speckle information. Traditionally, it needs a manual ROI selection prior to contour detection for a lesion. After performing our approach to this image, we finally obtain 20 nodes to represent all possible lesion's regions, where an image including the inclusion results like Fig. 7 is given in Fig. 10(b). Obviously, the real lesions should be in the detection list even many non-lesion regions are located. Because of the inherently un-uniform brightness property and the influence of speckle information, the real lesion may not be placed in front of the significance order. In this case, three most possible lesions placed in order 1, 8, 20 are shown in Fig. 10(c), 10(d), and 10(e) respectively.

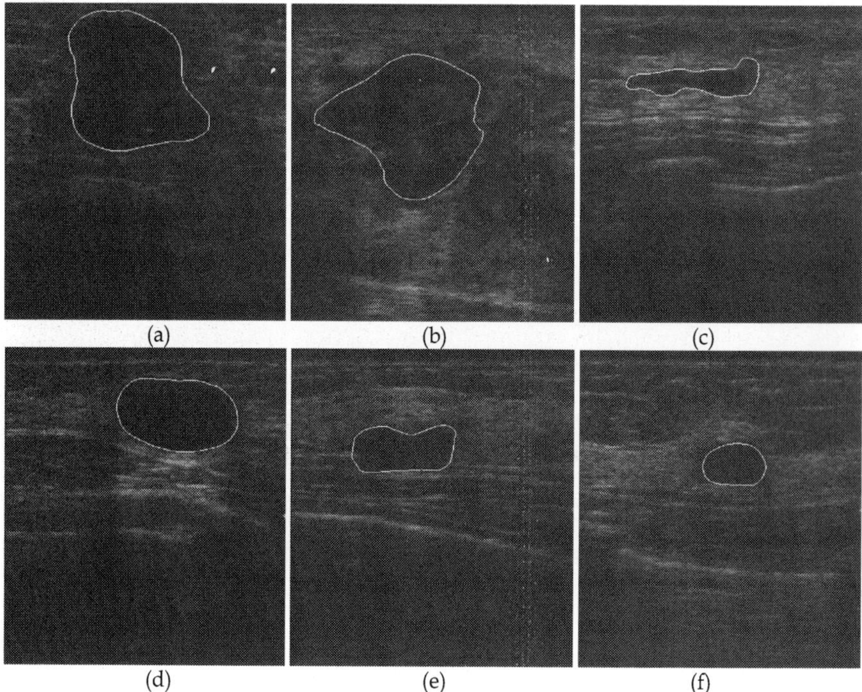

Fig. 9. Some other results. Here only the first place of detected regions in each image is displayed.

4. Conclusion

In this article, we have presented a simply but effectively fully automatic segmentation method for detecting lesions in ultrasonic images without the constraint of ROIs or initial seeds given. Based on the use of a binary tree structure and some postprocessings, multiple lesions can be detected and displayed in order for further visualization and inspection. Since experiments have confirmed the feasibility of the proposed approach, an e-service for ultrasonic imaging CAD system is worthy of being developed. In addition, the strategy of reducing non-lesion regions may also be an interesting topic; and will be further investigated and involved in this approach as a near future work.

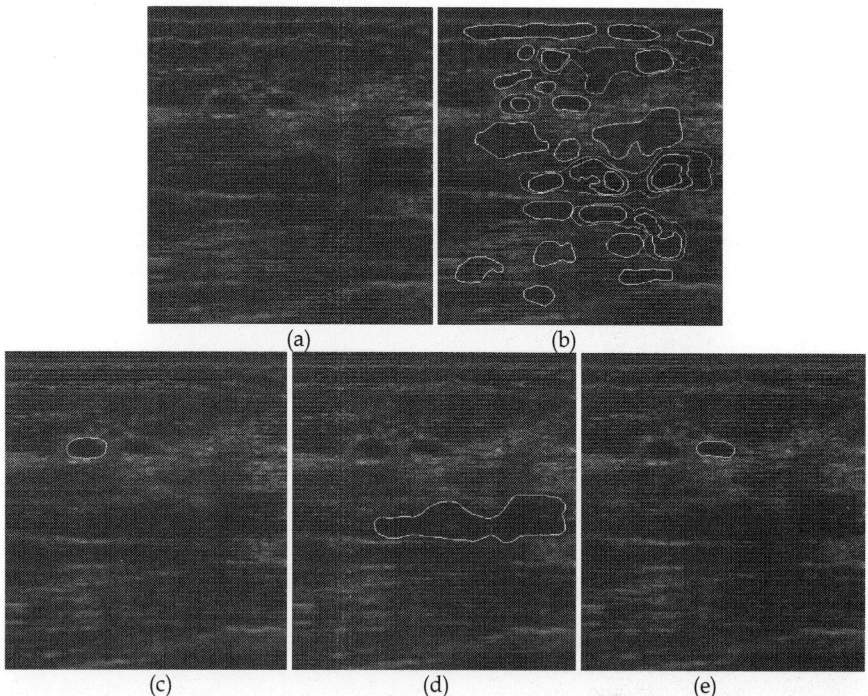

Fig. 10. (a) Ultrasonic image having multiple-lesion. (b) Contour all possible lesion's regions with inclusion results. (c)-(e) Three most possible lesions placed in order 1, 8, and 20.

5. Acknowledgments

This work was supported in part by the National Science Council, Taiwan, Republic of China, under Grant No. NSC 96-2221-E-155-057-MY3.

6. References

Aarnink, R.; Giesen, R.; Huynen, A.; de la Rosette, J.; Debruyne, F. & Wijkstra, H. (1994). A practical clinical method for contour determination in ultrasonographic prostate images, *Ultrasound Medical and Biology*, Vol. 20, pp. 705-717.

Abolmaesumi, P. & Sirouspour, M. R. (2004). An interacting multiple model probabilistic data association filter for cavity boundary extraction from ultrasound images, *IEEE Transactions on Medical Imaging*, Vol. 23, No. 6, pp. 772-784.

Akgul, Y.; Kambhamettu, C. & Stone, M. (2000). A task-specific contour tracker for ultrasound, In: *Proceedings of IEEE Workshop Mathematical Methods in Biomedical Image Analysis*, pp. 135-142, Hilton Head Island, South Carolina, USA, June 11-12 2000.

Chen, Y. S. & Lin, T. D. (1995). An iterative approach to removing the closure noise using disk expansion method, *IEEE Signal Processing Letters*, Vol. 2, No. 6, pp. 105-107.

Hamarneh, G. & Gustavsson, T. (2000). Combining snakes and active shape models for segmenting the human left ventricle in echocardiographic images, In: *Proceedings of IEEE Computers in Cadiology*, Vol. 27, pp. 115-118, Cambridge, Massachusetts, USA, September 24-27, 2000.

Ladak, H.; Downey, D.; Steinman, D. & Fenster, A. (1999). Semi-automatic technique for segmentation of the prostate from 2D ultrasound images, In: *Proceedings of IEEE BMES/EMBS Conference Serving Humanity, Advanced Technology*, Vol. 2, p. 1144, Atlanta, GA, USA, October 13-16, 1999.

Ladak, H.; Mao, F.; Wang, Y.; Downey, D.; Steinman, D. & Fenster, A. (2000). Prostate segmentation from 2D ultrasound images, In: *Proceedings of International Conference Engineering in Medicine and Biology*, Vol. 4, pp. 3188-3191, Chicago, IL, USA, July 23-28, 2000.

Richard, W. & Keen, C. (1996). Automated texture-based segmentation of ultrasound images of the prostate, *Computerized Medical Imaging and Graphics*, Vol. 20, pp. 131-140.

Yeh, C. K.; Chen, Y. S.; Fan, W. C. & Liao, Y. Y. (2009). A disk expansion segmentation method for ultrasonic breast lesions, *Pattern Recognition*, Vol. 42, No. 5, pp. 596-606.

## 18

Image Processing in Biology Based on the Fractal Analysis

István Sztojánov[1], Daniela Alexandra Crişan[2],
Cătălina Popescu Mina[3] and Vasilică Voinea[1]
[1]*Politehnica University of Bucharest*
[2]*Romanian-American University, Bucharest*
[3]*University of Bucharest*
Romania

1. Introduction

The state of the art of classification based on the fractal analysis with applications in biology will be presented. Fractal features describe closely the properties of natural forms. For this reason, the interest in this new mathematical field, fractal geometry, grows quickly. New techniques of fractal analysis are developed and these techniques prove their utility in real systems in various fields such as informatics, economics, engineering, medical screening and biology.

This chapter discusses problems of classification based on the fractal theory with applications in biology. Here are introduced the necessary notions for the defining of the fractals and their quantitative evaluation and an algorithm for fractal dimension computation based on biofractal contours processing is also presented. Concretely, there were extracted window-images from the interested area; the contours of the window-images were processed with the "box-counting" algorithm in order to establish the fractal dimensions for the analysed sections. The algorithm based on the „box-counting" method offers two major advantages: it is easy to implement in case of using a computer and can be applied for images no matter how complex.

The first application is dedicated to the analysis of the particularities of some species from Gentianaceae family, with the purpose of establishing their affiliation to the Gentiana genus, knowing the fact that, up to the present, there have been used only evaluations based on the distinctive morphological characteristics. Concretely, there were extracted window-images from the rind and the central cylinder of the root and stem and also from the mesophyll and leaf nervure/rib and those areas where analysed by using fractal techniques. We consider that the acquiring of samples from more sections of a species (the studied one) for the statistical processing of the data will lead for the first time in botany to very precise characterizations of that species.

The second applications use the same procedure in order to classify mammary tumours: benign or malign. The fractal dimension of the FAR (Focused Attention Region) is computed, by using the same box-counting algorithm. Depending on the size of the fractal dimension, a classification can be made: over 30 lesions cases with known diagnostic were tested and the results show that a threshold of 1.4 value can be used: over 90% malign cases have fractal dimensions above 1.4, while over 80% benign cases have fractal dimensions below 1.4.

The results are encouraging for the development of fractal techniques in biology domains.

2. Fractal analysis in biology

The fractal analyses proved their utility in biology and the necessary notions for the defining and the quantitative evaluation of the fractals will be presented; an algorithm for fractal dimension computation based on biofractal contours processing will be shown.

2.1 Biofractal and fractal dimension

Fractals are objects with irregular, auto-similar features, with details that can be noticed at any scale of representation. Biofractals are the fractal textures/contours in biology (tissues, neurons, leaves, etc.). The similarity between fractals and the natural objects suggests that fractal properties, such as fractal dimension, may be used as a classifier in biology.

In order to understand the surrounding world, the natural sciences have progressed by focusing on the simplest forms of representation, in accordance with the principle: simplicity explains complexity. Sometimes the researches turned away from the direct study of nature, of the details of reality and limited themselves to studies based on general, approximate and linear expressions.

In the '60s, a mathematician, Mandelbrot proposes to study the complex irregular forms in nature that he names fractals and founds the bases of fractal (non-Euclidan) geometry.

The appearance of fractal geometry marks the return of the scientific knowledge to the real world. It was rather easy to observe that the forms of rivers, mountains, the Earth in its details are of fractal type. Important examples of fractals in botany – that we shall name fitofractals - are the leafs of a tree, the structure of the tissue from a plant's stem or root section, the forms and contours of the cells etc.

With the aid of fractal geometry, the growth and ramification models from the plants world can be explained and reproduced (fig. 1.) by using strings of ordered characters and simple operations of translation and rotation (Lindenmayer & Prusinkiewicz, 1996).

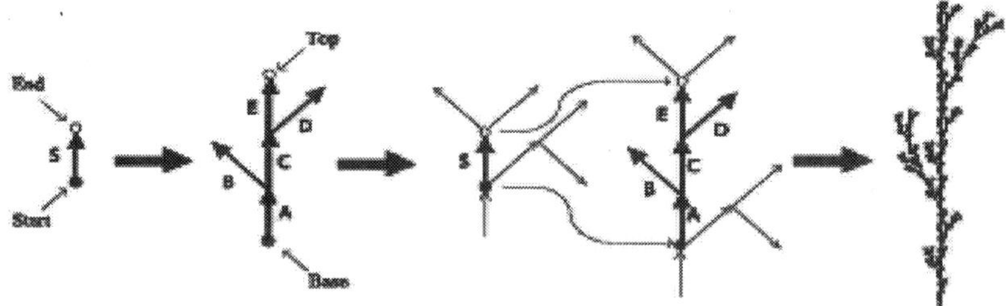

Fig. 1. The construction of an L-system that can be applied to ramification types of plants

An important feature of the fractal objects is the dependence between their dimension and the used measure unit (fig.2.). By choosing a finer measure unit, an irregular contour can be better approximated, with finer accuracy, and this is so because a finer measure unit better shows the objects details.

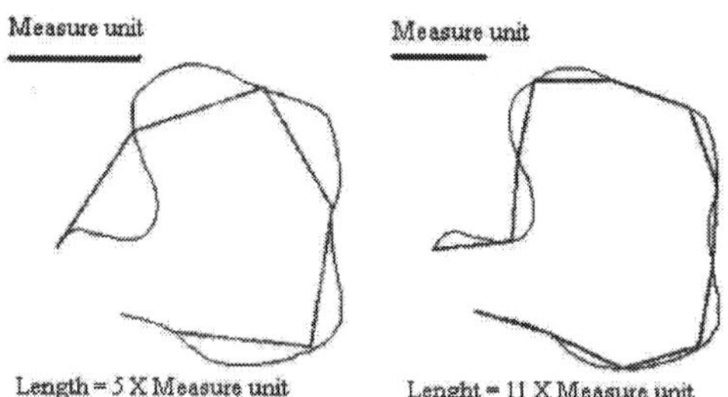

Fig. 2. The dependence of the length of a curve upon the used measure unit

Richardson noticed this fact for the first time. Desirous to know the length of the borderline between Spain and Portugal, he consulted the documents from the archives of both countries. In the Spanish encyclopaedia it was written that the borderline had a length of 987km, while in the Portuguese encyclopaedia the length was approximated to 1214km. The explanation of the strange phenomenon was that two different measure units were used: the smaller unit used by the Portuguese could go over more border details, and so they obtained a finer measurement.

This dependence from the used scale measure makes the fractal objects difficult to measure in the classic (Euclidian) geometry context.

The Euclidian dimension D is given by the number of coordinates needed to define any of the points of the object, or, more exactly, the dimension of the Euclidian space into which the analysed object can be submerged: the line in a plane, the cone in a three dimensional space.

The topological dimension T is defined by the local properties of the analysed object and corresponds to the concept that the dimension of a point is 0, the dimension of a line, thin curve is 1, the surfaces have the dimension equal with 2, volumes with 3 and so on, without taking into account any bigger dimension of the Euclidian space into which these forms were submerged.

With the apparition of the fractals, the characterization of a form by using its topological dimension (which is a whole number) proves its insufficiencies. That is why the notion – fractal dimension Df (real number) was introduced.

The German mathematician Felix Hausdorff defines a new concept for the topological spaces, in this way suggesting that the fractal dimension is proportional with the minimum number of spheres, of a given radius, needed for covering the measured object. To facilitate the computer work, the coverage is made with cubes instead of spheres.

Thus, for covering a curve of unity of length 1, $N(s)=1/s$ cubes of side s are needed, for covering a unity area surface there are needed $N(s)=1/s^2$ cubes of side s and finally, to cover a unity volume cube $N(s)=1/s^3$ cubes of side s are needed (fig 3).

By induction the relation below is verified as follows:

$$N(s) \sim 1/s^{Df},$$

where:
N(s) is the number of cubes of side s;
s is the scale coefficient or the length of the coverage of the cube's side;
Df is the Hausdorff's coverage dimension of the object.

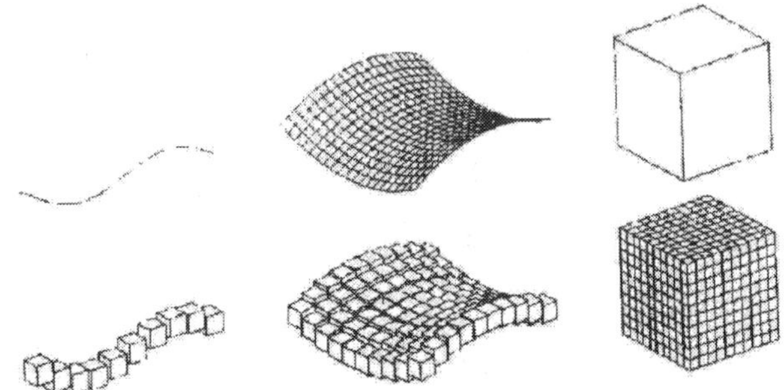

Fig. 3. Coverage of three Euclidian figures by using equal sides cubes

By applying logarithm to the relation above, we can deduce Df:

$$D_f = \frac{\log(N(s))}{\log(1/s)} \tag{1}$$

The fractal dimension Df is however difficult to calculate.

2.2 Algorithm for fractal dimension computation

There can be used many algorithms to calculate the fractal dimension and one of the easiest to implement is the box-counting algorithm.

The algorithm based on the "box-counting" method offers two major advantages: it is easy to implement in case of using a computer and can be applied for images no matter how complex.

The "box-counting" fractal dimension, derived from the Hausdorff coverage dimension is given by the following approximation:

$$D \approx \frac{\log(N(s))}{\log(1/s)} \tag{2}$$

It is expected, that for a smaller s, the above approximation should be better,

$$D = \lim_{s \longrightarrow 0} \log \frac{N(s)}{\log(1/s)} \tag{3}$$

If this limit exists, it is called the "box-counting" dimension of the measured object. Usually, this limit converges very slowly, that is why an alternative solution is used. Since the expression:

$$\log(N(s)) = D \cdot \log\left(\frac{1}{s}\right) \tag{4}$$

is the equation of a straight line of slope D, the "log-log" curve described by the points of the (log(N(s), log(1/s)) coordinates is plotted. Through linear regression (least squares method) the slope of the line that approximates the points' distribution is determined; this is the wanted fractal dimension.

Thus, the regression line has the form:

$$Y = a \cdot X + b \tag{5}$$

and the line slope (the value of the "a" coefficient), represents the fractal dimension:

$$a = D_f = \frac{n^2 \sum_{i=1..n} x_i y_i - \sum_{i=1..n} x_i * \sum_{i=1..n} y_i}{n^2 \sum_{i=1..n} x_i^2 - \left(\sum_{i=1..n} x_i\right)^2} \tag{6}$$

where: xi=log(1/s), and yi=log(N(s)).

The "box-counting" algorithm assumes to determine the fractal dimension according to the dependence of the object contour upon the used scale factor. It consists in successive image coverage with squares with equal sides (2, 4, 8, ...) and in counting every time the squares that cover the object contour.

The points of the coordinates (log(N(s)), log(1/s)), where s is the common side of the coverage squares, and N(s) the number of squares that contain any information, will be positioned approximately in a line and its slope will be the fractal dimension in the "box-counting" context. In a synthetic representation, the algorithm for determining the "box-counting" dimension for binary images is the following:

1. the original image (binary) is read;
2. the analysed region is selected;
3. the box-counting dimension is calculated by counting each time the number of cubes N(s) that contain at least a point of the form. Logarithm is applied to the obtained values then, they are graphically represented by a curve with a slope that is the box-counting dimension.

For an example of how the algorithm is used, we'll consider the image of a leaf (Fig. 4a) from which we'll extract a binary version by neglecting all the pixels over a certain luminosity (Fig. 4b).

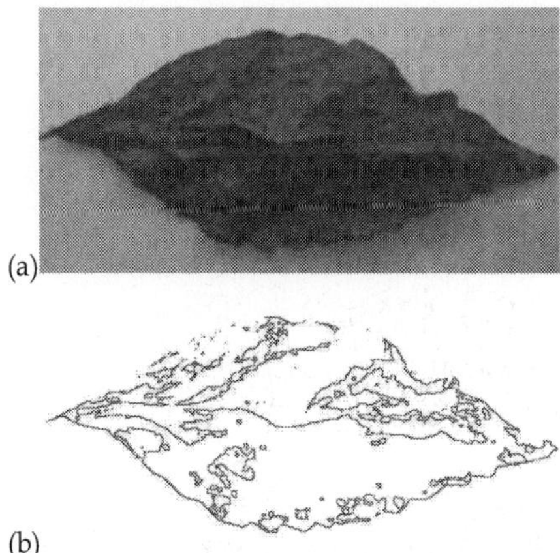

(a)

(b)

Fig. 4. (a) The initial image; (b) The binary (black-white) image version

Next, we'll apply the "box-counting" algorithm, described above, for different scale values s (only the squares that contain information are plotted, the ones that cover the leaf contour), by using an original software product, presented in detail in (Crisan, 2006).

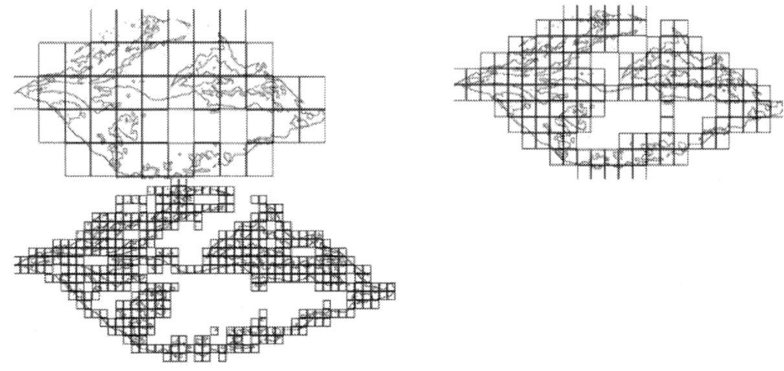

Fig. 5. Object coverage with squares of different side values – "s".

We obtain the values table and "log-log" curve from the figure below:

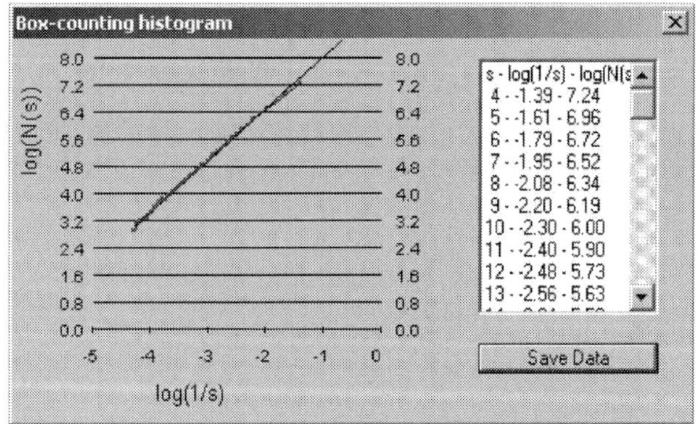

Fig. 6. The log-log curve and the s, log(1/s), log(N(s)) values.

By using the least squares method, with the pairs of points (log(N(s)), log(1/s)), the regression line with the slope 1.55 is determined. Thus, the fractal dimension for the studied leaf is 1.55.

3. Case studies

In the presented case studies we will focus on the results of our original work in the fractal applications in botany and medicine.

3.1 Fractal analysis in botany

The actual application is dedicated to analysing the particularities of some species from the Gentianaceae family, with the purpose of establishing their affiliation to the Gentina genus. For establishing the independent position of the Gentianopsis genus, respectively the Gentianella ciliata for the Gentiana genus, we have fractally analyzed the species Gentiana lutea and Gentianella ciliata. The analysed material was acquired from the transversal section made through the root, stem and leaf of the mentioned taxoms. The microscopical images of the extracted samples were analysed by using fractal techniques based on the "box-counting" algorithm in order to use other criteria than the morphological ones for establishing the position of the Gentiana, Gentianella and Gentianopsis genera in the Gentianaceae family.

3.1.1 Experimental processing

The Gentianaceae family was divided as time passed, in many genera (I. Prodan, 1939, Al. Beldie, 1979, Fr. Ehrendorffer, 1998, V. Ciocârlan, 2000); from these the Menyanthes and Nymphoides genera came from the initial family and formed a new family named Menyanthaceae. At the moment, in the Romanian flora there are recognized 8 genera of the gentinacee's family: Blackstonia, Centaurium, Comastoma, Gentiana, Gentianella, Gentianopsis, Lomantogonium, Sweertia (V. Ciocârlan, 2000), obtained by the separation of the central genus Gentiana that has 13 species, into Gentianella with 5 species and Gentianopsis with one species. In the reference paper Flora Europaea (T. G. Tutin, 1972), the Gentianopsis genus is included at Gentianella under the name of Gentianella cilliata. Today, the Gentiana genus has 19 species spread all over our country. We are mentioning that the separation of the Gentianella and Gentianopsis genera was made on pure morphological criteria (Ciocarlan, 2000; Kinker, 1994).

For establishing the independent position of the Gentianopsis genus, respectively of the Gentianella ciliata for the Gentiana genus, we have fractally analyzed the species Gentiana lutea and Gentianella ciliata. Taking into account that the fractal technique is used as premiere work in this field of botany, for verifying its "sensibility", we have compared the fractal dimensions of the 2 taxons from Gentianaceae with one from the Ranunculus genus from the Ranunculaceae family.

The analyzed material was acquired from the transversal section made through the root, stem and leaf of the mentioned taxoms. The microscopical images of the extracted samples were analyzed by using fractal techniques based on the "box-counting" algorithm in order to use other criteria than the morphological ones for establishing the position of the Gentiana, Gentianella and Gentianopsis genera in the Gentianaceae family. Concretely, there were extracted window-images from the rind and the central cylinder of the root and stem and also from the mesophyll and nervure/rib of the leaf. The contours of the window-images were processed with the "box-counting" algorithm in order to establish the fractal dimensions for the analyzed sections.

The images have been analyzed by using an original software system described in detail in [5] which implements the extended box-counting algorithm for gray-level shapes. These images are binarized by using different thresholds, the contour is traced, and then the box-counting fractal dimension is represented into a spectrum. Finally, the representative fractal dimension (where the fractal character is preponderant) is selected for each tissue.

3.1.2 Results

For Gentiana lutea - root, the fractal dimension of the rind is D11=1.71 and the central cylinder dimension is D12=1.80:

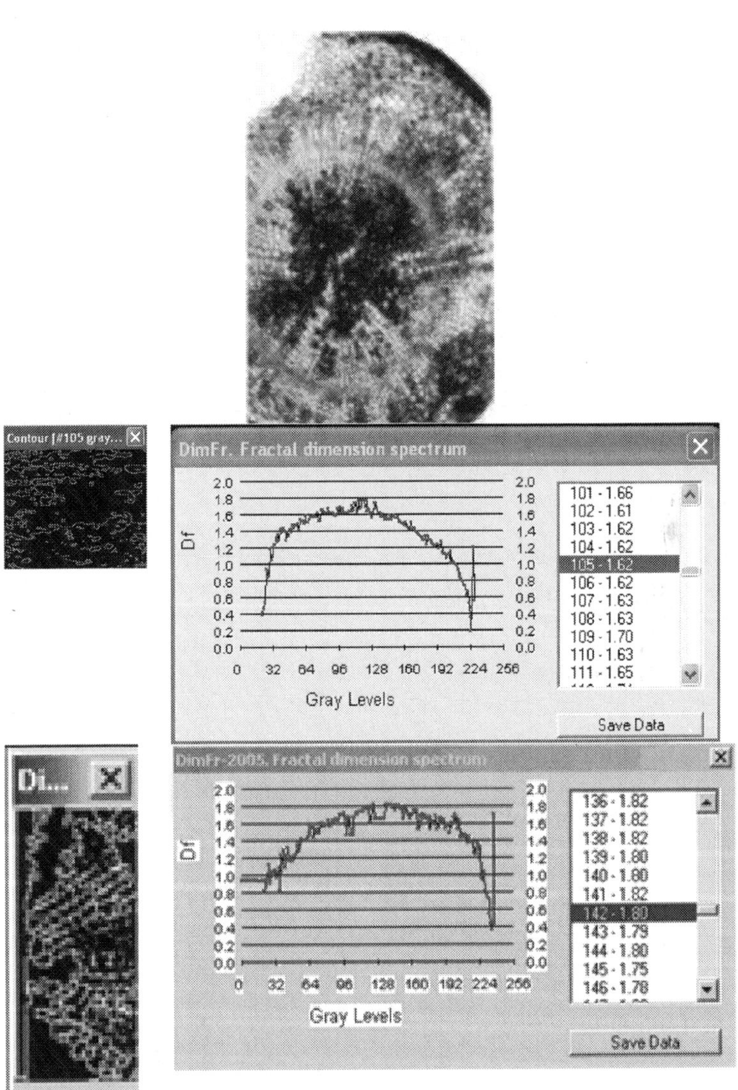

Fig. 7. Fractal dimensions of the root, in the rind and central cylinder oft Gentiana lutea.

For Gentiana lutea - stem, the fractal dimension of the rind is D21=1.63 and the dimension of the central cylinder is D22=1.75:

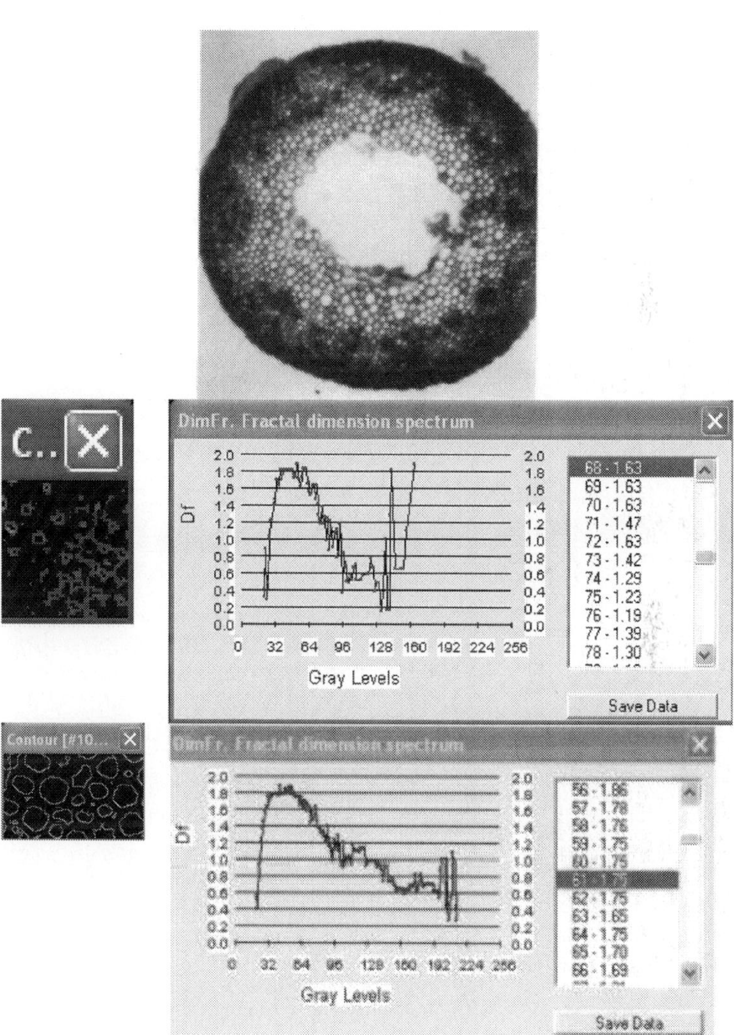

Fig. 8. Fractal dimensions for the stem in the rind and central cylinder for Gentiana lutea.

For Gentiana lutea - leaf, the fractal dimension of the mesophyll is D31=1.55 and the dimension of the vascular bundle is D32=1.69:

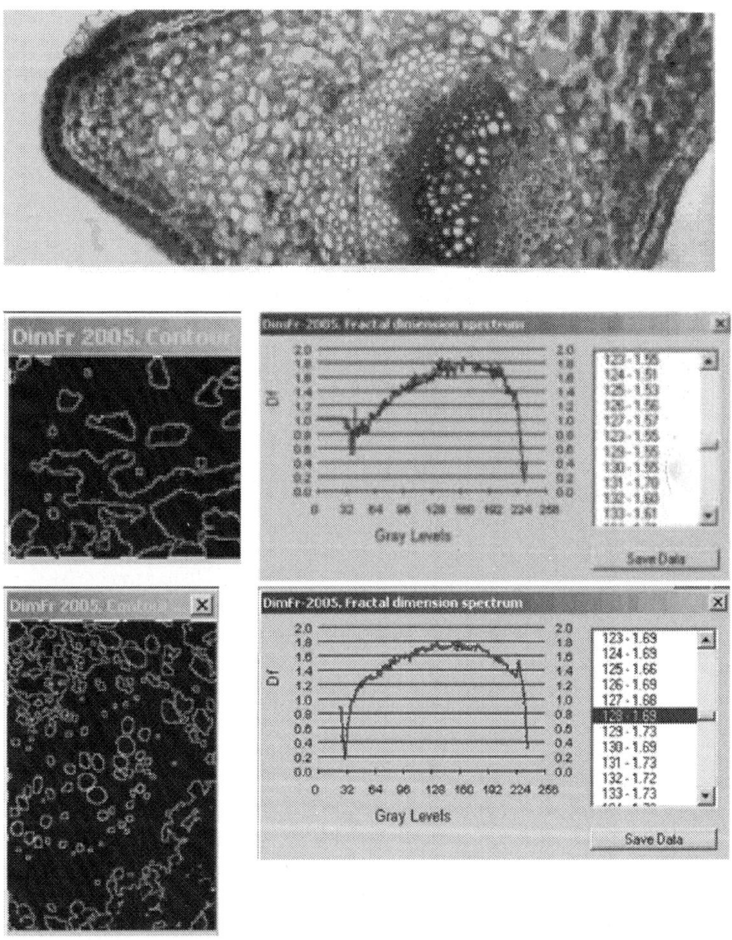

Fig. 9. Fractal dimensions for the leaf, in the mesophyll and vascular bundle for Gentiana lutea.

For Gentianella cilliata (Gentianopsis) - root, fractal dimension of the rind is D11=1.65 and the central cylinder dimension is D12=1.86:

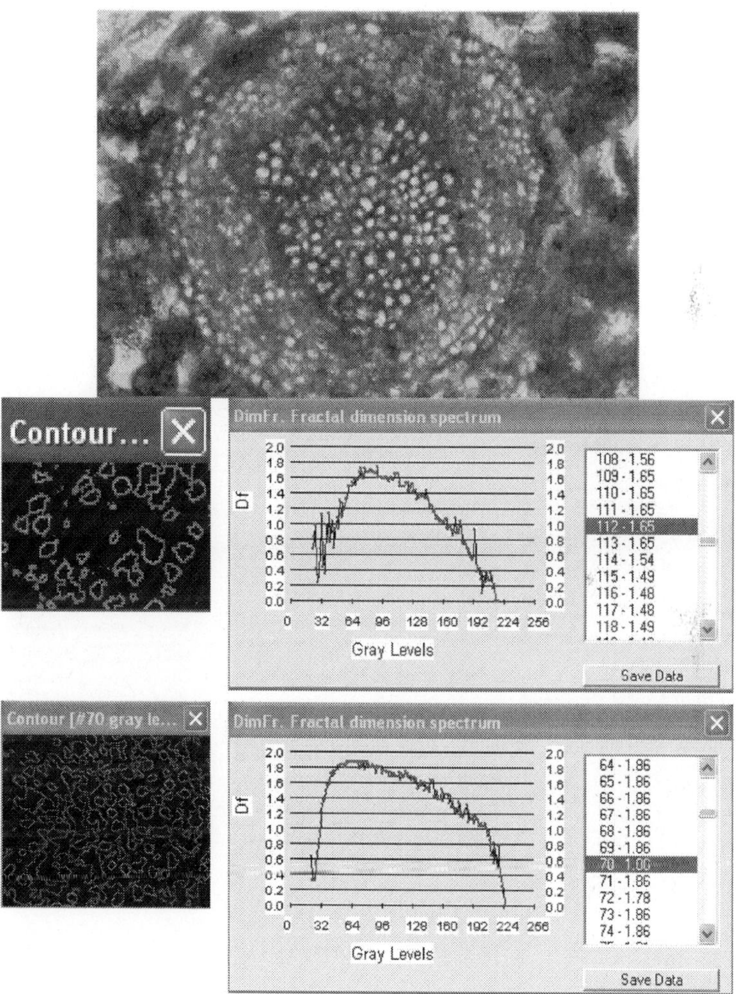

Fig. 10. Fractal dimensions for the root, in the rind and central cylinder for Gentianella cilliata (Gentianopsis).

For Gentianella cilliata (Gentianopsis) - stem, the fractal dimension of the rind is D21=1.62 and the dimension of the central cylinder is D22=1.78:

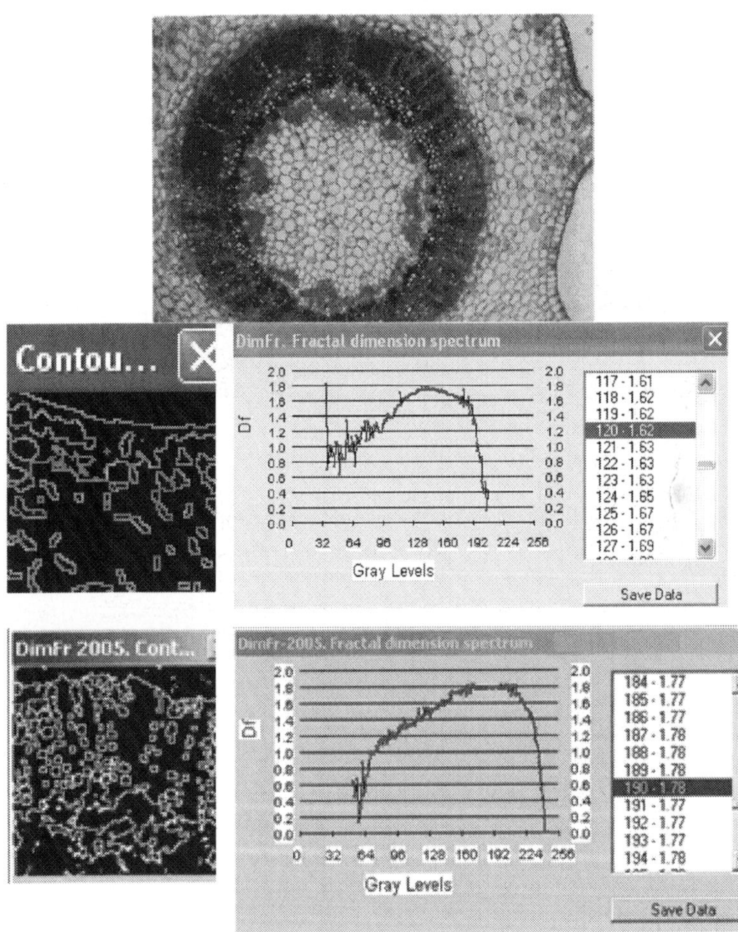

Fig. 11. Fractal dimensions for the stem in the rind and central cylinder for Gentianella cilliata (Gentianopsis).

For Gentianella cilliata (Gentianopsis) - leaf, the fractal dimension of the mesophyll is D31=1.58 and the dimension of the vascular bundle is D32=1.77:

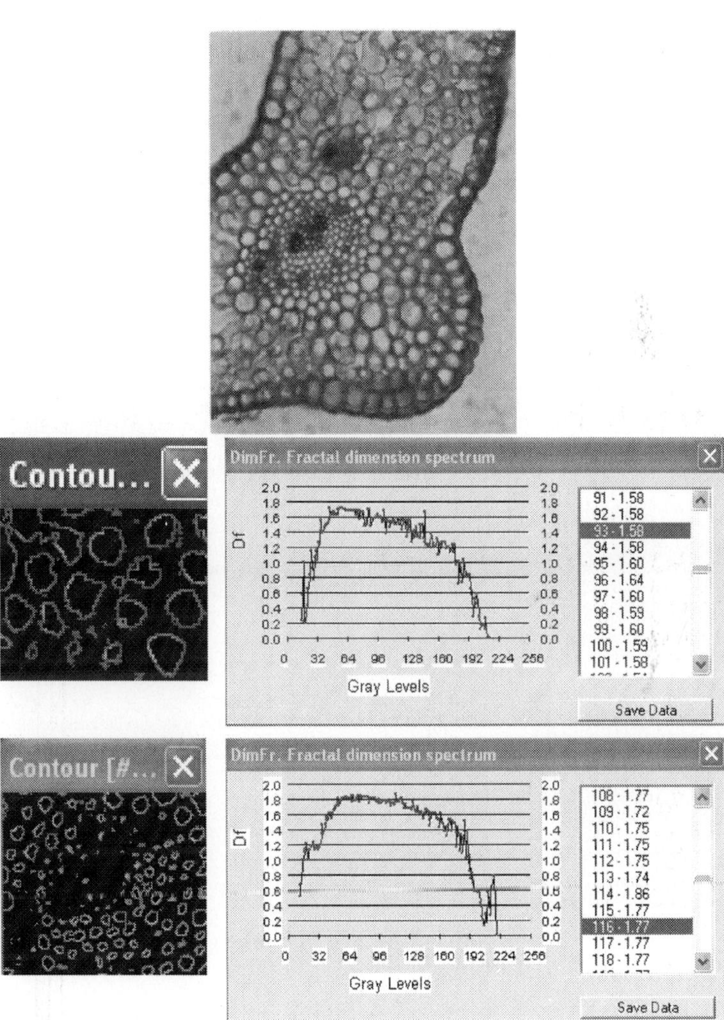

Fig. 12. Fractal dimensions for the leaf, in the mesophyll and vascular bundle for Gentianella cilliata (Gentianopsis).

For Ranunculus repens - root, the fractal dimension of the rind is D11=1.55 and the central cylinder dimension is D12=1.60:

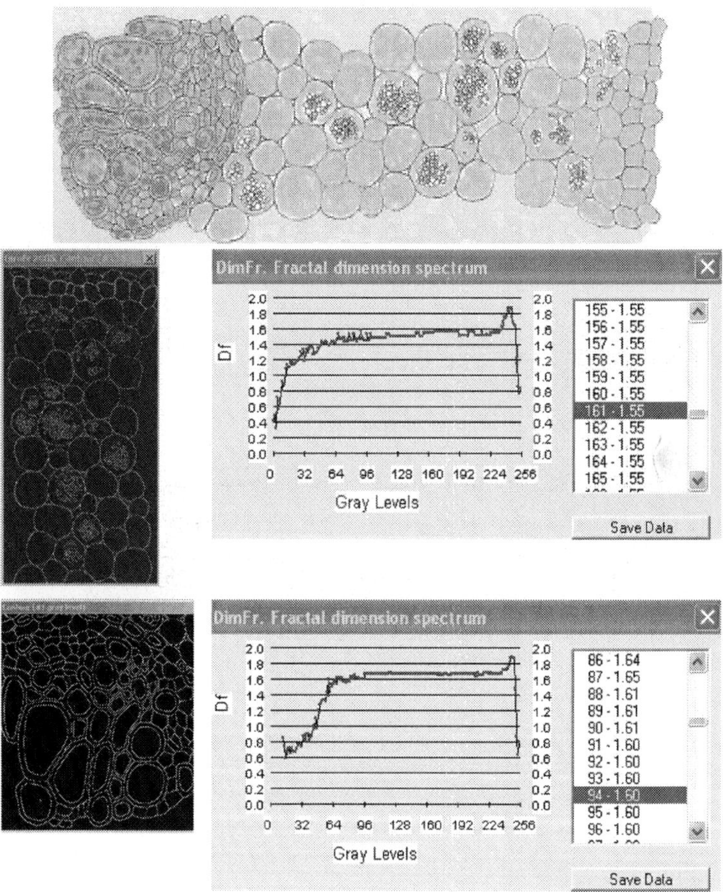

Fig. 13. Fractal dimensions for the root in the rind and central cylinder for Ranunculus repens.

For Ranunculus repens - stem, the fractal dimension of the rind is D21=1.52 and the dimension of the vascular bundle is D22=1.57:

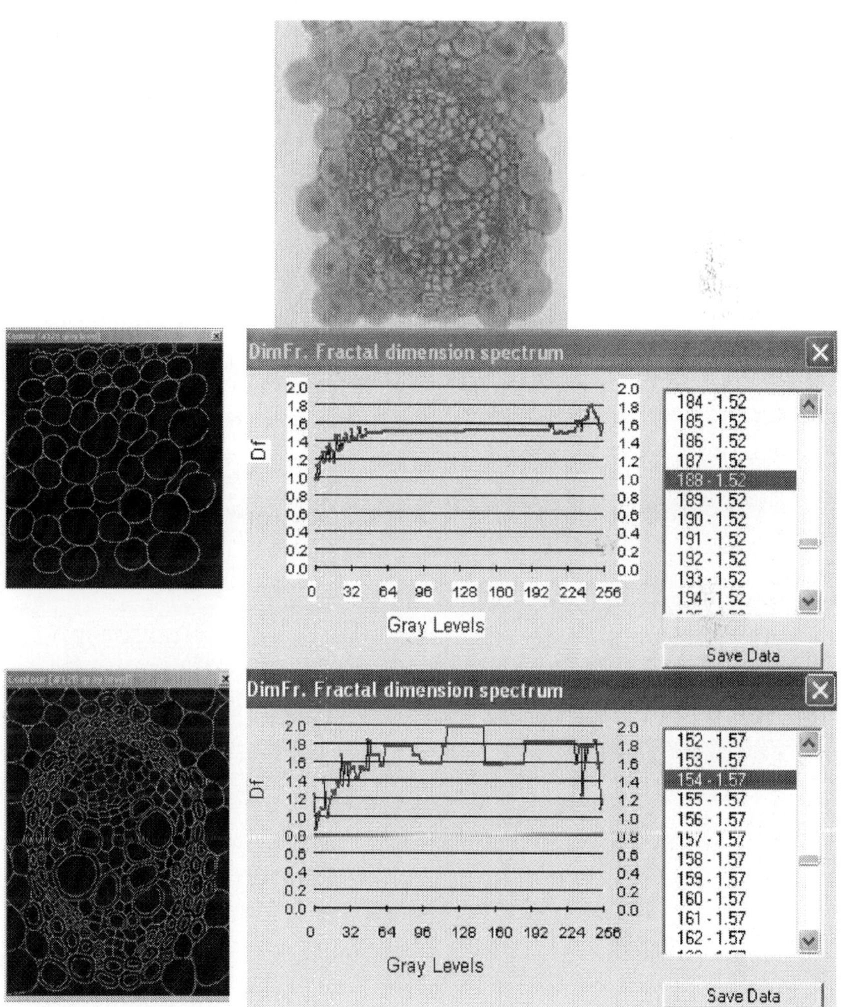

Fig. 14. Fractal dimensions for the stem, in the rind and vascular bundle for Ranunculus repens.

For Ranunculus repens - leaf, the fractal dimension of the mesophyll is D31=1.53 and the dimension of the vascular bundle is D32=1.58:

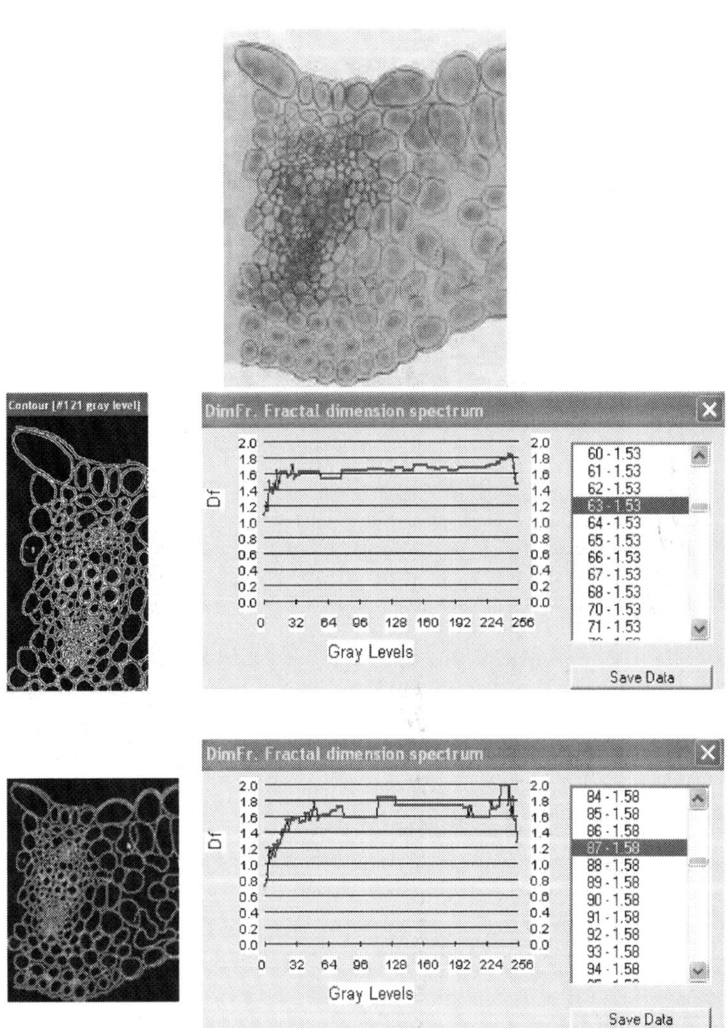

Fig. 15. Fractal dimension for the leaf, in the mesophyll and vascular bundle for Ranunculus repens.

Df	Root		stem		leaf	
	rind	central cylinder	rind	central cylinder	mesophyll	vascular bundle
Ranunculus repens	1.55	1.60	1.52	1.57	1.53	1.58
Gentiana lutea	1.62	1.80	1.63	1.75	1.55	1.69
Gentianella cilliata (Gentianopsis)	1.65	1.86	1.62	1.78	1.58	1.77

Table 1. Comparative table of the obtained data

In conclusion, the presented application, from biology is dedicated to analysing the particularities of some species from the Gentianaceae family, with the purpose of establishing their affiliation to the Gentina genus. To achieve this goal we have fractally analyzed microscopical images from the species of Gentiana lutea, Gentianella ciliata and Ranunculus repens.

The different positions of Gentianela ciliata (Gentianopsis) and Ranunculus repens can be observed. From our provisional observations it results that, from the fractal dimensions point of view (central cylinder - root, central cylinder - stem, vascular bundle - leaf), the separation of the Gentiana and Gentianopsis genera is justified.

The authors present for the first time in this field of botany a new method for differentiating some species of the Gentiana genus, by using the fractal analysis in order to establish the position of the Gentianella and Gentianopsis genera.

We consider that this paper opens new prospects in the botanical research domain and in biology in general.

3.2 Fractal analysis in medicine

Important results coming from the usage of fractal properties were obtained in medicine. Further on, some results in breast lesions classification will be presented.

Breast cancer is the most common women disease in modern world; statistics shows that a woman's lifetime risk of developing breast cancer is 1/8. Mammography is the most efficient tool for the detection and diagnosis of breast lesions. In the last decades, medical exams became a regular act; thus, the amount of mammograms interpreted by a radiologist increased dramatically. As a result, a focused effort initiated two decades ago, is under way to develop a Computer-Aided Diagnosis of Mammograms (CADM).

One of the most important components in a CADM is to classify the lesion. The similarity between the breast tissue and synthetically generated fractals shown in fig. 16 (Sari-Sarraf et al., 1996) suggests that the fractal properties, such as the fractal dimension, may be used as a classifier.

Fractal dimension measures the complexity of an object; it grows as the shape is more irregular, as it can be seen in the table below. This observation will be very useful in order to characterize mammographic lesions.

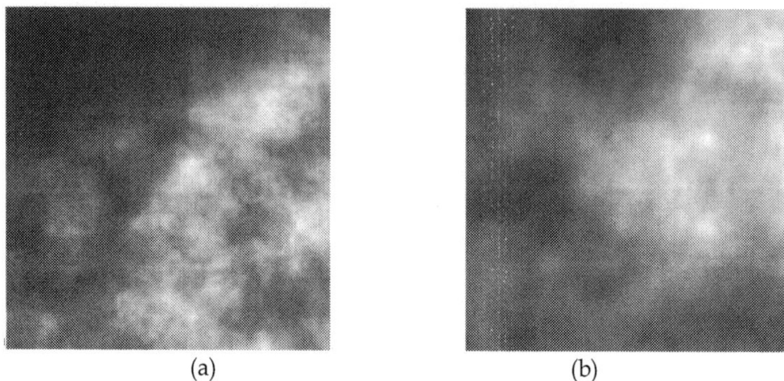

(a)   (b)

Fig. 16. The similarity between the breast tissue (a) and synthetically generated fractals (b)

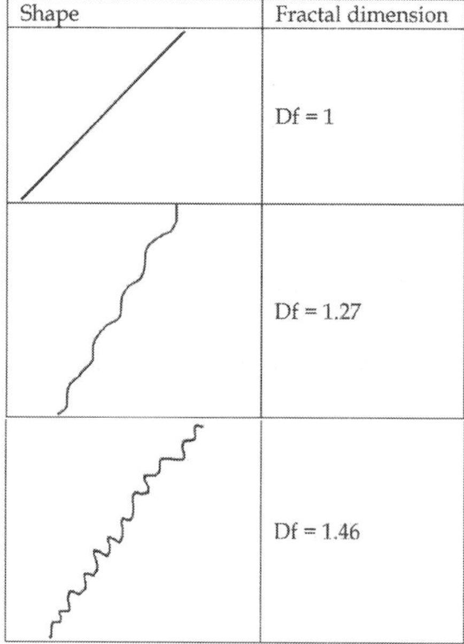

Shape	Fractal dimension
	Df = 1
	Df = 1.27
	Df = 1.46

Table 2. The fractal dimension grows as the shape is more irregular

3.2.1 BI-RADS classification

BI-RADS (Breast Imaging Reporting and Data System) is a very complex system proposed by The American College of Radiology (ACR) in order to classify mammographic lesions. The purpose of the BI-RADS system is to standardize mammography reporting in order to reduce confusion in breast imaging interpretations and facilitate outcome monitoring.

BI-RADS system consists of five categories from 1 to 5; each of them characterizes a kind of mammographic lesion and implies a certain action as a treatment. Shortly, the five categories are:

- BI-RADS 1 – the category is referring to negative cases
- BI-RADS 2 – also describes a negative lesion, but in this case the interpreter may wish to describe a finding
- BI-RADS 3 – the third category refers to a probably benign finding, in this case a short interval follow-up is suggested
- BI-RADS 4 – characterizes the lesions that do not have the characteristic morphologies of breast cancer but have a definite probability of being malignant. In those cases, the radiologist may appeal to a biopsy.
- BI-RADS 5 – characterizes the lesions having a high probability of being cancer

3.2.2 Hypothesis and experiments

When categorizing a mammographic anomaly, the radiologist has to observe several properties of the lesion:
- the contour's shape
- localization
- dimension
- density
- number and bilarity of anomalies
- presence or absence of associated microcalcifications.

One of the most important features is the contour's shape: a regular contour is associated to a benign case, while an irregular shape characterizes a malign lesion. As table 2 shows, the fractal dimension grows with the irregularity of the shape; this could be an essential observation in order to classify the BI-RADS 4 lesions, with no need for further investigations or biopsy. The fractal dimension may provide a tool for classification: the lesions with a regular contour are more probably benign, while the lesions with an irregular contour are more probably malign.

A statistical experiment was developed on a lot of 30 cases. The hypothesis was tested on these cases of BI-RADS 4 classified lesions, 18 benign cases and 12 cancers provided by the Medical Imaging Department of Fundeni Clinical Institute, of Bucharest.

Each mammogram was analysed by following these steps:

Step 1 - the radiologist traces a FAR (Focussed Attention Region), by using a mobile cursor. The size area can be of 64X64, 128X128, 256X256 or 512X512. The selection must contain the anomaly and it is based on the radiologist's experience. Budging the selection to the left or right, top or bottom will not influence the results of the analysis.

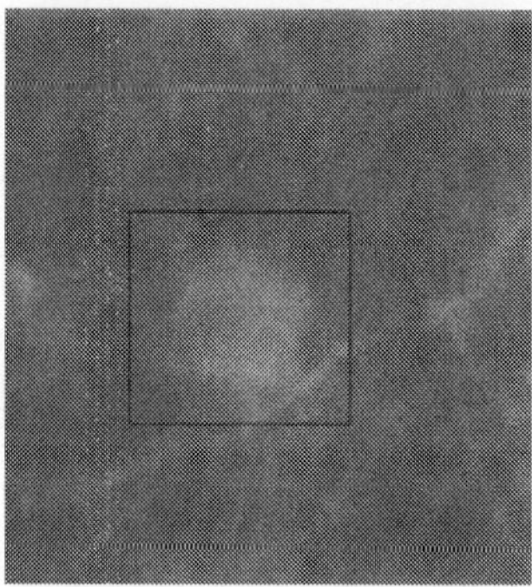

Fig. 17. A FAR traced by the radiologist.

Step 2 - the image is binarized by using a threshold between 1-255 gray level: all the pixels whose gray level is greater or equal to the threshold will be transformed into white pixels; the rest will become black. At this point, the forms inside the image are white on a black background.

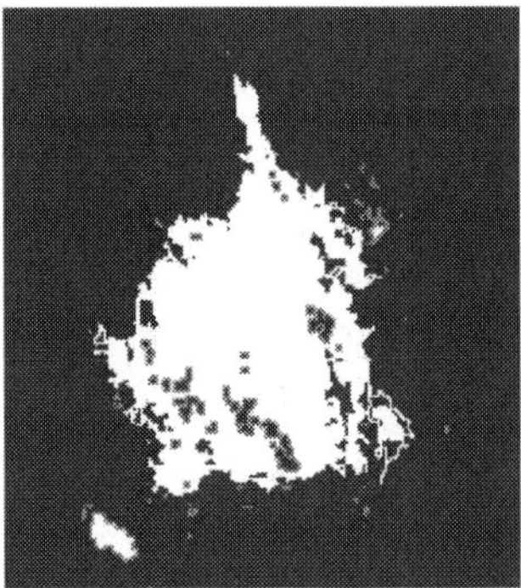

Fig. 18. The FAR is binarized; the white pixels are part of the form on a black background

Step 3 - the contour is automatically traced: once the image is binarized, the next step is to trace an outline of the white areas: all the white pixels which have at least one black neighbour will become part of the contour (every pixel has 8 neighbours: N, NE, E, SE, S, SV, V, NV). The rest of the pixels will be transformed into black pixels.

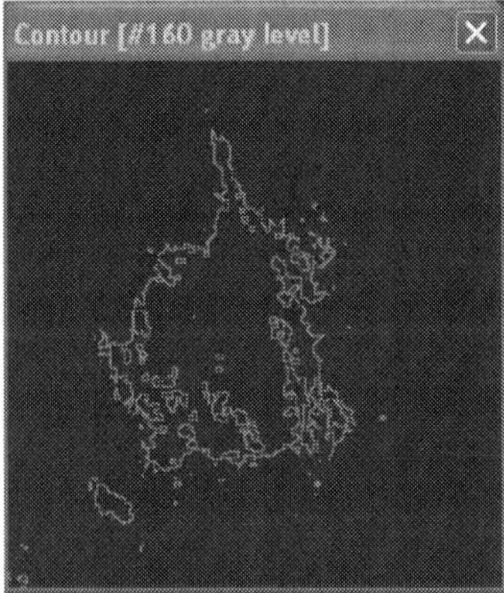

Fig. 19. The contour is traced - an outline of the white areas.

Step 4 - the fractal dimension of the outline will be computed by using the box-counting algorithm. The result will be 1.36.

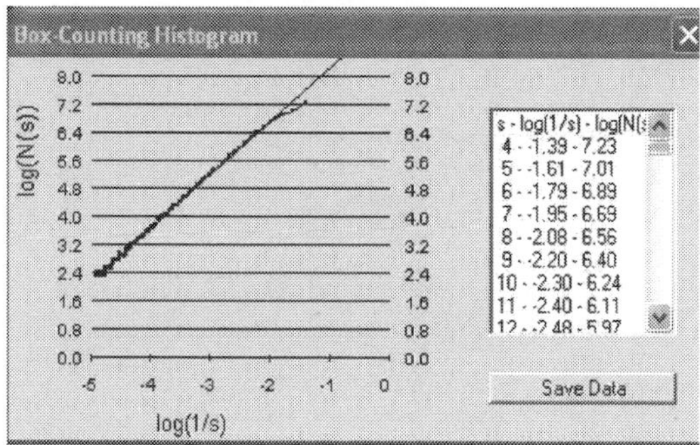

Fig. 20. The box-counting algorithm will provide the 1.36- fractal dimension.

The results of 30 cases of BI-RADS 4 classified lesions are as follows: the benign lesions have lower fractal dimensions, between 1-1.50, while malign lesion have higher dimensions, between 1.35-2.

Lesions	Fractal dimension	Cases
Benign(18 cases)	<1.4	16 (89%)
	>1.4	2 (11%)
Malign(12 cases)	<1.4	1 (8%)
	>1.4	11 (92%)

Table 3. The fractal dimensions on 30 mammographic lesions

In fig. 21 it is presented the statistical result based on the fractal study. The fractal dimensions corresponding to 16 benign cases are situated below the 1.4 – threshold, while only two benign cases have higher dimensions; meanwhile, 11 malign cases have higher fractal dimensions, above 1.4 and only one case is below the 1.4-threshold.

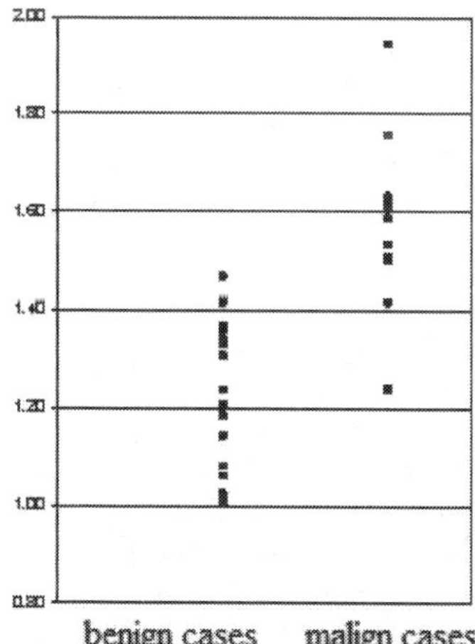

Fig. 21. The fractal dimensions distribution on 30 mammographic lesions.

3.2.3 Conclusions

The presented application, from biomedicine, involves non-invasive techniques based on the processing of mammographic images. The method allows the diagnosing of mammographic tumours and it is based on two observations:

- the fractal dimension grows as the irregularity of the object grows;
- regular outline of a lesion is associated to a benign lesion, while irregular outline is associated to a malign lesion.

The hypothesis that cancers have higher fractal dimensions than benign lesions was tested on 30 cases and the results are encouraging.

4. References

Anchisi A., A. Berlini, N. Cartasegna, F. Polani (2000), *"Genziane d'Europa"*, Oltrepo'Pavese

Andrei M. (1997), *"Morfologia Generală a Plantelor"*, Editura Enciclopedică , Bucureşti

Beldie Al. (1979), *"Flora României"*, Vol. II, Editura Academiei, Bucureşti

Ciocârlan V. (2000), „Flora Ilustrata a României. Pteridophyta şi Spermatophyta", Editura Ceres, Bucureşti

Crişan D.A. (2006), „Image processing using fractal techniques", Ed. Universitară, Bucureşti

Dobrescu R., C. Vasilescu (2004), "Interdisciplinary Applications Of Fractal And Chaos Theory", Academia Română, Bucuresti

Ehrendorfer Fr. (1998), „*Lehrbuch der Botanik*", (Ed. 34,) Gustav Fischer Verlag, Stuttgart

Kinsner W. (1994), *"A unified approach to fractal and multifractal dimensions"*, Technical Report, DEL94-4. Department of Electrical and Computer Engineering, University of Manitoba, Winnipeg, Manitoba, Canada

Lindenmayer A., Prusinkiewicz P. (1996), *"The Algorithmic Beauty of Plants"*, Springer-Verlag, Berlin,New York

Sari-Sarraf H., S. Gleason, K. Hutson, K. Hubner (1996), "A Novel Approach to Computed Aided Diagnosis of Mammographic Images", 3rd IEEE Workshop on Applications of Computer Vision

Tutin T. G., ş.a (1972), *"Flora Europaea"*, vol. 3, Press University, Cambridge

*** Breast Imaging Reporting Data System - http://www.birads.at

## 19

Image Recognition on Impact Perforation Test by Neural Network

Takehiko Ogawa
Takushoku University
Japan

1. Introduction

It is important to estimate the perforation characteristics of materials in the design of structures that collide with a flying object. Concretely, the perforation limit speed and the remaining speed of a material are evaluated by performing an impact perforation test (Backman & Goldsmith, 1978; Zukas, 1990). Then, a method for evaluating these parameters using successive images of the perforation process captured with a super-high-speed camera system has been researched in the mechanical and material engineering fields (Kasano, 1999; Kasano et al., 2001). In this method, a steel ball is shot into the material specimen as successive images are captured. Then, the characteristics of the material are estimated from the location of the steel ball and the behavior of the specimen. However, it is often difficult to observe these parameters because of the scattered fragments. Fragment scattering is especially observed in acrylic composites, ceramics, and their composite materials; these materials have high hardness and heat resistance. Therefore, it can be difficult to accurately evaluate the characteristics of the material.

On the other hand, neural networks are often used in an image recognition method (Bishop, 2006; Ripley, 2007). Because of their robustness, noise-proofing, etc., neural networks can be expected to correctly recognize an imperfect image. A multilayered neural network, in particular, can distinguish an unknown image by developing relationships between the input image and the distinction category through its mapping ability. Neural networks have been applied to impact perforation image processing in order to estimate the position of steel balls (Ogawa et al., 2003; Ogawa et al., 2006; Ohkubo et al., 2007).

The impact perforation image includes the scattered fragments; the obscurity and the difference in brightness depend on the experimental conditions of the specimen material and the difference in light. The input-output relationship is determined beforehand using the training data, and distinction is performed using the obtained input-output model for distinction by a multilayer neural network. In general, different data based on the material and environment are used in learning and for an actual distinction. It is possible to deal with a few differences between the learning and the distinction data in a robust neural network. To improve the estimation accuracy, it is necessary for the method to decrease the differences between the training and the distinction data and clarify the features between groups in the training data.

In this study, we examined the addition of an image preprocessing method to improve the learning method for impact perforation image processing using a neural network. The objective of this study was to improve the distinction ability by clarifying the features of the image and decreasing the differences between the training and the distinction data. First, preprocessing of the input image by gamma correction is introduced to clarify features between the distinction data groups of the image in the input image. Then, the incremental learning method, in which distinction data is added to the study data, is introduced to reduce the difference between input data. The effect of these two methods is confirmed by simulations carried out using actual impact perforation images.

2. Impact perforation test

The impact perforation test is a method in which a flying object such as a steel ball is shot into a material specimen to examine the perforation and destruction process. The system for the impact perforation test consists of a super high-speed camera used to observe the perforation process. With this system, we can observe the state before and after impact perforation by looking at successive images.

When a steel ball perforates through a plate, the residual velocity of the steel ball after the perforation is expressed by several characteristics: the strength of the board, rigidity, initial form, size, etc. For example, we can estimate the material properties using the impact velocity and residual velocity of the steel ball and the geometric properties of the material. Kasano et al. have researched methods for evaluating material properties by performing the impact perforation test based on the abovementioned principle. The residual velocity V_R is expressed by

$$V_R = F(a_1, a_2; V_i) \tag{1}$$

where a_1, a_2, and V_i represent the material properties, geometric properties of the material, and the initial velocity of the steel ball, respectively. We can estimate the material property a_1 if we know the initial velocity V_i, residual velocity V_R of the steel ball, and geometric property a_2. The perforation limit velocity is one of the important material properties and can be estimated by the initial and residual velocities obtained in the impact perforation test (Kasano et al., 2001).

As a measuring method for the velocity of a steel ball, we used the high-speed camera method because the perforated specimen's fragments have little influence. In this system, the steel ball launched from the shooting device perforates a monotonous material plate in the high-temperature furnace; pictures are taken of the event with the high-speed camera. The high-speed camera of this system can take pictures of four successive images. The experimental setup is shown in Fig. 1. We can measure the velocity of the steel ball with the high-speed camera from successive images of the perforation. However, the location of the steel ball cannot often be measured precisely by the fragments of the destroyed material in the perforation image of an actual material. In the current system, image classification for the impact perforation test is done visually. Therefore, classification is done from successive images, which is difficult because of the fragments of the material. Therefore, precise image clustering of the steel ball, background, and fragments is necessary. We propose using a neural network to classify these components in images degraded by fragments of the specimen. We show the image classification for the images degraded by the scattered material fragments can be performed accurately with a neural network.

Successive images of the impact perforation test with actual composite materials— carbon nitride (Si_3N_4) and alumina (Al_2O_3) specimens—are shown in Fig. 2. The numbers drawn in the figure show the photographed order. The image of Si_3N_4 specimen is so clear that we can sufficiently classify it visually. However, classifying the image of alumina is too difficult because of scattered fragments. The aim of this study is to localize the steel ball in these images accurately. The plate size, thickness of the specimen, impact velocity of the steel ball, and interframe time of successive images are shown in Table 1. The size of the steel ball was 5 mm in diameter and 0.5 g in mass.

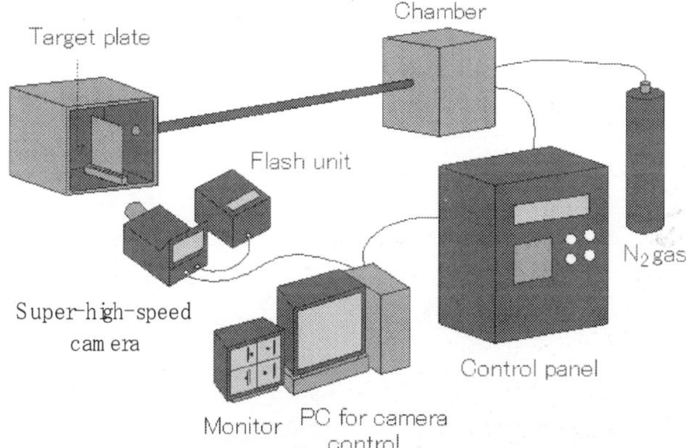

Fig. 1. Experimental setup of the impact perforation test.

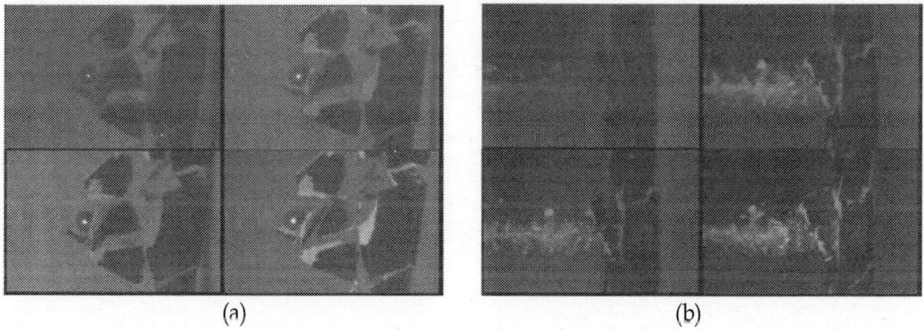

Fig. 2. Successive images obtained using super-high-speed camera in the impact perforation test performed with composite materials: (a) carbon nitride (Si_3N_4) and (b) alumina (Al_2O_3).

Material	Si_3N_4	Al_2O_3
Image size (pixel)	1172×770	1172×770
Specimen's size (mm)	80×50	80×80
Specimen's thickness (mm)	1.5	1.5
Initial velocities of the steel ball (m/s)	104.8	224.6
Interval time of successive images(μs)	50	50

Table 1. Parameters of the impact perforation test and its image.

3. Neural network for impact perforation image processing

In this study, we used a neural network to localize a steel ball in the impact perforation image. We used the three-layer feed-forward network. The input and output are preprocessed sub-images and distinguished results of the input sub-images, respectively. The sub-images are sequentially extracted and provided to the network. The network distinguishes whether the sub-image is a steel ball from the provided sub-images of the impact perforation image. The network estimates the steel ball's location from the sequential distinction of the steel ball.

The actual input of the network is each normalized pixel value in [0, 1], which is extracted from the whole image as a sub-image and compressed into 8 × 8 pixels via image compression. Image compression based on the two-dimensional wavelet transform was used in this study. The wavelet transform is a conversion with a lot of energy concentrations on the upper expansion coefficient (Goswami & Chan, 1999). Therefore, it compresses images with little loss of information. With the image sizes used in this study, the effect of using wavelet compression was not so large. However, because the effect of the image compression method causes changes in the sub-image size and so on, wavelet compression with the abovementioned advantage was used in this study. The eighth Daubechies basis function is concretely used; the octave of the image of the horizontal two steps and vertical two steps is divided; and the lowest region element (LLLL element) is used as a compressed image. In general, when the filter is processed to the image signal, the existence of the distortion at the edge of the image might be a problem. In a sub-image, filter processing by enhancing the processing area was not used because no remarkable distortions were seen. However, doing so may be necessary in the future according to the image size, kind of filter, etc.

The network architecture is shown in Fig. 3. The input-output characteristic of the neurons in the hidden and output layers is the sigmoid function expressed by

$$f_{(u)} = \frac{1}{1+e^{-u}} \tag{1}$$

where u denotes the weighted sum of the inputs. The neurons in the hidden and output layers output the weighted sum of the inputs after translation by the characteristic function of the sigmoid function. That is, the input-output relation is expressed by

$$y_i = f\left(\sum_{j=0}^{N} w_{ij}x_j\right) \tag{2}$$

where w_{ij}, x_j and y_i represent the interlayer weight, input, and output of each neuron, respectively. The threshold value is expressed by the special weight w_{i0} and the corresponding input is expressed by the constant input $x_0 = 1$.

In the learning phase, the network learns the sub-image of a steel ball and other subimages as learning data. The input for the network is the value of the normalized grayscale for the compressed sub-image; it is prepared for the steel ball and other components. The output of the network is expressed by two neurons. That is, the outputs are assigned $(O_1, O_2) = (1, 0)$ and $(O_1, O_2) = (0, 1)$ for the steel ball and other components, where the value of two neurons is assumed to be O_1 and O_2.

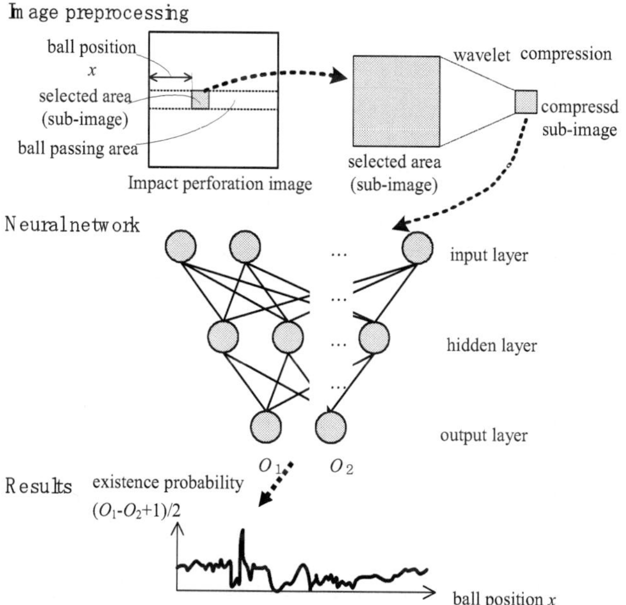

Fig. 3. Neural network architecture for localizing a steel ball in impact perforation images.

In the estimation phase, the sub-image sequence obtained by horizontally scanning the part of the impact perforation image which the steel ball passes is input to the network. The network is then expected to output the values $(O_1, O_2) = (1, 0)$ and $(O_1, O_2) = (0, 1)$ for the steel ball and other components, respectively. The network then outputs the existence probability for the steel ball at each sub-image position. The existence probability of the steel ball is expressed according to the normalized value of the difference between two neuron outputs, which is expressed as

$$O(x) = \frac{O_1(x) - O_2(x) + 1}{2}$$

(3)

where x denotes the horizontal position of the image. A position with a high existence probability is estimated to be the steel ball position. By sequential distinction of the steel ball at each position, the network estimates the steel ball location (Ogawa et al., 2003; Ogawa et al., 2006).

The purpose of this study was to estimate an indistinct steel ball position correctly by using a clear steel ball image. In other words, we estimated the position for a hidden steel ball based on the results for a confirmed steel ball. In actual estimation, the neural network distinguishes a steel ball position in the indistinct image by using the input-output relation obtained during the learning phase. Concretely, we aimed to correctly estimate the position of the steel ball in the impact perforation image of the alumina specimen by using the position from the silicon nitride specimen. The steel ball, background, and fragment subimages for the nitride silicon specimen were used as learning data. The steel ball position in the impact perforation image of the alumina specimen, in which the steel ball was hidden by the fragments of specimen, was estimated by the network after using the learning data. In other words, a simulation corresponding to the actual use of the network was carried out using images with normal and high levels of difficulty.

When different images are used for learning and estimation, the features — color, shape, and reflection — of the objects are different between the two images. For instance, it is difficult to estimate accurately based on features of the learned image because the features for the images of the alumina and silicon nitride specimens are different. To solve this problem, it is necessary to decrease the differences between the learning and estimation images and learn the features for the steel ball, background, and fragments sufficiently. In this study, we examine image preprocessing and the corresponding improvement in the learning method.

3.1 Preprocessing by gamma correction

In the impact perforation images, the steel ball, background, and fragments in the image are distinguished by the learned neural network. If the neural network can learn the correct group classifications with clear data, making distinctions with high accuracy becomes possible.

To clarify the input image, we convert the density distribution to express the features of the image. The density distribution of the image is expressed by the contrast, which is the ratio between the light and shade of the image. Contrast conversion is used to equate the contrast between different images. Contrast conversion includes linear and nonlinear density conversion and is used for each objective. In linear density conversion, part of the image information may be lost within the range of the upper and lower bounds of the density value for the original image, while the brightness of the present image can be easily converted. On the other hand, the advantage for nonlinear density conversion is that the contrast can be improved without losing image information. Gamma correction is a type of nonlinear density conversion with a high contrast improvement (Pratt, 2007). The general form of the gamma correction can be expressed by

$$Z' = Z_m \left(\frac{Z}{Z_m} \right)^{\gamma} \tag{4}$$

where Z', Z, and Z_m denote the density values obtained after processing, before processing, and the maximum, respectively. The contrast is converted by adjusting the value of γ in the gamma correction. The image lightens when $\gamma < 1$ and darkens when $\gamma > 1$. When $\gamma = 1$, the images before and after processing become the same because Z' becomes equal to Z. In this study, we examined making the steel ball, background and fragments of the impact perforation image clear by using gamma correction. In addition, we improved the estimated accuracy for the gamma value, which reduced the difference between the learning and estimation images.

3.2 Incremental learning by adding estimation data

The image is distinguished by applying the input-output relation obtained during learning to the estimation image for robustness of the neural network, even though the learning and estimation images are different in actual impact perforation image processing. One method to improve the distinction ability of the image is to reduce the difference between the learning and estimation data. In this study, both the learning and estimation data were composed of four sequential photographs. Therefore, images easy and difficult to distinguish may exist in the four estimation images. To improve the positional estimation accuracy, we used the incremental learning method (Sugiyama & Ogawa, 2001; Yamauchi & Ishii, 1995). Concretely, the data that is obtained with high accuracy in the first estimation are added to the learning data; the network then learns all data again. This method aims to restructure the input-output relation of the neural network by adding part of the estimation data to the learning data to reduce differences in the features for both images.

In this method, the estimation image is first distinguished by the neural network which goes through learning with only the learning data. The image data to be added as the learning data are decided by the distinction results, and the network goes through learning again. Then, distinction is carried out for the estimation images again by using the neural network that had gone through learning using both the learning and added estimation images. This procedure is as follows.

Step 1. The steel ball, fragments, and background are extracted from the learning image and used as learning data.

Step 2. The neural network learns.

Step 3. The position of the steel ball is estimated for the estimation image.

Step 4. The part of the image corresponding to maximum output is extracted and added to the learning image.

Step 5. Steps 2 to 4 are repeated.

From the viewpoint of the neural network model, the procedure feeds the obtained output result back to the input as input image data. In this study, the feedback is expressed as the addition of the training data without changing the network architecture. However, it is also possible to compose the model as a recurrent neural network with modules corresponding to the number of learning data sets.

4. Simulation

First, we examined the usual learning and estimation without gamma correction and incremental learning by using the neural network architecture explained in the previous section. During learning, the sub-images of the steel ball, background, and fragments for the impact perforation image of the silicon nitride specimen are learned to construct the input-output relation. Then, the steel ball position in the impact perforation image of the alumina specimen is estimated by the network.

The impact perforation image of the nitride silicon specimen in Fig. 2(a) was used as learning data. The image of the alumina specimen in Fig. 2(b) was used as the estimation data. The network used is shown in Fig. 3, and its parameters are shown in Table 2. The condition for finishing the learning was set to 15 000 iterations or 0.0001 of the output mean squared errors, and we confirmed the learning finished within the maximum number of iterations.

The estimation results for the steel ball positions in the impact perforation images of four alumina specimens are shown in Figs. 4(a)–(d). The upper rows of each result are subimages extracted at the vertical position to estimate the position; they are used as inputs. The lower rows of each result are the estimated steel ball positions, which represent the probability of existence of the steel ball. The steel ball positions estimated to be an actual image can be compared by contrasting the upper and lower rows. From Fig. 4(a), it is observed that the position of the steel ball cannot be estimated from the first image. From Figs. 4(b)–(d), it is found that the other three images are not accurately distinguished because there are many misjudgments and the output value of the steel ball part is too small. However, a candidate for the steel ball position is barely estimated. Consequently, a steel ball position not estimated enough by the original neural network that learned the image of the silicon nitride specimen is estimated from the image of the alumina specimen.

Image size	385 × 586
Sub-image size	32 × 32
Compressed image size for network input	8 × 8
Number of input neurons	64
Number of hidden neurons	12
Number of output neurons	2
Training gain	0.01
Mean squared error for attain	0.0001
Maximum training epoch	150000

Table 2. Network parameters

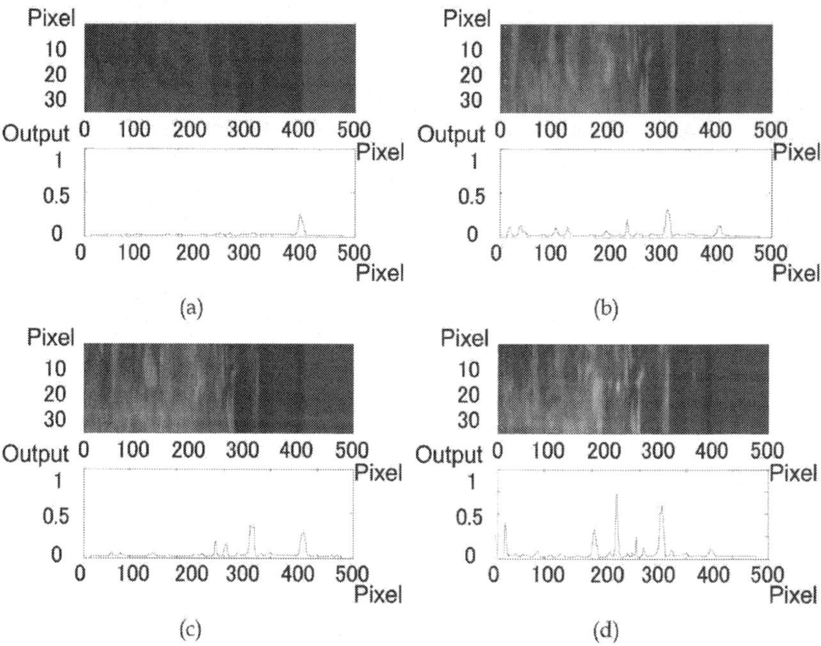

(a)

(b)

(c)

(d)

Fig. 4. Horizontally scanned images and network output indicating the ball location estimated using the usual network.

4.1 Results of gamma correction

The effect of image preprocessing by gamma correction was examined by carrying out a simulation. The second image of the silicon nitride specimen shown in Fig. 2(a) was used as the learning image. Further, the image of the alumina specimen shown in Fig. 2(b) was used as an estimation target. Gamma correction of $\gamma = 1.5$ was applied to both the learning image and the estimation image. The network architecture and the network parameters used in this simulation were the same as those used in the previous simulation, which are shown in Fig. 3 and Table 2, respectively. The condition for completing the learning was set to 15000 iterations or 0.0001 of the output mean-squared errors, which was the same as that mentioned in the previous subsection. As a result, we confirmed that learning was completed within the maximum number of iterations.

The estimated result of the position obtained using the images processed by gamma correction is shown in Fig. 5. The misjudgement is reduced overall, and in particular, it is found that image preprocessing has a significant effect on the result of the fourth image shown in Fig. 5(d). Moreover, the output corresponding to the steel ball approaches 1.0, and from the result of the third image shown in Fig. 5(c), it is observed that the steel ball recognition level improves. Consequently, the results, i.e., the improvements in the distinction performance of the steel ball and the reduction in the misjudgement, were obtained by gamma correction processing. However, it is necessary to examine the parameters of gamma correction, because the effect of image preprocessing seems not so large.

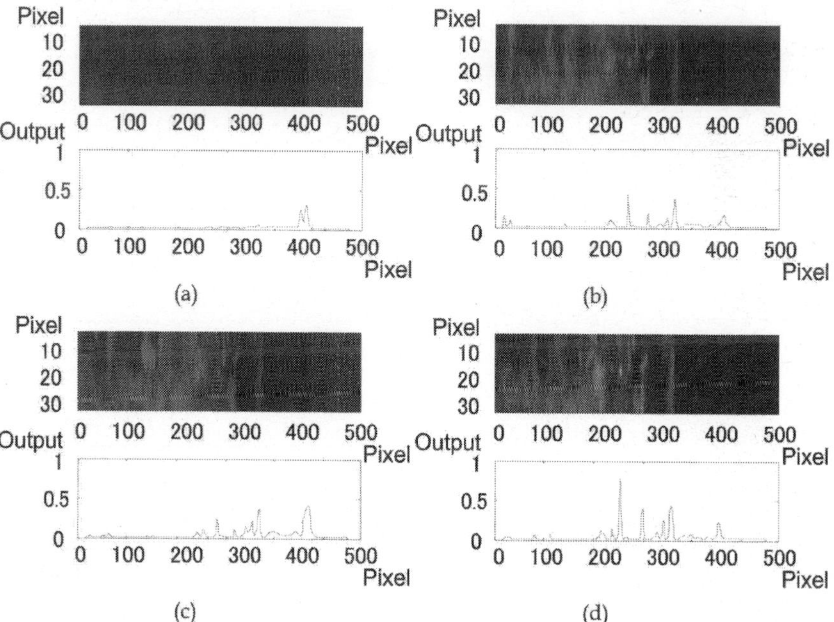

Fig. 5. Horizontally scanned images and network output indicating the ball location estimated using the network with gamma correction.

4.2 Results of incremental learning

The effect of incremental learning was examined by carrying out a simulation. Similar to the previous simulation, the second image of the silicon nitride specimen shown in Fig. 2(a) and the image of the alumina specimen shown in Fig. 2(b) were used as the learning and estimation images, respectively. In addition, gamma correction of $\gamma = 1.5$ was applied to the input images. The network architecture and the network parameters used in this simulation were the same as those used in the previous simulation, which are shown in Fig. 3 and Table 2, respectively. The condition for completing the learning was set to 15000 iterations or 0.0001 of the output mean-squared errors, which was the same as that mentioned in the previous subsection. As a result, we confirmed that the learning was completed within the maximum number of iterations.

We first did the usual learning and estimation. The result of this simulation is similar to that of the previous simulation showed in Fig. 5, which includes gamma correction. The image part corresponding to the maximum network output was extracted from the estimation image, and it was added to the learning image for carrying out incremental learning. We added four images to the learning image by repeating this procedure four times. The added four sub-images are shown in Fig. 6. Incremental learning was done in the same condition to finish the learning as usual learning. Then, we confirmed that the learning was completed within the maximum number of iterations.

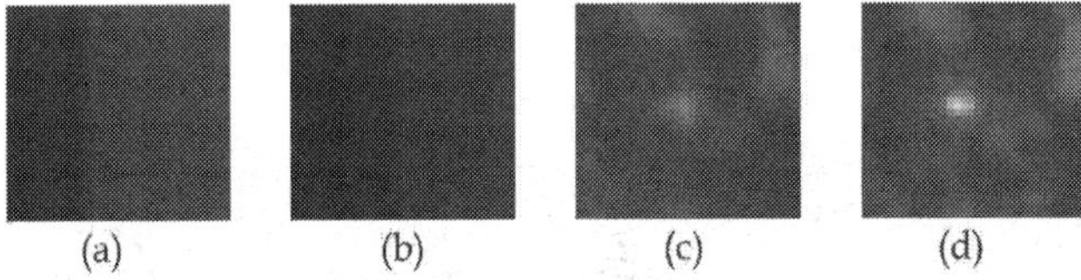

(a)   (b)   (c)   (d)

Fig. 6. Extracted sub-images for incremental learning.

The estimation results for the network with additional learning are shown in Fig. 7. The accuracy of steel ball recognition was improved greatly, and misjudgments were almost eliminated by adding a part of the estimation image to the learning image. It became possible to accurately estimate the position of the steel ball by the incremental learning method. The effectiveness of the proposed method was confirmed by these results.

5. Conclusion

In this study, a neural network was introduced for impact perforation image processing. Moreover, a preprocessing method of an image and a novel learning method of the neural network were introduced to improve distinction ability. Concretely, to clarify the features of an image, preprocessing of the input image by gamma correction was introduced. In addition, an incremental learning method, which adds a part of the estimation image to the learning image and relearns it, was introduced to improve the reduction in the distinction ability on the basis of the difference between the learning image and the estimation image. As a result, the accuracy of recognition of the steel ball was improved by preprocessing with gamma correction. Moreover, the position of the steel ball could be estimated correctly by adding additional learning data for a situation which had been estimated to be difficult in usual learning.

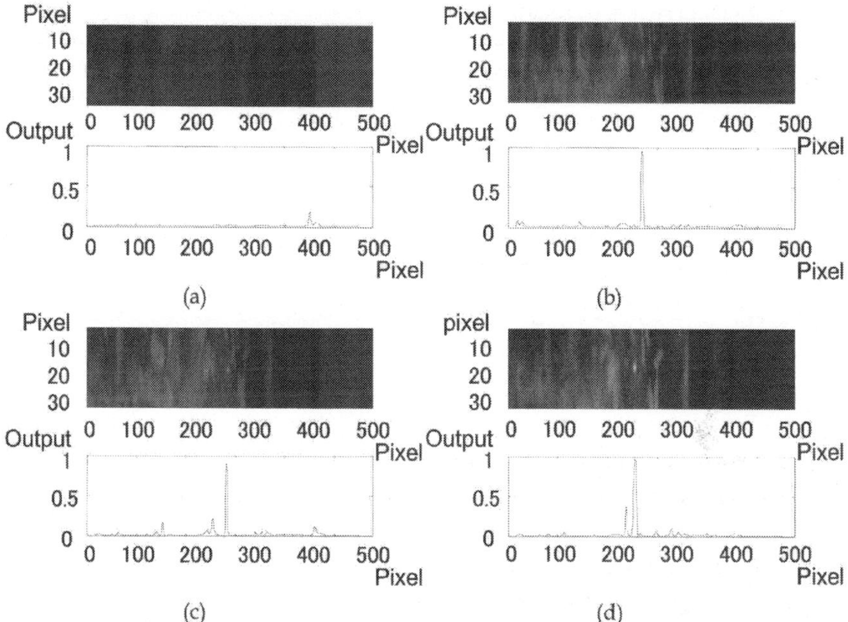

Fig. 7. Horizontally scanned images and network output indicating the ball location estimated using the network with gamma correction and additional learning.

In future, it is necessary to determine an appropriate parameter for gamma correction. In this study, we focussed on reducing the difference between the learning image and the estimation image by gamma correction. However, it is possible to aim at converting images that are easy to distinguish for further advanced work. In addition, it is also necessary to develop a selection method for the images used in incremental learning. In this study, an image was selected on the basis of the output value. A certain threshold value may have to be decided. Further, it is necessary to obtain more types of learning data for improving the generality of the estimation method.

6. References

Backman, M. E. & Goldsmith, W. (1978). The mechanics of penetration of projectiles into targets. *International Journal of Engineering Science*, Vol. 16, No. 1, pp. 1-99.

Bishop, C. M. (2006). *Pattern Recognition and Machine Learning*, Springer, ISBN: 978-0387310738, New York.

Kasano, H. (1999). Recent advances in high-velocity impact perforation of fiber composite laminates. *JSME International Journal A*, Vol. 42-2, pp. 147-157.

Kasano, H.; Okubo, T. & Hasegawa, O. (2001). Impact perforation characteristics of carbon/carbon composite laminates. *International Journal of Materials and Product Technology*, Vol. 16, No. 1-3, pp. 165-170.

Ogawa, T.; Kanada, H. & Kasano, H. (2003). Neural network localization of a steel ball in impact perforation images, *Proceedings of the SICE Annual Conference*, pp. 416-419.

Ogawa, T.; Tanaka, S.; Kanada, H. & Kasano, H. (2006). Impact perforation image processing using a neural network, *Proceedings of the SICE-ICASE International Joint Conference.* pp. 3762-3765.

Okubo, K.; Ogawa, T. & Kanada, H. (2007). Impact perforation image processing using a self-organizing map, *Proceedings of the SICE Annual Conference*, pp. 1099-1103.

Pratt, W. K. (2007). *Digital Image Processing*, John Wiley & Sons, ISBN: 978-0471767770, New Jersey.

Ripley, B. D. (2007). *Pattern Recognition and Neural Networks*, Cambridge University Press, ISBN: 978-0521717700, New York.

Sugiyama, M. & Ogawa, H. (2001). Incremental projection learning for optimal generalization. *Neural Networks*, Vol. 14, No. 10, pp. 53-66.

Yamauchi, K. & Ishii, N. (1995). An incremental learning method with recalling interfered patterns, *Proceedings of the IEEE International Conference on Neural Networks*, Vol. 6, pp. 3159-3164.

Zukas, J. A. (1990). *High Velocity Impact Dynamics*, John Wiley & Sons, ISBN: 978-0471514442, New York.

## 20

Analog-Digital Self-Learning Fuzzy Spiking Neural Network in Image Processing Problems

Artem Dolotov and Yevgeniy Bodyanskiy
Kharkiv National University of Radio Electronics
Ukraine

1. Introduction

Computational intelligence provides a variety of means that can perform complex image processing in a rather effective way. Among them, self-learning systems, especially self-learning artificial neural networks (self-organizing maps, ART neural networks, 'Brain-State-in-a-Box' neuromodels, etc.) (Haykin, 1999) and fuzzy clustering systems (fuzzy c-means, algorithms of Gustafson-Kessel, Yager-Filev, Klawonn-Hoeppner, etc) (Bezdek et al., 2005; Sato-Ilic & Jain, 2006), occupy a significant place as they make it possible to solve a data processing problem in the absence of a priori knowledge of it.

While there are many artificial neural networks that can be successfully used in image processing tasks, the most prominent of them are networks of a new, the third generation, commonly known as spiking neural networks (Maass & Bishop, 1998; Gerstner & Kistler, 2002). On the one hand, spiking neural networks are biologically more plausible than neural networks of the previous generations that is of fundamental importance for computational intelligence from theoretical point of view. On the other hand, networks of spiking neurons appeared to be computationally more powerful than conventional neural networks (Maass, 1997b). In addition, complex data processing via artificial neural networks of the second generation is time consuming due to multi-epoch learning; instead, spiking neural networks can perform the same processing tasks much faster as they require a few learning epochs only (Bohte et al., 2002; Berredo, 2005; Meftah et al., 2008; Lindblad & Kinser, 2005). All these facts are causing considerable interest in networks of spiking neurons as a powerful computational intelligence tool for image processing

Although spiking neural networks are becoming a popular computational intelligence tool for various technical problems solving, their architecture and functioning are treated in terms of neurophysiology rather than in terms of any technical sciences apparatus in the most research works on engineering subjects. Yet none technically plausible description of spiking neurons functioning has been provided.

In contrast to artificial neural networks, fuzzy logic systems are capable of performing accurate and efficient data processing under a priori and current uncertainty, particularly if classes to be separated overlap one another. Integrating artificial neural networks and fuzzy systems together allows of combining capabilities of both in a synergetic way (Jang et al., 1997), thus producing hybrid intelligent systems that achieve high performance and reliability in real life problems solving, particularly in image processing. Obviously, designing hybrid intelligent systems based on the new generation of artificial neural networks attracts both practical and theoretical interest.

In the present chapter of the book, analog-digital self-learning fuzzy spiking neural network that belongs to a new type of computational intelligence hybrid systems combining spiking neurons computational capabilities and fuzzy systems tolerance for uncertainty is proposed. It is demonstrated that both fuzzy probabilistic and fuzzy possibilistic approaches can be implemented on spiking neural network basis. A spiking neural network is treated in terms of well-known and widely used apparatus of classical automatic control theory based on the Laplace transform. It is shown that a spiking neuron synapse is nothing other than a second-order critically damped response unit, and a spiking neuron soma is a kind of threshold detection system. An improved unsupervised learning algorithm for the proposed neural network based on 'Winner-Takes-More' rule is introduced. Capabilities of the neural network in solving image processing problems are investigated. From theoretical point of view, the proposed neural network is another step toward evolution of artificial neural networks theory as a part of computational intelligence paradigm.

2. Formal models of spiking neurons

Biological neuron constructive features that are significant for the discussion that follows are sketched on Fig. 1 (Dayan & Abbott, 2001; Scott, 2002). As illustrated, neuron includes synapses, dendritic tree, soma and axon and its terminals. Synapse connects axonal terminals of a neuron with dendrites of another neuron. Soma processes incoming information and transmits it through axon and axonal terminals to synapses of the subsequent neurons. Neurons communicate one another by nerve pulses (action potentials, spikes).

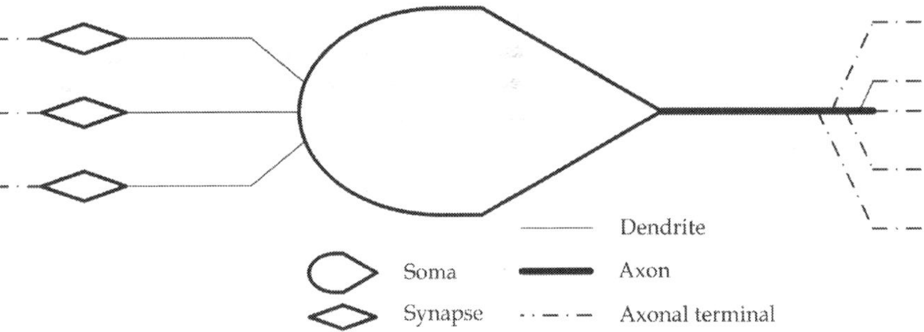

Fig. 1. Biological neuron

Neuron behaviour can be briefly described in the following way (Fig. 2). Spike arrived to synapse from presynaptic neuron generates postsynaptic potential (either excitatory or inhibitory – depending on synapse type). Postsynaptic potential reaches neuron soma through a dendrite and either increases membrane potential, or decreases it. Neuron soma accumulates all postsynaptic potentials incoming from different synapses. When membrane potential exceeds firing threshold, neuron fires and emits outgoing spike that moves through axon to postsynaptic neurons. Once neuron has fired, its soma produces spike after-potential, namely, the membrane potential drops steeply below the rest potential and then it ascends gradually to the rest potential back. Period when membrane potential is below the rest potential is called refractory period. Within this period, appearance of another spike is unlikely. If the firing threshold is not reached after arrival of a postsynaptic potential, membrane potential gradually descends to rest potential until another postsynaptic potential incomes.

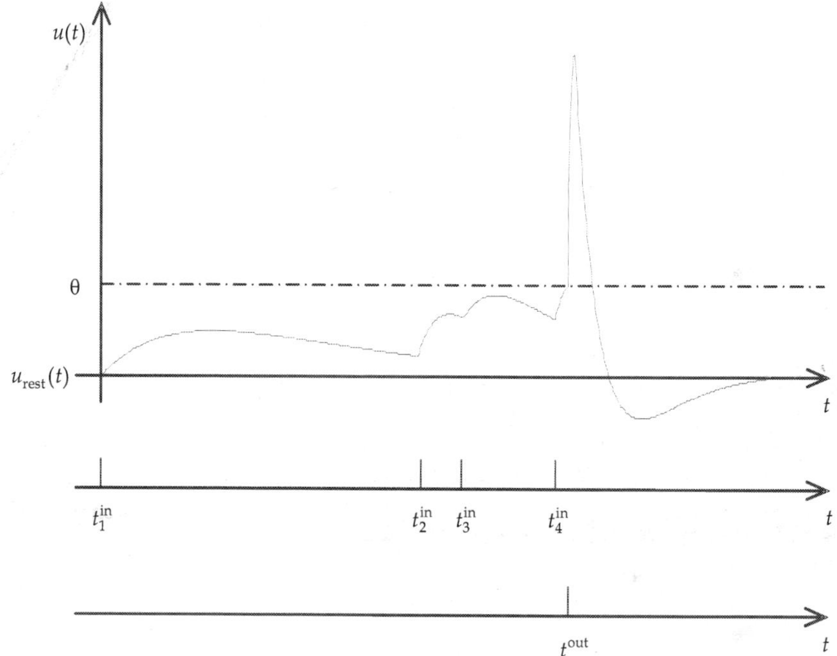

Fig. 2. Biological neuron behaviour: a) Dynamics of membrane potential $u(t)$ (θ is the firing threshold, $u_{rest}(t)$ is the rest potential); b) Incoming spikes; c) Outgoing spike

Traits of any artificial neural networks generation depend upon the formal model of biological neuron that is considered within scope of that generation. Any formal model treats biological neuron on a certain level of abstraction. It takes into account some details of biological neuron behaviour and features, but disregards other ones. On the one hand, prescribing complexity level of formal model sets computational and performance properties of artificial neural networks originated by that model. On the other hand, chosen level of abstraction of formal model defines how realistic artificial neural networks are.

Both the first and the second generations of artificial neural networks (Maass, 1997b) rest on the rate model that neglects temporal properties of biological neuron (Maass & Bishop, 1998). One of the essential elements for both generations is a neuron activation function. The rate model based on the threshold activation function (McCulloch & Pitts, 1943) gave birth to the first generation of artificial neural networks. Though such networks were capable of performing some elementary logic functions, their computational capabilities were very limited (Minsky & Papert, 1969). Replacing the threshold activation function with continuous one resulted in appearance of the second generation, that turned out to be significantly powerful than networks of the previous generation (Cybenko, 1989; Hornik et al., 1989). Nevertheless, neurons of the second generation are even far from real biological neurons than the first generation neurons since they ignore soma firing mechanism totally (Gerstner & Kistler, 2002). This gap is avoided in threshold-fire models (Maass & Bishop, 1998). One of such models, namely, the leaky integrate-and-fire model (Maass & Bishop, 1998; Gerstner & Kistler, 2002), is the basis for the third generation of artificial neural networks.

The leaky integrate-and-fire model is the one of the simplest and well-known formal models of a biological neuron that are used in different areas of neuroscience. It captures neuron behaviour described above except the neuron refractoriness. The model considers that on firing, membrane potential drops to the rest potential, not below it.

The spike-response model (Maass & Bishop, 1998; Gerstner & Kistler, 2002), another threshold-fire model, captures biological neuron behaviour more accurately. Besides postsynaptic potentials accumulating and spike firing, it models the neuron refractoriness also. This model will be used in the subsequent discussion.

It makes sense to mention here that computational neuroscience and computational intelligence sometimes understand spiking neurons in a different way. Spiking neuron in computational neuroscience is any model of biological neuron that transmits and processes information by spike trains. Within scope of computational intelligence, spiking neuron is a leaky integrate-and-fire model usually. This results from the fact that self-learning properties of spiking neurons are caused by capability of any threshold-fire model to detect coincidences in input signal. Since the leaky integrate-and-fire model is the simplest one among the threshold-fire models, there is no sense to use any complicated ones. Obviously, if any more complicated model reveals some particular properties that are useful for solving technical problems, the concept of spiking neurons will be extended in computational intelligence.

3. Self-learning spiking neural network

3.1 Introduction

Ability of spiking neurons to respond to incoming signal selectively was originally discovered by J. Hopfield in 1995 (Hopfield, 1995). He found that spiking neuron soma behaviour was similar to a radial basis function: the neuron fired as earlier as higher degree of coincidence of incoming spikes was; if the degree was sufficiently low, the neuron did not fire at all. And spiking neuron synapses appeared to be acting as a spike pattern storing unit: one was able to get a spiking neuron to fire to a certain spike pattern by adjusting synaptic time delays the way that they evened out (in temporal sense) incoming signal and made it to reach the neuron soma simultaneously. Spike pattern encoded in synaptic time delays of a neuron was called a center of spiking neuron in the following. Here it is worth to note that synchronization phenomena is of primary importance in nature (Pikovsky et al., 2001), particularly in the brain functioning (Malsburg, 1994).

The discovered capabilities of spiking neurons provided the basis for constructing self-learning networks of spiking neurons. Original architecture of self-learning spiking neural network and its learning algorithm, namely, a temporal Hebbian rule were introduced in (Natschlaeger & Ruf, 1998). The proposed self-learning network was able to separate clusters as long as their number was not greater than dimensionality of input signal. If clusters number exceeded number of input signal dimensions, spiking neural network performance decreased. This drawback was overcome by using population coding of incoming signal based on pools of receptive neurons in the first hidden layer of the network (Bohte et al., 2002). Such spiking neural network was shown to be considerably powerful and significantly fast in solving real life problems. Henceforward we will use this network as a basis for its further improvements and hybrid architectures designing.

3.2 Architecture

Self-learning spiking neural network architecture is shown on Fig. 3. As illustrated, it is heterogeneous two-layered feed-forward neural network with lateral connections in the second hidden layer.

The first hidden layer consists of pools of receptive neurons and performs transformation of input signal. It encodes an $(n \times 1)$-dimensional input sampled pattern $x(k)$ (here n is the dimensionality of input space, $k = \overline{1,N}$ is a patter number, N is number of patterns in incoming set) into $(hn \times 1)$-dimensional vector of input spikes $t^{[0]}(x(k))$ (here h is the number of receptive neurons in a pool) where each spike is defined by its firing time.

Spiking neurons form the second hidden layer of the network. They are connected with receptive neurons with multiple synapses where incoming vector of spikes transforms into postsynaptic potentials. Number of spiking neurons in the second hidden layer is set to be equal to the number of clusters to be detected. Each spiking neuron corresponds to a certain cluster. The neuron that has fired to the input pattern defines cluster that the pattern belongs to. Thus, the second hidden layer takes $(hn \times 1)$-dimensional vector of input spikes $t^{[0]}(x(k))$ and outputs $(m \times 1)$-dimensional vector of outgoing spikes $t^{[1]}(x(k))$ that defines the membership of input pattern $x(k)$.

This is the basic architecture and behaviour of self-learning spiking neural network. The detailed architecture is stated below.

3.3 Population coding and receptive neurons

The first hidden layer is constructed to perform population coding of input signal. It acts in such a manner that each dimensional component $x_i(k)$, $i = \overline{1,n}$, of input signal $x(k)$ is processed by a pool of h receptive neurons RN_{li}, $l = \overline{1,h}$. Obviously, there can be different number of receptive neurons h_i in a pool for each dimensional component in the general case. For the sake of simplicity, we will consider here that the number of neurons is equal for all pools.

As a rule, activation functions of receptive neurons within a pool are bell-shaped (Gaussians usually), shifted, overlapped, of different width, and have dead zone. Generally firing time of a spike emitted by a receptive neuron RN_{li} upon incoming signal $x_i(k)$ lies in a certain interval $\{-1\} \cup [0, t^{[0]}_{\max}]$ referred to as coding interval and is described by the following expression:

$$t^{[0]}_{li}(x_i(k)) = \begin{cases} \left\lfloor t^{[0]}_{\max}\left(1 - \psi\left(\left|x_i(k) - c^{[0]}_{li}\right|, \sigma_{li}\right)\right)\right\rfloor, & \psi\left(\left|x_i(k) - c^{[0]}_{li}\right|, \sigma_{li}\right) \geq \theta_{\text{r.n.}}, \\ -1, & \psi\left(\left|x_i(k) - c^{[0]}_{li}\right|, \sigma_{li}\right) < \theta_{\text{r.n.}}, \end{cases} \qquad (1)$$

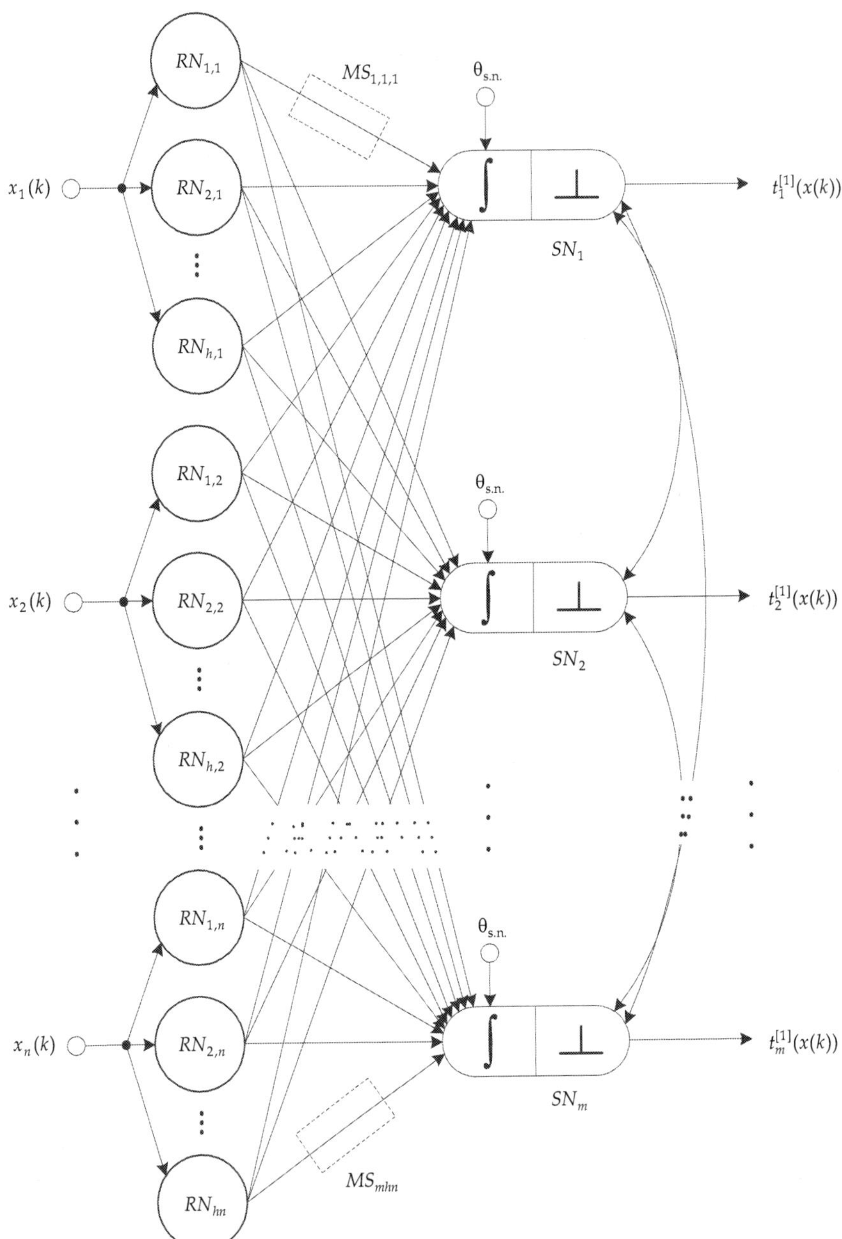

Fig. 3. Self-learning spiking neural network (spiking neurons are depicted the way to stress they act in integrate-and-fire manner)

where $\lfloor \bullet \rfloor$ is the floor function, $\psi(\bullet,\bullet)$, $c_{li}^{[0]}$, σ_{li}, and $\theta_{r.n.}$ are the receptive neuron's activation function, center, width and dead zone, respectively ($r.n.$ in the last parameter means 'receptive neuron'), -1 indicates that the neuron does not fire. An example of population coding is depicted on Fig. 4. It is easily seen that the closer $x_i(k)$ is to the center $c_{li}^{[0]}$ of receptive neuron RN_{li}, the earlier the neuron emits spike $t_{li}^{[0]}(x_i(k))$.

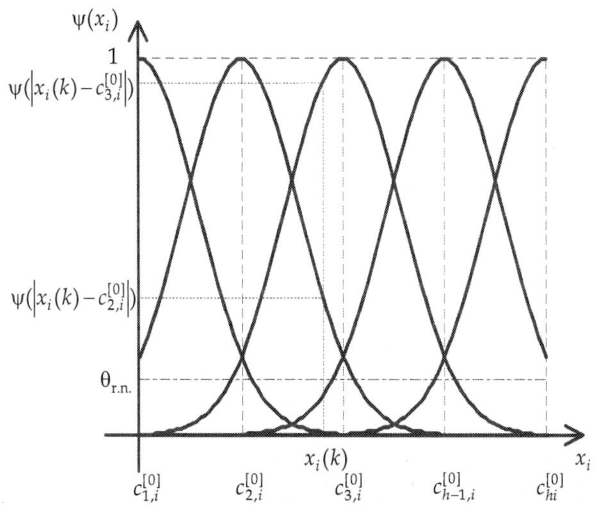

Fig. 4. An example of population coding. Incoming signal $x_i(k)$ fires receptive neurons $RN_{2,i}$ and $RN_{3,i}$. It is considered here that width of activation function of all receptive neurons within the pool is the same

In this work, we used Gaussian as activation function of receptive neurons:

$$\psi\left(\left|x_i(k)-c_{li}^{[0]}\right|,\sigma_{li}\right)=\exp\left(-\frac{\left(x_i(k)-c_{li}^{[0]}\right)^2}{2\sigma_{li}^2}\right).\tag{2}$$

There can be several ways to set widths and centers of receptive neurons within a pool. As a rule, activation functions can be of two types – either 'narrow' or 'wide'. Centers of each width type of activation function are calculated in different ways but in either case they cover date range uniformly. More details can be found in (Bohte et al., 2002).

3.4 Spiking neurons layer

Spiking neuron is considered to be formed of two constituents, they are: synapse and soma. As it was mentioned above, synapses between receptive neurons and spiking neurons are multiple structures. As shown on Fig. 5, a multiple synapse MS_{jli} consists of a set of q subsynapses with different time delays d^p, $d^p-d^{p-1}>0$, $d^q-d^1>t_{max}^{[0]}$, and adjustable weights w_{jli}^p (here $p=\overline{1,q}$). It should be noted that number of subsynapses within a multiple synapse are fixed for the whole network. Having a spike $t_{li}^{[0]}(x_i(k))$ from the li-th receptive neuron, the p-th subsynapse of the j-th spiking neuron produces delayed weighted postsynaptic potential

$$u_{jli}^p(t) = w_{jli}^p \varepsilon_{jli}^p(t) = w_{jli}^p \varepsilon\left(t - \left(t_{li}^{[0]}(x_i(k)) + d^p\right)\right), \tag{3}$$

where $\varepsilon(\bullet)$ is a spike-response function usually described by the expression (Natschlaeger & Ruf, 1998)

$$\varepsilon\left(t - \left(t_{li}^{[0]}(x_i(k)) + d^p\right)\right) = \frac{t - \left(t_{li}^{[0]}(x_i(k)) + d^p\right)}{\tau_{PSP}} \exp\left(1 - \frac{t - \left(t_{li}^{[0]}(x_i(k)) + d^p\right)}{\tau_{PSP}}\right) \times$$
$$\times H\left(t - \left(t_{li}^{[0]}(x_i(k)) + d^p\right)\right), \tag{4}$$

τ_{PSP} – membrane potential decay time constant whose value can be obtained empirically (PSP means 'postsynaptic potential'), $H(\bullet)$ – the Heaviside step function. Output of the multiple synapse MS_{jli} forms total postsynaptic potential

$$u_{jli}(t) = \sum_{p=1}^q u_{jli}^p(t). \tag{5}$$

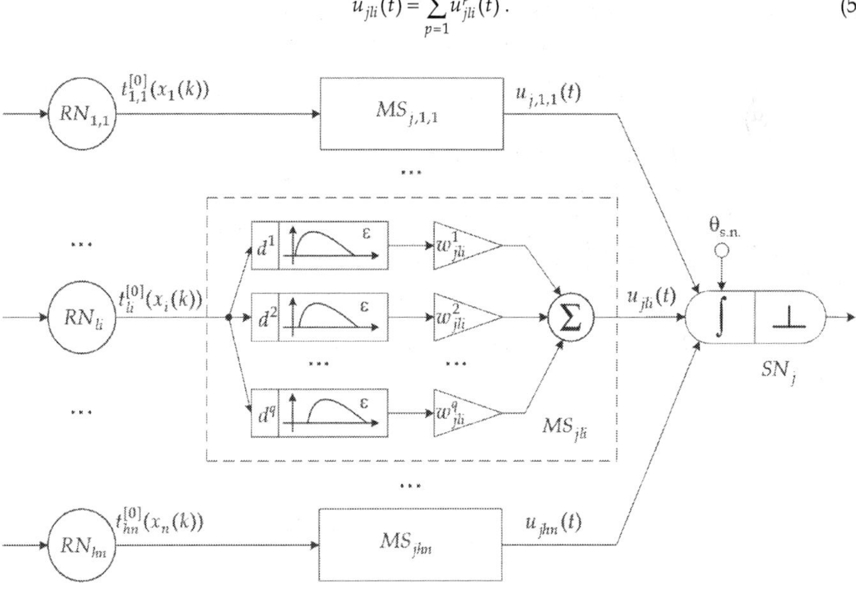

Fig. 5. Multiple synapse

Each incoming total postsynaptic potential contributes to membrane potential of spiking neuron SN_j as follows:

$$u_j(t) = \sum_{i=1}^n \sum_{l=1}^h u_{jli}(t). \tag{6}$$

Spiking neuron SN_j generates at most one outgoing spike $t_j^{[1]}(x(k))$ during a simulation interval (the presentation of an input pattern $x(k)$), and fires at the instant the membrane potential reaches firing threshold $\theta_{s.n.}$ (s.n. means here 'spiking neuron'). After neuron has fired, the membrane potential is reset to the rest value u_{rest} (0 usually) until the next input pattern is presented.

It is easily seen that the descried behaviour of spiking neuron corresponds to the one of the leaky integrate-and-fire model.

Spiking neurons are linked with lateral inhibitory connections that disable all other neurons to fire after the first one has fired. Thus, any input pattern makes only one spiking neuron to fire that is only one component of the vector of outgoing spikes has non-negative value. There can be cases when a few spiking neurons fire simultaneously for an input pattern. Such cases are rare enough, and their appearance depends directly on initial synaptic weights distribution.

3.5 Crisp data clustering

As it was mentioned above, a spiking neuron acts similarly to a radial basis function, and its response depends on degree of coincidence of the input. There was considered a spiking neuron center to describe such neuron behaviour in a convenient way (Natschlaeger & Ruf, 1998). In the general case, it is considered to possess the following property: the closer input pattern is to the neuron's center, the earlier output spike fires. Hence, a spiking neuron firing time reflects the similarity (Natschlaeger & Ruf, 1998) (or distance (Bohte et al., 2002)) between the input pattern and the neuron center. Degree of coincidence is utilized here as a similarity (distance) measure.

Center of spiking neuron is encoded in the synaptic time delays. They produce coincidence output (and in its terns it makes the soma to fire at the earliest possible time) if incoming pattern is similar to the encoded one. Thus, the learned spiking neuron can respond selectively to the input set of patterns. Data clustering in the described neural network rests on this property of spiking neuron. Input pattern fires the neuron whose center is the most similar (the closest) to it, and the fired spike prevents the rest neurons to fire through the lateral inhibitory connections. This way self-learning spiking neural network performs clusters separation if classes to be detected do not overlap one another.

One can readily see that the unsupervised pattern classification procedure of the spiking neurons layer is identical with the one of self-organizing maps (Kohonen, 1995).

4. Spiking neural network learning algorithms

4.1 Winner-takes-all

The purpose of an unsupervised learning algorithm of spiking neural network is to adjust centers of spiking neurons so as to make each of them to correspond to centroid of a certain data cluster. Such learning algorithm was introduced on the basis of two learning rules, namely, 'Winner-Takes-All' rule and temporal Hebbain rule (Natschlaeger & Ruf, 1998; Gerstner et al., 1996). The first one defines which neuron should be updated, and the second one defines how it should be updated. The algorithm updates neuron centers through synaptic weights adjusting, whereas synaptic time delays always remain constant. The concept here is that significance of the given time delay can be changed by varying corresponding synaptic weight.

Each learning epoch consists of two phases. Competition, the first phase, defines a neuron-winner. Being laterally linked with inhibitory connections, spiking neurons compete to respond to the pattern. The one wins (and fires) whose center is the closest to the pattern. Following competition phase, weights adjusting takes place. The learning algorithm adjusts synaptic weights of the neuron-winner to move it closer to the input pattern. It strengthens weights of those subsynapses which contributed to the neuron-winner's firing (i.e. the subsynapses produced delayed spikes right before the neuron firing) and weakens ones which did not contribute (i.e. the delayed spikes appeared right after the neurons firing or long before it). Generally, the learning algorithm can be expressed as

$$
w_{jli}^{p}(K+1) = \begin{cases} w_{jli}^{p}(K) + \eta_w(K)L(\Delta t_{jli}^{p}), & j = \tilde{j}, \\ w_{jli}^{p}(K), & j \neq \tilde{j}, \end{cases}
\tag{7}
$$

where K is the current epoch number, $\eta_w(\bullet) > 0$ is the learning rate (while it is constant in (Natschlaeger & Ruf, 1998), it can depend on epoch number in the general case; w means 'weights'), $L(\bullet)$ is the learning function (Gerstner et al, 1996), $\tilde{j}$ is the number of neuron that has won on the current epoch, Δt_{jli}^{p} is the time delay between delayed spike $t_{li}^{[0]}(x_i(k)) + d^p$ produced by the p-th subsynapse of the li-th synapse and spiking neuron firing time $t_j^{[1]}(x(k))$:

$$
\Delta t_{jli}^{p} = t_{li}^{[0]}(x_i(k)) + d^p - t_j^{[1]}(x(k)) .
\tag{8}
$$

As a rule, the learning function has the following form (Berredo, 2005):

$$
L(\Delta t_{jli}^{p}) = (1+\beta)\exp\left(-\frac{\left(\Delta t_{jli}^{p} - \alpha\right)^2}{2(\kappa-1)}\right) - \beta ,
\tag{9}
$$

$$
\kappa = 1 - \frac{v^2}{2\ln\left(\dfrac{\beta}{1+\beta}\right)} ,
\tag{10}
$$

where $\alpha < 0$, $\beta > 0$, v are the shape parameters of the learning function $L(\bullet)$ that can be obtained empirically (Berredo, 2005; Natschlaeger & Ruf, 1998). The learning function and its shape parameters are depicted on Fig. 6. The effect of the shape parameters on results of information processing performed by spiking neural network can be found in (Meftah et al., 2008).

Upon the learning stage, center of a spiking neuron represents centroid of a certain data cluster, and spiking neural network can successfully perform unsupervised classification of the input set.

4.2 Winner-takes-more

The learning algorithm (7) updates only neuron-winner on each epoch and disregards other neurons. It seems more natural to update not only spiking neuron-winner, but also its neighbours (Bodyanskiy & Dolotov, 2009). This approach is known as 'Winner-Takes-More'

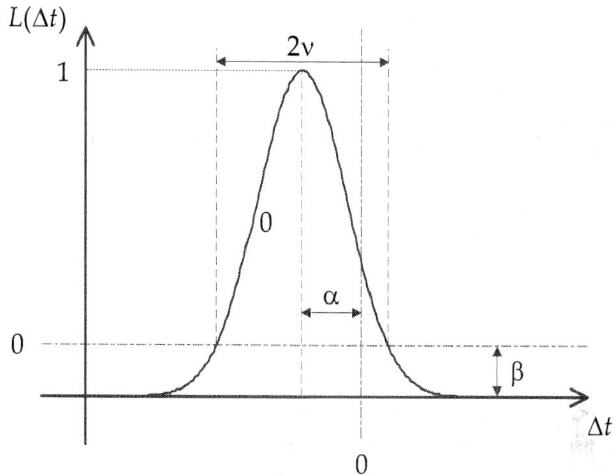

Fig. 6. Learning function $L(\bullet)$

rule. It implies that there is a cooperation phase before weights adjustment. Neuron-winner determines a local region of topological neighbourhood on each learning epoch. Within this region, the neuron-winner fires along with its neighbours, and the closer a neighbour is to the winner, the more significantly its weights are changed. The topological region is represented by the neighbourhood function $\varphi(|\Delta t_{\tilde{j}j}|)$ that depends on difference $|\Delta t_{\tilde{j}j}|$ between the neuron-winner firing time $t_{\tilde{j}}^{[1]}(x(k))$ and the neighbour firing time $t_{j}^{[1]}(x(k))$ (distance between the neurons in temporal sense) and a parameter that defines effective width of the region. As a rule, $\varphi(\bullet)$ is a kernel function that is symmetric about its maximum at the point where $\Delta t_{\tilde{j}j} = 0$. It reaches unity at that point and monotonically decreases as $\Delta t_{\tilde{j}j}$ tends to infinity. The functions that are the most frequently used as neighbourhood function are Gaussian, paraboloid, Mexican Hat, and many others (Bodyanskiy & Rudenko, 2004).

For self-learning spiking neural network, the learning algorithm based on 'Winner-Takes-More' rule can be expressed in the following form (Bodyanskiy & Dolotov, 2009)·

$$w_{jli}^{p}(K+1) = w_{jli}^{p}(K) + \eta_{w}(K)\varphi(|\Delta t_{\tilde{j}j}|)L(\Delta t_{jli}^{p}) , \tag{11}$$

where temporal distance $\Delta t_{\tilde{j}j}$ is

$$\Delta t_{\tilde{j}j} = t_{\tilde{j}}^{[1]}(x(k)) - t_{j}^{[1]}(x(k)) . \tag{12}$$

Obviously, expression (11) is a generalization of (7).

Analysis of competitive unsupervised learning convergence showed that width parameter of the neighbourhood function should decrease during synaptic weights adjustment (Cottrell & Fort, 1986). For Gaussian neighbourhood function

$$\varphi\left(\left|\Delta t_{\tilde{j}j}\right|, K\right) = \exp\left(-\frac{\left(\Delta t_{\tilde{j}j}\right)^2}{2\rho^2(K)}\right) \qquad (13)$$

width parameter ρ can be adjusted as follows (Ritter & Schulten, 1986):

$$\rho(K) = \rho(0)\exp\left(\frac{K}{\gamma}\right), \qquad (14)$$

where $\gamma > 0$ is a scalar that determines rate of neuron-winner effect on its neighbours. Noteworthily that exponential decreasing of width parameter can be achieved by applying the simpler expression instead of (14) (Bodyanskiy & Rudenko, 2004):

$$\rho(K) = \gamma\rho(K-1), 0 < \gamma < 1. \qquad (15)$$

Learning algorithm (11) requires modification of self-learning spiking neural architecture. Lateral inhibitory connections in the second hidden layer should be replaced with excitatory ones during the network learning stage in order to implement 'Winner-Takes-More' rule.

In the following sections, it will be shown that the learning algorithm based on 'Winner-Takes-More' rule is more natural than the one based on 'Winner-Takes-All' rule to learn fuzzy spiking neural network.

5. Spiking neural network as an analog-digital system

5.1 Introduction

Hardware implementations of spiking neural network demonstrated fast processing ability that made it possible to apply such systems in real-life applications where processing speed was a rather critical parameter (Maass, 1997a; Maass & Bishop, 1998; Schoenauer et al., 2000; Kraft et al., 2006). From theoretical point of view, the current research works on spiking neurons hardware implementation subject are very particular, they lack for a technically plausible description on a general ground. In this section, we consider a spiking neuron as a processing system of classical automatic control theory (Feldbaum & Butkovskiy, 1971; Dorf & Bishop, 1995; Phillips & Harbor, 2000; Goodwin et al., 2001). Spiking neuron functioning is described in terms of the Laplace transform. Having such a general description of a spiking neuron, one can derive various hardware implementations of self-learning spiking neural network for solving specific technical problems, among them realistic complex image processing. Within a scope of automatic control theory, a spike $t(x(k))$ can be represented by the Dirac delta function $\delta(t - t(x(k)))$. Its Laplace transform is

$$L\{\delta(t - t(x(k)))\} = e^{-t(x(k))s}, \qquad (16)$$

where s is the Laplace operator. Spiking neuron takes spikes on its input, performs spike–membrane potential–spike transformation, and produces spikes on its output. Obviously, it is a kind of analog-digital system that processes information in continuous-time form and transmits it in pulse-position form. This is the basic concept for designing analog-digital architecture of self-learning spiking neural network. Overall network architecture is depicted on Fig. 7 and is explained in details in the following subsections.

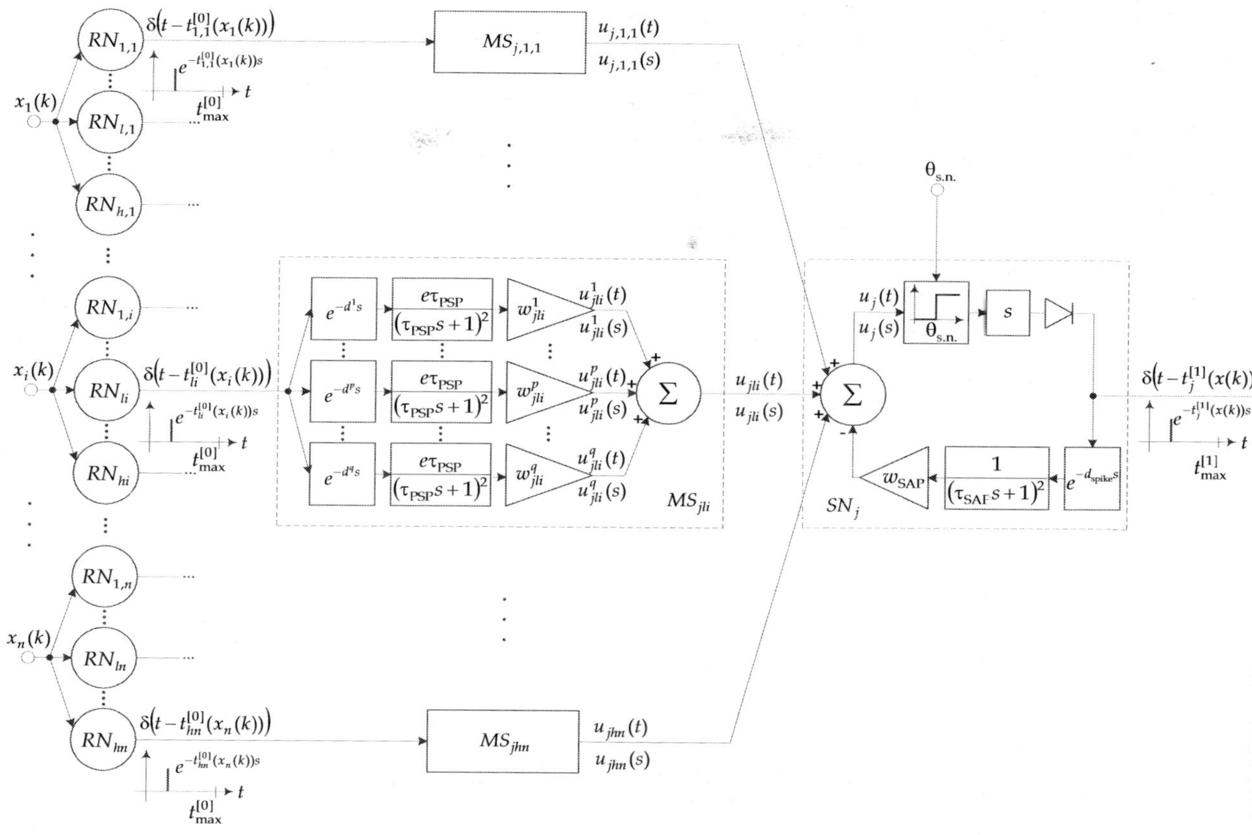

Fig. 7. Spiking neuron as a nonlinear dynamic system

5.2 Synapse as a second-order critically damped response unit

Multiple synapse MS_{jli} of a spiking neuron SN_j transforms incoming pulse-position signal $\delta\!\left(t - t_{li}^{[0]}(x_i(k))\right)$ to continuous-time signal $u_{jli}(t)$. Spike-response function (4), the basis of such transformation, has form that is similar to the one of impulse response of second-order damped response unit. Transfer function of a second-order damped response unit with unit gain factor is

$$\widetilde{G}(s) = \frac{1}{(\tau_1 s + 1)(\tau_2 s + 1)} = \frac{1}{\tau_4^2 s^2 + \tau_3 s + 1} , \tag{17}$$

where $\tau_{1,2} = \dfrac{\tau_3}{2} \pm \sqrt{\dfrac{\tau_3^2}{4} - \tau_4^2}$, $\tau_1 \geq \tau_2$, $\tau_3 \geq 2\tau_4$, and its impulse response is

$$\widetilde{\varepsilon}(t) = \frac{1}{\tau_1 - \tau_2}\left(e^{-\frac{t}{\tau_1}} - e^{-\frac{t}{\tau_2}}\right). \tag{18}$$

Putting $\tau_1 = \tau_2 = \tau_{PSP}$ (that corresponds to a second-order critically damped response unit) and applying l'Hôpital's rule, one can obtain

$$\widetilde{\varepsilon}(t) = \frac{t}{\tau_{PSP}^2} e^{-\frac{t}{\tau_{PSP}}} . \tag{19}$$

Comparing spike-response function (4) with the impulse response (19) leads us to the following relationship:

$$\varepsilon(t) = e\tau_{PSP}\widetilde{\varepsilon}(t) . \tag{20}$$

Thus, transfer function of the second-order critically damped response unit whose impulse response corresponds to a spike-response function is

$$G_{SRF}(s) = \frac{e\tau_{PSP}}{\left(\tau_{PSP}s + 1\right)^2} , \tag{21}$$

where SRF means 'spike-response function'.

Now, we can design multiple synapse in terms of the Laplace transform (Bodyanskiy et al., 2009). As illustrated on Fig. 7, multiple synapse MS_{jli} is a dynamic system that consists of a set of subsynapses that are connected in parallel. Each subsynapse is formed by a group of time delay, second-order critically damped response unit, and gain. As a response to incoming spike $\delta\!\left(t - t_{li}^{[0]}(x_i(k))\right)$, the subsynapse produces delayed weighted postsynaptic potential $u_{jli}^p(s)$, and the multiple synapse produces total postsynaptic potential $u_{jli}(s)$ that arrives to spiking neuron soma.

Taking into account (21), transfer function of the p-th subsynapse of MS_{jli} takes the following form:

$$U_{jli}^p(s) = w_{jli}^p e^{-d^p s} G_{SRF}(s) = \frac{\tau_{PSP} w_{jli}^p e^{1 - d^p s}}{\left(\tau_{PSP}s + 1\right)^2} , \tag{22}$$

and its response to a spike $\delta\!\left(t - t_{li}^{[0]}(x_i(k))\right)$ is

$$u_{jli}^p(s) = e^{-t_{li}^{[0]}(x_i(k))s} U_{jli}^p(s) = \frac{\tau_{PSP} w_{jli}^p e^{1-\left(t_{li}^{[0]}(x_i(k))+d^p\right)s}}{\left(\tau_{PSP}s+1\right)^2} . \tag{23}$$

So finally, considering transfer function of multiple synapse MS_{jli}

$$U_{jli}(s) = \sum_{p=1}^{q} U_{jli}^p(s) = \sum_{p=1}^{q} \frac{\tau_{PSP} w_{jli}^p e^{1-d^p s}}{\left(\tau_{PSP}s+1\right)^2} , \tag{24}$$

the Laplace transform of the multiple synapse output can be expressed in the following form:

$$u_{jli}(s) = e^{-t_{li}^{[0]}(x_i(k))s} U_{jli}(s) = \sum_{p=1}^{q} \frac{\tau_{PSP} w_{jli}^p e^{1-\left(t_{li}^{[0]}(x_i(k))+d^p\right)s}}{\left(\tau_{PSP}s+1\right)^2} . \tag{25}$$

Here it is worth to note that since it is impossible to use δ-function in practice (Phillips & Harbor, 2000), it is convenient to model it with impulse of a triangular form (Feldbaum & Butkovskiy, 1971) as shown on Fig. 8. Such impulse is similar to δ-function under the following condition

$$\lim_{\Delta \to 0} a(t, \Delta) = \delta(t) . \tag{26}$$

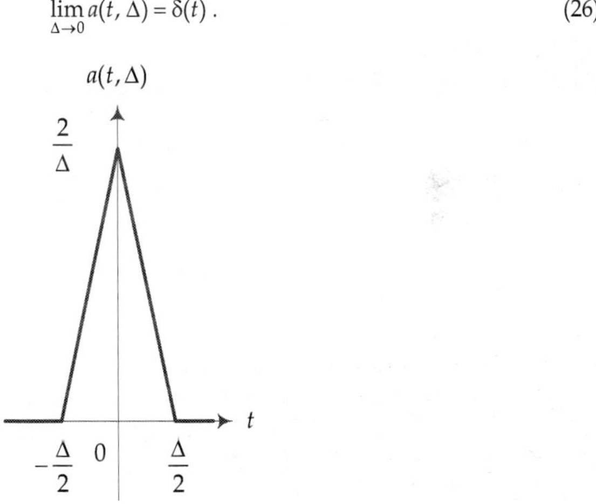

Fig. 8. Triangular impulse $a(t, \Delta)$

In this case, numerator of (21) should be revised the way to take into account finite peak of $a(t, \Delta)$ (in contrast to the one of the Dirac delta function).

5.3 Soma as a threshold detection unit

Spiking neuron soma performs transformation that is opposite to one of the synapse. It takes continuous-time signals $u_{jli}(t)$ and produces pulse-position signal $\delta\!\left(t - t_j^{[1]}(x(k))\right)$. In doing so, soma responds each time membrane potential reaches a certain threshold value. In other words, spiking neuron soma acts as a threshold detection system and consequently it can be designed on the base of relay control systems concept (Tsypkin, 1984). In (Bodyanskiy et al., 2009), mechanisms of threshold detection behaviour and firing process were described. Here we extend this approach to capture refractoriness of spiking neuron.

Threshold detection behaviour of a neuron soma can be modelled by an element relay with dead zone $\theta_{s.n.}$ that is defined by the nonlinear function

$$\Phi_{\text{relay}}\left(u_j(t), \theta_{s.n.}\right) = \frac{\text{sign}\left(u_j(t) - \theta_{s.n.}\right) + 1}{2} , \tag{27}$$

where sign $(\bullet)$ is the signum function. Soma firing can be described by a derivative unit that is connected with the element relay in series and produces a spike each time the relay switches. In order to avoid a negative spike that appears as a response to the relay resetting, a conventional diode is added next to the derivative unit. The diode is defined by the following function:

$$\Phi_{\text{diode}}\left(\delta\left(t - t^{[1]}_{\text{relay}}\right)\right) = \delta\left(t - t^{[1]}_{\text{relay}}\right) H\left(\delta\left(t - t^{[1]}_{\text{relay}}\right)\right), \tag{28}$$

where $t^{[1]}_{\text{relay}}$ is a spike produced by the derivative unit upon the relay switching.

Now we can define the Laplace transform of an outgoing spike $t^{[1]}_j(x(k))$, namely,

$$L\left\{\delta\left(t - t^{[1]}_j(x(k))\right)\right\} = e^{-t^{[1]}_j(x(k))s} = L\left\{\Phi_{\text{diode}}\left(sL\left\{\Phi_{\text{relay}}\left(u_j(t), \theta_{s.n.}\right)\right\}\right)\right\}. \tag{29}$$

As it was mentioned above, the leaky integrate-and-fire model disregards the neuron refractoriness. Anyway, the refractory period is implemented in the layer of spiking neurons indirectly. The point is that a spiking neuron cannot produce another spike after firing and until the end of the simulation interval since the input pattern is provided only once within the interval. In the analog-digital architecture of spiking neuron, the refractoriness can be modelled by a feedback circuit. As shown on Fig. 7, it is a group of a time delay, a second-order critically damped response unit, and a gain that are connected in series. The time delay defines duration of a spike generation period d_{spike} (usually, $d_{\text{spike}} \to 0$). The second-order critically damped response unit defines a spike after-potential. Generally, spike after-potential can be represented by a second-order damped response unit, but for the sake of simplicity, we use critically damped response unit as it can be defined by one parameter only, namely, τ_{SAP} (SAP means here 'spike after-potential'). This parameter controls duration of the refractory period. Finally, the gain unit sets amplitude of the spike after-potential w_{SAP}. Obviously, w_{SAP} should be much greater than any synaptic weight.

Thus, transfer function of the feedback circuit is

$$G_{\text{F.B.}}(s) = \frac{w_{\text{SAP}} e^{-d_{\text{spike}}s}}{\left(\tau_{\text{SAP}}s + 1\right)^2} , \tag{30}$$

where F.B. means 'feedback circuit', and transfer function of the soma is

$$G_{\text{soma}}(s) = \frac{G_{\text{F.F.}}}{1 + G_{\text{F.F.}} G_{\text{F.B.}}} , \tag{31}$$

where $G_{F.F.}$ is defined by (29) (F.F. means 'feed-forward circuit').

It is easily seen that the functioning of spiking neuron analog-digital architecture introduced above is similar to the spike-response model.

6. Self-learning hybrid systems based on spiking neural network

6.1 Fuzzy receptive neurons

A common peculiarity of artificial neural networks is that they store dependence of system model outputs on its inputs in the form of 'black box'. Instead, data processing methods based on fuzzy logic allow of system model designing and storing in analytical form that can be substantially interpreted in a relatively simple way. This fact arises interest in designing of hybrid systems that can combine spiking neural networks computational capabilities with capability of fuzzy logic methods to conveniently describe input-output relationships of the system being modelled. The present section shows how receptive neuron layers, a part of spiking neural network, can be 'fuzzified'.

One can readily see that the layer of receptive neuron pools is identical to a fuzzification layer of neuro-fuzzy systems like Takagi-Sugeno-Kang networks, ANFIS, etc. (Jang et al., 1997). Considering activation function $\psi_{li}(x_i(k))$ as a membership function, the receptive neurons layer can be treated as the one that transforms input data set to a fuzzy set that is defined by values of activation-membership function $\psi_{li}(x_i(k))$ and is expressed over time domain in form of firing times $t_{li}^{[0]}(x_i(k))$ (Bodyanskiy et al., 2008a). In fact, each pool of receptive neurons performs zero order Takagi-Sugeno fuzzy inference (Jang et al., 1997)

$$\text{IF } x_i(k) \text{ IS } X_{li} \text{ THEN OUTPUT IS } t_{li}^{[0]}, \tag{32}$$

where X_{li} is the fuzzy set with membership function $\psi_{li}(x_i(k))$. Thus, one can interpret a receptive neurons pool as a certain linguistic variable and each receptive neuron (more precisely, fuzzy receptive neuron) within the pool – as a linguistic term with membership function $\psi_{li}(x_i(k))$ (Fig. 9). This way, having any a priori knowledge of data structure, it is possible beforehand to adjust activation functions of the first layer neurons to fit them and thus, to get better clustering results.

6.2 Fuzzy clustering

Conventional approach of data clustering implies that each pattern $x(k)$ can belong to one cluster only. It is more natural to consider that a pattern can belong to a several clusters with different membership levels. This case is the subject matter of fuzzy cluster analysis that is heading in several directions. Among them, algorithms based on objective function are the most mathematically rigorous (Bezdek, 1981). Such algorithms solve data processing tasks by optimizing a certain preset cluster quality criterion.

One of the commonly used cluster quality criteria can be stated as follows:

$$E(\mu_j(x(k)), v_j) = \sum_{k=1}^{N} \sum_{j=1}^{m} \mu_j^\zeta(x(k)) \left\| x(k) - v_j \right\|_A^2 , \tag{33}$$

where $\mu_j(x(k)) \in [0,1]$ is the membership level of the input pattern $x(k)$ to the j-th cluster, v_j is the center of the j-th cluster, $\zeta \geq 0$ is the fuzzifier that determines boundary between

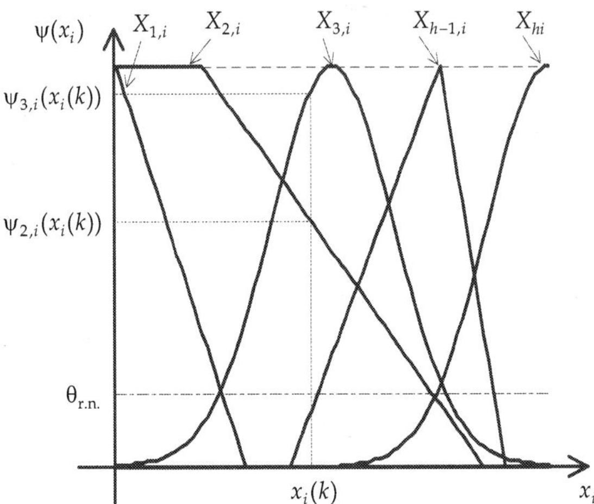

Fig. 9. Terms of linguistic variable for the i-th input. Membership functions are adjusted to represent a priori knowledge of input data structure. Incoming signal $x_i(k)$ fires fuzzy receptive neurons $FRN_{2,i}$ and $FRN_{3,i}$

clusters and controls the amount of fuzziness in the final partition, $\left\| x(k) - v_j \right\|_A$ is the distance between $x(k)$ and v_j in a certain metric, A is a norm matrix that defines distance metric. By applying the method of indefinite Lagrange multipliers under restrictions

$$\sum_{j=1}^{m} \mu_j\big(x(k)\big) = 1, \ k = \overline{1,N} , \tag{34}$$

$$0 < \sum_{k=1}^{N} \mu_j\big(x(k)\big) < N, \ j = \overline{1,m} , \tag{35}$$

minimization of (33) leads us to the following solution:

$$\mu_j\big(x(k)\big) = \frac{\left(\left\| x(k) - v_j \right\|_A^2 \right)^{\frac{1}{1-\zeta}}}{\sum_{\iota=1}^{m} \left(\left\| x(k) - v_\iota \right\|_A^2 \right)^{\frac{1}{1-\zeta}}} , \tag{36}$$

$$v_j = \frac{\sum_{k=1}^{N} \mu_j^{\zeta}\big(x(k)\big) x(k)}{\sum_{k=1}^{N} \mu_j^{\zeta}\big(x(k)\big)} \tag{37}$$

that originates the methods of so-called fuzzy probabilistic clustering (Bezdek et al., 2005). In the case when norm matrix A is the identity matrix and $\zeta = 1$, equations (36), (37) present hard c-means algorithm, and for $\zeta = 2$, they are conventional fuzzy c-means algorithm.

Efficiency of fuzzy probabilistic clustering decreases in the presence of noise. Algorithm (36), (37) produces unnaturally high degree of membership for outliers that are equidistant from clusters centers. This drawback is avoided by applying fuzzy possibilistic approach that is based on the following objective function:

$$E(\mu_j(x(k)), v_j) = \sum_{k=1}^{N}\sum_{j=1}^{m}\mu_j^{\zeta}(x(k))\|x(k)-v_j\|_A^2 + \sum_{j=1}^{m}\lambda_j\sum_{k=1}^{N}\left(1-\mu_j(x(k))\right)^{\zeta},\tag{38}$$

where $\lambda_j > 0$ is the scalar parameter that defines the distance at which membership level takes the value 0.5, i.e. if $\|x(k)-v_j\|_A^2 = \lambda_j$, then $\mu_j(x(k))=0.5$. Minimization of (38) with respect to $\mu_j(x(k))$, v_j, and λ_j yields the following solution:

$$\mu_j(k) = \left(1+\left(\frac{\|x(k)-v_j\|_A^2}{\lambda_j}\right)^{\frac{1}{\zeta-1}}\right)^{-1},\tag{39}$$

$$v_j = \frac{\sum_{k=1}^{N}\mu_j^{\zeta}(k)x(k)}{\sum_{k=1}^{N}\mu_j^{\zeta}(k)},\tag{40}$$

$$\lambda_j = \frac{\sum_{k=1}^{N}\mu_j^{\zeta}(k)\|x(k)-v_j\|_A^2}{\sum_{k=1}^{N}\mu_j^{\zeta}(k)}\tag{41}$$

that gives conventional possibilistic c-means algorithm if $\zeta = 2$ and A is the identity matrix (Bezdek et al., 2005).

After spiking neural network learning has been done, center $c_j^{[1]}$ of a spiking neuron SN_j represents center v_j of a certain data cluster, and its firing time $t_j^{[1]}(x(k))$ reflects distance $\|x(k)-v_j\|_A$ in temporal sense (Natschlaeger & Ruf, 1998; Bohte et al., 2002). This notion allows us of using self-learning spiking neural network output in fuzzy clustering algorithms described above. In order to implement fuzzy clustering on the base of the spiking neural network, its architecture is modified in the following way: lateral connections in the second hidden layer are disabled, and output fuzzy clustering layer is added next to spiking neuron layer. Such modification is applied to the spiking neural network on data clustering stage only. Output fuzzy clustering layer receives information on the distances of input patter to centers of all spiking neurons and produces fuzzy partition using either probabilistic approach (36), (37) as follows (Bodyanskiy & Dolotov, 2008a-b):

$$\mu_j(x(k)) = \frac{\left(t_j^{[1]}(x(k))\right)^{\frac{2}{1-\zeta}}}{\sum_{i=1}^{m}\left(t_i^{[1]}(x(k))\right)^{\frac{2}{1-\zeta}}},\tag{42}$$

or possibilistic approach (39)-(41) as follows (Bodyanskiy et al., 2008b):

$$\mu_j(x(k)) = \left(1 + \left(\frac{\left(t_j^{[1]}(x(k)) \right)^2}{\lambda_j} \right)^{\frac{1}{\zeta - 1}} \right)^{-1}, \tag{43}$$

$$\lambda_j = \frac{\sum_{k=1}^{N} \mu_j^{\zeta} \left(t_j^{[1]}(x(k)) \right)^2}{\sum_{k=1}^{N} \mu_j^{\zeta}(x(k))}. \tag{44}$$

Obviously, the learning algorithm (11) is more natural here then (7) since response of each spiking neuron within the second hidden layer matters for producing fuzzy partition by the output layer.

The advantage of fuzzy clustering based on self-learning spiking neural network is that it is not required to calculate centers of data clusters according to (37) or (40) as the network finds them itself during learning.

7. Simulation experiment

The proposed self-learning fuzzy spiking neural network was tested on the coloured Lenna image shown on Fig. 10a (USC-SIPI Image Database). The image is a standard benchmark that is widely used in image processing. The image has 3 layers (RGB) with spatial dimensions 512×512 so the set to process is formed of 262144 three-dimensional data points (n=3). The purpose was to separate classes by colour of pixels avoiding their spatial location. Obviously, some classes overlap one another as three RGB-components define a plenty of colours, and the boundary between colours is indistinct. There were considered 8 classes to be separated on the image (m=8). A certain grade of grey was assigned to each of the eight classes to visualize the obtained results. 30% of the image pixels were randomly selected to generate a training set (Fig. 10b).

Self-leaning fuzzy spiking neural network settings were set as follows (the most settings were taken from (Berredo, 2005)): time step is 0.1 sec, h=6, receptive neuron type – crisp, $\theta_{r.n.} = 0.1$, $t_{max}^{[0]} = 20$ sec, $\tau_{PSP} = 3$ sec, $q = 16$, $d^1 = 0$, $d^{16} = 15$, minimum value of a synaptic weight is 0, maximum value is 1, simulation interval length is 30 sec, $\eta_w = 0.35$, $\alpha = -2.3$ sec, $\beta = 0.2$, $v = 5$ sec, $\theta_{s.n.}(0) = 9$, $\theta_{s.n.}(K+1) = \theta_{s.n.}(K) + \dfrac{0.3 \cdot \theta_{s.n.}(K)}{K_{max}}$, $K_{max} = 3$, neighbourhood function – Gaussian, $\rho(0) = 6$, $\gamma = 0.5$, calculating $\rho(K)$ – expression (15), fuzzy clustering – probabilistic, $\zeta = 2$, defuzzification method – the largest value. Results of image processing produced by the spiking neural network on the 1st and the 3rd epochs are shown on Fig. 10c and Fig. 10d, respectively.

Fuzzy c-means algorithm was also trained over the same testing set ($\zeta = 2$, defuzzification method – the largest value). Results of image processing produced by the algorithm on the 3rd and the 30th epochs are shown on Fig. 10e and Fig. 10f, respectively.

Thus, self-learning fuzzy spiking neural network requires a number of epochs that is in an order less then conventional fuzzy c-means algorithm requires.

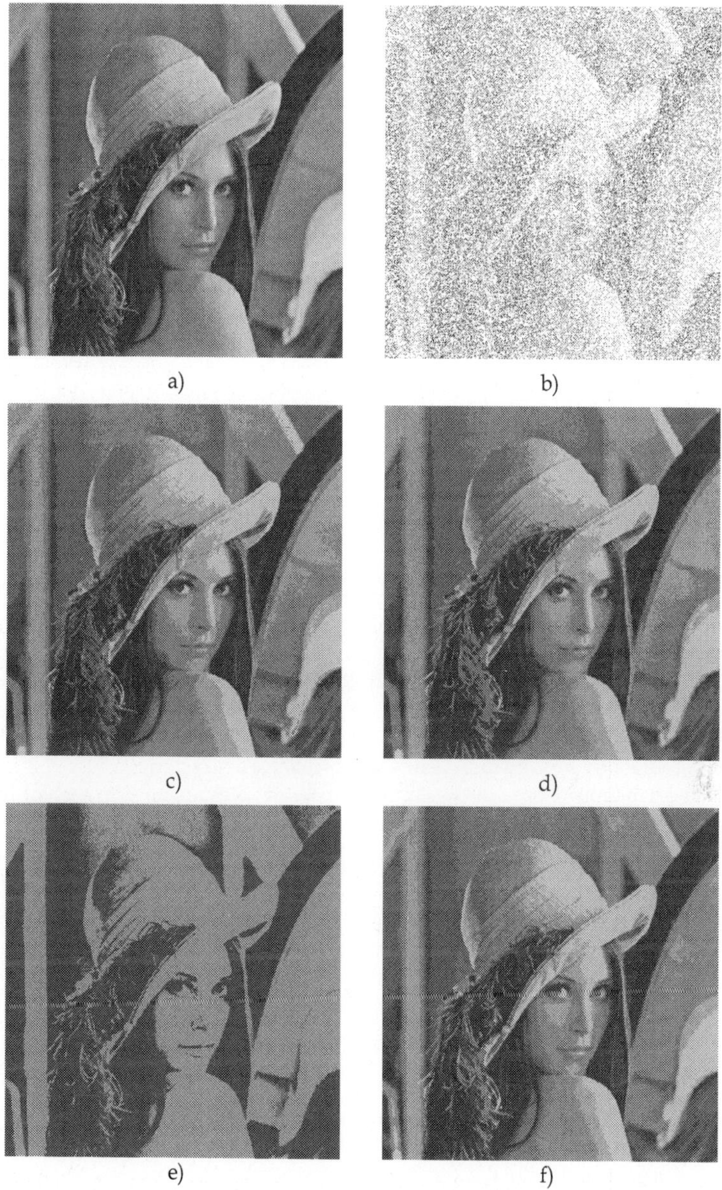

Fig. 10. The Lenna image processing: a) Original image; b) Training set (30% of the original image); c) The 1st epoch of self-learning fuzzy spiking neural network learning; d) The 3rd epoch of self-learning fuzzy spiking neural network learning; e) The 3rd epoch of fuzzy c-means learning; f) The 30th epoch of fuzzy c-means learning

8. Conclusion

Spiking neural networks are more realistic models of real neuronal systems than artificial neural networks of the previous generations. Nevertheless, they can be described, as it was shown in earlier sections, in a strict technically plausible way based on the Laplace transform. Spiking neural network designed in terms of transfer functions is an analog-digital nonlinear dynamic system that conveys and processes information both in pulse-position and continuous-time forms. Such precise formal description of spiking neural network architecture and functioning provides researchers and engineers with a framework to construct hardware implementations of various spiking neural networks for image processing of different levels of complexity.

Networks of spiking neurons introduced new, biologically more plausible essence of information processing and gave rise to a new, computationally more powerful generation of computational intelligence hybrid systems. In the present chapter, self-learning fuzzy spiking neural network that combined spiking neural network and fuzzy probabilistic and fuzzy possibilistic clustering algorithms was described as an example of such hybrid systems. It was shown that using of hybrid systems constructed on a spiking neural network basis made it possible to reduce number of learning epochs as compared to conventional fuzzy clustering algorithms. In addition, the way to 'fuzzify' spiking neural network architecture was demonstrated with consideration of a pool of receptive neurons to be a linguistic variable.

Although the temporal Hebian learning algorithm of spiking neural network is biologically plausible, even more realistic learning algorithm based on 'Winner-Takes-More' rule was proposed as its improvement.

Both theoretical innovations and simulation experiment presented in this chapter confirmed that self-learning spiking neural network and hybrid systems developed on its basis are powerful and efficient advanced tool of computational intelligence for data clustering and, particularly, for image processing.

9. References

Berredo, R.C.de (2005). *A review of spiking neuron models and applications*, M. Sc. Dissertation, Pontifical Catholic University of Minas Gerais, Belo Horizonte, http://www.loria.fr/~falex/pub/Teaching/disserta.pdf.

Bezdek, J.C. (1981). *Pattern Recognition with Fuzzy Objective Function Algorithms*, Plenum Press, ISBN 0-306-40671-3, New York.

Bezdek, J.C.; Keller, J.; Krishnapuram, R. & Pal, N.R. (2005). *Fuzzy Models and Algorithms for Pattern Recognition and Image Processing*, Springer, ISBN 0-387-24515-4, New York.

Bodyanskiy, Ye. & Rudenko, O. (2004). *Artificial Neural Networks: Architectures, Learning, Applications*, Teletekh, ISBN 966-95416-2-2, Kharkiv (in Russian).

Bodyanskiy, Ye. & Dolotov, A. (2008a). Image processing using self-learning fuzzy spiking neural network in the presence of overlapping classes, *Proceedings of the 11th International Biennial Baltic Electronics Conference "BEC 2008"*, pp. 213-216, ISBN 978-1-4244-2060-5, Tallinn/Laulasmaa, Estonia, October 2008, Tallinn University of Technology, Tallinn.

Bodyanskiy, Ye. & Dolotov, A. (2008b). A self-learning spiking neural network for fuzzy clustering task, *Scientific Proceedings of Riga Technical University, Computer Science*

Series: Information Technology and Management Science, Vol. 36, pp. 27-33, ISSN 1407-7493.

Bodyanskiy, Ye. & Dolotov, A. (2009). Hebbian learning of fuzzy spiking neural network based on 'Winner-Takes-More' rule, *Proceedings of the 11th International Conference on Science and Technology "System Analysis and Information Technologies",* p. 271, ISBN 978-966-2153-27-9, Kyiv, May 2009, ESC "IASA" NTUU "KPI", Kyiv.

Bodyanskiy, Ye., Dolotov, A. & Pliss, I. (2008a). Fuzzy receptive neurons using in self-learning spiking neural network, *Proceedings of International Scientific and Technical Conference "Automation: Problems, Ideas, Solutions",* pp. 12-14, ISBN 978-966-2960-32-7, Sevastopil, September 2008, Publishing House of SevNTU, Sevastopil (in Russian).

Bodyanskiy, Ye.; Dolotov, A.; Pliss, I. & Viktorov, Ye. (2008b). Fuzzy possibilistic clustering using self-learning spiking neural network, *Wissenschaftliche Berichte der Hochschule Zittau/Goerlitz,* Vol. 100, pp. 53-60, ISBN 3-9808089-9-9.

Bodyanskiy, Ye.; Dolotov, A. & Pliss, I. (2009). Self-learning fuzzy spiking neural network as a nonlinear pulse-position threshold detection dynamic system based on second-order critically damped response units, In: *International Book Series "Information Science and Computing": No. 9, Intelligent Processing,* K. Markov, P. Stanchev, K. Ivanova, I. Mitov, (Eds.), pp.63-70, Institute of Information Theories and Applications FOI ITHEA, ISSN 1313-0455, Sofia.

Bohte, S.M.; Kok, J.N. & La Poutre, H. (2002). Unsupervised clustering with spiking neurons by sparse temporal coding and multi-layer RBF networks, *IEEE Transactions on Neural Networks,* Vol. 13, pp.426-435, ISSN 1045-9227.

Cottrell, M. & Fort, J.C. (1986). A stochastic model of retinotopy: a self-organizing process, *Biological Cybernetics,* Vol. 53, No. 6, pp. 405-411, ISSN 0340-1200.

Cybenko, G. (1989). Approximation by superposition of a sigmoidal function, *Mathematics of Control, Signals, and Systems,* Vol. 2, pp.303-314, ISSN 0932-4194.

Dayan, P. & Abbott, L.F. (2001). *Theoretical Neuroscience: Computational and Mathematical Modeling of Neural Systems,* MIT Press, ISBN 0-262-04199-5, Cambridge.

Dorf, R.C. & Bishop, R.H. (1995). *Modern Control Systems,* Addison-Wesley, ISBN 0-201-84559-8, Reading.

Feldbaum, A.A. & Butkovskiy, A.G. (1971). *Methods of Automatic Control Theory,* Nauka, Moscow (in Russian).

Gerstner, W.; Kempter, R.; van Hemmen, J.L. & Wagner, H. (1996). A neuronal learning rule for sub-millisecond temporal coding, *Nature,* Vol. 383, pp.76-78, ISSN 0028-0836.

Gerstner, W. & Kistler, W.M. (2002). *Spiking Neuron Models: Single Neurons, Populations, Plasticity,* Cambridge University Press, ISBN 0-521-81384-0, Cambridge.

Goodwin, G.C.; Graebe, S.F. & Salgado, M.E. (2001). *Control System Design,* Prentice Hall, ISBN 0-13-958653-9, Upper Saddle Reiver.

Haykin, S. (1999). *Neural Networks: A Comprehensive Foundation,* Prentice Hall, ISBN 0-13-273350-1, Upper Saddle River.

Hopfield, J.J. (1995). Pattern recognition computation using action potential timing for stimulus representation, *Nature,* Vol. 376, pp. 33-36, ISSN 0028-0836.

Hornik, K.; Stinchombe, M. & White, H. (1989). Multilayer feedforward networks are universal approximators, *Neural Networks,* Vol. 2, No. 5, pp. 359-366, ISSN 0893-6080.

Jang, J.-Sh.R.; Sun, Ch.-T. & Mizutani, E. (1997). *Neuro-Fuzzy and Soft Computing: A Computational Approach to Learning and Machine Intelligence,* Prentice Hall, ISBN 0-13-261066-3, Upper Saddle River.

Kohonen, T. (1995). *Self-Organizing Maps,* Springer, ISBN 3-540-58600-8, Berlin.

Kraft, M; Kasinski, A. & Ponulak, F. (2006). Design of the spiking neuron having learning capabilities based on FPGA circuits, *Proceedings of the 3rd IFAC Workshop on Discrete-Event System Design "DESDes'06",* pp. 301-306, ISBN 83-7481-035-1, Rydzyna, September 2006, University of Zielona Gora Press, Zielona Gora.

Lindblad, T. & Kinser, J.M. (2005). *Image Processing Using Pulse-Coupled Neural Networks,* Springer, ISBN 3-540-28293-9, Berlin.

Maass, W. (1997a). Fast sigmoidal networks via spiking neurons, *Neural Computation,* Vol. 9, No. 2, pp. 279-304, ISSN 0899-7667.

Maass, W. (1997b). Networks of spiking neurons: the third generation of neural network models, *Neural Networks,* Vol. 10, No. 9, pp. 1659-1671, ISSN 0893-6080.

Maass, W. & Bishop, C.M. (1998). *Pulsed Neural Networks,* MIT Press, ISBN 0-262-13350-4, Cambridge.

Malsburg, C. von der (1994). The correlation theory of brain function, In: *Models of Neural Networks II: Temporal Aspects of Coding and Information Processing in Biological Systems,* E. Domany, J.L. van Hemmen, K. Schulten, (Eds.), pp. 95-119, Springer-Verlag, ISBN: 978-0-387-94362-6, New York.

McCulloch, W.S. & Pitts, W.A. (1943). A logical calculus of ideas immanent in nervous activity, *Bulletin of Mathematical Biophysics,* Vol. 5, pp. 115-133, ISSN 0092-8240.

Meftah, B.; Benyettou, A.; Lezoray, O. & QingXiang, W. (2008). Image clustering with spiking neuron network, *Proceedings of the International Joint Conference on Neural Networks "IJCNN 2008", part of the IEEE World Congress on Computational Intelligence "WCCI 2008",* pp. 681-685, ISBN 978-1-4244-1821-3, Hong Kong, June 2008, IEEE Press, Piscataway.

Minsky, M.L. & Papert, S.A. (1969). *Perceptrons: An Introduction to Computational Geometry,* MIT Press, ISBN 0-262-63022-2, Cambridge.

Natschlaeger, T. & Ruf, B. (1998). Spatial and temporal patterns analysis via spiking neurons, *Network: Computation in Neural Systems,* Vol. 9, No. 3, pp. 319-332, ISSN 1361-6536.

Phillips, C.L. & Harbor, R.D. (2000). *Feedback Control Systems,* Prentice Hall, ISBN 0-13-949090-6, Upper Saddle River.

Pikovsky, A.; Rosenblum, M. & Kurths, J. (2001). *Synchronization: A Universal Concept in Nonlinear Sciences,* Cambridge University Press, ISBN 0-521-59285-2, Cambridge.

Ritter, H. & Schulten, K. (1986). On the stationary state of Kohonen's self-organizing sensory mapping, *Biological Cybernetics,* Vol. 54, No. 2, pp. 99-106, ISSN 0340-1200.

Sato-Ilic, M. & Jain, L.C. (2006). *Innovations in Fuzzy Clustering: Theory and Applications,* Springer, ISBN 978-3-540-34356-1, Berlin.

Scott, A. (2002). *Neuroscience: A Mathematical Primer,* Springer, ISBN 0-387-95403-1, New York.

Schoenauer, T.; Atasoy, S.; Mehrtash, N. & Klar, H. (2000). Simulation of a digital neuro-chip for spiking neural networks, *Proceedings of the IEEE-INNS-ENNS International Joint Conference on Neural Network "IJCNN 2000", Vol. 4,* pp. 490-495, ISBN 0-7695-0619-4, Como, July 2000, IEEE Computer Society, Los Alamitos.

Tsypkin, Ya.Z. (1984). *Relay Control Systems,* Cambridge University Press, ISBN 0-521-24390-4, Cambridge.

USC-SIPI Image Database, the. Lenna, 4.2.04, *University of Southern California,* Signal & Image Processing Institute, Electrical Engineering Department, http://sipi.usc.edu/database/database.cgi?volume=misc&image=12.

## 21

Multichannel and Multispectral Image Restoration Employing Fuzzy Theory and Directional Techniques

Alberto Rosales and Volodymyr Ponomaryov
National Polytechnic Institute of México
México D.F.

1. Introduction

Satellite, Radar, Medical, High Definition Television, Virtual Reality, Electron Microscopy, etc. are some of the multispectral and multichannel image processing applications that need the restoration and denoising procedures, all these applications are part of a general image processing system scheme. All these images usually are corrupted by noise due to sensors influence, during transmission of the signals, or noise produced by environmental phenomena; these types of noise can be modelled as impulse noise, Gaussian noise, multiplicative (speckle) noise, among other. As a consequence, the application of image pre-processing (denoising) efficient schemes is a principal part in any computer vision application and includes reducing image noise without degrading its quality, edge and small fine details preservation, as well as colour properties.

The main objective of present work is to expose the justified novel approaches in restoration in denoising multichannel and multispectral images that can be used in mentioned applications. There exist in literature a lot of algorithms that process two dimensional (2D) images using fuzzy and vectorial techniques (Franke et al. (2000); Russo & Ramponi (1996); Schulte & De Witte & Nachtegael et al. (2007); Shaomin & Lucke (1994); Schulte & De Witte & Kerre (2007); Nie & Barner (2006); Morillas et al. (2006); Schulte & Morillas et al. (2007); Morillas et al. (2007; 2008); Camarena et al. (2008); Morillas et al. (2008; 2005); Ma et al. (2007); Amer & Schroder (1996)). The first approach presented above works in impulsive denoising scenario in 2D colour images. This filter uses fuzzy and directional robust technics to estimate noise presence in the sample to be processed in a local manner, employing fuzzy rules, the algorithm is capable to be adapted depending of quantity of noise detected agree to fuzzy-directional values computed under these fuzzy rules.

We compare the proposed 2D framework (*FCF – 2D*) with recently presented 2D *INR* filter based on fuzzy logic (Schulte & Morillas et al., 2007), this algorithm detects the noise and preserves the fine details in the multichannel image. There are other 2D algorithms that are also implemented and used in this work as comparative ones: *AMNF*, *AMNF*2 (Adaptive Multichannel Filters)(Plataniotis & Androutsos et al. (1997); Plataniotis & Venetsanopoulos (2000)); *AMNIF* (Adaptive Multichannel Filter using Influence Functions) (Ponomaryov & Gallegos et al. (2005); Ponomaryov et al. (2005)); *GVDF* (Generalized Vector Directional Filter) (Trahanias & Venetsanopoulos, 1996); *CWVDF* (Centered Weighted Vector

Directional Filters) (Lukac et al., 2004); and finally, *VMF_FAS* (Vector Median Filter Fast Adaptive Similarity) (Smolka et al., 2003). All these techniques described in the literature demonstrate the better results among a lot of other existed.

Most of mentioned above 2D techniques present good results in details preservation and noise suppression but they employ only one frame of a video sequence and principally can not use temporal information to distinguish noise or motion present in images and suppress the noise in a more effectively way, as well as preserve the fine details and chromaticity properties. This drawback can be efficiently solved applying the three dimensional (3D) algorithms.

It is known that the principal difference between noise suppression in still images and video sequences, where information from previous and future frames may also be available, consists of finding the efficient use of several neighbour frames during processing, taking into account a possible motion between frames. In this chapter, a novel scheme to characterize the difference between pixels is proposed introducing gradients that are connected with pixel angular directions, and additionally, robust directional processing techniques presented in (Ponomaryov, 2007) (Ponomaryov & Gallegos et al., 2006). The gathering of such two methods realizes suppression of a noise, as well as preservation of fine image details on base on designed fuzzy rules and the membership degree of motion in a 3D sliding-window. Important advantage of current filtering framework consists of using only two frames (past and present) reducing the processing requirements. We also realize the adaptation of several 2D algorithms in filtering of 3D video data: *MF 3F, VGVDF* (Trahanias & Venetsanopoulos, 1996), *VVMF* and *VVDKNNVMF* (Ponomaryov, 2007). Additionally, we have implemented the *VKNNF, VATM* (Zlokolica et al., 2006), and *VAVDATM* filters (Ponomaryov, 2007).

The video denoising can be realized in two forms: during temporal processing, or in spatio-temporal processing scheme (Zlokolica et al., 2005; Zlokolica et al., 2006), where additional 3D characteristics of a video sequence (motion and noise estimation) are researched and developed.

Fuzzy Logic techniques permits to realize 3D algorithms (Saeidi et al., 2006), assigning the adapted fuzzy weights for a mean weighted filter in video sequence denoising, or via the fuzzy gradient values on base the fuzzy rules and membership functions. Another algorithm (Zlokolica et al., 2006) applied in video sequences realizes the motion estimation employing a fuzzy logic scheme based on the gradients, which exploit only pixel magnitudes, and a spatiotemporal algorithm for noise suppression.

Many difficulties are met in image processing because the data, such as, distinction among edges, fine details, movements, noise, this yields a vague and diffuse knowledge in nature. Fuzzy set theory and fuzzy logic provides powerful tools to represent and process human knowledge in form of fuzzy *IF – THEN* rules. Whether a pixel is corrupted, or discriminating, or if a fine detail is present in a scene, are the examples where fuzzy approaches can be efficiently used (Schulte & Huysmans et al., 2006).

The fuzzy-directional proposed methodologies works in a 3D environment in a video colour denoising scheme. These algorithms make use of spatio-temporal information to detect motion and noise presence to take advantage of 2D methodologies working in 3D environment. One of the methodologies is used to smooth Gaussian noise (Fuzzy Directional Adaptive Recursive Temporal Filter for Gaussian Noise *FDARTF_G*) preserving fine details, edges and chromaticity properties, where the advantage of this 3D filter is the use of only two frames of a video sequence instead of three frames used by most 3D algorithms (*MF_3F, VGVDF, VVMF, VVDKNNVMF,* and *VAVDATM,* etc.). Another methodology (Fuzzy Temporal Spatial Colour Filter *FCF-3D*) operates the same way that *FDART_G* with some other ideas and modifications for impulsive denoising.

To justify the effectiveness of 3D technical proposals, the comparison with other filtering frameworks in video denoising were used (Zlokolica et al. (2006); Ponomaryov & Gallegos et al. (2006); Schulte & Huysmans et al. (2006); Schulte & Witte et al. (2006)). Reference filters: "Fuzzy Motion Recursive Spatio-Temporal Filter" (FMRSTF) (Zlokolica et al., 2006); an adaptation of FMRSTF employing only angles instead of gradients, named as "Fuzzy Vectorial Motion Recursive Spatio-Temporal Filter" (FVMRSTF); "Video Generalized Vectorial Directional Processing" (VGVDF) (Schulte & Huysmans et al., 2006), and also "Video Median M-type K-Nearest Neighbour" (VMMKNN) described in (Ponomaryov, 2007) were used as comparison in Gaussian denoising using numerous simulations and experiments.

The algorithms *MF_3F, VGVDF, VVMF, VVDKNNVMF, VKNNF, VATM,* and *VAVDATM* were used as comparative ones to evaluate *FCF – 3D* rendering.

Finally, multispectral image processing in different spectrum bands taken from Landsat 7, were used to evaluate the robustness of *FCF – 2D* against other filters studied.

Under various quality criteria and multiple numerical simulations, the denoising algorithms proposed demonstrate that the new framework, employing gradients and directional values, outperform analyzed methods in suppression of noise of different nature preserving important inherent characteristics of colour image and video data as well as in multispectral images. These criteria are Pick Signal to Noise Ratio (*PSNR*), Mean Absolute Error (*MAE*), and Normalized Colour Difference (*NCD*), which characterize noise suppression, edges and fine details preservation, and chromaticity properties preservation respectively.

The chapter is organized as follows: Sec. 2 presents the proposed schemes for simultaneous denoising processing of different kinds of noise: Gaussian and impulsive noises in 2D environments. Sec. 3 explains the Spatio-Temporal algorithm procedures to suppress Gaussian and impulsive noises, which employs two frames realizing the motion and noise detection. Sec. 4.1 describes the criteria to characterize the effectiveness of the approach in the image denoising, chromaticity preservation, and in reconstruction of fine details for each a frame. Sections 4.2 and 4.3 expose the experimental results in form of the objective and subjective measures presenting the effectiveness of several proposed approaches in suppression of noise and preservation of fine details and colours against other ones. A brief conclusion is drawn in Sec. 5.

2. Robust schemes applied for first frame of colour video sequences

2.1 First frame filtering

Here, the procedure consists of Histogram Calculation, Noise Estimation, and Spatial Algorithm Operations. A mean value $\bar{x}_\beta$ ($\beta = Red,Green,Blue$ in a colour image) is found in a 3×3 sliding processing window; later, the angle deviation between two vectors: the mean value $X = \{\bar{x}_{Red}, \bar{x}_{Green}, \bar{x}_{Blue}\}$, and the central pixel of the 3×3 sample $Y = \{x_{c(Red)}, x_{c(Green)}, x_{c(Blue)}\}$, is calculated as follows: $\theta_c = A(X,Y) = arccos\frac{(X \cdot Y)}{\|X\|\|Y\|}$, in this way, θ_c is the angle deviation of the central pixel with respect to a mean value indicating the similarity between neighbouring pixels and the central one.

To obtain the histogram suggests the interval [0,1]. Because the pixel magnitudes falls within 0 to 255, the maximum angle deviation between two pixels is achieved within the range of 0 or 1.57 radians ($[0,\pi/2]$), in this way, with the proposed interval, the angle deviations outside of [0,1] are eliminated of histogram process calculation. If $\theta_c \leq [F/255]$, the histogram is increased in "1" in "F" position, where "F" starts to increase from 0 to 255 with increasing magnitude steps of 1 for F, respectively, until it satisfies the condition, otherwise the increment is "0". Probabilities of occurrence for each value in the histogram are computed $p_j = \left(histogram_j \Big/ \sum_{j=0}^{255} histogram_j \right)$. After, the mean value $\mu = \sum_{j=0}^{255} j \cdot p_j$, the variance $\sigma_\beta^2 = \sum_{j=0}^{255} (j - \mu)^2 \cdot (p_j)$, and the standard deviation (SD) $\sigma_\beta' = \sqrt{\sigma_\beta^2}$, where SD is the Gaussian noise estimator proposed. This value will be used to smooth Gaussian noise for the first frame of a colour video sequence in a spatial filter.

Two processing windows: large 5×5, and centered within this, small 3×3 are employed in the procedure. Let denote as $\theta_i = A(x_i, x_c)$ the angle deviation x_i respect to x_c, where $i = 0, 1, \ldots, N - 1$, with $i \neq c$, $N = 8$ (3×3 window), and c =central pixel, as it is exposed in Fig. 1. To outperform our approach let identify uniform regions that should be processed by a fast algorithm reducing computational charge: fast algorithm is a *"Mean Weighted Filtering Algorithm"*. The IF-THEN rule that applies here is based on angle deviations to filter the first frame only: IF (θ_1 AND θ_3 AND θ_4 AND $\theta_6 \geq \tau_1$) OR (θ_0 AND θ_2 AND θ_5 AND $\theta_7 \geq \tau_1$) THEN *"MeanWeighted Filtering Algorithm"*, ELSE "Spatial Algorithm Operations", where τ_1 is a threshold defined as 0.1, this value was obtained during simulations. The "AND" operation is defined as "Logical AND", the "OR" operation is "Logical OR". Values $\theta_0, \theta_1, \ldots, \theta_7$ are angles within the 3×3 window defined in Fig. 1b).

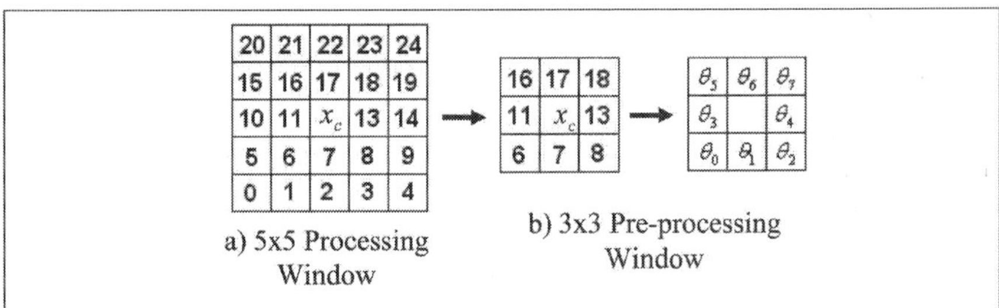

a) 5x5 Processing Window

b) 3x3 Pre-processing Window

Fig. 1. Different processing windows used in First Frame Filtering.

If *"Mean Weighted Filtering Algorithm"* is selected, this algorithm makes the processing fast enough and effective in the case of noise contamination in the uniform regions, and is defined as:

$$y_{\beta out} = \left[\sum_{i=0}^{N-1} x_{\beta i} \cdot \left(\frac{2}{(1 + e^{\theta_i})} \right) + x_{\beta c} \right] \Big/ \left[\sum_{i=0}^{N-1} \left(\frac{2}{(1 + e^{\theta_i})} \right) + 1 \right], N = 8, \text{ with } i \neq c. \qquad (1)$$

Using Eq. 1 is obtained a denoised pixel component output for each channel of the first frame of a colour video.

2.2 Spatial algorithm operations

The proposed spatial processing uses the procedure in each colour plane independently obtaining values SD (σ_β) that are adapted, forming local adaptive SD. The procedure to

receive σ_β is realized using 5×5 processing window (Fig. 1a)) in the following form:
$\sigma_\beta = \sqrt{\sigma_\beta^2} = \sqrt{\sum_{i=0}^{W}(x_{\beta i} - \bar{x}_{\beta 5x5})^2 \cdot (p_{\beta i})}$, and after, local adaptation is to adjust it as follows:
If $\sigma_\beta < \sigma'_\beta$, then $\sigma_\beta = \sigma'_\beta$, otherwise $\sigma'_\beta < \sigma_\beta$, where σ'_β was obtained in Sec. 2.1.

Let introduce for a central pixel $x_c = x(i, j)$ of a current sample the following neighbours in the eight directions: SW =South-West, S =South, SE =South-East, E =East, NE =North- East, N = North, NW =North-West, and W =West. Fig. 2 illustrates the cardinal directions. To obtain a similarity between the central pixel and the pixels in cardinal directions for each a plane ($\beta = R,G,B$), let perform the following equation:

$$\nabla_{(k,l)\beta}(i,j) = | \nabla_\beta(i+k, j+l) - \nabla_\beta(i,j) |, \text{where } k,l \in \{-1,0,1\}, \tag{2}$$

These gradients are called *"basic gradient values"*, and the point (i, j) is called *"the centre of the gradient values"*. Two *"related (rel) gradient values"* are used, permitting to avoid blur in presence of an edge. Finally, these three gradient values for a certain direction are connected into one single general value called *"fuzzy vectorial-gradient value"* under Fuzzy Rule 1 presented later.

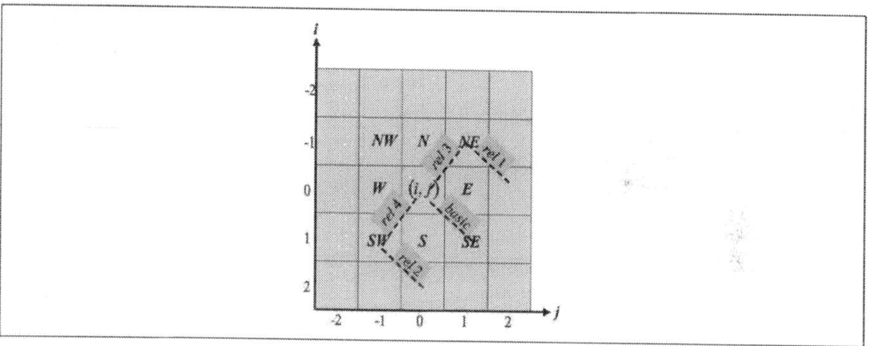

Fig. 2. Basic and related directions for gradients and angle variance (directional) values.

Now, let define $\gamma = \{NW,N,NE,E,SE,S,SW,W\}$, if $\nabla_{\gamma(\ell)\beta} < T_\beta$, where $\ell = \{basic, rel4, rel3\}$ as can be observed in Fig.2, for the "SE" direction only. Then, it is calculated the angle deviation in γ's directions for the basic and related magnitude component pixel values involved, where the threshold $T_\beta = 2 \cdot \sigma_\beta$ is selected according to the best performance criteria $PSNR$ and MAE.

Let define the membership function to obtain *"Basic and Related Vectorial-Gradient Values"*:

$$\mu_{NO\_NOISE} = \begin{cases} \max\{\alpha_{\gamma(\ell)\beta}, (1 - [\nabla_{\gamma(\ell)\beta}/T_\beta])\} & , \text{if} \nabla_{\gamma(\ell)\beta} < T_\beta \\ 0 & , \text{otherwise} \end{cases} \tag{3}$$

where μ_{NO_NOISE} characterizes membership value in NO_NOISE fuzzy set, this set implies that basic or related component of the pixels are probably free of noise and probably belongs to an edge or fine detail, and that might be important to take them into account in the denoising process; $\alpha_{\gamma(\ell)\beta} = \frac{2}{[1+\exp(\theta_{\gamma(\ell)\beta})]}$, and $\theta_{\gamma(\ell)\beta}$ is the angle deviation between vector pixels $[255, 255, x_{\gamma(\ell)\beta}]$ and $[255, 255, x'_{\gamma(\ell)\beta}]$ for each a component of a colour pixel. Finally, the process to obtain *"Fuzzy Vectorial-Gradient Values"* is defined as the Fuzzy Rule connecting Gradients with Vectorial values.

Fuzzy Rule 1: *Fuzzy Vectorial Gradient value* is defined as $\nabla_{\gamma\beta}\alpha_{\gamma\beta}$, in such a way:

IF ($\nabla_{\gamma(basic)\beta}$ IS NO NOISE AND $\nabla_{\gamma(rel4)\beta}$ is NO NOISE) OR ($\nabla_{\gamma(rel3)\beta}$ is NO NOISE AND $\nabla_{\gamma\beta D2}$ is NO NOISE) THEN $\nabla_{\gamma\beta}\alpha_{\gamma\beta}$ is NO NOISE.

The final step to filter out noise is realized using a Weighted Mean procedure with *Fuzzy Vectorial Gradient values* taken as fuzzy weights:

$$y_{\beta out} = \sum_{\gamma}(\nabla_{\gamma\beta}\alpha_{\gamma\beta}) \cdot x_{\gamma\beta} \Big/ \sum_{\gamma}(\nabla_{\gamma\beta}\alpha_{\gamma\beta}), \tag{4}$$

where $x_{\gamma\beta}$ represents each pixel within the pre-processing window used (Fig. 1b)).

2.3 Fuzzy 2D colour scheme in impulsive denoising

For impulsive noise suppression is necessary to consider not only one *"basic gradient value"* for any direction, but also four *"related gradient values"* (Fig. 2). Function $\nabla^{\beta}_{\gamma(\Im)}$ with $\Im =\{basic, rel1, rel2, rel3, rel4\}$ as illustrated in Fig. 2 for the *"SE"* direction only, where the gradient values for each a direction are shown, and parameter γ marks any chosen direction. The Fig. 2 exhibits the pixels involved in each of the directions. For example, for the "SE" direction (Fig. 2), the gradients are as follows: $\nabla^{\beta}_{(1,1)}x(0,0) = \nabla^{\beta}_{SE(basic)}$, $\nabla^{\beta}_{(0,2)}x(i-1,j+1) = \nabla^{\beta}_{SE(rel1)}$, $\nabla^{\beta}_{(2,0)}x(i+1,j-1) = \nabla^{\beta}_{SE(rel2)}$, $\nabla^{\beta}_{(0,0)}x(i-1,j+1) = \nabla^{\beta}_{SE(rel3)}$, and $\nabla^{\beta}_{(0,0)}x(i+1,j-1) = \nabla^{\beta}_{SE(rel4)}$.

Now that we have magnitude difference values, let proceed to obtain angle difference values. Let introduce the angle variance for each a channel in such a way $\theta^{\beta}_{\gamma(\Im)\Rightarrow SE(basic)} = arccos\left[\frac{2(255)^2+x^{\beta}_{(0,0)}\cdot x^{\beta}_{(1,1)}}{(2(255^2)+(x_{(0,0)})^2)^{1/2}\cdot(2(255^2)+(x_{(1,1)})^2)^{1/2}}\right]$. For example, in the "SE" direction, the "basic" and "related" vectorial values can be written as: $\theta^{\beta}_{(1,1)}x(0,0) = \theta^{\beta}_{SE(basic)}$, $\theta^{\beta}_{(0,2)}x(i-1,j+1) = \theta^{\beta}_{SE(rel1)}$, $\theta^{\beta}_{(2,0)}x(i+1,j-1) = \theta^{\beta}_{SE(rel2)}$, $\theta^{\beta}_{(0,0)}x(i-1,j+1) = \theta^{\beta}_{SE(rel3)}$, and $\theta^{\beta}_{(0,0)}x(i+1,j-1) = \nabla^{\beta}_{SE(rel4)}$ according to Fig. 2.

Figure 2 shows the pixels used in the processing procedure for the selected cardinal direction "SE" for the basic and four related components.

Let introduce fuzzy sets, BIG and SMALL that permit estimating the noise presence in a central pixel for window 5×5 (Fig. 2). A big membership level (near to value one) in the SMALL set shows that the central pixel is free of noise, and a large membership level in the BIG set demonstrates that central pixel is highly probably noisy. The Gaussian membership functions are used to calculate membership degrees for fuzzy gradient μ_{∇} and fuzzy vectorial μ_{θ} values:

$$\mu_{\nabla^{\beta}_{\gamma(\Im)}}(SMALL,BIG) = \begin{cases} 1, & \text{if}(\nabla^{\beta}_{\gamma(\Im)} < med2, \nabla^{\beta}_{\gamma(\Im)} > med1) \\ \left(\exp\left(-\left\{\frac{(\nabla^{\beta}_{\gamma(\Im)}-med2)^2}{2\sigma_1^2}\right\}\right)\right)\cdot\left(\exp\left(-\left\{\frac{(\nabla^{\beta}_{\gamma(\Im)}-med1)^2}{2\sigma_1^2}\right\}\right)\right) & \text{, otherwise} \end{cases} \tag{5}$$

$$\mu_{\theta^{\beta}_{\gamma(\Im)}}(SMALL,BIG) = \begin{cases} 1, & if(\theta^{\beta}_{\gamma(\Im)} < med4, \theta^{\beta}_{\gamma(\Im)} > med3) \\ \left(\exp\left(-\left\{\frac{(\theta^{\beta}_{\gamma(\Im)}-med4)^2}{2\sigma_2^2}\right\}\right)\right) \cdot \left(\exp\left(-\left\{\frac{(\theta^{\beta}_{\gamma(\Im)}-med3)^2}{2\sigma_2^2}\right\}\right)\right) & , otherwise \end{cases}, \quad (6)$$

where $med1 = 60, med2 = 10, \sigma_1^2 = 1000, med3 = 0.615, med4 = 0.1$, and $\sigma_2^2 = 0.8$ were obtained according to the best PSNR and MAE criteria results.

Fuzzy Rules in 2D Filtering

Let present novel fuzzy rules applied for gradient values and vectorial values in each channel.

Fuzzy Rule A introduces the membership level of $x^{\beta}_{(i,j)}$ in the set BIG for any γ direction:

IF ($\nabla^{\beta}_{\gamma\,(basic)}$ is BIG AND $\nabla^{\beta}_{\gamma\,(rel1)}$ is SMALL AND $\nabla^{\beta}_{\gamma\,(rel2)}$ is SMALL AND $\nabla^{\beta}_{\gamma\,(rel3)}$ is BIG AND $\nabla^{\beta}_{\gamma\,(rel4)}$ is BIG) AND ($\theta^{\beta}_{\gamma\,(basic)}$ is BIG AND $\theta^{\beta}_{\gamma\,(rel1)}$ is SMALL AND $\theta^{\beta}_{\gamma\,(rel2)}$ is SMALL AND $\theta^{\beta}_{\gamma\,(rel3)}$ is BIG AND $\theta^{\beta}_{\gamma\,(rel4)}$ is BIG) THEN $\nabla^{\beta F}_{\gamma}\theta^{\beta F}_{\gamma}$ *fuzzy gradient-directional value* is BIG. The operator AND outside of the parenthesis is applied as $min(A,B)$, and inside of the parenthesis is realized as A AND $B = A * B$.

Fuzzy Rule B presents the *noisy factor* (r^{β}) gathering eight *fuzzy gradient-directional values* that are calculated for each a direction as: IF *fuzzy gradient-directional values* $\nabla^{\beta F}_{N}\theta^{\beta F}_{N}$ is BIG OR $\nabla^{\beta F}_{S}\theta^{\beta F}_{S}$ is BIG OR $\nabla^{\beta F}_{E}\theta^{\beta F}_{E}$ is BIG OR $\nabla^{\beta F}_{W}\theta^{\beta F}_{W}$ is BIG OR $\nabla^{\beta F}_{SW}\theta^{\beta F}_{SW}$ is BIG OR $\nabla^{\beta F}_{NE}\theta^{\beta F}_{NE}$ is BIG OR $\nabla^{\beta F}_{NW}\theta^{\beta F}_{NW}$ is BIG OR $\nabla^{\beta F}_{SE}\theta^{\beta F}_{SE}$ is BIG THEN r^{β} (*noisy factor*) is BIG. The operation OR is introduced as $max(A,B)$.

The noisy factor is employed as a threshold to distinguish between a *noisy pixel* and a *free noise* one. So, if $r^{\beta} \geq 0.3$, the filtering procedure is applied employing the *fuzzy gradientdirectional values* as weights, in opposite case, the output is presented as unchanged central pixel: $y^{\beta}_{out} = x^{\beta}_{(i,j)} = x^{\beta}_{c}$ (Fig. 3).

For $r^{\beta} \geq 0.3$ (the value 0.3 was selected during simulations and is based on the best values for *PSNR* and *MAE* criteria), the fuzzy weights are used in the standard negator function ($\varsigma(x) = 1 - x, x \in [0,1]$) defined as $\zeta^{\beta F}_{\gamma} = 1 - \nabla^{\beta F}_{\gamma}\theta^{\beta F}_{\gamma}$, where $\nabla^{\beta F}_{\gamma}\theta^{\beta F}_{\gamma} \in [0,1]$. So, this value origins the fuzzy membership value in a new fuzzy set defined as "NO BIG" (noise free) where the fuzzy weight for central pixel in NO BIG fuzzy set is $\zeta^{\beta F}_{c=(0,0)} = 3 \cdot \sqrt{1 - r^{\beta}}$. Scheme showed in Fig. 3 performs denoising process using fuzzy values as fuzzy weights, where $\gamma \in \acute{\gamma}, \acute{\gamma} = \{NW,N,NE,E,SE,S,SW,W,$ and c(central pixel)$\}$.

So, the output's filtering result is formed by selecting one of the neighbouring pixels from the jth ordered values including central component, this procedure prevents the smoothing of a frame. The condition $j \leq 2$ permits to avoid selection of the farther pixels, but if $j \leq 2$ condition is not satisfied, it should be upgraded the total weight.

3. Spatio-temporal algorithm procedures to suppress noise

3.1 3D additive noise filtering

To avoid smoothing of fine details and edges, designing a temporal algorithm for motion detection in the past and present frames (t–1 and t frames) of a colour video sequence. A better preservation of the image characteristics (edges, fine details and chromaticity preservation) was obtained applying this scheme.

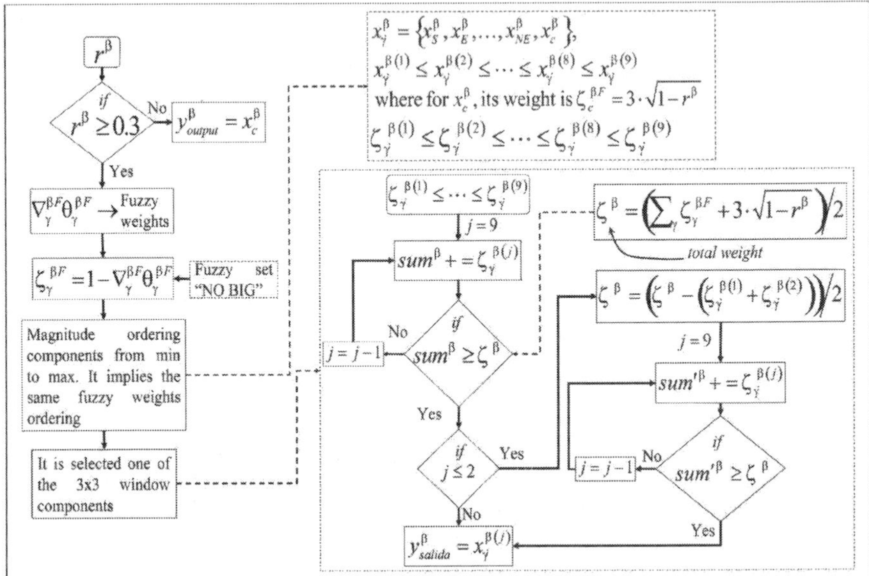

Fig. 3. Impulsive denoising scheme, using *fuzzy gradient-directional values* for the Spatial Filtering.

To characterize the similarity between two frames (*past* and *present* frames), it is necessary to obtain a relation of similarity between them. Using the gradient values and the angle deviations between pixels belonging to each frame, it is possible to compute a similarity level, which characterizes the motion and noise levels in the central sample in the present (t) frame.

The angle deviations and the gradient values related to a central pixel in the present frame respect to its neighbours from past frame are found accordingly to the first expression in equation 7(a):

$$
\begin{aligned}
&(\theta^1_{\beta i} = A(x^{t-1}_{\beta i}, x^t_{\beta c}), \nabla^1_{\beta i} = |\, x^{t-1}_{\beta i} - x^t_{\beta c}\,|),\ \text{(a)} \\
&(\theta^2_{\beta i} = A(x^{t-1}_{\beta i}, x^t_{\beta i}), \nabla^2_{\beta i} = |\, x^{t-1}_{\beta i} - x^t_{\beta i}\,|),\ \text{(b)} \\
&(\theta^3_{\beta i} = A(x^t_{\beta i}, x^t_{\beta c}), \nabla^3_{\beta i} = |\, x^t_{\beta i} - x^t_{\beta c}\,|),\ \text{(c)},
\end{aligned}
\tag{7}
$$

where $i = 0, \ldots, N-1$; $N = 8$, $x^t_{\beta c}$ is a central pixel channel in the present frame, and $t-1$ and t parameters mark the past and present frames, respectively. The angle and gradient values in both frames are calculated according to equation 7(b). Finally, the same parameters for the present frame are only employed, eliminating operations in past frame as in equation 7(c). This framework is better understood following Fig. 4.

The membership functions of fuzzy sets SMALL and BIG are defined similarly to equations (5) and (6):

$$
\mu_{SMALL(\chi)} = \begin{cases} 1, & \text{if } \chi < \mu_1 \\ \exp\left(-\left\{\dfrac{(\chi-\mu_1)^2}{2\sigma^2}\right\}\right), & \text{otherwise} \end{cases},
\tag{8}
$$

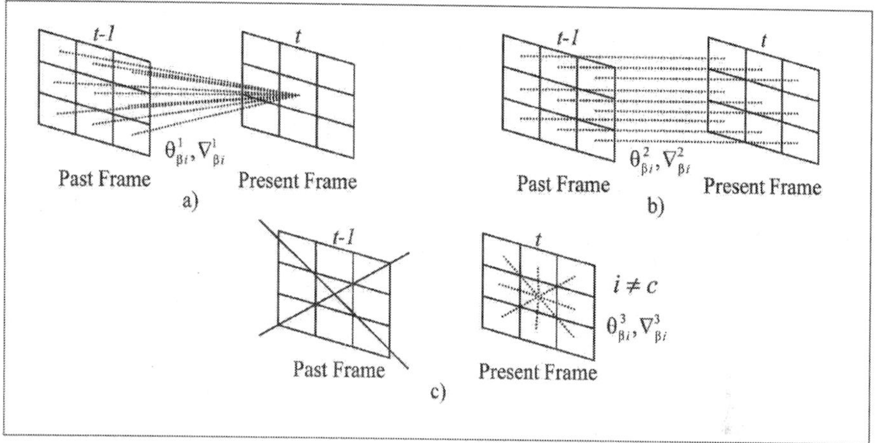

Fig. 4. Procedures used for angle and gradient values in neighbouring frames.

$$\mu_{BIG(\chi)} = \begin{cases} 1, & \text{if } \chi > \mu_2 \\ \exp\left(-\left\{\frac{(\chi-\mu_2)^2}{2\sigma^2}\right\}\right), & \text{otherwise} \end{cases} \tag{9}$$

where $\chi = \theta, \nabla$, with respective parameters $\mu_1 = \phi_1, \phi_2$, $\mu_2 = \phi_3, \phi_4$, and $\phi_1 = 0.2$, $\phi_2 = 60$, $\phi_3 = 0.9$, $\phi_4 = 140$, using $\sigma_2 = 0.1$ for ϕ_1 and ϕ_3, and using $\sigma_2 = 1000$ for ϕ_2 and ϕ_4 respectively.

The designed fuzzy rules are used to detect the *movement presence* and/or *noise* analyzing pixel by pixel. First, detecting motion relative to the central pixel in the present frame with the pixels in the past frame (Fig. 4(a)) are found. Secondly, the movement detection in respect to pixel by pixel in both positions of the frames (Fig. 4(b)) is realized. Finally, this procedure is only applied in the present frame using central pixel and its neighbours (Fig. 4(c)). These three movement values are used to define the parameter that characterizes the *movement/noise confidence*. The fuzzy rules presented below are illustrated in Fig. 5.

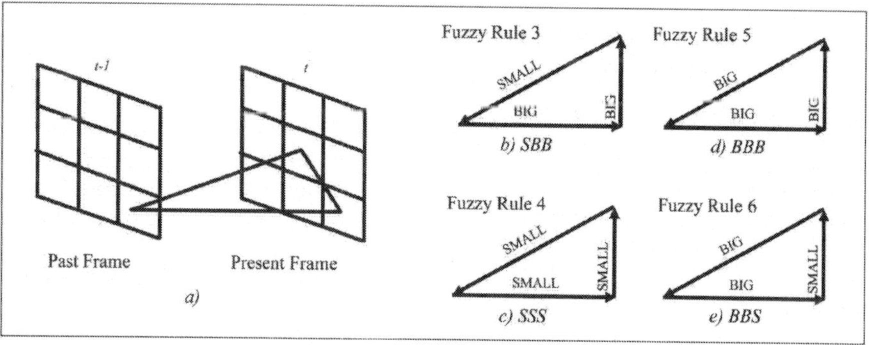

Fig. 5. **Fuzzy Rules** 3–6 in determination of the *movement/noise confidence* in past and present frames.

The following fuzzy rules were designed to detect changes in magnitude and angle deviations between the central and neighbour pixels in t and $t\text{–}1$ frames, this characterizes the motion and noise levels in the central pixel and its neighbourhood.

Fuzzy Rule 3: Definition of the *Fuzzy Vectorial-Gradient value* $SBB_{\beta i}$: IF $\theta^1_{\beta i}$ is SMALL AND $\theta^2_{\beta i}$ is BIG AND $\theta^3_{\beta i, i \neq c}$ is BIG AND $\nabla^1_{\beta i}$ is SMALL AND $\nabla^2_{\beta i}$ is BIG AND $\nabla^3_{\beta i, i \neq c}$ is BIG THEN $SBB_{\beta i}$ is true (Fig. 5b).

Fuzzy Rule 4: Definition of the *Fuzzy Vectorial-Gradient value* $SSS_{\beta i}$. IF $\theta^1_{\beta i}$ is SMALL AND $\theta^2_{\beta i}$ is SMALL AND $\theta^3_{\beta i, i \neq c}$ is SMALL AND $\nabla^1_{\beta i}$ is SMALL AND $\nabla^2_{\beta i}$ is SMALL AND $\nabla^3_{\beta i, i \neq c}$ is SMALL THEN $SSS_{\beta i}$ is true (Fig. 5c)).

Fuzzy Rule 5: Definition of the *Fuzzy Vectorial-Gradient value* $BBB_{\beta i}$. IF $\theta^1_{\beta i}$ is BIG AND $\theta^2_{\beta i}$ is BIG AND $\theta^3_{\beta i, i \neq c}$ is BIG AND $\nabla^1_{\beta i}$ is BIG AND $\nabla^2_{\beta i}$ is BIG AND $\nabla^3_{\beta i, i \neq c}$ is BIG THEN $SSS_{\beta i}$ is true (Fig. 5d)).

Fuzzy Rule 6: Definition of the *Fuzzy Vectorial-Gradient value* $BBS_{\beta i}$. IF $\theta^1_{\beta i}$ is BIG AND $\theta^2_{\beta i}$ is BIG AND $\theta^3_{\beta i, i \neq c}$ is SMALL AND $\nabla^1_{\beta i}$ is BIG AND $\nabla^2_{\beta i}$ is BIG AND $\nabla^3_{\beta i, i \neq c}$ is SMALL THEN $BBS_{\beta i}$ is true (Fig. 5e)).

The SD of the sample to a $3{\times}3{\times}2$ pre-processing window for each a colour channel in the past and present frames is calculated obtaining the parameter σ''_β, which is described as a *Temporal SD*. Procedure to calculate σ''_β is similar to used in Sec. 2.1, but applied for the $3{\times}3{\times}2$ samples. After that, we compare it with SD σ'_β obtained for Spatial Filter (Sec. 2.1) in a following way: *if* $\{(\sigma''_{red} \geq 0.4 * \sigma'_{red})$ AND $(\sigma''_{green} \geq 0.4 * \sigma'_{green})$ AND $(\sigma''_{blue} \geq 0.4 * \sigma'_{blue})\}$, *then* Fuzzy Rules 3, 4, 5, and 6 should be employed, otherwise, a *Mean Filter* must be performed. The AND operation is the "Logical AND" in presented above *if-then* condition. So, the application of the *Mean Filter Algorithm*: $\bar{y}_{\beta out} = \sum_{i=1}^{M} x_{\beta i} \big/ M$, $M = 18$ signifies that a uniform area is under processing.

The updating of the *Standard Deviation "SD"* that should be used in the processing of next frame is realized according to equation: $\sigma'_\beta = (\alpha \cdot (\sigma_{total}/5)) + ((1 - \alpha) \cdot \sigma'_\beta)$, where $\sigma_{total} = (\sigma''_{red} + \sigma''_{green} + \sigma''_{blue})/3$. Sensitive parameter "$\alpha$" is chosen: for *Mean Filter Algorithm* and fuzzy value SSS, $\alpha = 0.125$, and for fuzzy values SSB and BBS, $\alpha = 0.875$.

The consequences, which are applied to each fuzzy rule, are based on different conditions that might be present in the sample: *the sample is in movement*, or *the sample is noisy one*, or it is simply *free of noise and movement*. If conditions established in the Fig. 6 are satisfied, then, are performed the equations (10), (11), (12), and "**Procedure 1**" depending on the selected case.

$$y_{\beta out} = \frac{\sum_{i=1}^{\#pixels} x^{t-1}_{\beta i} \cdot SBB_{\beta i}}{\sum_{i=1}^{\#pixels} SBB_{\beta i}}, \text{or} \qquad (10)$$

$$y_{\beta out} = \frac{\sum_{i=1}^{\#pixels} 0.5(x^{t-1}_{\beta i} + x^{t}_{\beta i}) \cdot SSS_{\beta i}}{\sum_{i=1}^{\#pixels} SSS_{\beta i}}, \text{or} \qquad (11)$$

$$y_{\beta out} = \frac{\sum_{i=1}^{\#pixels} x_{\beta i}^{t} \cdot (1 - BBS_{\beta i})}{\sum_{i=1}^{\#pixels} (1 - BBS_{\beta i})} \tag{12}$$

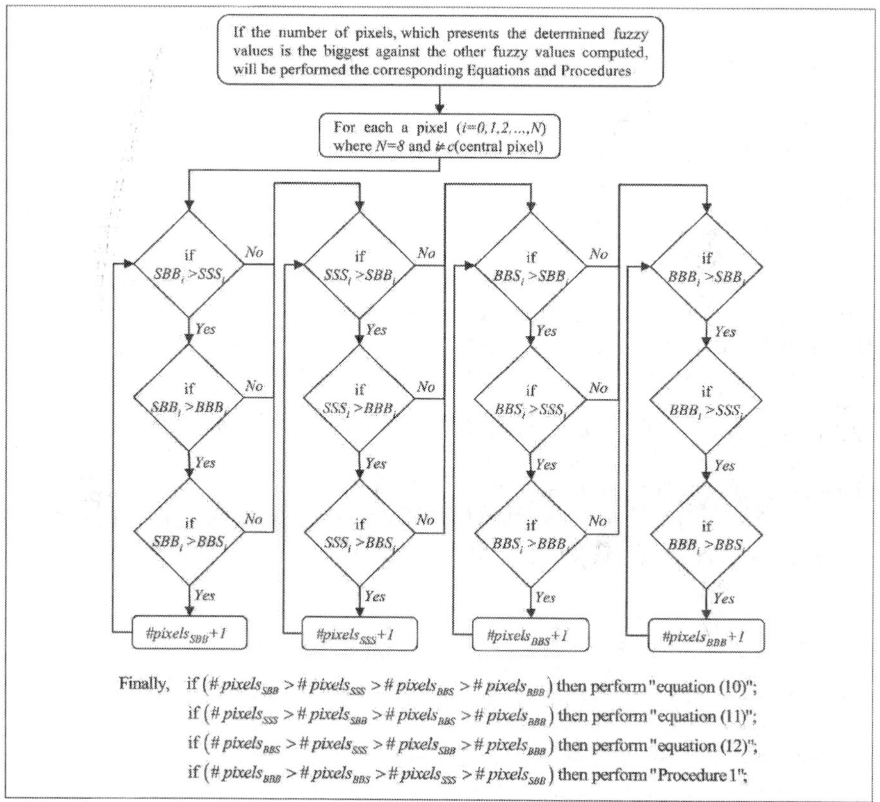

Fig. 6. Denoising scheme applied in 3D algorithm in case of *movement, noise, no movement, and no noise.*

Procedure 1: If the number of pixels with value $BBB_{\beta i}$ ($\#pixels_{BBB}$) is the largest reached, then consider the nine *Fuzzy Vectorial-Gradient values* obtained from *BBB*. It is selected the central value and three fuzzy neighbours values to detect motion. We conducted a combination of four subfacts, which are combined by a triangular norm defined as A AND $B = A *B$. The intersection of all possible combinations of *BBB* and three different degrees of membership BIG neighbours produces 56 values to be obtained. The values are added using an algebraic sum of all instances to obtain *the motion noise confidence*. This value is used to update the *SD* and get the output pixel using the following algorithm: $y_{\beta out} = (1 - \alpha) \cdot (x_{\beta c}^{t}) + \alpha \cdot (x_{\beta c}^{t-1})$ (α=0.875, if *motion_noise confidence*= 1; α=0.125, if *motion_noise confidence* = 0, and α=0.5, otherwise), where $x_{\beta c}^{t-1}$, and $x_{\beta c}^{t}$ represent each central pixel in the past and present frames that meets the conditions of the presented fuzzy rule.

If there is not exist the majority in pixels by any Fuzzy Rule calculated, it can be concluded that values of sample in the past and present frames have similarity nature. So, using only the central pixels from present and past frames, we can obtain an output's pixel,

$$y_{\beta out} = 0.5 \cdot x_{\beta c}^{t} + 0.5 \cdot x_{\beta c}^{t-1}, \text{ with sensitive parameter, } \alpha = 0.5. \qquad (13)$$

At final step, the algorithm employs the Spatial Filter proposed in Sec. 2 for smoothing the non-stationary noise left after preceding temporal filter. This can be done by a local spatial algorithm, which adapts to the structures of the image and the noise level corresponding to the spatial neighbourhood. This algorithm needs only the modification in its threshold value: $T_\beta = 0.25 \, \sigma'_\beta$.

3.2 Fuzzy Colour 3D Filter (FCF-3D) for impulsive denoising

Processing two neighbour frames (past and present) of a video sequence permits to calculate the motion and noise levels of a central pixel. A 5×5×2 sliding window, which is formed by the past and present frames, is employed, and the difference values among these frames are calculated, forming a *difference magnitude frame* "λ^β" and a *difference directional frame* "ϕ^β" related with differences only, as can be seen in Fig. 7:

$$\lambda_{(k,l)}^{\beta}[x_\beta^{t-1}(i,j), x_\beta^{t}(i,j)] = |\, x_\beta^{t-1}(i+k,j+l) - x_\beta^{t}(i+k,j+l)\,|, \qquad (14)$$

where $x_\beta^{t-1}(i,j)$ are pixels in $t-1$ frame of video sequence, and $x_\beta^{t}(i,j)$ show the pixels in t frame, with indexes $(k,l) \in \{-2,-1, 0, 1,2\}$ (Fig.7a)).

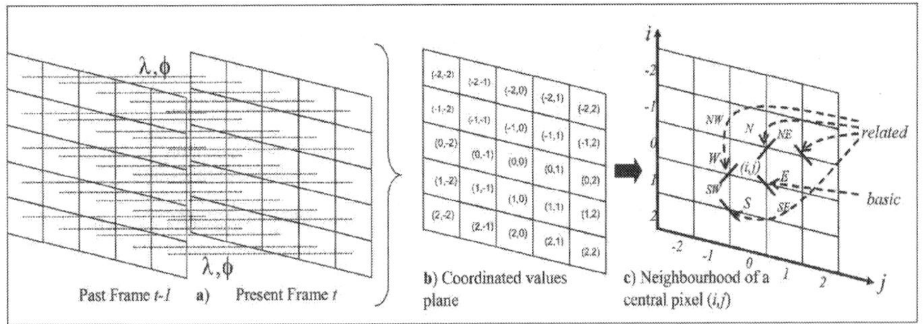

Fig. 7. a) Frames, b) Coordinated plane for *difference magnitude and directional values*, c) Neighbourhood pixels for central one.

Let calculate the absolute difference gradient values of a central pixel in respect to their neighbours for a 5x5x1 processing window (Fig. 7b) and Fig. 7c)). The *absolute difference gradient values* are calculated as in the following equation for only the $SE(basic)$ direction:

$$\nabla_{(1,1)}^{\prime \beta}\lambda(0,0) = \nabla_{SE(basic)}^{\prime \beta}, \ \nabla_{SE(basic)}^{\prime \beta} = |\, \lambda_{(0,0)}^{\beta} - \lambda_{(1,1)}^{\beta}\,| \qquad (15)$$

The same procedure should be repeated for all other basic and four related values in any direction. As in 2D framework (Sec. 2.1), calculate the *absolute difference directional values* of a central pixel with respect to its neighbours as an angle variance value among t-1 and t frames $\phi^{\beta}_{(k,l)}(x^{t-1}_{\beta}(i+k,j+l), x^{t}_{\beta}(i+k,j+l))$. Using angle variance value $\phi^{\beta}_{(k,l)}$, we can present the *absolute variance directional values* to the $SE(basic)$ direction only as:

$$\nabla^{''\beta}_{(1,1)}\phi(0,0) = \nabla^{''\beta}_{SE(basic)}, \quad \nabla^{''\beta}_{SE(basic)} = \mid \phi^{\beta}_{(0,0)} - \phi^{\beta}_{(1,1)} \mid \tag{16}$$

The same reasoning done for $\nabla^{'\beta}_{SE(basic)}$ regarding to $\nabla^{\beta}_{SE(basic)}$ (Sec. 2.3) can also be made for $\nabla^{''\beta}_{SE(basic)}$. Let employ the same Gaussian membership functions for fuzzy values as in the equations (5) and (6), introducing the *fuzzy gradient-directional difference values*. Numerical experiments realized in this case have given the values used for the functions described in equations (5) and (6): with $med3 = 0.1$, $med4 = 0.01$ according to the best *PSNR* and *MAE* criteria results.

Fuzzy Rules in 3D Impulsive Noise Suppression

The fuzzy rules used to characterize motion and noise levels in central pixel components are defined as follows:

Fuzzy Rule 1_3D determines the **FIRST 3D fuzzy gradient-directional difference** value as $(\nabla^{'\beta F}_{\gamma} \nabla^{''\beta F}_{\gamma})_{FIRST}$: IF ($\nabla^{'\beta}_{\gamma\,(basic)}$ is BIG AND $\nabla^{'\beta}_{\gamma\,(rel1)}$ is SMALL AND $\nabla^{'\beta}_{\gamma\,(rel2)}$ is SMALL AND $\nabla^{'\beta}_{\gamma\,(rel3)}$ is BIG AND $\nabla^{'\beta}_{\gamma\,rel4}$ is BIG) AND ($\nabla^{''\beta}_{\gamma(basic)}$ is BIG AND $\nabla^{''\beta}_{\gamma(rel1)}$ is SMALL AND $\nabla^{''\beta}_{\gamma(rel2)}$ is SMALL AND $\nabla^{''\beta}_{\gamma(rel3)}$ is BIG AND $\nabla^{''\beta}_{\gamma(rel4)}$ is BIG) THEN $(\nabla^{'\beta F}_{\gamma} \nabla^{''\beta F}_{\gamma})_{FIRST}$ is BIG. This fuzzy rule characterizes the confidence in the motion and noise in a central pixel due to neighbour fuzzy values in any γ direction. Operation "AND" outside of parenthesis is realized as $min(A,B)$.

Fuzzy Rule 2_3D defines the **SECOND 3D fuzzy gradient-directional difference** value as $(\nabla^{'\beta F}_{\gamma} \nabla^{'\beta F}_{\gamma})_{SECOND}$: IF ($\nabla\gamma(basic)^{'\beta}$ is SMALL AND $\nabla^{'\beta}_{\gamma\,(rel1)}$ is SMALL AND $\nabla^{'\beta}_{\gamma\,(rel2)}$ is SMALL) OR ($\nabla^{''\beta}_{\gamma}$ is SMALL AND $\nabla^{''\beta}_{\gamma(rel1)}$ is SMALL AND $\nabla^{''\beta}_{\gamma(rel2)}$ is SMALL) THEN $(\nabla^{'\beta F}_{\gamma(basic)} \nabla^{''\beta F}_{\gamma})_{SECOND}$ is SMALL. This fuzzy rule characterizes the confidence in the no movement and no noise in a central pixel in any g direction. So, the distinctness of the different area (uniform region, edge or fine detail), where a current central pixel component belongs, can be realized using this rule. Operation "OR" is calculated as $max(A,B)$; also, "AND" inside of parenthesis is defined as $A * B$.

Fuzzy Rule 3_3D defines the **motion and noise 3D confidence factor** r^{β}: IF (($\nabla^{'\beta F}_{SE} \nabla^{''\beta F}_{SE})_{FIRST}$ is BIG OR $(\nabla^{'\beta F}_{S} \nabla^{''\beta F}_{S})_{FIRST}$ is BIG OR . . . OR $(\nabla^{'\beta F}_{N} \nabla^{''\beta F}_{N})_{FIRST}$ is BIG) THEN r^{β} is BIG. So, Fuzzy Rule 3_3D permits to calculate the *fuzzy 3D movement noisy factor* and estimate the motion and noise levels presence in a central pixel component using fuzzy values determined for all directions.

Fuzzy Rule 4_3D defines the **no movement no noise 3D confidence factor** η^{β}: IF (($\nabla^{'\beta F}_{SE} \nabla^{''\beta F}_{SE})_{SECOND}$ is SMALL OR $(\nabla^{'\beta F}_{S} \nabla^{''\beta F}_{S})_{SECOND}$ is SMALL OR . . . OR $(\nabla^{'\beta F}_{N} \nabla^{''\beta F}_{N})_{SECOND}$ is SMALL) THEN η^{β} is SMALL. The fuzzy 3D no movement-no noisy factor allows the estimation of no movement and no noise levels presence in a central pixel component using fuzzy values determined for all directions.

The parameters r^β and η^β can be applied efficiently in a decision scheme (Fig. 8): If a central pixel component is *noisy*, or is *in movement*, or is a *free one* of both mentioned events. Fuzzy Rules from 1_3D to 4_3D determine the novel algorithm based on the fuzzy parameters.

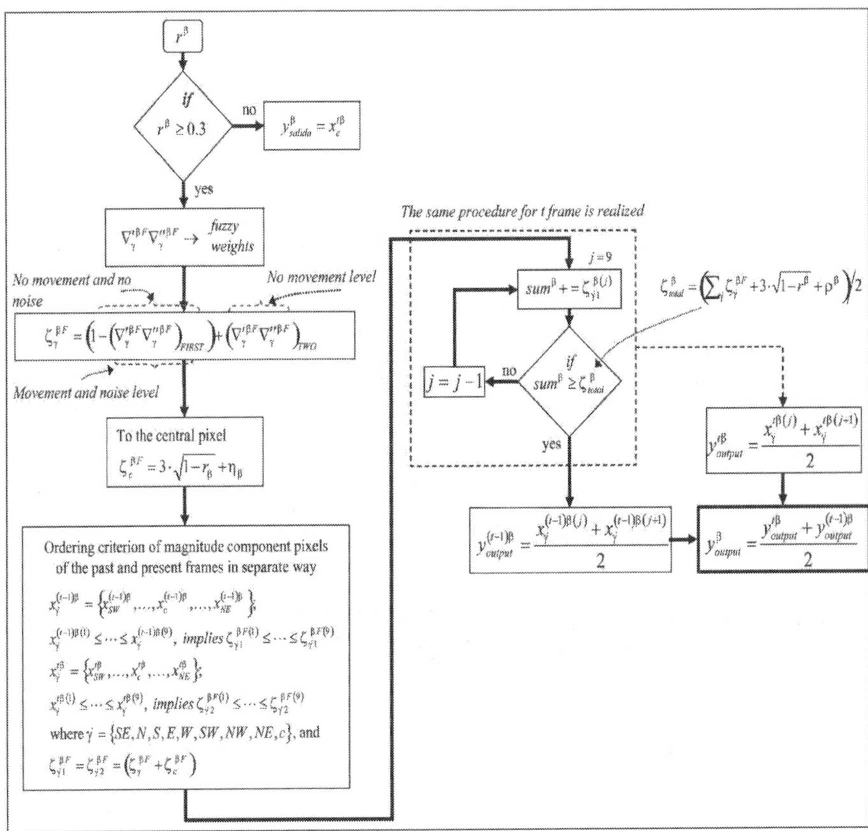

Fig. 8. Framework of the *FTSCF-3D* algorithm.

It should be chosen the *j–th* component pixel, which satisfies to the proposed conditions, ensuring that the edges and fine details will be preserved according to the selected sort ordering criterion in Fig. 8 in the selection of the nearest pixels to the central one in $t - 1$ and t frames.

Non-stationary noise that was not processed by the temporal filter, should be processed with the application of the *FCF-2D* designed in Sec. 2.3 that permits decreasing the influence of the non-stationary noise left by the temporal filter. As we are processing a frame that is free from noise, the spatial filter parameters change as follows:

- Condition $r^\beta \geq 0.3$ is changed to $r^\beta \geq 0.5$.

- The weight $\zeta^\beta = \left(\sum_\gamma \zeta_\gamma^{\beta F} + 3 \cdot \sqrt{1-r^\beta}\right)\big/2$ is rearranged as follows $\zeta^\beta = \left(\sum_\gamma \zeta_\gamma^{\beta F} + 5 \cdot \sqrt{1-r^\beta}\right)\big/2.$

- The central weight is modified according to $\zeta_c^{\beta F} = 5 \cdot \sqrt{1-r^\beta}$.

- If condition $sum^\beta \geq \zeta^\beta$ until $\zeta_\gamma^{\beta F(2)}$ is not satisfied, total weight is updated according to: $\zeta^\beta = \left(\zeta^\beta - \zeta_\gamma^{\beta F(1)}\right)\big/2.$

4. Experimental results

4.1 Objective and subjective performances

The proposed motion-detection approach has been evaluated using different objective and subjective criteria. $PSNR$ Criterion is commonly used as a measure of noise suppression:

$$PSNR = 10 \cdot \log\left[\frac{(255)^2}{MSE}\right] dB, \tag{17}$$

where the MSE (*Mean Square Error*) represents an objective measure of the square average deviation of an image estimation.

MAE criterion characterizes the edges and details preservation because it is well correlated with human visual system:

$$MAE = \frac{1}{M \cdot N} \sum_{i=0}^{M-1}\sum_{j=0}^{N-1}\left[\frac{\mid R(i,j) - R'(i,j) \mid + \mid G(i,j) - G'(i,j) \mid + \mid B(i,j) - B'(i,j) \mid}{3}\right], \tag{18}$$

The NCD (*Normalized Colour Difference*) measure estimates normalized perceptual error between two colour vectors in colour space $L * u * v$, and is suitable in a human perception sense. The perceptual error $\triangle E_{Luv}$ and $E_{Luv}^* = [(L^*)^2 + (u^*)^2 + (v^*)^2]$ vector magnitude of original image pixel no corrupted are used to define NCD:

$$NCD = \frac{\displaystyle\sum_{i=0}^{M-1}\sum_{j=0}^{N-1} \parallel \triangle E_{Luv} \parallel}{\displaystyle\sum_{i=0}^{M-1}\sum_{j=0}^{N-1} \parallel E_{Luv}^* \parallel}, \tag{19}$$

where M, N is the image size, $R(i, j)$, $G(i, j)$, $B(i, j)$ are pixel values (i, j) in the plane of the original image, and $R'(i, j)$, $G'(i, j)$, $B'(i, j)$ are pixel values (i, j) for filtered image in R, G and B colour planes.

We also use a subjective visual criterion presenting the filtered images and/or their error images for implemented filters to compare the capabilities of noise suppression and detail preservation. So, a subjective visual comparison of images provides information about the spatial distortion and artifacts introduced by different filters, as well as the noise suppression quality of the algorithm and present performance of the filter, when filtering images are observed by the human visual system.

4.2 Additive noise suppression results

Different colour video sequence *"Miss America"*, *"Flowers"* and *"Chair"* were used to rate the effectiveness of the proposed approach in suppression of additive noise and compare it with known techniques. They present different texture characteristics permitting a better understanding of the robustness of the proposed filtering scheme. Video sequences in the QCIF format (176×144 pixels) and in RGB colour space with 24 bits, 8 bits for each a channel were contaminated with Gaussian noise of different intensity from 0.0 to 0.05 in their SDs. The filtered frames were evaluated according to *PSNR, MAE, NCD* objective criteria, and also in subjective matter to justify the performance of the proposed filter.

The proposed Fuzzy Directional Adaptive Recursive Temporal Filtering for Gaussian noise named as *FDARTF_G* was compared with another similar one, the *FMRSTF*, which only employs the gradients. The next reference procedure, the *FVMRSTF* is some modification of *FMRSTF*, combining the gradients and angles in processing. Other two reference filters were: *VGVDF_G*, adapted to process three frames at a time, and the *VMMKNN* filter which has proven its efficiency in comparison with other filtering procedures in suppression of additive noise in grey images.

Other simulation results in Fig.9 expose the filtering performance along 43 frames of *Chair* sequence. One can clearly see that the *Chair sequence* processed by the designed procedure presents the best performance in *PSNR, NCD* and *MAE* criteria against other algorithms.

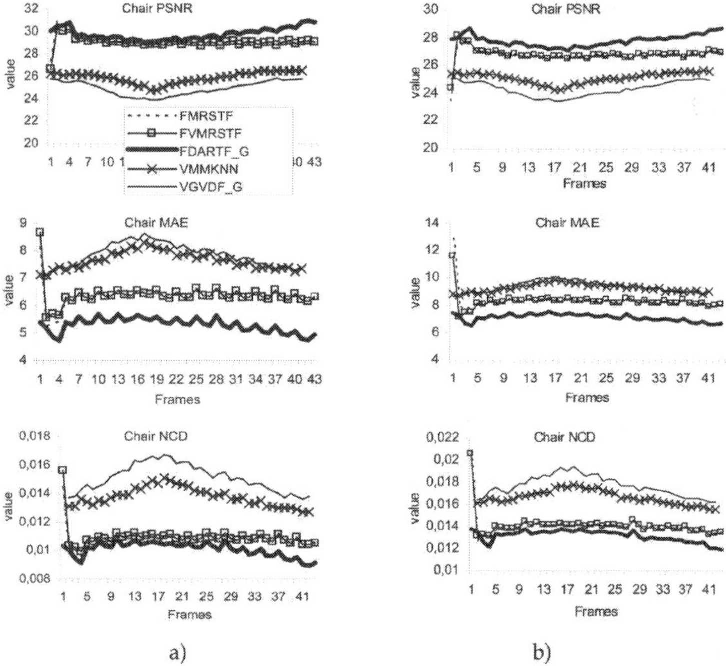

a)   b)

Fig. 9. *PSNR, MAE,* and *NCD* criteria for the first 43 frames of Chair colour sequence corrupted by noise, and processed by different algorithms. SD is equal: column a) 0.005, and column b) 0.01.

Criteria	Flowers Frame 20, Gaussian noise "SD"					Miss America Frame 20, Gaussian noise "SD"				
	FMRSTF	FVMRSTF	FDARTF.G	VMMKNN	VGVDF.G	FMRSTF	FVMRSTF	FDARTF.G	VMMKNN	VGVDF.G
SD = 0.005										
PSNR	26,192	26,007	27,309	25,348	25,46	29,926	29,905	32,51	29,799	30,658
MAE	9,628	9,825	8,503	8,777	8,959	5,818	5,826	4,459	6,178	5,549
NCD	0,016	0,017	0,015	0,015	0,017	0,02	0,02	0,016	0,021	0,02
SD = 0.01										
PSNR	24,363	24,34	25,717	24,629	24,723	27,686	27,681	30,059	27,612	28,655
MAE	11,932	11,971	10,438	9,916	10,15	7,477	7,5	6,069	8,143	7,213
NCD	0,0206	0,0208	0,0187	0,0169	0,0193	0,026	0,026	0,021	0,028	0,026
SD = 0.02										
PSNR	22,597	22,572	23,746	23,419	23.627	25,492	25,507	27,251	24,950	25,874
MAE	14,645	14,694	13,182	11,861	11.912	9,634	9,645	8,376	11,278	10,19
NCD	0,0251	0,0252	0,0234	0,0198	0,022	0,033	0,033	0,03	0,039	0,037
SD = 0.03										
PSNR	21,468	21,465	22,702	22.523	22.794	24,183	24,174	26,024	23,238	24,236
MAE	16,684	16,698	14,853	13.351	13.316	11,145	11,167	9,603	13,929	12,404
NCD	0,0285	0,0287	0,026	0,0217	0,0241	0,0384	0,0384	0,035	0,049	0,045

Table 1. Numerical results under different criteria for framework proposed and comparative ones.

Fig. 10 presents filtering results for one frame of sequence *Chair*, where the better preservation of the image details in the case of the proposed algorithm application is observed, denoting minus black dot points quantities in comparison with the second best filtering image results obtained in Fig. 10c). It is easy to see a better noise suppression observing uniform areas of the frame.

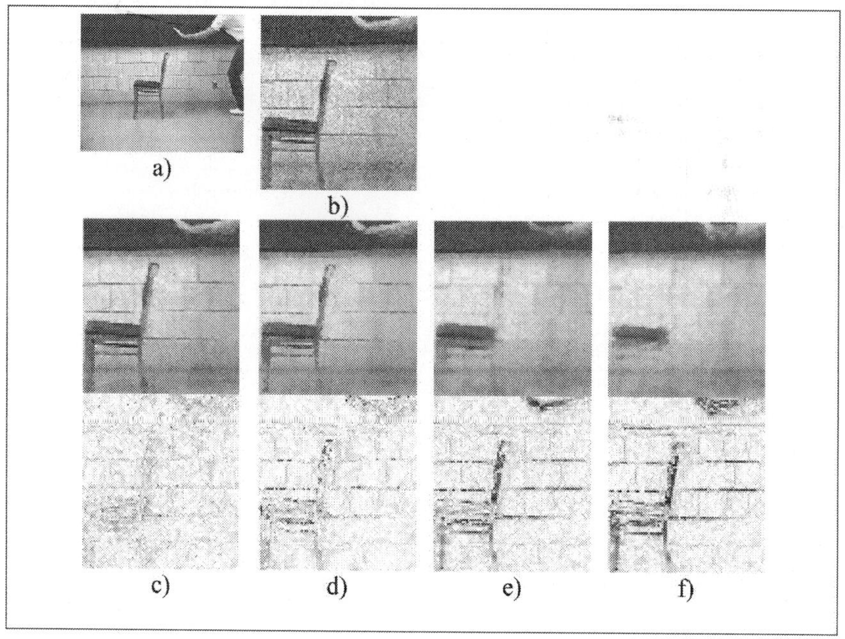

Fig. 10. Sequence Chair, frame 20; a) Original image, b) Zoomed image corrupted by Gaussian noise, *SD* = 0.005, c) *FMRSTF* filtered and error frames, d) filtered and error frames by proposed *FDARTF G*, e) *VMMKNN* filtered and error frames, f) *VGVDF G* filtered and error frames.

4.3 Impulsive noise suppression results

Test *Lena, Baboon,* and *Peppers* colour images and, also multichannel LandSat 7 satellite real-life images (320x320 pixels in RGB space, 24 bits) with different texture properties were used to evaluate 2D algorithms, as well as colour video sequence: *"Flowers"* and *"Miss America"* (QCIF format, 176x144 pixels in each a frame) were analyzed to characterize the performance of 3D designed filter. The frames of the video sequences were contaminated by impulsive noise with different percentages in independent way for each a channel. Table 2 presents *PSNR* and *MAE* criteria values for 2D designed algorithm against other existed ones exposing the better values in the case of low and middle noise intensity. The best performance is presented by designed scheme until 15% of noise intensity for Lena and until 10% for Baboon and Peppers colour images guaranteeing the robustness of novel framework because of different texture and chromaticity properties of the mentioned images. *MAE* criterion exposes that the best performance in preservation of the edges and fine details for mentioned images is demonstrated by designed method permitting to avoid the smoothing in wide range of noise intensity.

(%)Noise	FCF-2D	AVMF	AMNIF	CWVDF	VMF_FAS	INR
0	37,12/0,41	31,58/1,89	29,45/4,85	33,05/2,63	36,46/0,26	31,71/4,35
5	33,99/0.91	30,95/2,39	29,21/5,03	31,24/3,10	31,85/1,19	31,45/4,41
10	31,50/1,48	30,10/2,97	28,93/5,22	29,04/3,82	28,80/2,35	30,93/4,53
15	29,20/2.17	29,06/3,63	28,60/5,46	26,61/4,87	26,28/3,70	30,24/4,7
20	26,86/3.11	27,83/4,40	28,18/5,74	24,3/6,38	24,80/5,00	29,03/4,98
0	29,19/2,14	24,44/6,97	23,76/10,46	24,96/5,42	30,14/0,94	27,44/7,54
5	27,85/2.87	24,27/7,36	23,64/10,73	24,16/6,42	27,22/2,54	27,07/7,77
10	26,60/3,67	23,97/7,87	23,48/11,02	23,14/7,65	25,29/4,06	26,39/8,09
15	25,24/4,63	23,48/8,59	23,30/11,36	21,95/9,17	23,68/5,83	25,69/8,50
20	23,72/5,83	22,88/9,49	23,09/11,75	20,67/11,00	22,47/7,69	24,95/8,99
0	38,06/0,31	31,55/1,51	29,47/4,17	32,87/1,32	35,49/0,20	32,56/3,62
5	33,64/0,82	30,81/1,97	29,02/4,42	29,75/2,15	31,19/1,40	31,54/3,75
10	31,09/1,38	29,80/2,49	28,71/4,66	27,34/3,20	29,01/2,07	30,81/3,90
15	28,36/2,16	28,66/3,13	28,32/4,92	24,46/4,82	25,63/3,70	29,38/4,18
20	26,07/3,13	27,30/3,92	27,82/5,26	22,12/6,92	24,45/4,84	28,41/4,47

Table 2. *PSNR/MAE* criteria values for Lena, Baboon, and Peppers Images, respectively.

(%)Impulsive Noise	Multispectral image formed by 3, 2, and 1 Bands					
	GVDF		MMKNN		FCF-2D	
	MAE	PSNR	MAE	PSNR	MAE	PSNR
5	13,62	21,06	13,12	22,09	4,79	25,20
15	15,44	20,17	14,49	21,33	6,97	22,99
20	16,55	19,60	15,31	20,86	8,38	21,77
25	18,05	18,85	16,31	20,33	10,24	20,44
30	19,86	18,07	17,45	19,75	12,3	19,25
Multispectral image formed by 4, 3, and 2 Bands						
5	11,92	21,75	11,40	22,94	3,77	26,2
15	13,62	20,80	12,71	22,13	5,87	23,71
20	14,678	20,20	13,54	21,57	7,28	22,33
25	16,01	19,45	14,55	20,95	9,08	20,89
30	17,58	18,68	15,70	20,29	11,16	19,55
Multispectral image formed by 4, 5, and 3 Bands						
5	11,49	21,74	10,9	23,14	3,32	26,67
15	13,11	20,84	12,19	22,3	5,46	23,96
20	14,11	20,25	13,03	21,72	6,879	22,45
25	15,30	19,60	14,03	21,06	8,65	21,00
30	16,81	18,83	15,15	20,42	10,74	19,63

Table 3. *PSNR* and *MAE* measures for different algorithms applied in the Multispectral Images.

Table 3 exposes the multispectral filtering for real life images of the same scene received from the LandSat 7 satellite in seven different bands. Objective criteria *PSNR* and *MAE* were calculated using false colour in 321, 432 and 453 bands. Filtered multispectral images can be seen in Fig. 11 for the 432 Band.

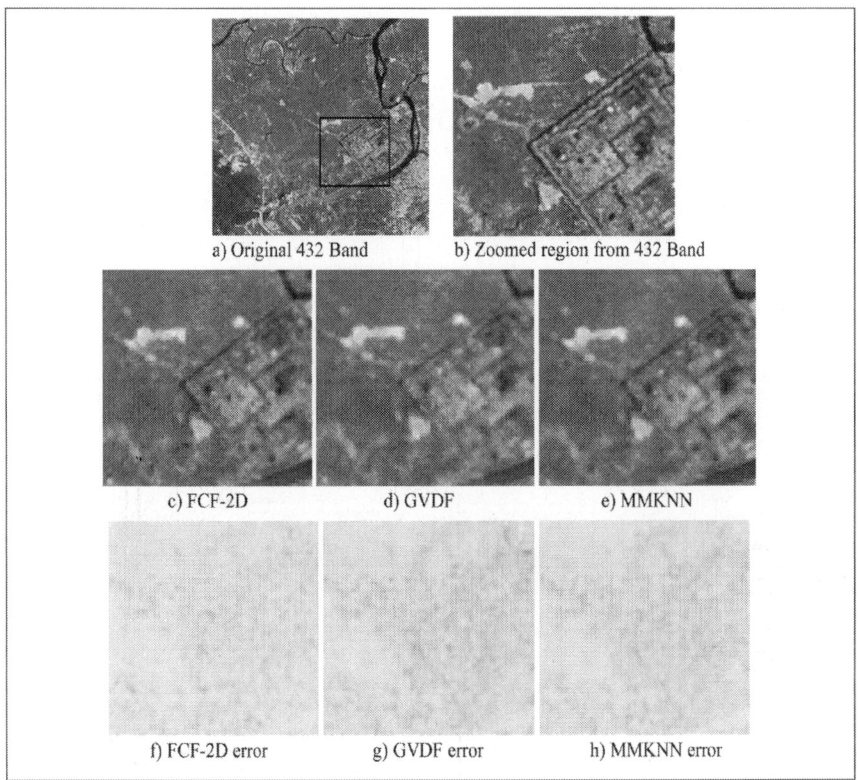

Fig. 11. Filtering and error image results in the 432 Band in a multispectral image.

In Table 4, one can see that the best performance is realized by novel 3D algorithm according to *MAE* criterion in wide range of noise contaminations, in opposite, in *PSNR* criterion values, the best performances for novel framework are found for middle, and in some cases, for high noise intensity. *NCD* criterion values exposed in the Table 5 characterize the best preservation in the chromaticity properties in wide range of noise corruption in Flowers video sequence realized by novel 3D filtering scheme confirming its robustness. Similar numerical results in less detailed video sequences, such as Miss America show that the designed algorithm demonstrates the best filtering performance in *NCD* values in wide range of noise corruption.

Subjective perception by human viewer can be observed in Fig. 12, showing in the zoomed filtered Flowers frame the better performance of the designed 3D framework in comparison with known methods, where it is clearly seen that novel algorithm preserves better the edges, fine details, and chromaticity properties against other filters.

(%)Noise	FCF-3D		MF_3F		VVMF		VVDKNNVMF		VGVDF		VAVDATM		VATM		KNNF	
	MAE	PSNR	MAE	PSNR	MAE	PSNR	MAE	PSNR	MAE	PSNR	MAE	PSNR	MAE	PSNR	MAE	PSNR
0	1,58	30,5	6,44	27,0	6,47	27.0	7,02	26,2	7,35	25,6	5,07	27,5	6,62	27,1	3,20	33,13
10	2,73	28,6	6,90	26,5	6,86	26,5	7,83	25,5	7,55	25,5	5,84	26,9	7,05	26,6	5,16	28,95
15	3,38	27,8	7,19	26,2	7,14	26,2	8,20	25,1	7,72	25,3	6,28	26,6	7,35	26,3	6,79	26,63
20	4,11	26,9	7,55	25,8	7,49	25,8	8,70	24,6	8,12	24,8	6,77	26,1	7,72	25,9	8,93	24,49
30	6,08	25,0	8,59	24,8	8,50	24,7	10,0	23,2	9,74	23,2	8,13	25,0	8,88	24,8	14,6	20,86

Table 4. *PNSR* and *MAE* criteria results for Flowers colour video sequence averaged per 100 frames.

(%)Noise	FCF-3D	MF_3F	VVMF	VVDKNNVMF	VGVDF	VAVDATM	VATM	KNNF
0	0,003	0,014	0,014	0,015	0,016	0,011	0,014	0,006
10	0,006	0,015	0,015	0,017	0,016	0,012	0,015	0,010
15	0,007	0,015	0,015	0,017	0,016	0,013	0,015	0,013
20	0,009	0,016	0,016	0,018	0,017	0,014	0,016	0,017
25	0,010	0,017	0,017	0,019	0,018	0,015	0,017	0,022
30	0,012	0,018	0,018	0,020	0,020	0,017	0,018	0,027

Table 5. *NCD* averaged values for Flowers colour video sequence.

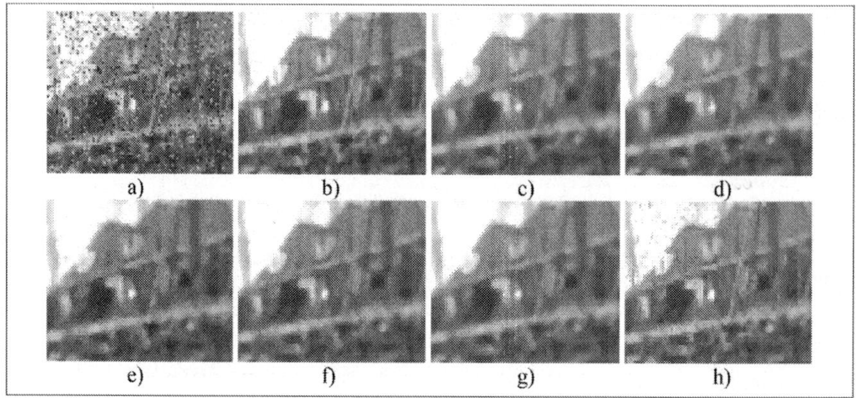

Fig. 12. a) Zoomed image region of 10*th* Flowers frame contaminated by impulsive noise of 15% intensity, b) Designed *FCF-3D*, c) *MF 3F*, d) *VVMF*, e) *VGVDF*, f) *VAVDATM*, g) *VATM*, h) *KNNF*.

Real-Time analysis was realized on the *DSP* (*TMS320DM642*, Texas Instruments) and is based on Reference Framework defined as *RF*5 (Mullanix & Magdic et al., 2003). Table 6 presents the processing times in some 2D and 3D algorithms, which have been implemented on *DSP*, demonstrating reliability of the proposed approach against better algorithms found in literature.

5. Conclusions

It has designed a novel structure of robust framework to remove impulse noise and additive noise in images and multichannel video sequences. Unlike existed techniques, the designed approach employs fuzzy and directional techniques to estimate motion and noise in the past and present frames showing good results. The designed fuzzy rules characterize the presence of motion and noise between the pixels in two frames (past and present frames). It has been demonstrated that the combined use of gradients and vectors improves the performance of the algorithm in comparison with cases where it is used any of this characteristics. The excellent performance of the new filtering scheme has been tested

Algorithm	Number of frames	Total Time	Max Time per frame (s)	Average Time (s)
2D Algorithms				
MF	20	0.062	0.0037	0.0031
VMF	20	0.552	0.0283	0.0278
VMF_FAS	20	41.116	2.093	2.055
AVMF	20	1.591	0.0805	0.0796
GVDF	20	117.382	5.887	5.869
CWVDF	20	58.18	5.806	2.909
FCF-2D	20	24.822	1.243	1.241
3D Algorithms				
MF_3F	20	0.114	0.0065	0.0057
VVMF	20	1.496	0.075	0.075
VATM	20	2.681	0.1347	0.134
KNNF	20	2.04	0.103	0.102
VGVDF	20	512.02	28.52	25.6
VAVDATM	20	497.356	25.551	24.867
FCF-3D	20	148.806	7.533	7.440

Table 6. 2D and 3D time processing on *DSP TMS320DM642*.

during numerous simulations in terms of objective criteria, as well as the subjective visual
perception where the filtered images are seen by human visual system.

6. References

Amer, A. & Schroder, H. (1996). A new video noise reduction algorithm using spatial
subbands, *ICECS*, vol. 1, 1996, pp. 45-48.

Camarena, G., Gregori, J., Morillas, V., & Sapena, S. (2008). Fast Detection and Removal of
Impulsive Noise Using Peer Groups and Fuzzy Metrics, *Journal of Visual
Communication and Image Representation*, Vol. 19, No. 1, 2008, pp. 20-29.

Franke, K., Kppen, M. & Nickolay, B. (2000). Fuzzy Image Processing by using Dubois and
Prade Fuzzy Norms, *Proceedings Pattern Recognition*, Vol. 3, 2000, pp. 514-517.

Lukac, R., Smolka, B., N. Plataniotis, K. & N. Venetsanopoulos, A. (2004) Selection Weighted
Vector Directional Filters, *Comput. Vision and Image Understanding*, Vol. 94, 2004, pp.
140-167.

Ma, Z. H., Wu, H. R. & Feng, D. (2007). Fuzzy vector partition filtering technique for color image
restoration, *Computer Vision and Image Un-derstanding*, Vol. 107, No. 1-2, 2007, pp. 26-37.

Morillas, S., Gregori, V. & Peris-Fajarnes, G. (2008). Isolating Impulsive Noise Pixels in Color
Images by Peer Group techniques, *Computer Vision and Image Understanding*,
Vol.110, No. 1, 2008, pp. 102-116.

Morillas, S., Gregori, V., Peris-Fajarns, G. & Latorre, P. (2005). A fast impulsive noise color
image filter using fuzzy metrics, *Real-Time Imaging*, Vol. 11, 2005, pp. 417-428.

Morillas, S., Gregori, V., Peris-Fajarnes, G. & Sapena, A. (2007). New Adaptive Vector Filter
Using Fuzzy Metrics, *Journal of Electronic Imaging*, Vol. 16, No. 3, 2007, pp. 033007.

Morillas, S., Gregori, V., Peris-Fajarnes, G. & Sapena, A. (2008). Local self-adaptive fuzzy
filter for impulsive noise removal in color images, *Signal Processing*, Vol. 88, No. 2,
2008, pp. 390-398.

Morillas, S., Gregori, V. & Sapena, A. (2006). Fuzzy bilateral filtering for color images,
Lecture Notes in Computer Science, Vol. 4141, 2006, pp. 138-145.

Mullanix, T., Magdic, D., Wan, V., Lee, B., Cruickshank, B., Campbell, A., DeGraw, Y. (2003).
Reference Frameworks for eXpressDSP Software: RF5, An Extensive, High Density
System (SPRA795A), *Texas Instruments*, 2003.

Nie, Y. & E. Barner, K. (2006). Fuzzy Rank LUM Filters, *IEEE Trans. on Image Processing*, Vol.
15, No. 12, 2006, pp. 3636-3654.

Plataniotis, K. N., Androutsos, D., Vinayagamoorthy, S. & Venetsanopoulos, A. N. (1997). Color Image Processing Using Adaptive Multichannel Filters, *IEEE Transactions on Image Processing*, Vol. 6, No. 7, 1997, pp. 933-949.

Plataniotis, K. N. & Venetsanopoulos, A. N. (2000). *Color Image Processing and Applications*, Springer Verlag, Berlin.

Ponomaryov, V. I. (2007). Real-time 2D-3D filtering using order statistics based algorithms, *Journal of Real-Time Image Processing*, Vol. 1, No. 3, 2007, pp.173-194.

Ponomaryov, V., Gallegos-Funes, F. & Rosales-Silva, A. (2005). Real-Time Color Image Processing Using Order Statistics Filters, *Journal of Mathematical Imaging and Vision Springer*, Vol. 23, No. 3, 2005, pp. 315-319.

Ponomaryov, VI., Gallegos-Funes, FJ. &Rosales-Silva, A. (2005). Real-time color imaging based on RM-filters for impulsive noise reduction, *Journal of Imaging Science and Technology*, Vol. 49, No. 3, 2005, pp. 205-219.

Ponomaryov, V., Gallegos-Funes, F., Rosales-Silva, A. & Loboda, I. (2006). 3D vector directional filters to process video sequences, *Lecture Notes in Computer Science*, 2006, Vol. 4225, pp. 474-480.

Russo, F & Ramponi, G. (1996). A Fuzzy Filter for Images Corrupted by Impulse Noise, *Signal Processing Letters*, Vol. 3, No. 6, 1996, pp. 168-170.

Saeidi, M., Saeidi, B., Saeidi, Z. & Saeidi, K. (2006). A New Fuzzy Algorithm in Image Sequences Filtering, *Circuits, Signals, and Systems*, 2006, pp. 531-105.

Schulte, S., De Witte, V., Nachtegael, M., V. der Weken, D. & E. Kerre, E. (2006). Fuzzy Two-Step Filter for Impulse Noise Reduction From Color Images, *IEEE Trans. on Image Processing*, Vol. 15, No. 11, 2006, pp. 3567-3578.

Schulte, S., De Witte, V., Nachtegael, M., Van Der Weken D. & E. Kerre, E. (2007). Fuzzy Random Impulse Noise Reduction Method, *Fuzzy Sets and Systems*, Vol. 158, No. 3, 2007, pp. 270-283.

Schulte, S., De Witte, V. & E. Kerre, E. (2007). A Fuzzy Noise Reduction Method for Color Images, *IEEE Trans. on Image Processing*, Vol. 16, No. 5, 2007, pp. 1425-1436.

Schulte, S., Huysmans, B., Pizurica, A., E. Kerre, E. & Philips, W. (2006). A new fuzzy-based wavelet shrinkage image denoising technique, *Lecture notes Comput. Sci.*, Vol. 4179, 2006, pp. 12-23.

Schulte, S., Morillas, S., Gregori, V. & E. Kerre, E. (2007). A New Fuzzy Color Correlated Impulse Noise Reduction Method, *IEEE Trans. on Image Proc.*, Vol. 16, No. 10, 2007, pp. 2565-2575.

Shaomin, P. & Lucke, L. (1994). Fuzzy filtering for mixed noise removal during image processing, *IEEE Fuzzy Systems*, Vol. 1, 1994, pp. 89-93.

Smolka, B., Lukac, R., Chydzinski, A., N. Plataniotis, K. & Wojciechowski, W. (2003). Fast Adaptive Similarity Based Impulsive Noise Reduction Filter, *Real-Time Imaging*, Vol. 9, No. 4, 2003, pp. 261-276.

Trahanias, P. E., Venetsanopoulos, A. N. (1996). Direccional Processing of Color Images: Theory and Experimental Results, *IEEE Transactions on Image Processing*, Vo. 5, No. 6, 1996, pp. 868-880.

Zlokolica, V., De Geyter, M., Schulte, S., Pizurica, A., Philips, W. & Kerre, E. (2005). Fuzzy Logic Recursive Motion Detection for Tracking and Denoising of Video Sequences, *IS&T/SPIE Symposium on Electronic Imaging, Video Communications and Processing 5685*, 2005, pp. 771-782.

Zlokolica, V., Schulte, S., Pizurica, A., Philips, W. & Kerre (2006). Fuzzy Logic Recursive Motion Detection and denoising of Video Sequences, *Journal of Electronic Imaging*, Vol. 15, No. 2, 2006, pp. 023008.

## 22

Fast Evolutionary Image Processing using Multi-GPUs

Jun Ando and Tomoharu Nagao
Yokohama National University
Japan

1. Introduction

In the realization of machine intelligence, image processing and recognition technologies are gaining in importance. However, it is difficult to construct image processing in each problem. In this case, a general-purpose method that constructs image processing without depending on problems is necessary.

On the other hand, Evolutionary Computation studies are widely applied to image processing. Evolutionary Computation is an optimizing algorithm inspired by evolutional processes of living things. We have previously proposed a system that automatically constructs an image-processing filter: Automatic Construction of Tree-structural Image Transformation (ACTIT). In this system, ACTIT approximates target image processing by combining tree-structurally several image-processing filters prepared in advance with genetic programming (GP), which is a type of Evolutionary Computation. We have proven that ACTIT is an effective method for many problems.

However, such complex image processing requires a great deal of computing time to optimize tree-structural image processing if ACTIT is applied to a problem that uses large and numerous images. Therefore, it is important to obtain fast evolutionary image processing. Some methods allow us to obtain fast processing, improve the algorithm, and implement fast hardware and parallel processing.

In this chapter, we employ a Graphics Processing Unit (GPU) as fast hardware to ACTIT for realization of fast image processing optimization. Moreover, the system calculates in parallel using multiple GPUs and increases in speed. We experimentally show that the optimization speed of the proposed method is faster than that of ordinary ACTIT.

This chapter is composed of the following. Section 2 discusses related works, ACTIT, General Purpose GPU (GPGPU), and parallel processing in Evolutionary Computation. Section 3 describes Multi-GPUs-ACTIT, which is the proposed system in this chapter. Section 4 experimentally shows that the proposed system is effective. Finally, section 5 describes our conclusions and future work.

2. Related works

2.1 ACTIT

ACTIT is a study of image processing using GP. It automatically constructs a tree-structural image transformation by combining several image-processing filters prepared in advance with GP by referring to training image sets. The individual in GP is a tree-structural image transformation. A tree-structural image transformation is composed of input images as terminal nodes, non-terminal nodes in the form of several types of image-processing filters, and a root in the form of an output image.

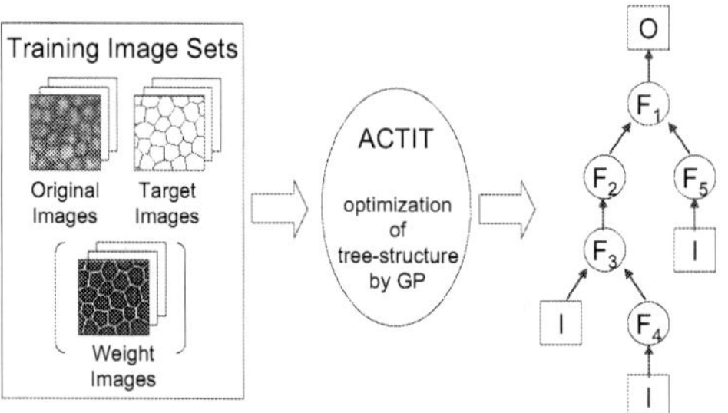

optimized tree-structural image transformation
(I: Input Image, O: Output Image, F_i: i-th Image-processing Filter)

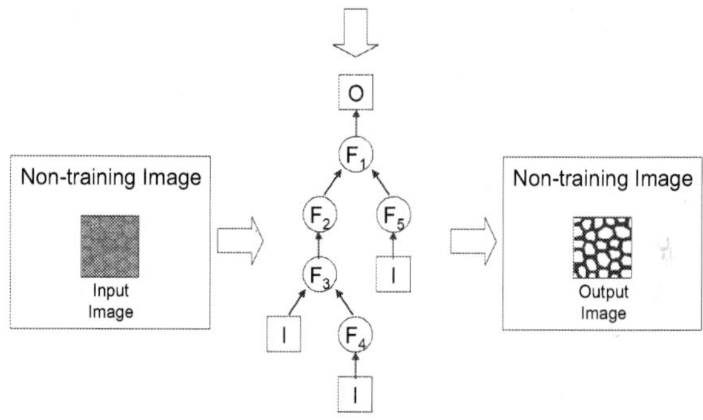

application of optimized tree-structural image transformation
to non-training image

Fig. 1. The processing flow of the ACTIT system.

Figure 1 shows the processing flow of the ACTIT system. Training image sets are prepared, including several original images, their target images and weight images that indicate the important degree of pixel. We set the parameters that GP uses to optimize the tree structure and feed the training image sets to ACTIT. Then, ACTIT optimizes the tree-structural image transformation by means of GP. As a result, we can obtain an optimized tree-structural image transformation that has maximum fitness.

The tree-structural image transformation applies a certain processing mechanism to images that have the same characteristics. If the constructed tree-structural image transformation is appropriate, we can expect similar effects to the images that have the same characteristics as those learned. We prove that ACTIT is an effective method for a number of problems, such as 2D image processing for the detection of defects and 3D medical image processing.

2.2 GPGPU

The computational power of GPU on general graphics boards has been improving rapidly. Simple computational power per unit time of GPU has previously been superior to that of

CPU. Past GPUs performed only fast fixed CG processing. However, the latest GPUs have graphics pipelines that can be freely programmed and replaced to perform complex CG processing. Thus, presently, in research that puts GPU to practical use for the general purpose of calculating, GPGPU is a popular technique.

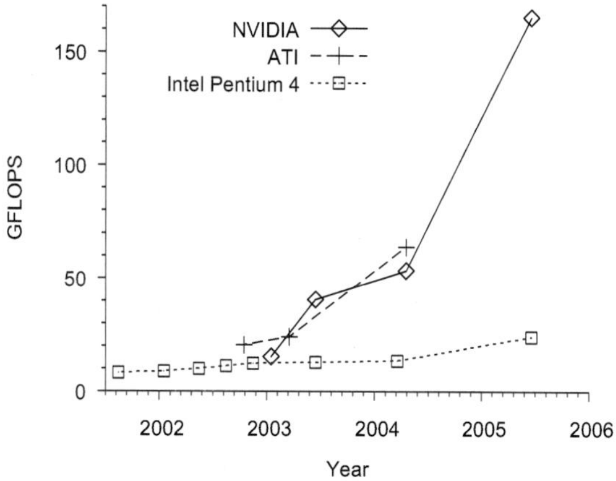

Fig. 2. The computational power of CPU and GPU in recent years.

2000	NVIDIA released DirectX 8 which supports programmable *shader* architecture for the first time.
2001	NVIDIA GeForce 3 series GPU, which actually supports programmable *shader* architecture, appeared.
2002	NVIDIA released the 3D graphics language, "Cg (C for graphics)".
2004	Research report on GPGPU, "GP2" is held in Los Angeles for the first time.
2005	GPGPU session is newly established at CG festival SIGGRAPH sponsored by the Association for Computing Machinery (ACM).

Table 1. The history of GPGPU.

Figure 2 shows the progress of the computational power of CPU and GPU over the past several years. Simple computational power per unit time of GPU has previously been superior to that of CPU during this time. The growth rate per year of GPU has also been superior to that of CPU.

Table 1 shows the history of GPGPU. Studies relating to GPGPU have only recently begun. NVIDIA GeForce 3 series GPU, which in practice supports programmable *shader* architecture, appeared in 2001. In 2002, NVIDIA released a high-level *shader* language Cg (C for graphics) and a toolkit that includes its compiler. Cg is a 3D graphics language similar to C language, and NVIDIA co-developed Cg with Microsoft. Formerly, it was necessary to code by hand with the assembly language to program using GPU. However, presently it is possible to generate an optimized code; GPU made by NVIDIA is the best technique for use with Cg. In 2005, GPGPU session was established at the CG festival SIGGRAPH, sponsored by the Association for Computing Machinery.

GPU programming is without doubt different from CPU programming. For instance, GPU does not have random access memory space that can be freely read and written to when it calculates. GPU has an architecture specializing in parallel processing. This means that GPU is a stream processor. Therefore, GPGPU is effective for applications that satisfy the following three demands:

- Processed data are of a huge size.
- There is little dependency between each data.
- The processing of data can be highly parallel.

Therefore, GPGPU is effective for calculating matrices, image processing, physical simulations, and so on. Recently, programming languages specializing in GPGPU, Sh, Scout and Brook have been released. In addition, in 2006, NVIDIA released CUDA (Compute Unified Device Architecture), which performs general-purpose applications on GPU. Thus it is now relatively easy to program with GPU.

2.3 Parallel processing in evolutionary computation

Many studies have proven the performance of genetic algorithm (GA) and GP in parallel. The following show the main parallel models in GA and GP.

1. Island model: In an island model (Fig. 3), the population in GA and GP is divided into sections of population (Islands). Each section of population is assigned to multiple processors and applied to normal genetic operators in parallel. Exchange of individuals between sections of population (Migration) is performed. Each section is independently evaluated. Therefore, we expect that each section retains the variety of the entire population.

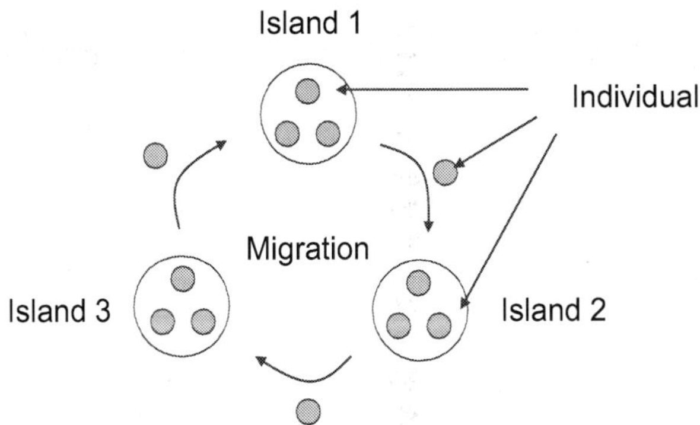

Fig. 3. Island model.

2. Master–slave model: In the master–slave model (Fig. 4), the fitness of individuals in GA and GP is calculated quickly in parallel. A master–slave model is generally composed of one control node (Master) and multiple calculation nodes (Slave). In this model, one control node performs genetic operators composed of selection, crossover, and mutation. Multiple calculation nodes share the task of calculating the fitness of individuals that consume computing time.

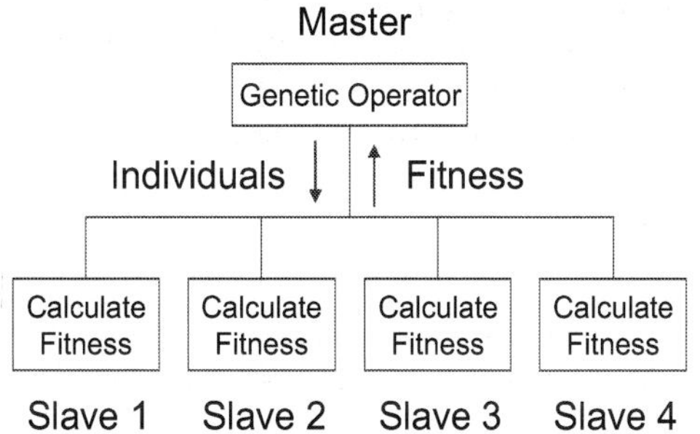

Fig. 4. Master-slave model.

3. Parallel-MGG model: The Parallel-MGG model (Fig. 5) is based on the master–slave model for fast processing. In the Parallel-MGG model, a control node sends two individuals as parents to calculation nodes. Each calculation node updates two individuals using Minimal Generation Gap (MGG) in parallel. A control node then receives two individuals of the next generation as children from each calculation node. In Parallel-MGG, the transport time between nodes is reduced because processing is asynchronous.

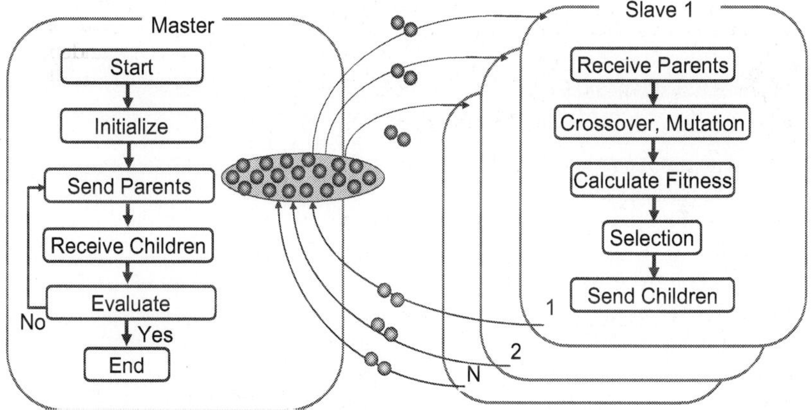

Fig. 5. Parallel-MGG model.

3. Fast evolutionary image processing

3.1 GPU-ACTIT

ACTIT requires a large amount of computing time to optimize tree-structural image processing when applied to a problem that uses large and numerous training image sets, because it needs to repeatedly create tree-structural image transformations and calculate their fitness. The computing time of the image transformation part of ACTIT accounts for 99% of the entire computing time. We therefore implement image-processing filters on programmable graphics pipelines of GPU for the purpose of reducing optimization time.

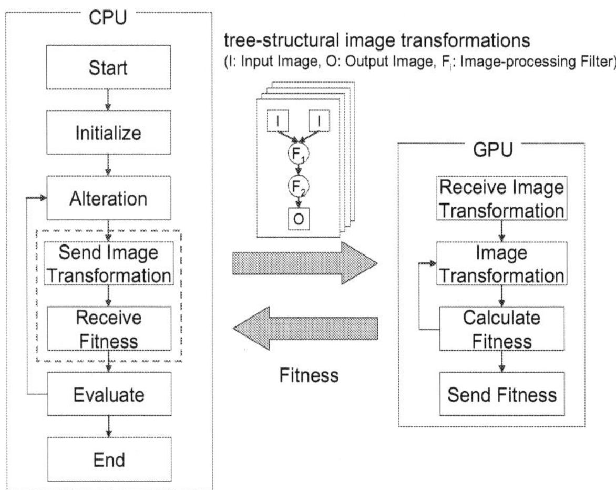

Fig. 6. GPU-ACTIT.

1. The parts of CPU and GPU: Figure 6 shows the processing flow of CPU and GPU for the proposed system. First, the system loads training image sets and image-processing filters, which are written in Cg and compiled to GPU during initialization. The system executes the alternation of generations part, composed of selection, crossover, and mutation operators, of GP on CPU. It then performs image transformation and calculates fitness on GPU.

    CPU indicates the image-processing filter and its target image that GPU executes from the image filters of tree-structural image transformation to GPU one by one during image transformation. GPU performs tree-structural image transformation according to CPU. GPU calculates the fitness of each individual, i.e., tree-structural image transformation from the difference between the target image and the output image that is a result of image transformation in calculating fitness part. These processes are repeated until the fitness of all updated individuals per iteration are calculated. CPU reads back the fitness from GPU immediately.

    The system repeats these processes until the fitness of the best individual becomes 1.0 or the iteration number becomes max. Finally, we obtain an optimized tree-structural image transformation that has maximum fitness. We can obtain faster ACTIT by reducing the number of transporting data between CPU and GPU by loading training image sets firstly and returning fitness at once. We almost allow GPU to perform processing which costs computing time.

2. Implement on GPU: Programs written for CPU cannot be applied to GPU directly, because GPU has some limitations over CPU. Therefore, we are currently implementing only simple image-processing filters on GPU. The following describes several image-processing filters implemented on GPU:

    - Calculation of current and neighboring pixels (Mean Filter, Sobel Filter, and so on).
    - Calculation of two images (Difference Filter and so on).
    - Calculation of mean, maximum, minimum value in the whole image (Binarization with Mean Value, Linear Transformation of Histogram, and so on).

Figure 7 shows a Binarization filter (mean value). We calculate fast mean value in the whole image with parallel reductions.

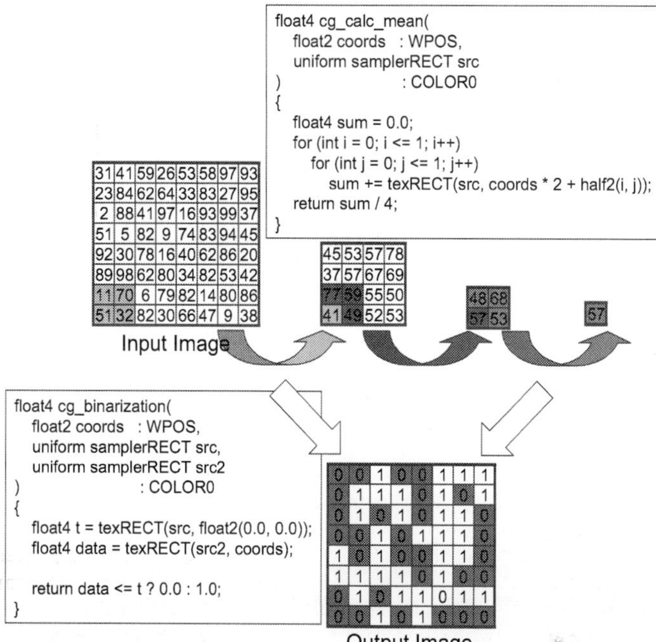

Fig. 7. Binarization filter (mean value).

3.2 Proposed parallel model

GPU-ACTIT is performed in parallel using multiple GPUs for fast processing. Parallel processing is effective for ACTIT, because the computing time of the parallelable part of ACTIT accounts for most of the entire computing time.

Figure 8 shows Multi-GPUs-ACTIT. The proposed system is composed of multiple PCs that have one GPU. The factors that prevent the system from achieving fast processing are synchronous time and transport time. There is no synchronous time, because processing is asynchronous in Parallel MGG. Moreover, we can improve Parallel MGG for the purpose of reducing transport time. In this new Parallel-MGG, the waiting buffer is located in each calculation node. The individual is sent to the waiting buffer in advance. Subsequent processing then starts as soon as the previous processing is finished, since the waiting buffer is utilized.

4. Experiments

4.1 Experimental setting

Here, we compare the optimization speed of the proposed system with ordinary ACTIT. The proposed system is composed of five PCs (one server and four clients) connected by a LAN network. Figure 9 shows the outside of the system.

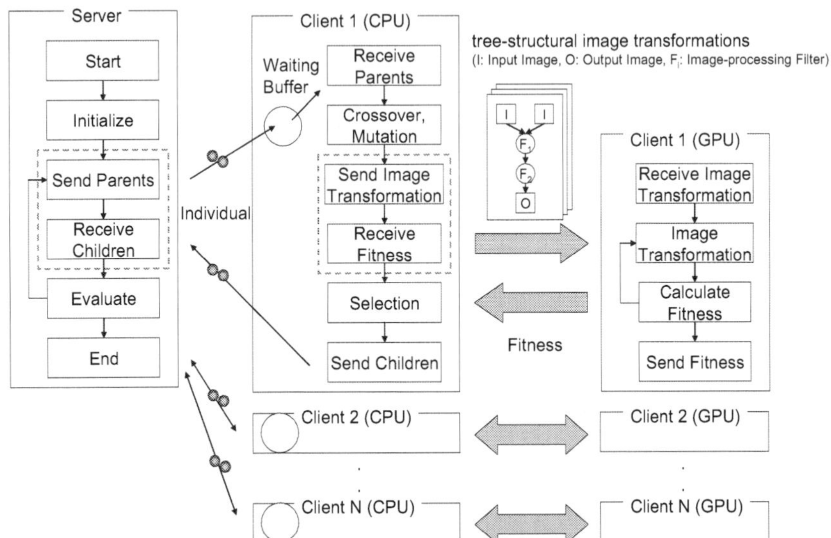

Fig. 8. Multi-GPUs-ACTIT.

Fig. 9. The outside of the system.

Table 2 shows the specifications of the PC used. Intel Core 2 Duo E6400 CPU and NVIDIA GeForce 7900 GS GPU are utilized in these experiments. We program with GPU using OpenGL and Cg.

We implement 37 types of one or two input and one output simple image-processing filters. GPU can calculate four planes (red, green, blue, and alpha) at the same time. Therefore, we prepare four training image sets. The dimensions of each image are 64×64, 128×128, 256×256, 512×512, and 1024×1024, respectively. GP parameters employ common values. The alternation model used by GP is MGG.

PC	DELL Dimension 9200
CPU	Intel Core 2 Duo E6400
RAM	2GB
Graphics Board	NVIDIA GeForce 7900 GS (G71)
Network	100Mbps Ethernet
OS	Microsoft Windows XP Professional SP2
Graphics API	OpenGL
Shader Language	Cg (C for graphics)

Table 2. Specifications of the PC used.

4.2 Experimental results

1. Comparison of ordinary CPU-ACTIT and one GPU-ACTIT: First, we compared the optimization speed of one GPU-ACTIT with ordinary CPU-ACTIT. Figure 10 and Table 3 show the experimental results. The horizontal axis denotes image size, and the vertical axis denotes optimization speed. In Fig. 10 and Table 3, values are based on the optimization speed of 1.0 for CPU-ACTIT using images of 64×64.

Image Size	CPU-ACTIT	GPU-ACTIT
64×64	1.0	6.3
128×128	0.7	21.1
256×256	0.9	73.3
512×512	1.1	102.0
1024×1024	1.3	104.3

Table 3. Details of experimental results of a comparison of CPU-ACTIT and GPU-ACTIT.

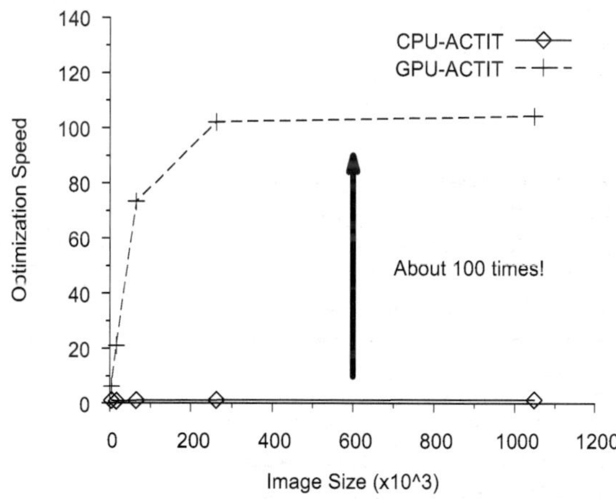

Fig. 10. Experimental results of a comparison of CPU-ACTIT and GPU-ACTIT.

The optimization of GPU-ACTIT was about 10 times faster than that of CPU-ACTIT with a small image, while it was about 100 times faster with a large image. It is well known that

GPU is effective when it uses large data. Therefore, the proposed method is very effective, because large and numerous training image sets tend to be used in real problems.

Next, we experimented to explain the influence of transporting data and synchronous time between CPU and GPU. Figure 11 shows details of the processing time. "GPU-ACTIT (inefficiently)" loads and reads images whenever it calculates the fitness of an individual. Loading and reading images influence the performance. As a result, the proposed method essentially performed the process that costs large computing time on GPU.

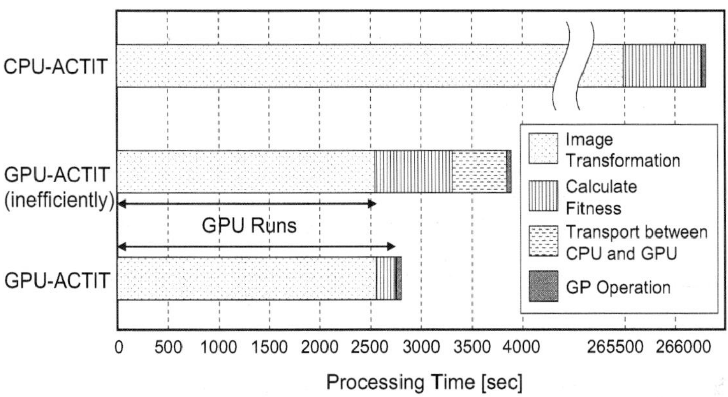

Fig. 11. Details of processing time.

2. Parallel of GPU-ACTIT: We compared the optimization speed of Multi-GPUs-ACTIT with one GPU-ACTIT. Parallel models used were master–slave, Parallel-MGG, and Parallel-MGG with waiting buffer. The number of GPUs was 1–4. Image size was only 512×512.

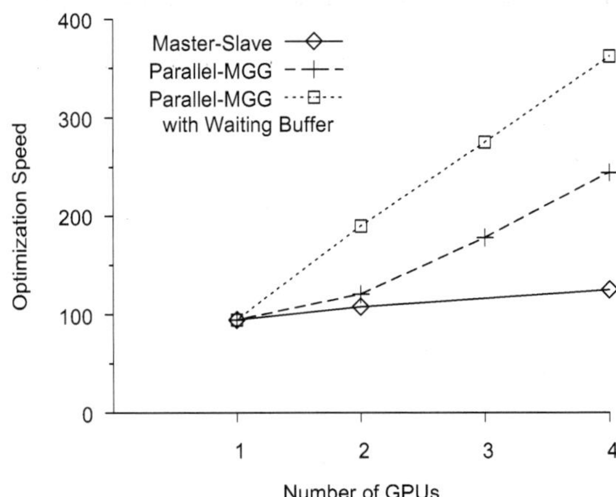

Fig. 12. Experimental results of Multi-GPUs-ACTIT.

Number of GPUs	CPU-ACTIT	Master-slave	Parallel-MGG	Parallel-MGG with Waiting Buffer
1	1.0	94.5 (1.0)	94.5 (1.0)	94.5 (1.0)
2	-	107.7 (1.1)	120.6 (1.3)	189.7 (2.0)
3	-	-	177.9 (1.9)	274.9 (2.9)
4	-	125.0 (1.3)	244.4 (2.6)	362.2 (3.8)

Table 4. Details of experimental results of Multi-GPUs-ACTIT.

Figure 12 and Table 4 show experimental results. The horizontal axis denotes the number of GPUs, and the vertical axis denotes optimization speed. In Fig. 12 and Table 4, values are based on the optimization speed of 1.0 for CPU-ACTIT using 512×512 images. Parenthetic values are based on the optimization speed of 1.0 for one GPU-ACTIT using 512×512 images.

The optimization of four GPUs-ACTIT was about 3.8 times faster than that of one GPU-ACTIT in the proposed parallel model. The optimization of four GPUs-ACTIT was about 360 times faster than that of CPU-ACTIT in the proposed parallel model. We experimentally showed that the proposed parallel method is efficient.

5. Conclusions

We employed GPU to ACTIT for the purpose of reducing optimization time. The proposed method essentially performed the process that costs large computing time on GPU. Moreover, we proposed an efficient parallel model and instructed GPU-ACTIT to perform in parallel using multiple GPUs for fast processing. The optimization of the proposed method was several hundred times faster than that of the ordinary ACTIT. We experimentally showed that the proposed method is effective.

In future work, we plan to implement complex filters for ACTIT using only CPU that can be implemented on GPU. We propose image-processing algorithms that are effective for GPGPU. We also aim to construct a fast evolutionary image-processing system.

6. References

Aoki, S. & Nagao, T. (1999). ACTIT; Automatic Construction of Tree-structural Image Transformation, *The Institute of Image Information and Television Engineers*, Vol.53, No.6, pp.888-894.

Buck, I.; Foley, T.; Horn, D.; Sugerman, J.; Fatahalian, K.; Houston, M. & Hanrahan, P. (2004). Brook for GPUs: Stream Computing on Graphics Hardware, *SIGGRAPH 2004*.

Erick Cantu-Paz. (1998). A survey of parallel genetic algorithms, *Calculateurs Paralleles*, Vol.10, No.2.

Fernando, R. & Kilgard, M. J. (2003). *The Cg Tutorial: The Definitive Guide to Programmable Real-Time Graphics*, the Addison Wesley, ISBN978-0321194961.

Fernando, R. (2004). *GPU Gems: Programming Techniques, Tips, and Tricks for Real-Time Graphics*, the Addison Wesley, ISBN978-0321228321.

Fung, J.; Mann, S. & Aimone, C. (2005). OpenVIDIA: Parallel GPU Computer Vision, *Proceedings of the ACM Multimedia 2005*, pp.849-852, Nov.6-11, Singapore.

GoldBerg, D. E. (1989). *Genetic Algorithms in Search, Optimization & Machine Learning,* the Addison Wesley, ISBN978-0201157673.

Holland, J. H. (1975, 1992). *Adaptation in Natural and Artificial Systems,* the Univ. Michigan Press, ISBN978-0472084609, MIT Press, ISBN978-0262581110.

Koza, J. R. (1992). *Genetic Programming on the Programming of Computers by Means of Natural Selection,* MIT Press, ISBN978-0262111706.

Mura, H.; Ando, J. & Nagao, T. (2006). A research on fast tree-structural image transformation using PC cluster, *The Institute of Image Information and Television Engineers Technical Report,* Vol.30, No.17, pp.87-88, Japan.

Nagao, T. (2002). *Evolutionary Image Processing,* Shokodo, ISBN978-4785690632, Japan.

Nakano, Y. & Nagao, T. (2006). Automatic Extraction of Internal Organs Region from 3D PET Image Data using 3D-ACTIT, *International Workshop on Advanced Image Technology 2006,* Jan.10, Okinawa, Japan.

Owens, J. D.; Luebke, D.; Govindaraju, N.; Harris, M.; Kruger, J.; Lefohn, A. E. & Purcell, T. J. (2005). A Survey of General-Purpose Computation on Graphics Hardware, *EUROGRAPHICS 2005.*

Pharr, M. & Fernando, R. (2005). *GPU Gems 2: Programming Techniques for High-Performance Graphics and General-Purpose Computation,* the Addison Wesley, ISBN978-0321335593.

Sato, H.; Ono, I. & Kobayashi, S. (1997). A New Generation Alternation Model of Genetic Algorithms and its Assessment, *The Japanese Society for Artificial Intelligence,* Vol.12, No.5, pp.734-744.

Tanese, R. (1989). Distributed Genetic Algorithms, *Proc. 3rd International Conference on Genetic Algorithms,* pp.434-439.

## 23

Image Processing:
Towards a System on Chip

A. Elouardi, S. Bouaziz, A. Dupret, L. Lacassagne,
J.O. Klein and R. Reynaud
Institute of Fundamental Electronics, Paris XI University, Orsay
France

1. Introduction

Many kinds of vision systems are available on today's market with various applications. Despite the wide variety of these applications, all digital cameras have the same basic functional components, which consist in photons collection, wavelength photons discrimination (filters), timing, control and drive electronics for the sensing elements, sample/hold operators, colours processing circuits, analogue to digital conversion and electronics interfaces (Fossum, 1997).

Today, robotics and intelligent vehicles need sensors with fast response time, low energy consumption, able to extract high-level information from the environment (Muramatsu et al., 2002). Adding hardware computation operators near the sensor increases the computations potentiality and reduces inputs/outputs operations towards the central processor unit.

The CCD technology have been the dominant tool for electronic image sensors during several decades due to their high photosensitivity, low fixed pattern noise, small pixel and large array sizes.

However, in the last decade, CMOS image sensors have gained attention from many researchers and industries due to their low energy dissipation, low cost, on chip processing capabilities and their integration on standard or quasi-standard VLSI process.

Still, raw output images acquired by CMOS sensors present poor quality for display and need further processing, mainly because of noise, blurriness and poor contrast. In order to tackle these problems, image-processing circuits are typically associated to image sensors as a part of the whole vision system. Usually, two areas coexist within the same chip for sensing and preprocessing that are implemented onto the same integrated circuit.

To face the high data flow induced by the computer vision algorithms, an alternative approach consists in performing some image processing on the sensor focal plane. The integration of pixels array and image processing circuits on a single monolithic chip makes the system more compact and allows enhancing the behavior and the response of the sensor. Hence, to achieve some simple low-level image processing tasks (early-vision), a smart sensor integrates analogue and/or digital processing circuits in the pixel (Burns et al., 2003, El Gamal et al., 1999, Dudek, Hicks, 2000) or at the edge of the pixels array (Ni, Guan, 2000). Most often, such circuits are dedicated for specific applications. The energy dissipation is weak compared to that of the traditional approaches using multi chip (microprocessor, sensor, logic glue ...etc) (Alireza, 2000). Noise and cross-talk can also be reduced through monolithic connections instead of off-chip wires.

Moreover, this chapter is built to get a conclusion on the aptitude of the retinas to become potential candidates for systems on chip, consequently to reach an algorithm-architecture and system adequacy. In this context, an application was selected making it possible to develop a conclusion on a partial integration of a system on chip. Hence this chapter focuses on the VLSI compatibility of retinas, more particularly, of integrating image processing algorithms and their processors on the same sensor focal plane to provide a smart on chip vision system (System on Chip). It discusses why the retina is advantageous, what elementary functions and/or operators should be added on chip and how to integrate image processing algorithms (i.e. how to implement the smart sensors). The chapter includes recommendations on system-level architectures, applications and discusses the limitations of the implementation of smart retinas, which are categorized by the nature of image processing algorithms, trying to answer the following questions:

- Why vision algorithms (image processing algorithms) should be implemented by the retinas?
- What algorithms and processing components should be put with retinas to provide a part or a whole system on chip?
- How to aggregate these processing operators (by pixel, by group of pixels, by column, by line or for the whole array)?
- What structures are the best suited for each class of image processing algorithms?

To sustain the discussion, we propose a system-level architecture and a design methodology for integrating image processing within a CMOS retina on a single chip. It highlights a compromise between versatility, parallelism, processing speed and resolution. Our solution aims to take also into account the algorithms response times, the significant resolution of the sensor, while reducing energy consumption for embedding reasons so as to increase the system performances.

We have done a comparison relating two different architectures dedicated for a vision system on chip. The first one implements a logarithmic APS imager and a microprocessor. The second involves the same processor with a CMOS retina that implements hardware operators and analogue microprocessors. We have modeled two vision systems. The comparison is related to image processing speed, processing reliability, programmability, precision, subsequent stages of computations and power consumption.

2. Systems description

2.1 On chip vision system: why smart retinas?

The smart retinas focus on analogue VLSI implementations even though hardware implementation of image processing algorithms typically refers to digital implementations. The main interest is to adjust the functionality and the quality of the processing. Compared to a vision processing system consisting of a combination of a CMOS imagers and a processor in separate chips, a smart retina provides many advantages:

- Processing speed: the information transfer occurs serially between the imager and the associated processor, while in smart sensor data can be processed and transferred in parallel. Consequently, the processing speed can be enhanced: parallel operations between image acquisition and processing occur without digital sampling and quantization.

- Single chip integration: a single chip implementation of smart sensors contains image acquisition, low and high-level image processing circuits. A tiny sized chip can do the equivalent work of a camera associated to a computer or a DSP.
- Adaptation: Conventional cameras have at best an automatic gain control with offset tuning at the end of the output data channel. In smart sensors, photodetectors and operators are co-located in the pixel for a local or global adaptation that enhances their dynamic range.
- Power dissipation: a large portion of the total power is due to off-chip connections. On-chip integration reduces power consumption.
- Size and Cost: Analogue implementations of image processing algorithms feature a more compact area than their digital counter part. This is a crucial design issue for smart sensors. While a simple computation of large digital bit consumes a large area for the component design, a simple analogue component with compact size can typically compute the equivalent operation. The single chip implementation of the sensor and the processor can reduce the system size. The compact size of the chip is directly related to the fabrication cost.

Although designing single chip sensors is an attractive idea and the integration of image sensing and analogue processing has proven to be very striking, it faces several limitations well described and well argued in (Alireza, 2000):

- Processing reliability: Processing circuits of smart sensors often use unconventional analogue circuits which are not well characterized in many current technologies. As a result, if the smart sensor does not take in account the inaccuracies, the processing reliability is severely affected.
- Custom designs: Unconventional analogue or digital operators are cells often used in implementation of smart sensors. Operators from a design library cannot be used, and many new schemes and layout have to be developed. Their design can take a long time and the probability of design errors is higher.
- Programmability: most smart sensors are not general-purpose devices, and are typically not programmable to perform different vision. This lack of programmability is undesirable especially during the development of a vision system when various simulations are required.

Even with these disadvantages, smart sensors are still attractive, mainly because of their effective cost, size and speed with various on-chip functionalities (Rowe, 2001, Seguine, 2002). Simply, benefits exist when a camera with a computer system are converted into a small sized vision system on chip (SoC).

2.2 Proof-of-concept: a retina based vision system
2.2.1 On-chip image processing: review of integrated operators on smart circuits

Many vision algorithms of on-chip image processing with CMOS image sensors have been developed (Koch, 1995, Kleinfelder, 2001): image enhancement, segmentation, feature extraction and pattern recognition. These algorithms are frequently used in software-based operations, where structural implementation in hardware is not considered. Here, the main research interest focuses on how to integrate image processing (vision) algorithms with CMOS integrated systems or how to implement smart retinas in hardware, in terms of their system-level architectures and design methodologies.

Different partitions for the architectural implementation of on-chip image processing with CMOS image sensors are proposed. The partition does not only take in account the circuit density, but also includes the nature of image processing algorithms and the choice of the operators integrated in its focal plane with the sensors. The difference between partitions is the location of the signal-processing unit, known as a Processing Element (PE); this location becomes the discriminating factor of the different implementation structures.

The pixel processing consists of one processing element (PE) per image sensor pixel. Each pixel typically consists of a photodetector, an active buffer and a signal processing element. The pixel-level processing promises many significant advantages, including high SNR, low power, as well as the ability to adapt image capture and processing to different environments during light integration. However, the popular use of this design idea has been blocked by the severe limitations on pixel size, the low fill factor and the restricted number of transistors in PE like the approach presented by P. Dudeck in (Dudek, 2000).

In a view of great block partitioning, a global processing unit can be instantiated, beside the array of sensors, from a library. This way to do is one of the obvious integration methods due to its conceptual simplicity and the flexibility of the parameterization of the design features. Each PE is located at the serial output channel at the end of the chip. There are fewer restrictions on the implementation area of the PE, leading to a high fill factor of the pixel and a more flexible design. However, the bottleneck of the processing speed of the chip becomes the operational speed of the PE, and therefore, a fast PE is essentially required. The fast speed of the PE potentially results in high complexity of design and the high power consumption of the chip (Arias-Estrada, 2001).

Another implementation structure is the frame memory processing. A memory array with the same number of elements as the sensor is located below the imager array. Typically, the image memory is an analogue frame memory that requires less complexity of design, area, and processing time (Zhou, 1997). However, this structure consumes a large area, large power and high fabrication cost. Structures other than frame memory face the difficulty in implementing temporal storage. The frame memory is the most adequate structure that permits iterative operation and frame operation, critical for some image processing algorithms in a real time mode.

2.2.2 PARIS architecture

PARIS (Parallel Analogue Retina-like Image Sensor) is an architecture for which the concept of retinas is modeled implementing in the same circuit an array of pixels, integrating memories, and column-level analogue processors (Dupret, 2002). The proposed structure is shown in figure 1. This architecture allows a high degree of parallelism and a balanced compromise between communication and computations. Indeed, to reduce the area of the pixels and to increase the fill factor, the image processing is centred on a row of processors. Such approach presents the advantage to enable the design of complex processing units without decreasing the resolution. In return, because the parallelism is reduced to a row, the computations which concern more than one pixel have to be processed in a sequential way. However, if a sequential execution increases the time of processing for a given operation, it allows a more flexible process. With this typical readout mechanism of image sensor array, the column processing offers the advantages of parallel processing that permits low frequency and thus low power consumption. Furthermore, it becomes possible to chain basic functions in an arbitrary order, as in any digital SIMD machine. The resulting low-level information extracted by the retina can be then processed by a digital microprocessor.

The array of pixels constitutes the core of the architecture. Pixels can be randomly accessed. The selected mode for the transduction of the light is the integration mode. Two vertical bipolar transistors, associated in parallel, constitute the photosensor. For a given surface, compared to classic photodiodes, this disposal increases the sensitivity while preserving a large bandwidth (Dupret, 1996) and a short response time can be obtained in a snapshot acquisition. The photosensor is then used as a current source that discharges a capacitor previously set to a voltage Vref. In some cases, the semi-parallel processing imposes to store intermediate and temporary results for every pixel in four MOS capacitors used as analogue memories (figure 2). One of the four memories is used to store the analogue voltage deriving from the sensor. The pixel area is 50x50 μm^2 with a Fill Factor equal to 11%.

This approach eliminates the input/output bottleneck between different circuits even if there is a restriction on the implementation area, particularly for column width. Still, there is suppleness when designing the processing operators' area: the implementation of the processing is more flexible relatively to the length of the columns. Pixels of the same column exchange their data with the corresponding processing element through a Digital Analogue Bus (DAB). So as to access any of its four memories, each pixel includes a bidirectional (4 to 1) multiplexer. A set of switches makes possible to select the voltage stored in one of four capacitors. This voltage is copied out on the DAB thanks to a bi-directional amplifier. The same amplifier is used to write the same voltage on a chosen capacitor.

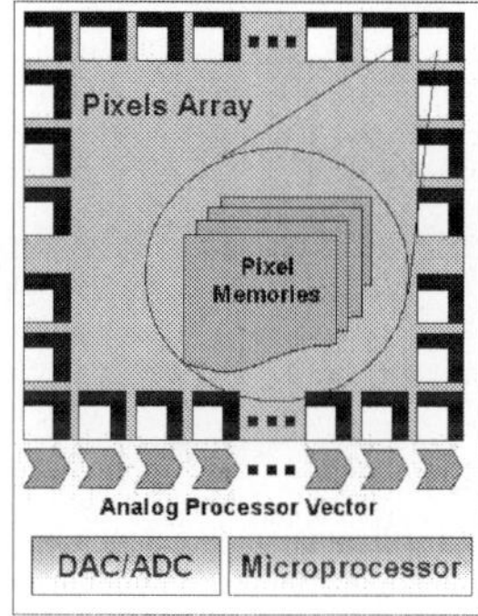

Fig. 1. PARIS architecture

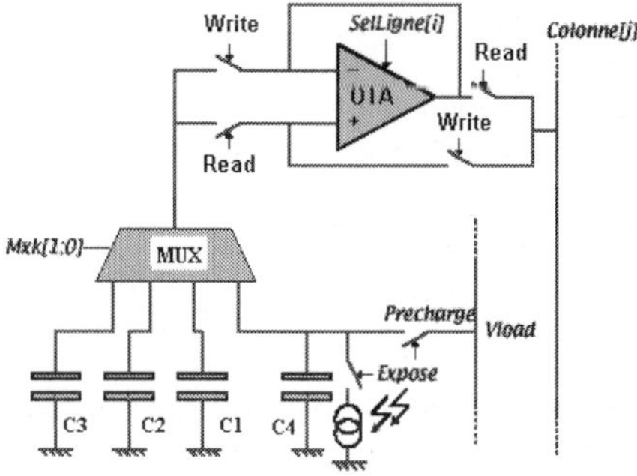

Fig. 2. Pixel scheme

The pixels array is associated to a vector of processors operating in an analogue/digital mixed mode (figure 3). In this chapter, we shall detail only the analogue processing unit: APU (figure 4). Each APU implements three capacitors, one OTA (Operational Transconductance Amplifier) and a set of switches that can be controlled by a sequencer.

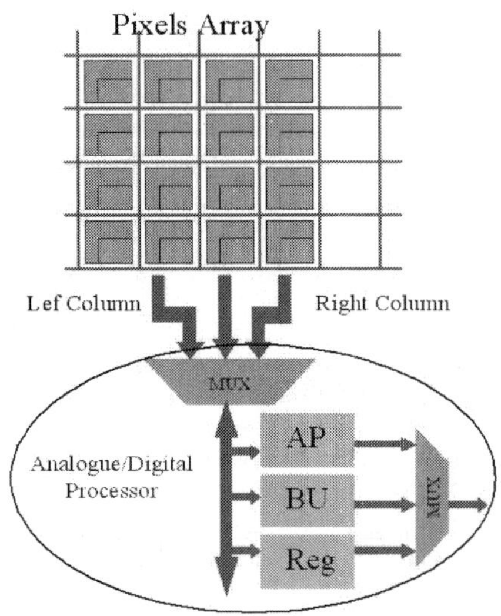

AP: Analogue Processor   **Reg**: Registers
BU: Boolean Unit   **Mux**: Multiplexer

Fig. 3. Analogue processor interface

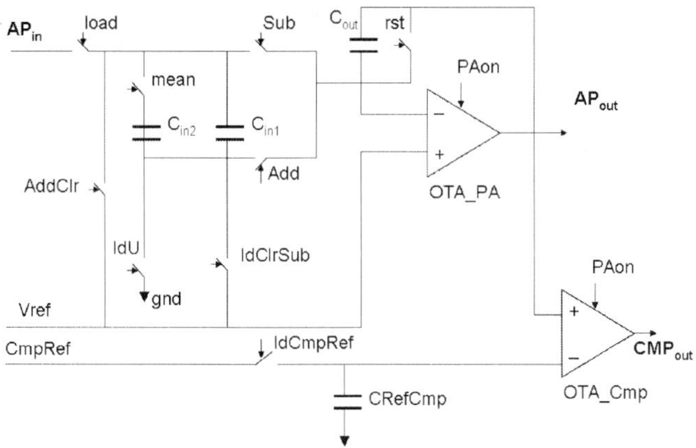

AP$_{out}$: Analogue Processor output   **AP$_{in}$**: Analogue Processor input
CMP$_{out}$: Comparator output

Fig. 4. Analogue-digital processor unit

Its functioning is much like a bit stream DAC: An input voltage set the initial charges in C_{in1}. The iterative activation of switches "mean" and/or "reset" reduces the amount of charges in C_{in1}. When "mean" is activated (C_{in1} and C_{in2} are connected together), and since C_{in1} and C_{in2} are at equal value, the charge in C_{in1} is divided by two. Iterating the operation N times, this step leads to a charge in C_{in1} of the form given by the equation (1):

$$Q_{in1} = \langle C_{in1} \cdot V_{in1} \rangle / 2^N \tag{1}$$

Thanks to the OTA, the remaining charge in capacitor C_{in1} is arithmetically transferred to Cout when switch "Add", or. "Sub" are "On". Therefore, the charges initially in C_{in1} are multiplied by a programmable fixed-point value. The capacitor C_{out} is so used as an accumulator that adds or subtracts charges flowing from C_{in1}. More detailed examples of operations can be found in (Dupret, 2000).

In order to validate this architecture, a first prototype circuit has been designed including 16x16 pixels and 16 analogue processing units. This first circuit allows validating the integrated operators through some image processing algorithms. Using a standard 0.6 µm CMOS, DLM-DLP technology, this prototype "PARIS1" is designed to support up to 256x256 pixels. Considering this architecture and the technology used, higher resolution retina would lead to hard design constrains such on pixel access time and power consumption. As to reduce costs the prototype implements 16x16 pixels with 16 analogue processors. Yet, this first circuit allows validating the integrated operators through some image processing algorithms like edge and movement detection. At a first order, the accuracy of the computations depends on the dispersion of the components values. The response dispersion between two APE units is 1%. A microphotography and a view of a first prototype of PARIS circuit are given in figure 5. The main characteristics of this vision chip are summarized in Table 1. Notice that the given pixel power consumption is its peak power i.e. when pixel is addressed. In other cases the OTA of the pixels are switched off and the pixel power consumptions is only due to C4 resetting. In the same way, when the Processing Unit is inactive its OTA is switched off. Hence, the maximum power of the analogue cells is: $C \cdot (P_{pixel} + P_{Processing\ Unit})$, where C is the chip number of columns.

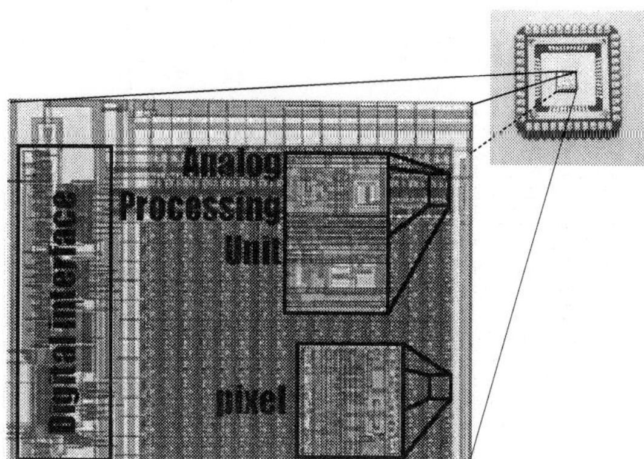

Fig. 5. Microphotography and a 16x16 pixels prototype of PARIS sensor

Circuit area (including pads)	10 mm²
Resolution (Pixels)	16x16
Number of APUs	16
Pixel Area	50x50 μm²
Area per Processing Unit	50x200 μm²
Clock Frequency	10 MHz
Processing Unit Power Consumption	300 μW
16 Pixels Line Power Consumption	100 μW

Table 1. Main characteristics of PARIS circuit

A finer analysis of the circuit performance (figure 6) shows that the time allocated to analogue operations is considerable. This problem can be solved in two ways. Either we increase the number of input in the analogue processor, or we give the opportunity to perform multiplications on a single clock (Moutault, 2000).

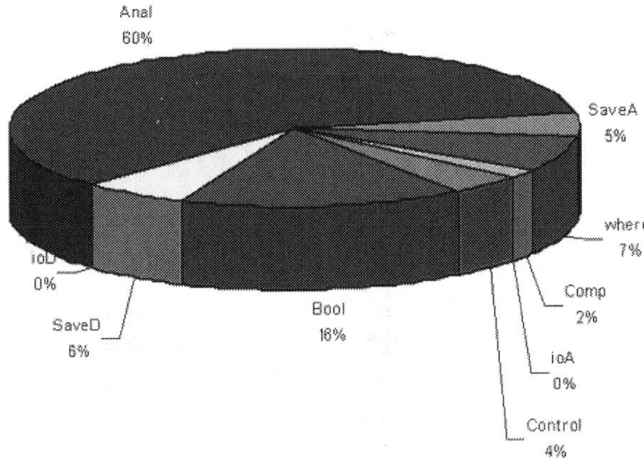

Fig. 6. Instructions occurrences based on multiples tests

2.2.3 Global architecture

To evaluate an on chip vision system architecture, we have implemented a vision system based on PARIS retina, implementing DAC/ADC converter and a CPU core: the 16/32-bit ARM7TDMI1 RISC processor. It is a low-power, general purpose microprocessor, operating at 50 MHz, developed for custom integrated circuits.

The Embedded ICE logic is an additional hardware that is incorporated with the ARM core. Supported by the ARM software and the Test Access Port (TAP), it allows debugging, downloading, and testing software on the ARM microprocessor.

The retina, used as a standard peripheral of the microprocessor, is dedicated for image acquisition and low-level image processing. The processor waits for the extracted low-level

---

[1] ARM System-on-Chip Architecture (2nd Edition), Steve Furber, September 2000.

information and processes them to give high-level information. The system sends then sequences of entire raw images.

With all components listed above, we obtain a system vision that uses a fully programmable smart retina. Thanks to the analogue processing units, this retina extracts the low-level information (e.g. edges detection). Hence, the system, supported by the processor, becomes more compact and can achieve processing suitable for real time applications.

The advantage of this architecture type remains in the parallel execution of a consequent number of low level operations in the array by integrating operators shared by groups of pixels. This allows saving expensive resources of computation, and decreasing the energy consumption. In term of computing power, this structure is more advantageous than that based on a CCD sensor associated to a microprocessor (Litwiller, 2001). Figure 7 shows the global architecture of the system and figure 8 gives an overview of the experimental module implemented for test and measurements.

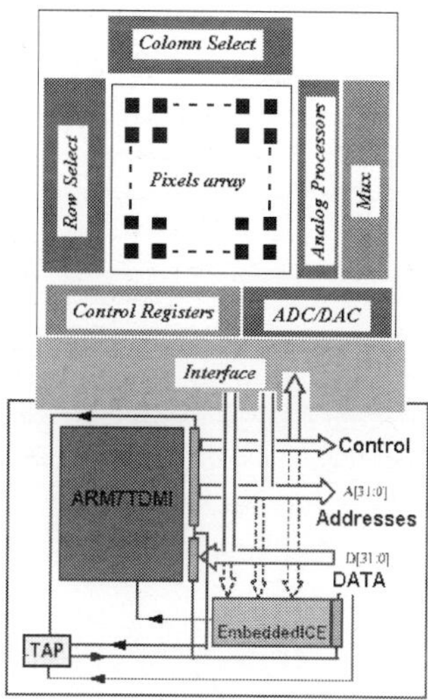

Fig. 7. Global architecture

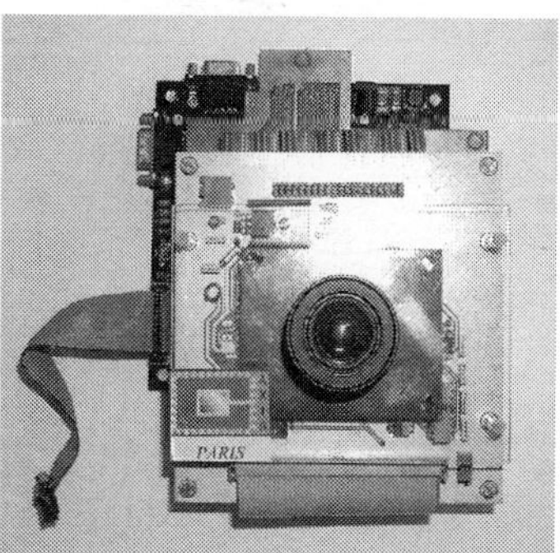

Fig. 8. Experimental module overview

2.3 Proof-of-concept: a vision system based on a logarithmic CMOS sensor

In recent years CMOS image sensors have started to attract the attention in the field of electronic imaging that was previously dominated by charge-coupled devices (CCD). The reason is not only related to economic considerations but also to the potential of realizing devices with imaging capabilities not achievable with CCDs. For applications where the scene light intensity varies over a wide range, dynamic range is a characteristic that makes CMOS image sensors attractive in comparison with CCDs (Dierickx, 2004, Walschap, 2003). An example is a typical scene encountered in an outdoor environment where the light intensity varies over a wide range, as, for example, six decades. Image sensors with logarithmic response offer a solution in such situations. However, many works (Loose, 1998) have been reported on high dynamic range CMOS sensor having a 130dB dynamic. These sensors may be the alternative to logarithmic CMOS sensors.

Since the sensor is a non-integrating sensor there is no control of the integration time. Because of the large logarithmic response the sensor can deal with images with large contrast without the need for iris control, simplifying the system vision. This makes this sensors very well suited for outdoor applications.

Due to the random access, regions of interest can to be read-out and processed. This reduces the image processing, resulting in faster and/or cheaper image processing systems.

We have modeled a vision system based on a logarithmic CMOS sensor (FUGA1000) (Ogiers, 2002) and an ARM microprocessor (the same used for the first vision system based on PARIS retina). The entire architecture is shown in figure 9. Figures 10.a and 10.b gives an overview of the CMOS sensor and the experimental module.

The CMOS sensor (FUGA1000) is an 11.5 mm (type-2/3") random addressable 1024 x 1024 pixels. It has a logarithmic light power to signal conversion. This monolithic digital camera chip has on-chip a 10 bit flash ADC and digital gain/offset control. It behaves like a 1 Mbyte ROM. After application of an X-Y address, corresponding to X-Y position of a pixel in the matrix, a 10 bit digital word corresponding to light intensity on the addressed pixel is returned.

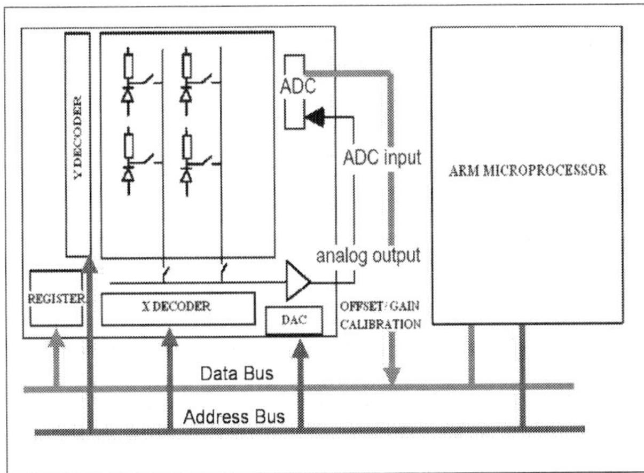

Fig. 9. Second architecture implementing a logarithmic CMOS sensor and an ARM7TDMI microprocessor

Even if the sensor is really random addressed, pixels do not have a memory and there is no charge integration. Triggering and snapshot (synchronous shutter) is not possible.

Fig. 10.a. Logarithmic CMOS sensor (1024x1024 pixels)

Fig. 10.b. Instrumental module overview with the CMOS sensor

3. Applications

3.1 Exposure time calibration algorithm

Machine vision requires an image sensor able to capture natural scenes that may have a dynamic adaptation for intensity. Reported wide image sensors suffer from some or all of the following problems: large silicon area, high cost, low spatial resolution, small dynamic range, poor pixel sensitivity, etc.

The primary focus of this research is to develop a single-chip imager for machine vision applications which resolves these problems, able to provide an on-chip automatic exposure time algorithm by implementing a novel self exposure time control operator. The secondary focus of the research is to make the imager programmable, so that its performance (light intensity, dynamic range, spatial resolution, frame rate, etc.) can be customized to suit a particular machine vision application.

Exposure time is an important parameter to control image contrast. This is the motivation for our development of a continuous auto-calibration algorithm that can manage this state for our vision system. This avoids pixels saturation and gives an adaptive amplification of the image, which is necessary to the post-processing.

The calibration concept is based on the fact that since the photo-sensors are used in an integration mode, a constant luminosity leads to a voltage drop that varies according to the exposure time. If the luminosity is high, the exposure time must decrease, on the other hand, if the luminosity is low the exposure time should increase. Hence lower is the exposure time simpler is the image processing algorithms. This globally will decrease response time and simplify algorithms. We took several measurements with our vision system, so that we can build an automatic exposure time checking algorithm according to the scene luminosity.

Figure 11 presents the variation of the maximum grey-level according to the exposure time. For each curve, we note a linear zone and a saturation zone. Thus we deduce the gradient variation (Δmax/Δt) according to the luminosity. The final curve can be scored out as a linear function (figure 12).

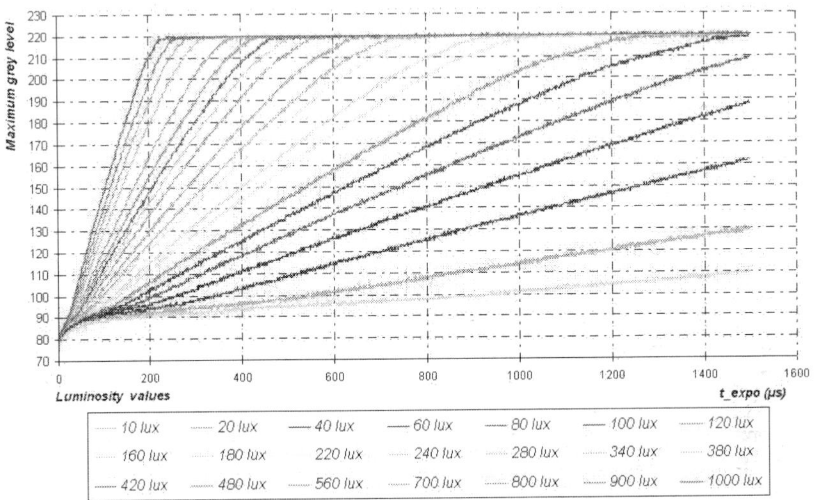

Fig. 11. Measured results (Maximum grey-level versus exposure time for different values of luminosity)

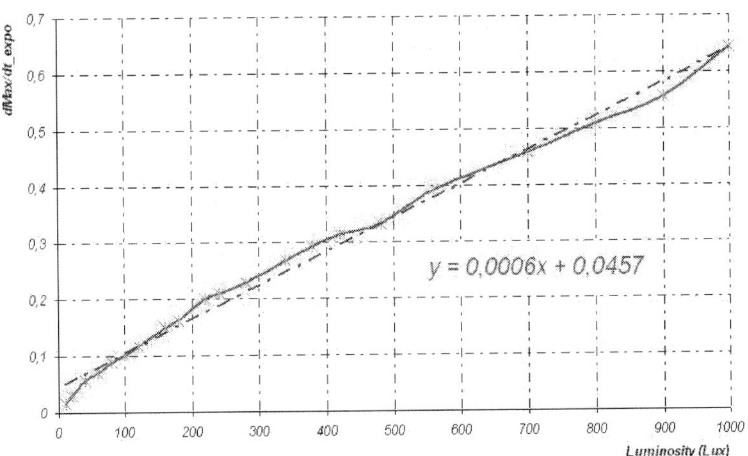

Fig. 12. Gradient variation according to the luminosity

The algorithm consists in keeping the exposure time in the interval where all variations are linear and the exposure time is minimal. Control is then initialised by an exposure time belonging to this interval. When a maximum grey-level is measured, the corresponding luminosity is deduced and returns a gradient value which represents the corresponding slope of the linear function. Figure 13 gives an example of images showing the adaptation of the exposure time to the luminosity.

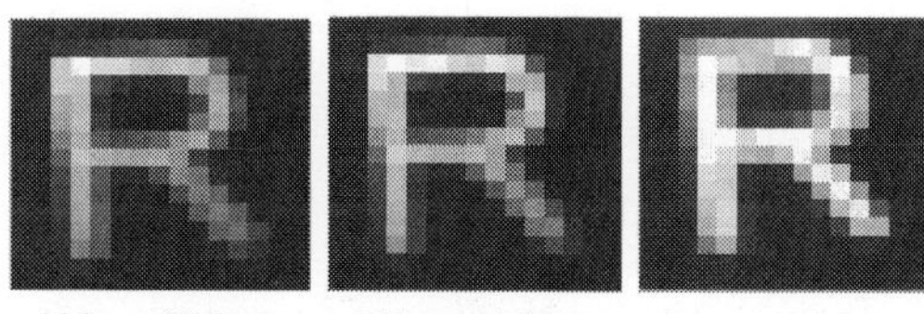

Fig. 13. Exposure time adaptation to the luminosity

3.2 On Chip image processing

Yet, in this chapter, we do not wish to limit implementations to application-specific tasks, but to allow for general-purpose applications such as DSP-like image processors with programmability. The idea is based on the fact that some of early level image processing, in the general-purpose chips, is commonly shared with many image processors, which do not require programmability on their operation.

These early level image processing algorithms, from the point of views of on-chip implementation, are relatively pre-determined and fixed, where their low precision can be compensated later by back-end processing. Here, we will investigate what image processing algorithms can be integrated on smart sensors as a part of early vision sequences and we will discuss their merits and the issues that designers should consider in advance.

General image processing consists of several image analysis processing steps: image acquisition, pre-processing, segmentation, representation or description, recognition and interpretation. The order of this image analysis can vary for different applications, and stages of the processes can be omitted. In image processing, the image acquisition is used to capture raw images from its input scene, through the use of video camera, scanners and, in the case of smart retinas, the solid-state arrays.

Local operation is also called mask operation where each pixel is modified according to the values of the pixel's neighbors (typically using convolution masks). In aspects of on-chip integration with image sensors, these operations provide advantages of real time process in image acquisition and processing, such as implementations of many practical linear spatial image filters and image enhancement algorithms. In addition, because the local operation is feasible for column structure implementations, low frequency processing is enabled and thus low power consumption is possible. However, since the local operations are based on a technique where local memory stores pixel values of the neighbors and processes them concurrently, implementation of the operation must contain some type of storage. Applications of local operations typically use an iterative technique for advanced image enhancement algorithms, which cannot practically be implemented on-chip. Nevertheless, in the case of column structure implementations, local operation still has a limitation on design area because of the restricted column width, even with flexible design area in the vertical direction. Therefore, in order to overcome these limitations, careful designs and system plans are required for the on-chip implementations.

In order to understand the nature of a local operation and to find an adequation relationship between algorithms and on chip architectural implementations, we will look into the main algorithms, grouped according to the similarity of functional processing. The diagram presented in figure 14 allows understanding the functioning of such architecture (where each column is assigned to an analogue processor). We chose a traditional example consisting of a spatial filter which is a 3x3 convolution kernel K, implementing a 4-connex laplacian filter. The convolution kernel K used is given by the table (2):

0	-1/4	0
-1/4	1	-1/4
0	-1/4	0

Table 2. Convolution kernel

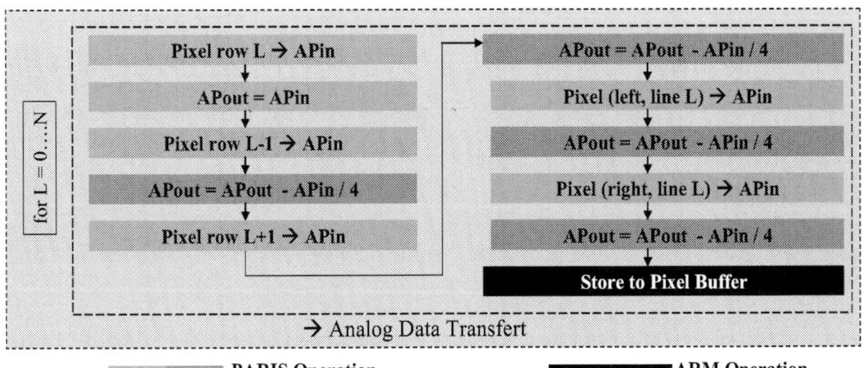

Fig. 14. Diagram of the K filter operation

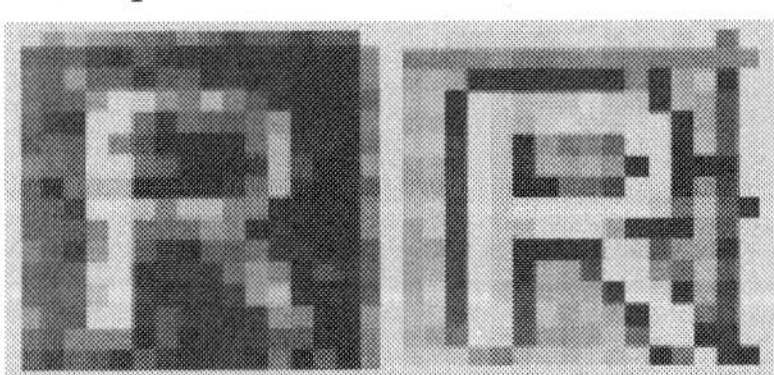

Fig. 15. Original image (left) and filtered image (right)

Pixels of the same line are simultaneously processed by the analogue processor (AP) vector and the computing is iterated on image rows. The arithmetic operations (division, addition) are carried out in analogue. The accumulation of the intermediate results is achieved in the analogue processor by using the internal analogue registers. Starting from an acquired image, the figure 15 shows the K filtering operation result of an NxN pixels image, obtained by PARIS1 when N=16. Such operation is achieved in 6887 µs. This computation time is globally due to:

$T= N. (T_{add} + 4.T_{div} + 4 T_{sub})$ where T_{add}, T_{div} and T_{sub} are the computation time, for one pixel, of the addition, division and subtraction operation. Of course, the computation time is proportional only to the number of rows in the sensor and more elaborated algorithms can be implemented similarly.

This operation can be carried out using the four analogue memories integrated in each pixel: for each subtraction and division and for each neighbour pixel, the result can be stored in one of the reports memories plans. Each memory can store an intermediate result. The final result can be obtained finally by a simple addition or subtraction achieved by the analogue processor vector. We obtain the filtered image by iterating on all array's rows. Such operation is processed in 6833 µs. This computation time is globally due to:

$T= N.(T_{add} + 4.T_{sub}) + N.T_{div}.$

This second method reduces the computing time and it is significant when the number of rows grows. Here for our example, it enabled us to reduce the computing time of 50µs for 16x16 pixels image. Saved time will be of 0.8ms for an image of 256x256 pixels. The control and addressing of the PARIS retina requires more ARM program computing resources to establish an FSM (Finite State Machine). PARIS retina can accept more control and addressing flow than what it is sent by the ARM programmed FSM controller. Hardware FSM version can deliver more control flow. So, our experimental results give low limit bandwidth of the retina control flow.

Opposite to integration that is similar to averaging or smoothing, differentiation can be used to sharpen an image leaving only boundary lines and edges of the objects. This is an extreme case of high pass filters. The most common methods of differentiation in image processing applications are first and second derivatives: gradient and laplacian operators. The difference filter is the simplest form of the differentiation with subtracting adjacent pixels from the centred pixel in different directions. The gradient filters represent the gradients of the neighbouring pixels (image differentiation) in forms of matrices. Such gradient approaches and their mask implementations are represented with various methods: Roberts, Prewitt, Sobel, Kirsch and Robinson.

With many different local operations in image processing algorithms, these operations can be categorized into three major groups: smoothing filters, sharpening filters and edge detection filters. Examples of the local operation algorithms are described in (Bovik, 2000).

We have successfully implemented and tested a number of algorithms, including convolution, linear filtering, edge detection, segmentation, motion detection and estimation. Some examples are presented below. Images are processed at different values of luminosity [60 Lux, 1000 Lux] using the exposure time self calibration. Figure 16 gives examples of processed images using the exposure time calibration algorithm.

3.3 Calibration of the CMOS sensor and off-chip image processing

The major drawback of the logarithmic sensor is the presence of a time-invariant noise in the images. The Fixed Pattern Noise (FPN) is caused by the non-uniformity of the transistors characteristics. In particular, threshold voltage variations introduce a voltage-offset characteristic for each pixel. The continuous-time readout of a logarithmic pixel makes the use of Correlated Double Sampling for the suppression of static pixel-to-pixel offsets quite impossible. As a result, the raw image output of such a sensor contains a large overall non-uniformity.

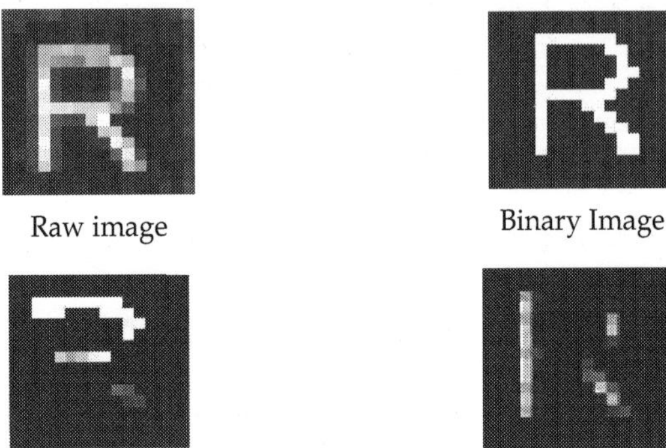

Raw image   Binary Image

Vertical Sobel filtered image   Horizontal Sobel filtered image

Fig. 16. Examples of image processing

The downstream system of the sensor is then used to compensate the FPN: as the FPN is static in time, a simple look-up table with the size of the sensor's resolution can be used for a first-order correction of each individual pixel. Higher-order corrections can be employed when the application demands higher image quality. The FPN noise is removed from the images by adding to each pixel value the corresponding offset.

For the CMOS/APS sensor, the FPN suppression is performed by the ARM microprocessor in real time and it is transparent (this operation can be achieved by an FPGA circuit for example). The sensor is shipped with one default correction frame. Figure 17 shows an image with the FPN and the image after the FPN correction.

The response of the logarithmic CMOS sensor typically is expressed as 50 mV output per decade of light intensity. After first order FPN calibration and using an ADC, a response non-uniformity of below 2mV remains, being quite constant over the optical range. This non-uniformity translates to about 4% of a decade. The temporal noise of the logarithmic sensor is about 0.2 mV RMS.

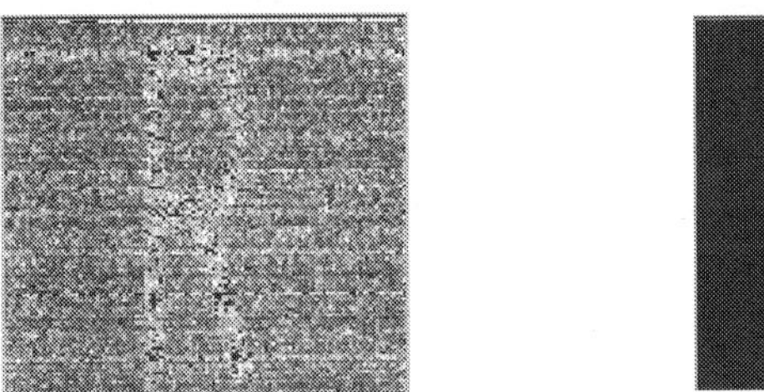

Fig. 17. Images with FPN (left) and with removed FPN (right)

For the FUGA1000 sensor based vision system, images are processed on the ARM microprocessor. We established several algorithms of image processing similar to those established for PARIS based vision system. Other more complicated algorithms which require diversified computing with exponential power were also established. We recall that to carry out comparisons relating to the processing times, we chose to use the same processor (ARM7TDMI) for the different implemented systems.

The filter we used has been designed by Federico Garcia Lorca (Deriche, 1990). This filter is a simplification of the Deriche filter (Garcia Lorca, 1997), the recursive implementation of the optimal Canny filter. The smoother is applied horizontally and vertically on the image, in a serial way. Then a derivator is applied. Garcia Lorca derivator is, after simplification of Deriche, derivator, a 3x3 convolution kernel instead of a recursive derivator.

$$y(n) = (1-\lambda)^2 x(n) + 2\lambda y(n-1) - \lambda^2 y(n-2) \text{ with } \quad \lambda = e^{-\alpha} \qquad (2)$$

X(n) is the pixel source value. Y(n) is the pixel destination value and n is the pixel index in a one dimensional table representing the image. λ is an exponential parameter allowing much more filtering flexibility, depending on the noise within the image. If the image is very noisy we use a very smoothing filter: $\alpha=[0.5,0.7]$ otherwise we use bigger values of α: $\alpha=[0.8,1.0]$. Figure 18 gives examples of smoothing filter and derivator filter implemented with the FUGA-ARM vision system and applied to 120x120 pixels images.

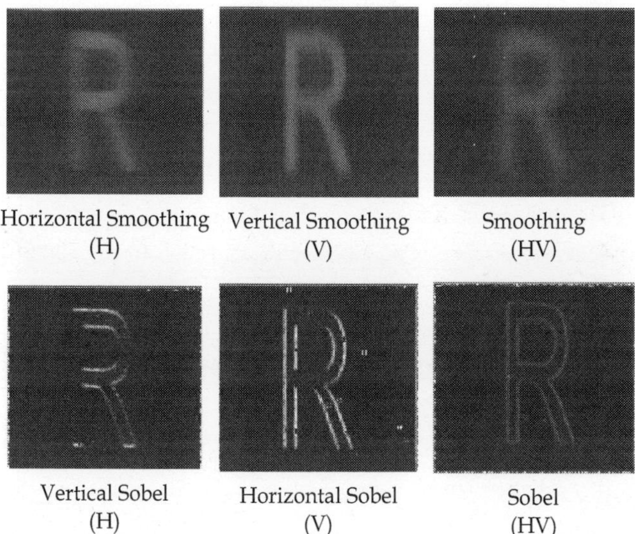

Fig. 18. Examples of image processing implemented with the FUGA1000 sensor based vision system

4. Comparison: standard CMOS sensors versus retina

The aim is to compare the vision system implementing the logarithmic CMOS imager (FUGA1000) and the ARM microprocessor with the one based on PARIS retina (see section B.2). This comparison is related to image processing speed, programmability and subsequent stages of computations.

We have used the edge detection algorithm and a Sobel filter algorithm to take several measurements of the computation times relating to the two architectures described bellow. For the retina based system, these computations are carried out by the analogue processors integrated on-chip. For the FUGA1000 sensor based system, these computations are carried out by the ARM microprocessor.

The two computation time graphics presented in the figure 19 translate the diverse computing times for different square sensor pixel resolutions for both systems. It is significant to note that the acquisition time of the frames is not included in these measurements in order to evaluate just the data processing computing time.

Times relating to the PARIS retina were obtained by extension of the data processing timing obtained from those of the first prototype (Dupret, 2002). Figure 20 presents the same kind of comparison between PARIS system and a third commercial camera system: EtheCam (Neuricam, Italy). This camera is based on a linear CMOS sensor and an ARM7TDMI microprocessor.

We deduce that the computation time for the FUGA1000 like system varies according to the pixels number N^2 (quadratic form). Hence, the computation time for Retina like system varies according to the number of line N (linear form) thanks to the analogue processor vector.

Consequently, the microprocessor of the FUGA1000 like system carries out a uniform CPP (Cycle Per Pixel) relative to regular image processing independently of the number of proceeded pixels. For PARIS like system, the CPP factor is inversely proportional to the number of lines N. Figure 21 shows the evolution of the CPP for PARIS and FUGA1000/ARM systems.

A characterization of the power consumption for PARIS based system has been achieved (Dupret, 2002). The total power of an NxN resolution and N analogue processing units is:

$$P = 100.N^2 + 300.N \qquad (3)$$

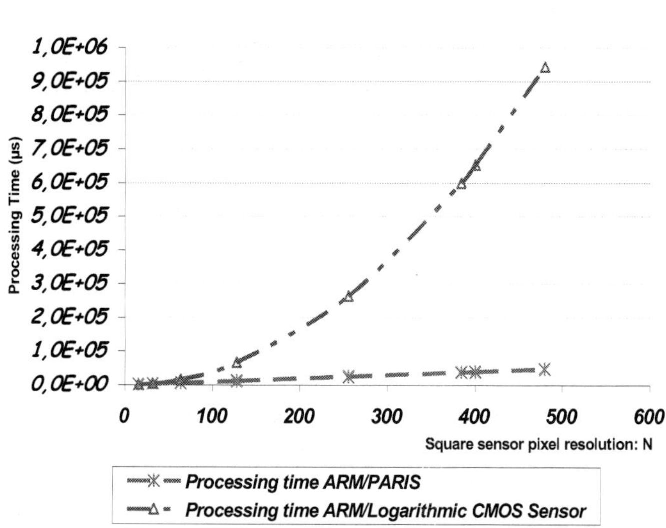

Fig. 19. Time processing of an edge detection: PARIS architecture versus ARM/Logarithmic CMOS sensor

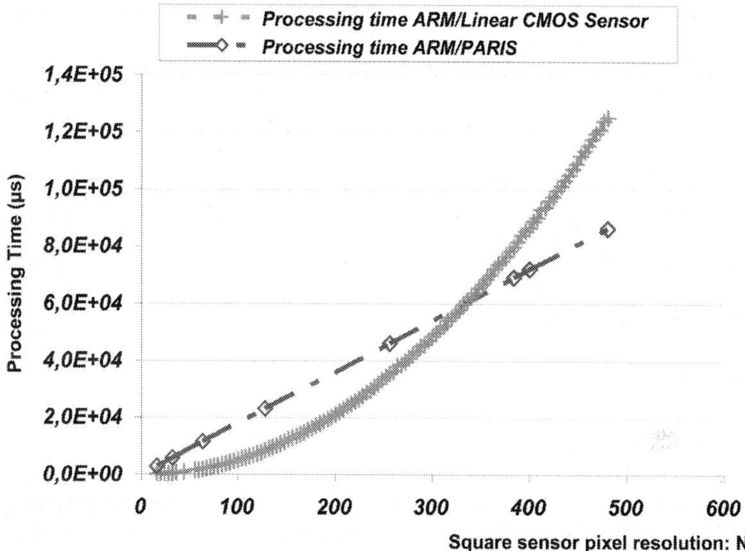

Fig. 20. Processing time of a Sobel operation: PARIS architecture versus ARM/Linear CMOS sensor

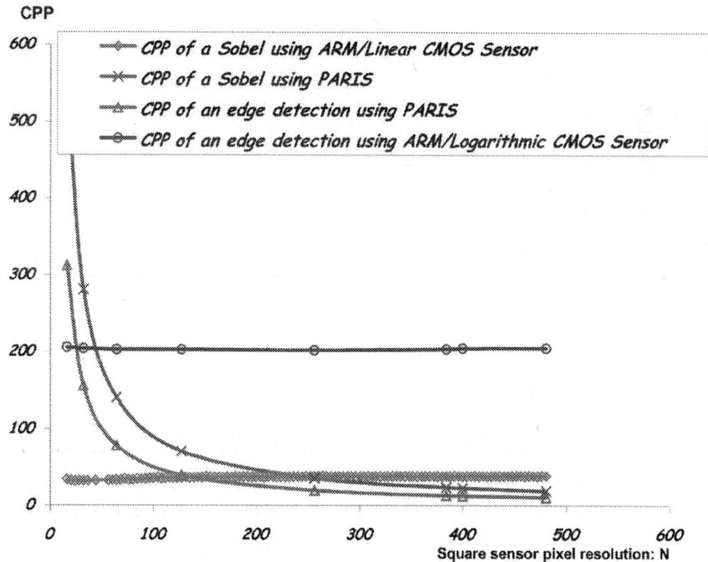

Fig. 21. Evolution of the CPP (Cycle Per Pixel) for PARIS and the ARM/CMOS architectures

When 100 µW is the power consumption per 16 pixels and 300 µW is the power consumption per analogue processing unit. The 16x16 pixels circuit has a consumption of

50.4 mW. The consumption of the FUGA1000 sensor is 0.25 mW per pixel and that of the ARM microprocessor is 14 mW (RAM, ROM and logic glue consumption are excluded). It gives 76.5 mW consumption for 16x16 pixels resolution.

Hence, When comparing the power consumption between the FUGA1000/ARM like system and the PARIS retina at 10 MHz frequency, we conclude that the on chip solution allows better performances and low power consumption.

5. Conclusion

When we wish to carry out real time image acquisition and processing, the hardware processing implementation with smart sensors becomes a great advantage. This chapter presents one experience of this concept named a retina.

It is concluded that on-chip image processing with retinas will offer benefits of low power consumption, fast processing frequency and parallel processing. Since each vision algorithm has its own applications and design specifications, it is difficult to predetermine optimal design architecture for every vision algorithm. However, in general, the column structures appear to be a good choice for typical image processing algorithms.

We have presented the architecture and the implementation of a smart integrated retina based vision system. The goal is the integration of a microprocessor in the retina to manage the system and to optimise the hardware resources use.

To exhibit the feasibility of the chosen approach, we have presented an algorithm for the exposure time calibration. It is obvious that an algorithm of objects tracking, for example, will be more complex since the interval between two images is important.

As a result, if it is possible to carry out processed images in a short time, between two processing, the relevant objects will be seen as "immobile objects". Therefore, applications involving these algorithms will be less complex and efficient to implement them on a test bench. Our implementation demonstrates the advantages of the single chip solution and contributes as a highlight. Hence, designers and researchers can have a better understanding of smart sensing for intelligent vehicles (Elouardi, 2002, 2004). We propose implementing such a system with high resolution starting from a complex application on an intelligent vehicle embedding smart sensors for autonomous collision avoidance and objects tracking.

6. References

Fossum R., "CMOS Image Sensors: Electronic Camera-On-A-Chip", IEEE Transactions on Electron Devices. Vol.44, No.10, pp.1689-98, Oct.97.

Muramatsu, et al., "Image Processing Device for Automotive Vision Systems". Proceeding of IEEE Intelligent Vehicle Symposium 2002, Versailles, France.

Burns R., Thomas C., Thomas P., Hornsey R., Pixel-parallel CMOS active pixel sensor for fast objects location, SPIE International Symposium on Optical Science and Technology, 3 - 8 Aug. 2003, San Diego, CA USA.

El Gamal A., et al, "Pixel Level Processing: Why, what and how?" SPIE Vol.3650, 1999, pp. 2-13.

Dudek P., Hicks J., "A CMOS General-Purpose Sampled-Data Analogue Microprocessor", Pro. of the 2000 IEEE International Symposium on Circuits and Systems. Geneva, Suisse.

Ni Y., Guan J.H., "A 256x256-pixel Smart CMOS Image Sensor for Line based Stereo Vision Applications", IEEE, J. of Solid State Circuits, Vol. 35 No. 7, Juillet 2000, pp. 1055-1061.

Alireza M., "Vision chips or seeing silicon", Technical Report, Centre for High Performance Integrated Technologies and Systems, The University of Adelaide, March 1997. Kluwer Academic Publishers, ed. I. 0-7923-8664-7. 2000.

Rowe A., Rosenberg C., Nourbakhsh I., "A Simple Low Cost Color Vision System," Technical Sketch Session of CVPR 2001, 2001.

Seguine D., "Just add sensor - integrating analogue and digital signal conditioning in a programmable system on chip," Proceedings of IEEE Sensors, vol. 1, pp. 665–668, 2002.

Koch C., Li H., "Vision Chips Implementing Vision Algorithms with Analogue VLSI circuits", IEEE Computer Society Press, 1995.

Kleinfelder S., Lim S., "A 10 000 Frames/s CMOS Digital Pixel Sensor". IEEE Journal of Solid-State Circuits, Vol. 36, N°. 12, Page 2049. December 2001.

Arias-Estrada M., "A Real-time FPGA Architecture for Computer Vision", Journal of Electronic Imaging (SPIE - IS&T), Vol. 10, No. 1, January 2001, pp. 289-296.

Zhou Z., Pain B., Fossum E., "Frame-transfer CMOS Active Pixel Sensor with pixel binning," IEEE Trans. On Electron Devices, Vol. ED-44, pp.1764-8, 1997.

Dupret A., Klein J.O., Nshare A., "A DSP-like Analogue Processing Unit for Smart Image Sensors", International Journal of Circuit Theory and Applications 2002. 30: p. 595-609.

Dupret A. et al, "A high current large bandwidth photosensor on standard CMOS Process" presented at EuroOpto'96, AFPAEC, Berlin, 1996.

Dudek P., "A programmable focal-plane analogueue processor array" Ph.D. thesis, University of Manchester Institute of Science and Technology (UMIST), May 2000.

Dupret A., Klein J.O., Nshare A., "A programmable vision chip for CNN based algorithms". CNNA 2000, Catania, Italy: IEEE 00TH8509.

Moutault S., et al, "Méthodologie d'analyse de performances pour les rétines artificielles". Report for Master graduation, IEF, Paris XI University. Orsay, 2000.

Litwiller D., "CCD vs. CMOS: Facts and Fiction". The January 2001 issue of PHOTONICS SPECTRA, Laurin Publishing Co. Inc.

Dierickx B., Bogaerts J., "Advanced developments in CMOS imaging", Fraunhofer IMS workshop, Duisburg, 25 May 2004.

Walschap T. et al, "Brain Slice Imaging: a 100x100 Pixel CIS Combining 40k Frames per Second and 14 Bit Dynamic Range", IEEE Workshop on CCD & AIS, Elmau, 15 17 May 2003.

Loose M., Meier K., Schemmel J., "CMOS image sensor with logarithmic response and self calibrating fixed pattern noise correction". Proc. SPIE 3410. ISBN 0-8194-2862-0, 1998, pp.117-127.

Ogiers W. et al., "Compact CMOS Vision Systems for Space Use". http://www.fillfactory.com/htm/technology/pdf/iris_cets.pdf

Bovik A., "Handbook of Image & Video Processing", Academic Press, 2000.

Deriche R., "Fast algorithms for low level-vision".IEEE Transaction of Pattern Analysis and Machine Intelligence, vol 12-1, 1990.

Garcia Lorca F., et al, "Efficient ASIC and FPGA implementation of IIR filters for real time edge detections", Proc. International Conference on Image Processing, IEEE ICIP 1997.

Elouardi A., Bouaziz S., Reynaud R., "Evaluation of an artificial CMOS retina sensor for tracking systems". Pro. of IEEE IV'2002, Versailles, France.

Elouardi A. et al, "Image Processing Vision System Implementing a Smart Sensor". Proceeding of IEEE Instrumentation and Measurement Technology Conference, IMTC'04. Pages 445-450. ISBN 0-7803-8249-8. May 18-20, 2004. Como, Italy.

Langeheine J., et all "A CMOS FPTA Chip for Hardware Evolution of Analogue Electronic Circuits" Proceedings of the 2001 NASA/DoD Conference on Evolvable Hardware, pages 172-175, IEEE Computer Society, 2001.

Schemmel J., Loose M., Meier K., "A 66 x 66 pixels analogue edge detection array with digital readout". Proceedings of the 25th European Solid-State Circuits 1999, Edition Frontinières, ISBN 2-86332-246-X, p. 298.

Lew Yan Voona L.F.C., et all, "Real-Time Pattern Recognition Retina in CMOS Technology" Proceedings of the International Conference on Quality Control by Artificial Vision – QCAV'2001, Vol. 1, pp. 238-242, Le Creusot, FRANCE, May, 2001.

Nudd G.R., et al., "A Charge-Coupled Device Image Processor for Smart Sensor Applications", SPIE Proc. Vol 155, pp.15-22, 1978.

Knight T., "Design of an integrated optical sensor with on-chip processing", PhD thesis, Dept. of Electrical Engineering and Computer Science, MIT, Cambridge, Mass., 1983.

Keast C.L., Sodini C.G., "A CCD/CMOS-based imager with integrated focal plane signal processing", IEEE Journal of Solid State Circuits, Vol. 28, No. 4, pp.431-7, 1993.

## 24

Acquisition and Digital Images Processing, Comparative Analysis of FPGA, DSP, PC for the Subtraction and Thresholding.

Carlos Lujan Ramirez[1], Ramón Atoche Enseñat[1]
and Francisco José Mora Mas[2]
[1]*Instituto Tecnológico de Mérida*
[2]*Universidad Politécnica de Valencia*
[1]*Mexico*
[2]*Spain*

1. Introduction

Given the need to reduce the time involved in image processing, we found that is necessary to use new methods to improve the time response. In our application of real time tracking of different species in the study of marine animal conduct, a reduction in the image processing time provides us with more information that allows us to better predict the animal's escape trajectory from a predator.

Nowadays, photographic cameras can deliver photographs in various formats, hence the need to provide them with pre-processing in order to deliver the required format. Although Photographic cameras are available that can deliver photos without pre-processing, the format provided is the Bayer format. A characteristic of this format is that we obtain the images almost directly from the CCD sensors and from the analogical to digital converter with no pre-processing. The only requirement is a deserialization step and registers in parallel whose role is to place the Bayer format image in a memory for the investigation (Lujan et al., 2007). In the initial method in our project, the camera is connected to a Frame Grabber which retrieves the image, converts it to RGB, changing it to a scale of greys and subsequently carries out the necessary processing, the first being the subtraction of the background from the image of the animals under study, followed by the application of blurring.

Subtraction of images is widely used when the aim is to obtain the animal's trajectory (Gonzales et al., 2002), however, we use it to leave only the animals under study, eliminating everything else. A low pass filter (Gonzales et al., 2002) (blurred) is used which unifies any division in some of the animals caused by the subtraction. Occasionally a shrimp would be divided in two due to the kind of background used, recognizing two shrimps instead of one, this error was resolved by the application of the blurring.

The new process would involve recovering the image and then to immediately carry out the image processing of subtraction and blurring, saving time by avoiding the use of a Bayer to RGB encoder and the frame grabber. We included a stage of image recovery by a number of deserielizors and registers in order to deliver the image in Bayer format.

For this investigation, an analysis will be performed on the third part of image processing which begins after the image has been stored in an FPGA. The two processing stages analyzed will be the subtraction between the background and the image where the animals under study are found, and the subsequent thresholding from the subtraction.

This will be implemented in four different systems, and the time and resources consumed will be analyzed; first in a PC computer with a Borland C++ program, second with an embedded microprocessor programmed in C++, third with a DSP also programmed in C++, and finally with a hardware designed in VHDL.

2. Camera link digital images acquisition.

The need to acquire images at high transfer rates, it takes us to use a camera with camera link interface, and then, to save time when recovering the image; we connect the camera with FPGA instead of use a frame grabber.

2.1 The standard camera link.

The protocol camera Link (Camera Link, 2000) is a communication interface for vision applications. The interface extends the basic technology of the channel link to provide a more useful specification for vision applications.

For many years, there has been a need for a standard method for communication in the scientific and industrial digital video market. The manufacturers of frame grabbers and cameras developed products with different connections, making cable production difficult for the manufacturers and very confusing for the consumers. A standard connection between digital cameras and frame grabbers is becoming more necessary as the data transfer rate continues to rise.

Increasingly diverse cameras and advanced data transmission signals have made a standard connection such as camera Link an absolute necessity. The camera Link interface reduces both the support time and the cost of Support. The normal cable will be able to manage the increased speed of the signal and the cable assembly will allow clients to reduce their expenses.

2.2 The standard ANSI/TIA/EIA-644

The LVDS is a pattern of data transmission that uses a balanced interface and a low voltage to solve many of the problems relating to existing technologies. The lower amplitude of the signal reduces the voltage used for the line circuits, and a balance in the signals reduces the coupling noise, allowing greater transfer rates.

The LVDS, standardized in TIA/EIA-644, specifies a maximum transfer rate of 1.923 Gbps. In practice however, the maximum transfer rate is determined by the quality of the communication media between the transmitter and the line receiver. Similarly, the length and characteristics of a transmission line condition the usable transfer rate to the maximum (Cole, E., 2002)(Texas Instruments, 2002).

National Semiconductor (National Semiconductor, 2006) developed the technology of channel link as a solution for flat screens, based on LVDS for the physical layer. The technology was later extended into a method for data transmission. The channel link comprises a pair of drivers in the transmitter and in the receiver. The driver accepts 28 data signals of simple terminal and one clock signal of simple terminal. The data are transmitted in series at a rate of 7: 1 in four lines, and together with the clock they form five differential pairs. Therefore, the receiver accepts the four pairs of data lines in LVDS plus one pair for the clock signal which will recover the 28 bits of data and the clock signal, as shown in Fig. 1.

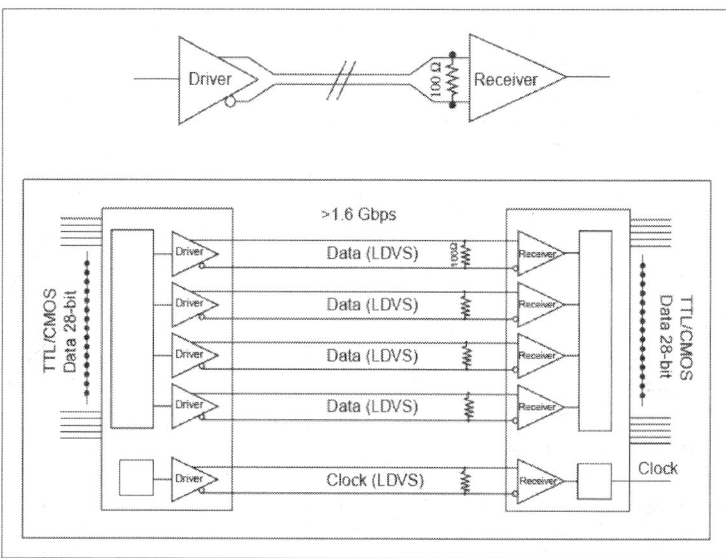

Fig. 1. Operation of channel Link

One of the benefits of the channel link transmission method is that it requires fewer conductors for transferring data. Five pairs of cables, therefore, can transmit up to 28 data bits. These cables reduce the size of the connector, allowing the manufacture of smaller cameras. Furthermore, the data transmission rate in the channel link chipset can reach 2.38 Gbits/s.

2.3 Camera connection for digital image acquisition

In the first time the camera was connected a Frame Grabber and this to the computer, we propose not to use the Frame Grabber on the other hand to use a FPGA for image recovery and storage in FPGA memory for later processing. Our advantages is a savings of Frame Grabber, because its cost is high, and on the other hand we gain the total control of the image storage.

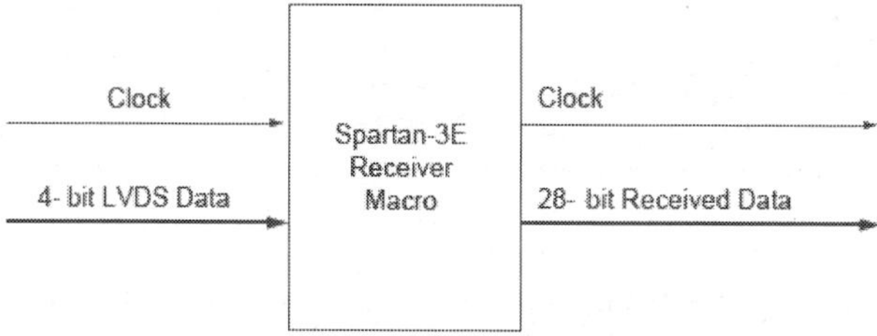

Fig. 2. Input and output receiver signals

Taking into account Sawyer implementation (2008) acquisition stage was redesigned, the FPGA was exchanged for a Virtex 4 FPGA, and a memory was added so that the image could be accessed by other devices.

The Figure 2 shows us the camera signals, which enter the receiver, and this provides us with the 28 bit data in parallel. These 28 bits are composed of 24 data bits and 4 control bits used to determine a valid pixel, an end of line and an end table. Fig. 2 shows how the camera signals enter to the receiver in serial form and the receiver gives us 28 data bits in parallel. These 28 bits are composed of 24 data bits and 4 control bits used to determine a valid pixel, an end of line and an end frame.

Logic Description

The logic for the receiver is simplified by using the cascadable IOB DDR flip-flops. The Fig. 3, shows the 4-bit interface.

Two bits of data are clocked in per line, per high-speed rxclk35 clock period, thus giving 8 bits (4-bit data width) of data to register each high-speed clock. Because this high-speed clock is a 3.5x multiple of the incoming slow clock, the bit deserialization and deframing are slightly different under the two alignment events described in "Clock Considerations." Basically, 28 bits (4-bit data width) are output each slow speed clock cycle. However, for 4-bit data width, the receiver captures 32 bits per one slow clock cycle and 24 bits the next. The decision as to which bits are output and when is made by sampling the incoming clock line and treating it as another data line. In this way, the multiplexer provides correctly deframed data to the output of the macro synchronous to the low speed clock.

There is no data buffering or flow control included in the macro, because this interface is a continuous high-speed stream and requires neither.

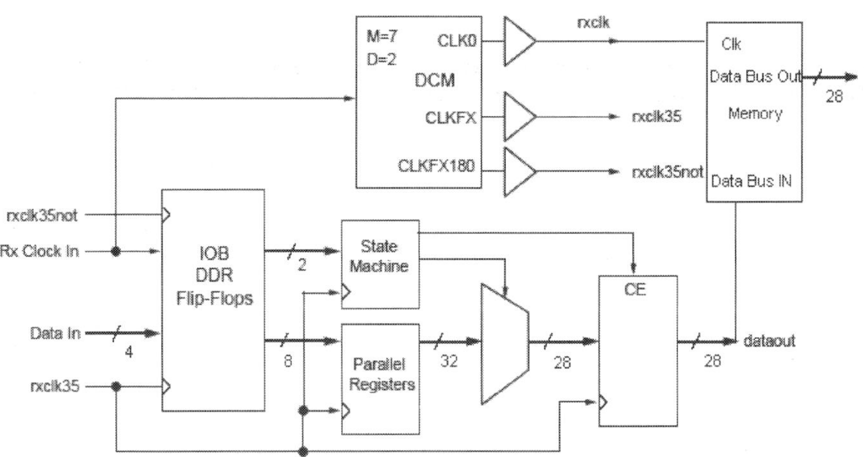

Fig. 3. Camera Link receiver implementation

It's important to be careful with the generation of the two clock signals rxclk35 and rxclk35not because the recovery of the correct images depends on them. The time diagram for these signals is shown in Fig. 4.

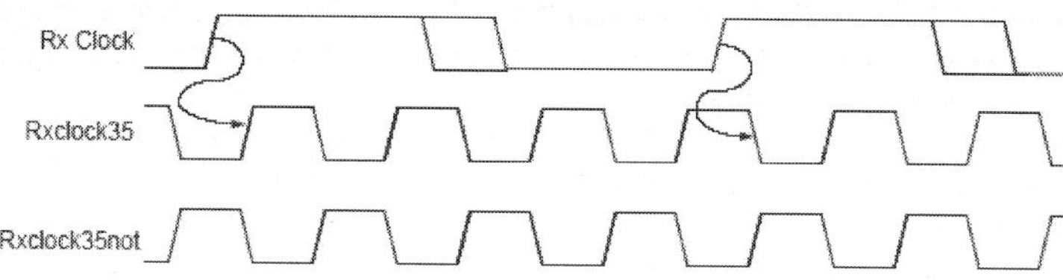

Fig. 4. Clocks wave form

The Fig. 5 shows us how the image data are transmitted through the camera link protocol.

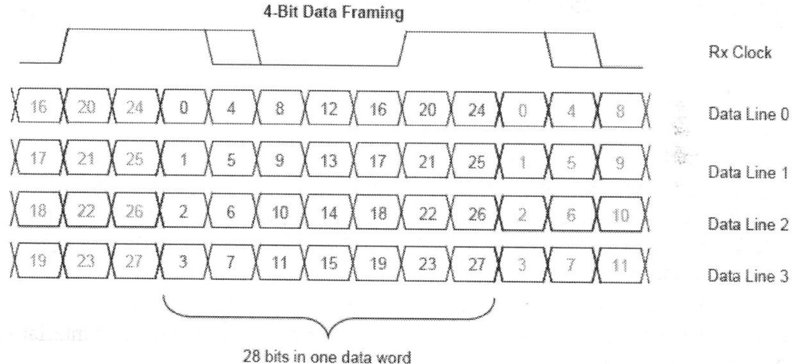

Fig. 5. Receive Data Formatting

Is very important to be careful with the placement of flip flops from deserializer, because the transfer rate of data depends of them. (Lujan et al., 2007). No use of FPGA resources (for example Digital Clock Managers in Xilixs architectures) for skew correction allows us to use in other applications that really need them.

Finally, the pixels of the digital image are stored in memory and this can be used by other devices for future processings.

In Fig. 6 shows an image of 720 x 480 pixels, recovered and stored in memory.

3. Digital images subtraction and thresholding

Two concepts that we use are defined below.

3.1 Image subtraction

The difference between two images $f(x,y)$ and $g(x,y)$ is expressed by:

$$o(i,j) = f(i,j) - g(i,j) \quad \forall i,j \tag{1}$$

This technique has several applications in segmentation and in image enhancement.

3.2 Thresholding

In order to understand this concept more clearly, we must first understand the concept of contrast amplification.

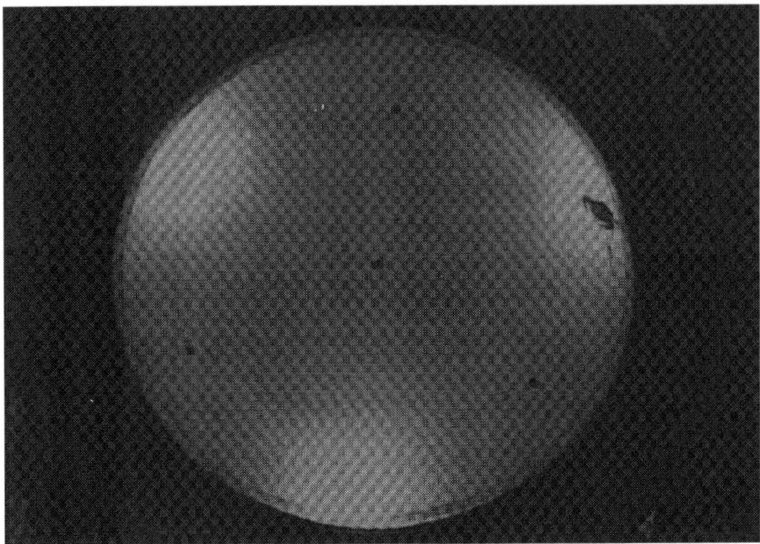

Fig. 6. Camera recovered image.

Images with poor contrast are often the result of insufficient or variable illumination, or are due to the non-linearity or small dynamic range of the image sensors. A typical example of transformation is shown in figure 7, which can be expressed by:

$$
v = \begin{cases} \alpha u & 0 \le u < a \\ \beta(u - a) + v_a & a \le u < b \\ \gamma(u - b) + v_b & b \le u < L \end{cases} \tag{2}
$$

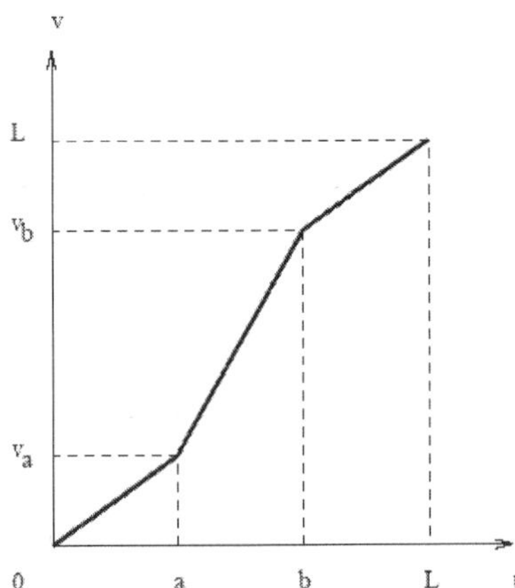

Fig. 7. Contrast amplification.

The slopes are taken greater than one in the regions in which contrast amplification is desired.

The parameters a and b can be estimated by examining the histogram of the image. For example, the intervals of grey level where the pixels occur with greater frequency must be amplified in order to enhance the visibility of the image.

A particular example of the above is when $\alpha = \gamma = 0$, this case takes de name of *cutoff*. This cutoff can be useful for instance, when we know that the signal is within the range [a,b].

Thresholding is a special case of cut model in which a binary image is obtained.

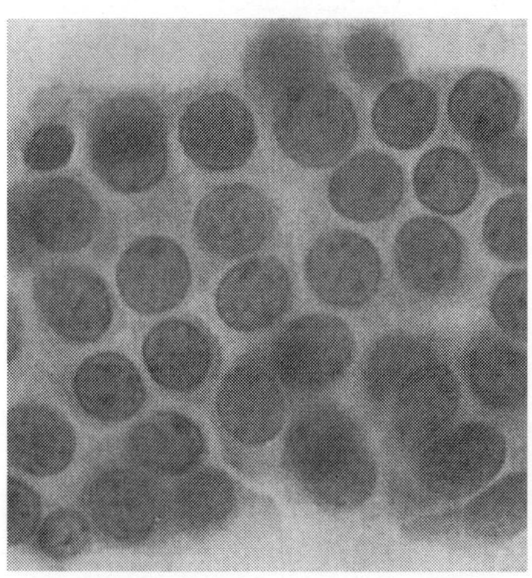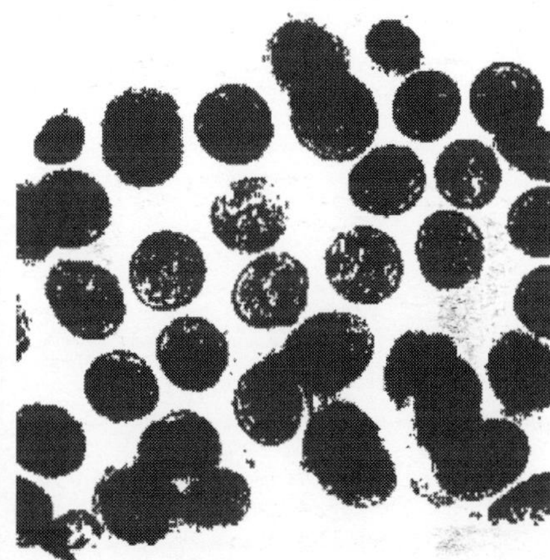

Fig. 8. Original Image and its thresholding by 150.

This can be expressed by:

$$v = \begin{cases} 0 & 0 \leq u < a \\ L & a \leq u < b \\ 0 & b \leq u < L \end{cases}$$

This model can be useful when we know that the image must be binary and when this has not been obtained by the process of digitalization. It can also be used in a segmentation process, as shown in Fig. 8.

4. Bayer format utilization for subtraction and blurring of images

4.1 Bayer format

At present, a large number of formats for storing digital images are available, however, most cameras capture the image in Bayer format (Bayer, 1976) which then passes through a converter and the image is delivered in the RGB format. The use of the Bayer color filter is a popular format for the digital acquisition of color images (National Semiconductor, 2006). A drawing of the color filters is shown in Fig. 9. Half the total number of pixels are green (G), while a quarter of the total are attributed to both red (R) and blue (B).

G	R	G	R
B	G	B	G
G	R	G	R
B	G	B	G

Fig. 9. Bayer Format.

In order to obtain the color information, the color image sensor is covered with a red, green, or blue filter, in a repetitive pattern. This pattern or sequence of the filters can vary, but the "Bayer" pattern is widely used, it is an arrangement of 2x2 repetitive and was invented by Kodak. Fig. 10 shows the positioning of the sensors and the representation of the color generated in the image.

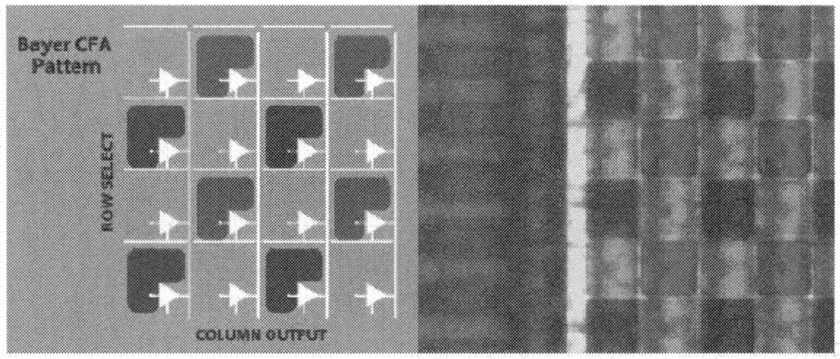

Fig. 10. Positioning of the sensors and their respective image

To obtain an image in bit map, a Bayer to RGB converter is required, there are several methods. The bilinear interpolation method together with that of linear interpolation was chosen; this correlation was taken into consideration as it presents better characteristics in comparison with others (Sakamoto et al, 1998). A brief description of the method is as follows.

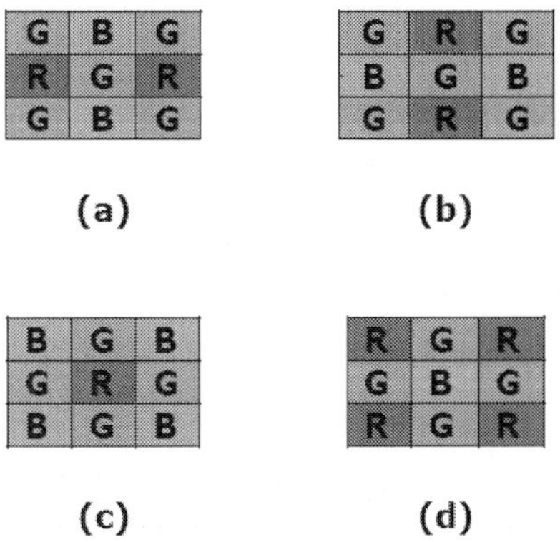

(a)   (b)

(c)   (d)

Fig. 11. Four possible cases for the interpolation of components R and B

The values of R and B are interpolated in a straight line from the closest neighbors of the same color. There are four possible cases, as shown in Fig. 11. The missing values of R and B are interpolated on a green pixel, see Fig. 11 (a) and (b), taking the mean values of the two closest neighbors with the same color. For example, in Fig. 11 (a), the value of the blue component on a G pixel will be the average of the blue pixels above and below the G pixel, while the value of the red component will be the average of the two red pixels to the left and right of the G pixel. In Fig. 11 (c) we can observe that, when the value of the blue component is interpolated for an R pixel, we take the average of the four closest blue pixels surrounding the R pixel. Similarly, to determine the value of the red component on a B pixel (Fig.11 (d)), we take the average of the four closest red pixels surrounding the B pixel.

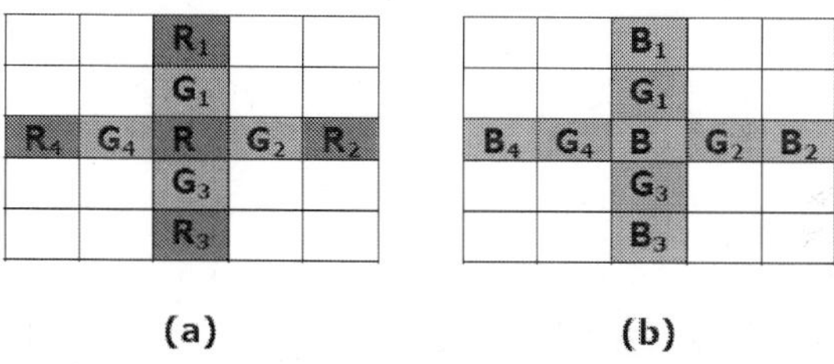

Fig. 12. two possible cases for the interpolation of the G component.

The part of the linear interpolation method dealing with the correlation is as follows:
In Fig. 12(a) the value of the green component is interpolated on a R pixel. The value used for the G component is:

$$G(R) = \begin{cases} (G_1 + G_3)/2, & \text{if } |R_1 - R_3| < |R_2 - R_4| \\ (G_2 + G_4)/2, & \text{if } |R_1 - R_3| > |R_2 - R_4| \\ (G_1 + G_2 + G_3 + G_4)/4, & \text{if } |R_1 - R_3| = |R_2 - R_4| \end{cases} \tag{3}$$

For Fig. 12 (b), the value of the green component is interpolated on a B pixel. The value used for the G component is as follows:

$$G(B) = \begin{cases} (G_1 + G_3)/2, & \text{if } |B_1 - B_3| < |B_2 - B_4| \\ (G_2 + G_4)/2, & \text{if } |B_1 - B_3| > |B_2 - B_4| \\ (G_1 + G_2 + G_3 + G_4)/4, & \text{if } |B_1 - B_3| = |B_2 - B_4| \end{cases} \tag{4}$$

4.2 Implementation of the Bayer to RGB converter in a DSP

In accordance with the method previously described, we implemented the converter in the DSP 6416 of Texas Instruments, operating at a frequency of 1GHz (Texas Instruments, 2008). A summary of the implementation is presented in Table 1.

Size in Bytes	total of instructions	CPU cycles	time
2448	28373352	37273108	37.27 ms

Table 1. results of the implementation in DSP 6416

In the input of the converter, we have a Bayer image with the characteristics shown in Fig. 9. After applying the converter, the output would be three matrixes with the characteristics shown in Fig. 13, in other words we would obtain an image three times the size of the input.

R	R	R	R		G	G	G	G		B	B	B	B
R	R	R	R		G	G	G	G		B	B	B	B
R	R	R	R		G	G	G	G		B	B	B	B
R	R	R	R		G	G	G	G		B	B	B	B

Fig. 13. Results of the converter: RGB image

4.3 Results obtained in the tracking of the shrimp and crab.

For the following of the shrimp and crab, the first step is to subtract the background from the image of the two animals under study. The results obtained from this process using two different methods are detailed below.

4.3.1 Subtraction of images with RGB format.

First, the background of the pond must be captured (without animals). Fig. 14 shows the background and Fig. 15 shows the animals (mat), both images in RGB format.

$$p\_image2 = mat - background \tag{5}$$

Once we have the two images, the subtraction of images is carried out (Fig. 16) using the equation (1), after which a blurring is applied (Fig. 17).

4.3.2 Subtraction of images with Bayer format.

The procedure is the same as for the previous images, but in this case using the images in Bayer format directly before passing them through the converter. Fig. 18 shows the background image, and Fig. 19 the image with the animals.

In Fig. 20 we can observe the result of the subtraction and in Fig. 21 the result after blurring.

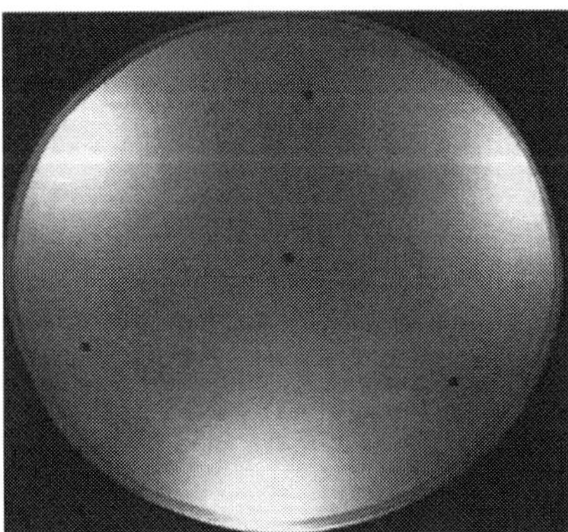

Fig. 14. Background with RGB format

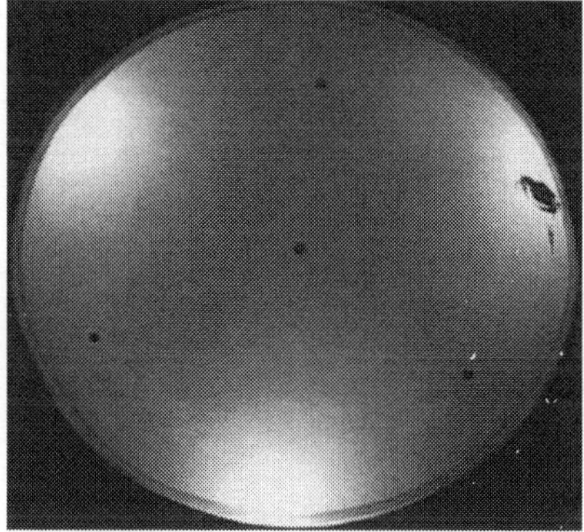

Fig. 15. Animals in the pond with RGB format

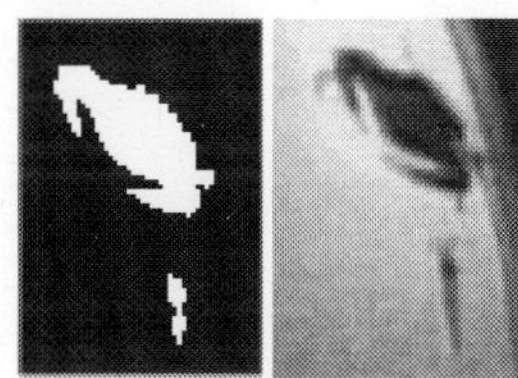

Fig. 16. Subtraction of images in RGB format

Fig. 17. Blurring of images in RGB format

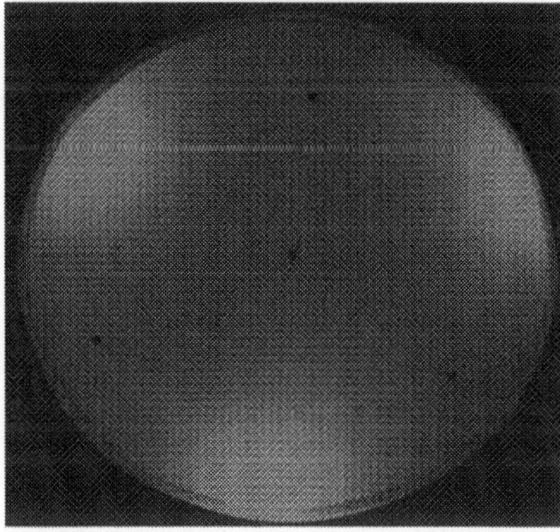

Fig. 18. Background of the pond

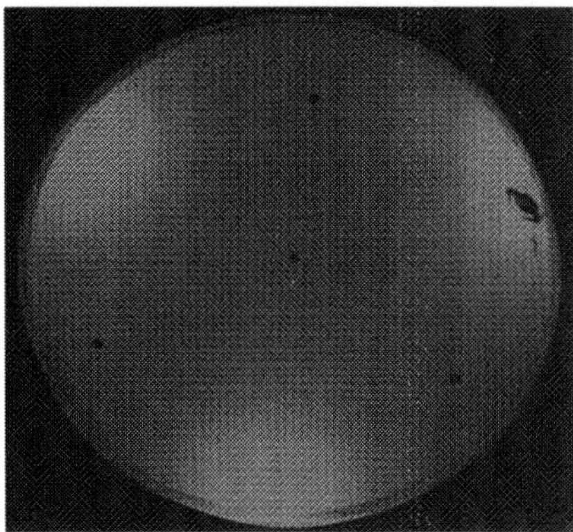

Fig. 19. Animals in the pond

Fig. 20. Subtraction of the images in Bayer format

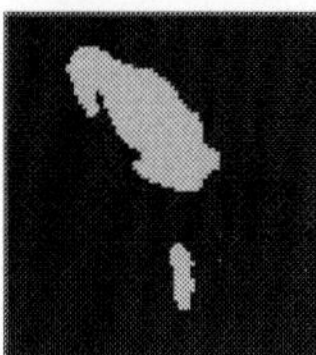

Fig. 21. Blurring of the images in Bayer format

5. Use and justification of the tools for digital images blurring and subtraction.

Once determined that is not necessary Bayer's conversion to RGB the next step is to determine the tool that it optimizes the time, to perform subtraction and blurring of the digital images.

The first objective is to separate the background from the objects to be detected. The method used to eliminate the background is that of image subtraction, in other words, the image of the scenery or background is subtracted from the images where the objects to be detected are found, obviously without the presence of the objects. The resulting image will conserve only those agents not found in the background image, which in this case will be the objects. The pixels not pertaining to the objects will remain in a range of values very close to zero and will be perceived in the image as dark or almost black colors.

The difference between two images f(x,y) and h(x,y), expressed as:

$$g(x,y) = f(x,y) - h(x,y) \tag{6}$$

The effect being that only the areas in which f(x,y) and h(x,y) are different will appear in the output image with enhanced details.

The Fig. 22, shows the images that must be subtracted in order to detect the objects, in this case the crab and the shrimp.

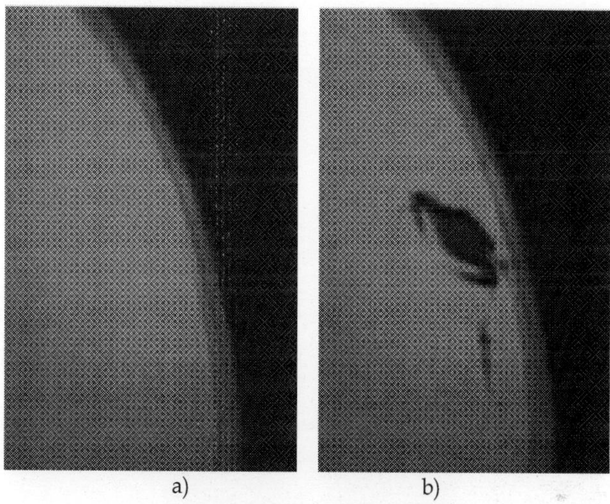

a)   b)

Fig. 22. In (a) we have the background image, in (b) the image with objects to be detected.

The result of the subtraction can be observed in Fig. 23.

Fig. 23. Result of the subtraction.

The next step is to binarize the image by a thresholding. This is achieved by fixing a constant value of brightness, which will serve as a threshold to be able to distinguish between the sections of the image pertaining to the background and those pertaining to the objects of interest. If the brightness level of the pixel under analysis is greater than the established threshold, its value will be modified and established with the maximum brightness value in an image with an 8 bit resolution, and this value is "255". If the brightness value is not greater than the threshold, its value will be modified to the minimum brightness value corresponding to deep black, i.e. "0". The result of the thresholding can be observed in Fig. 24.

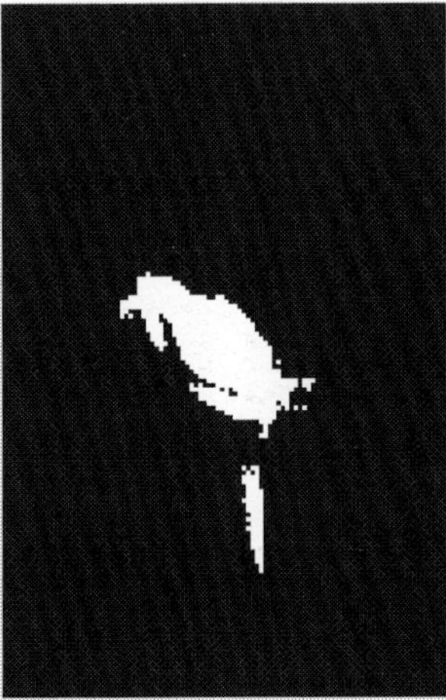

Fig. 24. Result of the thresholding

In every system in which the subtraction and thresholding were implemented, the results shown in the figures above were obtained.
Results obtained in the 4 systems implemented. For all cases the systems was implemented using an image of 102 x 150 pixels in Bayer format (Bayer, 1976)

5.1 With the Borland C++ Builder compiler in a PC.
After carrying out the implementation and executing it in the builder (2002), the next step was to measure the processing times for each process, resulting in 140 ms for the subtraction and 160 ms for the thresholding. An advantage of developing the segmentation algorithms in the Builder compiler is that they can be modified very easily and, as we are dealing with a programming language in C++, this makes the code more portable. Furthermore, a person with little knowledge of hardware development could develop the implementations, and even improve them since this tool is software orientated and an elemental knowledge of programming is sufficient. It is important to note that greater efficiency can be attained in execution times, although the main objective of using this code was its functionality rather than its efficiency. For example, predictive filtering and other techniques of algorithm development could be added. Similarly, the capacity to emigrate this code to other more

powerful programming tools, perhaps under other operating systems, could produce better results. This application was run in a computer with a 1.6 Ghz processor with which it could be possible to improve the performance by using computers with better processors.

5.2 With the Microblaze.

After downloading the project in the ML 401 board containing the "Microblaze microprocessor (Xilinx, 2002), the processing times were measured, both for the execution of the subtraction and thresholding only and for the execution of the same processes plus the blurring. In order to obtain the processing times, a flag was added to the main program which indicates when processing begins and which changes state when the execution of the segmentation algorithm ends.

The observation of the times required an oscilloscope where a testing point was placed on an output of the board and the measurement was taken. The results can be seen in Fig. 25.

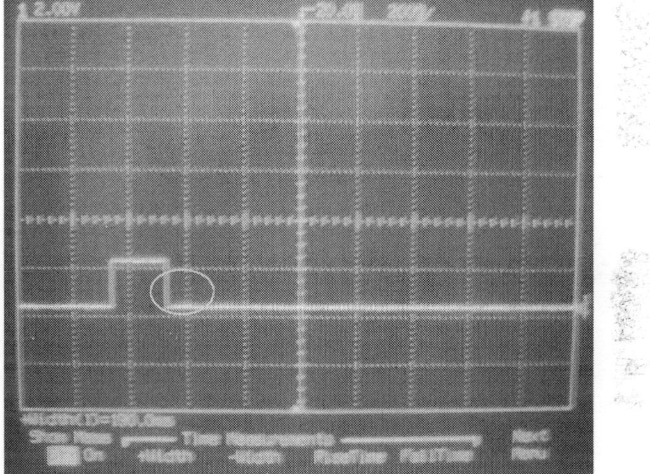

Fig. 25. Processing time of the process previously described.

The duration of the width of positive pulse observed in the above figure is the total processing time, and with a tool of the oscilloscope it was possible to measure the period of the positive pulse and the exact time was obtained. The legend +Width(1)=190.0ms can be observed in the lower left-hand corner of the screen, this is the time for the subtraction and thresholding.

An advantage of developing the algorithms in the EDK is that a C++ programming language is used to program the embedded microprocessor, again making the code more portable, however, it has some instructions reserved from the Xilinx. A greater knowledge of hardware design is also required in comparison with the Builder since a hardware platform must be elaborated; however, for the user who does not have this advanced knowledge, an assistant is provided to facilitate the development of the platform

For this implementation a 100MHz master clock is used, which is the oscillating crystal of the board used for this project. The results of the algorithms presented can be improved with the use of more powerful boards, such as faster clocks and boards that can handle these speeds.

Another way to improve these times is by using solid nucleus processors such as the Power PC, which has the advantage of being able to handle higher speeds and which has greater efficiency in clock cycles by instruction.

Resources used:

	Device Utilization Summary		
Logic Utilization	**Used**	**Available**	**Utilization**
Number of Slice Flip Flops	1,217	21,504	5%
Number of 4 input LUTs	1,639	21,504	7%
Logic Distribution			
Number of occupied Slices	1,353	10,752	12%
Number of Slices containing only related logic	1,353	1,353	100%
Number of Slices containing unrelated logic	0	1,353	0%
Total Number 4 input LUTs	1,977	21,504	9%
Number used as logic	1,639		
Number used as a route-thru	15		
Number used for Dual Port RAMs	256		
Number used as Shift registers	67		
Number of bonded IOBs	43	448	9%
Number of BUFG/BUFGCTRLs	3	32	9%
Number used as BUFGs	3		
Number used as BUFGCTRLs	0		
Number of FIFO16/RAMB16s	27	72	37%
Number used as FIFO16s	0		
Number used as RAMB16s	27		
Number of DSP48s	3	48	6%
Number of DCM_ADVs	1	8	12%
Number of RPM macros	1		
Total equivalent gate count for design	41,811		
Additional JTAG gate count for IOBs	2,064		

Table 2. Resources used by the FPGA.

5.3 With the processor designed in the Ise Foundation.

Once the complete electronic system(Xilinx,2006), had been elaborated and its functionality verified, the processing time of a 102 x 150 image was measured.

In order to obtain the processing times, a flag was added to the developed hardware which indicates when the image processing begins and when it ends. In this way the total time can be determined by measuring the time between each change in voltage level. The results are shown in Fig. 26.

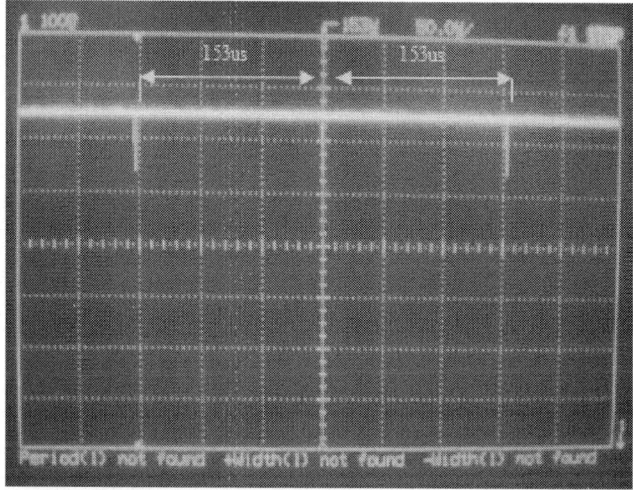

Fig. 26. Hardware processing time.

The time measured is 153us for each frame processed and is indicated in the above figure with arrows.

The results were also measured with the use of a tool within the Ise Foundation that generates a test bench with which it is possible to simulate the complete electronic system. To facilitate visualization, the necessary pines were added and, as can be observed, the processing time given is 153 us.

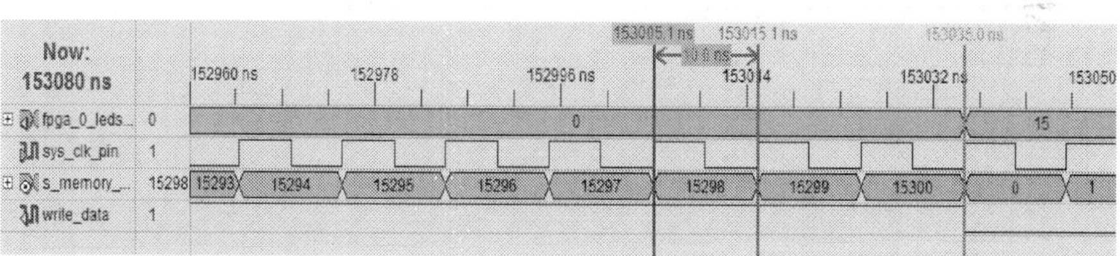

Fig. 27. Illustration of the processing time.

In the following table the resources used for the implementation of segmentation are specified.

One of the main benefits obtained from developing the segmentation algorithms in the hardware description language (HDL) is the parallelization of the processing, with which greater frame rates would be attained since it would be possible to increase the efficiency of instructions by clock cycles.

For this implementation a 100MHz master clock is used, which is the oscillating crystal in the board used for this project. The results of the algorithms presented could be improved by using more powerful boards, such as faster clocks and boards that can handle these speeds.

Logic Utilization	Device Utilization Summary		
	Used	Available	Utilization
Number of Slice Flip Flops	94	21,504	1%
Number of 4 input LUTs	163	21,504	1%
Logic Distribution			
Number of occupied Slices	100	10,752	1%
Number of Slices containing only related logic	100	100	100%
Number of Slices containing unrelated logic	0	100	0%
Total Number 4 input LUTs	175	21,504	1%
Number used as logic	163		
Number used as a route-thru	12		
Number of bonded IOBs	35	448	7%
Number of BUFG/BUFGCTRLs	2	32	6%
Number used as BUFGs	2		
Number used as BUFGCTRLs	0		
Number of FIFO16/RAMB16s	19	72	26%
Number used as FIFO16s	0		
Number used as RAMB16s	19		
Total equivalent gate count for design	2,193		
Additional JTAG gate count for IOBs	1,680		

Table 3. Resources used by the FPGA.

5.4 With the TMS320C6416" processor of Texas Instruments.

The subtractor and thresholder were subsequently used in the DSP 6416 of Texas Instruments, operating at a frequency of 1GHz (Texas Instruments, 2008). A summary of the implementation is described in Table 4.

Size in Bytes	Total of instructions	CPU cycles	Time
156	459754	506258	5.06 ms

Table 4. Resultados de la implementación en DSP 6416.

An advantage of developing the algorithms in the DSP is that a C++ programming language is used, which again gives more portability to the code, however, better results are obtained in comparison with the others implemented in C++, and in this case, an advanced knowledge of hardware design is not required, in contrast with the implementation in the Microblaze.

6. Conclusion

The image recovery is a fundamental part of the research, since all subsequent processes depend on it. To achieve this, departing from signals of Camera Link protocol, is very important to have a lot of care with the location of the receiver's flip-flops, to achieve the lowest possible skew, to reach the highest transfer rate, achieving even not to use the FPGA's resources of clock managing (DCM) and to have them available for future applications.

From the obtained results, we can appreciate that converting the images to RGB format is not necessary, in other words the images obtained from the cameras in Bayer format can be used directly. Furthermore, in images 16 and 20 we can appreciate that the subtraction is better in Bayer format since the result conserves the form of the shrimp more faithfully which is of great importance as this shape will be used to obtain the orientation of the shrimp.

With this we can avoid the entire code in the implementation of the Bayer to RGB converter, and more significantly, we can save time in the conversion, which is a critical parameter in real time following of animal trajectories.

All the tests conducted on the implementations demonstrated the functionality of each one of them as well as their technological expectations.

From the results, we can see that the best results are obtained with the implementation in an FPGA, however, the complexity of programming could be a limiting factor and any change in the hardware might represent another difficulty. The recommendation therefore is to work with the mixture of technologies; in processes requiring greater speed, the FPGA can be used and in processes where this not a critical factor the DSP can be used, thereby making use of the good results obtained in this investigation. With this combination it would be possible to optimise the whole system.

7. References

Bayer, B. E.; (1976) Color imaging array, U.S. Patent, 3971065.

Builder 6; (2002) Borland C++ Builder 6, 2002.

Camera Link; (2000) Specifications of the camera link, interface standard for digital camera and frame grabbers, Camera Link, October 2000.

Cole, E.; (2002) "Performance of LVDS with Different Cables", SLLA053B, Application report, Texas Instruments, February 2002

Gonzales, R.; Woods, R. (2002) "*Digital Image Processing*", Second Edition, Prentice Hall,

Lujan, C.; Mora, F.; Martinez J. (2007) "Comparative analysis between the Stratix II (Altera) and Virtex 4 (Xilinx) for implementing a LVDS bus receiver", Electrical and Electronics Engineering, 2007. ICEEE 2007 4th International Conference on 5 7 Sept. 2007, Page(s):373 - 376.

National Semiconductor, (2006) Channel Link Design Guide, National semiconductor, June 2006

Sakamoto, Nakanishi and Hase, "Software Pixel Interpolation for Digital Still Camaras Suitable for a 32-bit MCU", IEEE Transactions on Consumer Electronics, Vol. 44, No.4, November 1998.

Sawyer N. (2008) "1:7 Deserialization in Spartan-3E/3ª FPGAs at Speeds Up to 666 Mbps", XAPP485 (v1.2), Application notes, Xilinx, 27 May 2008.

Texas Instruments, (2002) "Interface Circuit for TIA/EIA-644 (LVDS)", SLLA038B, Application notes, Texas Instruments, September 2002.

Texas Instruments, (2008) "Fixed-Point Digital Signal Processor TMS320C6416", SPRS226K, Data Sheet, Texas Instruments, January 2008.

Xilinx, (2002) MicroBlaze Product Brief, USA, 2002.

Xilinx, (2006) ML 401/ ML 402/ ML 403 Evaluation Platform, User Guide, Xilinx, May 2006.

## 25

Hardware Architectures
for Image Processing Acceleration

Almudena Lindoso and Luis Entrena
University Carlos III of Madrid
Spain

1. Introduction

Achieving high performance has traditionally been a challenge in the image processing field. Even though many useful image processing algorithms can be described quite compactly with few operations, these operations must be repeated over large amounts of data and usually demand substantial computational effort. With the rapid evolution of digital imaging technology, the computational load of image processing algorithms is growing due to increasing algorithm complexity and increasing image size. This scenario typically leads to choose a high-end microprocessor for image processing tasks. However, most image processing systems have quite strict requirements in other aspects, such as size, cost, power consumption and time-to-market, that cannot be easily satisfied by just selecting a more powerful microprocessor. Meeting all these requirements is becoming increasingly challenging.

In consumer products, image processing functions are usually implemented by specialized processors, such as Digital Signal Processors (DSPs) or Application Specific Standard Products (ASSPs). However, as image processing complexity increases, DSPs with a large number of parallel units are needed. Such powerful DSPs become expensive and their performance tends to lag behind image processing requirements. On the other hand, ASSPs are inflexible, expensive and time-consuming to develop. The inherent parallelism in image processing suggests the application of High Performance Computing (HPC) technology (Marsh, 2005); (Liu & Prasanna, 1998). As a matter of fact, image processing and computer vision have been the most common areas proposed for the use of HPC. However, actual applications have been few because HPC has failed to satisfy cost, size or power consumption requirements that are usually required in most image processing applications (Webb, 1994).

Hardware acceleration is a suitable way to increase performance by using dedicated hardware architectures that perform parallel processing. With the advent of Field Programmable Gate Array (FPGA) technology, dedicated hardware architectures can be implemented with lower costs. In fact, FPGAs are the cornerstone of Reconfigurable Computing (Todman et al., 2005), a technology that offers unprecedented levels of performance along with a large flexibility. On the one hand, performance can be increased dramatically with the use of custom processing units working in parallel. These units can be mapped to a reconfigurable fabric to obtain the benefits of an application specific approach at the cost of a general purpose product. Cost and time-to-market are also greatly reduced as manufacturing is avoided and substituted by field programming. Finally, power consumption can be reduced as the circuitry is optimized for the application. Reconfigurable computing can also reduce the circuit size (and hence the cost) and provide additional flexibility by run-time reconfiguration. As a result, image processing performance can be improved by several orders of magnitude and becomes affordable for many applications (Memik, 2003); (Diaz et al., 2006); (Gupta et al., 2006); (Bowen & Bouganis, 2008); (Choi et al., 2006).

Modern FPGA devices currently include a large amount of general purpose logic resources, such as Look-Up Tables (LUTs) and registers. In addition, they commonly include an increasing number of specialized components such as embedded multipliers or embedded memories, which are very useful to implement digital signal processing functions. For instance, Xilinx devices include specialized blocks called DSP slices (Xilinx a, 2007). A DSP slice can perform a variety of multiply-accumulate (MAC) operations. Both the DSP-slice operation and the interconnection are programmable.

Many implementations of image processing algorithms on FPGAs have been proposed (Wisdom & Lee, 2007); (Koo et al., 2007); (Note et al., 2006). This chapter describes and analyzes hardware architectures for the acceleration of image processing algorithms. In particular, it focuses on filtering, convolution and correlation techniques, which are very commonly used in many image processing applications. These techniques are a primary target for hardware acceleration, as they are computationally expensive. As a matter of fact, the size of filters and correlation areas must be kept small in many cases in order to avoid introducing large performance penalties. Hardware acceleration can improve the trade-off between performance and complexity, enabling the use of larger filters and correlation areas.

In this chapter, two hardware architectures are described and discussed, based on the spatial domain and on the spectral domain, respectively. Both architectures can be easily parameterized to fit different applications and FPGA sizes. In addition, we show that the approach is not technology dependant and can be implemented in several FPGA technologies. Experimental results demonstrate that performance can be improved by more than two orders of magnitude with respect to a high-end microprocessor.

The integration of the hardware acceleration units with a controlling microprocessor is also studied. As the hardware acceleration units take on the most computationally expensive tasks, microprocessor requirements can be lowered. An architecture based on an embedded microprocessor and a hardware acceleration coprocessor is described. The coprocessor executes the computationally intensive image processing tasks under the control of the microprocessor. This architecture has been optimized for image processing and the hardware coprocessor is able to compute several critical operations for large data sets. The coprocessor architecture exploits the availability of high performance MAC modules in modern FPGAs.

The programming interface of the coprocessor has been optimized in order to reduce configuration time to a minimum. To this purpose, a simple configuration interface built upon the configurable fabric is used instead of the FPGA built-in fine grain configuration mechanism. This way, the performance improvements provided by the coprocessor can be fully exploited while a wide set of typical image processing functions for any image size can be mapped dynamically into the coprocessor.

The proposed coprocessor is dynamically reconfigurable during execution time. Reconfiguration is carried out by the embedded microprocessor, which can specify the image sizes and the operation to be performed by the coprocessor. As all coprocessor units execute basically the same operation, they can be configured in parallel. This approach combines the benefits of reconfiguration without decreasing performance, as the reconfiguration time has been optimized to complete the reconfiguration process in a few clock cycles. The whole system can be embedded into a single FPGA chip to implement a System on a Programmable Chip (SoPC).

This chapter is organized as follows; in section 2 image processing fundamentals are described, focusing on filtering, convolution, correlation and wavelet transform. Section 3 describes hardware architectures to accelerate the operations described in section 2 in spatial (subsection 3.1) and spectral domains (subsection 3.2). Experimental results obtained with the architectures are summarized in subsection 3.3. Section 4 describes the integration of a hardware coprocessor for image processing in a SoPC. Subsection 4.1 describes the image processing coprocessor and subsection 4.2 summarizes the experimental results obtained with the SoPC. Finally section 5 presents the conclusion of this chapter.

2. Image processing fundamentals

Image processing algorithms involve the repetition of some computations over large amounts of data. We will focus on linear filtering, convolution and correlation techniques, which are very commonly used in many image processing applications. Before going into implementation details, we need to establish the foundation of these techniques.

Linear filtering, convolution and correlation are strongly related concepts. They are typically defined by a sum of products, and can be implemented in a direct form by means of Multiply-Accumulate (MAC) operations. Alternatively, they can be described in the spectral domain and can be implemented using the Fast Fourier Transform (FFT). All these operations introduce a high computational load that is proportional to the size of the images considered.

2.1 Linear filtering, correlation and convolution

Filtering is one of the main techniques used in the field of image processing. Linear filters are a common type of filters that are computed as a linear operation on the pixels of an image. At any point (x,y) in the image, the response G(x, y) of the filter is the sum of products of the filter coefficients T(i,j) and the image pixels overlapped by the filter (Gonzales &Woods,1992):

$$G(x,y) = \sum_{i=0}^{N-1}\sum_{j=0}^{M-1} T(i,j)I(x+i,y+j) \tag{1}$$

The process of moving a filter mask over the image and computing the sum of products at each location is generally called correlation. Corrrelation is a function of the relative displacement (x,y) of the filter T with respect to the image I. Correlation with a discrete unit impulse mask yields a reversed version of the image. Alternatively, we can reverse the filter so that the operation with a discrete unit impulse mask yields the original image. This operation is called convolution and can be expressed as follows:

$$CV(x,y) = \sum_{i=0}^{N-1}\sum_{j=0}^{M-1} T(i,j)I(x-i,y-j) \tag{2}$$

The response of the filter can also be computed in the frequency domain, using the convolution and correlation theorems (Gonzales & Woods, 1992). The convolution theorem states that the Fourier transform of the convolution of two functions is equal to the point-wise product of the Fourier transforms of the two functions. The correlation theorem has a similar formulation, but the product in the frequency domain must be made with the complex conjugate of the Fourier transform of the filter to take reversing into account:

$$CC(x,y) = F^{-1}(F\,(T(x,y))^* * F\,(I(x,y))) \tag{3}$$

The interest of the correlation theorem lies in the use of the Fast Fourier Transform (FFT) in the previous formula. The complexity of the 2-D Discrete Fourier Transform (DFT) is in the order of $(MN)^2$, but the FFT reduces dramatically the number of multiplications and additions required to the order of $MN\log_2(MN)$. Thus, the correlation in the frequency domain using formula (3) is a good choice for a large filter size.

2.2 ZNCC

Cross-correlation, or simply correlation, is a measure of image similarity that is often used for image matching. In order to compensate differences in brightness, intensity, etc. of the images, a correlation measure that is invariant to affine transformations, such as Zero-Mean Normalized Cross-Correlation (ZNCC), must be used (Gonzales & Woods, 1992), (Crouzil et al., 1996). On the other hand, the measure must take into account the possible relative displacement between the images. Given two images T and I, ZNCC is given by the following formula:

$$ZNCC(p,q) = \frac{CC(T - \bar{T}, I(p,q) - \bar{I}(p,q))}{\left\| T - \bar{T} \right\| \cdot \left\| I(p,q) - \bar{I}(p,q) \right\|} \tag{4}$$

In equation 4, T and I are two images, usually called template and input images, respectively, $\bar{T}$ and $\bar{I}(p,q)$ are the mean values of the respective images and p and q are horizontal and vertical translations of the original input image.

When template images are previously processed, equation 4 can be simplified to equation 5 (Lindoso & Entrena, 2007). In this case, $\bar{T}$ =0 and $||T|| = \sqrt{NM}$, being N and M the dimensions of the considered template image.

$$ZNCC(p,q) = \frac{CC\,(p,q)}{\sqrt{NMSS(p,q) - S(p,q)^2}} \tag{5}$$

In equation 5, CC is the cross correlation, S is the sum of the input image pixels, SS is the sum of squares of the input image pixels. Formulae 6-8 describe CC, S and SS.

$$CC(p,q) = \sum_{i=0}^{N-1} \sum_{j=0}^{M-1} T(i,j)I(p+i,q+j) \tag{6}$$

$$S(p,q) = \sum_{i=0}^{i=N-1} \sum_{j=0}^{j=M-1} I(p+i,q+j) \tag{7}$$

$$SS(p,q) = \sum_{i=0}^{i=N-1} \sum_{j=0}^{j=M-1} I(p+i,q+j)^2 \tag{8}$$

2.3 Wavelet transform

The wavelet transform is the cornerstone of multiresolution processing. Wavelet transforms are based on small waves, called wavelets, of varying frequency and limited duration. Wavelet functions can be defined in many ways as long as the set of wavelet functions satisfies some scaling properties (Gonzales & Woods, 2008).
Given a set of wavelet functions

$$\varphi_{j,k,l}(x,y) = 2^{j/2} \varphi(2^j x - k, 2^j y - l)$$
$$\Psi^i_{j,k,l}(x,y) = 2^{j/2} \Psi^j(2^j x - k, 2^j y - l) \tag{9}$$

the 2-D Discrete Wavelet Function (DWT) of an image I is defined as follows

$$W_\varphi(j_0,k,l) = \frac{1}{\sqrt{MN}} \sum_{x=0}^{M} \sum_{y=0}^{N} I(x,y)\varphi_{j0,k,l}(x,y) \tag{10}$$
$$W_\Psi^i(j,k,l) = \frac{1}{\sqrt{MN}} \sum_{x=0}^{M} \sum_{y=0}^{N} I(x,y)\Psi^i_{j,k,l}(x,y) \qquad \text{i= H, V, D}$$

The results W_φ and W^i_Ψ are called the wavelet coefficients. The coefficients W_φ define an approximation of the image I at scale j_0. The coefficients W^i_Ψ define a detailed approximation of the image I for scales $j > j_0$ in horizontal, vertical or diagonal directions.
The 2-D DWT can be implemented using digital filters and downsamplers. More precisely, the wavelet functions define a low pass filter and a high pass filter that are used to extract the image components in the low and high frequency bands, respectively. The coefficients W_φ are obtained by low pass filtering in horizontal and vertical directions (LL filter), while the coefficients W^H_Ψ, W^V_Ψ, W^D_Ψ are obtained by different combinations of low pass and high pass filters, LH, HL, and HH, in order to show details in the horizontal, vertical and diagonal dimensions, respectively.

3. Hardware architectures

The image processing operations summarized in section 2 imply a large quantity of multiply-accumulation (MAC) operations. Microprocessors require several steps (instruction fetching, decoding, execution and write back) for every MAC operation. As these steps are performed sequentially, it is difficult to speed up the computation without architectural changes. To the contrary, FPGAs can provide high performance MAC computation with dedicated architectures that are able to perform several MAC operations at the same time.
In this section two different architectures are described. The architectures perform the computation of cross correlation (equation 6) in the spatial and spectral domains (Lindoso & Entrena, 2007). Other operations such as filtering and convolution can be considered as particular cases of cross-correlation. In the following subsections it will also be described how these architectures can be adapted to perform all the operations described in section 2.

3.1 Spatial architecture

Current FPGAs generally contain a large number of embedded multipliers that can be used for the implementation of MAC operations. A MAC operator module can be built with just a multiplier, an adder and several registers. Besides, modern FPGA families usually include dedicated modules for high performance MAC computation, such as the Xilinx DSP Slice (Xilinx a, 2007), or the Altera's DSP Block. (Altera, 2005).

The spatial architecture consists of a systolic array of MAC modules connected to a memory which contains the images, Figure 1. Inside the array, every MAC module performs the operation and passes the result to the next module in the same row. With this approach, a single data value is read from the input memory at every clock cycle, which is supplied to the first MAC module in each row. The last slice of every row produces the row computation result.

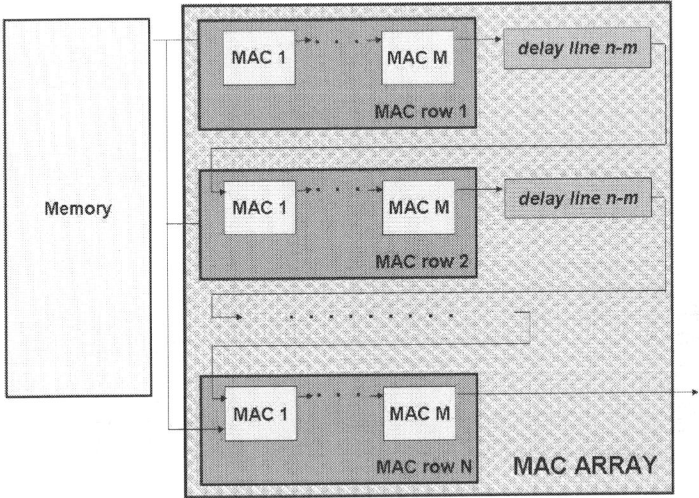

Fig. 1. Spatial architecture

The computation matrix results from the addition of N consecutive row results obtained at different times. This addition is performed by accumulating the row result to the next row. A delay line of N - M cycles is inserted for this purpose between the output of the last MAC module in a row and the input of the first MAC module in the next row, being N and M the size of the rows of I (input image) and T (template or filter coefficients) respectively.

Delay lines can be implemented as shift registers or FIFOs. The choice depends mainly on the selected technology and device, and may affect performance.

The proposed architecture can compute all the operations described in section 2. For CC computation, equation 6, first the template data are stored in the input registers of the MAC modules. After that, the input image is sent to the MAC array to perform the computation. For this purpose, two different data paths (input and template) can be used that may be governed by different clocks. The template path must disable its clock after data loading.

CC operation is quite similar to filtering (the template data can be considered as the filter coefficient matrix) and the computation process is completely equivalent. Convolution is also possible by reversing one of the images. Wavelet transform can be considered a multiresolution two-dimensional filtering with downsampling. The differences in this case are in the downsampling and the number of iterations required for completing the computation. For this iterative process, intermediate storage (results for each decomposition level) is required. A multiplexer between the MAC array and the memory is also required in order to choose the appropriate input data at every iteration.

This architecture can also compute SS and S as required for ZNCC, equation 5.

The proposed architecture is portable and scalable. Most FPGA technologies include high performance embedded MAC modules in advanced families (Xilinx a, 2007), but multipliers are available in any family and make possible the efficient implementation of MAC modules. The maximum size of the MAC matrix depends mainly on the resources available in the device chosen.

More formally, the correlation/filtering computation can be defined in a recursive manner as it is shown in equation 11:

$$R(i,p,q) = R(i-1,p,q) + \sum_{j=0}^{M-1} T(i,j)I(p+i,q+j) \tag{11}$$

where R(i, p, q) represents the result for the i first rows, R(-1, p, q) = 0 and CC(p, q) = R(N-1, p, q). By making the variable change t = i + p, we obtain:

$$R(i,t,q) = R(i-1,t-1,q) + \sum_{j=0}^{M-1} T(i,j)I(t,q+j) \tag{12}$$

This formula is implemented by the MAC array as follows. At each clock cycle, a new pixel I(t, q) is read from the memory, where the index t is incremented when the index q has completed a row of the image. The MAC module at position (i, j) has T(i, j) in one of the input registers and operates with the value of I that is also passed to the next MAC module in the row at each clock cycle. Then, at a particular clock cycle, given by t and q, each row is computing R(i, t, q) for a different value of i=0, ..., N-1. In other words, several row-operations are computed inside the MAC array at the same time. The result of the previous row, R(i-1, t-1, q), is added up at the beginning of each row. To this purpose, a delay line must be inserted, since R(i-1, t-1, q) was obtained during the computation of the previous row.

This approach allows completing the operation in a single memory pass, provided that the size of the MAC array is equal to the size of the template image. The MAC array can compute size(T) MAC operations in a single clock cycle. Therefore, in this case, the number of clock cycles required to complete all correlation computations is equal to the size of the input image plus the latency of a single row correlation. Usually, the latter is negligible. If the template image is larger than the number of available MAC modules, then the template image can be partitioned and operations are computed partially. For the general case, the total number of clock cycles can be estimated as:

$$Nclk = size(I) \times size(T) / size(MAC\ array) \tag{13}$$

In practice, the main timing bottleneck of this architecture may appear at the memory and the delay lines. FPGA families provide small, fast embedded RAM blocks (Xilinx a, 2004). Larger RAMs and FIFOs can be built by composing RAM blocks, at the expense of decreasing speed. This problem can be solved by dividing the memory clock frequency by two and doubling the data bus width. With this approach, every memory position stores two data values, corresponding to two consecutive pixels. The same approach can also be used for the delay lines. By doubling the data width of the delay lines, they can work at half the frequency and meet the data rate required by the MAC array.

3.2 Spectral architecture

Correlation can also be computed in the spectral domain, as formulated in equation 3. Computations in the spectral domain may be preferred in microprocessor oriented implementations because the number of MACs is reduced by using the FFT (Fast Fourier Transform). Equation 3 requires the computation of 3 two-dimensional Fourier transforms, two direct and one inverse. Assuming that the template T is stored after calculating its FFT, CC can be determined by computing only two two-dimensional FFTs, one direct and one inverse, and a complex multiplication. The Fourier transforms are implemented by two-dimensional FFT.

Figure 2 shows the architecture for the CC computation in the spectral domain. In this architecture a 1-D FFT array is used instead of a MAC array. The 1-D FFT array performs several 1-D FFT simultaneously.

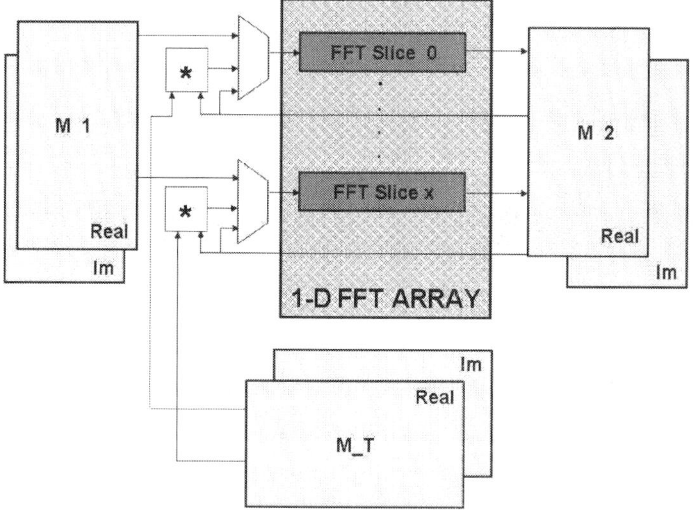

Fig. 2. Spectral correlation architecture

For CC computation, the images are split into rows or columns to perform parallel FFTs. The FFT modules compute the rows/columns FFTs, and are called FFT slices. The maximum number of FFT slices allocated depends on the image size and the device chosen for the implementation.

In this process three different memory blocks are required (Fig. 2): M1 for the storage of the input image and the result, M_T for the storage of FFT(T) and M2 for the storage of intermediate results. All those memories have the same size, which is the double of the input image size in order to store real and imaginary part of the FFT computation. It must be noted that the size of the input image and the template must be a power of 2 in order to compute the FFT. Zero padding is generally used if necessary to meet this requirement. Those three memories can be implemented with internal FPGA memory blocks.

In this architecture the computation of the two two-dimensional FFTs requires four iterations:

1.   Compute the FFT of the rows of M1 and store the result in M2.
2.   Compute the FFT of the columns of M2 and store the result in M1. After this iteration M1 stores FFT(I).
3.   Compute the inverse FFT of the rows of M1 multiplied by the conjugate of the corresponding elements of M_T, and store the result in M2.
4.   Compute the inverse FFT of the columns of M2 and store the result in M1.

Since every FFT slice consumes a large amount of resources, in most cases it will not be possible to allocate the number of FFT slices required to complete each iteration in one single step. The maximum number of FFT slices depends on the device available resources and is usually much smaller than the image size.

The memories M1 and M2 are divided into independent blocks in order to provide enough memory ports for each FFT slice. In order to avoid memory access collisions, memories are accessed diagonally by delaying the FFT slices with respect to each other.

The described architecture is useful for convolution and filtering in the spectral domain, and require just minor changes. In particular, convolution implementation is achieved by removing the conjugate operation at the output of M_T.

3.3 Experimental results

In this section the results obtained for several implementations of the architectures described in subsections 3.1 and 3.2 are analyzed. Only CC computation is reported, since other computations produce similar results.

FPGA and software implementations have been considered in order to stablish the speed up achieved with the proposed architectures. Experiments have been conducted with FPGAs from two different FPGA suppliers, namely Xilinx and Altera, in order to test the scalability and portability of the approach.

For the first set of experiments we selected a Xilinx Virtex 4 FPGA, namely XC4SX55-11 with 512 DSP slices. Xilinx V4 FPGA provides embeded high performance MAC modules called DSP slices (Xilinx a, 2007), that can be used for the spatial architecture and also to implement FFT slices in the spectral architecture. The SX subfamily is oriented to digital signal processing applications and contains a large number of DSP slices. Each DSP slice is able to perform many variations of MAC operations at very high speed (up to 500 MHz).

The image size considered is 256x256 pixels. For the device chosen, the maximum number of MAC modules in the spatial architecture is 512 and the maximum number of FFT slices in the spectral architecture is 16. The Fast Fourier Transform Core (Xilinx b, 2004) with radix 4 burst-I/O configuration has been used for the implementation of the FFT slices of the spectral architecture, computing 256 points FFTs.

The experimental results obtained with the Virtex 4 FPGA are summarized in Table 1.

Implementation	SW T_{CC} (ms)	HW T_{clk} (ns)	HW T_{CC} (ms)	Speed Up SW spatial	Speed Up SW spectral
Spatial T=12x12	62	2.477	0.162	240	383
Spatial T=16x16	110	2.438	0.160	244	688
Spatial T=20x20	172	2.490	0.163	239	1055
Spectral (16 FFT slices)	39	4.069	0.145	270	760

Table 1. Xilinx Virtex 4 performance results (spatial and spectral architectures).

Table 1 shows the performance measurements for the architectures and the speed-up achieved with respect to software implementations. For the spatial architecture, three different template sizes have been evaluated (12x12, 16x16, 20x20) as spatial architecture performance depends on the template size. For the spectral architecture only one implementation has been considered (16 FFT slices) because spectral architecture is not dependent on the template size as long as the template is smaller than the input image.

The second column of Table 1 shows the time required by the software implementations (SW Tcc). The reported SW Tcc time has been obtained in a PC equipped with a 3GHz Pentium IV processor and 1 Gbyte of memory. The third and fourth columns of Table 1 show respectively the minimum clock period (Tclk) and the time required to complete the computation of CC of the two images (HW Tcc) with the corresponding FPGA implementation. Finally, the last two columns of Table 1 show the speed-up of the proposed architectures with respect to the software implementations: spectral SW implementation (SW spectral) and spatial SW implementation (SW spatial).

The FPGA implementations achieve a remarkable speed-up of more than two orders of magnitude with respect to software implementations, as it is shown in the last two columns of Table 1. For instance, the spatial FPGA implementation for a 16x16 template performs 688 times faster than an equivalent software implementation and 244 times faster than a spectral implementation in a modern personal computer without loss of accuracy.

Analyzing the resource consumption, the spatial architecture has moderate resource consumption that increases with template size. The main limitation in the spatial architecture is the number of DSP slices available in the device chosen. Larger templates, such as 32x32, need to be partitioned, multiplying the processing time by the number of partitions. In any case, there is enough memory in the device to store the input image and implement the delay lines.

On the other hand, the spectral architecture consumes most of the FPGA resources, including logic, embedded memories and DSP slices, and is only slightly faster than the spatial implementation. The improvement is smaller than initially expected due to several reasons. First, the number of FFT slices that can be allocated is limited by FPGA resources. Second, the minimum clock period is larger than in the spatial architecture, as the critical delays are in the logic, rather than in other architectural elements. On the other hand, the spectral architecture must be applied on an image size that is a power of two and may be affected by rounding errors. If the input image is to be correlated with several templates (or several rotations of the same template), a large amount of memory is required, since the FFT of each template must be stored. Notwithstanding, the spectral architecture can be advantageous for large template sizes, as the processing time is independent of the template size.

In general, the spectral architecture is less versatile than the spatial one: the range of operations that can be implemented is reduced and the required resources are largely increased. The high amount of required resources provoques that the number of simultaneous FFT slices is considerably small in comparison with the images sizes. In this scenario, several iterations are required to perform a single operation, reducing considerably the speed-up.

The second set of experiments was performed with larger images. In this case we selected a ProcStar II board (Gidel, 2007) with 4 FPGAs. Each FPGA was an Altera Stratix II (Altera, 2007), namely EP2S60-5, and has on-board DDRII memory attached to it to store input and output data. The Altera Stratix II family is not oriented to digital signal processing applications. Each FPGA can implement up to 288 8-bit multipliers that can run at 450 MHz. The selection of a different technology in this case is just to prove the portability and scalability of the described architectures. Both sets of experiments can be performed on each technology and appropriate boards for them are commercially available.

The results obtained in these experiments are summarized in Table 2. In this case the template sizes are smaller since there are less multipliers available. However, the input images are much bigger. As a matter of fact, they must be stored in on-board memory, as they do not fit inside the FPGAs. Only spatial architecture has been considered. The first two columns show the template and input image combinations for each reported experiment. The third column shows the time required by a pure software implementation

Template Size	Input Image size	SW T_{CC} (ms)	HW T_{CC} (Theoretical) (ms)	HW T_{CC} (Experimental) (ms)	Speed up
8x12	1000x1000	631	1,90	3,5	179
8x12	2200X1000	1388	4,19	6,7	209
12x12	1000x1000	944	1,90	3,5	274
12x12	2200X1000	2077	4,19	6,8	307
16x16	1000x1000	1680	1,90	3,1	538
16x16	2200X1000	3695	4,19	7,0	526

Table 2. Altera Stratix II performance results (spatial architecture).

in a 3GHz Pentium IV processor and 1Gbyte of memory. The clock period of the FPGA implementation is 7,613 ns. In this experiment we are using FPGAs with the lowest speed grade that provoques an increase in the clock period with respect to the previous experiment. With this clock period, the fourth column shows the theoretical time required to complete the CC computation. However, in practice the time required is much longer (fifth column), because of the time needed to transfer the images to the memories and from the memories to the FPGA. Taking all data transfers into account results in as much as 84% time overhead with respect to the theoretical time. Notwithstanding, a speed-up of more than two orders of magnitude is still achieved even though data is stored in external memories and the chosen FPGAs have lower performance.

Experimental results demonstrate that the architecture is portable and scalable given the two FPGA implementations with different image sizes. The architecture can be adapted to any FPGA with or without high performance MAC modules and large speed up over software implementations can be achieved.

4. Image processing SoPC

In the previous section, we have shown hardware architectures for high performance image processing operations. The proposed architectures require an iteraction with other elements (microprocessor or PC) to control the data flow and to perform the rest of the algorithm operations. They can be considered as hardware coprocessors that accelerate a certain operation.

In this section the problem of the interaction with a microprocessor is solved within a System on Programmable Chip (SoPC) scenario. Inside a single FPGA, an embedded microprocessor is connected to a hardware coprocessor that accelerates the most complex operations. The analysis applies also to the case where a stand-alone microprocessor is used. However, SoPC presents advantages because the whole system is located in a single chip, decreasing size, cost and possibly power consumption.

A SoPC design requires an initial device choice in order to adapt the system to the avalaible embedded resources. It must be noted that existing FPGAs present similar options for communication buses and microprocessors. For this case study of a real system, a Xilinx Virtex 5 FPGA, XC5VSX50T, (Xilinx b, 2007) has been chosen. The system is intended for high performance image processing and consists of an embedded microprocessor, a hardware coprocessor that accelerates the critical operations, memories and communication buses between the elements.

Xilinx presents a range of posibilities for the embedded components (microprocessor and communication buses). In this case study, the architecture chosen is shown in Figure 3.

The main components of the system are the following (Fig.3):

- Microblaze soft microprocessor (Xilinx c, 2007), 32 bits wide, 100 MHz, that controls all the system elements, including coprocessor control and data interchange.
- OPB Bus. This is the main bus that is also used to interact with the coprocessor. Data interchange with the coprocessor is made through Direct Memory Access (DMA).
- Coprocessor, which is used for the most computationally expensive tasks.

The main component of the SoPC is the hardware coprocessor that makes possible the acceleration of image processing tasks. The image processing coprocessor is described in the following subsection.

4.1 Image processing coprocessor

The most common image processing operations require a large amount of MAC operations that can be executed in parallel to improve performance. The coprocessor has been designed using the spatial architecture, described in section 3.1, because its versatility along with smaller resources consumption.

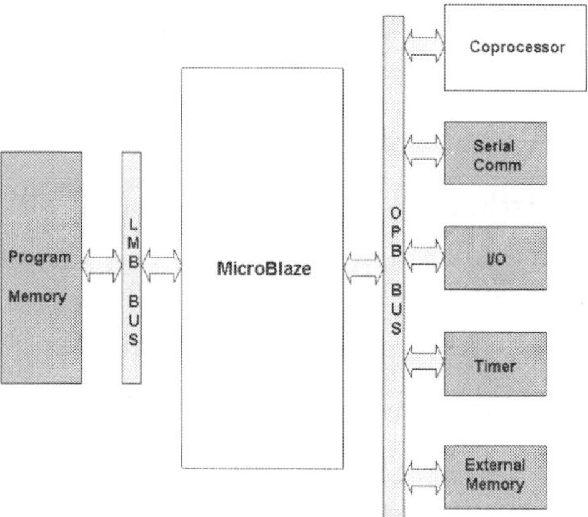

Fig. 3. SoPC architecture.

In order to broaden the number of operations performed, the coprocessor is dynamically reconfigurable. When the coprocessor is reconfigured, the architecture changes to fit the needs of the operation.

Reconfigurable architectures can be classified according to its reconfiguration depth. In this case, fine grain and coarse grain reconfiguration approaches can be considered. FPGAs support a fine grain reconfiguration mechanism. Fine grain reconfiguration provides higher versatility but typically requires large reconfiguration time, even in the case partial reconfiguration is used. On the other hand, coarse grain reconfiguration reduces the versatility but also reduces the reconfiguration time. Thus, an appropriate configuration depth balance must be found in order to achieve the best performance. For image processing purposes, coarse grain reconfiguration is much more efficient since the reconfiguration needs are actually small.

The configuration interface has been compacted to its maximum degree and it is acomplished directly by the embedded microprocessor with 4 transactions of 32 bits. In this approach all processing elements are configured to perform the same operation (MAC operation). The configuration interface can be extended, for instance, by configuring different operations at the processing elements. It must be noted that filter or template data are not considered part of the configuration data.

The coprocessor architecture is shown in Fig. 4. The basic elements of the architecture are: the MAC array, the control block and two I/O FIFOs for data interchange with the microprocessor through the OPB.

The control block manages the I/O FIFOs, the data transfer between the FIFOs and the MAC array, and the operation of the MAC modules. The control block also controls the clocks for the different elements in the coprocessor. In particular, the coprocessor must handle two data streams that use different clocks. The main data stream is used for image data and is typically controlled by a non-stopping clock. The secondary data stream is used to load filter coefficients or a correlation template. For the latter case, the clock is stopped when all the coefficients have been loaded in order to freeze the contents of the MAC array registers. This operation is required when a filter is computed in order to store the coefficients while the image data is passing through the MAC array.

The coprocessor contains a set of configuration registers that can be programmed by the microprocessor.

The configuration parameters are the following:

-   Operation performed by each MAC module.
-   Sliding window size. This parameter sets the MAC array dimensions and the length of delay lines.
-   Input data dimensions. This parameter sets the image dimensions over which the operations are performed.
-   Downsampling rate. This parameter sets the amount of data that is loaded into the output FIFO.
-   Control commands, such as coprocessor reset and start commands

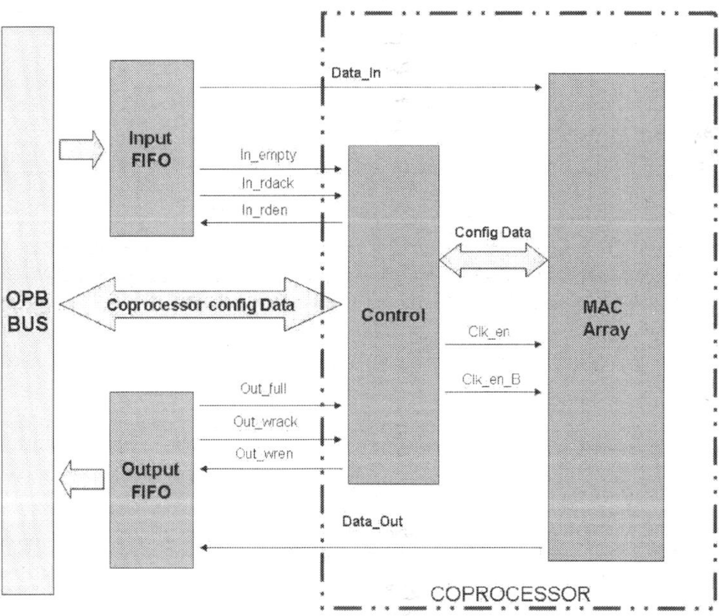

Fig. 4. Coprocessor architecture.

The configuration parameters are packed in 4 32-bit registers, so that full configuration of the coprocessor can be implemented in 4 OPB transactions. Once the coprocessor is programmed, data processing starts immediately as long as data is available at the input FIFO. The coprocessor works in parallel with the FIFO and stores output data at the output

FIFO. Input/output data are transferred from/to main memory by DMA without the intervention of the microprocessor.

The system has been validated with two types of image processing algorithms, described in section 2, which in turn require several coprocessor reconfigurations:

- Wavelet transform. This algorithm involves several two-dimensional filters of the image.
- Zero Mean Normalized Cross-Correlation (ZNCC). This algorithm involves cross-correlation as well as normalization. To this purpose, several reconfigurations of the coprocessor are required in order to compute cross-correlation, sum and sum of squares for sliding windows of the image.

4.2 Coprocessor operations
4.2.1 Wavelet computation

The dyadic wavelet transform involves spatial/spectral filtering that is performed by filtering and subsampling iteratively. The number of required iterations depends on the image size and wavelet level.

For this case study, two wavelet levels are computed. Usually wavelet is computed by detaching horizontal and vertical filters. However, two-dimensional filters are preferred as they can be processed faster by the coprocessor. On the other hand, two-dimensional filters are a common case in image processing applications. In this architecture, 4 two-dimensional filters are considered instead of 8 one-dimensional filters.

Filter coefficients and data are sent to the coprocessor in order to complete the computation. The first level of dyadic wavelet transform requires 4 different two dimensional filters computed over the whole image. Filters are computed and sent to the microprocessor in sequence.

To compute the second wavelet level, the input image is the LL filter result of the first level wavelet transform. This architecture could be optimized by computing several filters at the same time. This can increase performance but the data transfer will be penalized. In this architecture no additional elements are included for data transfer. Once the results are ready they are stored in the FIFO and sent to the microprocessor via OPB. If additional elements are included in order to store data and send it more efficiently, there will be a performance decrease and a connection penalty inside the coprocessor architecture. Adding additional connections can cause a loss in reconfiguration possibilities and a performance decrease inside the coprocessor for a considerable set of coprocessor operations.

4.2.2 ZNCC computation

CC, S and SS (equations 6-8) are computed separately by the coprocessor. Thus, the computation of ZNCC involves 3 reconfigurations. The relative displacement (p,q) that provides the maximum correlation is computed on the microprocessor by traversing the ZNCC results.

For all these operations, the MAC module array uses 4 rows of 48 MAC modules connected in pipeline. The horizontal dimension exploits the MAC column performance to its maximum degree. The vertical dimension has been fixed as the maximum available power of two in order to reduce the computational effort of the microprocessor. It must be noted that the image size is usually larger than the MAC array size. Then, partial results are accumulated by the microprocessor in order to complete the computation correctly.

4.3 Experimental results

The reconfigurable coprocessor performance has been measured for the proposed algorithms. Results were obtained with and without the coprocessor for comparison. In addition, software results were obtained with a PC Pentium IV, 3.2 GHz and 2 GB of RAM.

The coprocessor resource consumption is mainly driven by the MAC array size and the length of the delay lines. FPGA resource consumption is moderate. Half of the FPGA is still empty, so that more components could be added to the SoPC.

Accuracy of the SoPC results and the software results were analyzed without detecting accuracy loss in the considered algorithms.

The operating frequency of the SoPC is 100 MHz, which is Microblaze and OPB frequency.

Performance has been measured for the proposed algorithms. These measurements have been taken for the SoPC, Microblaze without coprocessor and a PC. Different image sizes and wavelet filter sizes have been considered.

Table 3 shows the performance results for the wavelet transform. The wavelet family used is Daubechies 2. These coefficients have been scaled in order to make efficient hardware computations. The results can be correctly rescaled by the microprocessor.

Table 3 shows that the SoPC is working much faster than Microblaze (up to 49 times faster) and slightly faster than the PC. Results show that the achieved speedup mostly depends on the MAC array size, with a clear trend to improve the speedup factor for larger array sizes.

For the two considered array sizes, no additional operations should be performed over the results because the whole two dimensional filters fit inside the coprocessor. If the considered filter size is larger than the available MAC array, the coprocessor would produce partial results and the final results must be computed by Microblaze. In spite of the penalty introduced in such a case by Microblaze computations, the overall SoPC performance will be highly increased because the speedup produced by a larger array size compensates this penalty.

Array Size	Image size	SoPC (ms)	Microblaze (ms)	PC (ms)
4x4	220x220	2.32	112.78	2.58
4x4	110x110	0.59	27.68	0.64
2x2	220x220	2.31	31.02	1.01
2x2	110x110	0.59	7.61	0.26

Table 3. Wavelet transform performance results.

Table 4 shows the performance results for CC. In this case, the SoPC has a much better performance than the other two systems. In particular, for the larger images sizes, the SoPC is 157 times faster than the Microblaze alone and about 3 times faster than the PC. For the considered array sizes the coprocessor is exploiting the MAC modules capacity to its maximum degree. Experimental results demonstrate that a not so powerful microprocessor, such as Microblaze, with the help of the proposed coprocessor can achieve better performance than a modern PC with a very powerful microprocessor.

Tables 5 and 6 show the performance results for S and SS, respectively. Results are quite similar to the results of Table 4. It can be seen that the SoPC performance is the same for the three computations, while the Microblaze and the PC reduce the time for SS and S. Thus, the speedup is proportional to the complexity of the operation.

Note that for CC, S and SS, the coprocessor can only be used for partial computations, as the maximum array size is 4x48. Also, in Tables 4, 5 and 6 it must be noted that when the array size is reduced to the half, the SoPC acceleration is not reduced in the same proportion. The reason is that the number of partial results also decreases and the effort performed by Microblaze is also reduced.

T size	I size	SoPC (ms)	Microblaze (ms)	PC (ms)
48x48	220x220	242	38047	684
48x48	110x110	33	5046	95
24x24	220x220	143	12405	223
24x24	110x110	28	2419	48

Table 4. CC performance results.

T size	I size	SoPC (ms)	Microblaze (ms)	PC (ms)
48x48	220x220	242	19813	634
48x48	110x110	33	2627	87
24x24	220x220	143	6460	214
24x24	110x110	28	1260	42

Table 5. S performance results.

T size	I size	SoPC (ms)	Microblaze (ms)	PC (ms)
48x48	220x220	242	21591	658
48x48	110x110	33	2863	94
24x24	220x220	143	7034	222
24x24	110x110	28	1370	47

Table 6. SS performance results.

Another experiment was performed with the SoPC, testing the performance for ZNCC for images of 560x400 pixels. ZNCC is computed using 3 coprocessor reconfigurations (CC, S, SS) and composing ZNCC result in the embedded microprocessor. Table 7 shows the performance results for SoPC, Microblaze without coprocessor and PC implementations.

Table 7 shows that SoPC reduces considerably the time required by Microblaze to accomplish the computation. Comparing SoPC and PC performance, a speed-up is observed for large templates. It must be noted that most of the time required for ZNCC computation is consumed by the tasks realized by Microblaze. Actually, when T=48x48, from the 632 ms required: CC takes 100 ms, S 87 ms and SS 87 ms, and the rest of the tasks performed by

Microblaze take 358 ms. When T=24x24, Microblaze time increases to 535 ms while the rest of the operations time is reduced slightly (CC=72, S=60, SS=60). In fact the low profile of the embedded microprocessor affects to the achieved speed-up over PC implementations. It must be noted that the performance with a SoPC containing a low profile embedded microprocessor can be even better that a PC Pentium IV.

T size	I size	SoPC (ms)	Microblaze (ms)	PC (ms)
48x48	560x400	632	28549	834
24x24	560x400	727	12166	392

Table 7. ZNCC performance results

5. Conclusion

Hardware acceleration using FPGAs provides a solution to improve the performance of image processing algorithms. In this chapter, hardware architectures for some of the most typical image processing algorithms, such as filtering, correlation and convolution have been presented. Several architectural options have been evaluated, including spectral or spatial architectures, hardware coprocessors or SoPC. These architectures exploit the increasing availability of specific resources in modern FPGAs, such as embedded multipliers and embedded memories, as well as the capabilities of FPGAs to efficiently implement some particular structures, such as delay lines or FIFOs. Experimental results demonstrate that all the presented solutions achieve up to 3 orders of magnitude speed up over equivalent software implementations. The proposed architectures are adaptable to many applications and to the needs of many image processing systems. The architectures are scalable for any FPGA family and adaptable to any FPGA vendor.

To further exploit hardware acceleration, an image processing reconfigurable hardware coprocessor is presented and integrated in a SoPC. This system can provide the flexibility of having a microprocessor that executes C code and take advantage of FPGA high performance for critical operations. Coarse-grain reconfigurability makes the coprocessor adaptable to many operations and algorithm changes without having a negative impact in the system performance. The approach can be easily extended to support other operations in the coprocessor.

6. References

Altera Corporation,(2005) Stratix Device Handbook: DSP blocks in Stratix & Stratix GX devices.

Altera Corporation, (2007), Stratix II Device Family Data Sheet.

Bobda, C. & Hartenstein R. W. (2007), *Introduction to Reconfigurable Computing Architectures, Algorithms and Applications*, Ed. Springer-Verlag, 2007.

Bowen, O. & Bouganis, C.S., (2008), Real-time image super resolution using an FPGA, *Proceedings International Conference on Field Programmable Logic and Applications*, 2008, FPL '08, pp: 89-94.

Choi, J. S.; Lim J. K.; Nam J. Y.; Ho Ha Y.,(2006) Image capture and storage system for digital TV without degrading image quality, *IEEE Transactions on Consumer Electronics*, vol. 52, Issue 2, pp:467 – 471.

Crouzil, A., Massip-Pailhes, L., Castan, S., (1996), A new correlation criterion based on gradient fields similarity, *Proceedings of the 13th International Conference on Pattern Recognition*, vol. 1, pp: 632 – 636

Diaz, J.; Ros, E.; Mota, S.; Pelayo, F.; Ortigosa, E. M.,(2006), Subpixel motion computing architecture, *IEE Proceedings -Vision, Image and Signal Processing,* Volume 153, Issue 6, pp:869 – 880.

Gidel Ltd., (2007), Gidel ProcStar II Data book.

Gonzales, R. C. & Woods, R. E., (1992), *Digital Image Processing*, Addison-Wesley, Reading, MA, 1992.

Gonzales, R. C. & Woods, R. E., (2008), *Digital Image Processing*, Pearson Prentice Hall, 2008.

Gupta, A. K., Nooshabadi, S., Taubman, D., Dyer, M.,(2006), Realizing Low-Cost High-Throughput General-Purpose Block Encoder for JPEG2000, *IEEE Transactions on Circuits and Systems for Video Technology*, Volume 16, Issue 7, pp: 843 – 858.

Koo, J. J.; Evans, A. C.; Gross, W. J., (2007), Accelerating a Medical 3D Brain MRI Analysis Algorithm using a High-Performance Reconfigurable Computer; *International Conference on Field Programmable Logic and Applications*, FPL 2007., pp:11 – 16.

Lindoso, A. & Entrena, L, (2007), High Performance FPGA-based image correlation, *Journal of Real Time Image Processing*, Vol. 2, Ed. Springer-Verlag, pp: 223-233.

Liu, W. & Prasanna, V.K., (1998) Utilizing the power of high-performance computing, *IEEE Signal Processing Magazine*, Volume 15, Issue 5, Page(s):85 – 100.

Marsh, P., (2005) High performance horizons [high performance computing], *Computing & Control Engineering Journal*, Volume 15, Issue 6, Page(s):42 – 48.

Memik, S.O., Katsaggelos, A.K., Sarrafzadeh, M., (2003),Analysis and FPGA implementation of image restoration under resource constraints, *IEEE Transactions on Computers*, vol. 52, Issue 3, pp: 390 – 399.

Note, J.-B.; Shand, M.; Vuillemin, J.E. ,(2006), Real-Time Video Pixel Matching, *International Conference on Field Programmable Logic and Applications*, FPL '06., pp:1 – 6

Todman, T.J., Constantinides, G.A.; Wilton, S.J.E., Mencer, O., Luk, W., Cheung, P.Y.K. (2005), Reconfigurable computing: architectures and design methods, *IEE Proceedings Computers and Digital Techniques*, vol 152, Issue 2, Mar 2005, pp:193 – 207.

Webb, J.A., (1994), High performance computing in image processing and computer vision, *Pattern Recognition, Proceedings of the 12th IAPR International Conference on Signal Processing*, Vol. 3 - Conference C, Page(s):218 – 222.

Wisdom, M. & Lee, P., (2007), An Efficient Implementation of a 2D DWT on FPGA, *International Conference on Field Programmable Logic and Applications*, FPL 2007., pp:222 – 227

Xilinx Inc., (2004), Block RAM (BRAM) Block (v1.00a), www.xilinx.com.

Xilinx Inc., Xilinx LogiCore, (2004), Fast Fourier Transform v3.0, www.xilinx.com.

Xilinx Inc., (2007), XtremeDSP for Virtex-4 FPGAs User Guide, www.xilinx.com.

Xilinx Inc., (2007), Virtex-5 Family overview: LX, LXT, and SXT Platforms, www.xilinx.com.

Xilinx Inc., (2007), Microblaze Processor Reference Guide, www.xilinx.com.

## 26

FPGA Based Acceleration
for Image Processing Applications

Griselda Saldaña-González and Miguel Arias-Estrada
Computer Science Department
National Institute for Astrophysics, Optics and Electronics (INAOE)
Puebla, Mexico

1. Introduction

Image processing is considered to be one of the most rapidly evolving areas of information technology, with growing applications in all fields of knowledge. It constitutes a core area of research within the computer science and engineering disciplines given the interest of potential applications ranging from image enhancing, to automatic image understanding, robotics and computer vision. The performance requirements of image processing applications have continuously increased the demands on computing power, especially when there are real time constraints. Image processing applications may consist of several low level algorithms applied in a processing chain to a stream of input images. In order to accelerate image processing, there are different alternatives ranging from parallel computers to specialized ASIC architectures. The computing paradigm using reconfigurable architectures based on Field Programmable Gate Arrays (FPGAs) promises an intermediate trade-off between flexibility and performance (Benkrid et al., 2001).

The present chapter is focused on how a well defined architecture can deliver high performance computing in a single chip, for image processing algorithms, in particular those based on window processing, i.e. convolution. The core architecture is a parallel processors array that can be the basis for processing several image algorithms based on window processing. The architecture is targeted to a single medium size FPGA device following the reconfigurable computing paradigm. The idea is to propose a platform that allows the acceleration of the computationally demanding part of a family of image processing algorithms.

The architecture introduces a new schema based on the use of local storage buffers to reduce the number of access to data memories and router elements to handle data movement among different structures inside the same architecture. These two components interact to provide the capability of processes chaining and to add flexibility to generalize the architecture functionality in order to constitute a versatile and scalable hardware platform.

The architecture copes with window-based image processing algorithms due to the fact that higher level algorithms use the low-level results as primitives to pursue cognitive level goals.

The contribution shows several variations of the architecture for convolution, 2D-filtering and motion computation. The motion computation correlation based algorithm and architecture are further detailed in order to show the flexibility on one of the most computational demanding algorithms in image processing.

The obtained results show the benefits that can be provided by a system implemented with FPGA technology and reconfigurable computing, since a high degree of parallelism and a considerable hardware resource reutilization is reached. Furthermore, with a standard medium size FPGA, a peak performance of 9 GOPS can be achieved, which implies operation in video rate speed.

Finally in this chapter some conclusions are presented emphasizing the key aspects of this approach to exploit both spatial and temporal parallelism inherent in image processing applications. The contribution concludes with some guidelines learned from the architecture design exploration. New opportunities, recommendations and future work are discussed.

2. Low-level image operators

Low-level image processing operators can be classified as point operators, window operators and global operators, with respect to the way the output pixels are computed from the input pixels (Umbaugh, 1998).

A window-based image operator is performed when a window with an area of w×w pixels is extracted from the input image and it is transformed according to a window mask or kernel, and a mathematical function produces an output result (Li & Kunieda, 1999). The window mask is the same size as the image window and their values are constant through the entire image processing. The values used in the window mask depend on the specific type of features to be detected or recognized. Usually a single output data is produced by each window operation and it is stored in the corresponding central position of the window as shown in Fig. 1.

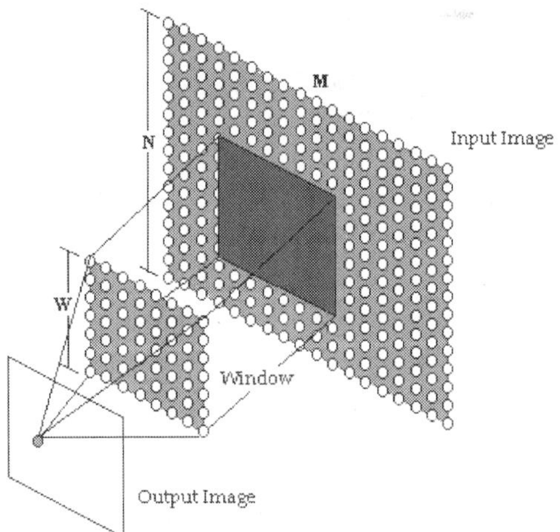

Fig. 1. Schematic representation of a window based operation

Window-based operations can be formalized mathematically as follows. Let I be an $M{\times}N$ input image, Y the output image, and W a $w{\times}w$ window mask. A window operation can be defined by Equation (1):

$$Y_{rc} = F(f(W_{ij}, I_{r+i,\ c+j}))\quad \forall (i,j) \in w \times w,\ \forall (r,c) \in M \times N \tag{1}$$

Where w_{ij} represents a coefficient from the window mask W, $I_{r+i,\ c+j}$ represents a pixel from a $w \times w$ window around the (r, c) pixel in the input image, f defines a scalar function, and F defines the local reduction function.

Window-based operators are characterized because the same scalar function is applied on a pixel by pixel way to each individual pixel of one or more input images to produce a partial result. Common scalar functions include relational operations, arithmetic operations, and logical operations. The local reduction function reduces the window of intermediate results, computed by the scalar function, to a single output result. Some common local reduction functions employed are accumulation, maximum, and absolute value. Scalar and local reduction functions form the image algebra to construct window-based image applications. In order to implement a flexible architecture these functions are considered (Torres-Huitzil & Arias-Estrada, 2005); (Ballard & Brown, 1982); (Bouridane et al., 1999).

3. Architecture description

The rectangular structure of an image intuitively suggests that image processing algorithms map efficiently to a 2D processors array, therefore the proposed architecture consists of a main module based on 2D, customizable systolic array of $w \times w$ Processing Elements (PEs) as can be observed in Fig. 2 diagram.

The main purpose of the architecture is to allow processes chaining, therefore the basic scheme shown in Fig. 2, can be replicated inside the same FPGA several times in order to process different algorithms independently. This processes chaining scheme provides the advantage of using a reduced bandwidth for communication between processing blocks since all of them are inside the same FPGA.

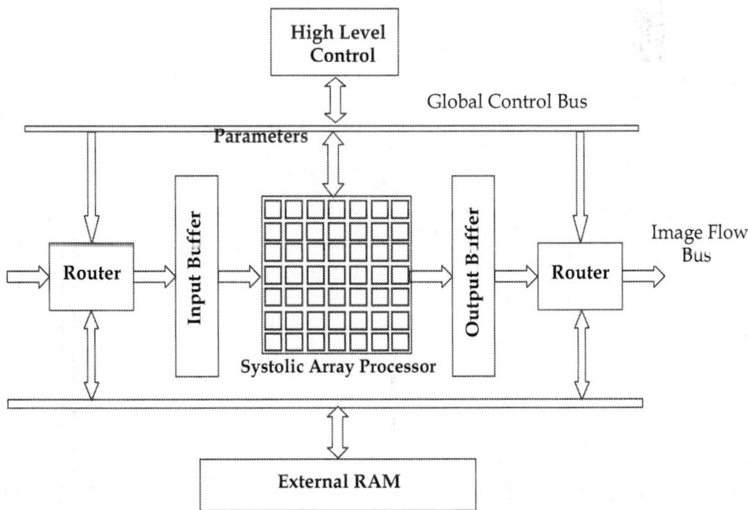

Fig. 2. Block diagram of the architecture

The simplified block diagram of the architecture shown in Fig. 2 comprises six main blocks:
- A high level control unit
- An external main memory
- A dedicated processor array
- Routers
- Image buffers
- Internal buses

High Level Control Unit: This unit could be placed in a host PC or embedded in the FPGA. The main purpose of the control unit is to manage the data flow and synchronize the different operations performed in the architecture. The high level controller starts and stops the operation in the system, furthermore, it is responsible of image capturing and displaying. From the PC it is possible to choose a particular operation that can be performed by the PEs in the systolic array, to coordinate operations and to manage bidirectional data flows between the architecture and the PC. From this unit, the user can select configuration parameters to customize the architecture functionality; the parameters include the size of the images to be processed, the coefficients for the mask to be used during processing and the kind of arithmetic to be employed between integers or fixed-point.

Main Memory: The memory in the architecture is a standard RAM memory for storing data involved in the computations. The data in the memory are accessed by supplying a memory address. The use of these addresses limits the bandwidth to access the data in the memory, and constrains the data to be accessed through only one memory port. Furthermore, the time to access the data is relatively long, therefore a buffer memory is included to store the data accessed from memory and to feed the processor array at a much higher rate. The buffers are used to re-circulate the data back to the processors, and they reduce the demand on main memory. An important issue to be solved is the allocation of area to implement data buffers. To obtain good performance one of the issues in the architecture design is, therefore, how to schedule the computations such that the total amount of data accesses to main memory is bounded.

Processor Array: The processor array is the core of the architecture where the PEs are organized in a 2-D systolic approach; and where the algorithms are executed. The processor array obtains image pixels from the buffers, and mask coefficients from memory to start a computation cycle. The processing array achieves a high performance due to a pipelined processing schema and local connections without long signal delays. The array organization with a small number of boundary (I/O) processors reduces the bandwidth between the array and the external memory units. The control unit specifies and synchronizes the actions to be performed in the PEs.

Routers: The Router unit is responsible for all data transfers in and out of the systolic array as well of interfacing processing modules to external memories. The data streams routers take data from/to input/output image memories and make explicit the data parallelism usually found in the image processing. The incoming data is stored in external memory RAM and data is brought into a set of internal buffers prior to be processed in parallel. The processed data by a processing block can be stored and then transmitted to an external memory output using a router.

Buffers: The purpose of the buffers is to supply data to the processors array and mask the long main memory latencies. The buffers have a fixed amount of storage to keep some rows of the input image or the intermediate data from a processing module. The storage buffers are organized in a First-Input, First-Output (FIFO) style. In each clock cycle, the data present at the buffers are sent to the processors array or to the main memory. Address decoding for the buffer is carried out using pointers that make reference to the buffer row that is being processed or being filled. These pointers allow a circular pattern in data movement inside the buffers. The buffer basically performs the following operations:

- Pre-fetches data from the main memory into its rows to hide the memory latency
- Reorders the information according to the processing needs of the algorithm to increase parallelism
- Stores intermediate information for its reutilization in subsequent processing blocks

Internal Buses: The global bus interconnects architecture elements to interchange back and forward control or configuration information, i.e. mask coefficients. In addition, this bus is connected to the high level control unit placed in a Host processor which is in charge of data and parameters transfer via Direct Memory Access (DMA) with the processor.

This architecture schema resembles a high level pipeline representation, formed of memory units and computing units. The architecture is intended for data communication among processes using data buffers abstraction. With these elements it is possible to chain processes since different processing blocks inside the same FPGA can carry out a different window-operator over the same data set. The results obtained by each block can be stored in the output image buffers and reused by subsequent processing blocks. This structure of cascading interconnection is a key feature of the architecture since it supplies generality to the array of processors, providing enough flexibility to run a variety of low-level processing algorithms and constitutes a platform to pursue the implementation of higher complexity algorithms.

3.1 Systolic array

The processor block of the architecture is shown in Fig. 3. In our implementation, the systolic array is a 7×7 set of configurable PEs. A window mask corresponds to the whole array, with every PE representing a pixel from the input image. The PEs array is vertically pipelined, PEs are activated progressively every clock cycle as shown in Fig. 4.

At every clock cycle all PEs in an array column receive the same column of image pixels but mask coefficients are shifted from left to right between the array columns to calculate the window operation. Partial results are shifted to a Local Data Collector (LDC) in charge of accumulate results located in the same column of the array and the captured results are sent to the Global Data Collector (GDC). The GDC stores the result of a window processed and sends it to the output memory buffer.

After a short latency period, all PEs in the array are performing a computation according to a control word. From that moment on, each new column of pixels sent to the array shifts the window mask to a new adjacent position until the whole image has been visited in the horizontal direction.

If reading image pixels from the buffer one row below, it is possible to cross the image in the vertical direction. The image buffer is updated during PEs operation, in a circular pipeline schema.

This image buffer was implemented with two port BlockRAM memories, where image pixels are stored as neighboring elements.

Routers take data from the input image memories and transfer them to the input buffers that store as many rows as the number of rows in the mask used for processing a window. An additional row is added to the buffer to be filled with new image data in parallel with the rows being processed; in this way the memory access time is hidden. Each time a window is

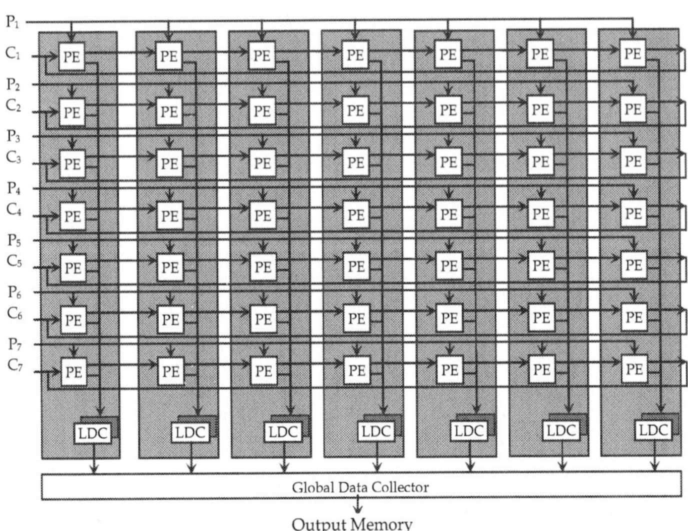

Fig. 3. 2D systolic array implementation

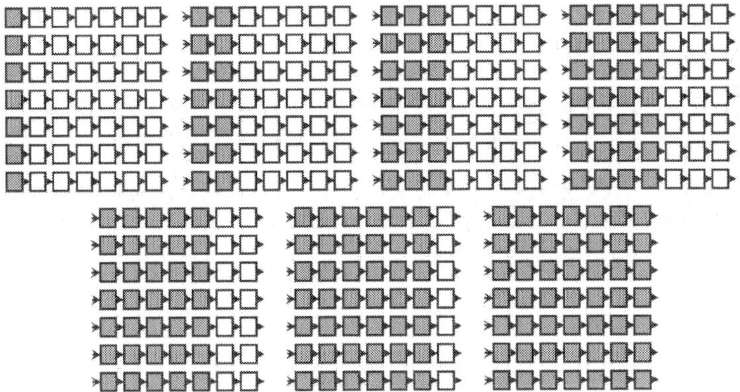

Fig. 4. PEs activation schema

slid in the vertical direction, a new row in the buffer is chosen to be refreshed with input image data, following a FIFO style. When the buffer end is reached, the first buffer row is reused following in this way the circular pattern as is represented in Fig. 5.

The coefficients of the window mask are stored inside the architecture in a memory bank that is able to shift data from one element to its neighbor. A shift register bank is distributed on internal registers of the processing elements to delay the mask coefficients.

In a similar way to the one used to read the input data, the memory containing the coefficients of the window mask of a window operator is read in a column-based scan. Fig.6 shows the reading process of the mask coefficients as time progresses. The coefficients are read sequentially and their values are transmitted to different window processors when an image is being processed.

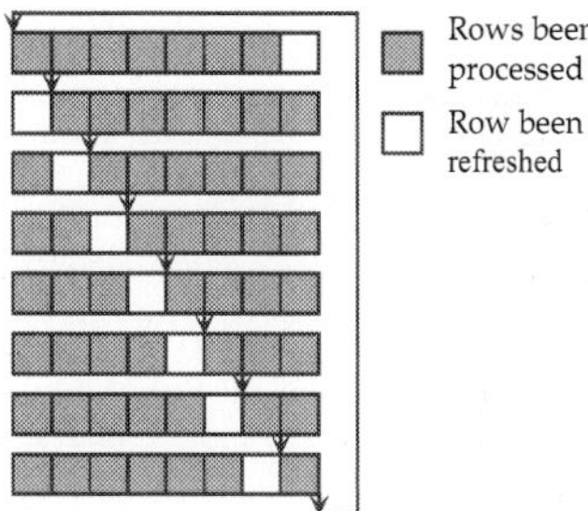

Fig. 5. Circular pipeline in the buffer memory

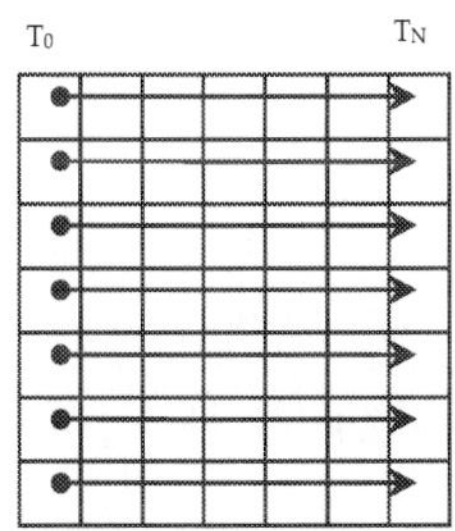

Fig. 6. Reading pattern for window mask

The reading process of the window mask coefficients and input image pixels requires a synchronization mechanism to match the operations sequence.

For simplicity the control unit for the systolic array has not been show in Fig. 2. This module is in charge of generating all the control and synchronization signals for the elements of the architecture.

The control unit synchronizes external memory, input and output buffers banks, and systolic array computations. The control unit indicates which processors execute an operation and when a result must be sent to the output storage elements. The control unit has been decomposed into local and simpler control circuits which are synchronized through a restricted set of signals. Therefore several distributed control sub-units exist in the systolic array to manage data flow in the PEs, to generate output memory addresses, and systolic array computations.

3.2 Processing element

Each PE has been specially designed to support the operations involved in most window-based operators in image processing: Multiplication, addition, subtraction, accumulation, maximum, minimum, and absolute value.

One processing element comprises one arithmetic processor (ALU) and a local reduction module (Accumulator) and can be configured by a control word selected by the user as can be observed in Fig. 7.

The PE has two operational inputs, incoming pixels from the input image (p) and coefficients from the window mask (w). Each PE has two output signals, the partial result of the window operation and a delayed value of a window coefficient (w_d) that is transmitted to its neighbor PE. For every clock cycle, each PE executes three different operations in parallel:

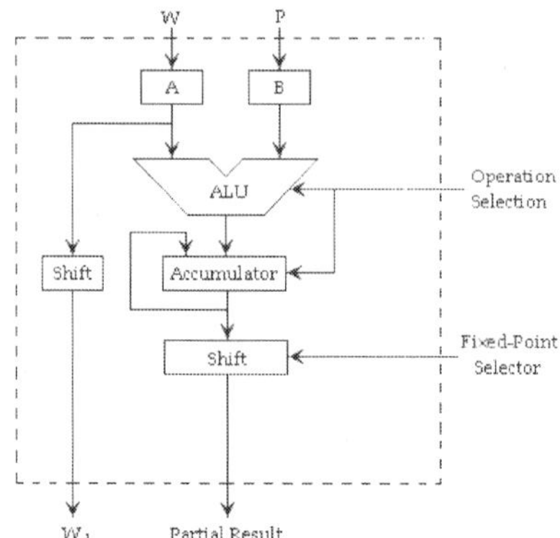

Fig. 7. Processing element implementation

- Computes the pixel by pixel value to be passed to the next computation cycle
- Integrates the contents of the outputs registers calculated at the previous clock cycle, with the new value produced in the arithmetic processor (ALU).
- Reads a new mask coefficient and stores it into the register. Then, transmits the previous coefficient to the next PE.

When the systolic pipeline is full a window output is obtained every cycle providing a throughput of 1.

4. Extension to the architecture for motion computation

In order to provide more capacity to the architecture and to turn it into a real platform, the basic structure has been modified to support the Motion Estimation (ME) algorithm. To implement ME in coding image applications, the most popular and widely used method, is the Full Search Block-Matching Algorithm (FBMA) (Gui-guang & Bao-long, 2004).

The FBMA divides the image in squared blocks, macro-block (MB), and compares each block in the current frame (reference block) with those within a reduced area of the previous frame (search area) looking for the best match (Kuhn, 1999). The matching position relative to the original position is described by a motion vector, as has been illustrated in Fig. 8.

$I_k(x, y)$ is defined as the pixel intensity at location (x, y) in the k-th frame and $I_{k-1}(x, y)$ is the pixel intensity at location (x, y) at the $k-1$-th frame. For FBMA motion estimation, $I_{k-1}(x, y)$, represents usually a pixel located in the search area of the size $R^2 = R_x \times R_y$ pixel of the reference frame and $I_k(x, y)$ belongs to the current frame. The block size is defined as $N^2 = N \times N$ pixel. Each individual search position of a search scheme is defined by $\overline{CMV} = (dx, dy)$.

The matching procedure is made by determining the optimum of the selected cost function, usually Sum of Absolute Differences (SAD), between the blocks (Saponara & Fanucci, 2004). The SAD is defined as:

$$SAD(dx, dy) = \sum_{m=x}^{x+N-1} \sum_{n=y}^{y+N-1} \left| I_k(m,n) - I_{k-1}(m+dx, n+dy) \right| \qquad (2)$$

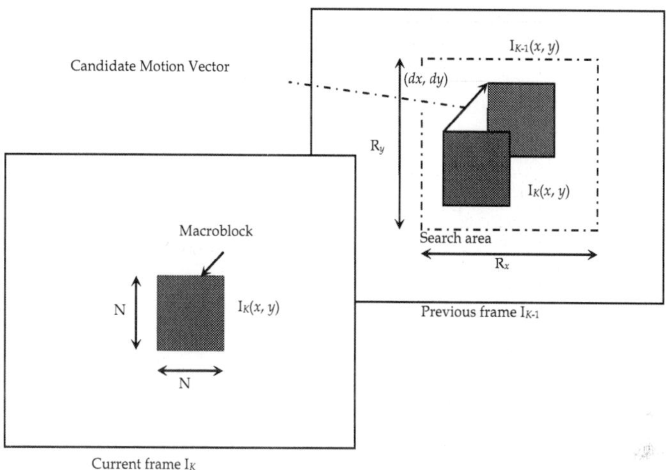

Fig. 8. Block-matching for motion estimation

$$\overline{MV} = \left(MV_x, MV_y\right) = \min_{(dx,dy)\in R^2} SAD(dx, dy) \qquad (3)$$

The motion vector $\overline{MV}$ represents the displacement of the best block with the best result for the distance criterion, after the search procedure is finished.

Due to the nature of Equation (2) the FBMA can be formulated as a window-based operator, though some aspects must be considered:

- The coefficients of the window mask are variable and new windows are extracted from the first image to constitute the reference block. Once the processing in the search area has been completed, the window mask must be replaced with a new one, and the processing goes on the same way until all data is processed.
- The different windows to be correlated are extracted in a column-based order from the search area to exploit data overlapping and sharing. The pixels are broadcasted to all the processors to work concurrently.

Based on these characteristics, the processing block has been modified to support SAD operation required for FBMA.

When the SAD value is processed, data is available in a row format therefore when blocks are processed vertically; previous read data in the search area are overlapped for two block search as shown in Fig. 9.

In order to reuse the image pixel available, the PE has been modified to work with a double ALU scheme to process two blocks in parallel. The final structure is observed in Fig. 10.

5. Performance discussion

In this chapter some representative algorithms based on windows-operators convolution, filtering, matrix multiplication, pyramid decomposition and morphological operators have been presented in order to validate the correct functionality of the proposed architecture and its generalization as a hardware platform. The technical data presented for each version

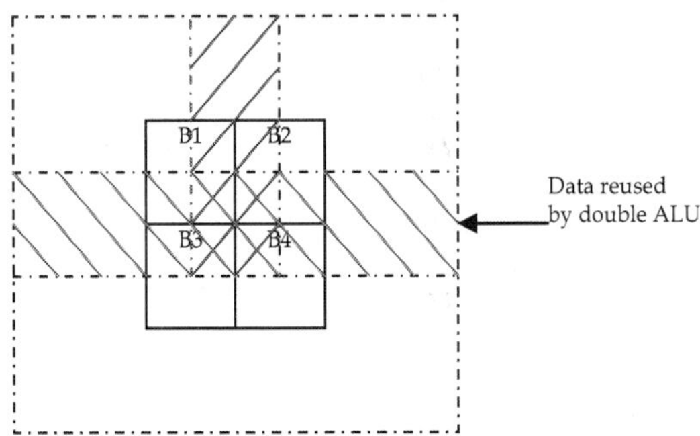

Fig. 9. Data overlapped between search areas in the horizontal and vertical direction for ME

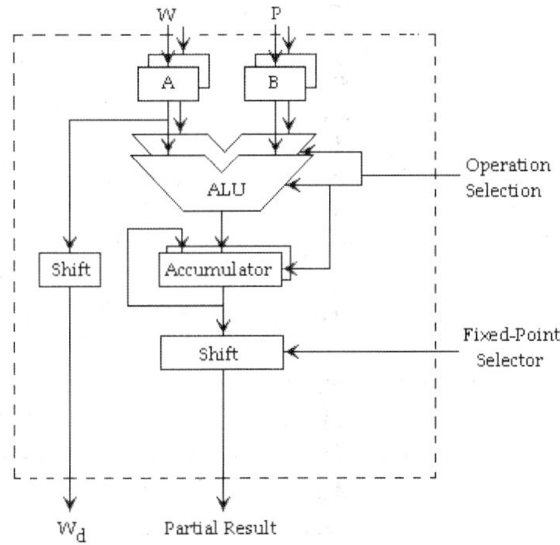

Fig. 10. PE modified structure to support ME algorithm

of the architecture constitute a measurement of its performance. The three main parameters considered are the speed, the throughput and the power consumption. Table 1 summarizes the results obtained for this set of algorithms.

Application	Number of Slices	Clock Frequency	Power Consumption
Convolution	11,969 out of 19200	66 MHz	2.017 W
Filtering	11,969 out of 19200	66 MHz	2.017 W
Matrix multiplication	11,969 out of 19200	66 MHz	2.017 W
Gaussian pyramid	11,969 out of 19200	66 MHz	2.017 W
Erosion	12,114 out of 19200	66 MHz	2.4 W
Dilation	12,074 out of 19200	66 MHz	2.017 W

Table 1. Summary of the architecture performance

From this table it can be observed little variations in the area occupied according to the algorithm being performed. These changes are due to the configuration selected for the PEs and the scalar operation being performed. However the performance and power consumption practically remain the same.

In order to establish the advantages of the presented architecture, the results obtained in Table 1 needs to be compared with previous implementations of image processing architectures; even though most performance metrics are rarely reported for architectures and systems in literature. This lack of standard metrics for comparison makes difficult to determine the advantages of a given system.

(DeHon, 2000) proposed a model to compute the hardware resource utilization in a system considering the fabrication technology. This model provides a standard metric that allows doing a fair comparison between systems measuring the silicon area in feature size units rather than in absolute units.

The silicon area required by the architecture is computed in terms of the feature size in λ. Considering data for the XCV2000E device and the results obtained by (DeHon, 2000) and (Torres-Huitzil, 2003) it is possible to present a comparison with previous architectures. For this purpose the execution time, given in milliseconds, and the silicon area occupied are considered as main metrics. The assessments were made considering that the systems deal with the same algorithm and they use the same image size. Table 2 presents the technical details for the chosen architectures.

System	Architecture	Application	Image Size	Timing	Silicon Area
(Rosas, 2005)	SIMD FPGA-based	3×3 Filtering	640×480	23.04 ms	Not reported
(Vega-Rodriguez, 2004)	FPGA-based	3×3 Filtering	640×480	868.51 ms	322 Gλ^2
(Torres-Huitzil, 2003)	Systolic FPGA-based	7×7 Generic Window-based Image operator	640×480	9.7 ms	15 Gλ^2
(Vega-Rodriguez, 2002)	Systolic FPGA-based	7×7 Median Filter	640×480	998.20 ms	1.41 Gλ^2
(Herrmann, 2004)	Von Newman	3×3 Generic Convolution	640×480	2863 ms	N/A
Proposed Architecture	Systolic	7×7 Generic Window-based operators	640×480	5 ms	26.7 Gλ^2

Table 2. Performance for different architectures

In summary, the proposed architecture provides a throughput of 5.9 GOPs for this set of algorithms on a chip area of 26.7 Gλ^2 with an estimated power consumption of 2.4 W running at 66 MHz clock frequency, which is a good compromise in area and power consumption for the attained performance. From these results it can be shown that it is possible to achieve real-time performance for applications based on windows operators. Furthermore, the capacity of generalization for the proposed schema has been established.

6. Implementation and results

For test and validation purposes, a RC1000 board from Celoxica that supports a XCV2000E XILINX Virtex-E FPGA with up to 2 million system gates, 640×480 gray-level images and sequences were used. Even though window masks of different size can be employed, only results for 7×7 are presented. Technical details for the implementation are shown in Table 3. The hardware resource utilization for the complete architecture is about 63% of total logic available in the FPGA.When the double ALU scheme is activated the Peak performance grows up to 9 GOPs.

Element	Specification
Virtex-E	XCV2000E
FPGA technology	0.18 μm 6-layer metal process
Number of PEs	49
Off-chip memory data buses	21 bit-address, 32 bit data
Internal data buses for ALUs	8 bits for fixed-point operations
Number of Block RAMs:	13 out of 160
Number of Slices	12,114 out of 19200
Number 4 input LUTs	19,163 out of 38,400
Number of Flip Flops	4,613 out of 38,400
Overall % occupancy	63%
Clock frequency	66 MHz
Estimated Power Consumption	2.4 W
Peak performance	~5.9 GOPs

Table 3. Technical data for the entire architecture

In order to prove the architecture versatility several window-based algorithms have been tested in the FPGA board, filtering, erosion, dilation, Gaussian pyramid, and matrix by matrix multiplication. Some images examples obtained during experiments are shown in Fig. 11.
Table 4 summarizes the technical details obtained for the motion estimation algorithm.

7. Conclusions and future work

In this paper a versatile, modular and scalable platform for test and implementation of low-level image processing algorithms under real-time constraints was presented.
The architecture consists of a programmable array of processors organized in a systolic approach. The implementation can achieve a processing rate of near 5.9 GOPs with a 66MHz clock frequency for the window processing. The performance increased to 9 GOPs for the motion estimation architecture extension. The high-performance and compact hardware architecture opens new and practical possibilities to mobile machine vision systems where size and power consumption are hard constraints to overcome.

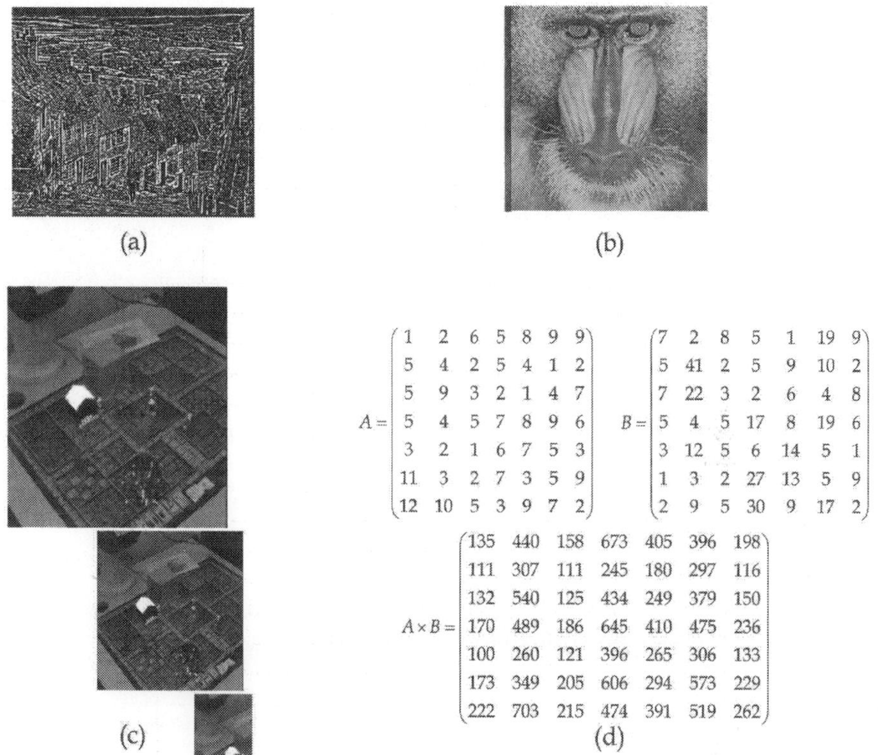

$$A = \begin{pmatrix} 1 & 2 & 6 & 5 & 8 & 9 & 9 \\ 5 & 4 & 2 & 5 & 4 & 1 & 2 \\ 5 & 9 & 3 & 2 & 1 & 4 & 7 \\ 5 & 4 & 5 & 7 & 8 & 9 & 6 \\ 3 & 2 & 1 & 6 & 7 & 5 & 3 \\ 11 & 3 & 2 & 7 & 3 & 5 & 9 \\ 12 & 10 & 5 & 3 & 9 & 7 & 2 \end{pmatrix} \quad B = \begin{pmatrix} 7 & 2 & 8 & 5 & 1 & 19 & 9 \\ 5 & 41 & 2 & 5 & 9 & 10 & 2 \\ 7 & 22 & 3 & 2 & 6 & 4 & 8 \\ 5 & 4 & 5 & 17 & 8 & 19 & 6 \\ 3 & 12 & 5 & 6 & 14 & 5 & 1 \\ 1 & 3 & 2 & 27 & 13 & 5 & 9 \\ 2 & 9 & 5 & 30 & 9 & 17 & 2 \end{pmatrix}$$

$$A \times B = \begin{pmatrix} 135 & 440 & 158 & 673 & 405 & 396 & 198 \\ 111 & 307 & 111 & 245 & 180 & 297 & 116 \\ 132 & 540 & 125 & 434 & 249 & 379 & 150 \\ 170 & 489 & 186 & 645 & 410 & 475 & 236 \\ 100 & 260 & 121 & 396 & 265 & 306 & 133 \\ 173 & 349 & 205 & 606 & 294 & 573 & 229 \\ 222 & 703 & 215 & 474 & 391 & 519 & 262 \end{pmatrix}$$

Fig. 11. Window-based algorithms implemented: (a) Filtering, (b) Morphologic Operators, (c) 2 level Gaussian pyramid, (d) Matrix Multiplication.

The configurable architecture developed can be use to support different algorithms based on windows processing such as generic convolution, filtering, gray-level image morphology, matrix multiplication and Gaussian pyramid. In addition the architecture provides support to the algorithm of motion estimation that is one of the most computationally demanding in video applications achieving bandwidth efficiency for both transmission and storage with reduced power consumption.

The programmability of the proposed architecture provides the advantage of being flexible enough to be adapted to other algorithms such as template matching and stereo disparity computation, among others. In this sense, considering the broad range of algorithms that can be implemented in the architecture, it is a convenient platform to develop and accelerate image processing applications under real-time constraints.

The platform has proven to be capable of handling a large amount of data with low area utilization, to benefit from parallelism as well as to attain a higher data transfer using a reduced bus bandwidth. The main focus has been placed on communication, and the possibility of processes chaining. Image buffers and Router elements allow cascade connection of several processing stages.

Element	Specification
Virtex-E	XCV2000E
FPGA technology	0.18 μm 6-layer metal process
Number of PEs	49
Off-chip memory data buses	21 bit-address, 32 bit data
Internal data buses for ALUs	8 bits for fixed-point operations
Number of Block RAMs:	18 out of 160
Number of Slices	12,100 out of 19200
Number 4 input LUTs	5,600 out of 38,400
Number of Flip Flops	7,742 out of 38,400
Overall % occupancy	65%
Clock frequency	66 MHz
Estimated Power Consumption	3 W
Peak performance	~9 GOPs

Table 4. Technical data for ME algorithm

The performance comparison with other existing architectures confirms the promising advantages of the proposed FPGA-based systolic architecture over other conventional approaches. Its performance has been evaluated for the previous window-based algorithms with excellent results that validate the proposed high-performance architectural model.

Furthermore, the design can be extended using dynamic reconfiguration techniques at high level, that is, the processor array could be reconfigured for different parts of a high level image processing chain, reusing the existing Routing, I/O Buffer and Data Flow Control structures. Dynamic reconfiguration allows modifying an application architecture at run time, therefore the platform capacities can be extended beyond what has been presented in this chapter without large increase in FPGA resource requirements. Selectively modification of the system operation at run time would allow the architecture to execute a sequence of different window-based operators to processes chaining, reusing the same hardware resources which implies a reduction in area occupancy and power consumption. This approach is currently been explored in order to determine its capacities.

8. References

Ballard, D. H. & Brown, C. M. (1982). *Computer Vision*, Prentice-Hall, Englewood Cliffs, NJ, USA

Benkrid, K., et all. (2001). High Level Programming for FPGA based Image and Video Processing using Hardware Skeletons, *Proceedings of the Symposium on Field-Programmable Custom Computing Machines*, pp. 219-226, ISBN: 0-7695-2667-5, April 2001, IEEE Computer Society, Washington, DC

Bouridane, A., et al (1999). A high level FPGA-based abstract machine for image processing, *Journal of Systems Architecture*, Vol. 45, No. 10, (April 1999), pp. 809-824, ISSN: 1383-7621

DeHon, A. (2000). The Density Advantage of Configurable Computing, *IEEE Computer*, Vol. 33, No. 4, (April 2000), pp. 41-49, ISSN: 0018-9162

Gui-guang, D. & Bao-long, G. (2004). Motion Vector Estimation Using Line-Square Search BlockMatching Algorithm for Video Sequences, *Journal on Applied Signal Processing*, Vol. 2004, No. 11, (January 2004), pp. 1750-1756, ISSN: 1110-8657

Herrmann, C. & Langhammer, T. (2004). *Automatic Staging for Image Processing*, Technical Report, Fakultät für Mathematik und Informatik, Universität Passau, Germany

Kuhn, P. (1999). *Algorithms, Complexity Analysis and VLSI Architectures for MPEG-4 Motion Estimation*, Kluwer Academic Publishers, ISBN-13: 978-0792385165, USA

Li, D., Jiang, L. & Kunieda, H. (1999). Design optimization of VLSI array processor architecture for window image processing, *IEICE Transactions on Fundamentals*, Vol. E-82-A, No. 8, (August 1999), pp. 1474-1484, ISSN: 0916-8508

Managuli, R., et al. (2000). Mapping of two dimensional convolution on very long instruction word media processors for real-time performance, *Journal of electronic Imaging*, Vol. 9, No. 3, (April 2000), pp. 327–35, ISBN: 10.1117/1.482755

Reuver, D. & Klar, H. A Configurable Convolution Chip with Programmable Coefficients, *IEEE Journal of Solid State Circuits*, Vol. 27, No. 7, (July 1992), pp. 1121-1123, ISSN: 0018-9200

Rosas, R. L., De Luca, A. & Santillan, F. B. (2005), SIMD architecture for image segmentation using Sobel operators implemented in FPGA technology, *Proceedings of the 2nd International Conference on Electrical and Electronics Engineering*, pp. 77-80, ISBN: 0-7803-9230-2, September 2005, IEEE Computer Society, Mexico

Saponara, S. & Fanucci, L. Data-adaptive motion estimation algorithm and VLSI architecture design for low-power video systems, *IEE Proceedings - Computers and Digital Techniques*, Vol. 151, No. 1, (January 2004), pp. 51-59, ISSN: 1350-2387

Torres-Huitzil C. (2003). *Reconfigurable Computer Vision System for Real-time Applications*, Ph.D. Thesis, INAOE, Mexico

Torres-Huitzil, C. & Arias-Estrada, M. (2005), FPGA-Based Configurable Systolic Architecture for Window-Based Image Processing, *EURASIP Journal on Applied Signal Processing*, Vol. 2005, No. 7, (January 2005), pp. 1024-1034, ISSN:1110-8657

Umbaugh, S.E. (1998). *Computer Vision and Image processing - a practical approach using CVIPtools*, Prentice Hall, ISBN-13: 978-0132645997, USA

Vega-Rodriguez, et al. (2002). An FPGA-based implementation for median filter meeting the real-time requirements of automated visual inspection systems, *Proceedings of the 10th Mediterranean Conference on Control and Automation*, pp. 131-136, July 2002, Lisbon, Portugal

Vega-Rodriguez, et al. (2004). An optimized architecture for implementing image convolution with reconfigurable hardware, *Proceedings of the World Automation Congress*, Vol. 16, pp. 131-136, ISBN: 1-889335-21-5, June-July 2004, Spain

Villasenor, J. & Hutchings, B., The flexibility of configurable computing, *IEEE Signal Processing Magazine*, Vol. 15, No. 5, (September 1998), pp. 67–84, ISSN: 1053-5888k

## 27

An FPGA-based Topographic Computer for Binary Image Processing

Alejandro Nieto, Víctor M. Brea and David L. Vilariño
Department of Electronic and Computer Science
University of Santiago de Compostela
Spain

1. Introduction

Initial processing steps in a computer vision system usually consist of low complex operations replicated on all the pixels of the image under processing. These operations are often very time consuming, particularly when they are executed on conventional serial computers. Every pixel-level processing represents millions of operations when moderate image sizes are considered. These processing stages provide the set of features of interest (object edges, movement, area, shape,…) with a considerable reduction of the data flow to subsequent processing stages. Higher level processing will benefit from such data to produce an abstract description of the scene and, if needed, to make a decision.

In visual processing, a great deal of computation is made on B/W images. This is particularly relevant for intermediate level image processing. Pattern recognition, texture detection and classification, or prediction and estimation of motion, are some examples of operations managing binary data. This fact has motivated an intense research focused on the design and implementation of efficient algorithms dealing with 1-bit data flows.

Traditionally, most of the algorithms in computer vision are executed on general-purpose computers using data from imagers as inputs. Recently, new bioinspired systems integrate together both sensing and processing stages, exploiting the massively parallelism inherent to early vision. These vision systems are usually analog or mixed-signal implementations allowing high density of integration as well as fast computation, with low/moderate accuracy. Often, these systems are not optimized to compute B/W images. Nevertheless, in some practical applications, (e.g., tracking with cellular active contours), the set of operations involving binary images are the main bottleneck from the time performance point of view. Keeping in mind the main constraints featuring integrated circuits: speed, area and reliability; the design of a special unit for binary image processing would be advantageous to be part of a complete computer vision system or even like an independent module.

As for the suitable hardware platform, the ever larger availability of hardware resources and faster clock signals on today FPGAs permit to do image processing with similar time-efficiency to that of custom ASICs from the recent past. Also, the time to market of FPGA-based systems clearly outperforms that of ASICs. Altogether makes FPGAs a good candidate to host proof-of-concept systems or even ended solutions.

In this chapter, a pixel-parallel binary image computer is approached. The architecture consists of a 2D array of processing elements based on the simple instruction and multiple data paradigm. The spatial arrangement allows to associate one processor to one pixel or to a reduced number of pixels of the image and consequently to exploit the inherent parallelism in visual computing. A 48x48 processor array has been implemented and tested on a Xilinx Virtex II FPGA. Several examples of practical applications are included to show the efficiency of the proposed system. In addition, based on the International Technology Roadmap for Semiconductors an estimate of how the increasing integration density will affect both FPGA and ASIC solutions is discussed. From this study, some conclusions about the capabilities of state-of-the-art or near-future generations of FPGA to host processor arrays with practical size are made.

2. Why a binary image computer?

The development of a computer vision application is divided into three stages. In the first, *low level vision*, acquisition and pre-processing are performed in order to highlight the features of interest to the specific application. The second, known as *mid-level vision*, has as goal to process information from the previous stage to extract a set of characteristics that define the problem to be solved: objects features, textures, edges, etc. The last stage, *high-level vision*, uses these results to obtain a more abstract description of the scene and makes decisions based on their content (Eklundh & Christensen, 2001).

The mid-level processing steps uses a lower knowledge of the domain of the problem and a significantly lower level of abstraction than the high level vision. In the same way, the data type used also differs. Low and mid-level processing images are represented by arrays, e.g., intensity values, while high level vision only uses the relevant data, usually in a symbolic fashion, greatly reducing the information used. These data represent some kind of knowledge, like the size of an object, its shape or its relationship with other objects. In the mid-level steps, the original image is processed in order to extract these features: segmentation, extraction of the number of objects, their shape, area, etc.

The amount of data to handle is very high, the operations that are performed have low complexity and they are massively parallel in a natural way, unlike what happens during the high level processing. The high computational effort, especially when dealing with high-resolution images or with applications with very demanding time requirements, involves processing millions of data per second. One strategy to tackle this computational power is the parallelization since the processing of each pixel is independent of each other, being this one of the main characteristics of mid-level image processing.

Another strategy to increase the time performance is to have an adequate representation of the data contained in the image arrays. In other words, the fewer the number of bits, the faster the processing. Thus, many algorithms employ gray-scale images instead of a color representation. A more aggressive optimization is to process binary images, i.e., 1 bit per pixel. Binary images are the simplest type of image. They have many other advantages, including easy acquisition, lower storage and transmission requirements and greater simplicity of the algorithms so they are widely used in many industrial and medical applications. It is true that in certain cases, such as the image segmentation in certain environments (Cheng et al., 2001) or the detection and treatment of shadows (Prati et al., 2003), using color images eases the resolution of the problem and can not be used representations in gray-scale or purely binary. However, there are problems that can be solved using only binary images (Szolgay & Tomordi, 1996) (Spiliotis & Mertzios, 1997) (Rekeczky, 1999) (Tseng et al., 2002). Moreover, many algorithms, including those processing color images have modules that use binary images (Garcia & Apostolidis, 2000) (Hsu et al., 2002) (Vilariño & Rekeczky, 2005) (Park et al. 2007).

A binary image can contain two types of information. On the one hand, a scene, i.e., partial information on the intensity of radiation can be stored. This information can come from a binary sensing or a transformation of an image, e.g. a thresholding or a halftoning of a gray-scale image. Furthermore, information contained in a binary image goes beyond shrinking the range to a 1-bit representation. The *active pixels* store information like edges, motion, occurrences of patterns, etc. This information enhances the original scene and speeds up the computation. Thus an algorithm can work with multiple binary images, representing the position of an object, the edges, and so on.

The retinal vessel-tree extraction algorithm (Alonso-Montes et al., 2008) is a good example of all the facts mentioned above. This approach is based on active contours, fitting the vessels from the outside. It consists of a controlled region growing started from seeds placed out of the vessels. The first step is a pre-segmentation of the vessels to obtain the guiding information for the active contour and its initial position. Next, the evolution is done. This algorithm was designed to operate in a pixel-parallel fashion. Some of the images, as the retinal image or the guiding information, are gray-scale images. Nevertheless, the contour evolution is performed using binary images because regions, contours, collision points, etc, only need 1 bit for its representation. In addition, as it can be extracted from (Alonso-Montes et al., 2008), the pre-segmentation step consumes the minor part of the computation. This algorithm was implemented in a vision chip (see Section 3) and this step consumes only the 3% of the time of the global computation. As a result, to speedup the computation is needed not only to pay attention to the more complex gray operations as additions or convolutions, but also to the simpler ones because in many algorithms they will limit the performance seriously.

3. Hardware for image processing

The most straightforward platform to implement a computer vision application is the personal computer. The main advantage of the *Microprocessors* is their versatility, the ability to perform many different tasks with a low cost. This permits any type of processing, although its performance is not always adequate. Even in this case it allows to simulate and study a wide range of applications, although the final implementation is done on another platform. The current trend is the growing number of processor cores due to the limitations in frequency scaling and power dissipation due to the transistor scaling (Creeger, 2005) (Schauer, 2008). They include parallel computation units to accelerate the computation, known as SIMD extensions (Gepner & Kowalik, 2006). Among other components in a personal computer, we must highlight the *Graphics Processing Units*, GPUs, because they reduce the workload of the main processor. Because of their specialization and because they include several hundred processing units, they have higher computing power. It is now possible to use them as generic accelerators using the concepts of GPGPU, *General Purpose GPU*. Nevertheless, they have certain limitations because of their fixed architecture, although the new families of graphics processors substantially improve its functionality (Owens et al., 2008) (Shen et al. 2005) (Soos et al., 2008).

A *Digital Signal Processor*, DSP, is a system based on a processor with an instruction set, hardware and software optimized for highly demanding applications with numerical operations at high speed. They are especially useful for processing analog signals in real time. They are systems that incorporate digital converter AD/DA for communication with the outside world (Tan & Heinzelman, 2003). Its flexibility comes from the ability to work with multiple data in parallel, its accuracy and expertise to the digital processing, and where the limitations of power and range are significant. However, it is not the most widely used platform for medium level operations by not being able to exploit the characteristics of such operations. However, for early vision tasks or higher-level, such as decoding or video compression, are a serious alternative to other platforms (Akiyama et al., 1994) (Hinrichs et al., 2000). A DSP reduces the hardware requirements by eliminating the no necessary hardware present in personal computers.

To meet the high computational cost of computer vision applications it might be necessary to perform the processing steps in the focal plane. A *Vision Chip* or a *Focal Plane Processor Array* is, in a generic way, an array of simple processors with an associated image sensor, with a one to one correspondence between processors and pixels of the image. These systems have a high performance and, if sensors are available, the bottleneck of uploading the image diminishes. Vision Chips work usually in SIMD mode. SIMD, *Single Instruction Multiple Data,* is a technique used to achieve a high degree of parallelism in data processing. This technique, originally used in supercomputers, is present now in all personal computers. The SIMD refers to an instruction set that are applied the same operation on a broad set of data. A single control unit manages the process and each processor operates on different data sets. They are executed synchronously in all the processors. This paradigm concerns only the way that the control over the operations is done, not the internal structure of the processing units or their spatial organization. Including local bus and distributed memory it evolves into Processors Arrays. The main limitation of Vision Chips is the reduced area available for each processor, cutting the resolution. However, the performance and power consumption achieved is difficult to obtain with other platforms (Linan et al., 2001) (Dudek, 2005) (Anafocus, 2007).

A *Field Programmable Gate Array*, FPGA, is a device that contains programmable logic components by the user. These components are formed by a set of logical blocks with a network of interconnections also programmable. In this way, the blocks are programmed to emulate complex combinational functions that are then chained together using interconnects as buses. The major advantage of FPGAs is their internal interconnect capability, with a complex hierarchy of connections optimized for specific functions. Moreover, they allow to develop a highly parallel hardware with a very low cost compared to an integrated circuit. As the description is done using *hardware description language*, HDL (Maginot, 1992), the designer does not have to worry about the low level electronics problems, reducing the time-to-market. Hence they are widely used in many areas as accelerators. The inclusion of specific hardware as dedicated multipliers or memory blocks, DSP or even microprocessor units, makes it possible to consider an FPGA a System on Chip with a reduced cost. Recent advances in their development lead to a similar performance to recent specific integrated circuits, but with a lower cost. For this, FPGAs are widely used in image processing tasks (MacLean, 2005). However, they have certain limitations, as it is necessary to design a new hardware, as well as control units, for each application, the designer must be an expert in hardware, software and the algorithm to be implemented. Besides, the performance will depend on the particular implementation done. It should be noted that when compared to the platforms described above, microprocessors, vision chips or other programmable systems, an FPGA implementation not only obliges to do an efficient adaptation of the algorithm, but also a new hardware design, so the required skill level is higher.

An *integrated circuit*, IC, is the miniaturization of an electronic circuit composed of semiconductor devices and passive components fabricated on a semiconductor surface. Its biggest advantage is the miniaturization, allowing building large systems with processing low power and area requirements and high throughput. An ASIC, *Application-specific integrated circuit*, is an IC designed for a particular use, but concepts like SoC (System on Chip), which integrate the whole system on a single chip, or SiP (System in Package), where multiple chips are piled up, are increasingly extended. They include, in general, a microprocessor or microcontroller, memory blocks, digital interfaces such as USB or Ethernet, analog modules, such as DACs, etc. They are designed from scratch and a large number of parameters can be modified. On some occasions, the CMOS technology provide component libraries which can greatly cut down the design time. Anyway, the design is costly in terms of time and manufacturing, and except when the number of units produced is high or when the application is very specific or it has very tight specifications, solutions as FPGAs become a serious alternative (Courtoy, 1998).

4. SIMD array for binary image processing

Low and medium image processing levels have an inherent high degree of parallelism at algorithmic level. This fact is exploited during the design and implementation of new hardware. The increase in parallelism is now in the leading-edge commercial microprocessors. The inclusion of multiple processor cores can greatly speed up computation. However, this is not enough when we talk about early vision. Moreover, the hardware specialization in floating point units is not fully suitable for image processing.

In a natural way, Single Instruction Multiple Data architecture is able to exploit such a massive parallelism. The creation of small processing units that only have to perform simple calculations in a matrix disposition, where each element of the matrix is associated with a pixel of the image, and with local connections matches the nature of early vision algorithms.

The relationship between the size and the computing power of the processing elements is critical. Small processing units allow bigger arrays at the expense of not being able to perform complex operations. Operations have to be segmented, increasing the number of required clock cycles, but with a higher level of parallelism. However, low complex Processing Elements, PEs, shorten the critical path of the design, decreasing the cycle time, so performance will not be heavily penalized with highly complex PE. In the latter, the level of parallelism is limited but complex operations can be performed easier. The complexity of the hardware and the computational power must be balanced. In the proposed architecture, an effort was made to use the smallest possible processor in order to increase parallelism and to build a large array. Being binary images, the complexity of the processing elements does not need to be high to perform an efficient computation.

4.1 The processing array

Fig. 1 shows schematically the processing array. The array is composed of a single type of processing elements, named as PE, as described below. The data flow in and out of a PE to the four nearest neighbors along the NEWS distribution network, a local communication system in four directions, north, east, west and south. It allows to interact through direct physical connections to the four cardinal points of each PE. To access to a farther PE, a strategy for moving data between PEs is needed.

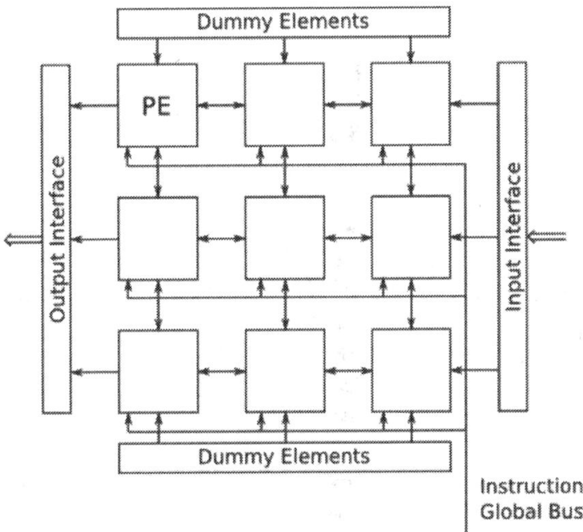

Fig. 1. The Processing Array schematic. Simple PE disposed regularly with local NEWS communication and a ring of dummy cells as boundary condition.

To obtain a full functionality, a cell ring of dummy cells that provides a configurable contour condition for the array was added. These cells are formed only by a memory element that takes values 0 or 1 depending on the algorithm being executed. If a not constant condition is necessary, i.e. varies pixel by pixel, the outer ring of PEs of the array can be used, the latter, at the cost of image resolution. Nevertheless, constant and homogeneous boundary conditions are usually the case.

The schematic of Fig. 1 shows that dedicated buses to load and download data are not present. The following approach is proposed: to use the existing local connections to perform shifts to upload and to download the data contained in the local memories of each PE. Thus, the global data buses are eliminated, being only necessary to design an interface between the array and the external memories, which stores the images, and to permit loading and unloading at one column per cycle. The interface is made by a series of multiplexers connected to the adequate input port of each PE which form the first column and allow to select between the value stored in the dummy ring (during processing) or the external memory (loading and unloading data). The output interface does not need additional hardware, since it is only necessary to connect the output of the PEs to the output bus. In this way, for an NxN array, N cycles are needed to upload or download an image.

Although this setting seems limited in terms of speed, the inclusion of the two interfaces gives the same speed as implementations which include rows and columns decoders. Both cases require as many accesses to the array as rows or columns. However, the input and output interfaces improve loading times allowing to download and to upload the current and the next image simultaneously, reducing the time by a factor 2. In contrast, the array random access is not permitted. In those cases where it is necessary to extract a concrete column of the array, shifts must be performed as many times as needed. However, despite this drawback, we achieve a significant improvement in the area consumed by the array and the processing speed.

Due to the simplicity of the PE, it is expected a great regularity in the design of the array. Even in programmable architectures such as FPGAs, an automatic *place & route* provides a good approximation to a topographic implementation without requiring manual intervention. With respect to a full custom implementation, it is also expected a high integration.

4.2 The processing element

The processing element, PE, is shown in Fig. 2. There are three main modules: the Logical Unit, the Memory Bank and the Routing Module. It can be checked that there is not an associated control module. The control is done globally and it is common to all of them, greatly decreasing the area. In this way, all the PEs run the same instruction synchronously. Using an appropriate set of instructions, the control unit can be implemented with very reduced hardware resources.

The Routing Module

The Routing Module acts as the interconnection between the PE and the rest of processing elements of the array. It consists of a multiplexer of four 1 bit inputs to the PEs located in the NEWS positions. A 2 bits signal controls the direction of communication, providing the value of one of the neighbors within the PE. The output provided by the PE always comes from a position of the Memory Banks, as it will be detailed later, so no additional logic is necessary for control.

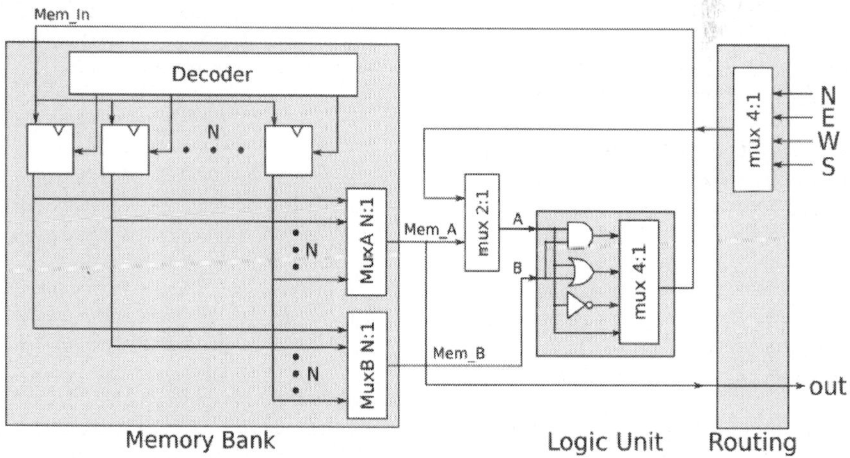

Fig. 2. Processing Element schematic. It is composed by three modules: The Memory Bank, the Logic Unit and the Routing Module.

This communication system is suitable for most of the low and mid-level operations as it can be extracted from the study of different algorithms in the literature or from the configuration of the coefficients in the templates listed on the Cellular Wave Computing Library (Kék et al., 2007). This library collects some of the most used templates in image processing on CNNs. Although the proposed architecture has a different operating mode than a CNN, its templates are fully representative of low-level image processing algorithms (Fernandez Garcia et al., 2008).

The Logic Unit

The Logic Unit performs only the most basic Boolean operations: *AND, OR* and *NOT*. In order to increase flexibility, the *Identity* operator is also included. With this set of operations, we can build any kind of binary operation instructions because it forms a functionally complete set.

The Logic Unit has two inputs for the 1-bit operands, labeled A and B, and one output, R, also 1-bit. The A operator drives the four operands, while the B, only drives the *AND* and *OR* gates. The multiplexer, controlled by a 2 bits signal, is responsible for providing the proper result in R.

Operands A and B have different origins. B is always a memory value, internal to the PE. However, A can be either an internal value or a value from one of the neighboring PEs obtained through the Routing Module. To select between these two options is necessary to add a 2:1 multiplexer (see Fig. 2) that selects the correct source of A. Thus, A is present in all operations while B is only required when the operation involving two operands.

It is interesting to highlight some of the functions of the *Identity* operator. Its main task is to act as data bus between the elements within the array and inside the PE. In this case, it serves to duplicate the value of a memory. It also stores the value of a neighbor in the PE local Memory Bank. Thus, we can move data across the array at a rate of one pixel per cycle. Thus, we are able to access elements that are not directly connected.

The architecture of the Logic Unit allows the addition of new operations easily. For example, an algorithm may need to perform a more complex operation many times. In that case it might be worthy to add an extra operator to boost speed. In return, the size of the multiplexer increases, as the size of the global control lines does. It is also possible to replace the Logic Unit with a *Look-Up Table* or a *ROM* that stores the appropriate outputs for certain inputs, thus emulating the overall operations of the Logic Unit. Our implementation has the potential to address complex operations with a reduced set of logic gates.

The Memory Bank

The Memory Bank consists of a set of 1-bit registers. It has just an entry, labeled *Mem_In,* of 1 bit and provides two simultaneous outputs, *Mem_A* and *Mem_B*, also 1-bit each.

The data input by *Mem_In* port is controlled by a decoder which activates the write signal in the register selected by an S-bit control signal, where S means 2^S=N, where N is the number of memory elements of the bank. An additional flag activates the writing on the Memory Bank. Thus the array can be blocked, holding its status, so interruptions in processing can be managed.

The two simultaneous outputs allow a flexible management of resources of the PE. On the one hand, they allow for internal operations to provide two operands to the Logic Unit. On the other hand, when the operation requires access to the neighborhood of the PE, an operand is provided *Mem_B* while the second comes from the Routing Module through the external 2:1 multiplexer. In this case it is necessary to provide an external output, determined now by *Mem_A*. Two N:1 multiplexers with S-bit control signals, *MuxA* and *MuxB*, provide this functionality.

The configuration of the Memory Banks acts as a dual-port memory allowing to simultaneous reads and writes on the same memory position. Thus, operations such *Register(2) = Register(1) OR Register(2)* are possible, reducing the amount of memory needed to implement the algorithms and the area of each PE.

Altogether, the necessary number of control bits is *3S+1*. This module is the most critical, since it consumes the greatest percentage of area of the PE. Its size might have to be shrunk to comply with the specific algorithm implementation. In this way, it also reduces the *fan-out* of the global interconnections, each buffering a smaller number of memory elements, increasing speed. The design of the decoder and the multiplexer will depend on the platform that is implemented, aiming at the greatest efficiency.

Functionality summary

In summary, the processing elements shown in Fig. 2 can:

- Select a neighbor
- Select two memory values
- Choose between two operation modes:
  - Two operands, one from the memory and other either from memory or an external element (AND, OR)
  - One operand from memory or from an external element (NOT, Identity)
- Write the result in the memory bank
- Provide a stable value as external output

The PE control

In order to increase the size of the array and as all PEs perform the same operation, it was decided to implement a global control system. It translates the high-level instruction into the signals arriving at each individual module of the PEs. This control can be implemented very easily if the instruction set is selected correctly.

	OP	A		B	R	OUT
		A_from	A_address	Address	address	address
nº bits	2	1	S	S	S	S

Table 1. Encoded instruction format for the Processing Element.

Table 1 outlines the encoding of the instruction format for the PE. The meaning of each segment is as follows

- *OP* segment encodes the operation performed by the Logic Unit. If there are specific operations its size must be adapted.
- *A* segment encodes the address of the first operand. It consists of two fields, *A_from* and *A_address*. The first is a 1-bit flag indicating if it comes from the local Memory Bank or from the Routing Module. The second, S-bit wide, has a double meaning according to the value of the flag above. If it comes from memory, it encodes the memory address. Otherwise, the two least significant bits encode the neighbor from which the data come.
- *B* encodes the address of the second operand, which always comes from the Memory Bank.
- *R* segment indicates the memory address where the result of the current operation is stored.
- *OUT* segment indicates the address inside the Memory Bank from where the data are to be provided to the array.

The total size of an instruction is 4S+3 bits. It should be noted that a 1 bit flag is needed to control the interruptions of the array, as specified above.

The instruction decoding of the control signals for the particular elements within each module is undertaken by the Global Control Module. From Table 1 it can be extracted that each field directly controls the elements of the PE, without needing decoding. Therefore, this module can be implemented only by distributing the coded instructions to the PEs. For example, the *OP* field encodes directly the multiplexer of the Logic Unit.

5. SIMD array programming

By the nature of the instruction set, a Boolean equation that means how each PE changes its value according to a given neighborhood must be found. This equation can be obtained in various ways: from the original image and the expected image, observing the differences between them; translating the effects of a mask or a filter; directly designing the Boolean equation, etc. Next, a selection of algorithms to test and show as the proposed system works is listed. The examples were extracted from the Cellular Wave Computing Library, CWCL, which collects the most used templates in image processing on CNNs. This selection is not a limitation because it is a widely used platform for these tasks, being a representative set of low-level image processing operators.

In terms of notation, the following variables are used to refer to the neighborhood of the central pixel, *c*: *n, nw, se,* etc. refer to *north, northwest, southwest,* etc. We will refer to instructions on the type *neighbor{address}*, for example *north{R2}*, meaning *access to the #2 memory address of the northern neighbor*. If a neighbor is not specified, it is understood that it is the local memory of the PE under study.

5.1 Binary edge detector

The well known edge detector is a good model to show how the architecture works. This operator corresponds to the binarized version of the edge detector present in the CWCL and follows the outline of Fig. 3, where the mask T is defined in Eq. (1).

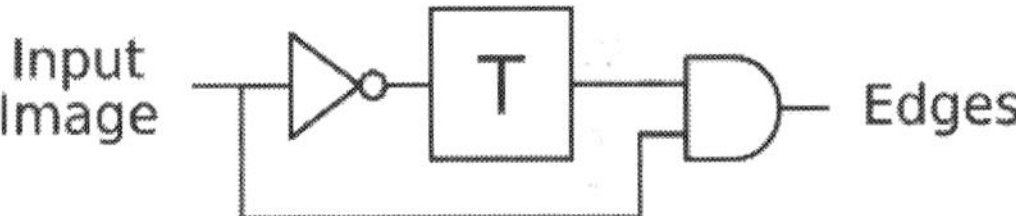

Fig. 3. Algorithm for the binary edge detection.

$$T : A = \begin{pmatrix} 0 & 1 & 0 \\ 1 & 0 & 1 \\ 0 & 1 & 0 \end{pmatrix}, I = -0,5 \tag{1}$$

The interpretation of this template is simple. Only when one or more neighbours *n, s, e* or *w,* are active, the central pixel is activated. This is equivalent to an *OR* between these four values. As the Logic Unit is not capable of operating simultaneously on the four neighbours, it is necessary to divide *T* into four sub-operations. Thus, in the first clock cycle the image is inverted. Then *T* is applied, requiring 4 clock cycles, to finally perform the *AND* between the previous results. Altogether, it takes 6 clock cycles. The pseudo-code is listed below:

- R0 ← input image
- inversion
  - R1 ← NOT R0
- template
  - R2 ← north{R1}
  - R2 ← R2 OR east{R1}
  - R2 ← R2 OR west{R1}
  - R1 ← R2 OR south{R1}
- and
  - R1 ← R0 AND R1

In this case, a four input *OR* may be implemented to enhance the speed in applications that require intensive use of edge detection. It clearly illustrates the possibilities of expanding the proposed Logic Unit for this architecture. Fig. 4 shows the application of this operator over a test image.

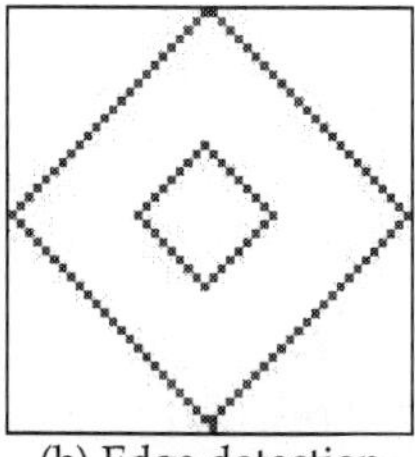

(a) Input image   (b) Edge detection

Fig. 4. Binary edge detection example.

5.2 Hole filling

The Hole Filling is an iterative operation. It is used to fill the holes in all the objects that are part of an image. In a synchronous architecture, as the proposed here, it is executed iteratively a number of times that can be fixed beforehand or determined during the execution. The first case is the most common and it is the considered here. The algorithm used is described in (Brea et al., 2006) and shown in Fig. 5, where T is the same template described above in Eq. (1).

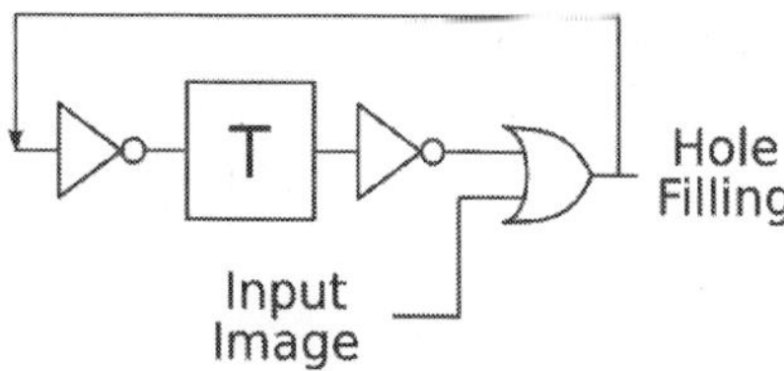

Fig. 5. Algorithm for the Hole Filling.

The pseudo-code of this operation is as follows:
- R0 ← input image
- 1st inversion
  - R1 ← NOT R0

- template
  - R2 ← north{R1}
  - R2 ← R2 OR east{R1}
  - R2 ← R2 OR west{R1}
  - R1 ← R2 OR south{R1}
- 2nd inversion
  - R1 ← NOT R1
- OR
  - R1 ← R0 OR R1

A complete iteration of the algorithm requires 7 clock cycles. The number of iterations needed depends on the shape of the image and its size. The result of applying it on a test image is displayed on Fig. 6.

5.3 Shortest path problem

Finally, an implementation of the algorithm that solves the problem of the minimum path was done. The application is significantly more complex than the other examples outlined previously and it illustrates the capability of the SIMD array.

The aim is to determine the shortest path between two points, avoiding a series of obstacles. It is based on the implementation discussed in (Rekeczky, 1999), which proposed a new approach to solve this problem by using CNN computing. In line with this strategy, a wave front with constant speed explores the labyrinth from the starting point. At each branching of the labyrinth, the wave front is divided. When two wave fronts are at an intersection, the first to reach will continue evolving while the rest remains static, avoiding the collision.

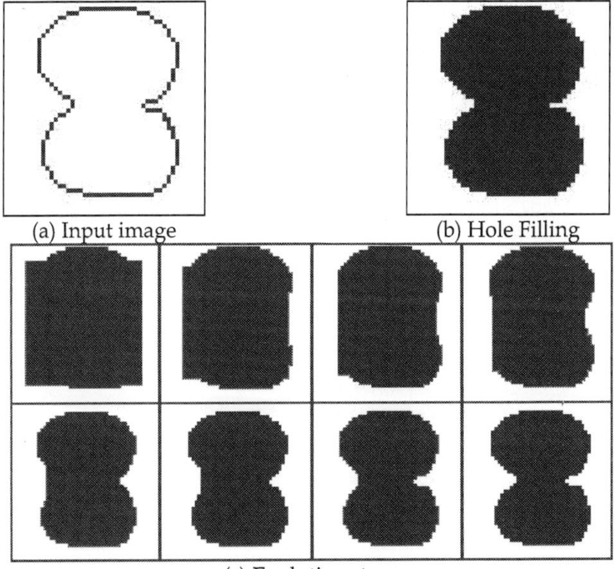

(a) Input image   (b) Hole Filling

(c) Evolution steps

Fig. 6. Hole Filling example.

Then, a prune of all paths is done, maintaining fixed the start and end points, which are external parameters of the system, so only the shortest path between those points remains.

The algorithm has two stages, both to carry out iteratively. The first stage, the exploration, is shown in Fig. 7. The templates T1 and T2 defined in Eqs. (2) and (3) along with its translation into Boolean equations.

$$T1 : A = \begin{pmatrix} 0 & 1 & 0 \\ 1 & 0 & 1 \\ 0 & 1 & 0 \end{pmatrix}, I = -0,5 \quad \Rightarrow \quad T1 = n + e + w + s \tag{2}$$

$$T2 : A = \begin{pmatrix} 0 & -1 & 0 \\ -1 & 0 & -1 \\ 0 & -1 & 0 \end{pmatrix}, I = -1 \quad \Rightarrow \quad T2 = \overline{n \cdot (w + s + e) + e \cdot (w + s) + w \cdot s} \tag{3}$$

The second stage, the pruning, is done executing iteratively T3, defined in Eq. (4). This template is equivalent to an AND between the labyrinth and explored the result of invert the application of T2 on the explored labyrinth, so the above equations will be used again.

$$T3 : A = \begin{pmatrix} 0 & 1 & 0 \\ 1 & 3 & 1 \\ 0 & 1 & 0 \end{pmatrix}, I = -2 \tag{4}$$

During the exploration phase, T1 requires 4 clock cycles, T2 9 cycles and the additional logic operations, 3 cycles. All in all, each iteration requires 16 cycles. The pruning phase is executed in 9 cycles, 8 for T2 and one for the additional operations. The number of necessary iterations for each stage depends on the labyrinth. Fig. 8 shows the different stages of each phase on a test labyrinth.

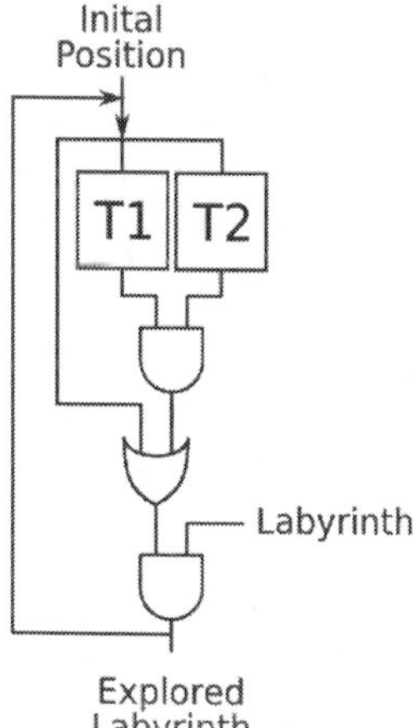

Fig. 7. Shortest path problem: exploration step.

The pseudo-code for both stages is shown bellow.

<table>
<tr><td valign="top">

Exploration step:
- R0 ← input image
- R1 ← start point
- Template T1
  - R2 ← north{R0}
  - R2 ← R2 OR east{R1}
  - R2 ← R2 OR west{R1}
  - R2 ← R2 OR south{R1}
- Template T2
  - R3 ← west{R1}
  - R4 ← R3 AND south{R1}
  - R5 ← R3 OR south{R1}
  - R3 ← R5 AND east{R1}
  - R3 ← R3 OR R4
  - R4 ← R5 OR east{R1}
  - R4 ← R4 AND north{R1}
  - R3 ← R3 OR R4
  - R3 ← NOT R3
- Final operations
  - R2 ← R2 AND R3
  - R2 ← R2 OR R1
  - R1 ← R0 AND R2

</td><td valign="top">

Pruning step:
- R7 ← end point
- Join start and end point images
  - R1 ← R1 OR R7
- Template T3
  - R3 ← west{R1}
  - R4 ← R3 AND south{R1}
  - R5 ← R3 OR south{R1}
  - R3 ← R5 AND east{R1}
  - R3 ← R3 OR R4
  - R4 ← R5 OR east{R1}
  - R4 ← R4 AND north{R1}
  - R3 ← R3 OR R4
  - R1 ← R1 AND R3

</td></tr>
</table>

6. Proof of concept: FPGA synthesis

In order to test and verify the functionality of the proposed architecture, a description in VHDL was made for a subsequent implementation on a programmable architecture, specifically on an FPGA.

6.1 Global system configuration

Fig. 9 displays the schematic view of the global configuration of the proposed architecture. As our emphasis has been put on the array, the global system architecture addressed here is not optimized and it is only intended as an operation tester of the processing array. It is made up of the following elements:

- Input and Output Memory Banks: to store images to be processed and the processed images. Both of them provide a column per clock cycle.
- Instruction Storage: it stores the decoded instructions, the value of the dummy ring for each instruction and the interrupt signal, *process*.
- Global Control: it synchronizes all existing modules. It consists of a finite state machine and the Instruction Decoder described above.
- Processing Array: has an input column data of the stored image in the memory bank and as output, a column of the processed image. The control is done through the current instruction from the Instruction Memory. The *process* signal controls interruptions of the array acting on the decoder of the Memory Bank of each PE.

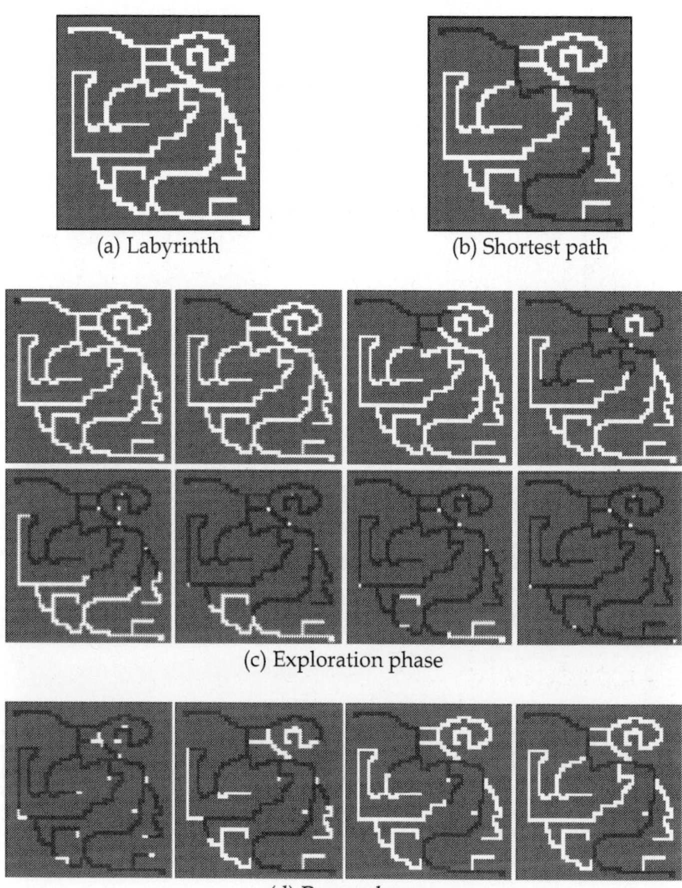

(a) Labyrinth
(b) Shortest path

(c) Exploration phase

(d) Prune phase

Fig. 8. Shortest path problem. Example

- Address Generator: it calculates the address of the next instruction to execute. It allows loops in order to iteratively execute blocks of instructions, reducing memory requirements for storing the instructions.

6.2 Implementation results

The selected platform was an RC2000 card from Celoxica, which comprises a card with a PMC RC2000 PCI controller, which allows to insert the card into the PCI bus of a PC, and an ADM-XRC-II board by Alpha Data, with the following features:

- Xilinx Virtex-II xc2v6000-4 FPGA
- 6 banks x 2MB RAM ZBT
- 2 banks x 4MB RAM ZBT
- External clocks: [40KHz - 100MHz] and [25MHz – 66MHz]

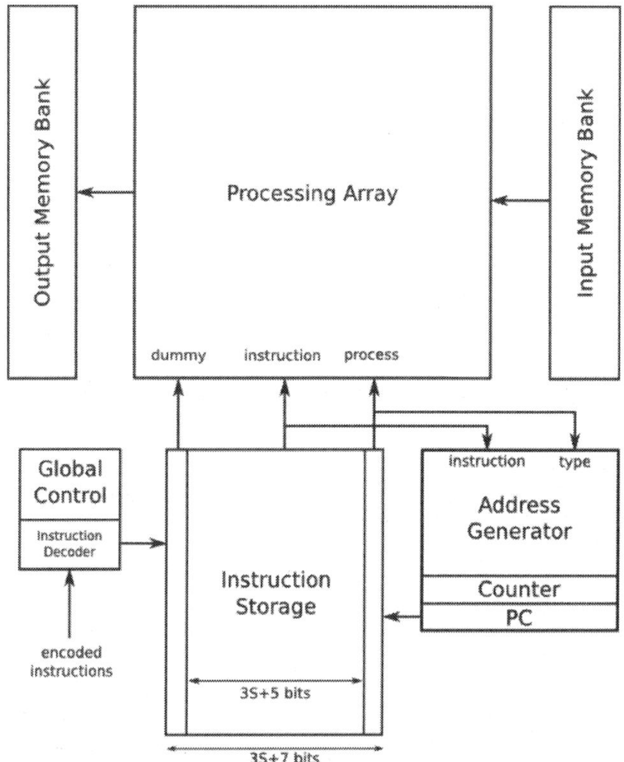

Fig. 9. Global system architecture.

The Xilinx Virtex-II xc2v6000 main characteristics are:
- 6M equivalent logic gates
- 33792 slices
- 1056Kbits of distributed RAM
- 144 dedicated multipliers
- 144 dedicated RAM blocks

The design and mapping process was done using the ISE 9.2i, from Xilinx.

The selected array for the synthesis has a size of 48x48 processing elements, with a Memory Bank of 8 bits per PE (S=3). The external memory banks were implemented using the dedicated RAM blocks of the FPGA. The main results are summarized in Table 2.

Occupied slices	26,428 (78%)
Slices Flip-Flops	20,165 (29%)
4-input LUTs	50,649 (74%)
Number of equivalent gates	527,716
Maximum frequency achieved	67,3MHz

Table 2. Main results of the FPGA implementation.

There are available resources on the FPGA which can increase the resolution of the array, the size of the PE memory, or the instruction storage. With the same configuration, the resolution can be increased to reach an array of 56x56 elements.

6.3 Tested algorithms: Summary of results

Table 3 gives a summary of processing times for each algorithm, considering only one iteration. The maximum working frequency for the Virtex-II FPGA xc2v6000 is 67.3MHz. It also includes the number of required memories for its implementation, including always the memory where the original image is stored and is not changed during processing, although this would not be necessary in all cases. It also includes results for other tested algorithms that have not been detailed in this chapter, but intended to illustrate more clearly the performance of the platform.

Algorithm	#cycles	Time (µs)	#memories
Edge detector	6	0.089	3
Hit and Miss	10	0.149	3
Hole Filling	7	0.104	3
Skeletonization	84	1.248	5
Shortest Path: exploration	16	0.238	6
Shortest Path: prune	9	0.138	4

Table 3. Processing times for the proposed sample algorithms. One iteration at 67,3MHz.

For the iterative algorithms, Table 4 shows the total execution times. The test images have the same size as the matrix, i.e., 48x48 pixels

Algorithm	#cycles	#iterations	Time (µs)
Array load/Donwload	1	48	0.71
Hole Filling	7	45	4.68
Skeletonization	84	40	49.93
Shortest Path: exploration	16	125	29.72
Shortest Path: prune	9	75	10.03

Table 4. Processing times for the iterative algorithms. One iteration at 67,3MHz.

7. Technology evolution: FPGA vs. ASIC

The impressive progress of new technologies, marked by Moore's Law (ITRS, 2007) allows increasingly integration density. This leads to more hardware resources with higher clock frequencies, increasing performance considerably. In this way, programmable systems such as FPGAs are able to get the same performance than recent past specific integrated circuits, IC, keeping the development times and the time-to-market at low(Nagy et al., 2006). In this section we examine the scaling possibilities of the SIMD architecture due to the technology evolution, both for FPGAs and ICs.

7.1 FPGA

The ever-increasing density of the CMOS technology market by the Moore's Law means that the designers can choose FPGAs as a proof of concept system (Lopich & Dudek, 2005) or even as an end system (Diaz et al., 2006). The time to market is another major reason why FPGAs are becoming increasingly competitive. A study based on the International Technology Roadmap for Semiconductors (ITRS) roadmap which estimates the increased logic capacity and speed of commercial FPGAs is shown below. Area reduction allows to integrate more logic. In this way, the parallelism that can be obtained with the proposed SIMD architecture will increase considerably, allowing large array sizes, so that the final solution could be based on an FPGA and not on an integrated circuit, cutting costs and design time. These results are shown in Fig. 10.

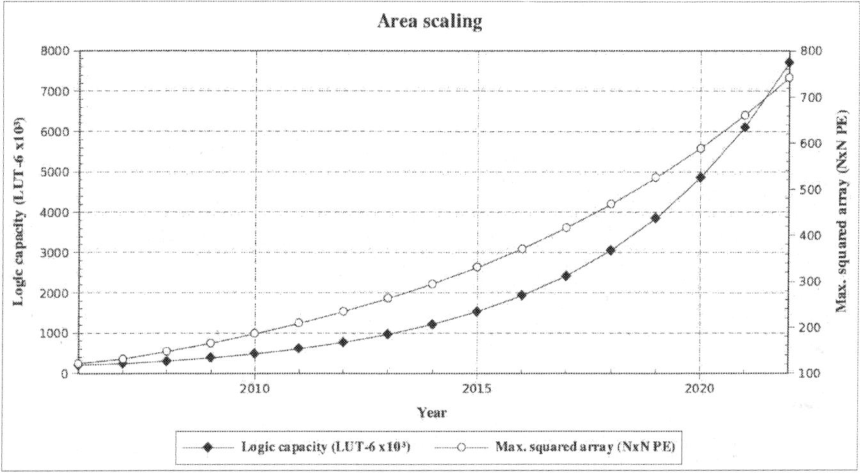

Fig. 10. Scaling of the FPGA logic capability. Logic capacity in thousands of 6-input LUTs. Maximum resolution of a square matrix, in number of PEs per row.

The method used for this estimate is as follows. Given the ability of the FPGA logic for a given year, the number of logic cells, and the prediction of the ITRS, the capacity of the FPGA logic cells for the target year is:

$$\text{capacity}_B = \text{capacity}_A \cdot \frac{Density_B}{Density_A} \cdot \frac{Die_B}{Die_A}$$

where the subscript A refers to the known year and B to the estimate year. As the ITRS shows, the chip size remains constant over the next years, thus simplifying the above equation. This study is based on the one detailed in (Varghese & Rabaey, 2001) and is a review of the last ITRS update (ITRS, 2007). This formula is valid only if the internal architecture of the FPGA does not change.

The selected FPGA to start this study with is one of the most advanced from Xilinx, a Virtex-5 XC5VLX330. The most salient characteristics are gathered in Table 5. This FPGA has more than 50,000 logic cells, CLBs, each composed of 2 slices, each one with 4 LUTs with 6 inputs and 4 Flip-Flops per slice. The logic contained in each CLB is summarized in Table 6. The technology used in the manufacturing process is 65nm at 1.0V with triple-oxide. We must emphasize that the Virtex 5 family changed its internal architecture from 4 input LUTs to 6 input LUTs, with respect to previous family (Cosoroaba & Rivoallon, 2006) (Percey, 2007).

CLBs array	LUT-6	Flip-Flops	Distributed RAM	Shift registers
240x108	207360	207360	3420 Kb	1710 Kb

Table 5. Virtex-5 XC5VLX330. Main hardware details.

Slices	LUT-6	Flip-Flops	Distributed RAM	Shift registers
2	8	8	256 bits	128 Kb

Table 6. Virtex 5 family. Hardware on each CLB.

With these data, whereas the number of basic elements of the selected FPGA is 207,000 in 2006, year that Xilinx introduced the Virtex 5 family, and assuming that the chip size remains constant, in 2010 it is possible to reach 481,000 elements. Fig. 10 shows the scaling of the current Virtex 5 family. The same figure includes what would be the maximum size of the SIMD processing array. This result should be taken as an upper bound and not as a precise value because they are not included the elements employed by control, memory instructions or even new features that may include newer FPGAs.

Concerning the Virtex 5 family, each Processing Element requires 8 Flip-Flops and 14 6-LUT, keeping the same characteristics as the detailed in the previous implementation. Therefore, the limiting factor is the number of available LUTs. Thus, it appears that using the 2009 technology node it would be possible to implement a QCIF array (144x176) and that before 2013 and 2019 it is feasible to process images of 256x256 and 512x512 pixels, respectively, without dividing them into sub-windows, with a PE per pixel.

7.2 ASIC

For certain applications, an FPGA-based solution can not meet the appropriate requirements such as higher performance, lower consumption and higher integration. One of its uses is as coprocessor in focal plane vision systems, accelerating the binary computation, where the integration with gray image processing units is necessary. Thus, it is interesting to discuss the features of a full custom implementation. An ASIC implementation for the Processing Element is proposed in this section in order to explore the possibilities of scaling along the ITRS predictions.

CMOS complementary logic with minimum size transistors will be used. This implementation is not optimal because using other CMOS logic families and specific design techniques, such as pseudo-nMOS or dynamic CMOS, a higher yield in both area and speed can be obtained. The different modules of the PE are conceived in the most straightforward manner. For example, a 2:1 multiplexer is formed by two 2-AND gates, an OR-2 and an inverter for the control signal. The features of the PE are the same as those detailed above: an 8-bit Memory Bank. A summary of the number of transistors per PE is given in Table 7.

	Routing	Memory Bank	Logic Unit	Other
No. of transistors	46	902	60	20

Table 7. Number of transistors for each Processing Element using CMOS logic.

It should be noted that the area occupied by the memory banks amounts to the 87% of the total area. Each memory element is formed by a D master/slave Flip-Flop with reset and enable signals. Clearly the selected implementation is not the best. Using RAM-based elements will considerably reduce the number of transistors. This module will require a greater effort during the design to optimize the area requirements. The adequate selection of the size of the Memory Bank for a particular implementation is critical.

To determine the area occupied by each PE is assumed, similarly as for programmable architectures, that the integration density predicted by the ITRS includes the parameters that limit it. To estimate the size of the processing array it will also be assumed that the buffering is negligible compared to the processing hardware. This will not affect the precision with which the results are expected.

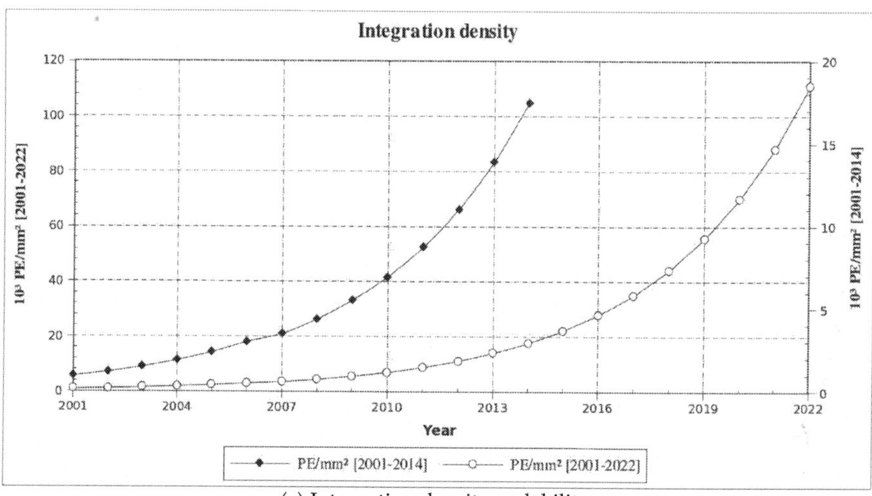

(a) Integration density scalability

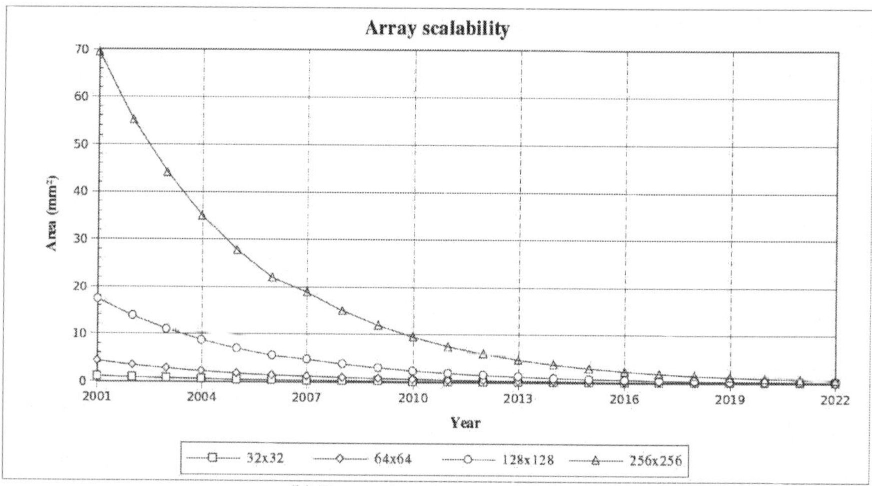

(b) Processing Array scalability

Fig. 11. Scalability of the ASIC implementation.

The results are summarized in Figs. 11.a and 11.b. The first one shows the maximum amount of PEs that a given technology is able to integrate by mm². To ease the visualization the figure also shows the Near Term Years expanded. The second figure displays, for some array sizes, the total area that would be occupied according to the technological process selected. The planned integration density will allow use a processing array as accelerator in general purpose visual processors with a very low cost in terms of area, even in high resolution. We emphasize that with the 2001 technology, an array of 128x128 elements needs 18mm2 and that, with the same area, it is possible to integrate an array of 256x256 elements in 2007. It should be remembered that this is only an estimation and that the design is not optimized. Just by using transmission gates for multiplexors and SRAM memories the area requirements are reduced by a factor of 5. With a more aggressive design strategy is feasible to reduce an order of magnitude in the occupied area.

8. Conclusions

The range of applications where binary images are used is very wide due to its particular characteristics, such as low storage and processing requirements or the simplicity of the algorithms. Many of early vision operations can be addressed using a small computer unit. Thus, the path to explore is to increase the parallelism. SIMD architectures, with simple processing elements arranged in a matrix topology with local connectivity between them, are able to efficiently exploit the characteristics of low and medium level operations.

For the development of the processing element, special attention was paid to the reduction of its size while maintaining a generic functionality. Furthermore, it is easy to extend its functionality for those critical operations of a given algorithm. A limited set of instructions allows to easily translate a mask or filter or to deduce the Boolean equation that governs the change of status of each pixel of the image according to its neighborhood.

Functionality and performance were verified using an FPGA, obtaining performance data that indicate that even on a programmable architecture, the efficiency is high. Furthermore, short term future FPGAs will allow to implement bigger arrays, achieving a higher degree of parallelism. In the same way, full-custom implementations allow to use the proposed Processing Array as co-processor on generic vision systems with low area requirements.

9. Acknowledgements

This work is funded by Xunta de Galicia under the project PGIDT06TIC10502PR

10. References

Alonso-Montes, C.; Ortega, M.; Penedo, M. & Vilarino, D. (2008). Pixel parallel vessel tree extraction for a personal authentication system. *IEEE International Symposium on Circuits and Systems. ISCAS 2008*. pp. 1596–1599.

Anafocus (2007). Eye-Ris v1.0/v2.0 datasheet. *Anafocus White Papers*. http://anafocus.com

Akiyama, T.; Aono, H.; Aoki, K.; Ler, K.W.; Wilson, B.; Araki, T.; Morishige, T.; Takeno, H.; Sato, A.; Nakatani, S. & Senoh, T. (1994). MPEG2 video codec using image compression DSP. *IEEE Transactions on Consumer Electronics,* pp. 466-472, Vol. 40, No. 3, August 1994

Brea, V.; Laiho, M.; Vilarino, D.; Paasio, A. & Cabello, D. (2006). A binary-based on-chip CNN solution for Pixel-Level Snakes. *International Journal of Circuit Theory and Applications,* pp. 383-407 Vol. 34(4), 2006

Cheng, H.; Jiang, X.; Sun, Y. & Wang, J. (2001). Color image segmentation: advances and prospects. *Pattern Recognition Letters.* pp. 2259–2281, Vol. 34, No. 12

Cosoroaba, Adrian & Rivoallon, Frédéric (2006). Achieving Higher System Performance with the Virtex-5 Family of FPGAs. *Xilinx White Papers,* July 2006

Creeger, M. (2005). Multicore CPUs for the masses. *Queue,* ACM New York, NY, USA

Diaz, J.; Ros, E.; Pelayo, F.; Ortigosa, E.M. & Mota, S (2006). FPGA-based real-time optical-flow system. *IEEE Transactions on Circuits and Systems for Video Technology,* pp. 274-279, Vol. 16, No. 2, February 2006

Eklundh, J.-O. and Christensen, H. I. (2001). Computer Vision: Past and Future. *Springer Berlin - Heidelberg.*

Fernandez Garcia, N.A.; Suarez, M.; Brea, V.M. & Cabello, D. (2008). Template-oriented hardware design based on shape analysis of 2D CNN operators in CNN template libraries and applications. *Proceedings of 11th International Workshop on Cellular Neural Networks and Their Applications,* pp. 63-68, July 2008

Garcia, C. & Apostolidis, X. (2000). Text detection and segmentation in complex color images. *Proceedings of IEEE International Conference on Acoustics, Speech, and Signal Processing.* pp. 2326–2329, Vol. 4, No. 6.

Gepner, P. & Kowalik, M.F. (2006). Multi-Core Processors: New Way to Achieve High System Performance. *International Symposium on Parallel Computing in Electrical Engineering,* pp. 9-13, 2006

Courtoy, M. (1998). Rapid system prototyping for real-time design validation. I*n Proceedings of 9th International Workshop on Rapid System Prototyping.* pp. 108–112.

Dudek, P. (2005). A general-purpose processor-per-pixel analog SIMD vision chip. *IEEE Transactions on Circuits and Systems I: Regular Papers [IEEE Transactions on Circuits and Systems I: Fundamental Theory and Applications],* pp. 13–20, Vol. 52, No. 1:

Hinrichs, W.; Wittenburg, J.P.; Lieske, H.; Kloos, H.; Ohmacht, M.; Pirsch, P. (2000). A 1.3-GOPS parallel DSP for high-performance image-processing applications. *IEEE Journal of Solid-State Circuits,* pp. 946-952, Vol. 35, No. 7, July 2000

Hsu, R.-L.; Abdel-Mottaleb, M. & Jain, A. (2002). Face detection in color images. *IEEE Transactions on Pattern Analysis and Machine Intelligence.* pp. 696–706, Vol. 24, No. 5.

ITRS (2007). International Technology Roadmap for Semiconductors. *http://public.itrs.net*

Kék, László; Karacs, Kristóf & Roska, Tamás (2007). Cellular wave computing library (templates, algorithms, and programs). Version 2.1. *Research report of Cellular Sensory and Wave Computing Laboratory CSW-1-2007,* (Budapest, 2007)

Linan, G.; Dominguez-Castro, R.; Espejo, S. & Rodriguez-Vazquez, A. (2001). Ace16k: An advanced focal-plane analog programmable array processor. *Proceedings of the 27th European Solid-State Circuits Conference. ESSCIRC 2001.* pp. 201–204.

Lopich, A. & Dudek, P., R. (2001). Architecture of asynchronous cellular processor array for image skeletonization. *Proceedings of European Conference on Circuit Theory and Design*, pp. III/81-III/84 , Vol. 3, August 2005

MacLean, W. (2005). An evaluation of the suitability of FPGAs for embedded vision systems. *International Conference on Computer Vision and Pattern Recognition*, pp. 131–138.

Maginot, S. (1992). Evaluation criteria of hdls: Vhdl compared to verilog, udl/i and m. *European Design Automation Conference*, pp. 746–751.

Nagy, Zoltán; Vörösházi, Zsolt & Szolgay, Péter. (2006). Emulated digital CNN-UM solution of partial differential equations. *International Journal on Circuit Theory and Applications*, pp. 445-470, Vol. 34, No. 4

Owens, J.D.; Houston, M.; Luebke, D.; Green, S.; Stone, J.E. & Phillips, J.C. (2008). GPU Computing. *Proceedings of the IEEE*, pp. 879-899, Vol. 96, No. 5, May 2008

Park, H. J.; Kim, K. B.; Kim, J. H. & Kim, S. (2007). A novel motion detection pointing device using a binary cmos image sensor. *IEEE International Symposium on Circuits and Systems. ISCAS 2007*. pp. 837–840.

Percey, Andrew (2007). Advantages of the Virtex-5 FPGA 6-Input LUT Architecture. *Xilinx White Papers*, December 2007

Prati, A.; Mikic, I.; Trivedi, M. & Cucchiara, R. (2003). Detecting moving shadows: algorithms and evaluation. *IEEE Transactions on Pattern Analysis and Machine Intelligence*. pp. 918–923, Vol. 25, No. 7

Rekeczky, Cs. (1999). Skeletonization and the Shortest Path Problem - Theoretical Investigation and Algorithms for CNN Universal Chips. *7th International Symposium on Nonlinear Theory and its Applications* (December 1999)

Schauer, B. (2008). Multicore Processors--A Necessity. *ProQuest*, September 2008

Shen, G.; Gao, G.P.; Li , S.; Shum, H.G. & Zhang, Y.Q. (2005). Accelerate video decoding with generic GPU. *IEEE Transactions on Circuits and Systems for Video Technology*, pp. 685-693, Vol. 15, No. 5, May 2005

Soos, B.G.; Rak, A.;Veres, J. & Cserey, G. (2005). GPU powered CNN simulator (SIMCNN) with graphical flow based programmability. *11th International Workshop on Cellular Neural Networks and Their Applications*, pp. 163-168, July 2008

Spiliotis, I. & Mertzios, B. (1997). A fast skeleton algorithm on block represented binary images. *Proceeding of the 13th International Conference on Digital Signal Processing*. pp. 675–678, Vol. 2.

Szolgay, P. & Tomordi, K. (1996). Optical detection of breaks and short circuits on the layouts of printed circuit boards using CNN. *Proceedings of the 4th IEEE International Workshop on Cellular Neural Networks and their Applications. CNNA-96*. pp. 87–92.

Tan, Edwin J. & Heinzelman, Wendi B. (2003). DSP architectures: past, present and futures. *SIGARCH Computer Architecture News*, pp. 6-19, Vol. 31, No. 3, New York, NY, USA

Tseng, Y.-C.; Chen, Y.-Y. & Pan, H.-K. (2002). A secure data hiding scheme for binary images. *IEEE Transactions on Communications*, pp. 1227–1231, Vol. 50, No. 8.

Varghese, George & Rabaey, Jan M. Name of paper (2001). *Low-Energy FPGAs, Architecture and Design*, Kluwer Academic Publishers

Vilariño, D. L. & Rekeczky, C. (2005). Pixel-level snakes on the CNNUM: algorithm design, on-chip implementation and applications. International Journal on Circuit Theory and Applications. pp. 17–51, Vol. 33, No. 1.